Bullying in Irish Education

*Perspectives in Research
and Practice*

Bullying in Irish Education

*Perspectives in Research
and Practice*

Mona O'Moore & Paul Stevens

EDITORS

CORK UNIVERSITY PRESS

First published in 2013 by
Cork University Press
Youngline Industrial Estate
Pouladuff Road, Togher
Cork, Ireland

British Library Cataloguing in Publication Data
A CIP catalogue record for this book is available from the British Library

ISBN 978–1–78205–043–8

Typeset by Carrigboy Typesetting Services
Printed by Gutenberg Press Ltd, Malta
www.corkuniversitypress.com

Contents

PART 1. PEER BULLYING IN IRISH EDUCATION

PART 2. PEER BULLYING IN OUT-OF-SCHOOL SETTINGS

PART 3. ADULT BULLYING IN EDUCATION

PART 4. PROMISING STRATEGIES FOR PREVENTION AND INTERVENTION

PART 5. BULLYING AND THE LAW

Tables

꧁꧂

Figures

Acronyms

ABC — Anti-Bullying Centre (Trinity College Dublin)
ACCS — Association of Community and Comprehensive Schools
ADHD — Attention Deficit Hyperactivity Disorder
AER — All England Law Reports
ASTI — Association of Secondary Teachers, Ireland
BoG — Board of Governors
BDI — Beck Depression Inventory
BOM — Board of Management
BVQ — Bully/Victim Questionnaire (Olweus)
CBCL — Child Behaviour Check List
CCMS — Council for Catholic Maintained Schools
CPSMA — Catholic Primary School Management Association
CYP — Children and Young People
DENI — Department of Education Northern Ireland
DES — Department of Education and Skills
ELB — Education and Library Board
ELR — European Law Review
ESRI — Economic and Social Research Institute
ETFO — Elementary Teachers' Federation of Ontario
EWHC — England and Wales High Court
EWO — Educational Welfare Officer
F2F — 'face to face'
FCR — Family Court Reporter
GCSE — General Certificate of Secondary Education
GLEN — Gay and Lesbian Equality Network
GMTV — Good Morning Television
HEA — Higher Education Authority
HSA — Health and Safety Authority
ICT — Information and Communications Technology
IEHC — High Court of Ireland
ILRM — Irish Law Reports Monthly
INTO — Irish National Teachers' Organisation
IP — Internet Protocol

IPPN	Irish Primary Principals' Network
IR	Irish Record
ISM	In-School Management
ISP	Internet Service Provider
ISPAI	Internet Service Providers Association of Ireland
IVEA	Irish Vocational Educational Association
IYF	Irish Youth Foundation
JMB	Joint Managerial Body
JMBSS	Joint Managerial Body for Secondary Schools
KLT	Kids' Life and Times
LAWSEQ	Lawrence Self-Esteem Questionnaire
LBGT	Lesbian, Bisexual, Gay and Transgender
MISP	Massage in Schools Programme
NATFHE	National Association of Teachers in Further and Higher Education
NAPD	National Association of Principals and Deputy Principals
NAQ	Negative Acts Questionnaire
NASUWT	National Association of Schoolmasters/Union of Women Teachers
NCB	National Children's Board
NCCA	National Council for Curriculum and Assessment
NEWB	National Educational Welfare Board
NIABF	Northern Ireland Anti-Bullying Forum
NIDD	National Intellectual Disability Database
NISRA	Northern Ireland Statistics and Research Agency
NPC	National Parents Council
NPC-PP	National Parents Council – Post-Primary
NPM	New Public Management
NUS	National Union of Students
OECTA	Ontario English Catholic Teachers' Association
OSSTF	Ontario Secondary School Teachers' Federation
PHSCE	Personal, Health, Social and Citizenship Education
PRS	Participant Role Scale (Salmivalli)
PSNI	Police Service of Northern Ireland
QB	Queen's Bench
RSE	Relationships and Sexuality Education
RTÉ	Radio Telifís Éireann
SMS	Short Message Service
SNA	Special Needs Assistant
SPHE	Social, Personal and Health Education
SST	Sexual, Sexist and Transphobic
TFPWB	Taskforce on the Prevention of Workplace Bullying

TLR	Times Law Reports
TUI	Teachers' Union of Ireland
UKSC	Supreme Court of the United Kingdom
UNESCO	United Nations Educational, Scientific and Cultural Organization
UNICEF	United Nations International Children's Emergency Fund
USI	Union of Students in Ireland
USS	Union of Secondary Students
VEC	Vocational Education Committee
WHO	World Health Organisation
WHS	Work Harassment Scale
YLT	Young Life and Times
YPBAS	Young Person's Behaviour and Attitudes Survey

Acknowledgements

We would like to express our gratitude to authors of individual chapters without whose commitment and assistance this book would not have been possible. Their families also deserve thanks for undoubtedly having had to compete for their time and attention. Special thanks to Professor Rory O'Moore and Dr Linda Stevens for their patience and support during the writing of this book.

With reference to Chapter 9 Paul Stevens would like to express his thanks to Irish Primary Principals' Network Director Mr Sean Cottrell, former IPPN President Mr Larry Fleming, IPPN Conference Organiser Ms Angela Lynch, IPPN support staff Ms Rachel Brannigan, Ms Louise O'Brien and Ms Jennifer McCarthy who supported and facilitated access to over 2,600 primary school principals. In addition, thanks to Professor Charlotte Rayner, Portsmouth Business School at the University of Portsmouth, England, Dr Sarah Branch, Griffith College, Brisbane, Australia, Dr Stephen Whitehead formerly of Keele University, Staffordshire, England and to Ms Fiona Mulvany for her helpful advice on data coding and statistical procedures.

In respect of Chapter 12 Mona O'Moore would like to express her sincere thanks to the Irish Council for Humanities and Social Sciences for their generous financial support of the evaluation of the ABC Whole School Community Approach to Bullying Prevention. She would like also to express her thanks to Colin Kirkham who has given so generously of his time in providing statistical support. In addition she would like to take the opportunity to thank Stephen Minton (Director of Training), all the trainers, staff and students who contributed to the development and evaluation of the ABC Whole School Community Approach.

Finally our sincere gratitude to Maria O'Donovan and Mike Collins of Cork University Press for their courtesy and unfailing assistance at all times.

Dedication

This book is dedicated to all who have experienced
bullying within our education system.

Declaration

The views expressed by individual authors do not
necessarily state or reflect those of the editors.

Notes on Contributors

Jackie Black, BSc (Hons), MPysch, BPsS, PsSI, has worked with both children and adults with intellectual and/or physical disabilities and has worked with adolescents and their families within a residential addiction treatment centre. She has recently completed an MSc in Health Psychology and also lectures part-time on the Diploma in Disabilities Studies with the Centre for Adult and Continuing Education at UCC.

Dr Declan Fahie is a qualified primary school teacher who has taught in Ireland, the UK and Italy. He holds an MEd and PhD from the School of Education, UCD. Declan is currently lecturing in Sociology of Education, Philosophy of Education and Research Methods at a number of colleges of education in Dublin. His research interests include teacher effectiveness, equality issues in education, gender roles in schooling and workplace bullying.

Seán Fallon, BA, HDipEd, MA, with colleague Mary Kent, helped start the 'Anti-Bullying Campaign' in Coláiste Éanna, Dublin in 2003. As coordinator of the programme he oversaw its evolution into a permanent, effective, positive feature of school life. He believed that, given the right tools and a template to use them, other teachers would be able and willing to reduce bullying in their schools. In 2008 he helped create the free www.antibullyingcampaign.ie website to give them this opportunity and already over 1,000 Irish secondary teachers have registered on the site. He retired in 2009 to devote more time to this work.

Claire Healy, BA in Applied Social Studies, worked as a social care worker for nine years with disadvantaged youth, primarily those who have experienced homelessness in Dublin city centre. In 2008 she graduated with an MEd in Aggression Studies from Trinity College. Her dissertation was a comparative study that looked at the relationship between self-esteem and bullying behaviour among young people out of home and young people in mainstream education. She began working as an intern at the Anti-Bullying Centre in Trinity College in October 2010 before starting work on the *Let me be ME!* project which looks at countering workplace bullying for people with intellectual disabilities.

Mary Kent, BA, HDipEd, MEd, is a doctoral student in the School of Education, Trinity College Dublin, where she completed an MEd (Aggression Studies). Her research interests include conflict, aggression and bullying in schools with particular emphasis on empowering students to resolve these issues peacefully. She was co-founder, with Seán Fallon, of the website www.antibullyingcampaign. ie, which grew out of the 'Anti-Bullying Campaign' programme they developed in Coláiste Éanna, Dublin where she holds the post of Anti-Bullying Coordinator. With colleagues in Spain and Norway, she is a member of the Comenius Sabona partnership, developing materials to teach peer mediation and conflict resolution skills in schools.

Dr Linda McGrath is a registered clinical psychologist and has worked in various disability services and schools for over twenty years. She is a graduate of University College Dublin (BA and MA) and undertook the DipClinPsych from the British Psychological Society at Trinity College Dublin. She is also a graduate of the University of Bangor (DClinPsych) where she undertook research into bullying among intellectual disabilities populations.

Dr Conor McGuckin is a full-time lecturer in the Psychology of Education at the School of Education, Trinity College Dublin. Conor coordinates the professional Masters programme in Educational Guidance and Counselling. He is co-director of the Inclusion in Education and Society research grouping at Trinity College Dublin, and is a Visiting Research Fellow of Glyndŵr University (Wales). Conor has published and consulted widely on the area of psychology applied to educational policy and processes, educational psychology, bully/victim problems among children and adults, special educational needs, psychometrics, and the scientific study of religiosity. He is also a co-director of Selection by Design, an innovative and leading provider of psychometric training and consultancy solutions.

Lian McGuire, BA, MEd, DipMed, has been the Administrator of the Anti-Bullying Research and Resource Unit in the School of Education, Trinity College Dublin since its inception in 1996. A trained mediator, she has worked extensively on the nationwide studies of both school and workplace bullying in Ireland carried out by the unit and has carried out surveys and authored reports for individual schools around the country.

Dr Stephen James Minton, BSc (Hons), MSc (Couns. Psychol.), PhD CPsychol, is a chartered psychologist with the British Psychological Society and a full-time lecturer in the psychology of education at the School of Education, Trinity College Dublin. He is the author of *Using Psychology in the Classroom* (Sage, 2012), and the co-author (with Professor Mona O'Moore) of *Dealing with Bullying in Schools: A Training Manual for Teachers, Parents and Other Professionals* (Sage, 2004), and *Cyber-Bullying: The Irish Experience* (Nova Science, 2011). He has been active as a researcher and practitioner in the field of anti-bullying since 2000. His research interests are in aggression studies (including the design, implementation and evaluation of whole school/community anti-bullying programmes), prejudice (including combating homophobia and alterophobia), and educational applications of existential and psychodynamic psychology.

Monica Monahan, MEd Aggression Studies, is a secondary school teacher with twenty-three years' teaching experience in schools in the Dublin area and the west of Ireland. Her special area of interest is teacher negative behaviours in the classroom and the impact of these behaviours on interpersonal relationships within the school community and eventual negative outcomes on teaching and learning. She remains committed to providing a voice for those in the school community who may become victims of these behaviours and to raising awareness about the importance of positive behaviour modelling within the school setting.

Genevieve T. Murray, BA, MSc, is a PhD student with the School of Education at Trinity College. Her research focuses on teacher-on-teacher workplace bullying in the Irish post-primary sector. She is a member of the Sociological Association of Ireland and the UCD Equality Society, where she was Auditor for 2008–9. She is at present lecturing on the Masters in Education (Aggression Studies) programme at Trinity College.

Orla Murray, BEd, MEd, is a primary school teacher based in Dublin. She is a member of the National Children's Strategy Consultation Oversight Committee, consulting with children and young people on the new National Children's Strategy (2011). Her main research interests are in alternative therapies which can help children overcome learning/behavioural difficulties. She is currently researching Animal-Assisted Therapy in order to improve literacy skills in children

Elaine O'Dowd has worked as a primary school teacher in Dublin since graduating from St Patrick's College of Education, Dublin with a BEd in 2004. She completed an MEd in Agression Studies in the School of Education at Trinity College Dublin in 2008. Her research involved an examination of the existence of bullying among the pupils in her own school and focused on strategies to counteract bullying and to increase its reporting by the students.

James O'Higgins Norman is a Senior Lecturer and Researcher in the School of Education Studies, Dublin City University, where he is also Chair of the initial teacher education programme. He has authored a number of books and reports on aspects of bullying, equality and well-being in schools. His research on homophobic bullying in secondary schools is considered to be seminal and led to a number of government initiatives to address bullying. He has presented conference papers on his research in Ireland, Australia, the UK, Finland and the USA. James is a co-founder of the Wellbeing, Interculturalism, Spirituality and Education Research (WISER) network which is based at Dublin City University.

Professor Mona O'Moore is the Founder and Director of the Anti-Bullying Research and Resource Centre in the School of Education in Trinity College Dublin. She is a graduate and Fellow of Trinity College, with an MA in Child and Educational Psychology from the University of Nottingham and PhD in Psychology from the University of Edinburgh. Prof. O'Moore also served as Head of the School of Education (2000–6) in Trinity College, and was a member of the ministerial working party that drew up the National Guidelines on Countering Bullying in Primary and Post-Primary Schools in Ireland in 1993. She was also a member of the Expert Advisory Group on workplace bullying (2005). She conducted the first nationwide study of both school and workplace bullying in

Ireland and has written widely on the subject of bullying, her most recent publication being *Understanding School Bullying: A Guide for Parents and Teachers* (Veritas, 2010).

Murray Smith, BL, MA (NUI), is a barrister at the Irish bar and a research assistant in the Anti-Bullying Centre, Trinity College Dublin. In the latter capacity he has been involved in research into school and workplace bullying. He has also been involved in policy development, having participated in most meetings of the Task Force on the Prevention of Workplace Bullying (1999–2001). He has lectured on law courses relating to property management, and has written articles for law journals concerning education and employment law.

Dr Paul Stevens has previously worked as a teacher and principal at primary level and has worked in postgraduate teacher education at third level. He has undertaken nationwide research into the bullying of primary principals in conjunction with the Irish Primary Principals' Network (IPPN). He is a graduate of Trinity College Dublin (BEd, MA, MLitt, PhD) and of Keele University (MBA) and is co-author of *Illusion or Inclusion: Educational Provision for Primary School Children with Mild General Learning Disabilities* (Blackhall Publishing, 2009). He is currently employed by the Inspectorate of the Department of Education and Skills and has recently completed an MSc in Learning and Teaching at Jesus College, University of Oxford.

Professor Keith Sullivan is the Statutory Professor of Education at NUI, Galway. He became interested in bullying when one of his children was being bullied. Dr Sullivan was educated at the University of Cambridge and the University of Leeds, England and at Concordia University, Canada. As recognition of his research and practical work in dealing effectively with bullying, he was appointed to the Charter Fellowship in Human Rights at Oxford University. He has written several books and numerous articles and presented lectures and workshops internationally on bullying and cyber-bullying.

Claire Sutton, BA Psych, MSc and currently studying for a D.PsychSc at University College Dublin, has previously worked as an assistant psychologist in an organisation providing services to children and adults with intellectual disabilities.

Madeleine Young was educated in London where she taught as an infant school teacher. She spent two years with the VSO scheme in Nigeria, training students to become primary teachers. From there she moved to Ireland and taught children with mild, moderate and severe learning disabilities and has since qualified with a BSc (Hons) in Psychotherapy and has her own practice, working with children, adolescents and adults. She completed an MEd at Trinity College where she researched the significance of mindfulness practices in a pre-school setting.

Preface

James O'Higgins Norman

Bullying in schools has received attention in research since the 1970s when Olweus began to study the issue in Sweden (1978). Internationally, the late 1980s and 1990s saw an increased awareness of the negative effects associated with school bullying and consequently there was an increase in the amount of research in this area in Ireland (O'Moore and Hillery, 1989), Scotland (Mellor, 1990), the Netherlands (Mooij, 1993), England (Whitney and Smith, 1993) and Australia (Rigby, 1998). The development in 1996 of the Anti-Bullying Centre at Trinity College was a significant moment in Irish education and now that the Centre has moved to Dublin City University we will ensure that bullying in schools remains on the agenda for researchers, teachers, parents and policy makers. The recent publication of the Action Plan on Bullying in January 2013 by the Minister for Education and Skills reflects a renewed concern about bullying in schools. The young person who is repeatedly bullied at school can experience anxiety, loss of confidence, loneliness and depression. This can result in punctuality problems, deteriorating academic attainment, poor attendance, truancy, early school leaving, mental health problems and even ideas of suicide (Parker and Asher, 1987; Sharp, 1995; Olweus, 1993; Rigby, 1998; Hunt and Jensen, 2006).

Many of the earlier studies of bullying relied on definitions that were based on the work of Olweus who defined school bullying as:

> ... when another student, or group of students, say nasty and unpleasant things to him or her. It is also bullying when a student is hit, kicked, threatened, locked inside a room, sent nasty notes, when no one ever talks to them or things like that. These things can happen frequently and it is difficult for the student being bullied to defend himself or herself. It is also bullying when a student is teased repeatedly in a nasty way. But it is not bullying when two students of the same strength have the odd fight or quarrel.

> Olweus, 1993, pp. 9–10

In essence, these earlier researchers understood bullying mostly in terms of *repeated aggressive behaviour* arising from a deliberate intent to cause physical or psychological distress to others. This has sometimes led to a tendency on the part of researchers, policy makers, teachers and parents to overly pathologise those who bully and those who are bullied (Kumpulainen, 2008; Pollastri et al., 2009). Such a focus on bullying *behaviour* ignores the reality that a huge amount of bullying occurs because of a lack of tolerance for diversity and as such constitutes a form of discrimination.

My own research on initiatives to address bullying in schools revealed that several schools are now rolling out innovative anti-discrimination initiatives aimed at eliminating bullying (O'Higgins Norman et al., 2010). The most successful initiatives focused on diversity education and were supported by school leadership. While leadership obviously includes school management, it also involves external agencies including government and inspectorates and internally other school leaders such as chaplains, guidance counsellors and year heads.

In summary, it is important that we understand bullying as both a sociological and a psychological problem. Such a shift in how we understand bullying involves a recognition that while certain individuals are more likely to bully, the context in which they exist can also contribute towards an environment where bullying is more acceptable. Young people are rarely bullied because they are perceived to be the same as others; rather, they are often bullied because they stand out for being different from their peers. This reality points to the need for schools to promote diversity as a 'normal' part of life. If young people in schools are provided with an opportunity to reflect on difference as a positive aspect of life, levels of violence and aggression and other forms of discrimination can decrease.

Given that there has been so much research on bullying in schools, it is important that any new publication on this topic moves the debate forward and enhances our knowledge and skills in this area. The chapters contained within this book reflect research by academics and practitioners in a variety of settings. As such, the book not only makes a very significant contribution to the established body of knowledge on bullying in schools but will assist teachers, parents and school managers to enhance their skills with new ways of addressing the issue. I am particularly delighted and commend the editors who have ensured that a whole-school and cross-community theme underpins the research reported on in this book. *Bullying in Irish Education* will help to broaden our understanding of bullying as an issue that should be treated as a psychological *and* sociological experience, thus expanding the discourse on bullying to include a consideration of bullying both as a form of aggression and discrimination.

REFERENCES

Hunt, R. and Jensen, J. *Education for All: The School Report* (London: Stonewall, 2006)

Kumpulainen, K. 'Psychiatric Conditions Associated with Bullying', *International Journal of Adolescent Medicine and Health*, 20, 2008, pp. 121–32

Mellor, A. 'Bullying in Scottish Secondary Schools', *Spotlights*, 23 (Edinburgh: Scottish Council for Research in Education, 1990)

Mooij, T. 'Working towards Understanding and Prevention in the Netherlands', in D. Tattum (ed.), *Understanding and Managing Bullying* (London: Heinemann, 1993)

O'Higgins Norman, J., Goldrick, M. and Harrison, K. *Addressing Homophobic Bullying in Second-Level Schools* (Dublin: The Equality Authority, 2010)

O'Moore, A.M. and Hillery, B. 'Bullying in Dublin Schools', *The Irish Journal of Psychology*, 10, 1989, pp. 426–41

Olweus, D. *Aggression in the Schools: Bullies and Whipping Boys* (Washington DC: Hemisphere-Wiley, 1978)

Olweus, D. *Bullying at School: What We Know and What We Can Do About It* (Oxford: Blackwell, 1993)

Parker, J.G. and Asher, S.R. 'Peer Relations and Later Personal Adjustment: Are Low-Accepted Children At Risk?' *Psychological Bulletin*, 102, 1987, pp. 357–89

Pollastri, A.R., Cardemil, E.V. and O'Donnell, E.H. 'Self-Esteem in Pure Bullies and Bully/Victims: A Longitudinal Analysis', *Journal of Interpersonal Violence*, 25, 2009, pp. 1489–502

Rigby, K. 'Peer Relations at School and the Health of Adolescents', *Youth Studies*, 17, 1998, pp. 13–17

Sharp, S. 'How Much Does Bullying Hurt? The Effects of Bullying on the Personal Well-Being and Educational Progress of Secondary-Aged Students', *Educational and Child Psychology*, 12, 1995, pp. 81–8

Whitney, I. and Smith, P.K. 'A Survey of the Nature and Extent of Bullying in Junior/Middle and Secondary Schools', *Educational Research*, 35, 1993, pp. 3–25

Introduction

Paul Stevens and Mona O'Moore

Bullying continues to occur in any context where human beings interact with each other. Despite every person's fundamental right to feel safe, bullying is a feature of everyday life for many in their homes, schools or places of work or study. Yes, undoubtedly, awareness has been raised and the successful work to date in addressing this insidious behaviour needs to be acknowledged, but bullying still remains a critical social issue often with serious negative consequences for its victims. The education sector is where much of the research began and strategies to counteract bullying have been implemented but it is also the sector where it continues to thrive and flourish.

Those involved in education form a significant sector of Irish society. Many attending or employed in education have fallen victim of, or at least witnessed, bullying behaviour. However, there are those who do not report bullying and who have dipped under the radar because of the culture of silence around bullying which prevails in Irish society.

There are those who understand that bullying is indeed a serious negative behaviour and acknowledge that it has the capacity to seriously impair or destroy lives. Others recognise it as a feature of life but really give it little thought or serious consideration until perhaps someone close to them experiences it. There are those who, sometimes correctly, claim that the term 'bullying' has become overused and hackneyed to put a serious label on or exaggerate an everyday behaviour which is part of the occasional negative interactions which happen between people. While this may occur to some degree, it in no way takes away from the reality of genuine bullying behaviour which occurs. Finally, there are those who feel 'it toughens us up' and that 'it is a part of the rough and tumble of life' and should be endured as it 'is character-forming'.

1

Not surprisingly, therefore, our collective response as a nation could at best be described as lukewarm. Yes, there has been a national response of concern when RTÉ screened a *Prime Time* programme on bullying and cyber-bullying. And yes, the news of Phoebe Prince's suicide and subsequent teenage suicides in this country were a wake-up call to everyone that serious action needed to be taken as a matter of priority. However, it seems that people's genuine emotional responses are quickly forgotten as some new news story takes precedence and the sense of urgency fades. Despite overwhelming evidence of bullying behaviour in Irish society, there still exists no specific legislation. While the Department of Education and Skills' newly launched Action Plan brings new hope, like so many critical issues in education, it is left to management authorities at local level, albeit with some guidance, to devise and implement policy. The result is that where the majority take this responsibility seriously, there is great variance in the manner in which bullying is addressed.

For the majority of those employed in education, there has been dialogue, debate and a genuine effort to address the issue. A crucial part of this work has included academic research to enhance understanding, pilot innovation and an evaluation of the effectiveness of strategies. This book is part of that process and for the first time brings to the fore current research on bullying in education. Some of the chapters are based on the work of postgraduate students who undertook the MEd in Aggression Studies at Trinity College Dublin while others are based on master's or doctoral research studies undertaken at universities elsewhere.

The book is divided into five sections. Part One (Chapters 1–5) focuses on peer bullying in education. In Chapter 1 O'Moore reports comprehensively on the incidence of bullying in Irish primary and second-level schools and explores victimisation in terms of age, gender, school location and highlights an increase in incidence between 1993 and 2006. In addition, she looks at cyber-bullying and its overlap with traditional bullying and advocates a whole-school community approach, as outlined later in Chapter 12. In the second chapter McGuckin examines similar themes for schools in Northern Ireland, a landscape with a unique ethno-political history. Interesting comparisons between Ireland and the UK are drawn, while the chapter also reviews the responses of government and non-governmental agencies in terms of curriculum and legislation and includes some practical steps to address the phenomenon. Minton, in the third chapter, outlines the background to society's prevailing attitude to non-heterosexual orientation. Through a survey of homophobic bullying he reveals the impact on the Lesbian, Bisexual, Gay and Transgender (LBGT) school-going population, again with specific recommendations to reduce the incidence and consequences of bullying. Chapter 4 addresses the issue of non-reporting and O'Dowd explores the factors which inhibit victims from telling. The final chapter in Part One is concerned with bullying among the third-level population and McGuire details attitudes, experiences and differing manifestations of bullying among the biggest single educational grouping in Irish society.

Part Two (Chapters 6–7) contains two chapters reflecting on bullying in less traditional educational settings. Firstly, Healy has undertaken a study examining bullying among out-of-school children. Her findings suggest a complex population with levels of bullying which are sometimes disturbing and for whom the implementation of anti-bullying strategies can prove challenging. She concludes that the issue of bullying among this particularly vulnerable population merits further investigation. McGrath, Black and Sutton present the results of a two-phase research project with adults with intellectual disabilities in educational settings, revealing factors associated with incidence and interesting implications for state and voluntary bodies providing such education.

The third part of the book (Chapters 8–11) addresses the issue of workplace bullying in the education sector. In Chapter 8, Fahie presents critical factors associated with the workplace bullying of primary school teachers and argues that the concept of new managerialism has negatively altered the work environment and thus has contributed to an increase in bullying among teachers. In contrast, Stevens explores the concept of managers themselves being victims of bullying in Chapter 9. His nationwide study of primary school principals reveals the who, why and where of bullying of primary school principals and articulates their concerns in terms of consequences and existing policy for the resolution of incidents. In the next chapter, G. Murray provides an international overview of bullying in the education sector together with three vignettes from three second-level teachers who have been subjected to bullying. Finally, Monahan's challenging research regarding teacher/student relationships poses key questions which require further dialogue and research.

Part Four deals with strategies for addressing bullying and contains six chapters. O'Moore opens this section with a chapter describing a successful whole-school community approach which was piloted in Donegal and, if implementation of such an approach was fully supported on a nationwide basis, could bring enormous benefits in terms of reducing levels of bullying in schools. Sullivan introduces Action Against Cyber-bullying (AAC), a programme with four related components which he has designed to assist schools to understand the nature of school-related cyber-bullying and to develop processes to counteract it effectively. Kent and Fallon provide details of a second-level anti-bullying campagin which offers schools online support and resources.

The three remaining chapters in this section describe small-scale research projects which may offer greater possibilities: the use of massage in schools by O. Murray; the concept of 'mindfulness' among children by Young; and the benefits of 'teaching thinking' using Edward de Bono's 'Six Thinking Hats' by Kent. These three alternative approaches could certainly play a role in reducing aggressiveness and therefore bullying behaviour and should be considered for further development.

In the final part of the book, Smith offers a comprehensive overview of aspects of the law which relate to bullying. The first section provides definitions of bullying and cyber-bullying. This is followed by a detailed analysis of legal and quasi-legal documents including constitutional, criminal and civil legislation together with Department of Education circulars. These are examined in terms of content and their implications for individuals and schools. Finally, he presents previous case law in eight areas pertinent to children, parents and schools. While all cases may not deal specifically with bullying, all have possible application to bullying scenarios.

It is hoped that this book will stimulate interest, initiate dialogue, increase public awareness and encourage further research. There is general agreement that a cohesive national strategy addressing bullying is the only way forward. Firstly, a cultural shift is required where the primary objective on a national basis is to reduce risk. Effective parenting and successful pre-school and primary education intervention are all vital where the establishment of bully and victim behaviour patterns can be prevented or at least reduced. Support must be provided to address the issue at second and third level together with a commitment to preserve dignity in the workplace. Secondly, despite a preventative approach at all levels, bullying will occur and therefore a clear strategy for responding to incidents must be in place. Thirdly, and critically, there needs to be adequate and effective support services for victims, perpetrators and their families.

Minister Fitzgerald of the Department of Children and Youth Affairs and Minister Ruairi Quinn of the Department of Education and Skills convened an Anti-Bullying Forum on 17 May 2012 to explore ways to prevent and counter bullying in schools. A Working Group was subsequently tasked by the ministers to develop an action plan on bullying and this was launched on 30 January 2013. It reflects great promise with many excellent recommendations for best practice for school communities. Together with the knowledge and insights to be gained from this book, it is hoped that the new Anti-Bullying Procedures for Primary and Post-Primary Schools launched by the Minister for Education and Skills, Ruairi Quinn will witness the creation of circumstances that will protect an individual's right to a safer learning and working environment. Although we are in a financial and economic quagmire, if those working in education become ever more vigilant and strive to tackle bullying, we should see, as stated by Minister Ruairi Quinn in the Anti-Bullying Action Plan, 'a culture that encourages respect, values, opinions, celebrates differences and promotes positive relationships'. For society, what can be of greater value?

CHAPTER ONE

The Prevalence of Bullying and Cyber-Bullying in Irish Schools

Mona O'Moore

INTRODUCTION

To be bullied can have serious implications for an individual's physical and mental health, not to mention the demand for professional services. Maria Lawlor (2006), child and adolescent psychiatrist with the North-Eastern Health Board has demonstrated with the help of two case studies just how costly bullying can be. Quite apart from the professional staff time – educational, clinical and psychiatric – that is usually required, there is also the hidden personal costs to the individual and their family. For example, Dr Lawlor reported on a clever, attractive 14-year-old who was bullied physically and psychologically during her second year at post-primary school. The victimisation resulted in her becoming depressed and suicidal and as a result she was referred to psychiatric services. The psychiatric assessment found the girl 'to be suffering from post-traumatic stress disorder symptoms, depression, suicide ideation, low self-esteem, and severe anxiety symptoms. She attended for treatment for over eighteen months and was treated with psychotherapy, family therapy, parental counselling, medication and liaison meetings with the school and health board personnel.' The other case which Dr Lawlor referred to was that of a 9-year-old who required eighty-one hours of outpatient therapy and a three-month admission to a paediatric unit. The total cost of treatment using 2004 rates was €101,000.

These case studies and others (Holmquist, 2010; O'Moore, 2010) are supported by a growing number of empirical studies. For example, Hawker and Boulton (2000) were able to draw the conclusion from their meta-analytic review of peer victimisation and psychosocial maladjustment that victimisation is associated with a pattern of distress that can no longer be ignored.

While most of the research literature on the consequences of victimisation relates to traditional bullying, referred to sometimes as face-to-face bullying, there is a growing literature to show that to be cyber-bullied may indeed accelerate and amplify the hurt associated with being targeted (Shariff, 2008; Kowalski and Limber, 2007; Kowalski et al., 2008; Hinduja and Patchin, 2009). Flanagan (2010) found that 33% of teenagers surveyed believed cyber-bullying to have a worse effect on victims than that of traditional bullying. The teens who have come to the attention of the media as having taken their lives as a result of suffering cyber-bullying provide strong support for this view (*Irish Times*, Weekend Review, 18 September 2010).

Research is also growing which links children who bully with externalising and internalising problems. Cook et al. (2010), the authors of a recent meta-analytic investigation of the predictors of bullying and victimisation in childhood and adolescence, describe the typical bully as one who 'exhibits significant externalising behaviour, has internalising symptoms, has both social competence and academic challenges, possesses negative attitudes and beliefs about others, has negative self-regulated cognitions, has trouble resolving problems with others, comes from a family environment characterized by conflict and poor parental monitoring, is more likely to perceive his or her school as having a negative atmosphere, is influenced by negative community factors, and tends to be negatively influenced by his or her peers' (pp. 75–6). This study gives support to a Finnish longitudinal study (Sourander et al., 2007) which found that frequent bullying predicted most types of crime, including violent crime. This was the case even after controlling for the parents' education level. Indeed Kumpulainen (2008) concluded that 'rarely does any single behaviour predict future problems as clearly as bullying does'. Worrying as these results are, the picture is even worse when account is taken of the distinct group of children and teenagers who both bully and are bullied (bully-victims). The Finnish researchers confirmed findings from earlier studies, such as those of Olweus (1993), O'Moore and Hillery (1991) and O'Moore and Kirkham (2001), showing bully-victims to be more prone to anti-social personality disorders and to suffer more psychiatric symptoms in later years. They found that 30% of the bully-victims suffered from some kind of adult psychiatric disorder. The disorders included anxiety, depression, psychosis and substance abuse. The boys who had been both frequent bullies and frequent victims suffered the worst outcomes (Sourander et al., 2007). In a subsequent study of cyber-bullying Sourander et al. (2010) were able to show that cyber-bullying and cyber victimisation are associated also with psychiatric and psychosomatic problems. The most troubled were once again those who were both cyber-bullies and cyber-victims.

With findings such as the aforementioned there is a clear case for urgent action to prevent the serious and persistent nature of bullying and cyber-bullying. However to implement effective prevention and intervention strategies an accurate picture of the nature and extent of bullying and victimisation is necessary. This chapter aims to examine, therefore, the prevalence of bullying and cyber-bullying in Irish schools.

It should be noted that the prevalence rates that are presented in this chapter are based on the concept of bullying as being defined as a form of aggression which is intentional and unprovoked as well as being repeated over time. There is also some form of imbalance of power, whether it be physical or psychological, between aggressor(s) and victim(s). This means that once-off or isolated acts of aggression are not regarded as bullying behaviour, which supports the definition of bullying by the Department of Education and Skills (see Chapter 18 for further details on definition of bullying). However, it is my personal opinion that consideration should be given to encapsulating into a definition of bullying isolated acts of anti-social aggression which are unjustified and serve to intimidate on an ongoing basis (see O'Moore, 2010 for further discussion of this viewpoint).

In presenting the overview of cyber-bullying in this chapter, the practice is seen as an extension of traditional bullying where computers, mobile phones and other electronic devices are used to send insulting, threatening and abusive comments or images. Again, as with traditional bullying, there is no universally accepted definition of cyber-bullying. However, it is generally accepted that the aggressive behaviour is deliberate, repeated and that the target(s) have difficulty defending themselves due to a power imbalance. However, insisting that a cyber attack has to be repeated over time to be defined as cyber-bullying is still open for debate by academics and practitioners in view of the fact that a single abusive message or image can stay online indefinitely and can be seen by multiple viewers (Kirwan and Power, 2012).

BULLYING OTHERS

In 2004, the World Health Organisation (WHO) reported that over one third of young people (35%) were involved in bullying others at least once during the previous couple of months. A further 11% bullied others frequently (i.e. two or three times or more during the previous couple of months). The rates varied substantially across countries and regions. The mean percentage for the three age groups of 11, 13 and 15 years in respect of occasional bullying were: 30%, 38% and 36% respectively. For frequent bullying the rates for the three age groups were: 9%, 12% and 13% respectively. The difference between girls and boys was discernible, especially for frequent bullying, and this was true for three quarters of the countries and regions which the WHO surveyed.

From Table 1.1 below it can be seen that the boys in Irish schools who participated in the WHO study are close to the international average rate. Like most of their transnational counterparts, they showed a higher rate of bullying than the girls. However, overall at both levels of frequency Ireland was in the lowest quartile across all age groups.

Table 1.1: Percentage of young people in Ireland who bullied others occasionally and frequently in the previous couple of months (WHO, 2004).

	GIRLS			BOYS		
	11 yrs	13 yrs	15 yrs	11 yrs	13 yrs	15 yrs
Bullied others occasionally	13.6	15.7	17.8	24.2	32.3	30.6
Bullied others frequently	1.4	2.3	3.0	5.9	8.0	8.2

VICTIMISATION

The World Health Organisation reported that over one third (34%) of all young people in the thirty-five participating countries admitted to being bullied at least once during the previous couple of months. The mean proportions for occasional victimisation for the three age groups studied were: 38% in 11-year-olds; 36% in 13-year-olds and 27% in 15-year-olds. For frequent victimisation 11% of young people reported being bullied this often, the rates being 15%, 14% and 10% for ages 11, 13 and 15. Once again the rates varied significantly by country and region.

From Table 1.2, which shows the WHO rates for Ireland for young people of eleven, thirteen and fifteen years of age it can be seen that the level of victimisation is lower than the international average. Of note, although Ireland is no exception, is the decrease in the level of victimisation with age at both levels of frequency.

Table 1.2: Percentage of Irish young people who have been bullied occasionally and frequently in the previous couple of months (WHO, 2004).

	GIRLS			BOYS		
	11 yrs	13 yrs	15 yrs	11 yrs	13 yrs	15 yrs
Victimised occasionally	30.5	22.7	18.2	29.8	32.1	23.1
Victimised frequently	9.0	7.1	4.7	11.3	11.5	5.9

BULLY-VICTIMS

Reference has been made earlier to the fact that there are children who are both bullied and who bully others (bully-victims). As the WHO study did not make the distinction between the children who were only bullied ('pure victims') and those who only bullied others (the 'pure bullies'), I have unfortunately no means of comparing the proportion of bully-victims in their study with previous or subsequent studies conducted in Ireland.

WHY DO COUNTRIES DIFFER IN THE EXTENT OF BULLYING?

Comparing prevalence rates for being bullied and bullying others within or across countries can be difficult. There are several reasons for this, the most common being differences of age, of reporting periods and definitions of bullying. However, the comparisons which I have made between our nationwide study and the later WHO study are, in my opinion, realistic as both studies used the same definition of bullying (which was that of Olweus, 1993), the same reporting periods (that of a couple of months preceding the study) and the same response options with regard to the level of involvement (i.e. occasional and frequent victimisation and bullying). However, there is no knowing whether the substantially lower rate of involvement in bullying either as victims or bullies that was found in the nationwide study is an underestimate. It is possible that the greater awareness of bullying that has taken place in schools in the intervening years has made it easier to report victim/bully problems. In any event the levels reported by either study reflect an unacceptable level of bullying among the Irish school-going population.

HAS THE INCIDENCE OF BULLYING IN IRELAND INCREASED OVER TIME?

This is a question that I am frequently asked. If we look to the WHO rates for Ireland and compare them with the nationwide study which I conducted some eight years earlier (O'Moore et al., 1997), there is evidence of a substantial increase among both girls and boys in both the rate of being bullied and of bullying others.

Victimisation

We found that approximately one in ten pupils (10.6%) from age 11 to 15 reported that they were bullied occasionally. In the intervening years this has been shown by the WHO to have risen to at least one in four (26%). For moderate victimisation and frequent victimisation we reported 2.8% and 1.9% respectively. This contrasts to the WHO rate of 8.2% for frequent victimisation. It should be noted that the WHO did not distinguish as I did between moderate (being bullied sometimes) and frequent victimisation (being bullied once a week or several times a week). Instead they combined the two levels of involvement, which may explain why their reported level of frequent bullying is so high. However, if we combine the moderate and frequent levels found in our nationwide study, we obtain a rate of 4.7%. This still indicates that the rate of frequent bullying has risen substantially over an eight-year period.

Bullying others

A rise in the involvement in bullying can be seen also when we compare the rates for bullying others. Our nationwide study found that among the 11–15-year-olds, 11.7% bullied others occasionally, 2.7% sometimes and 1.0% frequently. The WHO study showed the rates to have risen to 22.4% for occasional bullying of others and 4.8% for frequent bullying of others. This suggests a considerable increase in both occasional and frequent bullying.

If we now look beyond the WHO study which was conducted in 2001/2 to our most recent national study, named the ABC study, which I conducted together with Stephen James Minton in 2005 (Minton, 2007, 2010) we can make a comparison over time in respect of pure victims, pure bullies and bully-victims. See Table 1.3 on next page.

Table 1.3: Comparison of percentages of pupils reporting involvement in bullying during the last three months in the 2004–2005 'ABC' survey and in the 1993–1994 nationwide survey.

INVOLVEMENT	PRIMARY PUPILS		POST-PRIMARY PUPILS	
	Nationwide survey (1993–1994)	'ABC' survey (2004–2005)	Nationwide survey (1993–1994)	'ABC' survey (2004–2005)
As a victim only	17.1	21.2	11.5	15.2
As a bully only	12.3	6.8	10.8	13.5
As both a bully and a victim	14.1	7.3	4.1	7.7
Total Involvement	43.5	35.3	26.5	36.4

Primary school pupils

The results, as can be seen from Table 1.3 above, are very encouraging with regard to children attending primary schools. Overall there was a lower incidence of general involvement in bullying behaviour in the recent 'ABC' survey when we compare it with the 1993–1994 nationwide survey (35.3% versus 43.5% respectively). There were, in particular, lowered instances in the 'involvement as a bully only' (6.8% in the 'ABC' survey, versus 12.3% in the 1993 nationwide survey) and 'involvement as both a bully and a victim' category (7.3% in the 'ABC' survey, versus 14.1% in 1993 nationwide survey). However, the higher incidence of involvement as a 'victim only' (21.2%) in the 'ABC' survey when compared with the 1993 nationwide survey (17.1%) does present a cause for concern. The reasons are not obvious but one possibility may be that not enough attention was paid to the promotion of cultural diversity at the time when Ireland was becoming more multi-cultural and multi-denominational. O'Higgins Norman (2012), for example, is very much of the view that more needs to be done in schools to promote diversity as a 'normal' part of life. He believes that if young people are provided with an opportunity to reflect on difference as a positive aspect of life, levels of violence and aggression and other forms of discrimination can decrease.

Post-primary pupils

Pupils of post-primary in contrast to primary school pupils have shown a marked increase in their total involvement in bullying over ten years since the first study was conducted. In 1993/4 the level stood at 26.4% while in 2004/5 it had risen to 36.4%. Table 1.3 shows the percentage increase for victims, bullies and bully-victims over the ten-year period.

To conclude from the data that we have collected over the years on the prevalence of bullying in Ireland it would seem that there has been a decrease in the total involvement of bullying among children of primary school age, with the exception of pure victims. Unfortunately, the opposite is the case for post-primary school pupils. An increase was evident for all types of involvement, namely that of 'pure bully', 'pure victim' and 'bully-victim'. This trend may reflect that more work has been done at primary than at post-primary level to counteract the bullying. While the greater level of reporting among victims may seem to contradict this, it could be argued that the increased awareness of bullying over the years has enabled victims to more readily admit to being victims, thereby giving us a more accurate account of the level of victimisation. This may also explain the increase found among the post-primary pupils. Of course it is also possible that the heightened awareness may have the result of making 'bullies' feel somewhat more ashamed of their behaviour, prompting as a result a greater reluctance to admit to bullying. Were this the case, it may explain the decrease in 'bullying others' that we found among the primary school children. But it does not explain the increase found among the post-primary pupils. However, the questions which the findings raise point to the need to study changes in the extent and frequency of bullying from early school age to adulthood.

AGE DIFFERENCES IN VICTIMISATION AND BULLYING

As children grow older, victimisation tends to decrease. This is a universal phenomenon and Ireland is no exception. Using the data from O'Moore et al. (1997), Figure 1.1 presents the year differences (mean percentage rates) of those who are bullied only (pure victims), those who bully only (pure bullies) and those who both bully and are bullied (bully-victims) from third class in Irish primary schools through to sixth year in post-primary schools. For a detailed breakdown of the differences of girls and boys with age, see O'Moore (2010).

Unfortunately, it was not possible to sample children younger than eight as the questionnaires were not suitable for children younger than this. However, some children did report experiences that they had when they were even younger. A sixth-class pupil for example stated: 'when I was in baby infants I was bullied by two or three boys in sixth class.' However, where younger children have been represented in studies it has been found that they tend to be bullied more often than children in higher grades.

Figure 1.1: Percentage of victims, bullies and bully-victims from third class in primary school to sixth year in post-primary school.

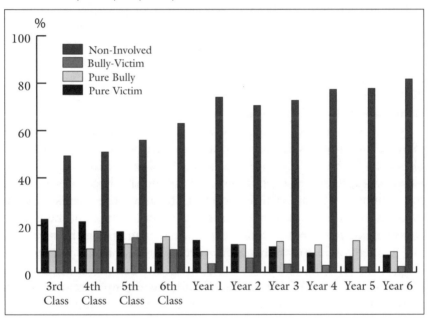

WHY IS THERE AN AGE DECLINE IN VICTIMISATION?

It has been shown that the age decline may be due to several factors (Smith, Madsen and Moody, 1999). These are as follows:

- young children are faced with more older children who can bully them.
- young children have not yet acquired the social skills and asser-tiveness skills to cope effectively with bullying incidents.

- young children have a different definition of what bullying is, which changes as they get older. Essentially 'their understanding of the term "bullying" may broadly encompass "something someone does that is nasty and hurts me" without any of the qualifications about repetition, inequality of power, or intent, which usually come into adult definitions or research questionnaires' (Smith and Levan, 1995). Guerin (2001) found also that children (aged 10–13 years) focus more on the effect on the victim and victim's interpretation of the incident. She found that less than 10% of the children surveyed found that aggressive behaviour needed to occur regularly in order for it to be defined as bullying.

While our results showed an overall decline from age 8 to 18 for pure victims it increased for boys in second year of post-primary school (approximate age being 13/14 years of age). This trend was also evident ten years later as reflected in the ABC study (Minton, 2007, 2010). As bullying that is experienced in early adolescence may be the worst and the most memorable to victims (Eslea and Rees, 2000), extra care needs therefore to be taken to minimise the risks of victimisation during early adolescence.

In contrast to the age decline in victimisation, there is a steady increase in pure bullies as they advance through primary school. However, by first year in post-primary school the incidence is almost halved but it increases again in second year and third year. Fortunately the number of bully-victims declines steadily from primary right through to sixth year in post-primary school although there is a considerable increase in second year, in particular among the boys.

The increase in the bullying of others which we found among the early adolescents in Ireland over a period of a decade is a worldwide phenomenon. The WHO (2004) found, for example, that bullying peaked at 13 years of age in twenty of the thirty-five countries in their survey. The reasons for this trend are not fully understood. Quite apart from blaming it on the surge of hormones that characterise adolescence at this age, it is thought that when they reach the higher grades they have more scope to target those younger than themselves. Evidence of this view can be gained from a third-year pupil in our nationwide study who reported that 'I bully first years because they are defenceless and I can take my anger out on them as well as their money.'

We found one third of Irish victims reported that they were bullied by pupils in higher classes. It is also not unimaginable that, for Ireland at least, the extra supervision and attention that is afforded pupils in first year of senior school may play a part in keeping the level of bullying down. Many first-year pupils tend not to know each other, as they come in from different primary schools, and in which case they may need some time before they can get a measure of each other's strengths and weaknesses. Lacking friends is a risk factor, Wang, Iannotti and Nansel (2009) having shown that having friends is associated with less victimisation. 'Bullies' will focus on the classmates for whom significant others do not care. Because children who bully are in pursuit of status and affection, they will therefore choose their potential victims so as to minimise loss of affection among their peers (Veenstra et al., 2010). Clearly it will take some time to work out the social status of each member of their class or year. It goes to show that bullying is very much a process and that much of peer interaction is about posturing and testing each other out to see who the easy targets may be.

GENDER DIFFERENCES IN VICTIMISATION AND BULLYING

The WHO study found that most countries 'show more similarity between the genders than the contrary and some show slightly more girls reporting victimisation'. However, both our large-scale studies carried out in Ireland (O'Moore et al., 1997; O'Moore and Minton, 2005; Minton, 2007, 2010) found as did Belgium (French) and Israel that significantly more boys than girls were bullied.

Figure 1.2: The level of victimisation among boys and girls from primary (class 3–6) to post-primary school (year 1–6).

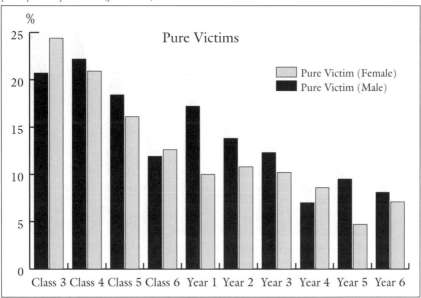

The differences in the level of victimisation between Irish boys and girls from third class in primary to sixth year in post-primary which were found in the nationwide study (O'Moore et al., 1997) can be seen in Figure 1.2 on previous page. The reasons for this trend are unclear. However, contributing to it may be society's attitude to aggression and any inequality of the sexes that may still prevail in Ireland. It is to be expected that there would be more male bullying in macho societies and that girls might under-report in cultures which conform to the more traditional gender stereotype. That inequality has powerful psychosocial effects has been demonstrated in a most convincing manner by Richard Wilkinson and Kate Pickett in their recent book *The Spirit Level* (Wilkinson and Pickett, 2009). They found that in the more unequal societies children experience more bullying, fights and conflicts.

Figure 1.3 below shows the gender differences in respect of bullying others from the age of 8/9 to 17/18 years of age. The frequency of the bullying of others is reported on in O'Moore et al. (1997). The higher proportion of male 'bullies' in each year group finds support in the WHO study referred to earlier. Essentially it found that 'in all countries and regions and for all age groups boys report bullying others more than girls'.

Figure 1.3: The level of bullying of others among boys and girls from primary (class 3–6) to post-primary school (year 1–6)

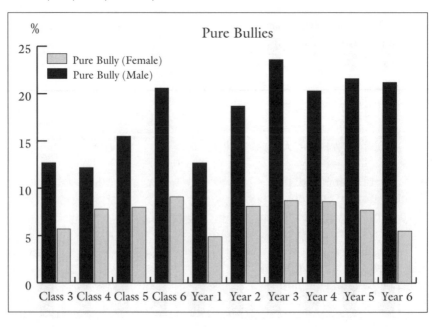

There are few prevalence studies with which to compare the level of bully-victims found in our nationwide study. However, Figure 1.4 shows that boys at all ages are more prone than are girls to being bully-victims. As bully-victims experience the worst of both worlds, it is good to see that there is a decline in both sexes with age, although second year is associated with an increase, especially among the boys. Ten years on has shown the same pattern of results as above, although overall there is evidence of fewer bully-victims at primary but more at post-primary school (Minton, 2007, 2010).

Figure 1.4: The level of bully-victims among boys and girls from primary (class 3–6) to post-primary school (year 1–6)

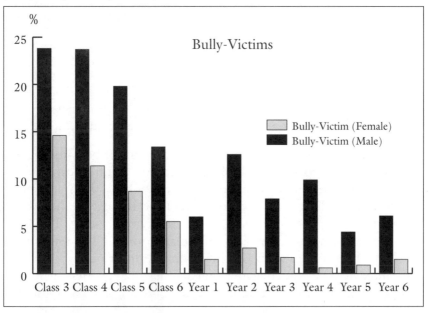

WHO CARRIES OUT THE BULLYING?

In Irish primary and post-primary schools we found that boys are bullied almost entirely by other boys, whereas girls are bullied by both boys and girls, although to a somewhat lesser extent to being bullied by other girls (O'Moore et al., 1997). When girls were bullied by boys, the bullying was predominantly dyadic (one boy against one girl). Over half the pupils (59%) were bullied by one individual in contrast to being bullied by a group of fellow pupils.

Table 1.4 below shows that the victims in both primary and post-primary were predominantly bullied by pupils from their own class. It can also be seen that pupils can be bullied by those younger than themselves, i.e. almost one in ten primary school children and almost one in twenty post-primary pupils. It is to be expected that to be bullied by someone younger may be more threatening to a child or teenager's self-esteem than it is to be faced down by a classmate of one's own age or older.

Table 1.4: Percentage of victims reporting in which class/year were the pupils by whom they were bullied.

	PRIMARY N = 3,101	POST-PRIMARY N = 1,775
In class or year where the bullies were in the victim's own class	56.5	46.3
In a different class but the same year	15.3	30.8
In years above	36.4	35.6
In years below	9.5	4.5

It is critical in our efforts to ascertain the amount of bullying in Irish schools that we do not overlook the fact that children can also be bullied by teachers and members of their family. A third-year pupil in our nationwide study, for example, had this to say: 'We have been bullied by a certain teacher. Since the first day of her class, I've been sitting on my own and she picks on me and others.' The few studies that have been undertaken on the victimisation of pupils by school staff indicate that the negative impact may be greater than that for peer victimisations (Khoury-Kassabri, Astor and Benbenishty, 2008). This was certainly evident in respect of some of the pupil response in our study. One pupil, for instance, who, while not herself bullied, nonetheless commented that 'Some teachers can be quite nasty and the person who is picked on is usually quite upset.' This sentiment was confirmed by the pupil, who wrote: 'One particular teacher picks on me regularly and she often has me in tears. She's a great teacher and I try my hardest but she has a very bad temper and she's impatient.' Because bullying by teachers tends to be a public degradation, it generates much publicity and for this reason it can become more humiliating than peer-on-peer bullying. Sadly it can also promote peer-on-peer bullying, as was pointed out by one second-year pupil who remarked: 'I think sometimes because a teacher bullies someone they think it is right and so they do it to someone else.'

In recognising that teachers can be guilty of bullying (see Chapter 11 in this book) it is equally important to not underestimate that teachers can also be bullied by pupils. They can be ridiculed, threatened or otherwise abused both online and face to face. The consequences of pupil-on-teacher bullying can be every bit as damaging to mental and physical health as teacher-on-pupil bullying.

WHERE BULLYING TAKES PLACE IN SCHOOL

In primary schools, we showed that the majority of children (74%) reported that they were bullied in the playground (O'Moore et al., 1997). The classroom was reported by the children (31%) as the next most likely place to be bullied. More primary school pupils (16%) reported that they were bullied 'in other places in the school' than they were in the corridors (7%).

In second-level schools, the most common place to be bullied is in the classrooms (47% of pupils). The next most likely place to be bullied was in the corridors (37%). Then there were 27% of post-primary pupils who said they were bullied in the playground and 15% who reported that they were bullied somewhere else in the school. The other places included: the toilets, changing rooms, locker areas, and dormitories in boarding schools. These findings are not unique to Ireland. Many other countries worldwide share a similar trend (Sullivan, 2000).

GOING TO AND FROM SCHOOL

Some 8% of primary school pupils and 2.8% of post-primary pupils reported that they were bullied 'sometimes or more often' on the way to and from school. An additional 11% of primary pupils and 6% of post-primary pupils stated that they had been bullied 'once or twice' on their way to or from school. The types of bullying involved a lot of physical attacks, such as being tripped, kicked and pushed to the ground and having one's money or personal belongings taken. The following are some examples:

> 'I would be walking down the road and some lads would hop on me and beat me up and sometimes they rob my money' (Post-primary second-year pupil).

'After school I've been bullied. I was thrown over a wall' (Primary fourth-class boy).

'Every time on my way home a bloke of 16 will hit me or kick me' (Post-primary first-year pupil).

There were also threats of violence. For example one girl reported the following:

'Two girls took me and my friend down to the field and said if we did not fight each other they would kill us and they tried to take our money. We managed to run away.' (Primary fourth-class girl).

Another girl had this to say: 'Outside school a girl chased me all the way home. She told me if she got me she was going to kill me. Since then every day that girl is at me.' (Primary fourth-class girl).

On occasions, belongings were set on fire. Thus books, schoolbags and overcoats were sometimes destroyed. One child even reported he was thrown in a river, others told that they were prevented from catching their buses or trains home. Some pupils even mentioned that they were sexually abused.

In relation to the extent of bullying others, 8% of primary school pupils and 4% of post-primary pupils admitted that they bullied others 'once or twice' on their way to and from school. Another 3% of primary and 1.3% of post-primary pupils said they bullied others 'sometimes or more often'. It is noteworthy that 33% of primary pupils and 26% of post-primary pupils who bullied in school reported that they also bullied on their way to and from school. Of those who bullied frequently in school, i.e. once a week or more, 64% of primary pupils and 59% of post-primary also bullied outside of school.

SCHOOL SPORTS

Taking part in sports offers children and adolescents great opportunities to develop new skills, to be part of a group, have fun, learn to win and lose and gain in confidence. Yet sadly much bullying occurs within the organised school sports environment causing children much distress and to quit their chosen sport. In our nationwide study, it was not uncommon to come across statements such as the following:

'I was punched and pushed and called all kinds of names and told by the person I'm going to get you and that you are dead. I am pushed to the ground at all games of football and have been kicked and my hair pulled.' (Primary fifth-class pupil)

'At football training I am better than a much older boy and he bullies me.' (Primary sixth-class pupil)

'At hurling training a boy would try to hit me with the ball when we are lining up to take shots.' (Post-primary first-year pupil)

'When I play rugby with the third years some of the players bully me after the match.' (Post-primary first-year pupil)

'I get called names about my weight but I like to take part in sports. They say that I have no right to do sport with my weight and size. I hate being slagged.' (Post-primary third-year pupil)

DO SCHOOLS DIFFER IN THE EXTENT OF BULLYING?

From the major Irish studies and the individual commissioned studies which our Trinity College's Anti-bullying Centre have conducted, the evidence points to considerable differences between schools in the level of bullying and victimisation. Possible reasons for this have been explored and these are reported on in some detail in O'Moore et al. (1997). The determinants which we examined were the following:

- school size
- class size
- ability grouping
- single-sex and co-educational
- advantaged/disadvantaged status
- location: rural/urban
- social composition of schools

Many other factors in addition to the above can be at play in determining school differences in the level of bullying, such as curricular activities, disciplinary measures and the values and attitudes of the school community. For further information on these factors, see Gittins (2006).

HOW MANY IRISH PUPILS ARE AFFECTED BY CYBER-BULLYING?

As cyber-bullying is a relatively new phenomenon, studies are only beginning to emerge. However, there is considerable urgency in finding effective preventative and intervention measures in view of the anonymous, instant and far-reaching communication capabilities of this form of bullying. The threat which it poses to schools in Ireland has already been noted (*Irish Times*, 18 May 2012).

Researchers have not yet reached a consensus on the definiton of cyber-bullying, this being one of the aims of the COST (European Coperation in Science and Technology) Action (IS0801) on Cyber-bullying which had 28 countries sharing experiences on cyber-bullying in educational settings. However, it has been defined as willful and repeated harm inflicted through the use of computers, cell phones and other electronic devices (Hinduja and Patchin, 2009).

The studies which have been conducted in Irish schools to date (Corcoran, Connolly and O'Moore, 2012; Flanagan, 2010; O'Moore and Minton, 2009; O'Moore, 2012; O'Neill, Grehan and Olafson, 2011) indicate that there are fortunately far fewer children and adolescents who are involved in cyber-bullying than in traditional bullying.

Building on the preliminary findings of O'Moore and Minton (2009) the complete data set on the 3,004 12–17-year-old pupils (1,009 girls and 1,995 boys), which formed part of a study commissioned by RTÉ's *Prime Time* programme (broadcast on 19 May 2008), showed that there were 18.3% of Irish pupils, almost one in five, who admitted to being involved in cyber-bullying either as pure victim (9.3%), pure bully (4.4%) or bully-victim (4.1%). Pure victims were those who reported that they were victims only and had therefore never bullied others. Pure bullies were those who bullied only and had therefore never been victimised. Bully-victims were the pupils who admitted to both bullying others as well as being bullied.

The rate for traditional bullying in comparison to cyber-bullying was nearly one in two (41.8% with 17.5% pure victims, 12.1% pure bullies and 12.3% bully-victims). There were 33.1% (39% girls and 29.9% boys) who were witness to and had knowledge of those who were traditionally bullied as compared to 28.4% of pupils (29.4% girls and 27.7% boys) who admitted to having knowledge of those who cyber-bullied. For details of the sampling and methodology see O'Moore (2012).

There are not many studies on cyber-bullying worldwide that have used the bullying classification of pure victims, pure bullies and cyber-bullies, which makes for limited cross-cultural comparisons with our Irish data. However, looking to Table 1.5, which lists those studies that have employed the same typology, we see that Canada and the USA report higher rates than Ireland. However, care needs to be taken when comparing these incident rates as differing definitions would have been used, as well as differing methodologies, reporting periods, age and sub-categories of cyber-bullying. Wang et al. (2009) have reported for example, how even within the USA the prevalence rates for cyber-bullying have ranged from 6% to 42%.

Table 1.5: Transnational percentage rates of cyber-bullying

TRANSNATIONAL STUDIES	CYBER-VICTIMS	CYBER-BULLIES	CYBER BULLY-VICTIMS
Ybarra and Mitchell (2004), USA	4.0	12.0	3.0
Li (2005), Canada	24.9	14.5	4.6
Kowalski and Limber (2007), USA	11.1	4.1	6.8
Ortega, Calmaestra and Mora-Merchan (2008), Spain	10.8	7.4	8.4
Hinduja and Patchia (2009), USA	10.0	8.0	5.0
Renati, Berrone and Zanetti (2009), Italy	7.0	6.0	6.0
Pyzalski (2010), Poland	6.5	19.5	6.0
Sourander et al. (2010), Finland	4.8	7.4	5.4
O'Moore (2012), Ireland	9.8	4.4	4.1

Of interest is to compare Ireland with Finland as both studies were carried out at around the same time in 2008. It is of note that while total involvement in cyber-bullying is almost identical for both countries (Finland: 17.6% and Ireland 18.3%) Ireland reports more cyber-victims than Finland with the situation reversed for the cyber-bullies. The reasons for this are not obvious. With the reporting periods being different (six months for Finland and a couple of months for Ireland) the expectation would be that Finland would report higher rates. As this was not the case it is, therefore, tempting to speculate whether Finnish adolescents may be more adept at dealing with cyber-bullying than their Irish counterparts or are there cultural differences in how they perceive and readily admit to victimisation and bullying?

Of great value for comparative purposes is the recent EU Kids Online report (Livingstone, Haddon, Görzig and Ólafsson, 2011).

Applying the same methodology and measurements in each of the twenty-five European Union countries surveyed, they found a wide variation in the prevalence of cyber-bullying across Europe with a range of 2% to 14%. O'Neill et al. (2011), reporting on Irish children aged 9–16 years, found only a small proportion (4%) were bullied online, or by mobile phone calls, texts or image/video texts. They reported, however, a sharp increase with age with 1% of 9–10-year-olds having been bullied on the internet as compared with 9% of 15–16-year-olds. Similarly they found 1% of 9–10-year-olds as compared to 10% of 15–16-year-olds having been subjected to hurtful or nasty behaviour by mobile phone calls, texts or image/video texts.

GENDER AND AGE DIFFERENCES IN CYBER-BULLYING

Gender

In contrast to traditional bullying where boys tend to be more involved in bullying than girls, the opposite, as can be seen from Table 1.6, was found to be true for cyber-bullying (O'Moore, 2012). In this we support the literature on cyber-bullying and it reinforces the view that cyber-bullying is especially attractive to girls as it tends towards the more indirect, non-physical and relational forms of bullying. Shariff (2008) is also of the opinion that cyberspace allows girls to break away from cultural and social non-feminist expectations and stereotypes.

Table 1.6: Percentage of pupils in Ireland reporting involvement in cyber-bullying behaviour

| INVOLVEMENT | GENDER | | TOTAL |
	BOYS	GIRLS	
As a victim only	6.9	15.6	9.8
As a bully only	4.9	3.5	4.4
As both a bully and a victim	3.9	4.5	4.1
Total Involvement	15.7	23.6	18.3

If you look again to Table 1.6 you will see that while there were almost three times as many girls than boys who were cyber-victims, there were fewer Irish girls than boys who admitted to being cyber-bullies. It should be noted that girls have been known to under-report the extent to which they conventionally bully and in which case this may also be true of their cyber-bully status in our study. Hinduja and Patchin (2009) report that in their review of cyber-bullying studies there was only one study, by Ybarra and Mitchell (2007), which found boys to be more likely to be the online perpetrators. Yet Wang et al. (2009) and Guarini, Brighiand and Genta (2010) have since shown that boys were more likely to be cyber-bullies. Thus it would appear that the relationship between gender and bullying is still open for debate.

Looking to the different forms of cyber-abuse that boys and girls use we found that girls were the primary targets of all forms of cyber-abuse with the exception of being subjected to mobile camera and video clips. There were 11% boys as compared with 8% girls who reported having been subjected to this form of cyber-bullying. While boys perpetrated all forms of cyber-bullying more than girls, it seemed that they relied more on the camera than on any of the other methods of electronic bullying. For example, 25.6% of boys had either taken or sent camera or video clips as compared to 15.7% who had sent text messages. Being noted for being less verbal in their behaviour than girls it is perhaps not surprising that they would prefer to convey their message by using the camera. After all, a picture can be very direct and has, as we all know, 'the power to tell more than a thousand words'. The fact that boys also tend to be more into things that are 'techie' means that the camera lends itself well in this respect. For a detailed breakdown of the different forms of cyber-bullying for boys and girls, see O'Moore (2012).

Age

When we examined our data as to whether the same age trend existed for cyber-bullying as it did for traditional bullying, the pattern was not so clear-cut. As we only have cyber-bullying data on post-primary school children, it is not possible to compare cyber-bullying with traditional bullying at the primary level of education. However, comparing first year through to fourth year shows that the significant increase that was typical of traditional bullying in second year of post-primary school was not found in respect of cyber-bullying. Some individual forms of cyber-bullying, however, did appear to reflect an increase in second year. For example, 19.7% of boys in second year as compared to 7.5% in first year reported that they had made a nasty, aggressive or threatening call to others from a mobile phone. Similarly 9.4% of second-year as compared to 4% of first-year pupils admitted to 'having sent a mobile phone camera picture of others that they would think is threatening or embarrassing'. Both boys and girls in second year as compared to the other three years also reported having the highest level of nasty, aggressive, threatening or embarrassing things posted about them on the internet. These findings lend support to O'Neill et al. (2011) in so much as they showed a substantial increase from age 11/12 to 13/14 in the level of online bullying and mobile phone calls, texts or image/video texts.

DO CYBER-BULLIES AND VICTIMS DIFFER FROM TRADITIONAL BULLIES AND VICTIMS?

Livingstone et al. (2011) have pointed out that there tends to be more cyber-bullying in countries where there is more bullying. They view, therefore, cyber-bullying and traditional bullying to be connected, 'part of a vicious cycle in which perpetrators reach their victims through diverse means and victims find it hard to escape' (p. 25). Our study found that over two thirds (67.4%) of cyber-bullies were also bullying their schoolmates in a traditional manner. Of note also was that almost one third of the cyber-bullies (32%) admitted to being traditional victims. Of the cyber-victims, the majority (71%) were traditional victims while well over one quarter (28.9%) were also traditional bullies. As investigation of cyber-bullying is at an early stage it is too soon to say whether cyber-bullying is to quote Li (2007), 'a new bottle but old wine'. Wang et al. (2009) believe there is a distinct difference based on the friendship patterns of those involved in cyber-bullying as compared with the more traditional forms of bullying, i.e. physical, verbal and relational. However, Corcoran et al. (2012) have shown that cyber-victims and traditional victims display similar patterns across personality and self-concept.

HOW IRISH VICTIMS RESPONDED TO CYBER-BULLYING

Victims responded to cyber-bullying in varying ways, ranging from doing nothing, getting really angry, to telling a friend or a parent or reporting the abuse to the service provider. Of the 564 victims in our study, only 16% (21% girls and 12% boys) asked the cyber-bully to stop. For example, one second-year boy remarked: 'I talked to him and then it stopped.' Another reported: 'I got aggressive and said leave me alone'. Worryingly, one pupil responded with: 'I cut myself.'

It is not clear whether the reason for choosing not to intervene may be personal or that they may simply not know the identity of the cyber-bully. We do know, however, that almost 7% were afraid to tell anyone, with little difference between the boys and girls. Telling friends (35%) was more common than telling parents (18%) with girls twice as likely as boys to confide in either of them. The fact that almost one third of pupils sent back an angry message indicates the lack of awareness of best practice in relation to dealing with cyber-bullying. On getting angry, one pupil remarked: 'I punched him.' Another said: 'I started a fight' and yet another stated: 'I broke his nose.'

More detail on the gender breakdown of the victims for the different forms of coping with cyber-bullying can be gained in O'Moore (2012).

HOW DO BYSTANDERS REACT TO CYBER-BULLYING?

We found that only a minority (1%) of the 859 pupils who were witness to cyber-bullying alerted a teacher or a parent to the fact that a pupil was being cyber-bullied. It was encouraging, however, that one in twenty pupils (6% girls and 5% boys) said they tried to stop the bullying. The methods of intervention among boys, however, tended to involve some form of verbal or physical aggression. One pupil remarked: 'I told the bully to "f" off.' Another said: 'I beat them up'. Yet another stated: 'I turned the bully into a victim.' The pupil responses essentially showed just how easily violence begets violence. However, there were pupils who stated that they reported the abuse to the social networking site such as Facebook. One such pupil remarked further that whereas 'schools should not need to ban websites they should, however, offer advice on how to use them properly and should offer support to victims of cyber-bullying and have an easy person to talk to about the matter'.

A positive feature of the responses given was that there were at least some pupils – if only 7%, with more girls (9%) than boys (5%) – who were willing to support the victim. One pupil remarked: 'I helped the person who was getting bullied and taught him how to respond.'

There were 6% of pupils, slightly more girls than boys, who were upset at what they witnessed but did nothing to stop it. A minority of pupils (0.55% girls and 1.5% boys) stated that they joined in the cyber-bullying and a further 3% (2% girls and 5% boys) admitted to having fun watching it.

WHAT DO PUPILS THINK OF CYBER-BULLYING?

On asking the 3,004 pupils what they thought about cyber-bullying, we found that less than half of the pupils (47% girls and 43% boys) thought it was wrong. There were those who thought it was stupid, pointless, distasteful, sickening, cynical and cowardly, and simply pathetic, with the latter pupil adding that, 'the bullies are just pathetic going to such extremes to put someone else through such misery.' One fourth-year pupil felt that sometimes arguments occur on the internet because people are too afraid to say certain things to people's faces.

There were one in five pupils who said cyber-bullying upset them, with more girls (25%) upset than boys (14%). Considerably more boys (10%) than girls (1%) thought it was part of life. Typical comments were: 'I think it is part of the risk of having a phone, email and personal page.'

PUPIL OPINIONS AS TO WHAT SCHOOLS CAN DO TO PREVENT AND DEAL WITH CYBER-BULLYING

When the pupils were asked for their opinion as to what schools can do to prevent and deal with cyber-bullying, they provided an extremely rich source of very insightful and practical ideas. The most popular response, given by 18% of the pupils, was that schools can do little to deal with cyber-bullying, the reason for this being, as one girl put it, 'schools do not have sufficient technology or resources to monitor the cyber-bullying'. Another girl had this to say: 'I do not believe it is up to the school but to the people within the year. If everyone stands up for one another there would be no cyber-bullying. The only problem is people are too scared to stand up for people because it means they might lose face or popularity.'

Other pupils put the onus on the service providers, saying, for example, that 'the internet is too large to be monitored by teachers or school personnel. It's up to the sites themselves to control what's being said on their site through administrators. It's entirely up to the pupils to go to teachers for help with things like this, individually.'

There were other responses to the one above which indicated that there was little realisation or appreciation of the difficulty or reluctance of pupils to report incidents of cyber-bullying. For example, one pupil was of the opinion that 'schools shouldn't butt their noses in at all; if someone wants help they'll ask.'

The fact that most cyber-bullying occurs outside of school was recognised by pupils as a major obstacle for schools wishing to tackle the problem.

Over one in ten pupils believed blocking websites would help to reduce cyber-bullying. A much smaller proportion of pupils suggested the blocking of internet access (4%) and the forbidding of mobile phones in school (8%). Three times as many girls as boys believed the banning of mobile phones in school would be an effective measure. Monitoring pupil activity was mentioned by 12% of the pupils, a view shared equally between the boys and girls. Of note was the considerably greater number of girls (14%) than boys (4%) who opted for 'raising awareness among pupils'.

One girl, for example, had the following to say:

> Schools can talk about cyber-bullying openly, explaining the effects it has on people and how any sort of bullying hurts. Schools can tell people how to react if they are cyber-bullied and who to tell. They could give suitable websites, maybe even a school chat room with real names, so friends can chat but at the same time be monitored.

Interestingly, more boys (13%) than girls (7%) suggested counselling. One boy, for example, wrote: 'Get a counsellor from the school who people trust to have an open door policy where pupils know they can go and talk to the counsellor if they are being bullied.' An equal proportion (9%) of boys and girls believed in punishing the bullies. One pupil, for example, was of the opinion that: 'as cyber-bullies are like all other bullies they enjoy trouble. The only way to stop them is to stand up to them.' Indeed, there were those who shared the following view: 'Schools in general are not tough enough on bullies, so the bullies are not afraid to bully. Maybe also give talks to parents on internet bullies.'

Punishments that the pupils had in mind varied from naming and shaming at assembly to suspension and expulsion. However, some pupils took a more restorative approach, suggesting that:

> The people should have a chat with the bully and ask why he/
> she is doing it and see if there's anything wrong with him/her
> and if he/she would like to talk about it.

Other suggestions given by the pupils included responding to reports of cyber-bullying incidents (4%). A suggestion-type box was mentioned on a few occasions which would allow teachers to act on the information given.

Confronting both the bullies and their parents was felt to be important by 3% of the pupils.

It is of note that only 4% of pupils (5% girls and 3% boys) in the study stated that they had no suggestions to offer or that they were indifferent to the problem of cyber-bullying. Indeed some pupils believed schools make matters worse. One pupil, for example, sadly said: 'Schools never make it better. I have seen many cases where schools make everything worse.' Perhaps with this in mind, some pupils appreciated the need for schools to take a more proactive and preventative approach to countering cyber-bullying. Examples of this viewpoint were as follows:

> I think the school should have a monthly interview with each
> pupil to ask how they are and to give them tips and guidelines to
> help stop or prevent cyber-bullying. They should only be ten–
> fifteen minutes long. There should also be an expert coming
> into the school every six months to talk about all aspects of
> bullying. (Post-primary third-year boy)

> Schools should become more aware of what pupils are doing
> and look out for people who look upset and unhappy. (Post-
> primary second-year boy)

Gender differences for all the above response categories are to be found in O'Moore (2012).

CONCLUSION

The results presented in this chapter show school bullying in our Irish schools to involve at least a third of our school-going population. In primary schools, it is safe to say that there are approximately one in six children who are bullied and one in eight who bully others. There is also one in seven who both bully and are bullied. In post-primary schools we may expect at least a further one in ten pupils who are bullied and one in ten who bully others. In addition, there is one in twenty-five who both bully and are bullied. Worryingly, the evidence points to an increase in bullying, in particular at post-primary level. Cyber-bullying further affects a substantial number of our pupils. While there is a considerable overlap in pupils who engage in traditional and cyber-bullying, our evidence points to there being at least one in five teens involved in cyber-bullying. Over 57% of incidents originate by mobile phones, with text-messaging being the most common form of cyber-bullying in and out of school.

As pointed out in the Introduction, there is no shortage of media reports of the cruel realities of bullying and the impact that peer rejection has on the mental health of children (*Irish Times*, 17 September 2010). These reports find support from the research literature which shows that victimisation is associated with mental health problems such as depression, low self-esteem, self-harming and suicide (Roland, 2002; Mills et al., 2004; McMahon et al., 2010). Studies are also drawing attention to the negative outcomes associated with pupils who bully, with bullying of others during childhood linked with social deviance in adolescence (Kumpulainen and Rasanan, 2000).

Also not to be overlooked is that pupils who both bully and are bullied have the greatest number of risk factors. They have both externalising and internalising problems, low self-esteem, poor social competence and inadequate social problem skills. They also perform poorly academically and suffer rejection and isolation by peers as well as being negatively influenced by the peers with whom they interact (Cook et al., 2010).

Given the associations between bullying and victimisation and mental health problems and poor educational performance, it is clear that greater efforts than are currently in place in Ireland today are needed to prevent and counter bullying behaviour in our schools. The Finnish longitudinal study has showed that when the information about frequent bullying and victimisation is used it could identify over a quarter of all those who developed a psychiatric disorder within ten to fifteen years (Sourander et al., 2000). Already in 1997, based on the prevalence of moderate to frequent bully-victims alone, I estimated that there were over 13,000 young people in Ireland (aged 8 to 18 years) who in all probability were in serious need of psychological intervention in order to prevent life-long behavioural, emotional and vocational difficulties (O'Moore et al., 1997). Since then the Growing Up in Ireland Study alone has estimated there to be 5,600 nine-year-old bully-victims (Williams et al., 2009).

Quite apart from the increase in the amount of traditional victimisation and bullying that has been noted in our schools in recent years, the advent of cyber-bullying is placing more and more children at risk. The current levels are already bad, and as younger and younger children are becoming more advanced technologically, cyber-bullying has the potential to grow. With one fifth (29%) of 9–10-year-olds in Ireland having their own social networking sites (O'Neill, 2011), it is hardly surprising to find cyber-bullying among primary-school children. Indeed, one school principal has commented that: 'I have dealt with some quite serious cases of text bullying among primary school children, some of quite overtly sexual nature between boys and girls' (McCabe, 2009).

As little in the way of what can be regarded as a comprehensive anti-bullying programme has been implemented nationally in Irish schools to date, the justification and urgency becomes ever greater to apply best practice in all our schools to reduce the level of all forms of bullying. This is not to undermine the significant support which the Department of Education and Skills has given to individual schools in countering bullying (Aherne and Courtney, 2012).

However, immediate attention needs to be paid to cyber-bullying. In view of the psychosocial risks associated with it (Sourander et al., 2010), in addition to our finding that victims of cyber-bullying rarely tell an adult and that only 1% of witnesses to cyber-bullying would tell an adult, strongly suggests that all current policies and prevention and intervention strategies must now pay particular attention to cyber-bullying. As pupils tend to have the finger on the pulse, it is important in any review of policy and procedures that they be given a voice.

Accepting that the whole-school community approach (see Chapter 12 of this book) has shown itself to be the most effective in reducing bullying behaviour nationally and internationally (Ttofi, Farrington and Baldry, 2008), it is critical that strategies be included to prevent and counter cyber-bullying. The voices which we have heard from the pupils in our study give strong support to the view held by Sourander et al. (2010) that 'there is a need to create cyber environments and supervision that provide clear and consistent norms for healthy cyber behavior'. This means that schools must devote time to raising awareness about cyber-bullying so that no member of the school community is left in any doubt as to what defines healthy cyber behaviour. There also needs to be strategies of support such as counselling for both victims and bullies. However, this is not to undermine the need for there to be consequences for incidents of cyber-abuse but schools should be mindful that consequences need not necessarily be punitive but rather restorative in nature (O'Moore, 2010).

In order for all of our schools in Ireland to invest in a whole-school community approach to bullying prevention, traditional and cyber, additional resources will naturally be required. However, the benefit to individuals and society will far outweigh the cost of psychiatric problems, anti-social behaviour, substance abuse and criminal behaviour, all of which are among the negative outcomes of bullying and victimisation. Thus to delay further in seeking the optimal mental and physical growth of our nation's children should no longer be an option. Our hopes must now lie with the implementation of the Action Plan on Bullying (DES, 29 January 2013), and the new Anti-Bullying Procedures for Primary and Post-Primary Schools, which resulted from the welcome commitment of Ruairí Quinn, Minister for Education and Skills, and Frances Fitzgerald, Minister for Children and Youth Affairs, to have their departments 'develop a roadmap on how best to tackle all forms of bullying in our schools' (Anti Bullying Forum, 17 May 2012).

REFERENCES

Aherne, S. and Courtney, P. 'How Does the DES Support Schools in Countering Bullying?' Paper presented at the Anti-Bullying Forum, Clock Tower, Department of Education and Skills, 17 May 2012

Cook, C.R., Williams, K.R., Guerra, N.G., Kim, T.E. and Sadek, S. (2010). Predictors of bullying and victimization in childhood and adolescence: A meta-analytic investigation, *School Psychology Quarterly*, 25:65–83

Corcoran, L. Connolly, I. and O'Moore, M. 'Cyber-Bullying in Irish Schools: An Investigation of Personality and Self-concept, *Irish Journal of Psychology*, 33, 2012, pp.153–65

Eslea, M., and Rees, J. 'At What Age are Children Most Likely to be Bullied at School?' *Aggressive Behaviour*, 27, 2000, pp. 419–29

Flanagan, M. 'Cyber-Bullying among Irish Teenagers', unpublished MEd (Aggression Studies) thesis, University of Dublin, 2010

Gittins, C. *Violence Reduction in Schools: How to Make a Difference* (Strasbourg: Council of Europe Publishing, 2006)

Guarini, A., Brighi, A. and Genta, M.L.G. 'Cyber-Bullying among Italian Adolescents', in J. Mora-Merchan and T. Jager (eds), *Cyber-Bullying: Cross-National Comparison* (Landau: Verlag Empirische Padagogik, 2010)

Guerin S. 'Examining Bullying in School: A Pupil-Based Approach', unpublished PhD thesis, University College Dublin, 2001

Hawker, D.S.J. and Boulton, M.J. 'Twenty Years' Research on Peer Victimisation and Psychosocial Maladjustment: A Meta-Analytic Review of Cross-Sectional Studies', *Journal of Child Psychology and Psychiatry*, 4, 2000, pp. 441–55

Hinduja, S. and Patchin, J.W. *Bullying Beyond the Schoolyard: Preventing and Responding to Cyber-Bullying* (Thousand Oaks, CA: Corwin Press, 2009)

Holmquist, K. (2010). Bullying in Ireland: Schools are in Denial, *The Irish Times Weekend Review*, 19 September 2010

Khoury-Kassabri, M., Astor, R.A. and Benbenishty, R. 'Pupil Victimisation by School Staff in the Context of an Israeli National School Safety Campaign', *Aggressive Behaviour*, 34, 2008, pp. 1–9

Kirwan, G. and Power, A. *The Psychology of Cyber Crime: Concepts and Principles* (Hershey, PA: IGI Global, 2012)

Kowalski, R.M. and Limber, S.P. 'Electronic Bullying among Middle School Pupils', *Journal of Adolescent Health*, 41, 2007, pp. 522–30

Kowalski, R.M., Limber, S.P. and Agatston, P.M. *Cyber Bullying: Bullying in the Digital Age* (Malden, MA: Blackwell, 2008)

Kumpulainen, K. 'Psychiatric Conditions Associated with Bullying', *International Journal of Adolescent Medicine and Health*, 20, 2008, pp. 121–32

Kumpulainen, K. and Rasanen, E. 'Children Involved in Bullying at Elementary School Age: Their Psychiatric Symptoms and Deviance in Adolescence', *Child Abuse and Neglect*, 24, 2000, pp. 1567–77

Lawlor, M. 'School Bullying Costs, *Irish Psychiatrist*, 7, 2006, pp. 111–15

Leymann, H. and Gustafsson, A. 'Mobbing at Work and the Development of Post-Traumatic Stress Disorder', *European Journal of Work and Organisation Psychology*, 2, 1996, pp. 251–275

Li, Q. 'New Bottle but Old Wine: A Research of Cyber-Bullying in Schools', *Computers in Human Behaviour*, 23, 2007, pp. 1777–91

Livingstone, S., Haddon, L., Gorzig, A. and Olafsson, K. *Risks and Safety on the Internet: The Perspectives of European Children. Full Findings* (London: LSE 'EU Kids Online' Survey, 2011)

McCabe, B. 'What Are We Doing to Our Children?' *Irish Times* 'Health Plus' supplement, 11 August 2009

McMahon, E.M., Reulbach, U., Keeley, H., Perry, I.J. and Arensman, E. 'Bullying Victimisation, Self-Harm and Associated Factors in Irish Adolescent Boys, *Social Science and Medicine*, XXX, 2010, pp. 1–4

Mills, C., Guerin., S., Lynch, E. and Fitzpatrick, C. 'The Relationship between Bullying, Depression and Suicidal Thoughts/Behaviour in Irish Adolescents, *Irish Journal of Psychological Medicine*, 21, 2004, pp. 12–116

Minton, S.J. 'Preventing and Countering Bullying Behaviour amongst Pupils in Irish Schools at a Nationwide Level', unpublished PhD thesis, University of Dublin, 2007

Minton, S.J. 'Pupils' Experiences of Aggressive Behaviour and Bully-Victim Problems in Irish Schools', *Irish Educational Studies*, 29, 2010, pp. 131–52

Minton, S.J. and O'Moore, A.M. 'The Effectiveness of a Nationwide Intervention Programme to Prevent and Counter School Bullying in Ireland', *International Journal of Psychology and Psychological Therapy*, 8, 2008, pp. 1–12

O'Higgins-Norman, J. 'Editorial', *Pastoral Care in Education. Special Issue: Violence and Aggression in School*, 30, 2012, pp. 83–5

Olweus, D. *Bullying at School: What We Know and What We Can Do About It* (Oxford: Blackwell, 1993)

O'Moore, M. *Understanding School Bullying: A Guide for Parents and Teachers* (Dublin: Veritas, 2010)

O'Moore, M. 'Cyber-Bullying: The Situation in Ireland', *Pastoral Care in Education: An International Journal of Personal, Social and Emotional Development*, 2012, pp. 209–23

O'Moore, A.M. and Hillery, B. 'What Do Teachers Need to Know?', in M. Elliot (ed.), *A Practical Guide to Coping for Schools* (London: Longman, 1991)

O'Moore, A.M., Kirkham, C. and Smith, M. 'Bullying Behaviour in Irish Schools: A Nationwide Study', *Irish Journal of Psychology*, 18, 1997, pp. 141–69

O'Moore, M. and Kirkham, C. 'Self-Esteem and its Relationship to Bullying Behaviour', *Aggressive Behaviour*, 27, 2001, pp. 269–83

O'Moore, M. and Minton, S.J. 'Evaluation of the Effectiveness of an Anti-Bullying Programme in Primary Schools', *Aggressive Behaviour*, 31, 2005, pp. 609–22

O'Moore, M. and Minton, S.J. 'Cyber-Bullying: The Irish Experience', in C. Quin and S. Tawse (eds), *Handbook of Aggressive Behaviour Research* (New York: Nova Science Publishers, 2009)

O'Neill, B., Grehan, S. and Olafson, K. *Risks and Safety for Children on the Internet: The Ireland Report* (London: LSE 'EU Kids Online' Survey, 2009)

Ortega, R., Calmaestra, J. and Mora-Merchán, J.A. 'Cyber-Bullying', *International Journal of Psychology and Psychological Therapy*, 8, 2008, pp. 183–92

Pyżalski, J., cited in Pyżalski, J. and Wojitasik, L. 'The Spotlight on Electronic Aggression and Cyber-Bullying in Poland', in J. Mora-Merchán and J.T. Jager (eds), *Cyber-Bullying: Cross-National Comparison* (Landau: Verlag Empirische Pädagogik, 2010)

Renati, R., Berrone, M. and Zanetti, A. 'How Does Cyber-Bullying Relate to Empathy and Social Functioning? An Investigation on a Sample of Italian Adolescents', *Proceedings of XIV European Conference on Developmental Psychology* (COST Workshop), Vilnius, Lithuania, 18–22 August 2009

Roland, E. 'Bullying, Depressive Symptoms and Suicidal Thoughts', *Educational Research*, 44, 2002, pp. 55–67

Rutter, M., Maughan, B., Mortimore, P., Ouston, J. and Smith, A. *Fourteen Thousand Hours: Secondary Schools and their Effects on Children* (Cambridge: Harvard University Press, 1979)

Shariff, S. *Cyber-Bullying: Issues and Solutions for the School, the Classroom and the Home* (New York: Routledge, 2008)

Smith, P.K. and Levan, S. 'Perceptions and Experiences of Bullying in Younger Pupils', *British Journal of Educational Psychology*, 65, 1995, pp. 489–500

Smith, P.K., Madison, K.C. and Moody, J. 'What Causes the Age Decline in Reports of Being Bullied at School? Towards a Developmental Analysis of Risks of Being Bullied', *Educational Research*, 41, 1999, pp. 367–85

Sourander, A., Helsteln, I., Helenius, H. and Piha, J. 'Persistence of Bullying from Childhood to Adolescence: A Longitudinal Eight-Year Follow-up Study', *Child Abuse and Neglect*, 24, 2000, pp. 873–81

Sourander, A., Jensen, P., Ronning, J.A., Niemela, S., Helenius, H., Sillanmaki, L, Kumulainen, K., Piha, J., Tamminen, T., Moilanen, I. and Almquist, F. 'What is the Early Adulthood Outcome of Boys who Bully or are Bullied in Childhood? The Finnish "From a Boy to a Man" Study', *Pediatrics*, 120, 2007, pp. 397–404

Sourander, A., Klomek, A.B., Ikonen, M., Lindroos, J., Luntamo, T., Koskelainen, M., Ristkari, T. and Helenius, H. 'Psychosocial Risk Factors Associated with Cyber-Bullying among Adolescents', *Archives of General Psychiatry*, 67, 2010, pp. 720–8

Sullivan, K. *The Anti-Bullying Handbook* (New York: Oxford University Press, 2000)

Ttofi, M.M., Farrington, D.P. and Baldry, A.C. *Effectiveness of Programmes to Reduce School Bullying*, report prepared for the Swedish National Council for Crime Prevention, 2008

Veenstra, R., Lindeberg, S., Munniksma, A. and Dijkstra, J.K. 'The Complex Relation between Bullying, Victimisation, Acceptance and Rejection: Giving Special Attention to Status, Affection and Sex Differences', *Child Development*, 81, 2010, pp. 480–6

Wang, J., Iannotti, R.J. and Nansel, T.R. (2009) 'School Bullying among Adolescents in the United States: Physical, Verbal, Relational, and Cyber, *Journal of Adolescent Health*, 45, 2009, pp. 368–75

Wilkinson, R. and Pickett, K. *The Spirit Level* (London: Allen Lane, 2009)

Williams, J., Greene, S., Doyle, E., Harris, E., Layte, R., McCoy, S., McCrory, C., Murray, A., Nixon, E., O'Dowd, T., O'Moore, M., Quail, A., Smyth, E., Swords, L. and Thornton, M. *Growing Up in Ireland: National Longitudinal Study of Children: The Lives of 9-Year-Olds* (Dublin: Department of Health and Children, 2008)

World Health Organisation 'Young People's Health in Context: Health Behaviour in School-Aged Children (HBSC) Study: Intermediate

Report from 2001/2002 Survey', *Health Policy for Children and Adolescents*, No.4 (2004)

Ybarra, M.L. and Mitchell, K.J. 'Online Aggressors/Targets, Aggressors and Targets: A Comparison of Associated Youth Characteristics', *Journal of Child Psychology and Psychiatry*, 45, 2004, pp. 1308–16

Ybarra, M.L. and Mitchell, K.J. 'Prevalence and Frequency of Internet Harassment Instigation: Implications for Adolescent Health', *Journal of Adolescent Health*, 41, 2007, pp. 189–95

CHAPTER TWO

Bullying in Schools in Northern Ireland

Conor McGuckin

INTRODUCTION

In compiling their cross-national perspective regarding f2f (face-to-face) bully/victim problems, while Smith et al. (1999) garnered country-specific 'situation reports' from those countries geographically close to Northern Ireland (i.e. England and Wales: Smith, 1999; Scotland: Mellor, 1999; Republic of Ireland: Byrne, 1999), no reference or consideration was made to bully/victim problems among children and young people (CYP) in Northern Ireland. In their supplement to Smith et al. (1999), McGuckin and Lewis (2003) noted that while Northern Ireland is 'geographically close' to these countries, it is also the case that, having endured the effects of over forty years of violent ethno-political conflict (see http://cain.ulst.ac.uk and http://www.incore.ulst.ac.uk for scholarly reviews and commentaries), the region is 'culturally distant' from them too. As such, McGuckin and Lewis (2003) asserted that any cross-national consideration of bully/victim problems among CYP that ignores possible differences between Northern Ireland and its close geographical neighbours may be limited. Unfortunately, like Smith et al. (1999), Mora-Merchan and Jäger (2011) also fail to understand the significance of omitting Northern Ireland from any presentation of data from the British Isles.

Considering the poor attention that has been paid to the experiences of CYP involved in bully/victim problems in Northern Ireland, this chapter presents a timely opportunity to outline the current knowledge regarding the nature, incidence, correlates and management of bully/victim problems among Northern Ireland's CYP.

HOW MANY CHILDREN AND YOUNG PEOPLE IN NORTHERN IRELAND ARE INVOLVED IN BULLY/VICTIM PROBLEMS?

In Northern Ireland, as elsewhere, much of the research exploring bully/victim problems has been largely sporadic in nature, providing a smorgasbord of results that in combination create a rich tapestry of findings from which is beginning to emerge a picture of the nature, incidence, correlates and management of bully/victim problems in the region (McGuckin and Lewis, 2006). However, it is important to note that this picture is based on only a few studies, with further research required to provide a better understanding of the problem. Indeed, with a lack of consensus among researchers, studies to date have differed in terms of the emphasis placed upon methodological issues such as the time-reference period for the events to have happened within (e.g., previous week, previous two months, previous year), and whether or not questionnaires were used that would allow for international comparisons (e.g. Callaghan and Joseph, 1995; Collins and Bell, 1996; Grant, 1996; Taylor, 1996; Collins, McAleavy and Adamson, 2002, 2004; Livesey et al., 2007; RSM McClure Watters, 2011).

From the published research to date regarding the nature and incidence of bully/victim problems, of note has been the robust methodological approach taken by three large-scale studies commissioned by the Department of Education for Northern Ireland (DENI) (Collins et al., 2002, 2004; Livesey et al., 2007; RSM McClure Watters, 2011). In doing so, these studies have provided useful data that allow for both local and international comparisons. Utilising Olweus' (1989) 'gold standard' Bully/Victim Questionnaire (BVQ) among a representative sample of 3,000 pupils from 120 schools (60 primary, 60 post-primary), Collins et al. (2002, 2004) found that 40.1% of primary school pupils claimed to have been bullied during the period of the study (March 2000–June 2000). While 26% of these pupils experienced bullying 'once or twice in the last couple of months', 6% reported that they had experienced it 'two or three times a month', with 5% reporting a frequency of 'about once a week', and a further 4% reporting a frequency of 'several times a week'. Among post-primary school pupils, the rate was 30.2% (20%: 'once or twice in the last couple of months'; 3%: 'two or three times a month'; 3%: 'about once a week'; and 4%: 'several times a week'). Indeed, 5% of the primary school pupils and 2% of the post-primary school pupils reported that they had suffered bullying for several years. Regarding taking part in bullying others at school, this was reported by approximately a quarter (24.9%) of the primary school pupils (22%: 'occasional'; 3%: 'frequent') and 29% of the post-primary school pupils (26%: 'occasional'; 3%: 'frequent'). A further group of bully-victims were identified: 15% among the primary school pupils and 12% among the post-primary school pupils. Questionnaires were also completed by staff within the participating schools, in relation to attitudes to and awareness of bullying, school anti-bullying policies and procedures and their training needs. Collins et al. (2002, 2004) also asserted that all of the evidence indicated that bullying was happening even in the best-regulated schools, was not age or gender-specific, and was sometimes underplayed by the schools and teachers.

Utilising the same methodology (with the addition of questions regarding cyber-bullying [data presented in a later section] and Section 75 of the Northern Ireland Act 1998 [The Stationery Office: TSO, 2003], which related to opinions on equality in relation to ethnicity, religion, and disability), Livesey et al.'s (2007) follow-up to the work of Collins et al. (2002, 2004) found similar prevalence rates. Of the 993 Year 6 primary school pupils surveyed, 43.3% indicated that they had been bullied to some degree 'in the past couple of months' (26.2%: 'once or twice'; 7.9%: 'two or three times a month'; 4.3%: 'about once a week'; 4.9%: 'several times a week'). Of the 1,319 Year 9 post-primary school pupils surveyed, 28.8% indicated that they had been bullied to some degree 'in the past couple of months' (21.1%: 'once or twice'; 2.6%: 'two or three times a month'; 2.3%: 'about once a week'; 2.7%: 'several times a week'). Regarding taking part in bullying others at school, this was reported by 22% of primary and post-primary pupils. Among the primary school pupils, while 17% said that they had been involved in bullying other pupils 'only once or twice', 5% reported that they had been involved in such behaviour 'two or three times a month or more frequently'. Among the post-primary school pupils, the figures were 19% and 3% respectively. Pupils were also categorised to one of four categories: (i) not bully or victim, (ii) victim, (iii) bully, or (iv) bully-victim, based on their answers to the two key questions as per Solberg and Olweus (2003) and Ahmed and Braithwaite (2004). Among the primary school pupils, 80.4% were not involved in bullying and were classified as 'not a bully or victim', 14.6% were categorised as a 'victim', 2.5% as a 'bully' and 2.5% were considered 'bully-victims'. In the post-primary sample, 90.3% were assigned as 'not a bully or victim', 6.9% were a 'victim', 2.1% were classified as a 'bully' and 0.7% were categorised as a 'bully-victim'.

Questions were also asked in relation to having a disability and being involved in bully/victim problems. In relation to having a disability, 16.3% of primary school pupils reported that they did have a disability. Livesey et al. (2007) reported that there was a significant association in frequency of victimisation and whether a pupil had a disability. When compared to those without a disability (40.4%), a larger percentage (58.5%) of those with a disability reported that they were a victim of bullying behaviour. A significant association was also found in relation to bullying other pupils, with a greater percentage of pupils with a disability (37.7%) reporting that they had bullied other pupils in comparison to those without a disability (19.1%). Among the post-primary sample, 5.9% reported having a disability, with similar significant associations being found in relation to reporting of having a disability and being a victim of bullying behaviour: 29.7% of those with a disability reported being a victim in comparison to 27.7% for those with no disability. Similarly, significant associations were also reported for reporting of a disability and involvement in bullying others, with a great percentage (35.4%) of pupils with a disability admitting bullying other pupils in comparison to those pupils (21.2%) with no disability.

Thus, Livesey et al.'s (2007) findings showed little change in the level of bully/victim problems reported by pupils compared to Collins et al.'s (2002, 2004) study five years previously. Indeed, Livesey et al. (2007) concluded that their findings were similar to the findings of Collins et al. (2002, 2004), suggesting that there are still challenges facing schools in relation to developing an anti-bullying culture and preventing bully/victim problems and protecting CYP who have been affected.

The third funded project (RSM McClure Watters, 2011) built upon the strong methodological and empirical base set by the previous two projects (e.g. Revised Olweus Bully/Victim Questionnaire, 1996). Similarly, it examined the nature and incidence of school bullying, included questions relation to disability and cyber-bullying (data presented in a later section), and saw the return of questionnaires to staff (similar to Collins et al., 2002, 2004). Questionnaires were completed by a representative sample of 904 primary pupils and 1,297 post-primary pupils, along with 58 primary teaching staff, 57 primary non-teaching staff, 56 post-primary teaching staff and 58 post-primary non-teaching staff. Furthermore, in an extension to the previous research, one senior teaching member of staff who had specific responsibility for pastoral care and one non-teaching member of staff were interviewed in each school sampled.

Within the primary school sample, 39.3% (n = 352) of pupils had been victimised in the previous two months (22.1%, n = 198: 'it has only happened once or twice'; 7.7%, n = 69: '2 or 3 times a month'; 4.6%, n = 41: 'about once a week'; 4.9%, n = 44: 'several times a week'), with 9.5% (n = 85) of these pupils experiencing bullying once a week or more often. Among post-primary school pupils, the rate of victimisation was 29.5% (n = 380: 18.4%, n = 238: 'it has only happened once or twice'; 4.3%, n = 55: '2 or 3 times a month'; 3.3%, n = 42: 'about once a week'; 3.5%, n = 45: 'several times a week').

In response to the question about bullying others, 21.5% (n = 193) of primary school pupils admitted being involved in this behaviour (17.6%, n = 158: 'it has happened only once or twice'; 2.2%, n = 20: '2 or 3 times a month'; 1.1%, n = 10: 'about once a week'; 0.6%, n = 5: 'several times a week'), and 1.7% (n = 15) of these pupils engaged in this behaviour once a week or more often. Among the post-primary school pupils, 17.8% (n = 230) reported that they did this 'once or twice', and 3.4% (n = 44) reported that they bullied others on a more frequent basis (1.6%, n = 21: '2 or 3 times a month'; 1.1%, n = 14: 'about once a week'; 0.7%, n = 9: 'several times a week').

Similar to the previous iteration of the study (Livesey et al., 2007), pupils were categorised as 'not a bully or victim', 'victim', 'bully', or 'bully-victim' based on their answers to the two key questions. In relation to primary school pupils, 80.2% were classified as being 'not a bully or victim', 15.8% as a 'victim', 2.6% as a 'bully', and 1.3% as a 'bully-victim'. Among the post-primary school pupils, 86.6% were categorised as being 'not a bully or victim', 9.9% as a 'victim', 2.3% as a 'bully', and 1% as a 'bully-victim' (note: while percentage values were reported for these groups, the number of pupils in each category was not reported).

Similar to Livesey et al. (2007), analysis was also conducted regarding the relationship between involvement in bully/victim problems and disability. Overall, 12.1% of primary school pupils and 6.2% of post-primary school pupils reported having a disability (note: while percentage values were reported for these groups, the numbers of pupils in each category was not reported). Among the primary school pupils, a large percentage of those that reported having a disability also reported that they had been victimised (44.3%, n = 47) compared to their non-disabled peers (38.6%, n = 300). A similar trend was evident among the post-primary school pupils, with 44.9% (n = 35) of those with a disability reporting being bullied compared to 28.2% (n = 337) for those without a disability. Furthermore, a greater percentage of those primary school pupils who had a disability reported being involved in bullying other students (27.8%, n = 30) than those without a disability (20.8%, n = 162). Similarly, 29.1% (n = 23) of those in post-primary school with a disability reported that they had bullied other pupils compared with 20.5% (n = 245) for those without a disability.

As previously mentioned, staff surveys were also conducted. In relation to the incidence of bullying over the past 'two or three years', the majority of primary school teaching (60%, n = 35) and non-teaching staff (65%, n = 37) considered it to be 'about the same'. Within the post-primary sample, the incidence was also considered to be 'about the same' by teaching (54%, n = 30) and non-teaching staff (52%, n = 29). In relation to cyber-bullying, 17 primary school teaching staff and 18 non-teaching staff stated that cyber-bullying and problems with Facebook and phones were becoming more common. In the post-primary school setting, almost three quarters of teaching staff and one-third of non-teaching staff noted that cyber-bullying was increasing.

In comparison to the two previous studies, the incidence rate in relation to victimisation and involvement in bullying others for primary school pupils and post-primary school pupils remained consistent, with only slight changes occurring. All three studies reported victimisation rates of approximately 40% among primary school pupils and 30% among post-primary school pupils, and participation in bullying others for both school groups of approximately 20%. Based on their research findings, RSM McClure Watters (2011) made some key recommendations, such as reminding schools to update their policies and involve parents and pupils, that DENI should provide guidance on the roles of staff in dealing with school bullying, and provide guidelines on addressing cyber-bullying for schools (see later sections).

In terms of McGuckin and Lewis' (2003) argument that it would be unwise to assume that incidence rates from the province would be the same as for close geographical neighbours, some useful comparisons can be made between, for example, the work of Collins et al. (2002, 2004) and the highly regarded data provided by O'Moore, Kirkham, and Smith's (1997) seminal nationwide survey among CYP in the Republic of Ireland, and Whitney and Smith's (1993) 'Sheffield' data from England (both also using Olweus' questionnaire).

In terms of victimisation, the rate among the primary school pupils (40.1%) reported by Collins et al. (2002, 2004) was higher than that in both the Republic of Ireland (31.3%: O'Moore et al., 1997) and England (37.0%: Whitney and Smith, 1993). A similar finding was found in relation to victimisation levels among post-primary school pupils – the rate of 30.2% in Northern Ireland was higher than that for the Republic of Ireland (15.6%) and for England (14%).

In relation to taking part in bullying others, while the rate of 24.9% reported by Collins et al. (2002, 2004) among the primary school pupils was higher than the rate of 16% reported by Whitney and Smith (1993) in their English study, it was marginally lower than the 26.4% reported in O'Moore et al.'s (1997) Irish study. Referring to post-primary school pupils, the Northern Irish data (29%) was significantly higher than the rates reported among both Irish (14.9%) and English (7%) samples.

Thus, it becomes evident that while the Republic of Ireland and England are close to Northern Ireland in terms of geography, differences in the incidence rates of bully/victim problems may be indicative of cultural differences between these jurisdictions. However, despite the fact that all of the studies were methodologically robust in terms of instrument used and sampling procedures applied, Collins et al. (2002) caution us to be careful in terms of these direct comparisons. For example, while their post-primary sample were aged 13–14 years, the age range in O'Moore et al.'s (1997) sample was 11–18 years, with O'Moore et al.'s (1997) lower incidence figures perhaps being a reflection of the larger age range and that bully/victim problems tend to decrease with age. Collins et al. (2002) also note that the data for the different studies were collected at disparate times (e.g. English data collected in 1990, Northern Ireland data collected in 2000).

While the commissioned research of Collins et al. (2002, 2004), Livesey et al. (2007) and RSM McClure Watters (2011) have provided important information on the *nature* and *incidence* of bully/victim problems among the province's CYP, they have not added to the knowledge of the *correlates* of involvement in such problems (e.g. physical and psychological health and well-being). So as to help increase knowledge in this area, McGuckin and colleagues have been 'setting the scene' for the dissemination of their important data, gathered from a sample of approximately 9,000 pupils representative of the diversity of Northern Ireland's educational provision. This data will add significantly to this previous knowledge regarding the *incidence* of bully/victim problems, as data was collected from a multi-indicator approach (i.e. different and concurrent measures of involvement in bully/victim problems).

The data will also extend this previous work by reporting upon the relationships between involvement in bully/victim problems and various indices of health and well-being (e.g. happiness, self-esteem, psychological well-being, physical well-being, depression) and individual difference variables (e.g. personality, religiosity). In preparation for this dissemination, McGuckin and colleagues have been making the consistent argument that the research agenda regarding explorations of bully/victim problems moving forward should have an agreed consistency in terms of definitional stance, research samples utilised, and methodology employed. In particular, they have been focusing on bringing order and understanding to the results from regular and rigorous surveys of the attitudes of CYP in Northern Ireland.

Every few years the Northern Ireland Statistics and Research Agency (NISRA) administers the Young Persons Behaviour and Attitudes Survey (YPBAS: see http://www.csu.nisra.gov.uk/surveys) to pupils in the first five years of secondary school (11–16 years old). On an annual basis, ARK (Access, Research, Knowledge: a joint research initiative between Queen's University Belfast and the University of Ulster: see http://www.ark.ac.uk) carries out the annual Young Life and Times (YLT) survey covering the views of 16-year-olds, and the newly implemented Kids' Life and Times (KLT) survey, focusing on children in the final year of primary school education (10–11 years old).

The analyses of data collected in these surveys has demonstrated that even when large-scale sampling procedures have been employed, the general absence of consistency regarding the questions posed and response options offered has resulted in a 'mishmash' of information about bully/victim problems that has not been easy to compare, either intra-survey across datasets, inter-survey, nationally, or internationally (YPBAS: McGuckin and Lewis, 2006; McGuckin, Cummins, and Lewis, 2008, 2009; YLT: McGuckin, Lewis and Cummins, 2010; McGuckin, Cummins and Lewis, 2010; KLT: McGuckin, Cummins and Lewis, 2010).

Working with ARK, McGuckin and colleagues have been striving to ensure that the questions posed in future YLT and KLT surveys are considerate of the international approach to assessing the incidence of bully/victim problems among school pupils (e.g. utilising questions and response options that mimic Olweus' questionnaire). Thus, while we are gaining a robust knowledge base of information regarding bully/victim problems among the province's CYP, the future development of this knowledge shows great potential, with the promise of additional research knowledge that is both theoretically and methodologically robust. In an era where intervention and prevention attempts must be (at best) 'evidence informed', only with such knowledge can we truly, as researchers, practitioners and policy makers, have confidence that our work is guided by the best available evidence.

OK, BUT WHAT ABOUT CYBER-BULLYING: IS THIS A PROBLEM AMONG CHILDREN AND YOUNG PEOPLE IN NORTHERN IRELAND?

Having considered the research evidence regarding the incidence of f2f bully/victim problems, it is apparent that such problems and experiences are 'persistent' for Northern Ireland's CYP. As noted at the start of the chapter, we are also increasing our knowledge of a new 'emerging' problem: cyber-bullying. Although this section is entitled 'cyber-bullying', it is important to note that, rightly or wrongly, this has been the adopted term across the international research, applied, policy, and legal fields to signify not just 'bullying' by cyber means but also 'victimisation' by these means. While I, like many others, refer to bully/victim problems (traditional / f2f), I feel that it would be more appropriate to talk in terms of 'cyber-bully/ victim problems'. In doing so, we would give full recognition to the victim as well as to the 'bullying' behaviours.

When asked about their experiences with the internet and related technologies, most young people rate their experiences positively (Kowlaski, Limber and Agatston, 2008). However, the undisputed benefits of the internet and modern communication technologies cannot be experienced by young people if the technological environment is unwelcoming or inhospitable. Unfortunately, cyber-bullying is '… the by-product of the union of adolescent aggression and electronic communication'. (Hinduja and Patchin, 2008, p. 131). Unlike f2f bully/victim problems, we have scant knowledge of how to counter the insidious effects of cyber-bullying. For example, such is the importance of these new communication channels that cyber-victims are often loathe to report incidents for fear, not of the cyber-bully's retaliation, but that their access to the technology will be withdrawn as a safety measure (Shariff, 2009).

WHAT DO WE KNOW ABOUT COMPUTER AND INTERNET USE BY CHILDREN AND YOUNG PEOPLE IN NORTHERN IRELAND?

The 2009 version of the highly important KLT survey among children in the final year of primary school education (10–11 years old) enquired about the role of new information and communications technologies (ICTs), such as mobile phones and the internet, in the lives of the 'Net Generation' (Lloyd and Devine, 2009).

The vast majority (93%) of the children reported that they had a mobile phone. In terms of the internet, 98% said that their family had at least one computer or laptop, with 94% reporting that these computers had an internet connection. Most (97%) reported that they used the internet at school, with a slightly lower proportion (91%) using it at home. The majority of internet users (86%) said they used it for schoolwork as well as for fun. In relation to 'social networking', despite the fact that the terms and conditions set out by the three main providers (Bebo, Facebook, MySpace) state that children using these sites must be aged 13 years or over, almost half (48%) of the children reported that they are on social networking sites like Bebo, Facebook or MySpace. Of those who said they were using these sites, 29% said they use them 'a lot'. In terms of friendships, 17% reported that the good friends they had included those they had met online, with 35% reporting that they had 'virtual' friends that they talked to online but did not meet face-to-face (boys: 41%; girls: 31%). Indeed, 8% of boys and 4% of girls said that they had at least 40 'virtual' friends that they did not meet face-to-face. With regard to internet safety, 35% of those with internet access at home said they had access in their bedroom. While this is suggestive of unsupervised access, most respondents (87%) did report that their parents or teachers had talked to them about internet safety (1 in 20 weren't sure). One in 10 children who used the internet in their bedroom reported that their parents or teachers had not talked to them about internet safety (boys: 14%; girls: 6%). Lloyd and Devine (2009) concluded that '... this Net Generation relies heavily on technology, which influences the way they think and behave in relation to leisure activities, communication and friendship.' (p. 3).

CYBER-BULLYING: HOW COMMON IS IT AMONG CHILDREN AND YOUNG PEOPLE IN NORTHERN IRELAND?

In extending the work of Collins et al. (2002, 2004), Livesey et al. (2007) included additional questions regarding victimisation and bullying via the use of mobile phones and/or computers. They found that 12.9% of Year 6 students (primary) and 7% of Year 9 students (post-primary) reported having experienced bullying via mobile phones. Bullying via computers was reported to be the least likely form of bullying (7.4% of Year 6, 4.4% of Year 9). The research confirmed that cyber-bullying was experienced by both primary- and post-primary-aged children in Northern Ireland, but suggested a higher prevalence rate in younger-aged children.

Following Livesey et al. (2007), RSM McClure Watters (2011) also enquired about cyber-bullying in their study. In relation to being a victim of cyber-bullying, 15.5% (n = 140) of primary school pupils reported that they had experienced this in the past couple of months, with 'I received a threatening message via IM, text, email' (6%, n = 54) and 'I received a message that showed people were talking about me nastily online' (6.1%, n = 55) being most commonly reported. Similar trends were reported among the post-primary sample, with 17% (n = 221) reporting cyber-bullying and 'I received a threatening message via IM, text, email' (5.3%, n = 69) and 'I received a message that showed people were talking about me nastily online' (5.5%, n = 71) being the most reported options. Text message (primary: 8.1%, n = 73; post-primary: 9.6%, n = 124) and social networking (primary: 5.9%, n = 53; post-primary: 10.6%, n = 138) were two methods of bullying most commonly reported by a victim, to bully them using a mobile phone or computer.

When answering the question about involvement in cyber-bullying other pupils in the past couple of months, 5.2% (n = 47) reported that they had engaged in this behaviour. Similar to the victim-focused question, the most frequent reported responses were: 'I sent him or her a threatening message via IM, text, email' (1.7%, n = 15) and 'I sent him or her a message that showed people were talking about him or her nastily online' (1.8%, n = 16). Similarly, 6.6% (n = 85) of post-primary school pupils reported being a cyber-bully, with 'I sent him or her a message with insults calling him or her gay (whether true or not)' (2.1%, n = 27) and 'I sent him or her a threatening message via IM, text, email' (1.9%, n = 25) the most common response. Similarly, text message (primary: 3.4%, n = 31; post-primary: 2.7%, n = 35) and social networking (primary: 2.1%, n = 19; post-primary: 3.2%, n = 42) were the two methods most commonly reported by a bully.

McGuckin et al. (2010) have reported upon the incidence of cyber-bullying among primary school pupils in Northern Ireland, as recorded by the 2008 and 2009 iterations of the KLT. In 2008, while 10.3% (n = 353) of the pupils reported that they had experienced this type of victimisation (i.e. by someone sending nasty texts or putting up bad things about you on the internet), 3.4% (n = 115) reported that they had victimised others in this manner. In 2009, 12.9% (n = 470) of the pupils reported that they had experienced this type of victimisation (the question relating to involvement in cyber-bullying others was not presented in 2009).

Using Smith et al.'s (2006) questionnaire (based on Olweus, 1989), the Northern Ireland Anti-Bullying Forum (NIABF: over 20 regional statutory and voluntary organisations acting together to end bully/victim problems among CYP in Northern Ireland) explored cyber-bullying, its forms, awareness and impact, among a sample of 163 students (11–18 years; male = 53%, n = 86, female = 47%, n = 77) in one post-primary school (NIABF: 2007). While 'traditional' forms of bullying were not widely reported within the school, 8% (n = 13) of the pupils reported having experienced cyber-bullying over this time period ('once or twice' [7%, n = 11]; 'once a week' [1%, n = 2]), a relatively high figure compared to the overall reported levels of bullying (14%, n = 22), suggesting that cyber-bullying was a more prevalent trend compared to the other, more traditional forms of bullying. Girls were significantly more likely to experience bullying, including cyber-bullying. Younger year groups had the greatest proportion of students who reported having experienced cyber-bullying. The perceived impact of cyber-bullying was believed by over half of the pupils to be similar to the traditional forms of bullying. However, bullying using phone picture and video clips was perceived as having more impact than the more traditional forms of bullying. The majority of students felt that banning the use of equipment such as computers and mobile phones in school would not assist in the prevention of cyber-bullying, or solve the problem. This latter finding has been recently supported by the empirical research of Steffgen, König and Pfetsch (2009).

Concluding that these findings were similar to previous English research (e.g. National Children's Home, 2002, 2005; Smith et al., 2006), NIABF (2007) consulted a group of young people, through Childline (a NIABF member organisation that provides confidential 24-hour telephone support to children), to explore their views on the findings of the research and to consider what their recommendations for further action would be. Overall, the group were not surprised at the findings and were able to provide their insight as to possible explanations. For example, the group agreed that banning electronic equipment was not a strategy to stop cyber-bullying and suggested this could cause further challenges. These included the practical safety aspect of having a phone (e.g. to make an arrangement with a family member) and a fairness or rights based approach given that teachers also allegedly use their phones during class lessons. A common theme ran throughout their recommendations, namely the need for partnership working with a view to stopping the cyber-bullying of CYP. Having considered the results of the research and the consultation process, NIABF recommended the following actions: (i) to raise awareness of cyber-bullying (as a theme) during Anti-Bullying Week 2007 in local communities, (ii) to explore parents'/carers' understanding of cyber-bullying, (iii) to develop awareness-raising resources focusing on cyber-bullying for school staff to deliver to students, and (iv) to develop awareness-raising training focusing on cyber-bullying for community organisations working with CYP.

Also utilising Smith et al.'s (2006) questionnaire, Espey, Duffy and McGuckin (under review) explored cyber-bullying among a sample of 757 Year 8 and Year 11 pupils in attendance at five second-level schools (age = 11–15 years [mean = 13.04 years]; male = 42.5%, n = 322, female = 57.5%, n = 435), representative of the diverse nature of second-level education in Northern Ireland (i.e. grammar, secondary, single-sex, mixed-sex, urban, rural). Focus groups were also carried out with two groups of students (n = 8 Year 8; n = 6 Year 11) and one group of teachers (n = 6). While the incidence of cyber-bullying (19.3%: victim = 11.9%; bully = 3.1%; bully/victim = 4.3%) was less frequent than f2f (52.1%: victim = 31.6%; bully = 6.8%; bully/victim = 13.7%), the levels were concerning. More girls were involved in cyber-bullying overall, with significantly more as cyber-victims. Greater numbers of Year 11 pupils were involved overall, with significantly more as cyber-bullies. Bullying via text message was the most common and bullying through videos on a mobile phone was perceived to be most harmful. Over one-quarter of cyber-victims did not know their cyber-bully(ies). Pupils suggested blocking messages/numbers as the best coping strategy and many cyber-victims did not tell about their experiences.

BULLYING AND CYBER-BULLYING IN NORTHERN IRELAND:
A MANAGED RESPONSE

As noted by McGuckin and Lewis (2003), action aimed at preventing bully/victim problems in Northern Ireland's schools has traditionally come from three areas: government (DENI), local education and library boards (ELB: geographical area of centralised administration), and the independent and voluntary sector (e.g. night classes, community drama groups). The issue has been given considerable attention and significance by a range of strategic policy documents at both the UK level (Department for Education and Skills, 2004) and more locally by the Northern Ireland Assembly (Office of First Minister and Deputy First Minister, 2006), where emphasis is placed on children and young people having rights to a safe and respectful educational environment. Indeed, DENI's (2001) 'Pastoral Care in Schools: Promoting Positive Behaviour' document deals explicitly with good discipline and includes a section on bullying and how schools should develop an anti-bullying policy (which they are legally obliged to have).

DENI have extended their involvement and approach to dealing with bully/victim problems in Northern Ireland's schools. In 2004, at the request of DENI, Save the Children (a charitable organisation and member of NIABF) brought together representatives from organisations across Northern Ireland to establish a regional Anti-Bullying Forum (http://www.niabf.org.uk). During the first year, representatives of the forum worked to ensure a wide range of organisations were included, and engaged with other locally based groups working on similar issues. The forum is comprised of regional statutory and non-statutory organisations who are involved in the reduction of bully/victim problems. DENI funds a Regional Coordinator post attached to the NIABF which is involved in delivering a three-year Anti-Bullying Strategy that includes the development, implementation and promotion of models of good practice, developing parental partnerships, website development and an annual Anti-Bullying Week.

For example, the 2009 Anti-Bullying Week had a theme of 'Travelling to and from school, free from bullying'. Associated activities included the dissemination of anti-bullying resource packs for schools. NIABF worked with a group of young people from the National Children's Bureau (NCB: a member of NIABF) to develop a series of television advertisements, which were broadcast locally on UTV (Ulster Television) and nationally on GMTV (Good Morning

Television UK) during the week. These young people also helped develop a 'Top Tips' leaflet, offering practical advice on how to stay safe from bullying on the way to and from school. The tips were adapted into radio messages which were played on Cool FM (a local Belfast-based radio station). Translink, Northern Ireland's integrated bus and rail public transport company, provided advertising space in rail and bus stations.

NIABF also constitutes task groups to deal with particular issues. For example, in 2009, three task groups looked at the issues of homophobic bullying, disabilist bullying, and the need for specific resources for the pre-school sector and what this might entail.

As the main thrust against bully/victim problems in Northern Ireland, DENI and the NIABF are constituent members of the British and Irish Anti-Bullying Forum (BIABF). With members from the lead government and non-government agencies across the five jurisdictions (i.e. Northern Ireland, Republic of Ireland, England, Wales and Scotland), the BIABF meets twice yearly to share information and best practice in the area. For example, with some Forum members being heavily involved in EU-commissioned research projects regarding a managed response to cyber-bullying, policy makers in Northern Ireland are being kept abreast of latest developments regarding prevention and intervention in the area. For example, the recently completed CyberTraining Project (funded by the EU Lifelong Learning Programme: [Project No.142237-LLP-1-2008-1-DE-LEONARDO-LMP] http://cybertraining-project.org) has provided a well-grounded, research-based training manual on cyber-bullying for trainers. The manual includes background information on cyber-bullying, its nature and extent in Europe, current projects, initiatives and approaches tackling the cyber-bullying problem, best practice Europe-wide, as well as practical guidance and resources for trainers working with the target groups of: (i) pupils, (ii) parents, and (iii) teachers, schools and other professionals. The manual concludes with a comprehensive compilation of supporting references, internet links, and other resources for trainers. The outputs from another EU-supported project (COST Action IS0801: http://sites.google.com/site/costis0801) will also prove beneficial in this area.

As well as the support offered to the NIABF, DENI also offers assistance to those providing help and support to CYP who are affected by bully/victim problems (e.g. Childline). Since September 2007, the independent schools' counselling service has been available in all grant-aided post-primary schools, allowing pupils to speak to a trained counsellor about their concerns or fears around bullying.

The service is currently provided by three organisations (New Life Counselling, Counselling 4 Youth, and North Down Familyworks). While currently available to young people in Northern Ireland (who may self refer, or be referred by teachers), DENI is considering extending the service to other pupils (i.e. primary and special sectors). In addition, DENI provides support to CYP via dedicated teachers who are given enhanced training to recognise and support young people in crisis, including those who are victims of bullying.

In addition to the DENI and NIABF response, the ELBs have established an Inter-Board Anti-Bullying Group (hosted by NIABF), which is currently developing a common approach to tackling bully/victim problems in Northern Ireland's schools. Each ELB has a designated officer who works with schools to tackle the issue through assisting in the development of whole-school policies and supporting individual pupils who have been victims of bullying.

At the curriculum level, 'The Revised Curriculum for Northern Ireland' (introduced in 2007/2008) should enhance personal awareness among CYP of the stressors in their lives and their capacity to deal with them. At primary school level, a new area of learning called 'Personal Development and Mutual Understanding' has been introduced. At post-primary, 'Learning for Life and Work' has been introduced. These new areas of learning include Relationships and Sexuality Education (RSE) and Citizenship Education where pupils will explore, respectively, issues such as developing positive relationships and also diversity and respect for others, including those of differing sexual orientation. Young people are also encouraged to examine the organisation and structures of society and relationships.

BULLYING AND CYBER-BULLYING IN NORTHERN IRELAND: THE LEGAL RESPONSE

In terms of the management of bully/victim problems, legislation was introduced in Northern Ireland in 2003 (The Education and Libraries [Northern Ireland] Order 2003: DENI, 2003) which requires all schools to have a specific standalone anti-bullying policy (specifically Articles 17, 18 and 19). The implementation of this new legislation and accompanying guidance from DENI should serve to copper-fasten McGuckin and Lewis' (2008) finding that, in the absence of legislation, the vast majority of schools were proactive in the management of such problems.

Article 17 of the Order relates to the 'Welfare and Protection of Pupils' and places a statutory duty upon boards of governors (BoGs) 'to safeguard and promote the welfare of registered pupils at the school at all times when the pupils are on the premises of the school; or in the lawful control or charge of a member of the staff of the school'. Accompanying guidance (DENI, 2003 [para. 4]) states that pupil welfare embraces all aspects of pastoral care, child protection, pupil behaviour, health and well-being, safety and security. The guidance also reflects that this new duty makes explicit an implied duty of care which is already exercised by school managers and provides BoGs with the legal basis for taking an active interest in all aspects of a school's activities that promote pupil welfare (DENI, 2003 [para. 3]).

Article 18 of the Order relates to 'Child Protection Measures' and requires the BoGs of all grant-aided schools to ensure that they have a written child protection policy. This policy must reflect any guidance issued by DENI, the ELB where the school is located and, where appropriate, the Council for Catholic Maintained Schools (CCMS). The BoG is required to determine the measures to be taken by all persons associated with the school to protect pupils from abuse and to review these measures from time to time. 'Abuse', as defined in the legislation, includes sexual abuse and abuse causing physical or mental harm to a child. In 1999, DENI published a booklet entitled 'Pastoral Care in Schools: Child Protection' – this is *the* principal guidance issued by DENI in this area and contains advice and procedures for handling child protection issues in grant-aided schools.

Article 19 of the Order amends Article 3 of the Education (Northern Ireland) Order 1998, which is the primary legislation dealing with school discipline/promoting positive behaviour (DENI, 2001). Article 19 places new duties upon the school, as follows: '(i) the BoG shall consult with registered pupils and their parents before making or revising the school's disciplinary policy, (ii) the principal shall determine measures to be taken to prevent all forms of bullying among pupils, and (iii) the principal shall consult with registered pupils and their parents before deciding upon measures to encourage good behaviour and to prevent bullying.' Accompanying guidance (DENI, 2003 [paras. 14 and 15]) recommends that all schools will need to be satisfied that their current discipline/promoting positive behaviour policy deals with the prevention of bullying in a sufficiently clear and robust way to satisfy this legal requirement. Any revision of existing school disciplinary/promoting positive behaviour policies must be preceded by a consultation exercise with registered pupils and their parents.

As well as the Articles within the 2003 Order, DENI (2007) issued a circular in relation to the acceptable use of the internet and digital technologies in schools. The circular re-emphasised that BoGs of grant-aided schools have a duty to safeguard and promote the welfare of pupils (Article 17) and to determine the measures to be taken at the school to protect pupils from abuse (Article 18), and that in the exercise of those duties, BoGs must ensure that their schools have a policy on the safe, healthy, acceptable and effective use of the internet and other digital technology tools. The BoGs are also guided to ensure the active promotion of safe and acceptable working practices for all staff and pupils – a measure that will serve to reassure parents and guardians. The circular contains a section on child protection, bullying and harassment – with specific advice on dealing with cyber-bullying incidents. The guidance also has sections relating to management responsibilities in school, best practice codes for safe internet use, internet safety education for people using school ICT resources and information on social software, including internet chat rooms, instant messaging technology and social networks. As with the iterative development and implementation of any good policy, it is also pointed out that it is essential that school policy and practices be kept under frequent review as new challenges, threats and legal requirements emerge regularly. This is made explicit in terms of the statutory duty under Article 18 and the need to revise child protection policies to ensure that they reflect recent DENI guidance on this issue.

In terms of criminal law, there are three pieces of legislation which may provide protection from cyber-bullying: (i) Protection from Harassment (Northern Ireland) Order 1997, (ii) Malicious Communications (Northern Ireland) Order 1988, and (iii) The Communications Act 2003.

While the Protection from Harassment (Northern Ireland) Order 1997 was passed following concern that stalking was not well dealt with under existing legislation, the Act goes beyond the issue of stalking and covers harassment in a wider sense. Article 3 of the Order states that it is unlawful to cause harassment, alarm or distress by a course of conduct and states that 'A person must not pursue a course of conduct (a) which amounts to harassment of another, and (b) which he knows or ought to know amounts to harassment of the other.' In terms of dealing with perpetrators of harassment, Article 4 provides that a person guilty of an offence of harassment under

Article 3 shall be liable, on summary conviction, to imprisonment for a term not exceeding six months, or a fine not exceeding £5,000, or both. The legislation provides that a civil claim may also be brought by a victim in the High Court or County Court and that damages may be awarded for any anxiety caused by harassment and any financial loss resulting from harassment. The court may also grant a restraining order which shall prohibit the defendant from pursuing any further conduct which amounts to harassment or will cause a fear of violence. If without reasonable excuse the defendant does anything which breaches the court order, this will amount to a criminal offence and the defendant shall be liable, on summary conviction, to imprisonment for a term not exceeding six months, or a fine not exceeding £5,000, or both.

Under the Malicious Communications (Northern Ireland) Order 1988 it is an offence to send an indecent, offensive or threatening letter, electronic communication or other article to another person with intent to cause distress or anxiety. Under section 43 Telecommunications Act 1984 it is a similar offence to send a telephone message which is indecent, offensive or threatening. Both offences are punishable with up to six months' imprisonment and/or a fine not exceeding £5,000.

The most recent piece of legislation relevant to the issue of cyber-bullying, the Communications Act 2003, deals specifically with the improper use of a public electronic communications network. Section 127 of the Act provides as follows: '1. A person is guilty of an offence if he (a) sends by means of a public electronic communications network a message or other matter that is grossly offensive or of an indecent, obscene or menacing character; (b) causes any such message or matter to be so sent. 2. A person is guilty of an offence if, for the purpose of causing annoyance, inconvenience or needless anxiety to another, he (a) sends by means of a public electronic communications network a message that he knows to be false; (b) causes such a message to be sent; or (c) persistently makes use of a public electronic communications network. A person guilty of an offence under this section shall be liable, on summary conviction, to imprisonment for a term not exceeding six months or to a fine not exceeding £5,000, or to both.'

BULLYING AND CYBER-BULLYING IN NORTHERN IRELAND: THE IMPORTANT SUPPORTING ROLE OF THE POLICE SERVICE OF NORTHERN IRELAND (PSNI)

In their excellent factsheet concerning cyber-bullying and the law in Northern Ireland, NIABF very usefully point out the role of the Police Service of Northern Ireland (PSNI) and encourage parents/ carers to make contact and seek support from the PSNI when bullying occurs. The guidance highlights that contact, at an initial level, can be with the community and school officer or the crime prevention officer who is placed in each policing district. The factsheet offers guidance in relation to the importance of highlighting any evidence which may exist (e.g. downloaded website pages, text messages, or other notes). In consideration of the ethno-political context of Northern Irish society, the guidance offers the important reminder that where there are any specific references to religious, sectarian, racist, disablist or homophobic comments, it is important that these are highlighted to the PSNI as the incident may be considered a 'hate incident/crime'. In terms of the impact on the victim, the guidance also indicates the importance of informing the PSNI of any impact the incident(s) has had on the daily life of the child or young person. In terms of investigation, it is pointed out that the PSNI officer will make enquiries, speak to the child/young person (with appropriate supervision), and try to establish any offending or 'at risk' behaviour by the person involved. In terms of outreach activity, it is noted that the PSNI have a framework called the Youth Diversion Scheme, which allows for both types of behaviour to be addressed. The PSNI also deliver an educational programme entitled Citizenship and Safety Education, which incorporates lessons on 'Internet Safety' and 'Bullying' and can support schools/parent groups in delivering information on both subjects.

BULLYING AND CYBER-BULLYING IN NORTHERN IRELAND: FUTURE DIRECTIONS

From research studies among CYP in Northern Ireland, we know that while 'traditional' forms of bully/victim problems continue to be pervasive, cyber-bullying is an emerging form of peer aggression among this 'always on' (Belsey, 2004) generation, with involvement in such problems having a deleterious effect on health and well-being. With all of the legislative and practical support available to them, it would be an opportune time for schools to re-evaluate and update their policies and procedures in this area. Indeed, a follow-up to McGuckin and Lewis' (2008) pre-legislation survey would be most welcome – one that enquires not only about the management of f2f and cyber-bullying, but one that explores the knowledge, attitudes and management of other expressions of this peer aggression (e.g. disablist bullying: Purdy and McGuckin, 2011; sexist, sexual and transphobic (SST) bullying: DfES (Department for Education and Skills, 2010). The role of school management and the school community, as well as the input from psychologists and other professionals, is becoming even more important, as our 'digital natives' continue to develop in a fast-changing world. Everyone with an interest in the safety and well-being of children should re-double efforts in terms of prevention and intervention (see Smith, Pepler and Rigby, 2004 and Farrington and Ttofi, 2010 for scholarly reviews), especially in relation to the newly emerging cyber-bullying phenomena. Indeed, it is not only schools that need to be aware of the impact of cyber-bullying, all parents and adults with an interest in the safety and well-being of children should re-double efforts to understand the world of the 'net generation' (Lloyd and Devine, 2009). As a cautionary note about cyber-safety to the large proportion of adults who are 'digital migrants': if you don't understand it, you can't teach it!

REFERENCES

Ahmed, E., and Braithwaite, V. 'Bullying and Victimisation: Cause for Concern for Both Families and Schools' *Social Psychology of Education*, 7, 2004, pp. 35–54

ARK Northern Ireland, 'Kids' Life and Times Survey, 2008', http://www.ark.ac.uk/ylt/2008/ [accessed 10 January 2011]

ARK Northern Ireland, 'Kids' Life and Times Survey, 2008', http://www.ark.ac.uk/ylt/2009/ [accessed 10 January 2011]

Belsey, B. 'Cyber Bullying: An Emerging Threat to the 'Always On' Generation' (2004), http://www.cyber-bullying.ca/pdf/Cyber-bullying_Article_by_Bill_Belsey.pdf [accessed 22 December 2011]

Byrne, B. 'Ireland', in P.K. Smith, Y. Morita, J. Junger-Tas, D. Olweus, R. Catalano and P. Slee (eds), *The Nature of School Bullying: A Cross-National Perspective* (London and New York: Routledge, 1999)

Callaghan, S. and Joseph, S. 'Self-Concept and Peer Victimisation among Schoolchildren', *Personality and Individual Differences*, 18, 1995, pp. 161–3

Campbell, M.A. 'Cyber Bullying: An Old Problem in a New Guise?', *Australian Journal of Guidance and Counselling*, 15, 2005, pp. 68–76

Collins, K., and Bell, R. 'Peer Perceptions of Aggression and Bullying Behaviour in Primary Schools in Northern Ireland', *Annals of the New York Academy of Science*, 794, 1996, pp. 77–9

Collins, K., McAleavy, G. and Adamson, G. *Bullying in Schools: A Northern Ireland Study. Research Report Series No. 30* (Bangor, Northern Ireland: Department of Education for Northern Ireland, 2002)

Collins, K., McAleavy, G. and Adamson, G. 'Bullying in Schools: A Northern Ireland Study', *Educational Research*, 46, 2004, pp. 55–71

Department of Education for Northern Ireland, *Pastoral Care in Schools: Child Protection, Circular Number 1999/10* (Bangor, Northern Ireland: Department of Education, 1999)

Department of Education for Northern Ireland, *Pastoral Care in Schools: Promoting Positive Behaviour* (Bangor, Northern Ireland: Department of Education, 2001)

Department of Education for Northern Ireland, *Welfare and Protection of Pupils: Education and Libraries (Northern Ireland) Order 2003, Circular Number 2003/13* (Bangor, Northern Ireland: Department of Education, 2003)

Department of Education for Northern Ireland, *Acceptable Use of the Internet and Digital Technologies in Schools, Circular 2007/01* (Bangor, Northern Ireland: Department of Education, 2007)

Department for Education and Skills (DfES), *Every Child Matters: Change for Children* (Nottingham: DfES, 2004)

Department for Education and Skills (DfES), *Guidance for Schools on Preventing and Responding to Sexist, Sexual and Transphobic Bullying. Safe to Learn: Embedding Anti-Bullying Work in Schools* (Nottingham: DfES, 2010)

Espey, K., Duffy, J. and McGuckin (under review), *Cyber-Bullying among Northern Irish Post-Primary School Students*

Farrington, D.P. and Ttofi, M.M. 'School-Based Programs to Reduce Bullying and Victimisation', *Campbell Systematic Reviews*, 2009:6, 10.4073/csr.2009.6

Grant, M. 'Bullying: A Review of the Literature and Results of a Pilot Study', unpublished masters thesis, University of Ulster at Magee College, Londonderry, 1996

Hinduja, S. and Patchin, J.W. 'Cyber-Bullying: An Exploratory Analysis of Factors', *Deviant Behaviour*, 29, 2008, pp. 129–56

Kowalski, R.M., Limber, S.P. and Agatston, P.M. *Cyber Bullying: Bullying in the Digital Age* (Malden, MA: Blackwell, 2008)

Livesey, G., McAleavy, G., Donegan, T., Duffy, J., O'Hagan, C., Adamson, G. and White, R. *The Nature and Extent of Bullying in Schools in the North of Ireland. Research Report No. 46* (Bangor, Northern Ireland: Department of Education for Northern Ireland, 2007)

Lloyd, K. and Devine, P. 'The Net Generation', *ARK Research Update 62* (Belfast: ARK, 2009), http://www.ark.ac.uk/publications/updates/update62.pdf [accessed 17 January 2011]

Malicious Communications [Northern Ireland] Order 1988, http://www.legislation.gov.uk/nisi/1988/1849/contents [accessed 17 January 2011]

McGuckin, C. and Lewis, C.A. 'A Cross-National Perspective on School Bullying in Northern Ireland: A Supplement to Smith et al. (1999)', *Psychological Reports*, 93, 2003, pp. 279–87

McGuckin, C. and Lewis, C.A. 'Experiences of School Bullying in Northern Ireland: Data from the Life and Times Survey', *Adolescence*, 41, 2006, pp. 313–20

McGuckin, C. and Lewis, C.A. 'Management of Bullying in Northern Ireland Schools: A Pre-Legislative Survey', *Educational Research*, 50, 2008, pp. 9–23

McGuckin, C., Cummins, P.K. and Lewis, C.A. 'Bully/Victim Problems in Northern Ireland's Schools: Data from the 2000 Young Persons' Behaviour and Attitude Survey', *Individual Differences Research*, 6, 2008, pp. 280–8

McGuckin, C., Cummins, P.K. and Lewis, C.A. 'Bully/Victim Problems in Northern Ireland's Schools: Data from the 2003 Young Persons' Behaviour and Attitude Survey', *Adolescence*, 44, 2009, pp. 347–58

McGuckin, C., Cummins, P.K. and Lewis, C.A. 'Experiences of School Bullying, Psychological Well-being and Stress in Northern Ireland: Data from the 2005 Young Life and Times Survey', *Research in Education*, 83, 2010, pp. 54–66

McGuckin, C., Cummins, P.K. and Lewis, C.A. 'F2f and Cyber-Bullying among Children in Northern Ireland: Data from the Kids' Life and Times Surveys', *Psychology, Society and Education*, 2, 2010, pp. 67–78

McGuckin, C., Lewis, C.A. and Cummins, P.K. 'Experiences of School Bullying, Psychological Well-being and Stress in Northern Ireland: Data from the 2004 Young Life and Times Survey', *Irish Journal of Psychology*, 31, 2010, pp. 53–61

Mellor, A. 'Scotland', in P.K. Smith, Y. Morita, J. Junger-Tas, D. Olweus, R. Catalano, and P. Slee (eds), *The Nature of School Bullying: A Cross-National Perspective* (London and New York: Routledge, 1999)

Mora-Merchan, J. and Jäger, T. (eds), *Cyber-Bullying: A Cross-National Comparison* (Landau: Verlag Emprische Padagogik, 2010)

National Children's Home, *NCH National Survey 2002: Bullying*, http://www.nch.org.uk/itok/showquestion.asp?faq=9andfldAuto=145) [accessed 20 July 2009]

National Children's Home, *Putting U in the Picture: Mobile Phone Bullying Survey* (2005), http://www.filemaker.co.uk/educationcentre/downloads/articles/Mobile_bullying_report.pdf [accessed 17 January 2011]

Northern Ireland Anti-Bullying Forum, *Cyber Bullying: How Common Is It? A Sample Survey Investigating Cyber Bullying, its Forms, Awareness and Impact, and the Relationship between Age and Gender in Cyber Bullying* (2007), http://www.niabf.org.uk/cms/images/stories/documents/resources/cyber_bullying-_how_common_is_it.pdf [accessed 17 January 2011]

O'Moore, A.M., Kirkham, C. and Smith, M. 'Bullying Behaviour in Irish Schools: A Nationwide Study', *Irish Journal of Psychology*, 18, 1997, pp. 141–69

Office of the First Minister and Deputy First Minister (OFMDFM), *Our Children and Young People: Our Pledge (The ten-year strategy for children and young people in Northern Ireland)* (Belfast: OFMDFM, Children and Young People's Unit, 2006)

Olweus, D. *Bully/Victim Questionnaire For Students* (Bergen: Department of Psychology, University of Bergen, 1989)

Patchin, J.W. and Hinduja, S. 'Bullies Move Beyond the Schoolyard: A Preliminary Look at Cyber-Bullying', *Youth Violence and Juvenile Justice*, 4, 2006, pp. 148–69

Protection from Harassment [Northern Ireland] Order 1997

Purdy, N. and McGuckin, C. 'Disablist Bullying: An Investigation of Student Teachers' Knowledge and Confidence' (Armagh, Northern Ireland: The Standing Conference on Teacher Education North and South (SCoTENS), 2011)

RSM McClure Watters, *The Nature and Extent of Pupil Bullying in Schools in the North of Ireland*, vol. 56 (Bangor, Northern Ireland: Department of Education for Northern Ireland, 2011)

Shariff, S. *Confronting Cyber-Bullying: What Schools Need to Know to Control Misconduct and Avoid Legal Consequences* (New York: Cambridge University Press, 2009)

Smith, P.K., Morita, Y., Junger-Tas, J., Olweus, D., Catalano, R. and Slee, P. (eds), *The Nature of School Bullying: A Cross-National Perspective* (London and New York: Routledge, 1999)

Smith, P.K., Pepler, D.J. and Rigby, K. (eds), *Bullying in Schools: How Successful Can Interventions Be?* (Cambridge: Cambridge University Press, 2004)

Smith, P.K., Mahdavi, J., Carvalho, M. and Tippett, N. *An Investigation into Cyber-Bullying, its Forms, Awareness and Impact, and the Relationship between Age and Gender in Cyber-Bullying*. Research Brief No. RBX03-06 (London: DfES, 2006)

Solberg, M.E. and Olweus, D. 'Prevalence Estimation of School Bullying with the Olweus Bully/Victim Questionnaire', *Aggressive Behaviour*, 29, 2003, pp. 239–68

Steffgen, G., König, A. and Pfetsch, J. 'Does Banning Cell Phones in Schools Reduce Cyber-Bullying? *COST ACTION IS0801 Workshop*.

Cyber-Bullying: Definition and Measurement (Vilnius, Lithuania: Mykolas Romeris University, 2009)

Taylor, A. 'Comparison Study of Bullying Rates in Three Schools with Anti-Bullying Programs and Three Control Schools with No Anti-Bullying Programs in Northern Ireland', unpublished masters thesis, University of Ulster at Jordanstown, Belfast, Northern Ireland, 1996

The Communications Act [UK] 2003, http://www.legislation.gov.uk/ukpga/2003/21/contents [accessed 17 January 2011]

The Northern Ireland Act 1998 (Designation of Public Authorities) (Belfast: The Stationery Office, 2003)

Whitney, I. and Smith, P.K. 'A Survey of the Nature and Extent of Bullying in Junior/Middle and Secondary Schools', *Educational Research*, 35, 1993, pp. 3–25

Ybarra, M.L. and Mitchell, K.J. 'Online Aggressor/Targets, Aggressors, and Targets: A Comparison of Associated Youth Characteristics', *Journal of Child Psychology and Psychiatry*, 45, 2004, pp. 1308–16

Ybarra, M.L., Mitchell, K.J., Wolak, J. and Finkelhor, D. 'Examining Characteristics and Associated Distress Related to Internet Harassment: Findings from the Second Youth Internet Safety Survey', *Pediatrics*, 118, 2006, pp. 1169–77

Ybarra, M.L. and Mitchell, K.J. 'Prevalence and Frequency of Internet Harassment Instigation: Implications for Adolescent Health', *Journal of Adolescent Health*, 41, 2007, pp. 189–95

CHAPTER THREE

Homophobic Bullying in Schools in Ireland

Stephen James Minton

CONTEXTS AND DEFINITIONS

Norman, Galvin and McNamara (2006) have asserted that homophobic bullying is not simply another type of bullying, but rather it is linked to certain sections of society's prevailing negative attitudes towards people of non-heterosexual sexual orientation. It should be noted, therefore, that homosexuality was decriminalised in Ireland as recently as 1993, with male homosexual intercourse having been criminalised in Ireland under the Offences against the Person Act of 1861 and Criminal Law Amendment Act of 1885. Enactment of both Acts preceded Ireland's independence from Great Britain; they became part of Irish law in 1922. David Norris (now a senator) challenged the constitutionality of the provisions of these Acts in 1984, on the grounds that as a gay man his constitutional right to privacy (which, he argued, was implied) was compromised by the criminalisation of homosexuality. While Norris was unsuccessful in both the High Court and the Supreme Court in Ireland, the European Court of Human Rights ruled that the criminalisation of homosexuality did breach his right to privacy under Article 8 of the European Convention on Human Rights (which was not, however, part of Irish law at the time). Homosexuality was legalised with the passing of the Criminal Law (Sexual Offences) Act of 1993 (Bacik, 2004).

Decriminalisation of male homosexual intercourse has not in itself, of course, brought about equality. However, over the last two decades, other legal reform has taken place. It is, for example, illegal (under the Employment Equality Act of 1998 and the Equal Status Act of 2000) to discriminate on the grounds of sexual orientation in the areas of employment, vocational training, advertising, collective agreements, the provision of goods and services, and other publicly available opportunities, and the Prohibition of Incitement to Hatred Act of 1989 outlaws incitement to hatred based on sexual orientation (Government of Ireland, 2010 a, b and c). However, section 37 of the Employment Equality Act (Government of Ireland, 2010a) states that if religious organisations, medical institutions or educational institutions want to maintain their religious ethos then it is *not* illegal under section 37 for them to discriminate regarding employment. Given that over 90% of schools in Ireland and most of the teacher-training colleges in Ireland are under Roman Catholic control (Bacik, 2004), this has been an issue of concern for Lesbian, Gay, Bisexual and Transgender (LGBT) teachers, not to mention the potential for shaping school climate. The Civil Partnership and Certain Rights and Obligations of Cohabitants Act of 2010 (Government of Ireland, 2010d), which came into effect on 1 January 2011, provides for certain rights (e.g. home protection, maintenance, pension entitlements) of unmarried participants in long-term cohabiting relationships (whether same-sex or opposite-sex). However, it falls short of guaranteeing the same rights to same-sex couples as heterosexuals enjoy. It does not provide for same-sex couples to be legally married; nor can civil partners adopt jointly, or have joint guardianship over children they raise together. The Act does provide for same-sex couples who are legally married or have formed a civil union in other jurisdictions to have their partnership recognised in Ireland.

Hence, while certain legal reforms have taken place, *homophobia* remains a pervasive attitude in a number of sections of society, some of which exert considerable influence and power. Bacik (2004) cites some of Chief Justice O'Higgins' comments in his judgement in the Supreme Court against David Norris' challenge: that homosexuality had been regarded from the '... earliest days with a deep revulsion as being contrary to the order of nature, a perversion of the biological functions of the sex organs and an affront both to society and to God ... it remains the teaching of all Christian Churches that homosexual acts are wrong' (p. 137). Bacik notes that such comments '... for the majority make bizarre reading today, being based upon the sort of Victorian notions of morality upon which the legislation [that Norris was challenging] was founded' (2004, p. 136); it is to be recalled that these comments were made as recently as 1984 by a Supreme Court judge (i.e. the highest court in the land) in his ruling against legal reform.

Homophobia itself has been defined as '... the fear of being labelled homosexual and the irrational fear, dislike or hatred of gay males and lesbians' (Blumenfeld and Raymond, 1998; in Norman, Galvin and McNamara, 2006, p. 36). Homophobic bullying in schools is perhaps the clearest manifestation of this attitude among young people (or, at least, school-going young people) in Ireland. In publications that appeared in 2006 and 2008 respectively, two sets of Irish researchers – Norman, Galvin and McNamara (2006, p. 43) and Minton, Dahl, O'Moore and Tuck (2008, p. 178) – cited the following UK definition of homophobic bullying as being acceptable:

Homophobic bullying takes place where general bullying behaviour such as verbal and physical abuse and intimidation is accompanied by or consists of the use of terms such as gay, lesbian, queer or lezzie by perpetrators

(Warwick et al., 2001)

Elsewhere, in discussing homophobic bullying in schools in Ireland, my colleagues and I have found it useful to divide homophobic bullying into two sub-types. Firstly, there is the type of homophobic bullying that underpins the (often aggressive) heteronormativity of the school environment – 'heteronormative bullying'; secondly, there is the active persecution of known lesbian, gay, bisexual and transgender persons – and, although we noted that '... one hardly needs to construct a specific term', we referred to this sub-type as 'sexual orientation-based bullying' (Minton et al., 2008, p. 179). However, it is to be acknowledged that there is considerable potential for overlap between the two sub-types. For example, aggressive heteronormativity in schools frequently takes the form of the use of homophobic pejoratives; Thurlow's study of English and Welsh secondary schools (2001) found that homophobic pejoratives accounted for 10% of the pejoratives generated by his sample, and almost all of Hunt and Jensen's (2006) sample of 1,145 LGBTQ (lesbian, gay, bisexual, trans and queer) participants had '... heard words and phrases such as "dyke", "poof" and "you're so gay" used in a derogatory way' (Hunt and Jensen, 2006; in Clarke, Ellis, Peel and Riggs, 2010, p. 165). In an environment where the use of homophobic pejoratives among students is persistent (as Duncan (1999), Chang and Kleiner (2001) and Mac an Ghaill, Hanafin and Conway (2004), in the UK, USA and Ireland respectively, have indicated it is) and remains unchallenged, it is perhaps predictable that verbal aggression often degenerates further into physical acts of assault and bullying. One study in Iowa, USA recorded that the average high school student hears anti-gay epithets around twenty-five times per day, yet teachers who hear these words fail to respond 97% of the time (Flannery, 1999; in Chang and Kleiner, 2001). A number of researchers (Duncan, 1999; Thurlow, 2001; Warwick et al., 2001; and O'Moore and Minton, 2004) have commented that homophobic epithets are not always meant literally – i.e. are not always targeted at known LGBT people – but instead serve to build in-group and out-group identities, by norming along stereotypical gender lines (hence, are heteronormative (Minton et al., 2008)). Nevertheless, the rigid heteronormative climate is oppressive to LGBT individuals, whether they are open about their sexuality or not. As respondents in a survey conducted by my colleagues and I (see below, section on 'Research into Homophobic Bullying in Schools in Ireland') said (Minton et al., 2008, pp. 183–4):

> Homophobic attitudes are very prevalent in all-boys schools, irrespective of your sexual preference.

> Physical bullying both before AND after they knew I was gay. It's just that kind of school.

> People constantly shout at me 'gay', 'fag' ... and a lot of the guys, joking, ask me for oral sex ... it makes me feel very uncomfortable ... and although they are loud and open in their abuse, no teacher has ever stopped it or drawn attention to it ... it's as if it's normal, and acceptable!

Being subject to physical violence was reported by 14% of the LGBT high school students in Chang and Kleiner's US (2001) study; threats of violence were commonplace towards those deemed 'gay' (regardless of their actual orientation) in Duncan's UK study (1999). In Ireland, not only have gay individuals been assaulted and even killed (including the tragic case of a murdered gay man in Fairview Park, Dublin in 1983), but the Hirschfield Centre (gay resource) was burnt down in 1988 (Bacik, 2004). Mayock, Bryan, Carr and Kitching (2009) cite Savin-Williams (1990) and Mac an Ghaill (1994) in making the point that LGBT school-goers have been thus far an 'invisible minority' and 'one of the most significant "at-risk" groups of adolescents', and Remafedi (1987) and Elia (1993) in arguing that '... classrooms have been identified as the most homophobic of all environments' (p. 26). The reflection is thus prompted: given this background, one might expect homophobic bullying in schools in Ireland to be frequent, but the question is, just how frequent is it?

RESEARCH INTO HOMOPHOBIC BULLYING IN SCHOOLS IN IRELAND

Much empirically driven research material exists on bullying in *general* in Irish schools, and how to prevent it – as the content of the rest of this book indicates – but much less is known about *homophobic bullying,* and the bullying of LGBT young people in Irish schools (Minton et al., 2008, p. 177). An important study that attempted to address this knowledge gap was Norman's investigation of 725 SPHE (Social, Personal and Health Education) teachers' views and perceptions of homophobic bullying (Norman, 2004; Norman and Galvin, 2006). It was found that 79% of the teachers in the sample were aware of verbal homophobic bullying, and 16% were aware of physical bullying related to homophobia; however, 90% of the teachers responded that their school's anti-bullying policy did not cover homophobic bullying. O'Higgins-Norman (2008) questioned the extent to which the Relationships and Sexuality Education (RSE) component of SPHE meets the needs of all second-level school students in Ireland, as there is '… silence on certain behaviours'; he argued that this, and '… the absence of any teaching about sexual orientation contributes to homophobic bullying among students in Irish schools' (p. 69).

A few years ago, my colleagues and I conducted an exploratory survey of the experiences of homophobic bullying among 123 LGBT young people in Ireland. We found that 22% of the sample reported not feeling safe on their way to/from school; 79.9% had been called nasty names, teased or made fun of in the previous three months; 71.2% had been called nasty names, teased or made fun of on the grounds of their sexual orientation in the previous three months; and that 50% had been bullied in the previous three months. In terms of the latter figure, it was recalled that the proportion of post-primary students reporting having been bullied in the previous three months in the general school-going population was found to be around one in six (according to O'Moore's nationwide survey of bullying behaviour (O'Moore, Kirkham and Smith, 1997)). We concluded that the LGBT population is one that is 'at risk' of being bullied in school, and that the issue of homophobic bullying should be included as a matter of concern in teachers' pre- and in-service training (Minton et al., 2008).

An important empirical contribution to the literature on homophobic bullying in Ireland came courtesy of the Supporting LGBT Lives project (Mayock et al., 2009), in which 1,100 participants (14–73 years [mean = 30.5 years]; 64% male, 34% female, 2% other [primarily transgender or gender queer]; over 80% gay or lesbian, 10% bisexual, less than 1% heterosexual) completed online surveys, and 40 participants were interviewed in depth. The study examined an array of factors that impinged upon the mental health and well-being of LGBT people, including experiences at school and bullying. Essentially, 58% of the sample, and over half of the current school-goers in the sample (which comprised less than 5% of the online sample) reported the existence of homophobic bullying in their schools. Over half reported having been called names relating to their sexual orientation or gender identity by fellow students, and 8% reported being subjected to the same by members of school staff. Some 40% reported having been subjected to verbal threats on the basis of being or being thought to be LGBT by fellow students, and 4% reported being subjected to the same by members of school staff. Twenty five per cent reported having been physically threatened on the basis of being or being thought to be LGBT by fellow students, and 1% reported being subjected to the same by members of school staff. In an earlier study of 362 LGBT individuals under the age of 25 conduced in Northern Ireland (Carolan and Redmond, 2003), findings were broadly similar, with 44% of the sample reporting having been bullied at school because of their sexual orientation. In terms of teacher responses, Mayock et al. (2009) found that many of their participants described:

> ... direct efforts on the part of certain school authorities or personnel to prevent, 'silence' or render invisible LGBT expression in schools ... most of the narrative commentary on official school responses to homophobic bullying characterised it as non-existent, ineffective, or complicit with a culture of hostility towards LGBT students (p. 67).

In terms of the effects of homophobic bullying at school, Mayock et al. (2009) found that 20% of their sample had missed school because they felt threatened or were afraid of getting hurt at school because they were LGBT; 5% had actually left school early because of homophobic bullying. In the words of one of their participants (a 23-year-old gay man):

I left school because of the hurt and suffering I got in school, and the teachers didn't care, as I think it was a case of 'well they call him gay and he probably is gay, so why should we step in, 'cos they aren't saying anything wrong' attitude towards gay people ... even though I wasn't out at school. I was forced to leave at my junior cert, due to the abuse I got ... jumped on, called puff, queer etc (p. 68).

Outside of school, Mayock et al. (2009) document reports of the day-to-day victimisation of LGBT people, with 80% of their sample reporting having been verbally abused, 40% having been threatened with physical violence, and 25% having been punched, kicked or beaten because of their LGBT identity. In the aforementioned Northern Ireland study, Carolan and Redmond (2003) found that 35% of their sample had been physically abused, and 65% had been verbally abused. For many LGBT people, then, bullying (in the sense of being the target of repeated and unprovoked acts of aggression) does not end on leaving school. It is small wonder in my view, then, that Mayock et al. (2009) found that 86.3% of their sample had suffered from depression, 27% had self-harmed, and 18% had attempted suicide, and that in Carolan and Redmond's (2003) study, 21% of their sample had been medicated for depression, 26% had self-harmed, and 29% had attempted suicide. These effects seem not to be precipitated by being part of a minority, but rather by being part of a minority that is at risk of abuse. Again, in the words of another of Mayock et al.'s (2009) participants (a 28-year-old lesbian):

I've been suicidal many times ... It's not because I'm a lesbian but because of how I've been treated in my life as a lesbian. School was terrible and then to get badly bullied in work was horrible (p. 102).

Following Mayock et al.'s (2009) study, the self-reported experiences of homophobic bullying (current and retrospective) of LGBT people was known, but what remained unknown was the relationship between sexual orientation and bullying in the general school-going population. However, in May 2010, 824 fifth-year (age ca. 16–17 years) secondary school students (341 male [41.4%], 483 female [58.6%]), at nine schools covering the entire geographical area of the Republic of Ireland, completed an English-language translation of a questionnaire previously used in a large-scale empirical study in Norway (Roland and Auestad, 2009). Some 3,046 (1,583 male, 1,463 female) tenth-grade students (ca. 17–18 years of age) participated in Roland and Auestad's (2009) study. In total 7.3% of heterosexual boys, 23.8% of bisexual boys, 48% of homosexual boys, 5.7% of heterosexual girls, 11.5% of bisexual girls, and 17.7% of homosexual girls had been bullied in the previous two to three months. The highest rates of anxiety and depression of all were found among bullied bisexual and homosexual students. Roland and Auestad (2009) also noted that their study had:

> ... shown that bisexual and homosexual students, especially boys, are very strongly over-represented in both being bullied ... being exposed to bullying has a more negative effect on bisexual and homosexual students than it does on heterosexuals (Roland and Auestad, 2009, p. 80).

In the Irish comparative study, it was found that whereas 32.9% of heterosexual males and 20.1% of heterosexual females reported having been bullied in the previous couple of months, and 9.9% and 1.5% respectively reported having been 'frequently' (that is to say, once a week or more often) so, 62.5% of non-heterosexual males and 66.7% of non-heterosexual females reported having been bullied in the previous couple of months, and 37.5% and 20.8% respectively reported having been frequently so. In other words, greater proportions of non-heterosexual males and females reported having been bullied than was the case for their heterosexual counterparts (Minton, 2011). In fact, non-heterosexual females were statistically significantly more likely to report having been bullied than were heterosexual females or females in general. However, the number of non-heterosexual males in the sample was too small to accurately calculate statistical significance (Minton, 2011).

RESOURCES FOR YOUNG PEOPLE AND SCHOOLS

It can be seen from past research, including that outlined above, that homophobic bullying is frequent and pervasive, and that LGBT young people are more frequently bullied than other young people; furthermore, young people who experience homophobic bullying are more likely to attempt suicide (BeLonG To, 2012). BeLonG To, Ireland's first designated lesbian, gay, bisexual and transgender youth project (Barron and Collins, 2005, p. 7), which has been operational since 2002, has been instrumental in ensuring the provision of services to young LGBT people who have been affected by homophobic bullying, and in the development and provision of resources and training to school personnel who wish to address LGBT issues and concerns (including homophobic bullying) in schools. In October 2006, BeLonG To and the Equality Authority made an attempt to raise awareness of LGBT issues in general, and homophobic bullying in schools in particular, through the dissemination to all schools in Ireland of a pack containing posters, postcards, and a leaflet entitled *Making Your School Safe for Lesbian, Gay, Bisexual and Transgender Students*. The project was supported by the two secondary school teachers' trade unions in Ireland (the Association of Secondary Teachers in Ireland (ASTI) and the Teachers' Union of Ireland (TUI)), the USS (Union of Secondary Students), the NAPD (National Association of Principals and Deputy Principals), the NPC-PP (National Parents' Council Post-Primary), Pobal, and An Garda Síochána (BeLonG To/The Equality Authority, 2006).

BeLonG To's 'Stop Homophobic Bullying in Schools' campaign was highlighted in the National Youth Council of Ireland's Active Youth Participation Report of 2008 as a case study of best practice, and in a 2009 Committee of the Council of Europe as an example of 'Good Practice' in addressing LGBT inequality in schools (BeLonG To, 2010). Developing from this, BeLonG To launched its first annual 'Stand Up! LGBT Awareness Week' in 2010, which was aimed at creating positive understanding of LGBT young people and their issues, with a focus on homophobia, transphobia and exclusion in schools, youth clubs and local areas, and tackling homophobic and transphobic bullying. It was held on 9–18 April 2010, and took place mainly in youth services around Ireland; everyone was encouraged to 'show your support for your lesbian, gay, bisexual and transgender friends' and, 'don't stand for homophobic bullying' (BeLonG To, 2010). It is no exaggeration to talk of the short film (*Stand Up! Don't Stand for Homophobic Bullying*) that accompanied the 2011 'Stand Up!' campaign as having 'gone viral'; at the time of writing (June 2012), it has received over one million views on YouTube. In the 2012 'Stand Up! Week' (launched by the Minister for Education and Skills), a pack (comprising a DVD and printed materials) was sent to every post-primary school in Ireland. 'Stand Up!' has, deservedly so, been internationally recognised by UNESCO, and that organisation's recent *Global Good Practice and Policy Manual on Education Sector Responses to Homophobic Bullying* (launched 16 May

2012 has been much informed and driven by researchers and activists in Ireland (BeLonG To, 2012).

The Gay and Lesbian Equality Network (GLEN) (founded in 1987) has funding from the Health Services Executive to '… promote awareness and develop responses to the factors that lead to poor mental health among lesbian and gay people' (Barron and Collins, 2005, p. 7), and has been particularly active in an advocacy and reformatory role in its work with educational partners. Following the publication of *Supporting LGBT Lives* (Mayock et al., 2009), GLEN, the ASTI and the TUI jointly published a resource for teachers entitled *Teachers Supporting Diversity: Lesbian, Gay and Bisexual Students* (GLEN, ASTI and TUI, 2009). The aims of the resource were to support teachers in recognising, affirming and supporting diversity (including the diversity of sexual orientations) and challenging name-calling and homophobic bullying. It was distributed to all schools nationwide (GLEN, ASTI and TUI, 2009). A similar resource, aimed at principals and school leaders, was authored by the Department of Education and Science and GLEN; entitled, *Lesbian, Gay and Bisexual Students in Post-Primary Schools: Guide for Principals and School Leaders*, it was distributed to all schools nationwide (Department of Education and Science and GLEN, 2010). This resource was published in association with a number of the key stakeholders in secondary education in Ireland – the ACCS (Association of Community and Comprehensive Schools), ASTI, the IVEA (Irish Vocational Educational Association), the JMBSS (Joint Managerial Body for Secondary Schools), the NAPD, the National Parents' Council (Post-Primary), and the TUI. The resource advocated that '… specific reference to homophobic bullying within the school's Anti-Bullying Policy' be included, and that schools should '… develop and/or maintain a zero tolerance approach to the use of anti-gay language that is pejorative or derisive in all areas of school' (Department of Education and Science and GLEN, 2010, p. 13).

It would seem that in very recent years, that such research, advocacy and activism is bearing fruit. O'Higgins-Norman et al.'s (2010) report on *Addressing Homophobic Bullying in Second-Level Schools* included six case study schools, selected from thirty, who were '… involved in trying to specifically address homophobic bullying'. Post-primary schools in Ireland were officially instructed to specifically reference homophobic bullying in their anti-bullying policies in 2010 (O'Higgins-Norman et al., 2010). Finally, in May 2012, the Department of Education and Skills convened an Anti-

Bullying Working Group, whose first task was to develop concrete strategies to combat homophobic bullying (BeLonG To, 2012) and the Department of Education and Skills' Action Plan launched in January 2013 places specific emphasis on addressing homophobic bullying.

RECOMMENDATIONS

In closing this chapter, I should like to make five general recommend-ations (aimed principally at policy makers and school management staff, but also school teaching staff and teacher-trainers) concerning preventing and countering homophobic bullying in schools in Ireland:

(i) Include homophobic bullying explicitly in school anti-bullying strategies.

Research evidence, quite simply, does not support the position that in addressing bullying behaviour in general one is simultaneously addressing the issue of homophobic bullying. Canadian researchers Mishna, Newman, Daley and Solomon (2009) have correctly stated that 'the preponderance of bullying research does not address sexual orientation as a possible factor' (p. 1598). Their compatriot, Gerald Walton, asserts that, 'Even though homophobia is a promin-ent feature of schoolyard bullying, it is also one of the most unchallenged forms of bullying' (2006, p. 13); furthermore, he argues that apparently non-targeted anti-bullying interventions in schools may be hampered by deficits of homophobia, heterosexism and heteronormativity (Walton, 2006). Hence, as well as schools specifically referencing homophobic bullying in their anti-bullying policies, it is recommended that 'general' anti-bullying programmes that are developed for use in schools should *meaningfully* address homophobic bullying as a *specific* issue. This should be reflected in the design, implementation (including resources formulation of policies, management and teaching staff, parents and community members and especially young people) and evaluation of such programmes. It will be recalled that a key point was made by the Department of Education and Science in the guidelines for principals and school leaders it co-authored with GLEN (2010) (see above, section on 'Resources for Young People and Schools'), when these bodies also advocated that:

(ii) Schools should develop and/or maintain a zero tolerance approach to the use of anti-gay language that is pejorative or derisive in all areas of school.

Homophobic bullying also raises key issues for pre- and in-service teacher training and the school curriculum:

(iii) Challenging heterosexism, homophobia and transphobia should be a key feature of pre- and in-service teacher training.

Mayock et al. (2009), citing evidence from Macintosh (2007), state that:

> ... Teacher education programmes should offer courses that will assist both early and in-career educators in taking action to challenge heterosexism, homophobia and transphobia in their schools and classrooms. Such interventions should not comprise 'one-off' anti-homophobia lectures and workshops addressing LGBT issues, which are likely to further marginalise LGBT youth, but rather be infused throughout teacher education programmes (p. 26).

(iv) The opportunity provided by subjects such as SPHE (Social, Personal and Health Education) and RSE (Relationships and Sexuality Education) to recognise and affirm non-heterosexual orientations should be actualised.

Mayock et al. (2009) found that '... the topic of sexual orientation is all but invisible within school-based Relationships and Sexuality Education in Ireland' (p. 33); they also quote Kiely (2005; in Mayock et al, 2009, p. 27), who states that '... the presumption of all students as heterosexual pervades the materials ... students identifying as gay, lesbian or bisexual ... are not likely to have their sex education needs met in the kind of programme provided.' Therefore, Mayock et al. (2009) state elsewhere (p. 26):

> The formal school curriculum, and Social, Personal and Health Education (SPHE) and Relationships and Sexuality Education (RSE) in particular, should provide far greater scope for the exploration of minority sexuality and gender identity. In order to realise this, LGBT identities should be infused throughout the

RSE curriculum. LGBT identities should be equally validated through the informal curriculum such as school events.

O'Higgins-Norman's (2008) comments that '... the absence of any teaching about sexual orientation contributes to homophobic bullying among students in Irish schools' (p. 69) will perhaps also be recalled.

(v) Homophobic bullying is everyone's problem – entire school communities should be involved in acting against it.

If we have attitudes such as prejudice (e.g. homophobia) and discriminatory and persecutory actions such as bullying in our society, then it is because we as a society have not acted sufficiently against them. A saying that is often attributed to the great Irish philosopher Edmund Burke (1729–1787) is that, 'It is necessary only for the good man to do nothing for evil to triumph' (O'Donoghue, 1999, p. 99). BeLonG To's campaigns against homophobic bullying in schools have consistently highlighted that there is a need for everyone to act against it. The whole-school approach, with which the reader will be familiar from other chapters within this book, has an obvious application in preventing and countering homophobic bullying too. Indeed, the efforts of the 'Stand Up!' campaign should be applauded and centrally supported, potentially including the development of an evaluated, evidence-based whole-school or whole-school/ community programme specific to anti-homophobic bullying, to be implemented on a pilot and eventually nationwide basis.

REFERENCES

Bacik, I. *Kicking and Screaming: Dragging Ireland into the 21st Century* (Dublin: The O'Brien Press, 2004)

Barron, M. and Collins, E. 'Responding to the Needs of Vulnerable Lesbian, Gay, Bisexual and Transgendered Youth'. Presented to the Irish Association of Suicidology Fifth Annual Conference, Dublin, December 2005

BeLonG To Professional, 'Supporting Lesbian, Gay, Bisexual and Transgender Young People in Ireland' (2010), http://www.belongto. org/pro [accessed 6 January 2011]

BeLonG To, 'Combating Homophobic and Transphobic Bullying in Schools'. Presented to the Department of Education and Skills Anti-Bullying Forum, Dublin, May 2012

BeLonG To and the Equality Authority, 'Making Your School Safe for Lesbian, Gay, Bisexual and Transgender Students' (2006), http://www.glen.ie/education/pdfs/Making_Your_School_Safe_EN.pdf [accessed 7 January 2011]

Carolan, F. and Redmond, S. *shOUT. The Needs of Young People in Northern Ireland who Identify as Lesbian, Gay, Bisexual or Transgender* (Belfast: YouthNet, 2003)

Chang, C.W. and Kleiner, B.H. 'New Developments Concerning Discrimination and Harassment of Gay Students', *International Journal of Sociology and Social Policy*, vol. 21, no. 8, 2001, pp. 108–15

Clarke, V., Ellis, S.J., Peel, E. and Riggs, D.W. *Lesbian, Gay, Bisexual, Trans and Queer Psychology: An Introduction* (Cambridge: Cambridge University Press, 2010)

Department of Education and Science and GLEN (Gay and Lesbian Equality Network), *Lesbian, Gay and Bisexual Students in Post-Primary Schools: Guide for Principals and School Leaders* (Dublin: Department of Education and Science and GLEN, 2010)

Duncan, N. *Sexual Bullying: Gender Conflict and Pupil Culture in Secondary Schools* (London: Routledge, 1999)

GLEN (Gay and Lesbian Equality Network), ASTI (Association of Secondary Teachers Ireland) and TUI (Teachers' Union of Ireland) (TUI), *Teachers Supporting Diversity: Lesbian, Gay and Bisexual Students* (Dublin: GLEN, ASTI and TUI, 2009)

Government of Ireland, Employment Equality Act (1998), in the *Irish Statute Book* (Dublin: Office of the Attorney General, 2010a) http://www.irishstatutebook.ie/1998/en/act/pub/0021/index.html [accessed 10 January 2011]

Government of Ireland, Equal Status Act (2000), in the *Irish Statute Book* (Dublin: Office of the Attorney General, 2010b) http://www.irishstatutebook.ie/2000/en/act/pub/0008/index.html [accessed 10 January 2011]

Government of Ireland, Prohibition of Incitement to Hatred Act (1989), in the *Irish Statute Book* (Dublin: Office of the Attorney General, 2010c), http://www.irishstatutebook.ie/1989/en/act/pub/0019/index.html [accessed 10 January 2011]

Government of Ireland, The Civil Partnership and Certain Rights and Obligations of Cohabitants Act (2010), in the *Irish Statute Book* (Dublin: Office of the Attorney General, 2010d), http://www.irishstatutebook.ie/pdf/2010/en.act.2010.0024.pdf [accessed 26 June 2012]

Mac an Ghaill, M., Hanafin, J. and Conway, P.F. *Gender Politics and Exploring Masculinities in Irish Education* (Dublin: National Council for Curriculum and Assessment (NCCA), 2004)

Mayock, P., Bryan, A., Carr, N. and Kitching, K. *Supporting LGBT Lives: A Study of the Mental Health and Well-Being of Lesbian, Gay, Bisexual and Transgender People* (Dublin: GLEN and BeLonG To, 2009)

Minton, S.J. 'Experiences of and Perspectives on Homophobic Bullying among a Sample of Upper Secondary School Students in Ireland', presented at the 15th European Conference on Developmental Psychology, Bergen, Norway, 23–27 August, 2011

Minton, S.J., Dahl, T., O'Moore, A.M. and Tuck, D. 'An Exploratory Survey of the Experiences of Homophobic Bullying among Lesbian, Gay, Bisexual and Transgendered Young People in Ireland', *Irish Educational Studies*, vol. 27, no. 2, 2008, pp. 177–91

Mishna, F., Newman, P.A., Daley, A. and Solomon, S. 'Bullying of Lesbian and Gay Youth: A Qualitative Investigation', *British Journal of Social Work*, vol. 39, no. 8, 2009, pp. 1598–614

Norman, J. *A Survey of Teachers on Homophobic Bullying in Irish Second-Level Schools* (Dublin: Dublin City University, 2004)

Norman, J. and Galvin, M. *Straight Talk: An Investigation of Attitudes and Experiences of Homophobic Bullying in Second-Level Schools* (Dublin: Department of Education and Science Gender Equality Unit, 2006), http://www.dcu.ie/education_studies/schooling_sexualities/documents/schoolingsexualities-phase2report.pdf [accessed 12 January 2011]

Norman, J., Galvin, M. and McNamara, G. *Straight Talk: Researching Gay and Lesbian Issues in the School Curriculum* (Dublin: Department of Education and Science Gender Equality Unit, 2006)

O'Donoghue, B. (ed.), *Oxford Irish Quotations* (Oxford: Oxford University Press, 1999)

O'Higgins-Norman, J. 'Equality in the Provision of Social, Personal and Health Education in the Republic of Ireland: The Case of Homophobic Bullying?', *Pastoral Care in Education*, vol. 26, no. 2, 2008, pp. 69–81

O'Higgins-Norman, J., Goldrick, M. and Harrison, K. *Addressing Homophobic Bullying in Schools* (Dublin: The Equality Authority, 2010)

O'Moore, A.M., Kirkham, C. and Smith, M. 'Bullying Behaviour in Irish Schools: A Nationwide Study', *Irish Journal of Psychology*, vol. 18, no. 2, 1997, pp. 141–69

O'Moore, A.M. and Minton, S.J. *Dealing with Bullying in Schools: A Training Manual for Teachers, Parents and Other Professionals* (London: Paul Chapman Publishing, 2004)

Roland, E. and Auestad, G. *Seksuell Orienteering og Mobbing* (Stavanger, Norway: Universitetet i Stavanger, Senter for Atferdsforskning [*Sexual Orientation and Bullying* (Stavanger, Norway: University of Stavanger, Centre for Behavioural Research, 2009)]

Thurlow, C. 'Naming the "Outsider Within": Homophobic Pejoratives and the Verbal Abuse of Lesbian, Gay and Bisexual High-School Pupils', *Journal of Adolescence*, 24, 2001, pp. 25–38

UNESCO, *Education Sector Responses to Homophobic Bullying* (Paris: UNESCO, 2012)

Walton, G. 'H-Cubed: A Primer on Bullying and Sexuality Diversity for Educators', *Professional Development Perspectives*, 6, 2006, pp. 13–20

Warwick, I., Aggleton, P. and Douglas, N. 'Playing it Safe: Addressing the Emotional and Physical Health of Lesbian and Gay Pupils in the UK', *Journal of Adolescence*, 24, 2001, pp. 129–40

CHAPTER FOUR

The Challenges of Non-Reporting of Bullying

Elaine O'Dowd

INTRODUCTION

In Ireland it is compulsory for schools to have anti-bullying policies outlining the procedures a school will adopt to prevent and deal with aggressive behaviour. Nevertheless, bullying continues to be a widespread problem in schools (O'Moore and Minton, 2003). One major reason for the high prevalence of bullying in schools is the reluctance to tell, which has been found to increase for every year that a child grows older (O'Moore, Kirkham and Smith, 1997).

This chapter will report on a study that was conducted to examine the reasons which children gave for keeping their victimisation a secret. Having greater insight into the reasons for non-reporting will help measures to be developed and implemented which can challenge the strong reluctance to report bullying.

The study was carried out with a fifth and sixth class in a girls' primary school in 2008 and formed part of an MEd (Aggression Studies) with the School of Education, Trinity College Dublin (O'Dowd, 2009).

The study gathered information about where bullying occurs, what forms it takes, who it involves, what strategies the girls adopt to deal with it and who they inform about bullying. It also determined the level of non-reporting of bullying, why it exists and what the girls feel needs to change so that reporting bullying would be an agreeable option to them.

While the research to be presented in this chapter is confined to one school, it is hoped that it may highlight the policies and practices that may exist in schools with established anti-bullying policies, which hinder the reporting of bullying.

PREVIOUS RESEARCH

In recent years, there have been numerous studies carried out to ascertain the levels of bullying in schools. Figures vary from country to country, however; at least 5% of pupils in primary and secondary schools are bullied weekly or more often in countries all over the world (Roland and Galloway, 2002; Cowie, Jennifer and Sharp, 2003; Ortega, del Rey and Férnandez, 2003).

Much research to date has revealed a profound reluctance to report bullying on the part of bullied students (Olweus, 1993; Whitney and Smith, 1993; Rigby, 1997; Ortega and Lera, 2000; Smith and Shu, 2000; Rigby and Barnes, 2002; O'Moore and Minton, 2004). There appears to be a stigma attached to telling (Whitney and Smith, 1993; Rigby, 1997).

Findings also suggest a steady downward trend of the self-reporting of victimisation between the ages of 8 and 16 (Olweus, 1993; Whitney and Smith, 1993; O'Moore, Kirkham and Smith, 1997; Smith and Shu, 2000). Despite this apparent decline in reporting bullying, Childline shows a peak of reporting bullying between ages 11 and 13 (LaFontaine, 1991). Salmivalli (2002) found that while there was a decrease in the frequency of self-reported victimisation with age, no decline in peer-evaluated victimisation was observed. It therefore appears the decline is in fact only in the actual reporting of bullying, not in its perpetration. Therefore, James et al. (2006) suggest that relying on reported levels of bullying may not give a complete picture of the current situation.

Rivers and Smith (1994) found not telling was particularly likely in cases of indirect bullying, which is probably more disputable and harder to prove than physical bullying. This can include spreading rumours, breaking confidences, criticising clothing, appearance or personality, exclusionary behaviours, writing abusive messages, prank phone calls, infiltration of friendship groups, verbal/non-verbal gestures, sarcasm, etc. (Owens, Shute and Slee, 2000). Such bullying is more commonly found among girls and rarely takes place in the public arena, so it can be harder to detect (Besag, 2006).

In primary school, pupils are significantly more likely to tell someone at home that they have been bullied than to tell their teacher (Whitney and Smith, 1993; Genta et al., 1996; O'Moore, Kirkham and Smith, 1997; Smith and Shu, 2000; O'Moore and Minton, 2004).

Olivier and Candappa (2007) report that the reluctance to tell adults particularly teachers, increases with age, although the likelihood of telling friends remains high. Tisak and Tisak (1996) contend that younger students feel more comfortable involving adults. However, the probability of all victims telling someone increases with the frequency of being bullied (Whitney and Smith, 1993).

Smith and Shu (2000) discovered there was a small risk of things getting worse when teachers were told about the bullying. However, for those who had told a teacher, the outcome was usually positive (Smith and Shu, 2000). Menesini et al. (1997) report that children show more confidence in teachers than in other children that they will try to stop bullying.

Telling often means acting against a peer culture that discourages 'telling tales' to adults or engaging in help-seeking behaviours (Olivier and Candappa, 2007, p. 71). Children can be frightened to tell or may not have the confidence to tell. Telling leaves children open to the risks of losing friends, the bully denying the bullying, being made fun of if parents come into the school and experiences of not being believed (O'Moore, 2010).

Rigby (1997) suggests that victims often prefer to suffer the indignity of being bullied rather than the indignity of having someone intervene on their behalf. O'Donnell (1995) discusses how victims feel ashamed, rejected and want or feel obliged to show self-reliance. Victims can believe they are social failures and seeking help would confirm the taunts of inadequacy they receive while being bullied (Besag, 2006). Vulnerable children sometimes justify being bullied by believing they have brought it on themselves (Fitzgerald, 1999). O'Moore and Minton (2004) suggest some victims thrive on their victim status and telling may endanger this position.

Olivier and Candappa (2007) suggest children are reluctant to tell their parents about bullying as they fear they will respond insensitively or excessively, making matters worse. They also worry that talking about the victimisation at home could trigger family arguments (Olivier and Candappa, 2007). O'Moore and Minton (2003) also suggest that some children feel it is better to tell teachers if the bullying is in school, as they could be in trouble with their parents for not telling them sooner, or because their parents may not believe them. However despite the outlined difficulties in reporting to parents, telling parents is still perceived as a safer option than reporting to a teacher. Olivier and Candappa (2007) discuss how children perceive that schools take bullying more seriously if parents raise the issue of bullying at school than if they do so. Also Rigby (1997, p. 241) makes the point that 'Parents listen sympathetically without the slightest hint of blame.'

Telling teachers has been described as risking 'double jeopardy in two respects' in that the victim may not be believed by the teacher and telling may result in reprisals from bullies (Olivier and Candappa, 2007, p. 79). This fear of retaliation for reporting bullying is widely supported (Sharp and Smith, 1994; Smith and Shu, 2000; O'Moore and Minton, 2004). O'Moore and Minton (2003, p. 84) emphasise how 'Too many children stay silent for lack of a sympathetic ear and action that puts a stop to violence'. According to Whitney and Smith (1993) only half of bullied primary school pupils felt able to talk to teachers about the problem. This fear of reporting may reflect a lack of confidence in teachers' motivation or ability to help effectively in a way that protects their safety (McLeod and Morris, 1996; Menesini et al., 1997; Cowie and Olafsson, 1999; Smith and Shu, 2000; O'Moore and Minton, 2004).

Naylor and Cowie (1999) discuss how, in deciding whether telling a teacher is a viable option to children, children are influenced by their experiences of how effectively teachers have dealt with bullying previously. Rigby and Barnes (2002) found that for 10% of victims, things got worse after telling someone. Smith (2003) mentions how teachers often do not notice what is going on or intervene too late. When teachers are present and witness bullying as it occurs but take no action, this may be seen as 'tacit approval' and bullying tends to intensify (Berkowitz, 1973 cited in Hersov and Berger, 1978, p. 121; Alsakar, 2004; Stevens, Van Oost and De Bourdeaudhuij, 2004).

If teachers question children engaged in bullying as a group, this may result in the victim (or witnesses) being afraid to tell the full story (Fitzgerald, 1999). The victimised student must be able to trust that adults both want and are able to give them any help needed (Olweus, 1993). Smith (1997) emphasises how when teachers create an appropriate climate, where children can discuss their feelings, children are more able to tell when they are bullied.

McLeod and Morris (1996) report that Childline is a successful means for children to report bullying. With Childline children have control over the pace of disclosure and involvement in any subsequent action that is taken, which appears to be appealing to victims (McLeod and Morris, 1996).

Trying to combat the reluctance to tell has proved extremely difficult to date. Elsea and Smith (1998) found that after three years of school bullying intervention, children were still more likely to tell at home than school. Cowie (2000) discusses how even in schools with a well-developed policy and a system of peer support, victims are unable to seek help.

According to O'Moore and Minton (2003), anti-bullying initiatives so far have achieved little or no increase in the number of victims who tell either a teacher or a parent about being bullied. They suggest that encouraging children to tell of their own or their peers' victimisation is possibly the 'single greatest challenge for professionals who wish to develop or conduct anti-bullying programmes' (O'Moore and Minton, 2003, p. 70).

THE RESEARCH QUESTIONS

This study set about clarifying the types of bullying that girls are engaged in, the roles they adopt in bullying situations, the levels of non-reporting that exist and their opinions on what needs to change to increase the reporting of bullying. The study focused on four research questions:

- In what ways are girls involved in bullying at school?
- What types of bullying are girls most likely to report?
- Why do girls not tell about bullying?
- What does a teacher need to do to increase 'telling' in relation to bullying?

RESEARCH METHODOLOGY IN THE PRESENT STUDY

This study used a mixed methods approach using aspects of both quantitative and qualitative research with fifty-six girls in fifth and sixth classes in an urban primary school.

The 'Olweus Bully/Victim Questionnaire (BVQ)' (Olweus, 1996) self-report questionnaire was used to elicit the incidence of bullying over the previous three months at school as victims, bullies or both. Questions also yielded information on the types of bullying in which the children are engaged, how often it occurs, where it happens and whether they tell anyone about it. The questionnaire also examined the responses of the teachers and students, how they feel when they see others being bullied and their impressions of what adults and children at school do to stop or prevent bullying.

In addition to the Olweus Bully/Victim Questionnaire, the children were presented with researcher-created stories outlining three girls' experiences of bullying. The first was about physical bullying, the second about relational/emotional bullying and the third about e-bullying. The children listened to each story and wrote whether they believed the person in the story should report their victimisation and whether they would tell, if they were in a similar situation. They were then asked whether they had experienced similar bullying, did they tell and what were the reasons for telling or not telling about being bullied. The information allowed an examination of the types of bullying the children had experienced, whether they would tell about bullying, which types of bullying they had or had not reported and what influenced their decisions to report bullying or not.

The third research tool used was the 'Salmivalli et al. (1996) Participant Role Scale' (Samivalli PRS). This is a method for determining what role children are perceived to adopt in bullying situations, according to their peers, and in their own opinion. It is therefore a self-, and peer-report, questionnaire. Each child completes a questionnaire rating, on a three-point scale, how often each of their classmates engage in forty-eight different activities. These activities are broken down into five scales. By calculating class average scores for each scale and the average score of each child on each scale, the participant role they adopt is determined. These roles are Bully, Reinforcer of the Bully, Assistant of the Bully, Defender of the Victim and Outsider. On separate questionnaires, the children name who they believe are victims of bullying. If more than 30% nominates a child as a victim then that is their allocated role. This questionnaire allows for comparison between the roles the children believe they adopt and the roles their classmates believe they play. Comparing the outcomes of this scale with the other research tools used in this study allowed the researcher to explore whether the same children emerged as victims and bullies.

The final part of the research involved individual interviews with the girls to gain more detailed information about the bullying which they have experienced and/or witnessed in school. The girls had the opportunity to express how they felt about reporting, how effective telling had been in the past and what they believed needed to change to make telling a real option for victims. They were then asked to discuss who they believed could stop bullying and to evaluate the effectiveness of how bullying is currently dealt with at school.

RESULTS AND DISCUSSION

Telling about bullying

In this study of fifty-nine students, the most common response for children who had been bullied was to tell someone. Out of the twenty-six girls who reported having been bullied over the previous three months, 81% had told someone while 19% had not told anyone. This 19% is a considerably lower percentage of children not telling than was found in previous studies. Ortega and Lera (2000) reported that 60% of victims did not report their being bullied, 50% reported not telling in Olweus (1993) and 30% reported not telling in Smith and Shu (2000). Therefore the 'profound reluctance to tell' that has been reported elsewhere was not found (O'Moore and Minton 2004, p. 21). However the higher percentage of reporting of bullying in this study could be due to the fact that it is an all-female sample since Smith and Shu (2000) report girls are more likely to cry or ask for help than boys and are less likely to fight back.

From the interviews it emerged that six children would not tell anyone about being bullied. Only one of these children was being bullied and hadn't told. There were another three children who had actually told in the past but claimed that they wouldn't tell if it happened again, which indicates that telling did not have the desired effect in the past.

O'Moore, Kirkham and Smith (1997), Smith and Shu (2000) and Olivier and Candappa (2007) discovered a decline in the reporting of bullying by victims with increasing age. The decline in reporting was also evident in the present study, with more girls reporting bullying in fifth class than in sixth. Clearly younger children, as pointed out by Tisak and Tisak (1996), feel more comfortable involving adults.

According to Whitney and Smith (1993) the probability of all victims telling someone increases with the frequency of being bullied. In this research, this was evident as the children who had not told about their being bullied were children whose victimisation lasted less than a month. Any child that was bullied for a longer period of time had reported it to someone.

Olivier and Candappa (2007) found the most popular method of dealing with bullying was to stand up for oneself. However in this study, only four girls (6%) reported that they would do this.

Who the children tell

According to the Olweus BVQ, out of the twenty-six girls who reported having been bullied, 85% had told their parents or guardians, 75% told their friends, 29% told their teacher, 25% told another adult at school, 20% told their siblings and 20% told somebody else. These findings show that the children were almost three times more likely to tell their parents than their teacher and more than twice as likely to tell their friends than their teacher.

Across the hypothetical stories, parents were also the most likely person to be told as between 50–70% of the children reported they would tell their parents. However, only 10–25% said they would tell their teacher about their being bullied. The children who experienced physical bullying were the most likely to confide in their teacher about the problem. Confronting the bully directly, telling their siblings and talking to their friends also received some mention.

The higher level of reporting to parents rather than to teachers was also found in the interviews. Out of the fifty-nine children, twenty-two (43%) said that they had, or would, tell a teacher, while thirty-five (69%) mentioned telling their parents. A further nine (18%) said they would, or had, told their friends, five (10%) mentioned that they would tell the principal and four (8%) said they would tell the teacher on yard duty.

This preference for telling parents is similar to the findings of others (Whitney and Smith, 1993; O'Moore, Kirkham and Smith, 1997). However, the percentage of those who told their parents (85% in the Olweus BVQ) is a great deal higher than that which was found in O'Moore, Kirkham and Smith's (1997) nationwide study. They found that 50% of fifth and 46% of sixth class victims had told their parents, while 34% of fifth and 26% of sixth class victims had told their teachers. Smith and Shu (2000) discovered 16% of victims told their siblings, which is slightly lower than the 20% reported in this research. The percentage of victims who reported their bullying to their friends in this study (75% in the Olweus BVQ) was also a great deal higher than the 43% found by Smith and Shu (2000).

Differences were found between what the children said they would do if they were being bullied and what they actually did in the hypothetical story responses. The children were more likely to report that they would tell rather than telling in reality, which was also found by O'Moore and Minton (2003). Some children also discussed how they would tell their friends to report their victimisation to an adult and yet would not do likewise in a similar situation.

The types of bullying that have been or would be reported

From the hypothetical aspect in the story responses, the girls revealed they would be least likely to report emotional bullying whereas they were equally likely to report physical and cyber-bullying. When it came to actual reporting, it emerged that the children reported emotional bullying less often than physical and cyber-bullying, which were both reported equally. The fact that emotional bullying in the hypothetical stories gave rise to higher reporting than physical and cyber-bullying may be somewhat spurious as emotional bullying was the most common form of bullying depicted in the stories. With more children experiencing it, it is not unreasonable that a higher number of children would report it. This supports Rivers and Smith's (1994) findings that not telling is particularly likely in cases of indirect bullying such as emotional bullying as it can be disputed and is harder to prove than physical bullying.

In the interviews, a large number, twenty-five (49%), said they would find all types of bullying easy to talk about. However, for eight girls (16%), physical bullying would be harder to discuss and for five (10%), verbal bullying would be hard. The girls who said physical bullying would be harder to report explained that this was because they feared the violence would worsen. There were two girls (4%) who mentioned how physical bullying would be taken seriously, which would mean that parents would come into the school and the perpetrator would get into trouble, which they didn't seem to want because of the reprisals. For those children who believed verbal bullying would be harder to report, they explained that they worried their teachers or classmates might start to believe the taunts from others and question whether there was something wrong with them that excused the bullying.

Reasons for not reporting bullying

There were nine children (18%) who mentioned that they wouldn't report bullying as it could worsen if they told. This indicates that some children are doubtful of the school's ability to deal with bullying in a way that protects their safety (O'Moore and Minton, 2004). This fear of retaliation for telling about bullying is heavily supported (Sharp and Smith, 1994; Smith and Shu, 2000; O'Moore and Minton, 2004; Olivier and Candappa, 2007).

O'Donnell (1995) and Besag (2006) discuss how victims feel ashamed, rejected and want or feel obliged to show self-reliance, as seeking help would confirm the feelings of inadequacy they develop through the experience of being bullied. Rigby (1997) discusses how victims often prefer to suffer the indignity of being bullied rather than the indignity of someone intervening on their behalf. In this study, two children (4%) mentioned that they would be embarrassed to admit that they were being bullied.

There were two children (4%) who believed the girls in the stories should try to be friends with the bullies. Regardless of how badly they were treated, they believed they should not resort to behaving negatively towards others. Another girl (2%) felt it was just not right to tell on others. Besag (2006) reports a similar finding in that girls are wary of disclosing bullying as they worry about the possible consequences for the bullies.

It was found that two girls (4%) wouldn't tell about their friends bullying them. According to one girl, this was because one day they could be friends again and if they told, this would not be able to happen. O'Moore and Minton (2003) also report such findings as they explain telling leaves children open to the risk of losing friends.

There was one girl (2%) who claimed she hadn't told about being bullied because she did not believe the bullying was serious enough to report. Another (2%) reported that she would ignore the bullies, and two (4%) said they would just move on and make new friends. Some girls said that they would advise their friend to ignore the bully and to walk away. However, ignoring the bully in this study is a strategy that is used considerably less than in other studies. Smith and Shu (2000) reported that 66% ignore the bully while Salmivalli, Karhunen and Lagerspetz (1996) found that nonchalance was perceived as a more successful strategy for coping with bullying than retaliation or helplessness.

According to Olivier and Candappa (2007, p. 71), telling is often a decision to go against a peer culture that discourages 'telling tales' to adults or engaging in help-seeking behaviours. In the story responses, one child (2%) mentioned that adults give out to children for telling tales and so would not report her victimisation.

O'Moore and Minton (2003) discuss how the fear of being made fun of if parents come into the school can deter children from reporting victimisation. There were three children (6%) who discussed not wanting to be called names such as a 'rat' in the interviews and gave this as a reason for not reporting bullying.

However, one child (2%) in particular outlined how shameful the feeling of being a rat would be, regardless of whether anyone ever called her one, which was also discussed by Rigby and Barnes (2002). Fear of not being able to use their social networking sites was the reason given by two girls (4%) who would not report their cyber-bullying victimisation to their parents.

Telling at home

One of the most dominant reasons given for telling about bullying at home was because their parents would come in to talk to the teacher about the bullying and it would be resolved. In this situation, it was perceived that bullying would be taken more seriously by the school than if they spoke to the teacher themselves; this finding supports those of Olivier and Candappa (2007). There was one child (2%) who mentioned how in this situation she couldn't be called a 'rat' since she wouldn't be seen talking to the teacher.

There was another child (2%) who seemed to want to tell at home so that she could be comforted without the need of any action being taken. One girl (2%) discussed how she would be believed at home but was unsure if she would be believed in school. There was one child (2%) who discussed feeling more comfortable talking to her parents while another (2%) emphasised that her parents care about her. A further ten (20%) explained that they're closer to their parents, they know them the best and they understand them. It was also mentioned that in their homes they could report the bullying more privately than at school.

However, one sixth-class girl (2%) said that she would not tell about being bullied at home as she feared that her parents would take the bullying too seriously. This fear that parents might respond insensitively or excessively, and so make matters worse, was also identified by Olivier and Candappa (2007).

Telling friends

Similar to the findings of Olivier and Candappa (2007), some girls believe their friends are the best people to report bullying to as they do not need to be convinced that they are telling the truth. In the Olweus BVQ, 75% of those bullied reported it to their friends.

Telling the teacher on 'yard' (playground)

In the school, the existing policy was that the teacher supervising in the playground dealt with disputes that arose in the playground. This policy caused problems for four children (8%) and served to ensure some bullying went unreported. If the bullying was not dealt with adequately in the playground, the children saw little point in reporting the bullying to their own class teacher. It appeared that the girls believe the teachers are more likely to intervene in bullying that occurs in the classroom compared to in the playground, which was also the case in Pepler et al. (2004).

Telling the teacher

When the children discussed their experiences of telling the teacher about bullying, a recurring theme was that some children (four–8%) believed teachers needed to do more than talk to the bullies just once. Sometimes the bullying would stop for them, but the aggressive behaviour would then be directed at somebody else. There were eight children (16%) who implied that teachers sometimes avoid dealing with bullying.

In response to the question 'How often do teachers or other adults at school try to put a stop to bullying?' only 29% had confidence that teachers would try to stop bullying. This could be seen to influence the girls' decision to tell, since the highest number of children that didn't tell about their being bullied were children who believed teachers don't consistently try to stop bullying. And conversely, the higher number of children that had told someone about their being bullied were children who thought teachers often tried to stop bullying. This lack of consistency emerged not only in the frequency of attempts made to stop bullying, but also in the quality of the response made, which some children felt was dependent on the teacher's attitude towards, and relationship with, the children involved. For this reason, three children (6%) saw no point in telling teachers about their being bullied. Therefore in a way the staff may 'contribute to the silence' (O'Moore and Minton, 2003, p. 84).

In response to the question 'How often do students try to put a stop to bullying?' only 11% reported that they 'almost always' try. Twice as many children thought the teachers 'almost always' try to stop bullying than do students. Therefore the children perceive that adults make a greater effort than children to stop bullying. In the interviews, of those girls who believed it was possible to stop bullying, eighteen (35%) named the teachers as being capable of stopping bullying, nine (18%) mentioned their parents and four (8%) named their friends. Nevertheless, this belief in the teachers' ability to stop bullying is not reflected in the figures for those who would tell, or had told, a teacher about their being bullied.

When the children were asked, 'Overall, how much do you think your teacher has done to stop or prevent bullying in the past couple of months?' in the Olweus BVQ the replies varied greatly between the two classes, with sixth class perceiving that the teacher more regularly attempted to stop bullying than fifth class. This highlights that differences can exist in the efforts made by teachers or in the attitudes towards what is being done to stop bullying, as the teachers vary. The author believes that participating in the bullying research may have influenced the author's teaching and interactions with the children. This could indicate that increased knowledge of bullying has a direct effect on the children in the class.

There were two girls (4%) who stated that if the teachers really tried, they could stop bullying. Such a lack of confidence in adults' motivation to help effectively has received much coverage (McLeod and Morris, 1996; Menesini et al., 1997; Cowie and Olafsson, 1999; Smith and Shu, 2000). This lack of effort could be reflected in the children's responses in the Olweus BVQ. Out of the nine children who claimed to have engaged in bullying behaviour, only 22% had been spoken to about their behaviour at school, while 25% had been spoken to at home. This could suggest that bullying goes on undetected or that the teachers and parents do not take action. This situation could also reflect a casual and ambiguous attitude to bullying behaviour (Askew, 1989 cited in O'Moore, Kirkham and Smith, 1997).

There was one child (2%) who reported in the story responses that she had told the teacher in the past about being bullied but would not tell again. This may indicate that the bullying was not dealt with effectively. However, sometimes when children told in the past, it had led to a positive outcome in that the bullying stopped; this was also found by Smith and Shu (2000).

Children's suggestions for increasing telling

The suggestions for what a teacher could do to make it easier to tell included talking to the bully, asking the bully why exactly they are bullying and talking to both the victim and the bully. One girl suggested that the teacher remove the children from the classroom rather than talking to them in front of the class. Another suggested talking to the bully and victim separately, as in the No Blame Approach (Maines and Robinson, 1992). This idea has been previously identified by Fitzgerald (1999).

IMPLICATIONS

While the research sample in this study was confined to just one school and making generalisations beyond the school would be inappropriate, there are some lessons to be learned.

Inconsistencies arose within the research which highlighted that aggressive behaviours within the school can be viewed and classified differently by all parties. The responses to bullying therefore varied and the children were at times doubtful of the willingness of adults to intervene. This appeared to affect the levels of reporting and indicated the need for a community approach to defining bullying and developing and implementing school policies.

In Ireland, the Stay Safe Programme is the main programme used in schools to tackle bullying. This programme concentrates mostly on physical aggression. However, due to the high levels of other forms of bullying reported in the present study, schools may need to review their anti-bullying programme and tailor it to reflect all of the bullying experiences of the children.

The systems for sharing information about bullying, both between parents and teachers and among staff members, that are in place in the present study appeared to lack coherence and played a part in the non-reporting of bullying. This implies that there needs to be a concrete transfer of information about conflicts that arise in schools (particularly in the playground) from one teacher to the next and a universal system in place to document and track the children involved in bullying.

It also emerged that there was a lack of opportunities to report bullying to the adults at school confidentially. This appeared to cause the children to be hesitant about reporting victimisation and definitely needs attention.

Therefore, even though, as was the case in the reported school, anti-bullying policies have been in place in schools for many years, they need to be reviewed regularly in order to improve the safety and happiness of the students. Existing policies may serve to ensure the continuation of bullying and its non-reporting. Thus schools must consider their policy more carefully and review its practices regarding bullying in order to promote a culture of disclosure.

RECOMMENDATIONS

School community

- The whole school community should be involved in the development of a definition of bullying to ensure that everyone operates from the same point of reference. All members should also be involved in the formulation and review of the school policy.
- All members of the school should be educated about the negative effects of bullying. Negative attitudes towards the reporting of bullying need to be challenged to ensure the adults do not neglect the experiences of the children in their care.
- Schools must instil confidence in their pupils that they will take the bullying seriously.
- Schools should examine the forms of bullying that are being experienced by their pupils and tailor their anti-bullying programmes to include the forms of bullying that are prevalent and relevant to the children.
- Schools should examine the consequences that follow the reporting of bullying in the school to ensure they do not discourage it from being reported as was the case with cyber-bullying in the reported study.
- In the playground there needs to be careful monitoring and consistent supervision. Information about conflicts that arise in the playground needs to be documented and shared systematically with other teachers.
- Frameworks need to be in place so parents can share their information about bullying with the school.
- A room could be introduced where children know that they may talk confidentially to their teacher at specific times, as necessary.
- Peer support means training children to take active roles in finding solutions to conflicts that arise among their peers, such as Quality Circles, Conflict Mediation, Circle of Friends and buddy systems (Cowie and Sharp, 1992 cited in Smith et al., 2004; Sharp and Smith, 1994; Smith, 2003; Ortega, 1998, cited in Smith et al., 2004). These approaches require children

to engage in active listening, problem-solving, showing empathy, providing a support system, participating in conflict resolution and responding to the needs and feelings of others. According to Cunningham et al. (1998), 80% of disputes mediated by peers result in long-lasting agreements.

Teachers

- Teachers should endeavour to create genuine relationships with the children and adopt humanistic approaches to dealing with bullying which may help the children feel more comfortable about confiding in teachers. This could include the No Blame Approach, whereby teachers elicit the causes and events of bullying without placing blame on any party, or The Method of Shared Concern where students work in collaboration to find solutions to conflicts (Pikas, 1989; Maines and Robinson, 1992; Besag, 2006). Employing such methods would necessitate staff training.
- Teachers ought to listen to and respect the wishes of children, where possible, when implementing the next step in dealing with the bullying.
- Whole-class anti-bullying activities, which aim to improve social interactions within a class, might prove beneficial. These could include role-play, circle-time, co-operative learning and multicultural activities (Elliott, 2003).
- Training the children in how to be a good friend could also be advantageous in reducing bullying, as Olivier and Candappa (2007) suggest that anti-bullying strategies which support friendship networks are likely to be of considerable value.

Parents

- Parents could create parent circles to develop common attitudes towards bullying and become aware of what they can do to tackle bullying. They could also examine their own behaviour to ensure they are adequate role models for their children with regard to bullying behaviours.

CONCLUDING REMARKS

In this research, the girls showed an acute awareness of the barriers that exist to eradicating bullying in the school and encouraging its reporting. The girls also offered realistic insights into changes that could be made to practices which had not been given attention to in the school. Therefore the researcher suggests that enabling children to voice their opinions and present their ideas could be a successful way forward for addressing situations of bullying and increasing the levels of reporting aggressive behaviours in schools.

REFERENCES

Alsakar, F.D. 'Bernese Programme against Victimisation in Kindergarten and Elementary School', in P.K. Smith, D. Pepler and K. Rigby (eds), *Bullying in Schools: How Successful Can Interventions Be?* (Cambridge: Cambridge University Press, 2004)

Besag, V.E. *Understanding Girls' Friendships, Fights and Feuds: A Practical Approach to Girls' Bullying* (Maidenhead, Berkshire: Open University Press, 2006)

Cowie, H. and Olafsson, R. 'The Role of Peer Support against Bullying', *School Psychology International*, 20, 1999, pp. 96–105

Cowie, H. 'Bystanding or Standing By: Gender Issues in Coping with Bullying in English Schools', *Aggressive Behavior*, 26, 2000, pp. 85–97

Cowie, H., Jennifer, D. and Sharp, S. 'School Violence in the United Kingdom: Addressing the Problem', in P.K. Smith (ed.), *Violence in Schools: The Response in Europe* (London: Routledge Falmer, 2003)

Cunningham, C., Cunningham, L., Martorelli, V., Tran, A., Young, J. and Zacharias, R. 'The Effects of Primary Division, Student-Mediated Conflict Resolution Programs on Playground Aggression', *Journal of Child Psychology and Psychiatry*, 39, 1998, pp. 653–62

Elliott, G.P. *School Mobbing and Emotional Abuse* (New York: Brunner-Routledge, 2003)

Elsea, M. and Smith, P.K. 'The Long-Term Effectiveness of Anti-Bullying Work in Primary Schools', *Educational Research*, 40, 1998, pp. 203–18

Fitzgerald, D. *Bullying in our Schools: Understanding and Tackling the Problem* (Dublin: Blackhall Publishing, 1999)

Genta, M.L., Menesini, E., Fonzi, A. Constabile, A. and Smith P.K. 'Bullies and Victims in Schools in Central and Southern Italy', *European Journal of Psychology of Education*, 11, 1996, pp. 97–110

Hawkins, D.L., Pepler, D. and Craig, W. 'Peer Intervention in Playground Bullying', *Social Development*, 10, 2001, pp. 512–27

Hersov, L.A. and Berger, M. *Aggression and Antisocial Behaviour in Childhood and Adolescence* (Oxford: Pergamon Press, 1978)

James, D.J., Lawlor, M., Flynn, A., Murphy, N., Courtney, P. and Henry, P. 'One School's Experience of Engaging with a Comprehensive Anti-Bullying Programme in the Irish Context: Adolescent and Teacher Perspectives', *Pastoral Care*, 24, 2006, pp. 39–48

La Fountaine, J. *Bullying, the Child's View: An Analysis of Telephone Calls to Childline about Bullying* (London: Calouste Gulbenkian Foundation, 1991)

Maines, B. and Robinson, G. *The No Blame Approach* (Bristol: Lame Duck Publishing, 1992)

McLeod, M. and Morris, S. *Why Me? Children Talking to Childline about Bullying* (London: Childline, 1996)

Menesini, E., Elsea, M., Smith, P.K., Genta, M.L., Giannetti, E., Fonzi A. and Costabile, A. 'Cross-National Comparison of Children's Attitudes towards Bully/Victim Problems in School', *Aggressive Behavior*, 23, 1997, pp. 245–57

Naylor, P. and Cowie, H. 'The Effectiveness of Peer Support Systems in Challenging School Bullying: The Perspectives and Experiences of Teachers and Pupils', *Journal of Adolescence*, 22, 1999, pp. 467–79

Olivier, C. and Candappa, M. 'Bullying and the Politics of "Telling"', *Oxford Review of Education*, 33, 2007, pp. 71–86

Olweus, D. *Bullying at School: What We Know and What We Can Do About It* (Oxford: Blackwell, 1993)

Ortega, R. and Lera, M.J. 'The Seville Anti-Bullying in School Project', *Aggressive Behavior*, 26, 2000, pp. 113–23

Ortega, R., del Rey, R. and Férnandez, I. 'Working Together to Prevent School Violence: The Spanish Response', in P.K. Smith (ed.), *Violence in Schools: The Response in Europe* (London: Routledge Falmer, 2003)

Owens, L., Shute, R. and Slee, P. '"Guess What I Just Heard": Indirect Aggression among Teenage Girls in Australia', *Aggressive Behavior*, 26, 2000, pp. 67–83

O'Donnell, V. (1995) *Bullying: A Resource Guide for Parents and Teachers*, Dublin: Attic Press

O'Dowd, E. 'An Analysis of the Lack of Reporting Bullying by Girls', unpublished MEd thesis, Trinity College Dublin, 2010

O'Moore, M. *Understanding School Bullying: A Guide for Parents and Teachers* (Dublin: Veritas, 2010)

O'Moore, M. *Cyber-Bullying among a Sample of 2,974 Junior Cycle Post-Primary Students in Ireland* (Dublin: Anti-Bullying Centre, 2012)

O'Moore, A.M., Kirkham, C. and Smith, M. 'Bullying Behaviour in Irish Schools: A Nationwide Study', *Irish Journal of Psychology*, vol. 18, no. 2, 1997, pp. 141–69

O'Moore, A.M. and Minton, S.J. 'The Hidden Voice of Bullying', in M. Shevlin and R. Rose (eds), *Encouraging Voices: Respecting the Insights of Young People who Have Been Marginalised* (Dublin: National Disability Authority, 2003)

O'Moore, A.M. and Minton, S.J. *Dealing with Bullying in Schools: A Training Manual for Teachers, Parents and Other Professionals* (London: Paul Chapman Publishing, 2004)

Pepler, D.F., Craig, W.M., O'Connell, P., Atlas, R. and Charach, A. 'Making a Difference in Bullying: Evaluation of a Systematic School-Based Programme in Canada', in P.K. Smith, D. Pepler and K. Rigby (eds), *Bullying in Schools: How Successful Can Interventions Be?* (Cambridge: Cambridge University Press, 2004)

Pikas, A. 'The Common Concern Method for the Treatment of Mobbing', in E. Roland and E. Munthe (eds), *Bullying: An International Perspective* (London: David Fulton, 1989)

Rigby, K. *Bullying in Schools and What to Do About It* (London: Jessica Kingsley Publishers, 1997)

Rigby, K. and Barnes, A. 'The Victimised Student's Dilemma: To Tell or Not to Tell', *Youth Studies Australia*, vol. 21, no. 2, 2002, pp. 33–6

Rivers, I. and Smith, P.K. 'Types of Bullying and their Correlates', *Aggressive Behavior*, 20, 1994, pp. 359–68

Roland, R. and Galloway, D. 'Classroom Influences on Bullying', *Educational Research*, 44, 2002, pp. 299–312

Salmivalli, C., Lagerspetz, K., Bjorqvist, K., Ostermann, K. and Kaukiainen, A. 'Bullying as a Group Process: Participant Roles and their Relations to the Social Status within the Group', *Aggressive Behavior*, 22, 1996, pp. 1–15

Salmivalli, C., Karhunen, J. and Lagerspetz, K.M.J. 'How Do Victims Respond to Bullying?', *Aggressive Behavior*, 22, 1996, pp. 99–109

Salmivalli, C. 'Is There an Age Decline in Victimization by Peers at School?', *Educational Research*, 44, 2002, pp. 269–77

Sharp, S. and Smith, P.K. *Tackling Bullying in Your School* (London: Routledge, 1994)

Smith, P.K. 'Bullying in Schools: The UK Experience and the Sheffield Anti-Bullying Project', *Irish Journal of Psychology*, 18, 1997, pp. 191–201

Smith, P.K. *Violence in Schools: The Response in Europe* (London: Routledge Falmer, 2003)

Smith, P.K., Sharp, S., Eslea, M. and Thompson, D. 'England: The Sheffield Project', in P.K. Smith, D. Pepler and K. Rigby (eds), *Bullying in Schools: How Successful Can Interventions Be?* (Cambridge: Cambridge University Press, 2004)

Smith, P.K. and Shu, S. 'What Good Schools Can Do About Bullying: Findings from a Survey in English Schools after a Decade of Research and Action', *Childhood*, 7, 2000, pp. 193–212

Stevens, V., Van Oost, P. and De Bourdeaudhuij, I. 'Interventions against Bullying in Flemish Schools: Programme Development and Evaluation', in P.K. Smith, D. Pepler and K. Rigby (eds), *Bullying in Schools: How Successful Can Interventions Be?* (Cambridge: Cambridge University Press, 2004)

Tisak, M.S. and Tisak, J. 'Expectations and Judgements Regarding Bystanders' and Victims' Responses to Peer Aggression among Early Adolescents', *Journal of Adolescence*, 19, 1996, pp. 383–92

Whitney, I. and Smith, P.K. 'A Survey of the Nature and Extent of Bullying in the Junior/Middle and Secondary Schools', *Educational Research*, 35, 1993, pp. 3–25

CHAPTER FIVE

Third-Level Students' Experiences of Bullying in Ireland

Lian McGuire

A THIRD LEVEL OF BULLYING

It is, unfortunately, apparent that we, as a society, have a tendency to go from teaching our children that they matter as individuals, to introducing them to a working world where they can be told 'you are merely a cog in the wheel', and what they feel really isn't that important after all. Even if unspoken, this shift in philosophical ethos from school to workplace, as regards how we treat and regard others, is clear, placing functionality and what is easiest or most profitable before respect and attempting to do what is right. From personal experience with victims of workplace bullying, it is the (often brutal) realisation of this that can cause the greatest damage and sense of betrayal.

Given the emphasis placed on the importance of the ethos/philosophy of an organisation by many researchers and practitioners within the field of bullying and aggression, it is interesting to note how little attention, in regard to bullying, has ever really been given to one of the prime areas of our society most responsible for formulating, influencing and disseminating the philosophies we as a society live by.

McCarthy et al. (2001) state that bullying is an age-old societal problem, beginning in the schoolyard and often progressing to the boardroom; yet, while there is an increasingly large amount of data on school and workplace bullying, it is really quite notable the paucity of data that exists on what is, frequently, the link between the two. Research into the experiences and attitudes of third-level students towards bullying, both traditional and cyber-bullying, is negligible in the extreme.

It is within third-level institutions that many school leavers will have their views of the world, and those within it, shaped to a far more adult degree. Yet while their peers within the workforce are, at all levels and areas, questioned and analysed about their experiences of bullying, and what might or might not be done about it, those most likely to become the managers of businesses, formulate economic, social or philosophical theory, or create whole new areas of industry are overlooked in regards to their experiences of bullying and what their attitudes towards it might be.

This is a notable omission simply because, outside of our school and working population, our student population is one of the biggest single groupings in our society. In Ireland there are approximately 250,000 college-level students (USI, 2010), which amounts to 5.9% of our population as a whole. This places Ireland well ahead of the 2–4% of many other European Union countries such as the UK, France, Italy and Germany (Eurostat, 2010), and comparable with Russia and the USA (US Department of Education, 2010) in terms of percentage student population.

Southern (2009), in her analysis of the lack of data on bullying among third-level students, suggests that, in addition to the size of student population and the link between school and workplace, the change in higher education has led to what she terms 'massification'; or a workplace-style orientation and competition between institutions changing the values of the university, where an expectation of value for money alters the behaviour of students, which results in stressors more akin to a working individual than had been the student experience prior to this.

Ross et al. (1999) point out that university students comprise a sector of the populace uniquely exposed to pressure, especially so in the case of first-year students. The shift from school to student life consists of considerable upheaval, with many students living away from home and taking on the responsibilities that come with adult life for the first time, not least monetary issues, both in terms of their fees and day-to-day living costs. Friendships made and cemented during school life are dispersed, established social networks broken, and new ones constructed, all while students deal with the twin pressures of high academic achievement and future career goals (Vaez et al., 2004).

These are considerable stressors; and stress as Leymann (1992), Zapf et al. (1995) and Vartia (1996) indicate, can not only be a result of bullying but a prime cause of it, with severe stress factors leading to frustration and the need to let out one's feelings, which in turn can lead to psychological terror.

There have, of course, been studies of bullying in third-level institutions (Lewis, 1999; Lewis, 2004; Lipsett, 2005; Twale et al., 2008), but their focus has always been on staff concerns. Yet while concerted efforts continue to be made to study the experiences of school goers and workers, and attempts to prevent and combat bullying situations are ongoing, with between three and seven study years ahead of them, the student population, rather than being a focus of similar studies, has been by and large ignored and left to its own devices.

EXISTING LITERATURE AND STUDIES OF THIRD-LEVEL STUDENT BULLYING

There exists no current research on the level of bullying among third-level students in Ireland. However, a survey of student experiences carried out by the National Union of Students (NUS, 2008) in the UK indicated that 7% had experienced bullying, 79% of whom stated that the bullying had involved a fellow student but had not been reported to the institution.

Of the little existing literature on the extent of bullying among college students anywhere in the world, the prime example is that of the study carried out in Rowan University, New Jersey (Chapell et al., 2004) on a sample of 1,025 undergraduate students along the lines of the gender breakdown of the student body. The study found that male college students engaged in significantly more bullying than females, but that males and females were bullied equally. A quarter reported having been bullied by another student, while a fifth reported having been bullied by a lecturer. Just 5% of those sampled stated that they themselves bullied other students occasionally or frequently. The authors found that across the undergraduate years, the bullying did not continue the pattern of decreasing so often found in the latter years of secondary school, and instead found it steady and more in line with that which occurs in the workplace.

While the study did not examine the types of bullying involved, being focused solely on the overall occurrence rate, the authors expressed disquiet at the prevalence of lecturer-to-student bullying, which they also felt partially supported the Olweus (1999) hypothesis that lecturers who bully act as role models in promoting bullying among students. Following a number of secondary school shootings involving bullied students, and in the wake of these results and the knowledge that over one million American students carry firearms, the authors strongly recommended that the issue of bullying on college campuses receive greater attention from other researchers and the authorities. This is something that, it would appear from the lack of further studies, has not occurred.

However, a follow-up study by Chapell et al. (2006) of 119 undergraduates, looking at their experiences across elementary school, high school and college, found a positive correlation between having been bullied in school and later in college, and similarly bullying in school and then in college. This study also looked at the typology of bullying (though not cyber-bullying), finding that, as with students in primary and secondary education, verbal bullying in college was the most prevalent, followed by social-relational bullying, with physical bullying being the least common form. Male college students bullied more, both verbally and physically, than females. In regards to lecturer-to-student bullying, verbal bullying was found to be the predominant form, with social bullying second. There was almost no physical bullying from lecturers to students, though two students reported being physically bullied by sports coaches on campus.

A study of cyber-bullying among physics freshmen and those freshmen involved in the Physical Education Department was carried out in Aristotle University, Thessalonica (Gountsidou, 2009) to see whether there was a significant difference in the rate of cyber-bullying among those who spent more time in front of computers versus those regarded as athletes. Those in the Physics Department experienced slightly more bullying across the seven categories applied (pictures via mobile phones, Short Message Service [SMS], email, Microsoft Network [MSN]/Yahoo Messenger, internet, chatroom, phonecall bullying) than did those in Physical Education, though bullying via phone was the most prevalent form for both. Interestingly, there were differences in the experiences of the two groups in terms of the other types of cyber-bullying; for example, the second most prevalent form differed significantly between the two, with Physics students experiencing more bullying via chat rooms, while Physical Education students experienced more bullying via SMS.

In Selcuk University in Turkey, Dilmac (2009) carried out a study on predictors of cyber-bullying on 666 undergraduate students across the Faculty of Education and found that a quarter of students reported engaging in cyber-bullying at least once, while over half reported being victims of cyber-bullying at least once in their lifetime. Males engaged in cyber-bullying more than females, but female students were exposed to cyber-bullying more frequently than males.

Suicidal ideation rates found in studies on campuses around the world over the course of an academic year (Rudd, 1989; Schweitzer et al., 1995; Zhang and Jin, 1996; Shur-Fen Gau et al., 2008); and depression rates in universities around Europe (Mikolaczyk, 2007), for female and male students respectively, give cause for concern about the vulnerability of third-level students to stress. In Ireland, a study of medical and business students from Trinity College and University College Dublin (Curran et al., 2009) returned a range of suicidal ideation of 5.9% within a single month, with a quarter of those students surveyed registering as depressed on the Beck Depression Inventory (BDI), also within that month.

Like Chapell et al. (2006) in regards to bullying rates on campus, Curran et al. express grave concern at the rates of suicidal ideation in colleges, with the latter pointing out that while suicide rates among young adults elsewhere in northern Europe have stabilised or declined, the rate among Irish 15–24-year-olds has increased. It is yet to be seen whether there may be a correlation between the two.

THE RESEARCH QUESTIONS

As established, data on bullying among third-level students is rare, with little or no study on the matter having been carried out in Ireland before. The research that has taken place elsewhere has indicated that both traditional and cyber-bullying exists, is a problem on third-level campuses around the world, and that there is a need for similar research in this country.

Therefore, this study, which formed part of an MEd in Aggression Studies with the School of Education, Trinity College Dublin (McGuire, 2010), focused on the following questions:

1) To what degree is bullying prevalent in Irish third-level institutions?
2) What is the nature of the bullying that exists?
3) Is cyber-bullying an issue in Irish colleges?
4) How have students coped with bullying?
5) Do students have faith in their institutions to help them in such situations?
6) What, if any, are their experiences of bullying in school, and in the workplace?

RESEARCH METHODOLOGY IN PRESENT STUDY

The author implemented a quantitative study of third-level students, which endeavoured to provide an overview of the situation for students across as many institutions and regions as possible, piloting the study online with the co-operation of the USI (Union of Students in Ireland). The questionnaire was designed in five sections, intending to retrieve data on: students' personal details; their current perceptions of college life; their views on definitions of bullying and aggression as pertaining to both traditional and cyber-bullying; their experiences of both traditional and cyber-bullying; and their experiences, if any, of bullying in school or in the workplace.

The research tool employed was a self-report questionnaire comprising fifty-three questions designed by the author in conjunction with the Anti-Bullying Research Centre, which was translated into an online format via SurveyMonkey, and launched on the USI's website by its chief and regional welfare officers in conjunction with Student Mental Health Week (9–13 November 2009).

The definition of traditional bullying used in this study was as follows:

> We define bullying as a situation where one or several individuals persistently over a period of time perceive themselves to be on the receiving end of negative actions from one or several persons, in a situation where the target of bullying has difficulty in defending him or herself against these actions. We will not refer to a one off incident as bullying.
>
> (Einarsen and Skogstad, 2000)

For the purposes of this study cyber-bullying was defined as follows:

> Cyber-bullying is defined as intentional and harassing acts via electronic forms, often repeatedly. The seven categories of cyber-bullying are as follows: text-message (also called SMS), taking/publicizing photos or videos using mobile, phone calls (via mobile), e-mail, chat-room, instant messaging (IM), and on websites, such as YouTube or Facebook.
>
> (O'Moore and Minton, 2009)

RESULTS AND DISCUSSIONS

A total of 378 individual responses were received during a period from 9 November 2009 to 31 January 2010, a total of eighty-four days, resulting in a response rate of 4.5 per day. As the average hit rate on the USI website is eighty-one hits per month, or an average of 2.7 hits per day, this resulted in a hit rate on the website which averaged out as twice that which it would normally receive. As expected with an online survey, there was a falloff in terms of numbers who began the questionnaire and those who completed it (63.5%/n = 240).

PROFILE OF RESPONDENTS

Of the 378 responses received, 143 (37.8%) were male while 235 (62.2%) were female, a level of response that is almost identical to that experienced in the study of bullying in Rowan University (63% female/37% male) (Chapell et al., 2004).

The make-up of the age range (i.e. 62% between 18 and 21 years of age) and current year of the respondents (i.e. first year undergraduate (35.2%), second years (27.8%), third years (18.0%) fourth years (12.7%) and postgraduate students (6.3%)) roughly corresponded with the statistical breakdown of postgraduate and undergraduate students in Ireland carried out by the HEA (Higher Education Authority, 2009). Similarly, the spread of students across the faculties, with Arts/Humanities students making up the largest number, followed by Engineering/Maths and Sciences, and then Health Sciences, was to be expected, given that it too follows the HEA breakdown of allocation of students across the major third-level institutions. This dominance of the Arts/Humanities students was highlighted further by the fact that Law, Business and Arts students alone made up almost 25% of the total number of respondents.

The vast majority of students (88%) were Irish, though the presence of nineteen other nationalities (12% of respondents) showed both a broad range of nationality within the third-level education system in Ireland and differing cultural experience within the survey, though the ethnic make-up, with just 4% of respondents made up of other ethnicities outside of 'White', was not as diversified.

Overall, the spread of the students' age, faculties and course years in the present study was reflective of the current make-up of the greater student body at large in Ireland, indicating that the survey was successful in targeting a representative sample. However, the sample in comparison to the number of students overall in Ireland is small; and therefore caution must be taken in that regard.

STUDENT EXPERIENCES OF COLLEGE LIFE

An overview of students' social lives in college would seem to concur with Curran et al. (2009) that the drinking culture is alive and well among Irish students, with activity circling around the pub and nightclubs remaining at the top of favoured activities with 80% of students naming it so. Similarly, their contention that the level of stress and depression is high on Irish campuses could well be borne out by the fact that almost 60% of the students who participated in this study felt under pressure to succeed in their studies; almost half of the students had considered leaving college at some point, while almost 15% of the students found college life very isolating.

Students' dissatisfaction with both the level of information available to them in their institutions to help them solve their problems (20%), and with actually obtaining help to do so (15–22%), could be helping to exacerbate this sense of isolation, and certainly contrasts with their level of dissatisfaction with the students' union for the same purpose, which lay at only 7%. The fact that so many students were unhappy with getting help for scholastic problems (15%) or with difficulties with other students (17%) within their institutions would certainly increase their sense of isolation in college. In addition, the fact that 22% of all students (n = 69) who took this survey were not only unhappy with the level of help available to deal with difficulties with staff members, but would therefore appear to have actually *had* problems with staff members across their college, appears a cause for concern.

STUDENT EXPERIENCES WITH COLLEGE STAFF

Not surprisingly then, 13% of students were unhappy with the treatment they received from the college itself, and 14% were unhappy with the atmosphere they experienced within their school or department. More specifically, 8% were dissatisfied with the treatment they received at the hands of departmental staff, while 6% were unhappy with the treatment received from their tutors. This sense of dissatisfaction within specific areas of the college, and with regards to the help available to students, is reflected subsequently with the 15% of students who were unhappy with how conflicts were resolved in their college.

Unhappiness with college staff and procedure was further highlighted when one looks at the negative behaviours most frequently experienced by students. There were 34% of students who cited 'unfair marking' as *the* most widely experienced negative behaviour in college; 27.5% reported having experienced a 'hostile reception when they approached a tutor or staff member with a problem'; 18% maintained that they had had their work ignored by their tutors; while 15% said they had been subject to persistent unwarranted criticism of their work. These are somewhat startling numbers, and would certainly go some way to explaining the level of dissatisfaction with help available for dealing with problems with staff members.

This sense of dissatisfaction with the atmosphere, treatment and conflict resolution methods, in addition to the negative behaviours experienced at the hands of staff, would indicate that colleges have some work to do in regards to creating more confidence with staff and the institution as a whole, if they are to help students and combat bullying behaviour. Such findings would be in line with those studies carried out on the best methods to combat bullying in school (Smith and Sharp, 1994; Roland and Munthe, 1997; Smith, Pepler and Rigby, 2004; Ttofi and Farrington, 2009), wherein a whole-school approach, incorporating the school ethos and staff behaviours among others to create a safe, open atmosphere were among the best in fostering confidence in staff and reducing levels of bullying.

STUDENT EXPERIENCES WITH THEIR PEERS

With regard to their experiences with their peers, exclusion appears to be the prime negative behaviour most experienced by students, with 33% of all respondents alleging to have experienced it. The total is high, especially when compared to 22% of respondents reporting the same negative behaviour in the National Survey of Bullying in the Workplace (O'Moore, 2001). But with a looser organisational framework than either school or work, with students not at such close quarters to one another, and with far less monitoring of behaviour meaning that such deliberate open exclusion would not be so easily noticed, it is perhaps not surprising to find that this is the case.

Similarly, the differing make-up of college and the workplace appears to play a part in the 24% of students (n = 76) who experienced unwanted sexual attention, as compared to the 6% of those in the workplace study who complained of unwanted sexual attention/harassment. Though the increased rate is understandable given the far more social element of college life as compared to working life, where college mates would be viewed as prospective partners far more than work colleagues, it would appear that sexual aggression is definitely an issue among students in Ireland.

Students' experiences of hurtful teasing and taunting were also higher (28%) than in the workplace (23%), as was the percentage of students subjected to obscene or offensive language (32%), though this was more in line with the 29% experienced by those in the workplace, perhaps because of a peculiar prevalence and tolerance of swearing in Irish society. The experience of the spread of gossip and rumours was also very slightly higher in college (23%) than in the workplace (22%), while threats of violence or physical abuse were almost identical across both areas (6%). As these forms of negative behaviours can often be far better hidden than the deliberate open exclusion of an individual, it could be suggested that the differing structures of college and work may play less of a part in their prevalence, and help explain the lower declination rates.

STUDENT ATTITUDES TO BULLYING DEFINITIONS AND POLICY

When it came to defining bullying, there was far more disagreement with the traditional definition (13%) than that given for cyber-bullying (1.3%). Whereas the definition of cyber-bullying appeared to take into account one-off incidents, the definition of traditional bullying by Einarsen and Skogstad (2000) did not, and as was highlighted in students' responses that many had either witnessed or experienced one-off incidents and felt strongly that it warranted inclusion in any definition. Their view finds support with O'Moore and Minton (2004) and O'Moore (2010), who find an isolated incident, such as a threat, can serve to intimidate on an ongoing basis and can be described as bullying.

Similarly, student responses in regards to whether their college had a policy in relation to bullying or not highlighted the fact that colleges, even if they had such an anti-bullying policy, were doing a poor job in advertising the fact. Almost two-thirds of all respondents had no idea as to its existence, findings which concurred with the author's overview of colleges in regards to the ease of access to an institution's anti-bullying policies, as noted in the review of current literature.

STUDENT EXPERIENCES OF BULLYING

The prevalence rates of bullying revealed in the survey show that bullying is an issue within Irish third-level institutions. Some 14% of students have been bullied in a traditional manner during their time in college, while 21% have witnessed traditional forms of bullying while in college. From a review of the few other surveys on third-level bullying that have been carried out, Ireland compares favourably with those from the US (Chapell et al., 2004), which reported a 24% incidence rate of student bullying, and a 61% witness rate. However, the 14% prevalence rate among students in Irish colleges is twice that reported by the NUS (2008) in the UK, where 7% of students surveyed reported that they had experienced bullying in college.

Within the US study, males and females were bullied equally. However, the NUS study in the UK indicated (without giving specific statistics) that the vast number of those who stated they were bullied were female. The results of this Irish study, therefore, appear to be in line with the results of the UK survey, as 82% of respondents who said they were bullied were female. However, this percentage was reduced to 66.6% when subsequent questions gave specific examples of bullying, causing the number of male respondents to increase from 18% to 33.3%.

Students initially answering 'no' to being bullied and then proceeding to respond affirmatively to questions relating to specific forms of bullying supports the author's experience of gender differences while working with the Anti-Bullying Centre, TCD, and raises a possible issue. Quite frequently, in dealing with individuals who are bullied, male clientele will report that they 'didn't realise it was bullying' until it was pointed out to them by someone else or that they read something wherein they saw the kinds of behaviours involved and applied it to themselves. Given that, according to Galdas, Cheater and Marshall (2005), women are more likely to respond to stressful life events than men and that health matters is one of their prime interests (Berger, 2002), it could be posited that, in general, female respondents may have a stronger insight into what constitutes bullying.

In addition, the difference between 'negative behaviours', as previously outlined in the survey, and 'the types of bullying experienced' is something that sometimes needs to be distinguished for the general public, and it may be that, as was the case with Dilmac's (2009) study of third-level cyber-bullying, the provision of a typology of bullying behaviours as a guide, immediately prior to the initial question 'Have you been bullied?' might provide for more accuracy of response.

STUDENT EXPERIENCES OF CYBER-BULLYING

In terms of cyber-bullying, whereas 55% of students claimed to have experienced cyber-bullying in Dilmac's (2009) study, the prevalence rates in this study were far lower, with just 3.5% of students reporting that they had experienced cyber-bullying. The Turkish study, it must be noted, did not solely focus on college experience alone, asking students if they had ever experienced cyber-bullying in their 'lifetime', allowing for far more scope. However, the study in Aristotle University, Thessalonica (Gountsidou, 2009) also showed a far higher incidence rate (34% of Physics students/23% of Physical Education students) of cyber-bullying, indicating that the prevalence rate in Irish campuses is either quite low or that a more in-depth study on cyber-bullying alone needs to be carried out. Given the rate of cyber-bullying in Irish post-primary schools (O'Moore, 2012) with one in seven students (13.9%) reporting having been bullied online and one in four (26.6%) having been subjected to abusive text messaging in and out of school, it would seem the latter is more likely to be the case.

REPORTING BULLYING

Both in regards to cyber-bullying and traditional bullying, female students proved more likely to tell others about the issues affecting them than their male counterparts, who proved equally reluctant to tell whether they were bullied in a traditional manner (50%) or cyber-bullied (50%). In both types of bullying, and across the gender groups, telling friends was the most favoured option, with both displaying a marked reluctance to tell their tutors, college staff or the students' union. Most notable perhaps, though, was their reluctance to speak to their classmates about what was going on, either because they felt they could be of no help to them or because the perpetrator came from within that group. This low rate of reporting finds support in the literature on school bullying (O'Moore, Kirkham and Smith, 1997) and the workplace (O'Moore, 2001). Reasons for non-reporting at school level (see Chapter 4 of this book) can undoubtedly also be applied to the third-level experience.

WHO BULLIES?

In terms of traditional bullying, the possibility that the bully came from within the respondent's group is heightened by students reporting that they were most likely to have been bullied by other students (86% of those traditionally bullied). However, the fact that 24% of those bullied in a traditional manner reported that it was perpetrated by teaching staff would appear to further underline the levels of dissatisfaction students had previously indicated with college staff. Though they did not name the perpetrators, 66% of cyber-bullied students said they knew who they were, with 33% stating that there was more than one perpetrator and 33% that there was one perpetrator alone.

Female students who were bullied in a traditional manner were more likely to be frequently bullied than males. In addition, as at post-primary level in Ireland (O'Moore, Kirkham and Smith, 1997), female students were more likely to be bullied by females, and males by males, while female students were far more likely to be bullied by both men and women than their male counterparts, a pattern which finds further support in such studies as Rodkin and Berger (2008), Craig et al. (2001) and Russell and Owens (1999). Finally, group bullying was far more common in college (89% of those who had been bullied) than one-on-one bullying (11%).

TYPES OF BULLYING

As with Chapell et al. (2006), third-level students who were bullied in a traditional manner reported verbal (55%) and exclusionary bullying (52%) as the most prevalent forms of bullying they experienced. While students at post-primary level in Ireland (O'Moore, Kirkham and Smith, 1997), and adults in the workplace (O'Moore, 2001), also named verbal bullying as the most prevalent form of bullying they experienced, the tactic of exclusion appears to be at a much higher level in college (55%) than in post-primary school (9%) and even above that found in the workplace (41%). Physical bullying was among the lowest of those types of bullying reported (16%); and, when placed alongside post-primary students (22%) and workplace percentages (13%), there appears to be a steady decline as the age of the respondents increases. As there was a gender bias in the sample, it might explain why exclusion was the most prevalent form of bullying among third-level students. Social manipulation has been identified to characterise women more than men (Bjorkqvist, Osterman and Hjelt-Back, 1994).

Again, students (25% of those bullied in a traditional manner) highlighted a level of institutionalised bullying in the forms of over-load of work, withholding of information, or being given no tasks. As regards cyber-bullying, prank phone calls (50% of total cyber-bullied) was the most prevalent form experienced by Irish students, followed by nasty text messages (43%) and insults on a website (43%), which is in keeping with the Thessalonica study (Gountsidou, 2009) as well as other studies (Smith et al., 2006; O'Moore, 2012). Apart from 'happy slapping' (assaulting an unwitting victim while others record the event on a camera phone), which was experienced by male students only, there appears little difference in the types of cyber-bullying experienced in terms of gender.

BULLYING AND ETHNICITY

Keeping in mind the small numbers of respondents from the ethnicities involved, black (33%) and mixed race (33%) students were most at risk of being bullied in a traditional manner, but only white students were cyber-bullied. Similarly, only white Irish students were subjected to frequent traditional bullying.

BULLYING: YEAR AND DISCIPLINE

In keeping with Chapell et al.'s (2004) findings, unlike school bullying, bullying in college did not decline in later years; third-year undergraduates reported the highest level of experiences of traditional bullying (20% of total who had been bullied), while second-year undergraduates had the highest incident rate of cyber-bullying (33% of total who had been cyber-bullied). Engineering/Maths/Science students had the highest percentage of traditionally bullied victims within their number (18%), while all faculties reported identical incident rates of cyber-bullying (33%), though postgraduate students reported no incidents at all of cyber-bullying, perhaps due to a more advanced age and slightly lower familiarity with technology. At this stage it is only possible to speculate about the differences found. Only further research will account for these differences found between the year of study and discipline, whether they are of significance and what the reasons for the differences may be.

BULLYING AND FRIENDS

Underlining that there is safety in numbers, and perhaps also helping to account for their greater number, students bullied in a traditional manner proved more likely to have no friends (5.3% of such students) than cyber-bullied students (0%), over half of whom (55%) reported having many friends, compared to 42% of traditionally bullied students. Cyber-bullied students also reported having generally more active social lives than their traditionally bullied counterparts, with 18% of those bullied in a traditional manner stating that they did not go out much, while no student who was cyber-bullied reported not going out, a pattern also found to characterise second-level students (Wang et al., 2009).

BULLYING AND SCHOLASTIC DISSATISFACTION

While students who were bullied reported a higher level of scholastic dissatisfaction (16%) than non-bullied students (10%), interestingly cyber-bullied students reported no level of scholastic dissatisfaction, though they were far more likely to consider quitting college (89%) than those traditionally bullied (62%) and those who were not bullied (46%), which could perhaps underline how much more debilitating cyber-bullying can be to the individual in terms of trying to find an escape.

COPING WITH BULLYING

Both genders were more likely to seek help from the college administration when it came to cyber-bullying than traditional bullying. This would seem to indicate that there is less faith in the institutions to deal with forms of bullying where there is no obvious 'trail', such as e-mails, texts, web entries, etc. This lack of faith in the college staff and setup is also apparently reflected in the fact that not one student who had been bullied, in either form, approached their tutors for help with these issues; and only a small percentage of male students who had been bullied in a traditional manner (11%) made any use at all of the colleges' bullying contacts, though this could be, at least in part, because, much like a bullying policy, many students were unaware of their existence. In any event, the fact that so many students chose avoidance as their prime method of coping with bullying, in either its traditional form (74%) or cyber-bullying (69%), and so few chose to use any of the institutional avenues does indicate a problem, at the very least, with students' perceptions of and confidence in their college's ability to help them resolve their problems.

EFFECTS OF BULLYING

Unsurprisingly, students who were either bullied in a traditional manner (88% of those bullied) or cyber-bullied (83% of those bullied) agreed that the most profound effect of the bullying on them was a great amount of stress. Those who were bullied in a traditional manner reported that their enjoyment of the subject they were studying and their motivation to work in college had been reduced to a greater extent than among those students who were cyber-bullied. At first glance it would seem that this would naturally be the case, seeing as those who were victimised in a traditional manner would be more aware of who it was that was bullying them than those who were cyber-bullied, and would therefore find class and college a more uncomfortable place to work and study. However, as cyber-bullied students reported being marginally more afraid to go to college (59%) than students bullied in a traditional manner (53.5%), it might be posited that the larger reduction in subject enjoyment and work motivation among traditional students could be directly linked to the experiences of bullying by staff reported by them.

Male students in both cyber-bullying and traditional bullying situations reported higher levels of feelings of isolation and feeling helpless than did female students. Similarly their social lives were more likely to have been affected, and they were more likely to have to go for medical treatment and counselling than their female peers. While female students were not as affected by the cyber-bullying as their male counterparts, they reported higher levels of stress. They also reported a greater reduction in motivation to work when bullied in a traditional manner than did male students.

Not unexpectedly, bullying also increased the likelihood of students considering quitting college. While 49% of respondents had reported thinking of leaving college at some time, this increased to 63% for the student bullied in a traditional manner, and jumped to 89% for cyber-bullied students, although cyber-bullied students did not consider it as frequently as students bullied in a traditional manner.

BULLYING AND CYBER-BULLYING OTHERS

In respect of traditional bullying, only 2% of respondents admitted that they had bullied someone else in college, though no one admitted to doing so by themselves. Of those that bullied, the vast majority (80%) were male. Interestingly however, a slightly higher percentage of respondents (3%) admitted to cyber-bullying, with more female students (62.5%) than male (37.5%) declaring that they had cyber-bullied other students. These findings for cyber-bullying, in terms of gender, are in contrast to the findings of the Nationwide Study on School Bullying (O'Moore, Kirkham and Smith, 1997), where more post-primary school boys than girls bullied one another, and the Dilmac study (2009), where male third-level students cyber-bullied others more than female. Though the sample is very small, and caution should therefore be taken in terms of its meaning, it could be argued that, in keeping with the studies on girls and bullying (Bjorkqvist and Niemela, 1992; Besag, 2006), the extra 'level' of removal from one's target found in cyber-bullying would be in line with the types of bullying favoured by girls; and one might expect to see a higher prevalence rate among female perpetrators.

BULLYING IN SCHOOL AND COLLEGE

Almost 40% of all respondents had been bullied while in school, with slightly more female students (41%) than male students (37%) reporting this to be the case. A further 7% had both been bullied and bullied others (8.5% male/5.7% female), while 2% admitted to bullying others in school (2.4% male/1.3% female).

Results from this survey proved to be in line with the correlation found by Chapell et al. (2006), with 50% of those bullied in a traditional manner in college having been bullied in school, and a further 5% of those bullied in college having bullied others in school. In addition, 60% of those who bullied others in a traditional manner in college had also bullied someone in school, with a further 20% of 'traditional' bullies in college having themselves been bullied while in school. In terms of cyber-bullying 44% of those cyber-bullied in college had been bullied in school, while 22% had taken part in bullying others. No one who cyber-bullied others in college had bullied others in school, though 25% had themselves been bullied.

RECOMMENDATIONS

In carrying out what the author regards as one of the first studies into bullying and aggression among third-level students, the temptation was there to garner as much detail as possible from the students. However, the length of the survey (fifty-three questions in total), coupled with the brevity of attention recorded in web surfers (Akami, 2006), may have caused the 36% falloff in respondents from 378 initially to 240 latteraly.

Further research on a greater sample size from around the country would allow for more in-depth exploration of the differences in levels of bullying and negative behaviours found here in the varying disciplines and year of study, as well as the social differences apparent between victims of traditional bullying and cyber-bullying, and help to ascertain their significance. A survey of tutors, contact and administrative staff would also be beneficial in order to ascertain staff experiences of student-to-student bullying and aggression, their perceptions of same, and any difficulties they have found in helping to cope with it.

A specific study on cyber-bullying at third level would allow for deeper examination of students' attitudes towards cyber-bullying and their perceptions of who is bullying them and why, as well as allowing for further study on the gender differences in cyber-victimisation and coping.

Given the number of students who were revealed in this study to have been bullied in school and then bullied in college, a longitudinal approach, following individuals from school through college and perhaps into the workplace, would allow researchers to assess the propensity for bullying/being bullied, and assess changing attitudes towards bullying and cyber-bullying.

CONCLUSION

With reports among peers of high levels of negative behaviours such as exclusion, unwanted sexual attention and teasing and taunting, combining with the number of students who felt they were under a great deal of pressure to succeed, found college isolating, and had considered dropping out of college, a picture emerges of a student body in Ireland that is under considerable stress even without bullying being a factor. Coupled with student unhappiness with their colleges' ability to help them resolve their personal and scholastic problems, it would seem advisable, especially in an economic environment that is unstable and where success in college more than ever may determine success in securing employment, that colleges look again to both the level of help made available to students to help them cope with stress, and their own structures in regards to dealing with specific issues.

This is especially the case when it comes to students reporting difficulties with staff. The very fact that nearly a quarter of all those students who took this survey reported they were unhappy with their institutions' help in resolving problems with staff points towards a level of conflict with the staff which is a cause for unease. Unfair marking, hostile receptions, work ignored by tutors and persistent unwarranted criticism of work were widely reported, to the extent that it would seem that it would be beneficial for third-level institutions to survey their students as to their interactions with college staff to a more in-depth level, and perhaps consider consulting student representatives to work towards creating a transparent and fair way to hear and deal with such issues.

This is not the only area that colleges may wish to review. The lack of confidence students had in their college to help resolve issues was massively underlined by the fact that no bullied student sought their tutors' help in trying to deal with that bullying. Indeed, the rate of seeking help for bullying from any of the colleges' avenues was very low, to the point of being alarming. However, if the rate of conflict between staff and students reported is accurate, it comes as no surprise that this is the case. Colleges are not run on egalitarian lines, and the power resides almost entirely with academic and administrative staff. As such, if students do not feel that they can resolve their conflicts with staff in a fair and impartial manner, then it is unlikely that they will have much faith in the same staff to help them resolve issues with their peers.

With well over 65% of students having no idea whether their college had a policy on bullying or not, it is quite clear that colleges in Ireland have more to do in clarifying and advertising their stance on bullying and harassment within their walls. It is crucial that they do so for both students and staff. In order for students to have faith in their institutions, first the college itself, and then its staff, must set the tone, starting with their own behaviour to one another and to the students, otherwise they risk legitimising aggressive behaviour through indifference, causing the problem to spiral and become almost the norm (Twale et al., 2008).

That there is a problem to worry about is clear, as, despite the relatively small numbers involved, the results of this initial study into bullying among third-level students in Ireland indicate that bullying and cyber-bullying both exist and are a problem for students on Irish campuses. The effects of bullying or cyber-bullying on students are clearly stated here, including reduced enjoyment of college life, reduced motivation to work, higher levels of stress, increased visits to GPs, and greater weight given to thoughts of dropping out of college, and students clearly feeling they cannot turn to the college in most cases.

Colleges, like schools and workplaces, have an obligation to students and staff alike in regard to their health and safety, and must look to putting the same effort into combating bullying. From this study, both in terms of bullying and cyber-bullying, colleges are experiencing the same types of bullying and negative behaviours as Irish schools or workplaces, but at differing levels. As it stands, from this study, it appears that Southern (2009) is correct, and third-level institutions are closer in tone to workplaces than schools, in both their attitudes to students and their efforts to highlight and combat bullying. For while the creation of bullying policies and the designation of contact staff are welcome, there is little point in simply putting in place these options without knowing the true nature and extent of the issue, so that solutions can be found to target, prevent and combat the problem. To do otherwise is simply placing a generic and limited fix to what can be a very specific and chronic problem.

Bullying is an organic thing, often changing and developing in nature, as evidenced by the rise of cyber-bullying, and it can morph in nature in response to the tactics brought in to combat it. Therefore, these tactics too must be organic and fluid in nature, capable of changing as the issues change. Highlighting the issue of bullying, creating an atmosphere where talking about it is encouraged, where dignity and respect is fostered, training staff to deal with bullying issues and to set an example, putting in place impartial mediators, working with student bodies, creating mentoring programmes to help reduce isolation and stress and other situations which may cultivate bullying, all can help to create an ethos that will show that bullying is not tolerated, and foster a confidence in students to come forward to try and deal with it, before their health and studies diminish and they consider dropping out of college.

There are 250,000 students in Ireland, and by any standards this study is small, touching barely a fraction of the current student body. However, the results gleaned within this piece of work do indicate that there is an issue worth investigating. Therefore, it is to be strongly recommended that third-level institutions, as a whole, follow in the footsteps of schools and workplaces in Ireland and carry out a comprehensive national study in the near future.

REFERENCES

Akami Technologies, Press Release: 'Akamai and JupiterResearch Identify "4 Seconds" as the New Threshold of Acceptability for Retail Web Page Response Times' (2006), http://www.akamai.com/html/about/press/releases/2006/press_110606.html [accessed 10 May 2010]

Berger, S. 'Women Embrace Technology: The Number of Female Web Surfers Grow Faster Than Overall Internet Population', *Par Excellence* (2002), http://www.parexcellencemagazine.com/technology/executive-women-using-technology/166-women-embrace-technology-the-number-of-female-web-surfers-grow-faster-than-overall-internet-popu-lation-.html [accessed 10 May 2010]

Besag, V.E. *Understanding Girls' Friendships, Fights and Feuds: A Practical Approach to Girls' Bullying* (Maidenhead, Berkshire: Open University Press, 2006)

Björkqvist, K. and Niemelä, P. (eds), *Of Mice and Women: Aspects of Female Aggression* (San Diego: Academic Press, 1992)

Bjorkqvist, K., Osterman,K. and Hjelt-Back, M. 'Aggression among University Employees', *Aggressive Behavior*, 20, 1994, pp. 173–84

Chapell, M., Casey, D., De la Cruz, C., Ferrell, J., Forman, J., Lipkin, R., Newsham, M., Sterling, M. and Whittaker, S. 'Bullying in College by Students and Teachers', *Adolescence*, 39, Spring 2004, pp. 53–64

Chapell, M.S., Hasselman, S.L., Kitchin, T. and Lomon, S.N. 'Bullying in Elementary School, High School and College', *Adolescence*, 41, 2006, pp. 633–49

Craig, W.M., Pepler, D., Connolly, J. and Henderson, K. 'Developmental Context of Peer Harassment in Early Adolescence: The Role of Puberty and the Peer Group', in J. Juvonen and S. Graham (eds), *Peer Harassment in School: The Plight of the Vulnerable and Victimized* (New York: Guilford Press, 2001)

Curran, T.A., Gawley, E., Casey, P., Gill, M. and Crumlish, N. 'Depression, Suicidality and Alcohol Abuse among Medical and Business Students', *Irish Medical Journal*, 103, 2009, pp. 249–51

Dilmac, B. 'Psychological Needs as a Predictor of Cyber-Bullying: A Preliminary Report on College Students', *Educational Sciences: Theory and Practice*, 9, 2009, pp. 1307–25

Einarsen, S. and Skogstad, A. *Det Gode Arbeidsmiljø: Krav og Utfordringer* (*The Good Work Environment: Demands and Challenges*) (Bergen: Fagbokforlaget Vigmostad and Bjørke AS, 2000) (in Norwegian)

Eurostat: European Commission, *Your Key to European Statistics* (2010), http://epp.eurostat.ec.europa.eu/portal/page/portal/statistics/ themes [accessed 15 January 2011]

Galdas, P.M., Cheater, F. and Marshall, P. 'Men and Health Help-Seeking Behaviour: Literature Review', *Journal of Advanced Nursing*, 49, 2005, pp. 616–23

Gountsidou, V. 'Cyber-Bullying at the Tertiary Education: ABSTRACT', presented at COST Action IS0801 Workshop, Mykolas Romeris University, Vilnius, Lithuania, 22–3 August 2009

Higher Education Authority, 'Student Statistics' (2009), http://www.hea.ie/en/node/1312 [accessed 15 January 2011]

Lewis, D. 'Workplace Bullying: Interim Findings of a Study in Further and Higher Education in Wales', *International Journal of Manpower*, 20, 1999, pp. 106–19

Lewis, D. 'Bullying at Work: The Impact of Shame among University and College Lecturers', *British Journal of Guidance and Counselling*, 32, 2004, pp. 281–99

Leymann, H. *Fran mobbing till Utslagning i Arbetslivet* [*From Bullying to Exclusion in Working Life*] (Stockholm: Publica, 1992a)

Lipsett, A. 'Bullying Rife Across Campus', *Times Higher Education*, 16 September 2005

McCarthy, P., Rylance, J., Bennett, R. and Zimmermann, H. *Bullying: From Backyard to Boardroom*, 2nd edn (Sydney: The Federation Press, 2001)

McGuire, L. 'Bullying and Cyber-Bullying among Third-Level Students in Ireland', unpublished MEd thesis, Trinity College Dublin, 2010

Mikolajczyk, R.T., Maxwell, A.E., El Ansari, W., Naydenova, V., Stock, C., Ilieva, S., Dudziak, U. and Nagyova, I. 'Prevalence of Depressive Symptoms in University Students from Germany, Denmark, Poland and Bulgaria', *Journal of Social Psychiatry and Psychiatric Epidemiology*, vol. 43, no. 2, 2008, pp. 105–12

National Union of Students (NUS), *Student Experience Report* (p. 25) http://www.nus.org.uk/PageFiles/4017/NUS_StudentExperience Report.pdf [accessed 15 January 2011]

O'Moore, M. *Summary Report on the National Survey on Workplace Bullying in Ireland* (Dublin: ABC, Trinity College, 2001)

O'Moore, M. *Understanding School Bullying: A Guide for Parents and Teachers* (Dublin: Veritas, 2010)

O'Moore, M. 'Cyberbullying: The Situation in Ireland', *Pastoral Care in Education: An International Journal of Personal, Social and Emotional Development*, 30, 2012, pp. 209–23

O'Moore, M., Kirkham, C. and Smith, M. 'Bullying Behaviour in Irish Schools: A Nationwide Study', *Irish Journal of Psychology*, 18, 1997, pp. 141–69

O'Moore, M. and Minton, S.J. *Dealing with Bullying in Schools: A Training Manual for Teachers, Parents and Other Professionals* (London: Paul Chapman Publishing, 2004)

O'Moore, M. and Minton, S.J. 'Cyber-Bullying: The Irish Experience', paper presented to COST Action IS0801 Workshop, Mykolas Romeris University, Vilnius, Lithuania, 22–3 August 2009

Olweus, D. 'Norway', in P.K. Smith, Y. Morita, J. Junger-Tas, D. Olweus, R. Catalano and P. Slee (eds), *The Nature of School Bullying: A Cross-National Perspective* (London and New York: Routledge, 1999)

Rodkin, P.C and Berger, C. 'Who Bullies Whom? Social Status Asymmetries by Victim Gender', *International Journal of Behavioural Development*, 32, 2008, pp. 473–85

Roland, E. and Munthe, E. 'The 1996 Norwegian Programme for Preventing and Managing Bullying in Schools', *Irish Journal of Psychology*, 18, 1997, pp. 233–47

Ross, S.E., Niebling, B.C. and Heckert, T.M. 'Sources of Stress among College Students', *College Student Journal*, June 1999

Rudd, M.D. 'The Prevalence of Suicidal Ideation among College Students', *Suicide and Life-Threatening Behaviour*, 19, 1989, pp. 173–83

Russell, A. and Owens, L. 'Peer Estimates of School-Aged Boys' and Girls' Aggression to Same- and Cross-Sex Targets', *Social Development*, 8, 1999, pp. 364–79

Schweitzer, R., Klayich, M. and McLean, J. 'Suicidal Ideation and Behaviours among University Students in Australia', *Australian and New Zealand Journal of Psychiatry*, 29, 1995, pp. 473–9

Shur-Fen Gau, S., Chen, Y.Y., Tsai, F.J. and Lee, M.B. 'Risk Factors for Suicide in Taiwanese College Students', *Journal of American College Health*, 57, 2008, pp. 135–43

Smith, P.K., Mahdavi, J., Carvalho, M. and Tippett, N. 'An Investigation into Cyber-Bullying, its Forms, Awareness and Impact, and the Relationship between Age and Gender in Cyber-Bullying', Research Brief No. RBX03-06 (London: DfES, 2006), http://publications.dcsf.gov.uk/eOrderingDownload/RBX03-06.pdf [accessed 15 January 2011]

Smith, P.K., Pepler, D. and Rigby K. (eds), *Bullying in Schools: How Successful Can Interventions Be?* (Cambridge: Cambridge University Press, 2004)

Smith, P.K. and Sharp, S. (eds), *School Bullying: Insights and Perspectives* (London: Routledge, 1994)

Southern, L. 'University: A Bully-Free Environment?', paper presented to the 1ˢᵗ Global Conference on Bullying and the Abuse of Power: From the Playground to International Relations, Salzburg, Austria, 6–8 November 2009

Ttofi, M.M. and Farrington, D.P. 'What Works in Preventing Bullying: Effective Elements of Anti-Bullying Programmes', *Journal of Aggression, Conflict and Peace Research*, 1, 2009, pp. 3–24

Twale, D.J. and De Luca, B.M. *Faculty Incivility: The Rise of the Academic Bully Culture and What to Do About It* (San Fransisco: John Wiley & Sons, 2008)

Union of Students in Ireland (USI), 'About Us' (2010), http://www.usi.ie/about-usi.html [accessed 15 January 2011]

US Department of Education, Research and Statistics website (2010), http://www2.ed.gov/rschstat/statistics/resources/edpicks.jhtml?src=ln [accessed 15 January 2011]

Vaez, M., Kristenson, M. and Laflamme, L. 'Perceived Quality of Life and Self-Rated Health among First-Year University Students: A Comparison with their Working Peers', *Social Indicators Research*, 68, 2004, pp. 221–4

Vartia, M. 'The Sources of Bullying: Psychological Work Environment and Organisational Climate', *European Journal of Work and Organisational Psychology*, 5, 1996, pp. 203–14

Wang, J., Iannotti, R.J. and Nansel, T.R. 'School Bullying among Adolescents in the United States: Physical, Verbal, Relational and Cyber', *Journal of Adolescent Health*, 45, 2009, pp. 368–75

Zapf, D., Knorz, C. and Kulla, M. 'Causes and Consequences of Various Mobbing Factors at Work', Proceedings: Seventh European Congress of Work and Organisational Psychology, Gyor, Hungary, April 1995

Zhang, J. and Jin, S. 'Determinants of Suicide Ideation: A Comparison of Chinese and American College Students', *Adolescence*, 31, 1996, pp. 451–67

CHAPTER SIX

Bullying Behaviours Among Out-of-School Children

Claire Healy

INTRODUCTION

School bullying in Ireland has deservingly received much attention in recent years. Leading bullying researchers have worked tirelessly to see that we as a nation learn from the awful tragedies that have befallen some of our children and youth as a result of bullying. A shift in attitude is slowly taking place; bullying is being viewed less as 'character building' and 'harmless' and more as something catastrophic to the well-being of those being victimised. Great efforts have consequently been made also by school personnel, parents and students themselves who are determined to stamp out bullying and find effective ways of dealing with the issue. It is now mandatory for every school to have an anti-bullying policy in place, so that acts of violence and aggression (psychological or physical) cannot be permitted to go on unchallenged.

While these developments are certainly good news, what about those children and young people who are already alienated from school and society? Despite the progress made in relation to school bullying, bullying among young people out of home and school has received little research attention. However, it would be foolish to assume bullying is not a problem for this group. Having worked with young people out of home for a number of years, the writer was disturbed by the prevalence of bullying, aggression and low self-esteem that existed among these young people. More worryingly, these issues have not seemed to receive the attention or priority they deserved and necessitated. Research regarding this group more often than not relates to drug usage, educational attainment, poverty or criminal activity. While these topics are of course very valid and worthy of research, one could argue they are not of any more importance than the issues concerning this study. Studies from other countries provide some shocking results and prove that bullying is a significant problem among young people in care and homeless youth.

PREVIOUS RESEARCH

Stephenson (2002) found bullying to be a common occurrence in the fourteen children's homes he visited in north-east England. He reported that as many as 55% of young people were involved in bullying within the residential home in the last month. Twenty-five per cent said they had been bullied, 20% admitted to bullying others and 10% said they were involved as both a victim and bully. Forty per cent of the young people said they were also involved in bullying at school as well as in the residential home and sadly, of the 25% who said they had been bullied in the children's home, 24% said they were also bullied at school. Barter (2003) looked at how young people in residential care experience peer violence. She discovered over three-quarters of the young people interviewed had been involved in physical assaults, either as victims (56%) or perpetrators (35%), 73% of which were classified as high-level physical violence, such as knife attacks or severe beatings. While some of these assaults were isolated incidents, others were less fortunate, experiencing very regular bullying. Nearly half of the young people experienced non-contact violence, the most common forms being the destruction of property, threats of physical injury and controlling behaviour which dictated how one was 'allowed' to behave.

Ofsted (2008), the Office for Standards in Education, Children's Services and Skills in England, asked children and young people living away from home (in children's care homes, boarding schools, residential special schools, residential further education colleges, foster care, adoption placements or residential family centres) for their views on bullying. Twenty per cent of children reported they sometimes get bullied while 14% stated they got bullied often or most of the time. Fifty-five per cent reported being bullied at school while 24% stated they were bullied at home. In response to being asked what happened the last time they were bullied, 42% reported being subject to name-calling, 25% reported being hit, while 15% stated they were beaten up. The children living in children's care homes were more likely to have been physically bullied than those living in foster care.

Sinclair and Gibbs (1998), as part of a wider-scale study of the effectiveness of residential care, looked at bullying among residents. They found 41% of young people were bullied prior to living in the residential unit and nearly 44% while living there. They discovered just over half of those with a history of victimisation prior to being admitted to care were bullied again while living in the residential unit. Age and reason for admission into care had significant bearing on who was and was not bullied. Seventy per cent of 12-year-olds and younger reported being bullied after arrival while, interestingly, young people in trouble outside of the unit seemed to escape most victimisation. Thirteen per cent of young people had experienced unwelcome sexual behaviour from other residents. In Barter's study, reports of this kind of behaviour were low but perceived as deeply traumatic. Worryingly, half of these incidents went unreported to any member of staff or social work professional (Barter, 2003).

The trend continues into secure accommodation for young males, with some alarming results. Kidscape, the UK charity established to prevent bullying and child abuse, carried out a survey of young offenders and found 100% had been involved in bullying in some way (Elliot, 2002). Ireland and Monaghan (2006) carried out a survey on juvenile (12–17-year-olds) and young offenders (18–21-year-olds) from a secure care unit in the United Kingdom. They discovered 27% of offenders were classified as pure bullies, 25% were involved in the dual role of bully and victim, 19% were pure victims while 29% were not involved. At the Glenthorne Centre in Birmingham, 47% of the young people in secure care were reported to regularly bully their peers and 56% were frequent victims of bullying. Twenty-seven per cent of the young people had no involvement in bullying as victim or perpetrator, which meant 64% of those who bullied were also victims of bullying (Browne and Falshaw, 1996).

Connell and Farrington's (1996) study of young offenders in Canada found that 70% of the young people were involved in bullying, 45% as bullies and 25% as victims; surprisingly no one reported to be both a victim and a bully. Most of the victims said they experienced bullying every day, all had experienced verbal threats or insults, while 60% had been punched or hit. Similarly, Browne and Falshaw (1996) report 58% of all bullying incidents were violent assaults, while 42% were of an intimidatory nature. Connell and Farrington (1996) discovered that of those who admitted to bullying, 66% had also been bullies in their previous custodial facilities. Rather tellingly, all the bullies had previously been in custodial care, while none of the victims had.

BACKGROUND OF THE OUT-OF-HOME GROUP

The out-of-home young people who participated in this study no longer live at home due to family problems or due to their own challenging behaviour. Many of them have spent substantial periods away from the family home and instead have been cared for in substitute care such as foster care or residential care. The young people in this study have varied care histories and reside in temporary accommodation. Some are newly homeless, some have several failed care placements and some young people have had no fixed care placement for some time, resulting in a great deal of time being spent on the streets while they access accommodation on a nightly basis. Some young people live in temporary accommodation for a short period, as a stop-gap before they move on to a more settled environment, such as long-term residential care or semi-independent living. However, other young people live in temporary accommodation because all other services available to them have been exhausted; these young people have little accommodation options available to them.

Many of these young people have fallen behind in their schooling as a result of not being in full-time education for many years. They often have few skills and limited future employment opportunities. By their very nature, young people out of home are transient and have become used to little structure; at times they have chosen to disengage with the various care services and are absent for sometimes days at a time. The majority of these young people are going through a particularly tough time and some find themselves on a path of self-destruction, demonstrated by their very reckless behaviour. Family relationships can be very complex for this group; despite the possibility they may be out of home due to their own behaviour, there can still be great resentment and hurt at not being allowed live in the family home. This resentment is even greater again if the young person's actions are not responsible for this decision. Perhaps as a result of some or all of these factors, engaging in very risky behaviour is commonplace among those who seek to gain affirmation through a 'street' culture. This chapter reports on findings from a study which investigates the extent and nature of bullying among young people out of home as compared with young people attending mainstream second-level education. It also reviews the role self-esteem plays in young people who participate in bullying.

THE STUDY

The study, which formed part of an MEd in Aggression Studies at the School of Education, Trinity College Dublin (Healy, 2008), focused on answering the following questions:

- What is the extent and nature of bullying among young people living out of home?
- Does the self-esteem of young people out of home differ to that of young people in mainstream education?

A total of thirty young people participated in this study; they ranged in age from 14 to 17 years. The out-of-home group consisted of ten young people – four males and six females. The school sample consisted of twenty students, two students for every participating young person out of home. The school students were matched with the out-of-home sample in terms of age and gender. The young people out of home who co-operated in this study resided in one of four residential units which cater for young people who are newly homeless, those who have had several care placements and young people who have had no fixed care placement for some time. The young people in the school group attend a south inner-city Dublin co-educational school consisting of approximately 120 students. A simple random sampling approach (the lottery method) was used to choose an appropriate school. Five schools were chosen and contacted. However, none of the schools contacted agreed to take part, citing different reasons. On this basis, purposive sampling was employed to pick a school. These students were picked out by the principal based on the information given to him by the researcher.

RESEARCH METHODOLOGY

In order to investigate the young people's experiences of bullying behaviour, a questionnaire, developed as part of a follow-up study to the Nationwide Survey of Bullying at School in Ireland, was used (Minton and O'Moore, 2008). This questionnaire was adapted from the Olweus Self-Report Bullying Questionnaire (1996) to allow for examination of the extent and nature of once-off aggressive acts as well as bullying behaviours. However, this chapter will only examine bullying behaviours for the purpose of this study. Three extra questions were added to provide information on bullying within the residential units. The following definition of bullying was included in the questionnaire:

We say a young person is being bullied when he or she is singled out in an unpleasant way, and is picked on again and again, by another young person or several young people. For example, it is bullying when a young person has nasty or unpleasant things said to him or her, or is hit, kicked, threatened, locked inside a room, sent nasty notes, or when no one ever talks to him or her, and things like that. These things can happen often and it may be difficult for the young person being bullied to defend him or herself.

(Minton and O'Moore, 2008, p. 2)

The self-esteem of the young people was assessed using the Piers Harris 2, the second edition of the Piers Harris Children's Self-Concept Scale (Piers and Herzberg, 2007). The Piers Harris 2 assesses self-esteem globally and in six different domains, reflecting the assumption that self-concept is multi-dimensional. The domains are: Behavioural Adjustment (fourteen items); Intellectual and School Status (sixteen items); Physical Appearance and Attributes (eleven items); Freedom from Anxiety (fourteen items); Popularity (twelve items) and finally Happiness and Satisfaction (ten items). It is a self-report questionnaire with sixty short statements which express how a person may feel about themselves. Interviews were used as a means of collecting qualitative data. These were conducted on an individual basis by the researcher and involved the use of a dictaphone to record the conversation. The interviews were semi-structured and ranged in duration from five minutes to fifteen minutes.

The questionnaires were administered on an individual basis with each young person. Each participant received clear instructions on what the study was about, what it hoped to achieve and what would be expected of them prior to taking part. The importance of their honesty and the confidentiality was clearly communicated. The questionnaires were administered without a time limit and anonymously. Participants were only asked to provide the name of their school or residential unit and the date at the time of completing the questionnaire. The researcher remained in the vicinity in case any clarification was needed, which was sometimes the case with some of the younger participants.

The individual interviews were conducted after the completion of the two questionnaires, one relating to bullying and the other self-esteem. They ranged in duration from five minutes to fifteen minutes and were semi-structured in nature. They explored the young people's experiences of bullying more closely and the feelings surrounding the involvement in such behaviour. The young people were told at the onset of the interview the sort of questions they would be asked, they were informed they could speak from their own experiences of bullying if they had any or they could talk from their own opinions.

RESULTS

Bullying behaviours

Over half of the out-of-home young people (six out of ten) reported to have bullied another young person, while four admitted to being bullied in the past three months. There were only three young people out of home who were not involved in bullying as either a victim or a bully. Three were classified as pure bullies, one as a pure victim and three as bully/victims. In contrast to the percentage involved in bullying among the out-of-school young people, there were 30% of students in school who reported to be involved in bullying; of these four were pure victims, two were pure bullies and two were bully/victims. The findings suggest young people out of home suffer more victimisation and bully others more than their school-going peers. While there are some minor discrepancies as to the frequency of bullying, the findings in relation to young people out of home are however primarily in support of those from previous research. The findings also show the nature of bullying experienced by young people out of home is similar to that in previous studies (Ombudsman for Children and Young People, 2012; Mayock and O'Sullivan, 2007; Ireland and Monaghan, 2006; Mayock and Vekic, 2006; Barter, 2003; Elliot, 2002; Stephenson, 2002; Sinclair and Gibbs, 1998; O'Moore, Kirkham and Smith, 1997; Browne and Falshaw, 1996; Connell and Farrington, 1996). This indicates bullying is a significant problem for young people out of home. The findings in relation to bullying among the school group are in excess of those reported in the nationwide survey by O'Moore, Kirkham and Smith (1997) with regards to victims and bully/victims. The present findings indicate 10% of schoolgoers are involved in bullying as both a bully and victim, a larger number than what was reported in O'Moore et al.'s (1997) nationwide survey (4%).

Self-esteem and bullying behaviour

This study's findings clearly show there is a strong relationship between self-esteem and bullying behaviour. Table 6.1 demonstrates global self-esteem decreases considerably with involvement in bullying behaviour. While pure bullies appear to fare quite well with the second highest global self-esteem mean score, it is the pure victims who come out the worst, with the lowest mean score for global self-esteem. The findings in relation to victims are consistent with those from previous studies (O'Moore and Kirkham, 2001; Austin and Joseph, 1996; Callaghan and Joseph, 1995; Neary and Joseph, 1994; O'Moore and Hillery, 1991; Rigby and Slee, 1992; Rigby and Slee, 1993). Analysis of the cluster scales for pure victims are chiefly in support of previous studies (O'Moore, 2002; O'Moore and Kirkham, 2001). Young people in the out-of-home group who had been victimised indicated they were the unhappiest, with a noticeably lower score than their school-going peers. This finding is consistent with Rigby and Slee (1992). The results indicate that out-of-home victims of bullying have greater feelings of failure across all domains, while their school-going peers share this sense of failure in Behavioural Adjustment, Physical Appearance and Attributes, Intellect and School Status and Popularity.

Table 6.1: Mean cluster and Global Self-Esteem scores for young people out of home and school-going students who are not involved in bullying, pure victims, pure bullies and bully/victims.

CLUSTER SCALES	NOT INVOLVED IN BULLYING		PURE VICTIMS		PURE BULLIES		BULLY/ VICTIMS	
	Home N=3	School n=12	Home n=1	School n=4	Home n=3	School n=2	Home n=3	School n=2
Global	47.3	47.6	30	42.5	44.6	43	35.3	43
Behavioural Adjustment	39.3	52.3	37	41	34.3	35	29	46
Physical Appearance and Attributes	47.3	46.8	38	45	55	55	44	49
Intellect and School Status	48.6	48	36	43	45.6	38	34	44.5
Freedom from Anxiety	52	44.6	28	46.5	51	48.5	40.3	41.5
Popularity	59.3	55.3	41	44.2	56.7	54.5	51.6	45.5
Happiness and Satisfaction	51	49.6	33	50	50	55	39.6	45

Home = Out-of-Home Young People

The findings in relation to bullies indicate pure bullies have a relatively positive view of themselves. However, with a lower global self-esteem score, this view is still poorer than those not involved in bullying (O'Moore and Kirkham, 2001; O'Moore and Hillery, 1991). The findings for pure bullies presented are in support of O'Moore and Hillery (1991); Austin and Joseph (1996); Mynard and Joseph (1997) and O'Moore and Kirkham (2001), who found pure bullies were less well behaved, had lower scholastic competence and were less popular than those not involved in bullying. While pure bullies do not view themselves to be as popular as their peers who are not involved in bullying, they still view their popularity in a favourable light. These findings support Salmivalli (1998), who found pure bullies to be confident in their physical attractiveness and popularity. She puts forward the notion that pure bullies may have an unrealistic view of themselves with regards to popularity because classmates do not show their obvious disapproval of the bullies' actions; the bully then misconstrues this as support for his/her actions and thus popularity. Olweus (1993) and O'Moore and Kirkham (2001) found that adolescents who bully show little anxiety; this is in line with this study's findings from both groups, in particular out-of-home pure bullies. With some of the highest scores of all young people surveyed, pure bullies are very happy and satisfied with their current situation, especially so in the case of the school pure bullies.

O'Moore and Kirkham (2001), O'Moore and Hillery (1991), Olweus (1993), Austin and Joseph (1996) and Mynard and Joseph (1997) found young people involved in the dual role of bully/victim had significantly lower global and domain scores than pure bullies or victims. The presented findings in relation to bully/victims are not consistent with this view. Overall bully/victims from both groups seemed to fare better in many of the cluster scales, as well as global self-esteem, than their pure victim peers; this was the case for both groups although the gap was much smaller for the school group. According to Mynard and Joseph (1997), what sets bully/victims apart from their peers is their low levels of social acceptance. The bully/victims in this study, while scoring lower than those not involved in bullying for popularity, still view themselves as more popular than their pure victim peers. These differences may in part be due to the small numbers in some of the categories, which may have left some results a bit skewed. O'Moore and Kirkham (2001) posed that differences such as this may also be due to different researchers using different criteria to classify bully/victims. Both

Austin and Joseph (1996) and Mynard and Joseph (1997) placed children in their bully only group who were high bully, low victim while this present study, in line with O'Moore and Kirkham (2001), placed children in the pure bully group only if they had not been victimised even once or twice.

Outcome of individual interviews

The interview data highlighted the very different attitudes to bullying among the two groups and demonstrated an extremely high tolerance towards violent behaviour. This was particularly true for the young people out of home, but not exclusively so. Six of ten young people out of home stated they had no choice in the level of violence they were involved in. It seems if a disagreement ensued between a young person and his or her peers, then one automatically had to 'sort out' the situation. As one 14-year-old girl put it, 'you have to stand up for yourself and that's it ... you have to fight or you get killed. As long as you can say you fought someone ... if you don't fight you're gonna have the same people after you again and again' (Annie: Out-of-Home group). It seems the worst possible image one could portray was that of someone weak: 'if you even let a person know for a second that you're afraid then you're a goner' (Sabrina: Out-of-Home group). Young people who engaged in the Ofsted (2008) study agreed and felt that unless one was seen as a good fighter or good at defending oneself then they would be vulnerable to being picked on.

A third of the out-of-home young people liked the excitement fighting gave them. However, it was evident some young people did not feel they had a choice in participating in violence: 'I don't want to be that person but I don't know what else to do' (Liz: Out-of-Home group); 'I know it's not right but I don't have any other choice' (Marie: Out-of-Home group). According to Mayock and O'Sullivan (2007), most of the exploitation experienced by young people out of home and especially those involved in the 'street scenes' was at the hands of their peers. They reported little loyalty and fights often starting between 'friends' over money, drugs and possessions. Verbal and physical attacks from peers were common, as were incidents of one's clothing or property being stolen. Mayock and Vekic (2006) agree and state bullying is a significant problem for many out-of-home youth in hostels and street-based settings.

Some young people, three from both groups, felt they had no alternative but to bully others; they felt if they didn't then they too would be bullied. As one bully/victim despondently put it, 'you have to do some things just to get by' (Marie: Out-of-Home group). Rather tellingly, one pure bully explained: 'you sort of have to fight for it, fight to not have to be bullied' (Sinead: Out-of-Home group). Another pure bully explained: 'it's either bully or get bullied ... people that do bully, they only bully because their friends tell them to' (Anthony: School group). Some young people, again three from both groups, felt it was necessary to bully to defend one's name and as a form of protection from being bullied. This sentiment is echoed by reports from homeless youths (Ombudsman for Children and Young People, 2012) who state it is imperative that an image of toughness is maintained; to be perceived as weak would automatically mean one was open to being bullied. Further validation is provided by Elliott (2002), who found many young offenders became involved in gangs, fighting and bullying others so as not to become victims themselves. Sometimes it is easier to be a bully than be bullied; according to the young people in the Ofsted (2008) report, many felt young people engage in bullying because they fear they will be bullied if they don't.

The interviews demonstrated very clearly that violence and aggression are very familiar to many of the young people out of home. It seemed to be a way of life for them, something they had grown up with and to which they had become very accustomed. Seven out of ten young people spoke about involvement in violence in a very natural manner; and five of these seven felt violence was the answer to even the smallest of life's problems: 'if you're out on the road and someone says something to you, then you're gonna fight them' (Sabrina: Out-of-Home group); 'if someone went off with me fella, I'd definitely give her a straightner' (Liz: Out-of-Home group).

Five of the ten young people out of home spoke about the ways things operated within many of the residential units where they lived. What they described was something akin to a social hierarchy which all young people had to adhere to. As one young man put it, 'if one is older and they're here longer, they feel they have more rights than someone new coming in' (Niall: Out-of-Home group); another young man stated, 'that's the way it is, it happened to me when I first started going through places like this, everyone has a place' (Simon: Out-of-Home group). What this involves is 'knowing one's place', 'not getting too big for one's boots' and doing whatever those at the top tell you to do.

It seems these requests from those at the top can be quite demanding, as one young person explains: 'Like [they might be asked to] rob phones or that or give someone a hiding, that kinda thing'; she also explains that those at the bottom of this social hierarchy have little choice in their actions as to not comply would mean 'they would have been seen as little outcasts' (Sinead: Out-of-Home group). These five young people all admitted it was the youngest or the newest into the care system that experiences the most victimisation: 'they're easy targets cos they're not going to really fight back for themselves cos they're only straight out of home' (Liz: Out-of-Home group). This notion of 'pecking orders' was strongly supported by Barter (2003), who found not only were these factors present in all but one of the residential units she visited but victimisation had a direct bearing on one's position in the social hierarchy.

Similarly, this was also the case for teenage male offenders, who indicated that much of the bullying took place as part of an initiation process. New residents were bullied by those who were there the longest and one's bullying reputation (either as victim or bully) from previous custodial facilities indicated whether they would be bullied or not. Bullying was seen by the majority as a normal part of life in custody (Connell and Farrington, 1996). Browne and Falshaw (1996) saw bullying as interactive, with one main manipulator at the top of the social hierarchy escaping all victimisation but responsible for much of the bullying, the opposite being true for those in the most subordinate positions. The 'top dog', according to Barter (2003), was characterised as someone who yielded considerable power and influence over his or her peers and sometimes staff. Intimidation and a reputation for violence were seen as a crucial element in exercising this power. Sinclair and Gibbs (1998) found there to be a culture of bullying behaviour, akin to the William Golding novel *Lord of the Flies*. They discovered the younger and less streetwise young people were humiliated and bullied by older, more delinquent residents in some of the residential units.

In strong contrast to the young people out of home, eleven out of twenty school students felt bullying was wrong, while six of these eleven openly stated they hated bullying. Even though people tried to bully, there appeared to be a strong resistance to it from some young people. One young person explained: 'a lot of people in this school stand up to bullys, like they don't let them bully them' (Sarah: School group). Nine students felt a duty to stop bullying if they saw it happening; perhaps their sense of justice trickled over into their willingness to intervene if they saw someone being picked on. Intervention for school students did appear to be strongly correlated with age, as all nine young people who said they would unconditionally intervene were 17 years of age and so the eldest of the group. While many of the older students felt happy to intervene if they saw someone being bullied, this was not the case for the younger ones; eight out of twenty said they would not intervene as they feared the bully would turn on them. The young people from the out-of-home group had more complex reasons for not intervening; some felt it was none of their business, some felt people should stand up for themselves, some felt they would intervene if they liked the victim, while others said they would if it happened in the unit. However, the same underlying fear emerged from all the young people who admitted a reluctance to intervene, a fear of the bully and what would happen next.

Eleven out of twenty school students and four out of ten young people out of home spoke about the influence of one's peer group and how that sometimes affected how one behaved towards others. Some young people felt having friends protected one from being picked on and reported that those who were bullied had no friends as nobody stood up for them. Other young people spoke about a strong affiliation and loyalty to their friends even if it involved doing something one really didn't want to do. As one young person out of home stated, 'if your mate is getting beat around you can't just leave them there, you have to finish it off' (Marie: Out-of-Home group). Again it seems defending one's friends was not optional, it was expected, and if one didn't follow through then there would be repercussions: 'they'd probably turn on me, there'd be loads of hassle ... people wanting to fight ya' (Marie: Out-of-Home group). Wanting to impress one's friends and wanting to fit in were frequently cited as reasons why a young person would bully another.

DISCUSSION

The findings create quite a dark picture for the young person out of home and indicate involvement in bullying is a significant problem not only for the individuals involved but also for service providers. The question remains as to why young people out of home are involved in more bullying than their school-going peers. This is especially so when one takes into account that the school group was matched with the residential group in terms of age, gender and socio-economic background.

Supervision of environments frequented by children and adolescents is commonly held as central to discouraging bullying behaviours (see Olweus, 1993; Elliott, 2002). It is possible that young people out of home spend so much time away from adult supervision and in the company of their peers that this leads them to become involved to such a degree in these activities. As the individual accounts demonstrated, young people out of home place great value on their friendships; perhaps they feel a sense of belonging to a group who has shared experiences. However, as Mayock and O'Sullivan (2007) state, while young people out of home 'can identify with each other's experiences, more often than not, street youth stress the exploitative nature of these friendships' (2007, p. 66). However, the findings show bullying is also a reality within the different units. Mayock and Vekic (2006) found that while bullying was persistent in many hostels young people stayed in, there appeared to be an inability of service providers to address and effectively deal with the situation. According to Olweus (1993), there is little point in having supervision if one (in this case care staff) is not going to intervene 'quickly and decidedly' in bullying situations.

And herein lies the problem. While most residential units may have a policy on bullying the reality is quite different. The measures used in schools to combat and address bullying are not always appropriate in the residential environment, which aims to be the young person's home. Residential care provides care for often troubled young people, and challenging and aggressive behaviours are very common. If a bully refuses to stop bullying or if he or she is in complete denial about their involvement, the bully cannot be forced to address the problem. While expulsion of the bully can be used as an absolute last resort by schools, the same option is usually neither available nor appropriate for the young people in care. It is obviously a very complex situation and warrants some creative, realistic and rehabilitative measures to address it.

Olweus (1993) points to the family as an influence on bullying, stating that there are certain child-rearing practices which create aggressive children. He describes a combination of too little love, too much freedom, 'power-assertive' child-rearing methods which rely on physical punishment and a temperament for 'hot-headedness'. Salmivalli (1998) suggests that bullies do not perceive themselves to be accepted and respected members of their families and that often their experience of family relationships is quite negative, a finding that is supported in Connolly and O'Moore (2002). According to Berk (2006), children who have been abused have been repeatedly exposed to opportunities that teach them to use aggression as a means of problem-solving. Individual accounts from the young people were in support of this postulation. One young person explains her mother's reaction when she returned home after a physical fight as a 10-year-old: 'she wasn't really shocked, she always says you have to stand up for yourself or people will walk all over ya' (Sinead: Out-of-Home group).

There is, however, something disturbing about the findings. While a huge number reported to be involved in aggressive behaviours, many of these denied any involvement in bullying, particularly as a victim. Although all these young people may not perceive themselves to be victims of bullying, there are some indications that there may have been some down-playing of the extent of one's victimisation due to the stigma attached to the victim status among the young people out of home. One young person's disgust was evident when asked how she thought it felt to be bullied:

> I would say they go home and cry. What else can you do if you can't stand up for yourself? Like I'd say they're raging with themselves, like their confidence and self-esteem would be really bad because how are you supposed to walk around if you're not able to stand up for yourself?
>
> (Sabrina: Out-of-Home group).

Later when asked what she would do to stop bullying if she was a teacher in a school, she stated: 'I'd laugh if someone came and told me they were being bullied. I'd say to them "what are you doing", I'd think they were a f**king idiot' (Sabrina: Out-of-Home group).

While few young people were as articulate in expressing their feelings about victims of bullying, this attitude was sadly not isolated. There seemed to be a general feeling that one had to stand up for oneself and if one didn't, it was one's own fault if picked on. Maintaining an image of toughness was crucial for survival. Ireland and Monaghan (2006) and Mayock and O'Sullivan (2007) found the young people they spoke to tended to aggress towards each other as a means of preventing their own victimisation and communicating the message that they were not passive individuals. Elliott (2002) stated that the young offenders she spoke to felt bullying and violence were an integral part of life in which they did not have a choice to participate, while Mayock and Vekic (2006) found a strong theme of survival from the young people they interviewed, who seemed to feel they had to constantly defend themselves. Sadly, the aggression and violence they were exposed to appeared to be a continuation of abuse or neglect they experienced as young children.

CONCLUDING REMARKS

The findings of this study indicate bullying is a considerable problem for young people out of home. This would indicate further that the self-esteem of most of these young people is affected and quite possibly leading them into some very high-risk behaviour external to the bullying. Indeed, the one thing that stands out from all the findings is the climate of violence, aggression and bullying that seems to surround the young people in this study, especially those out of home. Olweus (1993) states there is a direct relationship between involvement in crime and bullying. This view is echoed by Elliott (2002), who found unchecked school bullying encouraged bullies to believe their behaviour can get them exactly what they want without fear of repercussions. So, clearly, bullying can be viewed as a societal problem as well. As if it was needed, this provides even more reason to tackle this problem.

However, tackling bullying does not have to involve the process of placing blame. Interventions that focus on punitive measures are being recognised as unhelpful in effectively addressing and combating bullying. Instead, rehabilitative methods are thought to be the way forward. Programmes such as Restorative Justice or Aggression Replacement Training use tools such as role-playing to prepare the young person for testing situations. The young person is re-taught alternatives to bullying aggressive behaviour and more effective ways to cope with how he or she feels. This may then have a knock-on effect and result in more positive relationships with one's family, school, peers and society. There is no reason why the progress that has been made in addressing school bullying cannot be made with regards to bullying among children and young people in other environments.

The findings provide evidence of what might previously have been regarded as biased opinion. It is clear this is an area which would greatly benefit from a larger-scale study that would further investigate bullying among young people out of home and school. It is only by finding out what exactly the situation is that we can implement effective interventions to tackle this very complex problem. While some of the young people in this study were complacent about their involvement in such a degree of aggression, service providers cannot afford to be content with the status quo. These are not adults who have years of life experience behind them, they are children caught up in an adult world of fighting, violence and retaliation.

REFERENCES

Austin, S. and Joseph, S. 'Assessment of Bully/Victim Problems in 8 to 11 Year Olds', *British Journal of Educational Psychology*, 66, 1996, pp. 447–56

Barter, C. 'Young People in Residential Care Talk about Peer Violence', *Scottish Journal of Residential Child Care*, 2, 2003, pp. 39–50

Berk, L.E. *Child Development*, 7th edn (Boston: Pearson, 2006)

Browne, K. and Falshaw, L. 'Factors Related to Bullying in Secure Accommodation', *Child Abuse Review*, 5, 1996, pp. 123–7

Callaghan, S. and Joseph, S. 'Self-Concept and Peer Victimization among Schoolchildren', *Personality and Individual Differences*, 18, 1995, pp. 161–3

Connell A. and Farrington, D. 'Bullying among Incarcerated Young Offenders: Developing an Interview Schedule and Some Preliminary Results', *Journal of Adolescence*, 19, 1996, pp. 75–93

Connolly, I. and O'Moore, M. 'Personality and Family Relations of Children who Bully', *Personality and Individual Differences*, 35, 2002, pp. 559–67

Elliott, M. *Bullying: A Practical Guide to Coping for Schools*, 3rd edn (London: Pearson Education/Kidscape, 2002)

Healy, C. 'The Relationship between Self-Esteem and Bullying Behaviours: A Comparative Study of Young People in Mainstream Education and Young People out of Home', unpublished MEd thesis, Trinity College Dublin, 2008

Ireland J. and Monaghan R. 'Behaviours Indicative of Bullying among Young and Juvenile Male Offenders: A Study of Perpetrator and Victim Characteristics', *Aggressive Behavior*, 32, 2006, pp. 172–80

Mynard, H. and Joseph, S. 'Bully/Victim Problems and their Association with Eysenck's Personality Dimensions in 8 to 13 Year-Olds', *British Journal of Educational Psychology*, 67, 1997, pp. 51–4

Mayock, P and Vekic, K. *Understanding Youth Homelessness in Dublin City: Key Findings from the First Phase of a Longitudinal Cohort Study* (Dublin: Children's Research Centre, Trinity College Dublin, 2006)

Mayock, P. and O'Sullivan, E. *Lives in Crisis: Homeless Young People in Dublin* (Dublin: The Liffey Press, 2007)

Minton, S.J. and O'Moore, A.M. 'The Effectiveness of a Nationwide Intervention Programme to Prevent and Counter School Bullying in Ireland', *International Journal of Psychology and Psychological Therapy*, 8, 2008, pp. 1–12

Neary, A. and Joseph, S. 'Peer Victimization and its Relationship to Self-Concept and Depression among School Girls', *Personality and Individual Differences*, 16, 1994, pp. 183–6

Ofsted, *Children on Bullying: A Report by the Children's Rights Director for England* (2008), http://www.ofsted.gov.uk/resources/children-bullying [accessed 26 June 2012]

Olweus, D. *Bullying at School: What We Know and What We Can Do About It* (Oxford: Blackwell, 1993)

Olweus, D. *The Revised Olweus Self-Report Bullying Questionnaire* (Bergen, Norway: Research Centre for Health Promotion (Hemil Centre), 1996)

Ombudsman for Children and Young People, 'Homeless Truths: Children's Experiences of Homelessness in Ireland' (2012), http://www.oco.ie/assets/files/issues/HomelessTruths/HomelessTruthsWEB.pdf [accessed 26 June 2012]

O'Moore, A.M. 'Teachers Hold the Key to Change', in M. Elliott (ed.), *Bullying: A Practical Guide to Coping for Schools*, 3rd edn (London: Pearson Education Limited, 2002)

O'Moore, A.M. and Hillery, B. 'What Do Teachers Need to Know?' in M. Elliot (ed.), *A Practical Guide to Coping for Schools* (London: Longman, 1991)

O'Moore, A.M., Kirkham, C. and Smith, M. 'Bullying Behaviour in Irish Schools: A Nationwide Study', *Irish Journal of Psychology*, 18, 1997, pp. 141–69

O'Moore, A.M. and Minton, S.J. *School Bullying Questionnaire* (Dublin: The Anti-Bullying Centre, Trinity College, 2000)

O'Moore, M. and Kirkham, C. 'Self-Esteem and Its Relationship to Bullying Behaviour', *Aggressive Behavior*, 27, 2001, pp. 269–83

Piers, E.V. and Herzberg, D.S. *Piers-Harris 2: Piers-Harris Children's Self-Concept Scale*, 2nd edn (Los Angeles: Western Psychological Services, 2007)

Rigby, K. and Slee, P. 'Dimensions of Interpersonal Relations among Australian Children and Implications for Psychological Well-Being', *Journal of Social Psychology*, 133, 1992, pp. 33–42

Rigby, K. and Slee, P. 'The Relationship of Eysenck's Personality Factors and Self-Esteem to Bully-Victim Behaviour in Australia', *Personality and Individual Differences*, 14, 1993, pp. 371–3

Salmivalli, C. 'Intelligent, Attractive, Well-Behaving, Unhappy: The Structure of Adolescents' Self-Concept and its Relations to their Social Behaviour', *Journal of Research on Adolescence*, 8, 1998, pp. 333–54

Sinclair, I. and Gibbs, I. *Children's Homes: A Study in Diversity* (Chichester: Wiley Publishers, 1998)

Stephenson, P. 'Bullying in Children's Homes', in M. Elliott (ed.), *Bullying: A Practical Guide to Coping for Schools*, 3rd edn (London: Pearson Education Limited, 2002)

CHAPTER SEVEN

Bullying of Adults with Intellectual Disabilities in Educational Settings

Linda McGrath, Jackie Black and Claire Sutton

INTRODUCTION

Bullying behaviour can be witnessed across all age levels, social strata and societies. It is not a new phenomenon, but research into this area is relatively new. Initially, such research focused on bullying in relation to children (Olweus, 1978; Farrington, 1993; Smith and Sharp, 1994), although over the last thirty years or so there has been increasing interest in adult bullying, particularly in the workplace (Einarsen, Raknes and Matthiesen, 1994; Groeblinghoff and Becker, 1996; McCarthy, Sheehan and Kearns, 1995; O'Moore, Lynch and Nic Daeid, 2003). While studies have shown that people with an intellectual disability are at an increased risk of victimisation (Bryen et al., 2003; Sobsey and Mansell 1997; Valenti-Hein and Schwartz, 1995; Wilson and Brewer, 1992), there has been little systematic research undertaken to date that has examined bullying in relation to children or adults with an intellectual disability in terms of definition, prevalence, characteristics and outcomes. The few studies that have been undertaken suggest that they are at an increased risk of being involved in bullying (Baladerian, 1994; Byrne, 1994; Glumbic and Zunic-Pavlovic, 2010; Mencap, 1999, 2007; Nabuzoka, Whitney, Smith and Thompson, 1993; O'Moore and Hillery, 1989; Whitney, Smith and Thompson, 1994).

In order to fully understand the complexities of bullying, Olweus (1994) and Atlas and Pepler (1998) recommend using a systemic-ecological framework which encompasses personal characteristics and environmental factors. Many researchers have attempted to identify the characteristics associated with both bullies and victims. Power and control are central themes in bullying. Bullies have been described as having a tendency to be hot-tempered, impulsive and having a low tolerance for frustration (Olweus, 1993). Most bullies appear to have a positive attitude towards violence (Carney and Merrell, 2001) and use bullying to gain dominance. They tend to have a lack of empathy for their victims (Beale, 2001). Swanson and Malone (1992) carried out a meta-analysis of eighty-one studies which indicated that children with an intellectual disability were more likely to be rated as aggressive, immature and to suffer from personality problems than their peers.

Victims tend to be small in stature or frail compared to bullies (McNamara and McNamara, 1997), may be unsuccessful at sports (Olweus, 1993) and less popular and more isolated than their peers (Smith and Sharp, 1994). Many of these characteristics are over-represented in an intellectual disability population. Rinaldi (1992) suggests that adolescents with intellectual disabilities have less social experience to develop their social skills, and Griffiths (1994) reports that it is difficult for them to interpret social situations and learn appropriate behaviours because of their problems with symbolic representation and difficulties understanding cause and effect. Valance, Cummings and Humphries (1998) reported that studies indicate that children with an intellectual disability have poor social skills and tend to display less assertive behaviour than their peers. Some studies have found that children with intellectual disabilities have fewer friends (Dixon, Smith and Jenks, 2004; Nabuzoka, 2000) and are more likely to be socially rejected by their peers without an intellectual disability (Greenham, 1999).

Environmental factors contributing to bullying in schools include school ethos (Olweus, 1993), the presence and implementation of anti-bullying programmes and policies, and trained and motivated staff (Smith and Sharp, 1994). Factors such as the culture of the organisation, male/female ratio and policies all have an impact on bullying in the workforce. Sobsey and Calder (1999) reported that people with an intellectual disability are at an increased risk of violence because of a number of factors, including their family's isolation from their communities and extended families, placement in foster care homes, group homes and institutions and their limited life choices. The abuse of vulnerable adults in institutional settings is well documented (Cambridge, 1998; White, 2003). Not only is there a higher incidence of victimisation in this population, but the abuse often goes unreported, or is discounted when it is reported (Bryen, 2002; Petersilia, 2001).

In Ireland, over 8,000 adults and 400 children with intellectual disabilities live in full-time care facilities. Another 20,000 attend on a part-time or occasional basis (Hawkins, 2009). Although new national standards have now been published for care in these homes, there has not been a date set for regulation of these standards because of the current economic climate. In order to reduce the prevalence of bullying and minimise the effects of bullying, many schools have introduced anti-bullying policies and programmes. Many of these use strategies devised by Olweus (1993) and implemented widely in Scandinavia, but they have been adapted to suit the needs of the different schools. Likewise, many organisations are now aware of the negative effects of bullying on their workforce and have introduced anti-bullying policies and procedures to deal with the problem.

There is a scarcity of published research on the outcomes of bullying intervention for individuals with intellectual disabilities. The one available study in Ireland (McGrath, Jones and Hastings, 2009) does suggest, however, that specially designed intervention programmes can be effective in reducing levels of bullying.

INTELLECTUAL DISABILITY IN IRELAND

There are currently no comprehensive official statistics on the prevalence of intellectual disability in the Republic of Ireland. The latest figures released by the National Intellectual Disability Database (NIDD) (Kelly, Kelly, Maguire and Craig, 2008) recorded that 26,023 individuals in the Republic of Ireland were registered as having an Intellectual Disability in December 2008. This represents a prevalence rate of 6.14 per 1,000 of the population of Ireland. Intellectual disability is estimated on a scale ranging from mild to moderate to severe to profound, as defined by the WHO International Classification of Diseases, tenth edition (ICD-10). Of these 26,023 individuals with an intellectual disability, 8,579 individuals were registered as having a mild diagnosis of intellectual disability, 10,249 a moderate diagnosis, 4,037 a severe diagnosis, 1,001 a profound diagnosis and 2,157 individuals with the level of diagnosis not verified. The ages of individuals registered showed 1,272 were aged 0–4 years, 7,874 aged 5–19 years, 13,852 aged 20–54 and 3,025 aged 55 years and over.

Within this population of 26,023 individuals registered with NIDD, 97.7% were in receipt of a service. Within the three main service provisions, 17,120 attended day services and 7,982 received five or seven-day residential services with 308 residing in psychiatric hospitals.

However, these figures do not give us an accurate overview, for several reasons. Firstly, the NIDD is a voluntary database so families are not required to submit information; secondly, pre-school children who are not in receipt of services or children who have not been assessed will not be included; thirdly, there are many adults, particularly those with a mild intellectual disability, who are not in receipt of services and who are not on the database.

THIS STUDY

In view of the fact that there is little information available with regards to bullying and intellectual disability, particularly in relation to adults, this study set out to gather data both on a local and a national level. One of the difficulties encountered is that there is no universal definition of bullying. The emphasis on early research in this area was on physical bullying and verbal taunting (Olweus, 1978). However, subsequent research recognised the importance of indirect bullying such as social exclusion (Bjorkqvist, Lagerspetz and Kaukiainen, 1992). Therefore, for the purposes of this study, bullying was defined as including both direct and indirect bullying (including texting and exclusion). The definition also allowed for individual or group bullying. The study was conducted in two phases. The first phase involved obtaining information about the nature and frequency of bullying as identified by adults with an intellectual disability in an educational setting. Although there has been little research in relation to adults with an intellectual disability some studies carried out in relation to bullying of children with intellectual disabilities in a school setting have reported that teachers tend to seriously underestimate the frequency with which children with special needs both bully and are bullied (de Monchy, Jan Pijl and Zandberg, 2004) and therefore it was decided to also obtain both parents' and staff's perceptions.

The second part of the study involved surveying other organisations on a national level that provide day services to adults with intellectual disabilities. The primary aim was to gather information in relation to prevalence or estimated prevalence of bullying, the existence of policies on bullying and use of intervention programmes.

PHASE 1

Participants

Participants all attended day services that provided a variety of educational programmes for adults with a broad range of intellectual disabilities. Programmes included rehabilitative training, occupational training, life skills training, supported employment and recreational activities. Of the 112 service users in the organisation, 77 participated. They ranged in age from 18 years to 66 years. Forty were male and thirty-seven were female. All participants were recorded as having a 'mild' or 'moderate' intellectual disability. Twenty service users were either unavailable or did not wish to take part and fifteen service users were unable to take part because of their level of intellectual functioning or poor communication skills.

In addition to service users, all parents of the seventy-seven participants were asked to take part in a semi-structured telephone interview. Sixty-five parents agreed to take part. Thirty-seven staff members who worked directly with the participants were also interviewed.

Procedure

Service users were all invited to take part in a series of workshops which discussed the topic of bullying. During these workshops, the definition of bullying was explained explicitly through role play, discussion and story-telling. Service users were invited to take part in a research project to look at bullying within the organisation. Those who agreed to take part in the project were met on an individual basis to complete a questionnaire. All of the questions were read by the researcher, who clarified any uncertainty in terms of wording. Participants were given the option of the information remaining confidential. If bullying was reported, participants were given the option of discussing this with the psychologist or staff member of their choice.

All parents of the seventy-seven participants were contacted by letter informing them of the research project and advising them that the researcher would be in touch shortly to invite them to take part in a phone interview. Sixty-five parents agreed to take part in the project.

Staff were all contacted by memo and invited to take part in the research project. Thirty-seven out of forty-four staff were available and agreed to participate.

Assessment Tool

Three separate but similar questionnaires were devised and piloted for the service users, parents and staff. The questionnaires contained a definition of bullying which included physical aggression, verbal abuse, texting, damage to property and exclusion. There was a combination of closed and open-ended questions.

Results

Forty-two per cent of the seventy-seven service users reported that they had been bullied in the last year, with 54% reporting that this occurred on a daily or weekly basis. Forty-one per cent reported that they had been bullied by more than one person. Interestingly, families identified only 19% of these same participants as having been bullied. The majority of parents were unaware that their sons/daughters had been bullied in the previous year. In relation to staff, they too seemed to be unaware of the extent of bullying and they only identified 34% of these same participants as having been bullied. Such results show a discrepancy between self-reported rates of victimisation and both parents' and staff's perceptions of bullying.

In addition to the above, parents identified another 1% of participants as having been bullied, although they did not report it themselves. Staff identified another 22% of participants as victims, although again they did not report this themselves. These figures further demonstrate the different perceptions of participants, parents and staff as to who has actually been bullied.

In relation to who carried out the bullying, 16% of participants identified themselves as bullies. Parents only identified 8% of these same participants as bullies and staff only identified 25% of this group. Both parents and staff also identified other participants in the study as bullies although they did not identify themselves as bullies, with parents identifying another 1% and staff identifying another 10% of participants. Again, there is a considerable discrepancy between these three sets of results.

The study also reported on the prevalence of bully-victims (participants who are both bullied themselves and bully other participants). Ten per cent of participants identified themselves as bully-victims. Parents did not identify anyone in this category. Staff identified 25% of these same participants as being bully-victims, and also identified a further 9% of service users who did not report being a bully-victim. As with the reporting of victimisation and bullying, there is a discrepancy between the self-reporting of service users, their families and staff.

When looking at who carries out the bullying, Figure 7.1 shows that the majority of participants (81%) identified other service users as the main perpetrators of bullying.

Figure 7.1: Service user questionnaire: who carried out the bullying

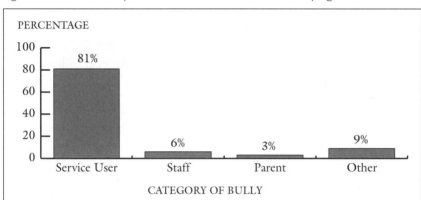

Similar to service users, 81% of the parents interviewed identified service users as the main perpetrators and 75% of staff identified them as the main perpetrators.

In relation to where the bullying takes place, as can be seen from Figure 7.2 below, the majority (69%) of participants reported that bullying primarily occurs within the Day Services Centre (Centre).

Figure 7.2. Service user questionnaire: location of bullying

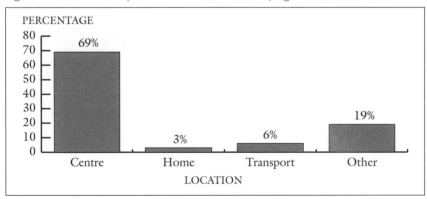

Similarly, 56% of parents reported that they felt that the Day Services Centre was the location where most bullying occurred and 94% of

staff perceived bullying to primarily take place in the Day Services Centre.

Seventy-one per cent of participants availed of a residential or respite service. Of these, 9% reported being bullied in a residential or respite house. Parents only identified 20% of these participants as having been bullied but also identified a further 7% of participants. Staff did not identify any of the participants who reported having been bullied in this setting but identified another 1% of participants as having been bullied.

When examining what form the bullying took, the majority of participants (84%) reported that the bullying is primarily verbal in nature, with only 28% of participants reporting physical bullying. See Figure 7.3 below:

Figure 7.3: Service user questionnaire: form of bullying

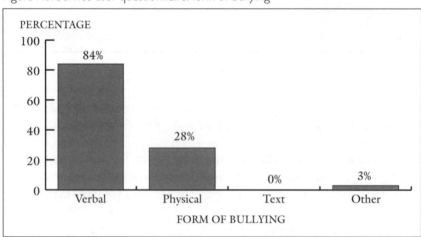

Examples of verbal bullying identified included teasing, name-calling and ordering someone around. Examples of physical bullying identified included pushing, hitting and knocking to the ground.

Similarly, 75% of parents and 84% of staff identified verbal abuse as the primary form of bullying. Interestingly, although 71% of service users reported owning a mobile phone, no service user reported being bullied by text.

With regards to addressing the bullying, 28% of participants who had been bullied tried to defend themselves. Twenty-five per cent told a staff member and 22% told someone other than a staff member. A worrying 44% reported that they did nothing or just walked away. In 50% of the cases, the bullying did not stop. Similar findings were found when interviewing staff members, as 73% of staff had tried to deal with the bullying themselves but the bullying had not stopped in over 43% of the cases.

Fifty-six per cent of participants who reported being bullied worried that the bullying would occur again in the future. Similarly, 69% of parents and 63% of staff were concerned that the bullying would reoccur. When asked what they thought would help prevent bullying reoccurring in the future, participants identified that the support of other service users and staff would be a help and also training in how to handle bullying themselves.

Parents suggested that more contact with staff would be beneficial, as well as higher levels of supervision and assertiveness training. Staff identified the importance of self-advocacy groups, assertiveness training, closer supervision, more individual contact time with staff and being able to opt out of certain situations or groups.

PHASE 2

Participants

Seventy-four organisations were identified as providing day services (with an educational component) for adults with an intellectual disability. Letters were sent to these organisations outlining the proposed research and asking them to complete an anonymous questionnaire. After follow-up, forty-two (55%) organisations had completed and returned the questionnaire.

Assessment tool

A questionnaire was devised and piloted on a small sample of four organisations. After minor alterations it was distributed by post to the seventy-four organisations providing day services. The questionnaires were accompanied by a covering letter explaining about the proposed research. The questionnaire was comprised of eight questions (both Yes/No and open-ended questions) concerning the topic of bullying.

Results

Over 90% of the respondent organisations reported that they considered bullying to occur within their day service. Despite this, however, only 7% had attempted to measure the prevalence of bullying. Forty-three per cent reported that they considered bullying to occur 'occasionally', 29% reported that they considered bullying to occur 'often' and 5% reported that they considered bullying to occur 'very frequently'. Fifty-two per cent reported that their organisation had an anti-bullying policy for service users and 45% reported that their organisation ran anti-bullying intervention programmes for service users. Only 29% reported that they had access to adequate resources in relation to bullying and intellectual disability. Over 97% reported that they would consider using an anti-bullying programme specially designed for adults with an intellectual disability if it were available.

DISCUSSION AND RECOMMENDATIONS

There is a scarcity of research in relation to bullying and an intellectual disability population but the limited research that does exist identifies them as a vulnerable population with both personal characteristics and environmental factors contributing to their being at an increased risk of involvement in bullying as victims, bullies and bully-victims. This small-scale research supports these findings, as 42% of the seventy-seven service users who participated in the study reported that they had been bullied in the last year, with 54% of them reporting that this occurred on a weekly or daily basis. Sixteen per cent identified themselves as bullies and 10% as bully-victims. In addition to this, over 90% of the forty-two service providers nationally who participated in the study reported that they considered bullying to occur within their day service. This highlights the need for more in-depth, long-term and large-scale research in relation to bullying and intellectual disability in terms of increasing our understanding of prevalence rates, precipitating factors both psychological and environmental, and the short- and long-term consequences for bullies, victims and bully-victims as well as bystanders.

One of the most salient findings of this study was the inconsistency between the participants' self-reports of bullying and that of their parents and staff. This raises questions about the reliability of self-reports and the awareness of parents and staff about bullying behaviour. Undoubtedly, self-report forms specifically designed for an intellectual disability population need to be devised and standardised, but other measures for identifying the prevalence should also be explored. These could include peer reports, observations and parent and staff reports. The challenge would be to see how these different perspectives could be combined and analysed to give an accurate picture of bullying behaviour.

Of particular concern arising from this study is the fact that 44% of participants who reported having been bullied coped by doing nothing or walking away. However, regardless of whether they acted or not, in 50% of cases the bullying did not stop and the victims were worried that they would be bullied again, signifying perhaps that they may lack the skills or strategies for coping with bullying behaviour.

Similarly, 69% of parents and 63% of staff reported that they were concerned that the bullying would reoccur. There is a need for service users to be made aware of their right to personal safety. Service users should be trained in self-advocacy and/or be part of advocacy groups. Access to an advocate is also desirable. The Citizens Information Act 2007 gave the Citizens Information Board legislative responsibility for the development and delivery of advocacy services specifically for people with disabilities. In response, the Citizens Information Board initiated the Advocacy Programme for People with Disabilities in the Community and Voluntary Sector. A pilot scheme provided funding and support to forty-six representative advocacy projects for people with disabilities around the country. This scheme ends in 2010 but our findings would suggest that it is important that it is further developed and expanded on a national basis.

With only half of the organisations surveyed having an anti-bullying policy, it is essential that anti-bullying policies which are service user friendly are put in place. This may necessitate them being available in several formats, for example visual, written, auditory, and multimedia, so that service users can readily access and understand them.

In addition, training needs to be made available to staff. This should include definitions of bullying, causes, prevalence, consequences, etc. with reference to latest research findings. Staff need to be trained to be more open and available in relation to disclosures and given strategies which assist in prevention and resolution.

Given the discrepancy in perceptions highlighted in this research, parents and guardians need to be involved. They need to be aware of all the issues around bullying and engage in dialogue with their sons/daughters, providing support and information. Good communication with the service provider should enhance confidence that the issue will be dealt with in a confidential and effective manner. Ongoing communication is essential as the bullying may reoccur.

Another issue of concern arising from this study is the fact that the majority (69%) of participants reported that bullying primarily occurs within the Day Services Centre. Organisations with similar facilities need to ensure that suitable staff are selected and placed appropriately within the organisation, that they are adequately trained, have access to policies, guidelines, etc. Of primary importance is that they have good communication skills and foster positive relationships with service users. In turn, ongoing support and supervision of staff is crucial. Finally, the ethos of the organisation is important and a mission statement reflecting the service users' right to safety should be considered. However, practice must reflect policy.

Feedback from the organisational survey indicated that over 90% of service providers estimate that bullying is occurring in their day services. However, despite this only 7% had attempted to measure it. Results suggest that this may be as a consequence of many factors including lack of appropriate tools and methods to measure bullying, lack of prioritisation or lack of access to appropriate intervention programmes. However, it is reassuring to note that over 97% of organisations reported that they would be interested in acquiring and implementing specially designed intervention programmes should they become available.

CONCLUDING REMARKS

It is with increasing frequency that we read about bullying cases concerning schools or the workplace, yet to date legal cases regarding bullying and intellectual disability are a rarity. This, combined with the limited research available and the results of this small-scale study, suggests that bullying in this area is perhaps not being taken seriously enough. The lack of resources is lamentable, but it is encouraging to note that the majority of organisations surveyed would be interested in implementing specifically designed programmes.

Given these findings, this issue needs to be prioritised on the agendas of umbrella organisations of which disability services are members. A national working party needs to be established to review and develop user-friendly policies that include assessment, implementation and evaluation in an effort to reduce bullying levels among this particularly vulnerable population. In the meantime, unless bullying is comprehensively addressed, organisations providing disability services will fail to meet the needs of vulnerable populations.

REFERENCES

Atlas, R.S. and Pepler, D.J. 'Observations of Bullying in the Classroom', *Journal of Educational Research*, 92, 1998, pp. 86–99

Baladerian, N.J. 'Intervention and Treatment of Children with Severe Disabilities who Become Victims of Abuse', *Developmental Disabilities Bulletin*, 22, 1994, pp. 93–9

Beale, A.V. 'Bullybusters: Using Drama to Empower Students to Take a Stand against Bullying Behaviour', *Professional School Counseling*, 4, 2001, pp. 300–6

Bjorkqvist, K., Lagerspetz, K.M.J. and Kaukiainen, A. 'Do Girls Manipulate and Boys Fight? Developmental Trends in Regard to Direct and Indirect Aggression', *Aggressive Behavior*, 18, 1992, pp. 117–27

Bryen, D.N. 'End the Silence', *Issues in Special Education and Rehabilitation*, 17, 2002, pp. 7–17

Bryen, D.N., Carey, A. and Frantz, B. 'Ending the Silence: Adults who Use Augmentative Communication and their Experiences as Victims of Crimes', *Augmentative and Alternative Communication*, 19, 2003, pp. 125–34

Byrne, B. 'Bullies and Victims in a School Setting with Reference to Some Dublin Schools', *Irish Journal of Psychology*, 15, 1994, pp. 574–86

Cambridge, P. 'The Physical Abuse of People with Learning Disabilities and Challenging Behaviours: Lessons for Commissioners and Providers', *Tizard Learning Disability Review*, 3, 1998, pp. 18–25

Carney, A.G., and Merrell, K.W. 'Bullying in Schools: Perspectives on Understanding and Preventing an International Problem', *School Psychology International*, 22, pp. 364–82

de Monchy, M., Pijl, S.J. and Zandberg, T. 'Discrepancies in Judging Social Inclusion and Bullying of Pupils with Behaviour Problems', *European Journal of Special Needs Education*, 19, 2004, pp. 317–30

Dixon, R., Smith, P.K. and Jenks, C. 'Bullying and Difference: A Case Study of Peer Group Dynamics in One School', *Journal of School Violence*, 3, 2004, pp. 41–58

Einarsen, S., Raknes, B.I. and Matthiesen, S.B. 'Bullying and Harassment at Work and their Relationship to Work Environment Quality: An Exploratory Study', *European Journal of Work and Organisational Psychology*, 5, 1994a, pp. 383–401

Farrington, D.P. 'Understanding and Preventing Bullying', in M. Tonry (ed.), *Crime and Justice*, vol. 17 (Chicago: University of Chicago Press, 1993)

Glumbic, N. and Zunic-Pavlovic, V. 'Bullying Behavior in Children with Intellectual Disability', *Procedia Social and Behavioral Sciences*, 2, 2010, pp. 2784–8

Greenham, S.L. 'Learning Disabilities and Psychosocial Adjustment: A Critical Review', *Child Neuropsychology*, vol. 5, no. 3, 1999, pp. 171–96

Griffiths, M. *Transition to Adulthood: The Role for Young People with Learning Disabilities* (London: NFER-Nelson, 1994)

Groeblinghoff, D. and Becker, M. 'A Case Study of Mobbing and the Clinical Treatment of Mobbing Victims', *European Journal of Work and Organisational Psychology*, 5, 1996, pp. 277–94

Hawkins, M. 'Who Protects Our Most Vulnerable?', *Irish Farmers Journal*, 27 June 2009, http://www.inclusionireland.ie/WHOPROTECTS OURMOSTVULNERABLE.asp [accessed 17 January 2011]

Kelly, F., Kelly, C., Maguire, G. and Craig, S. *Annual Report of the National Intellectual Disability Database Committee*, HRB Statistics Series 6 (Dublin: Health Research Board, 2008)

McCarthy, P., Sheehan, M. and Kearns, D. *Managerial Styles and their Effects on Employees' Health and Well-Being in Organisations Undergoing Restructuring* (Brisbane: Griffith University, School of Organisational Behaviour and Human Resource Management, 1995)

McGrath, L., Jones, R.S.P. and Hastings, R.P. 'Outcomes of Anti-Bullying Interventions for Adults with Intellectual Disabilities', *Research in Developmental Disabilities*, 31, 2009, pp. 376–80

McNamara, B. and McNamara, F. *Keys to Dealing with Bullies* (Hauppauge, NY: Barron's, 1997)

Mencap, *Living in Fear* (London: Mencap, 1999)

Mencap, *Bullying Wrecks Lives: The Experiences of Children and Young People with a Learning Disability* (2007), http://www.mencap.org.uk/displaypagedoc.asp?id=164 [accessed 17 January 2011]

Nabuzoka, D., Whitney, I., Smith, P. and Thompson, D. 'Bullying and Children with Special Educational Needs', in D.P. Tattum (ed.), *Understanding and Managing Bullying* (Oxford: Heinemann School, 1993)

Nabuzoka, D. *Children with Learning Disabilities: Social Functioning and Adjustment* (Oxford: BPS Blackwell, 2000)

Olweus, D. *Aggression in the Schools: Bullying and Whipping Boys* (Washington, DC: Hemisphere, 1978)

Olweus, D. *Bullying at School: What We Know and What We Can Do About It* (Oxford: Blackwell, 1993)

Olweus, D. 'Annotation: Bullying at School: Basic Facts and Effects of a School-Based Intervention Program', *Journal of Child Psychology and Psychiatry*, 35, 1994, pp. 1171–90

O'Moore, A.M. and Hillery, B. 'Bullying in Dublin Schools', *Irish Journal of Psychology*, 10, 1989, pp. 426–41

O'Moore, M., Lynch, J. and Nic Daeid, N. 'The Rates and Relative Risks of Workplace Bullying in Ireland, a Country of High Economic Growth', *International Journal of Management and Decision Making*, 4, 2003, pp. 82–95

Petersilia, J. 'Crime Victims with Developmental Disabilities: A Review Essay', *Criminal Justice and Behaviour*, 28, 2001, pp. 655–94

Rinaldi, W. *Working with Children with Moderate Learning Difficulties* (London: ICAN, 1992)

Round Table Solutions, 'Evaluation of the Programme of Advocacy Services for People with Disabilities in the Community and Voluntary Sector' (2010), http://www.citizensinformationboard.ie/publications/advocacy/evaluation_of_advocacy_services_for_people_with_disabilities_2010.pdf [accessed 17 January 2011]

Smith, P.K. and Sharp, S. (eds), *School Bullying: Insights and Perspectives* (London: Routledge, 1994)

Sobsey, D. and Mansell, S. 'Teaching People with Disabilities to be Abused and Exploited: The Special Educator as Accomplice', *Developmental Disabilities Bulletin*, 25, 1997, pp. 77–93

Sobsey, D. and Calder, P. 'Violence against People with Disabilities: A Conceptual Analysis', unpublished manuscript, National Research Council, Washington, DC, 1999

Swanson, H.L. and Malone, S. 'Social Skills and Learning Disabilities: A Meta-Analysis of the Literature', *School Psychology Review*, 21, 1992, pp. 427–42

Valance, D.D., Cummings, R.L., and Humphries, T. 'Mediators of the Risk for Problem Behavior in Children with Language Learning Disabilities', *Journal of Learning Disabilities*, 31, 1998, pp. 160–71

Valenti-Hein, D. and Schwartz, L. *The Sexual Abuse Interview for those with Developmental Disabilities* (California: James Stanfield Company, 1995)

White, C., Holland, E., Marsland, D. and Oakes, P. 'The Identification of Environments and Cultures that Promote the Abuse of People with Intellectual Disabilities: A Review of the Literature', *Journal of Applied Research in Intellectual Disabilities*, vol. 16, no. 1, 2003, pp. 1–9

Whitney, I., Smith, P. and Thompson, D. 'Bullying and Children with Special Education Needs', in P. Smith and S. Sharp (eds), *School Bullying: Insights and Perspectives* (London: Routledge, 1994)

Wilson, C. and Brewer, N. 'The Incidence of Criminal Victimisation of Individuals with an Intellectual Disability', *Australian Psychologist*, 27, 1992, pp. 114–17

World Health Organisation, *International Statistical Classification of Diseases and Related Problems*, 10th revision, volume 1 (Geneva: WHO, 1996)

CHAPTER EIGHT

Workplace Bullying and Primary School Teachers: The Role of Managerial Discourses

Declan Fahie

INTRODUCTION

> ... It's like a cancer ... a tumour eating at you ... you get no rest. It's always there at the back of your mind. I just can't stop thinking about [the principal] ... You know, if I pass the school in the car I feel like throwing up ... That's after four years! The place still makes me want to vomit.

> (Sinead)

Sinead (names and identifying details have been changed to protect the anonymity of interviewees) taught in the same primary school for most of her career and, as she states herself, 'loved every single minute of it'. Like many of those working in schools in Ireland, she regarded her job as more than just 'work'; she saw it as integral to her sense of self and, during her time in this school, worked happily with a close-knit team of other committed professionals. The appointment of a new principal, however, brought with it a profound transformation of the atmosphere within the school. What had been, for many years, a relaxed, fulfilling place to work was abruptly altered into one fraught with tension, discord and conflict. Ultimately, Sinead, along with several of her colleagues, left the school as a direct result of the negative interpersonal interaction between the new principal and staff. She has recently secured employment in another school. The teachers' testimonies cited in the chapter are selected from a series of twenty-four in-depth interviews of self-identifying victims of workplace bullying who are, or have been, employed within the Irish primary school system.

Sinead's experience typifies that of thousands of others working as professional educators, whose lives have been affected by their experience of workplace bullying (INTO, 2006). It is against this backdrop that this chapter examines the phenomenon of adult bullying within the Irish primary school system. The critical role of what has come to be known as managerialist discourses is considered, specifically within the context of a perceived correlation between these neo-liberal perspectives and the development or maintenance of bullying dynamics.

WORKPLACE BULLYING IN EDUCATION

National and international research has consistently cited education as a 'high risk' profession in terms of prevalence of workplace bullying (Zapf et al., 2003; Di Martino et al., 2003; Economic and Social Research Institute, 2007; Blase et al., 2008; Zapf et al., 2011). In many cases, Hubert and Van Veldhoven (2001) for example, no clarification as to what constitutes 'education' is offered, and one must assume that it includes all those working in the field of education from pre-school to third and, indeed, fourth level. In this context, there is a small, but growing, body of research into workplace bullying across all sectors of education (for example, Twale and DeLuca, 2008; McKay et al., 2008; Association of Secondary School Teachers Ireland, 2008; Noble, 2009; Fahie, 2010; Riley at al., 2011; De Wet, 2011). American studies by Blase (1991), Blase and Blase (2002, 2003 and 2006) and Blase, Blase and Du (2008) focus on the experiences of teachers as victims of bullying at the hands of school principals. Blase and Blase (2002 and 2006) found that 'principal mistreatment' resulted in significant harmful effects for teachers in terms of the physical, psychological and emotional well-being resulting in feelings of humiliation, self-doubt, lowered self-esteem, fear, anger, post-traumatic stress disorder and a range of physiological responses. They also reported a deterioration in relationships with fellow teachers, a compromised collective decision-making process in the school and negative consequences for the teachers' instructional work in classrooms. Reflecting other research by Dake et al. (2004) and Cemaloglu (2011), they stress the need for positive, effective leadership as a means of counteracting this behaviour and argue that schools promote a culture which serves to ignore conflicts, in the hope that they resolve themselves.

A further study by Blase et al. (2008) suggests that bullying of teachers by school principals should be considered one of the most significant contributory factors to escalating stress levels among teachers. In this context, they claim that 76.7%, of their sample of 172 teachers, reported that they would leave their school because of the ongoing treatment at the hands of the principal. Some 49.4% of the teachers wanted to leave teaching altogether because of their experiences. In terms of coping strategies, the study found that teachers, by and large, employed passive coping strategies (avoiding the principal, rationalising their behaviour) rather than actively engaging in resolution processes. The five 'Principal mistreatments' most commonly cited as causing intense harm were: 1) Intimidation, 2) Failure to recognise or praise work-related achievements, 3) Lack of support in confrontation with students or parents, 4) Unwarranted reprimands and 5) Unreasonable demands. Critically, the teachers surveyed for the study were questioned about their perception of the possible reasons behind such behaviour. Sixty-one per cent of the sample blamed 'school-level politics' (Blase et al., 2008, p. 285).

Meanwhile, Cemaloglu (2007) surveyed 315 primary school teachers in Turkey. This study revealed that 50% of the sample were bullied and found no significant relationship between bullying exposure levels and gender or age. The most common types of behaviour experienced by these teachers were being ordered to do work below your level of competence (Cemaloglu, 2007, p. 794). An Estonian study by Koiv (2006) suggested that verbal assault was the most common tactic of interpersonal conflict between teachers and detailed how teachers in this study reported insults, offensive remarks and shouting as the most common forms of bullying behaviours.

While there has long been anecdotal evidence of unhealthy staff relationships in a number of schools around Ireland, the trade union for primary teachers in Ireland, the Irish National Teachers' Organisation (INTO), was the first to publish tangible evidence regarding the phenomenon of workplace bullying in Irish primary schools (INTO, 2000). Following a random survey of 402 teachers the following behaviours were noted (see Table 8.1).

Table 8.1: Most common bullying behaviours experienced (2000)

	BULLYING BEHAVIOURS (n = 417)	YES
1	Verbally Abused	25%
2	Undermined	15%
3	Ignored/Excluded	14%
4	Shouted At	12%
5	Publicly Humiliated	12%
6	Intimidated	12%
7	Physically Abused	3%

(Adapted from *Staff Relations: A Report on Adult Bullying in Schools*, INTO, 2000)

These behaviours triggered stress (41%), low self-esteem (24%), low motivation (15%) and depression (11%), among respondents. Interestingly, 50% of those surveyed reported that they were aware of colleagues being bullied in their school and 16% said they would leave their school, if they could, because of the bullying behaviour. In a follow-up survey by the union in 2006, which surveyed 1,219 randomly selected members, when asked if they had been bullied or harassed in their work situation, 44% replied Yes. This is an inherent flaw in this research as bullying and harassment are considered different constructs within the Irish legal system. Furthermore, this question was not posed as part of the 2000 survey, thus making comparisons impossible.

Table 8.2 details the most frequent behaviours experienced (in descending order of frequency). No percentage details were provided. Again, stress, low self-esteem and low motivation were cited as the most common repercussions for this behaviour (INTO, 2006).

Table 8.2: Most common bullying behaviours experienced (2006)

1	Being Undermined
2	Intimidated
3	Ignored/Excluded
4	Shouted at
5	Public Humiliation
6	Physically Abused
7	Threat of Losing Job
8	Verbally Abused

(Adapted from *Bullying and Harassment in the Workplace*, Survey Results, INTO, 2006)

Focusing specifically on workplace bullying in Irish primary schools, Fahie (2010) revealed evidence of the traumatic effect of such behaviours. In this study, teachers and principals detailed how their personal and professional lives were profoundly compromised by the interpersonal disputes within schools and the coping mechanisms employed by these individuals to deal with these experiences. The study suggests that the current managerial structures in primary schools need to be examined, particularly in the context of training and awareness among those in positions of authority within individual schools and within the education system in general. Fahie (2010) highlighted a number of critical factors which may facilitate the development of workplace bullying dynamics in schools; they include Leadership, Communication, Organisational Structures, Organisational Culture and the over-zealous application of New Managerialist Imperatives. An impairment in any one, or more, of these factors has been shown to foster tensions and conflict within the workplace and has been cited as having a central role within bullying dynamics. Each of these factors plays a significant role in the development or maintenance of a bullying dynamic (see Figure 8.1).

Figure 8.1: Contributory factors in the development of a workplace bullying dynamic

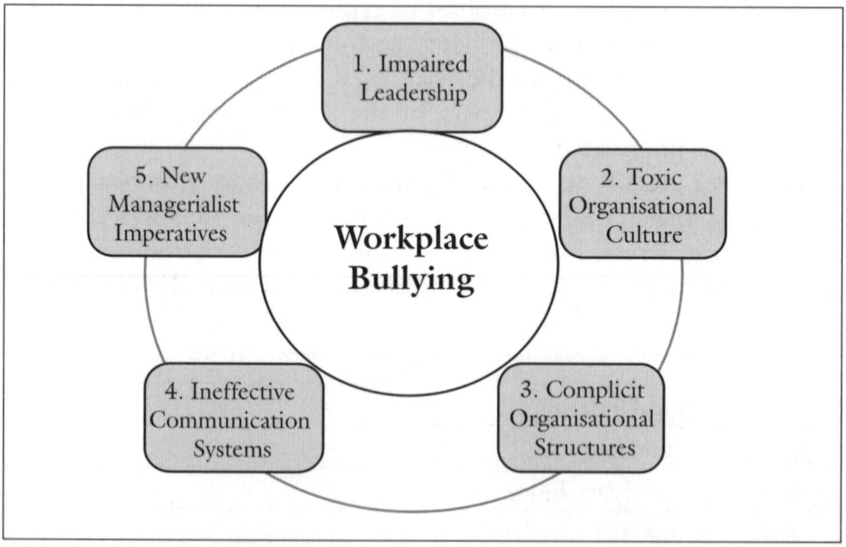

Indeed, the relationship between these first four factors (Leadership, Communication, Organisational Structures and Organisational Culture) and the incidence of workplace bullying has been the subject of considerable research in recent years (Dale and Burrell,

2008; Lutgen-Sandvik and McDermott, 2008; Caponecchia and Wyatt, 2011; Duffy and Sperry, 2012). However, in order to develop a more nuanced understanding of the phenomenon of workplace bullying in Irish primary schools, this chapter will focus specifically on the fifth factor referred to above: New Managerialist Imperatives, i.e. the tensions that have arisen in recent years as a result of the influence of neo-liberal perspectives and philosophies on the education sector.

NEW MANAGERIALISM

It has been argued that the work of the teacher in the twenty-first century differs fundamentally from that of even ten or twenty years ago (Fullan, 2003; Shapiro and Gross, 2008; Drudy, 2009; National Council for Curriculum and Assessment, 2010). Commentators have argued that new curricula, globalisation, information technology, increased parental expectations, the mainstreaming of special needs children and performance appraisal are just some of the changes which have impacted fundamentally on the nature of teaching (Hargreaves and Fink, 2006; Glanz, 2006; Hargreaves, 2007; Stoll et al., 2007). Ireland has not been immune to these seismic changes within the field of education (O'Sullivan, 2005; Lynch and Moran, 2006; Grummell et al., 2009a, 2009b). In the context of workplace bullying in education, it may be reasoned that if routine and consistency provide security, then change, by its very nature, can lead to anxiety and uncertainty. In such an atmosphere, tensions and conflict can easily manifest. Indeed, it has been argued that change itself constitutes a major causal factor in the escalation of tensions and anxieties brought about by increased pressures and changes in the workplace (Rayner et al., 2002; McCarthy and Mayhew, 2004; Weinberg and Cooper, 2007; Twale and De Luca, 2008; Salin and Hoel, 2011). New Managerialism may be considered the official manifestation of this focused and systemic impetus towards change, and what follows is a brief consideration of the phenomenon. The analysis will explain the extent to which New Managerialism may be seen as a contributory factor in the development of a bullying dynamic in schools, particularly in relation to its impact on school organisational culture through the fostering of a more competitive internal climate, potentially leading to increased rivalry, tensions and conflict.

New Managerialism (also known as New Public Management (NPM), e.g. Fitzsimons (1999), and Neoliberalism (Davies and Bansel (2007)) or simply Managerialism is the term used to describe the application of private-sector modes of management to public-sector bodies, ostensibly in an effort to improve accountability, efficiency and value for money. It is 'a system of government invented during the Thatcher and Reagan years ... [which] is characterised by the removal of power from the knowledge of practising professionals to auditors, policy makers and statisticians' (Davies, 2003, p. 91). It is a perspective which views surveillance, control and managing as central to productivity and, thus, to economic prosperity. Professional autonomy is eroded as the worker is reconstituted through a neoliberal discourse as a legitimate subject by internalising the panoptic monitoring (Foucault, 1991) it implies through self-surveillance, as a result of which the subject adapts their own behaviour against a set of internalised rules and regulations. Critically, these rules and regulations have been constituted through the new discourse as inevitable and logical (Zemblyas, 2006). In so doing, the worker accepts them as a 'given', resulting in self-monitoring, self-motivating, flexible workers for whom resistance would be unthinkable – such is the potency of the discourse of inevitability within the new managerial schema. Indeed, Zemblyas (2006) warns that research into workplace practices can easily be 'hijacked' and employed as technologies of power which, paradoxically, can be used to reinforce the managerialist discourse. In this context, resistance itself can be presented as an indication of the workers' ineffectiveness and proof of their incompetence or laziness. Resistance to such control is difficult, however, as New Managerialism presents itself as a model of efficiency and any resistance to it may be seen as an absurd attack on rationality and order. Therefore, it requires great fortitude and self-belief to overcome the overwhelmingly legitimate authority (Weber, 1978) exercised in these situations. This points towards a central tension at the heart of New Managerialism with its practice of centralised decentralisation (Court, 2004). On the one hand, regulatory structures are imposed upon personnel in an attempt to control and manage their working day while, on the other, it is predicated on the existence of an independent, self-determining and autonomous worker with free choice who operates on the basis of self-interest or egotism towards the attainment of rewards and the avoidance of sanctions.

Davies and Bansel (2007) argue that New Managerialism, and the neoliberal discourses which underpin it, are examples of the Foucauldian concept of governmentality (Foucault, 2003; Devine et al., 2011). This refers not only to the systems of governance within the political sphere but also to the ways in which the behaviour, opinions, attitudes and perspectives of individuals or groups can be controlled, altered, manipulated and, ultimately, directed. New Managerialism manages to subtly coerce workers to constitute themselves as appropriate and appropriated subjects within a world order defined by the managerialist system. Bansel et al. (2008) see managerialism as a system of government which formalises, expands and structures technologies of regulation and compliance in order to measure, examine, reward and punish.

As part of the public service, the education system has not been immune to the effects of these changes and neoliberal discourses are an increasing feature of modern education systems as governments and commercial interests turn to education as a means of fostering or boosting economic growth (Olssen, 2006; Drudy, 2009). Within education, New Managerialism is exemplified by a perceived change in emphasis by governmental policy-makers from an almost paternalistic or benevolent model – in which education was acknowledged as being central to a complex matrix of relationships founded on a premise of 'the common good', to a more pragmatic business model which places absolute emphasis on returns (O'Sullivan, 2005; Grummell et al., 2009a, 2009b). These returns may be seen in terms of the quantifiable and verifiable benefit to each individual and, crucially, to those in control of the allocation of funding. It is a functionalist philosophy which sees education as having a central role in the maintenance of an economically viable society.

Bansel (2007) argues that neoliberal discourses see education as central to the actualisation of their philosophy and may be considered as a technology of production in this context. He is critical of the manner in which individuals are constituted as 'subjects of choice' by these neoliberal discourses, suggesting that this notion of choice is spurious and is, in itself, a technology of control. For Zemblyas (2006), neoliberal discourses are designed implicitly or explicitly to constitute workers as docile, productive and adaptable. This managerialist discourse subjectifies workers as good/successful based on the capacity or enthusiasm to embrace the changing needs of the organisation which employs them and upon their ability to adapt and be flexible team players, 'regulating' themselves as constantly improving workers. Technologies of work and power are, therefore, aligned with technologies of self and technologies of success such that the self and the organisation are seen to share the same goals which are, in turn, inextricably linked to economic success and personal fulfilment. Resistance to such a doctrine is constituted by such discourses as unreasonable, irrational and counter to the 'greater good'.

Like Grummell et al. (2009a, 2009b) and Blackmore (2004), O'Brien and Down (2002) contend that Managerialism undermines the traditional caring and nurturing character of education and, in so doing, transforms it into a clinical, customer-driven service provider. This is at the kernel of the hostility surrounding the introduction of such methods into the educational discourse. This has serious implications for education in that by reconstituting education as an economic good, as a service that can be bought and sold and measured, education is reduced to being a product, resulting in 'exposure to competition, increased accountability measures and the implementation of performance goals' (Davies and Bansel, 2007, p. 252).

There are obvious implications for any study of workplace bullying in schools from the managerialist discourse. Unhappy teachers, working under increased pressure in a hostile environment, may well experience increased vulnerability to bullying from superiors for improved results, or from equally stressed colleagues who project their own difficulties onto others (Troman, 2000; Wornham, 2003; Johnson, 2005). Coupled with increased expectations from parents and, indeed, pupils, the potential for interpersonal conflict among teaching staff may be high.

NEW MANAGERIALISM AND IRISH EDUCATION

> I suppose it's true to say that teachers are under more pressure today than before. There's a lot expected from them. Parents want more, the department wants more ... and children have changed too. You have to be accountable for everything. You have to keep records for years in case you're sued!

> (Conor)

Conor, an experienced principal, is highly critical of what he considers to be intrusions into the professional life of teachers. Increased paperwork, he argues, and 'red tape' cause high levels of frustration for staff and management alike. He is particularly critical of the tensions which arise in respect of promoted posts in schools, which he sees as a common cause of frictions and conflict. 'They're [posts of responsibility] a diplomatic nightmare, trying to keep everyone happy. Someone is always disappointed ... and they blame the principal ...' (Conor).

Furthermore, Conor is wary of any increased responsibility being placed upon principals to formally, and systematically, evaluate the performance of teachers. He foresees potential difficulties, particularly in the context of increased numbers of bullying allegations should such initiatives come to fruition.

While it has been argued that the influence of New Managerialism on the Irish education system has, in general, been limited (O'Sullivan, 2005; Grummell et al., 2009a and 2009b), the Irish primary and secondary systems were always highly standardised in terms of curricula, examinations, etc. It is within the higher education sector in the Republic of Ireland that the effect of neoliberal, New Managerialist policies and practices has been most profound (Lynch, 2006; Grummell et al., 2009a and 2009b). Within this framework of control, paradoxically, individual schools operated under high levels of autonomy and, consequently, schools varied greatly in terms of organisation, academic climate, disciplinary climate, degrees of interaction between staff and pupils and parental involvement (Smyth, 1999, p. 41). However, increased legislation, including the Education Act (1998), Employment Equality Act (1998), Equal Status Act (2000), Education Welfare Act (2000) and Education for Persons with Special Educational Needs Act (2004), together with bureaucratic regulation has also become a feature of the Irish education system (Grummell et al., 2009a, 2009b), thus suggesting an intensification of market influences within Irish education.

There has been a move, argues O'Sullivan (2005), away from a traditional theocratic paradigm – of church control, whose aims and objective are based on 'unchanging principles based on a Christian view of human nature and destiny' (O'Sullivan, 2005, p. 112) – to a mercantile paradigm as the market and economic forces attempt to restructure the aims and objectives of education across all sectors of the system. In this context, for example, Lynch and Moran (2006) argue that a market philosophy revealed itself in Ireland during the economic boom of recent years in terms of middle-class parents deliberately utilising their considerable economic (and, indeed, cultural) capital to secure private education for their offspring, thus securing their class ambitions.

Indeed, as far back as the early 1990s it was recognised that there was a shift towards increasing external control and surveillance in the education sector in Ireland. Reflecting the concept of globalisation already alluded to, the Irish National Teachers' Organisation noted then that:

> 'Governments of industrialised nations are systematically encroaching upon the teaching/learning process through the promulgation of such technical control procedures as prescribed curricula expressed in terms of aims and objectives, attainment targets and performance indicators, the national testing of pupil performances through the use of standard attainment tests and profile components, the merit related appraisal of teacher performance, the privatisation of the system of school inspections, the mandating of school planning procedures and the reporting of school performance.'
>
> (INTO, 1992, p. 3)

Much of what is alluded to in the above quote has come to pass in the primary education system. It may be argued that, in comparison to the amount of direction and regulation in previous curricula, for example, the revised primary curriculum (1999) signifies increased control and influence by the state over another essential aspect of primary education – what and how to teach. Wong (2008) has argued that increased control and 'market mentality' (p. 276) has impacted negatively on the workplace practice as teachers and their sense of their own professionalism. This is particularly apparent, within the Irish context, in the contested areas of internal promotions within schools.

Undeniably, the application of business/market mores to education has been best reflected in the introduction of a form of middle management in Irish schools. Referred to as 'Special Duties Posts' or 'Graded Posts', these promotional posts may be viewed as another layer of middle management administration within schools. Introduced following negotiations under the Irish government's *Programme for Competitiveness and Work* (1994), more teachers were made eligible for promotion to posts of responsibility; such posts bring with them, along with extra duties, an increase in salary. O'Connor (2005) indicates that there is a level of ambiguity as to the exact specification of the duties. This lack of clarity can lead to tensions, she argues, especially in larger schools where there are demonstrably poor communication structures. She also argues that competition for such posts is negligible and posts are still afforded to those with greatest seniority rather than those who may have other qualities or attributes (O'Connor, 2005). Hilda, a retired teacher with over thirty years' experience, recounts her story:

> The whole posts [of responsibility] thing was a disaster ... there was no job description. No discussion. We were just told that there would be interviews the day after tomorrow. None of us had time to apply. It didn't matter anyway, the job was gone ... That's when the s**t hit the fan ... when I complained. I suddenly became the worst in the world and all the nastiness started ...
>
> (Hilda)

While it has been recognised that all teachers have a role to play in terms of school leadership (Liebermann and Miller, 2004), it is the school principal who is responsible for implementing change (Fink, 2005), thus leading to increased stress and workload (Glanz, 2006). Hargreaves and Fink (2006) detail how new managerialist practices have led to situations whereby principals have left the profession because of the increased stress of dealing with such problems. As Fullan (2003) notes about the discouragement and impotence felt by many principals in the face of increased accountability and bureaucracy:

> When so many demands are placed on the Principalship, it is not just the sheer amount of work that is the problem, but it is also the inconsistent and ambiguous messages. Take control, but follow central directives; make improvements, but run a smooth ship ...
>
> (Fullan, 2003, p. 22)

The critical role of the leader in preventing or interceding in workplace bullying disputes cannot be underestimated (O'Dea and Flint, 2003; Padilla et al., 2007; Yamada, 2008). It may be argued that the increased pressures placed upon principals by the tenets of New Managerialism cause a dislocation between the moral imperative of the principal to intervene and their ability to do so. Ineffective or passive leadership can lead to a stressful work environment for all, along with role ambiguity, conflict and, ultimately, bullying (Skogstad et al., 2007). Deirdre is the recently appointed principal of an urban school. She maintains that one teacher, an unsuccessful candidate for his job, actively undermines her position, leaving her isolated and unsure how to progress.

It's a lonely place to be. I'm in my office, trying my best to do my job … I know that she's outside – stirring it. Trying to make trouble. She gathers a crowd around her, turns on the waterworks and then I'm made out to be the big bad wolf … All because I won't let her get her own way.

(Deirdre)

The relevance of New Managerial structures to the bullying discourse is that the increased accountability, surveillance and monitoring which are fundamental features of this system may be catalysts in the creation of a bullying dynamic. Furthermore, an unscrupulous manager or principal may use them to harass or bully a subordinate. In many ways, these systems may become means of demonstrating and exercising authority and, if wielded unjustly, may result in bullying behaviour and tensions rather than increased productivity or efficiency. Liam, a teacher in his thirties, recounts how the principal in his school exploited his professional authority and, in so doing, demonstrated his power/control. This ongoing zealous and targeted application of official rules and regulations Liam found to be belittling and demeaning. Liam has recently left teaching.

My notes were checked every week by him. Every mistake or spelling or grammar was marked … like a child. No one else had this level of scrutiny. Just me. The inspector had said that my notes were perfect (during a whole-school evaluation). But he loved doing it. Reading my notes slowly. Sighing. It was his way of making sure I knew he was boss …

(Liam)

CONCLUSION

New Managerialism, or more accurately the behaviours that New Managerialism validates and endorses, must be acknowledged as playing a subtle, though important, role in the prevalence and incidence of workplace bullying in Irish primary schools. While in no way underestimating the fundamental, pivotal influence of Leadership, Communication, Organisational Structures and Organisational Culture in the ultimate development of a bullying dynamic, this chapter highlights a link between New Managerialism and workplace bullying, a relationship which, hithertofore, has received little attention.

The discourse of silence which surrounds workplace bullying augments the sense of isolation and vulnerability felt by targets of workplace bullying (Fahie, 2010). Targets feel unable to challenge the behaviours as to do so reconstitutes them as 'moaners' or 'victims'. New Managerialism seems to sanction this notion, thus setting in motion an unrelenting cycle of abuse, suppression, vulnerability and further abuse. Such was the experience of Anna, the final interviewee, whose testimony ends this chapter.

> Who do you turn to? I felt like a fool. My husband kept telling me to stand up to [her principal]. But I couldn't. I couldn't talk to anyone on the staff. I was so ashamed. I've worked hard my whole life. I'm more qualified ... but she gave it [the post of assistant principal] to [her colleague]. It's so unfair ... and now I'm the one who's being isolated and attacked because I spoke up ... It's so unfair. My heart is broken ...

(Anna)

REFERENCES

Aquino, K. and Thau, S. 'Workplace Victimization: Aggression from the Target's Perspective', *Annual Review of Psychology*, 60, 2009, pp. 717–41

ASTI (Association of Secondary Teachers Ireland), *Bullying of Teachers: Report of the Sub-Committee on the Bullying of Teachers* (Dublin: ASTI, 2008)

Bansel, P. 'Subjects of Choice and Lifelong Learning', *International Journal of Qualitative Studies in Education*, 20, 2007, pp. 283–300

Bansel, P., Davies, B., Gannon, S. and Linnell, S. 'Technologies of Audit at Work on the Writing Subject: A Discursive Analysis', *Studies in Higher Education*, 33, 2008, pp. 673–83

Bansel, P., Davies, B., Laws, C. and Linnell, S. 'Bullies, Bullying and Power in the Contexts of Schooling', *British Journal of Sociology of Education*, 31, 2009, pp. 59–69

Blackmore, J. 'Quality Assurance Rather than Quality Improvement in Higher Education?' *British Journal of Sociology of Education*, 25, 2004, pp. 383–94

Blase, J. 'The Micropolitical Perspective', in J. Blase (ed.), *The Politics of Life in Schools: Power, Conflict and Cooperation* (Thousand Oaks, CA: Corwin Press, 1991)

Blase, J. and Blase, J. 'The Dark Side of Leadership: Teacher Perspectives of Principal Mistreatment', *Educational Administration Quarterly*, 38, 2002, pp. 671–727

Blase, J. and Blase, J. *Breaking the Silence: Overcoming the Problem of Principal Mistreatment of Teachers* (Thousand Oaks, CA: Corwin Press, 2003)

Blase, J. and Blase, J. 'Teachers' Perspectives on Principal Mistreatment', *Teacher Education Quarterly*, Fall 2006, pp. 123–42

Blase, J., Blase, J and Du, F. 'The Mistreated Teacher: A National Study', *Journal of Educational Administration*, 46, 2008, pp. 263–301

Caponecchia, C. and Wyatt, A. *Preventing Workplace Bullying* (London: Routledge, 2011)

Cemaloglu, N. 'The Exposure of Primary School Teachers to Bullying: An Analysis of Various Variables', *Social Behaviour and Personality*, 35, 2007, pp. 789–802

Cemaloglu, N. 'Primary Principals' Leadership Styles, School Organizational Health and Workplace Bullying', *Journal of Educational Administration*, 49, 2011, pp. 495–512

Court, M. 'Using Narrative and Discourse Analysis in Researching Co-Principalships', *Journal of Qualitative Studies in Education*, 17, 2004, pp. 579–96

Dake, J.A., Price, J.H., Telljohann, S.K. and Funk, J.B. 'Principals' Perceptions and Practices of School Bullying Prevention Activities', *Health Education and Welfare*, 31, 2004, pp. 372–87

Dale, K. and Burrell, G. *The Spaces of Organisation and the Organisation of Space* (Basingstoke: Palgrave Macmillan, 2008)

Davies, B. 'Death to Critique and Dissent? The Policies and Practices of New Managerialism and of Evidence-Based Research', *Gender and Education*, 15, 2003, pp. 91–103

Davies, B. and Bansel, P. 'Neoliberalism and Education', *International Journal of Qualitative Studies in Education*, 20, 2007, pp. 247–59

Devine, D., Grummell, B. and Lynch, K. 'Crafting the Elastic Self? Gender and Identities in Senior Appointments in Irish Education', *Gender, Work and Organisation*, 18, 2011, pp. 631–49

De Wet, C. 'The Professional Lives of Teacher Victims of Workplace Bullying: A Narrative Analysis', *Perspectives in Education*, 29, 2011, pp. 66–77

DiMartino, V., Hoel, H. and Cooper, C.L. *Preventing Violence and Harassment in the Workplace* (Dublin: European Foundation for the Improvement of Living and Working Conditions, 2003)

Drudy, S. 'Education and the Knowledge Economy: A Challenge for Ireland in Changing Times', in S. Drudy (ed.), *Education in Ireland: Challenge and Change* (Dublin: Gill & Macmillan, 2009)

Duffy, M. and Sperry, L. *Mobbing Causes, Consequences and Solutions* (Oxford: Oxford University Press, 2012)

Einarsen, S., Aasland, M.S. and Skogstad, A. 'Destructive Leadership Behaviour: A Definition and Conceptual Model', *Leadership Quarterly*, 18, 2007, pp. 207–16

Fahie, D. 'An Analysis of Workplace Bullying in Irish Primary Schools', unpublished PhD thesis, University College Dublin, 2010

Fitzsimons, P. *Managerialism and Education* (1999), http://www.ffst.hr/ENCYCLOPAEDIA/doku.php?id=managerialism_and_education [accessed 18 January 2011]

Foucault, M. *Discipline and Punish: The Birth of the Prison* (London: Penguin Books, 1991)

Foucault, M. *Madness and Civilisation* (London: Routledge, 2001)

Foucault, M. *Society Must be Defended* (London: Penguin/Allen Lane, 2003)

Fullan, M. *The Moral Imperative of School Leadership* (Thousand Oaks, CA: Corwin Press, 2003)

Glanz, J. *Instructional Leadership* (Thousand Oaks, CA: Corwin Press, 2006)

Grummell, B., Devine, D. and Lynch, K. 'Appointing Senior Managers in Education: Homosociability, Local Logics and Authenticity in the Selection Process', *Educational Management Administration & Leadership*, 37, 2009a, pp. 329–49

Grummell, B., Devine, D. and Lynch, K. 'The Care-Less Manager: Gender, Care and New Managerialism', *Higher Education Gender and Education*, 21, 2009b, pp. 191–208

Hargreaves, A. 'Sustainable Professional Learning Communities', in L. Stoll and L.K. Seashore, *Professional Learning Communities: Divergence, Depth and Dilemmas* (Maidenhead, Berkshire: Open University Press, 2007)

Hargreaves, A. and Fink, D. *Sustainable Leadership* (San Francisco: Jossey-Bass, 2006)

Health and Safety Authority, *Report on the Prevention of Workplace Bullying* (Dublin: The Stationery Office, 2001)

Health and Safety Authority, *Code of Practice on the Prevention of Workplace Bullying* (Dublin: The Stationery Office, 2002)

Health and Safety Authority, *Work-Related Stress: A Guide for Employers* (Dublin: Health and Safety Authority, 2002)

Health and Safety Authority, *Report of the Expert Advisory Group on Workplace Bullying* (Dublin: Health and Safety Authority, 2005)

Hubert, A.B. and van Veldhoven, M. 'Risk Sectors for Undesirable Behaviour and Mobbing', *European Journal of Work and Organizational Psychology*, 10, 2001, pp. 415–24

INTO (Irish National Teachers' Organisation), *Professionalism in the 1990s* (Dublin: INTO, 1992)

INTO (Irish National Teachers' Organisation), *Staff Relations: A Report on Adult Bullying in Schools* (Dublin: INTO, 2000)

INTO (Irish National Teachers' Organisation), 'Workplace Bullying Survey Results' (2006), unpublished report presented at the INTO Equality Conference on Dignity at Work, Tullamore, Co. Offaly, 9 March 2007

Johnson, H. 'Are You Happy? The Question that the Education Leadership and Management Field Rarely Asks', *Management in Education*, 19, 2005, pp. 21–4

Koiv, K. 'Teachers as Multi-Target Victims of Bullying in School Settings', paper presented at the 5th International Conference on Workplace Bullying, Trinity College Dublin, June 2006

Lieberman, A. and Miller, L. *Teacher Leadership* (San Francisco: Jossey-Bass, 2004)

Lutgen-Sandvik, P. 'The Communicative Cycle of Employee Emotional Abuse', *Management Communication Quarterly*, 16, 2003, pp. 471–501

Lutgen-Sandvik, P. 'Take This Job and … : Quitting and Other Forms of Resistance to Workplace Bullying', *Communication Monographs*, 73, 2006, pp. 406–33

Lutgen-Sandvik, P. and McDermott, V. 'The Constitution of Employee-Abusive Organizations: A Communication Flows Theory', *Communication Theory*, 18, 2008, pp. 304–33

Lynch, K. 'Neo-Liberalism and Marketisation: The Implications for Higher Education', *European Educational Research Journal*, 5, 2006, pp. 1–17

Lynch, K. and Moran, M. 'Markets, Schools and the Convertibility of Economic Capital: The Complex Dynamics of Class Choice', *British Journal of Sociology of Education*, 27, 2006, pp. 221–35

McCarthy, P. and Mayhew, C. *Safeguarding the Organization against Violence and Bullying: An International Perspective* (Basingstoke: Palgrave Macmillan, 2004)

McKay, R., Huberman Arnold, D., Fratzl, J. and Thomas, R. 'Workplace Bullying in Academia: A Canadian Study', *Employee Response Rights Journal*, 20, 2008, pp. 77–100

National Council for Curriculum and Assessment, *Curriculum Overload in Primary Schools: An Overview of National and International Experiences* (2010), http://www.ncca.ie/en/Curriculum_and_Assessment/Early_Childhood_and_Primary_Education/Primary_School_Curriculum/PSN_Curriculum_Overload/Overview_national_international_experiences.pdf [accessed 17 January 2011]

Noble, K. *Understanding Workplace Bullying in Early Childhood Contexts* (Saarbrucken: VDM, 2009)

O'Brien, P. and Down, B. 'What are Teachers Saying about New Managerialism?', *Journal of Educational Enquiry*, 3, 2002, pp. 111–33

O'Connell, P.J., Calvert, E. and Watson, D. *Bullying in the Workplace: Survey Reports, 2007. Report to the Department of Enterprise, Trade and Employment* (Dublin: ESRI (The Economic and Social Research Institute), 2007)

O'Connor, B. 'A Mixed Methodology Study of In-School Management Practice in Irish Primary Schools', unpublished MEd thesis, University College Dublin, 2005

O'Dea, A. and Flint, R. *The Role of Managerial Leadership in Determining Workplace Safety Outcomes*, Health and Safety Executive Research Report RR044 (2003), http://www.hse.gov.uk/research/rrpdf/rr044.pdf [accessed 17 January 2011]

Olssen, M. (ed.), *Michel Foucault: Materialism and Education* (Boulder, CO: Paradigm Publishers, 2006)

O'Sullivan, D. *Cultural Politics and Irish Education since the 1950s: Policy Paradigms and Power* (Dublin: Institute of Public Administration, 2005)

Padilla, A., Hogan, R. and Kaiser, R.B. 'The Toxic Triangle: Destructive Leaders, Susceptible Followers, and Conducive Environments', *The Leadership Quarterly*, 18, 2007, pp. 176–94

Rayner, C. 'Reforming Abusive Organizations', in V. Bowie, B.S. Fisher and C.L. Cooper (eds), *Workplace Violence Issues, Trends, Strategies* (Abingdon, Devon: Willan Publishing, 2005)

Rayner, C., Hoel, H. and Cooper, C.L. *Workplace Bullying: What We Know, Who is to Blame, and What Can We Do?* (London: Taylor & Francis, 2002)

Riley, D., Duncan, D.J. and Edwards, J. 'Staff Bullying in Australian Schools', *Journal of Educational Administration*, 49, 2011, pp. 7–30

Shapiro, J.P. and Goss, S.J. *Ethical Educational Leadership in Turbulent Times: (Re)Solving Moral Dilemmas* (New York: Lawrence Erlbaum Associates, 2008)

Skogstad, A., Einarsen, S., Torsheim, T., Schanke Aasland, M. and Hetland, H. 'The Destructiveness of Laissez-Faire Leadership Behaviour', *Journal of Occupational Health Psychology*, 12, 2007, pp. 80–92

Salin, D. and Hoel, H. 'Organisational Causes of Workplace Bullying', in Einarsen, S., Hoel, H., Zapf, D. and Cooper, C.L. (eds), *Bullying and Harassment in the Workplace: Developments in Theory, Research and Practice* (Boca Raton, FL: CRC Press, 2011)

Smyth, E. *Do Schools Differ?* (Dublin: Oak Tree Press, 1999)

Stoll, L. 'School Culture: Black Hole or Fertile Garden for School Improvement?' in J. Prosser (ed.), *School Culture* (London: Sage, 1999)

Stoll, L., Robertson, J., Butler-Kisher, L., Sklar, S. and Whittingham, T. 'Beyond Borders: Can International Networks Deepen Professional Learning Communities', in L. Stoll and L.K. Seashore, *Professional Learning Communities: Divergence, Depth and Dilemmas* (Maidenhead, Berkshire: Open University Press, 2007)

The Samaritans, *Stressed Out: A Study of Public Experience of Stress at Work* (2007), http://www.samaritans.org/pdf/SamaritansStressReport1207.pdf [accessed 17 January 2011]

Troman, G. 'Teacher Stress in the Low-Trust Society', *British Journal of Sociology of Education*, 21, 2000, pp. 331–53

Twale, D.J. and De Luca, B.M. *Faculty Incivility: The Rise of the Academic Bully Culture* (San Francisco: Jossey-Bass, 2008)

Weber, M. *Economy and Society, Volume 1* (Berkeley: University of California Press, 1978a)

Weber, M. *Economy and Society, Volume 2* (Berkeley: University of California Press, 1978b)

Weinberg, A. and Cooper, G. *Surviving the Workplace: A Guide to Emotional Well-Being* (London: Thompson Learning, 2007)

Wong, J.L.N. 'How Does the New Emphasis on Managerialism in Education Redefine Teacher Professionalism? A Case Study in Guangdong Province of China', *Educational Review*, 60, 2008, pp. 267–82

Wornham, D. 'A Descriptive Investigation of Morality and Victimisation at Work', *Journal of Business Ethics*, 45, 2003, pp. 29–40

Yamada, D. *Workplace Bullying and Ethical Leadership*, Legal Studies Research Paper Series, Research Paper 08-37 (Boston: Suffolk University Law School, 2008)

Zapf, D. and Gross, C. 'Conflict Escalation and Coping with Workplace Bullying: A Replication and Extension', *European Journal of Work and Organizational Psychology*, 10, 2001, pp. 497–522

Zapf, D., Einarsen, S., Hoel, H. and Vartia, M. 'Empirical Findings on Bullying in the Workplace', in S. Einarsen, H. Howl, D. Zapf and C.L. Cooper, *Bullying and Emotional Abuse in the Workplace* (London: Taylor & Francis, 2003)

Zapf, D., Escartin, J., Einarsen, S., Hoel, H. and Vaartia, M. 'Empirical Findings on Prevalence and Risk Groups of Bullying in the Workplace', in S. Einarsen, H. Hoel, D. Zapf and C.L. Cooper, *Bullying and Harassment in the Workplace: Developments in Theory, Research and Practice* (Boca Raton, FL: CRC Press, 2011)

Zemblyas, M. 'Work-Based Learning, Power and Subjectivity: Creating Space for a Foucauldian Research Ethic', *Journal of Education and Work*, 19, 2006, pp. 291–303

CHAPTER NINE

The Bullying of Primary School Principals in Ireland

Paul Stevens

INTRODUCTION

Bullying is increasingly being recognised as a serious problem in the workplace context. Over the last two decades, employers, trade unions and professional organisations have become critically aware of behaviours which undermine the integrity and confidence of employees and reduce efficiency. These employees describe how bullying affects them physically and psychologically, with stress, depression and low self-esteem being commonly reported. This phenomenon has achieved growing recognition and researchers have reported disturbing findings regarding the negative consequences for organisations and individuals. Despite the emergent body of research, still relatively little is known about the nature of bullying by subordinates – sometimes referred to as 'upwards bullying'. Indeed, the focus of workplace bullying research has primarily been on downwards bullying (by managers) and, more recently, on horizontal bullying (by colleagues).

Research into bullying behaviour in Ireland has focused primarily on children in primary and secondary schools (Minton and O'Moore, 2004, 2007; O'Donnell, 1995; O'Moore and Minton, 2002, 2004, 2005; O'Moore et al., 1997). However, the subject of adult workplace bullying in Ireland is receiving increasing attention and recognition (Coyne et al., 2000; Sheehan, 1999), with a number of major surveys of bullying in the workplace being conducted (O'Connell and Williams, 2001; O'Connell et al., 2007; O'Moore et al., 2003). Two of these surveys have identified that the education sector is the second most common work environment in which bullying occurs. O'Connell and Williams (2001) (n=5,252) suggest a national general incidence of 7%, with a reported 12% in the education sector. Similarly, O'Connell et al. (2007) (n=3,579) record a nationwide incidence of 8% and 14% among education employees. These findings mirror international research where employees in the education sector experience higher rates of bullying when compared with those employed in other fields (e.g. Australia: Vickers, 2001; McCarthy et al., 2003; Finland: Bjorkqvist et al., 1994; the Netherlands: Hubert and van Veldhoven, 2003; the UK: Ironside and Seifert, 2003; Lewis, 2003; the USA: Price Spratlen, 1995). However, what these findings do not reveal is the degree to which different employees within this sector are bullied. Furthermore, it has been shown that teachers in China (McCormack et al., 2006), the UK (Edelmann and Woodall, 1997; NASUWT, 1996) and the USA (Blase and Blase, 2003) have specifically been targets of workplace bullying. A number of studies have reviewed the bullying of Irish teachers at primary (Fahie, 2007a, 2007b; INTO, 2000a, 2007; Kitt, 1999) and at second level (ASTI, 1999; O'Moore, 1999; O'Moore et al., 2003; TUI, 1999a, 1999b) but do not specifically review the bullying of school principals.

Research in educational leadership and management indicates that the role of the Irish primary school principal is becoming more diffuse and increasingly complex (Irish Primary Principals' Network [IPPN], 2006a), with the issue of interpersonal relationships and conflict resolution being one of the most challenging aspects of the role (Morgan and Sugrue, 2008). One question in the IPPN's 2008 pre-conference survey (IPPN, 2008a) revealed that 13% of primary principals reported that they had been subjected to workplace bullying. This, combined with a reported increase in the number of principals seeking assistance in dealing with this matter (Murray, 2009), strongly suggests that this is an issue meriting further investigation.

To date the main thrust of research into workplace bullying has focused on managers as perpetrators. However, Branch et al. (2003) contend that managers are increasingly vulnerable to workplace bullying by staff, a phenomenon referred to as 'upwards bullying'. Despite the limited usage of this term (Lewis and Sheehan, 2003; McCarthy et al., 2002), there is growing general agreement that managers can indeed be targets of bullying behaviours (CMI, 2005; Zapf et al., 2002). However, occurrences of 'upwards bullying' are rarely reported (Rayner et al., 2002) and are often presented anecdotally or as single cases (e.g. Braverman, 1999). Branch et al. (2006, 2007) argue that this phenomenon needs to be acknowledged and researched fully to enable organisations to understand the complexity of bullying more completely.

This chapter reports on some key findings from recent research (Stevens, 2010, 2012) involving over 700 primary school principals employed in national schools who are members of the Irish Primary Principals' Network.

TOWARDS A DEFINITION

Workplace bullying incorporates a range of inappropriate behaviours in the place of work, from low-intensity behaviours often termed incivility to higher aggressive and violent behaviours. In previous research several different definitions have been proposed and indeed different concepts have been used to describe the phenomenon such as 'mobbing' (Leymann, 1996; Zapf et al., 1996), 'emotional abuse' (Keashly, 1998), 'bullying' (Einarsen and Skogstad, 1996; Vartia, 1996), 'victimisation' (Einarsen and Raknes, 1991, 1997) and 'harassment' (Brodsky, 1976). In the absence of a universal description and irrespective of the differing labels or terminology, researchers are in agreement that bullying behaviour comprises the systematic persecution of a colleague, subordinate or superior, which, if unaddressed, may be the source of severe psychological, psychosomatic or health problems for the victim.

In the Irish context bullying is defined as *repeated*, *persistent* and *negative acts* towards one or more persons, which involve a power imbalance and thus create a hostile work environment:

> By bullying I mean repeated inappropriate behaviour, direct or indirect, whether verbal, physical or otherwise, conducted by one or more persons against another or others, at the place of work and/or in the course of employment, which could reasonably be regarded as undermining the individual's right to dignity at work. An isolated incident of the behaviour described in this definition may be an affront to dignity at work but is not considered to be bullying.
>
> (O'Connell et al., 2007, p. 33.)

Despite the limited usage of the term 'upwards' bullying (Lewis and Sheehan, 2003; Rayner et al., 2002), there is general agreement in literature that managers can be subject to bullying by subordinates. Within general definitions, the concept of upwards bullying is sometimes implied. For instance, Einarsen et al. (2003) refer to the 'systematic mistreatment of ... a superior' (p. 3) while Einarsen (2000) mentions 'mobbing by ... a subordinate' (p. 380). The general definition for bullying is equally applicable to upwards bullying. Power, dependency and change may also be factors. Of particular interest is the element of power. Given that school principals have been granted legitimate authority, the power balance which is an essential component of bullying must be created by a means other than formal position. Salin (2001) describes a situation 'how superiors can be put into a position in which they cannot defend themselves and how bullying alters power relations' (Salin, 2001, p. 435). In summary, there are a number of elements which are key to defining upwards bullying. These are frequency, duration, and nature of behaviours, intentionality and power imbalance involving a subordinate. Branch et al. (2006) concur and also identify isolation, resentment, difference, lack of clear structures and effective policies as frequent antecedents of upwards bullying.

PREVIOUS RESEARCH

Incidence

A large number of studies have been undertaken to examine the incidence of workplace bullying in different countries and among differing occupations. However, there are several issues that make comparisons difficult. Definition, strategies for identifying victims, and criteria regarding duration are factors which hinder accurate comparisons. These combined with differing methodologies and varying response rates, result in a wide range of reported incidence. However, in order to acquire a general overview, twenty-six previous studies over a fourteen-year period were reviewed with a wide range of reported incidence ranging from 2.9% to 38% with a mean incidence rate of 12%.

Research specifically examining bullying in the education field reveals that incidence rates are higher than in other employment sectors (Kitt, 1999). The two major Irish studies (O'Connell and Williams, 2001; O'Connell et al., 2001) place the education sector as the second highest occupational category to experience workplace bullying. Of particular note are the high incidence levels reported by the two surveys in primary education with 41% of primary teachers experiencing bullying in 2000 (INTO, 2000a) and 44% reporting such behaviour seven years later (INTO, 2007). Alas, no information is available from these studies as to what degree this data applies specifically to principals.

Gender

Gender is also an area of particular research interest. Some research shows lower occurrences of bullying where equal numbers of men and women are employed (O'Moore et al., 2003). Conversely, other studies highlight much greater levels of bullying in single-sex-dominated occupations (Archer, 1999; Djurkovic et al., 2004; Quine, 2001). Men in male-dominated occupations are more likely to experience higher levels of physical and verbal aggression (Hubert and van Veldhoven, 2001) compared with the passive aggressive types of behaviours reported in female-dominated occupations (Hockley, 2002).

It is evident that women are more likely to be bullied than men (Leymann and Gustafsson, 1996; O'Moore et al., 1998a; Zapf, 1999a; Zapf et al., 1996). For example, Salin's research (2003) reported 43% male victims and 57% female victims. WBI (2007) reported similar findings, although Rayner (1997) found more male (53%) than female victims (47%).

In the Irish context, O'Connell et al. (2007) confirm that males are more likely to be bullied by other males and females are more likely to be bullied by other females. According to O'Moore (2000), there is more bullying in organisations that employ primarily females, and given primary education is predominantly a female occupation, it will be interesting to review levels of bullying in terms of gender. However, the three previous studies in primary education (INTO, 2000b, 2007; Fahie, 2007a) reveal no information in this regard.

Effects of bullying

Previous research also illustrates that bullying has been found to have significant consequences for those experiencing or witnessing the practice, as well as the organisation for which they work. These consequences include physical and psychological effects in addition to affecting the victim's capacity to work and personal life. Effects of bullying also influence victims in terms of absenteeism, resignation and retirement.

A number of studies have shown significant relationships between exposure to bullying and the victim's health and well-being (Brodsky, 1976; Einarsen and Hellesøy, 1998; Einarsen et al., 1994a, 1994b, 1996; Mikkelsen, 2001; Zapf et al., 1996). Fatigue and chronic fatigue syndrome (Einarsen and Mikkelson, 2003), weakness and sleeplessness (Brodsky, 1976), musculoskeletal pains (Einarsen et al., 1996), headaches, stomach disorders and rashes (O'Moore et al., 1998b; Vartia, 2001) and cardiovascular disease (Kivimaki et al., 2000) are all physiological symptoms which highly correlate with workplace bullying.

An increase in stress levels among victims is also a common theme in research findings (Hansen et al., 2006; Zapf, 1999b; O'Moore, 1998; Vartia, 2003) and a significant contributor to ill-health (Kile, 1990). Primary teachers are particularly vulnerable to stress and anxiety (Boyle et al., 1995; Capel, 1991; Friesen et al., 1988). In Ireland, O'Connell et al. (2007) clearly report that the experience of bullying is associated with higher stress levels, while in another study 41% of teachers cite stress as a distinct outcome of bullying (INTO, 2000a). The health effects of workplace bullying in Ireland resulted in 19% of victims taking medication and 17% attending their doctor (O'Moore, 2000).

There is strong agreement among researchers that the range of psychological effects on victims can be enormous (Randall, 1997), in addition to psychosocial problems (Niedl, 1995) such as post-traumatic stress disorder (PTSD) (Leymann and Gustaffson, 1996). These psychological responses include anger, anxiety and panic attacks (Adams, 1992; Leymann, 1997), self-hatred (Bjorkqvist et al., 1994), helplessness and shock (Janoff-Bulman, 1989), insecurity and suspiciousness (Thylefors, 1987), lowered self-confidence (Price Spratlen, 1995), depression (Leymann, 1990; Einarsen et al., 1996) and even suicide (Leymann, 1992; Einarsen and Mikkelsen, 1999; Mikkelsen, 2001). Furthermore, continued exposure to workplace bullying has been shown to result in personality changes (Leymann and Gustafsson, 1996) and a risk of psychiatric illness (Romanov et al., 1996). Irish research concurs with these international findings. O'Moore et al. (1998b) revealed that victims of workplace bullying reported anxiety (90%), depression (87%), lower self-confidence (73%) and isolation (70%).

Being bullied at work reduces organisational satisfaction and commitment (Hoel and Cooper, 2000) and increasing absenteeism

(Vartia, 2003) and the likelihood that employees will leave through resignation and early retirement. Bullying increases a victim's intention to leave (Djurkovic et al., 2004), increases staff turnover (Begley, 1998) and therefore incurs substantial costs for organisations (Waldman et al., 2004).

Previous Irish research also indicates that workplace bullying has affected victims' capacity to work. O'Connell and Williams (2001) and O'Connell et al., (2007) report that 42.6% and 48.3% of the Irish workforce are affected respectively. Of particular note is that one third (31%) of teachers were found to be negatively affected in the workplace by the phenomenon (INTO, 2000a).

One of the most obvious manifestations of victims' capacity to work is employee absenteeism. Kivimaki et al. (2000) reported that victims are five times more likely to be absent than non-bullied colleagues, while Hoel and Cooper (2000) observed that victims take, on average, an additional seven days per annum. Findings also suggest that levels of absenteeism tend to be higher among males (Einarsen and Raknes, 1991) and that victims are more likely to under-report their own illness (Johns, 1994). In terms of Irish research, O'Moore (2000) found that nearly a third of victims had taken sick leave while O'Connell et al. (2007) reported a more conservative absenteeism rate of 19%. It is interesting to note that the self-reported absenteeism rates for bullied teachers are significantly lower, at 5% (INTO, 2000a) and 7% (INTO, 2007).

A more serious consequence that also arises is that the bullied employee considers resignation or actually resigns. Research shows that the numbers considering resignation (Keashly and Jagatic, 2000; Hoel and Cooper 2000) is much higher than those who actually exit their posts (Quine, 1999; Vartia, 1993). In essence, people leave out of despair (Einarsen et al., 1994a) and/or as a positive coping strategy (Zapf and Gross, 2001) although it may not be an option for some due to the lack of job opportunities (Tepper, 2000), particularly in the current limited employment market. In addition, some victims may be reluctant to leave until justice is done (Kile, 1990). Ireland's bullying research reveals similar results. In the general workforce, 58% of victims considered resignation while 15% actually resigned (O'Connell et al., 2007). In 2000, 16% of bullied teachers considered resignation with exactly half (8%) leaving (INTO, 2000a). Seven years later, 17% considered resignation with 11% actually following through (INTO, 2007).

THE RESEARCH QUESTIONS

There is also a growing body of research in Ireland with limited data available in the education sector. The small number of studies involving primary teachers do not differentiate between principals and teachers and hence provide no specific information on the bullying of principals. Given that their current working environment is ripe for bullying and there are anecdotal reports of bullied principals (Herron, 2007; IPPN, 2008a), this is an issue requiring further examination. Therefore, this study focused on five research questions:

- What is the incidence of upwards workplace bullying among primary principals?
- Who are the bullies, how do they bully and why?
- How does upwards workplace bullying affect principals?
- How do principals respond to upwards workplace bullying?
- Do existing structures and policies resolve bullying behaviour?

RESEARCH METHODOLOGY

In gathering data to answer these questions, a survey questionnaire was developed in conjunction with the IPPN and piloted with a group of principals. The definition of bullying employed in previous Irish workplace bullying surveys (O'Connell and Williams, 2001; O'Connell et al., 2007) was selected for this research. Using the online survey software SurveyMonkey, a web-based link containing the questionnaire was e-mailed to the 2,693 principals on the IPPN's database. Following a number of follow-up strategies, the survey acquired 795 responses. Face-to-face interviews were subsequently conducted with thirty principals who indicated a willingness to discuss in detail their experiences of workplace bullying.

Data checking and cleaning revealed forty-nine partially completed or duplicated responses which were eliminated, resulting in a final dataset of 746 unique records. This represents a final response rate of 28%, which is considered very acceptable for web-based surveys (Sue and Ritter, 2007). The data was exported to and analysed using the data analysis software package SPSS.15.

RESULTS AND DISCUSSION

Profile of principals

Thirty-eight per cent of the sample which completed the online questionnaire consisted of male principals while 62% were female, broadly corresponding to the 42% male and 58% female principals employed nationwide in 3,160 national schools. In terms of experience, 30% had less than five years' experience, 25% had six to eight years, 28% were employed as principals for eleven to twenty years while 17% had in excess of twenty years' experience. The mean number of years experience for the sample was 11.5 years. Over half the respondents (55%) were employed as administrative principals while the remaining 45% worked as principals with teaching duties.

Principals' perceptions of their role

In building a profile of the respondents, principals' views regarding a number of key areas were requested. Over 13% of principals considered themselves to be part of a minority grouping. Principals considered their role to be very stressful. Only 2% of respondents described the role as 'stress–free', while a further 28% stated it was 'mildly stressful'. Under half (46%) considered the job to be moderately stressful and a quarter of respondents (24%) viewed their role as 'highly stressful'. Therefore, 70% of Irish principals considered their role to be stressful. Such findings are in keeping with international research, which directly links the role with stress (Carr, 1994; Friedman, 2002; Sarros, 1988) and specifically the stress associated with being an administrative principal (Jones, 1999; Pascal and Ribbins, 1998; Torelli and Gmelch, 1993). Indeed these findings confirm previous suggestions that Irish principals are subject to constant stress (IPPN, 2004a) from 'mundane pressure and relentless struggle' (O'Reilly, 2007). Many of the qualitative responses and subsequent interviews of thirty principals highlighted and detailed high levels of perceived stress.

Over half of the respondents (61%) viewed the pressure of work as too intense, while 37% felt less comfortable in their role than twelve months previously, which reinforces principals' reported concerns regarding increasing levels of job intensity identified in previous research (IPPN, 2004a, 2006b).

Finally, over two-thirds (69%) of principals considered that parents had become more demanding during the previous twelve-month period. Many of these principals detailed the manner in which parents had become more taxing, the majority of whom cited that difficult interpersonal parental relationships had increasingly contributed to their personal workplace stress, similar to the findings of Jones (1999).

Incidence of workplace bullying among primary principals

When examining data to establish the incidence of workplace bullying in this study, two approaches were adopted. This was undertaken as a precaution as there was a possibility that the survey could possibly attract a greater number of responses from bullied compared with non-bullied principals. Firstly, incidence was reviewed in terms of the total sample (n=2,693) and secondly in terms of the total number of respondents (n=743).

A total of 307 principals stated they had been bullied within the last twelve months. In relation to the total sample, the incidence is 11%, which is highly consistent with previous research for the general incidence of workplace bullying (Hoel et al., 2001; zur Mühlen et al., 2001; Vartia, 1996), the incidence of upwards bullying (Bjorkqvist et al., 1994; Nieldl, 1995a; Einarsen and Skogstad, 1996) and the incidence of bullying in educational settings (Matthiesen et al., 1989; O'Connell and Williams, 2001; O'Connell et al., 2007). In addition, this incidence figure of 11% correlates closely with the reported incidence (13%) quoted by IPPN (2008a) and the reported incidence (11.1%) for secondary school teachers (O'Moore, 1999).

The incidence of bullying calculated on the number of respondents (307 bullied principals out of 743 respondents) is 41%. While this figure initially appears high, previous research into bullying specifically among primary teachers reveals equally high incidence levels. Two independent studies (INTO, 2000a and INTO, 2007) revealed workplace bullying incidence of 41% and 44% respectively. Given the close similarity between the 41% of this study when compared with these two previous studies, it could reasonably be assumed that this figure accurately reflects incidence among primary principals.

The who, how and why of workplace bullying

Principals who are bullied report that over two-thirds of this upwards bullying comes from teachers with whom they work. Deputy principals, assistant principals, special duties teachers and assistant teachers constitute the greatest number of perpetrators (68%) in the principal's workplace. The second most likely perpetrators are parents, accounting for 38% of bullies. Also of significance is the high level of bullying (29%) principals endure from board of management (BoM) members, who essentially are in situ to assist and support the principal in the day-to-day management of the school.

The model of distributed leadership introduced in primary schools in 1998 (Ó'Diomsaigh, 2000) through the establishment of posts of responsibility was created to assist with the increasing demands on principals (Travers and McKeown, 2005). It is of serious concern therefore that 41% of bullying emanates from categories of staff whose responsibilities include supporting the principal. Of particular note and worry is the fact that a quarter of bullied principals (27%) perceive that they are bullied by their deputy principals. Given that the designated duties of the deputy principals specifically include deputising for, working with and supporting the principal, being bullied by one's deputy can only be undermining and adversely affect a principal on a range of levels. These findings suggest a serious malfunction of the middle management structure in primary schools.

Principals also appear to be subjected to significant levels of bullying from the voluntary boards of management which have ultimate responsibility for school management. Chairpersons (13%), BoM parents' representatives (14%), BoM teachers' representatives (5%) and other BoM members (6%) are all cited as sources of bullying for principals.

Non-teaching staff are much less likely to be identified as perpetrators by principals. The reported rates of bullying among these staff were: SNAs (9%); secretaries (6%) and caretakers (2%). Similarly, bullying behaviour by those with whom the principal had external relationships was relatively low. Principals reported bullying by the inspectorate at 4% (comparable with 2% cited by Fahie, 2007b) and special educational needs organisers (SENOs) at just 1%.

Finally, although the bullying of principals by their pupils has received some attention (Kigotho, 2000; Pervin and Turner, 1998), the level of bullying by pupils in this study is encouragingly low. Only 3% of principals reported pupil bullying, compared with earlier reports of 7% (Fahie, 2007b; TUI, 1996b). Data from the interview process suggests that these cases occurred in schools where senior pupils present with challenging behaviour.

Despite evidence in some studies that females are more likely to be bullied than males (Salin, 2003; Zapf, 1999a), this study found no significant gender differences, with 41% male and 41% female principals claiming to be bullied. This is consistent with international studies for workers (Mikkelsen and Einarsen, 2002; Leymann, 1993a; Niedl, 1995b) and primary teachers (Cemaloglu, 2007) and Irish studies examining bullying in education (O'Connell et al., 2007; O'Moore, 1998).

Forms of bullying behaviour

Over half of bullied principals (58%) report they are undermined. This is the single greatest reported negative behaviour experienced by principals and is consistent with the 2006 survey of primary teachers (INTO, 2007). It is also cited by Fahie (2007b) as a frequent bullying behaviour and was the second most common behaviour in the nationwide survey of O'Connell et al. (2007). Qualitative data defined undermining as a variety of negative behaviours including overtly or covertly challenging the authority of the principal. Of equal concern are the other behaviours experienced. The next five most common types of bullying experienced by principals were: ignoring requests/proposals (50%); unreasonable blame (48%); repeated criticism (44%); devaluing principals' work (43%) and rumour, gossip or ridicule (42%). Naturally, these negative behaviours all have major implications on the principal's performance and mirror the findings of previous Irish research (INTO, 2007; O'Connell et al., 2007; O'Moore, 1998). Principals were also subjected to verbal abuse (32%) which included shouting, intimidating tone of voice, and using foul and abusive language. A small number of interviewed principals reported highly offensive language, personal insults and sexual innuendo. The strategies of withholding important information (28%), false accusations (27%), exclusion (27%) and deliberate overloading (27%) were all cited as negative bullying behaviours experienced by principals. To a lesser degree, principals reported being bullied through unreasonable requests (23%), humiliation (22%), threats (16%) and intrusion (15%).

Physical abuse as a form of bullying is rare (1.3%), confirming reports by the *Irish Independent* (2007). Similarly, the extent of sexual abuse was low (1%), as previously indicated by Donnelly

(2007) and Walshe (1998) (4%). One-third of respondents (34%) reported being bullied weekly, while almost a quarter (24%) indicated that they were subjected to bullying almost daily. A small minority (five teachers) indicated a frequency of a number of times per day. Just over a fifth (22%) reported monthly bullying and a further 19% less frequently. These findings corroborate the results of O'Connell et al. (2007), who reported bullying on a weekly (23%), monthly (26%) and occasional basis (27%).

Perceived reasons for bullying

Principals consider that the primary reason for bullying is connected to interpersonal behaviour (39%), while personality clash (23%) is also identified as a source of negative behaviours. Principals perceive that bullying can occur as a result of them engaging in their professional duties. The implementation of policies (25%), requesting teacher documentation (23%) and addressing teacher professional competence (17%) are all identified as key sources of bullying of principals by teachers.

Organisational issues are also seen as contributory factors. Class allocation (20%), discipline issues (13%), special education issues (12%), timetabling (10%) and the allocation of resource teaching (RT) and learning support (LS) duties (9%) are all perceived as organisational matters which can be a catalyst for workplace bullying.

The issue of staff appointments is one that can have contentious outcomes. Being newly-appointed to the position of principal can be a reason for being bullied. Twenty five per cent of respondents cited this as a contributory factor in the bullying behaviour to which they had been subjected. The 'disappointed candidate' has previously been identified in bullying literature as a possible perpetrator (McElduff, 2007). Unsuccessful candidates for the position of principal frequently hold the post of deputy principal and this study has already identified how 27% of deputies bully their principals.

According to principals, parents tend to engage in bullying behaviours when they have specific school-related issues about which they are unhappy. The three most common reasons, as perceived by principals, are displeasure at principals' decisions (33%), issues concerning pupil discipline (15%) and criticism of educational provision (15%). A minority of principals (8%) are bullied by parents in an effort to have their child transferred to a different class. Teacher professional competence and teacher interpersonal behaviour are minor reasons (6% in each case) for parents to subject principals to bullying behaviours.

Workplace bullying: its effects on principals

Without doubt, respondents in this study consider that the bullying to which they are subjected has serious effects in terms of emotional well-being, health and capacity to perform work. Over two-thirds (67%) of principals experienced feeling anxious, which is considerably lower than the 90% reported by O'Moore et al. (1998). Over half (57%) reported feeling unhappiness as an outcome of being bullied, with loss of self-confidence also being regarded as a serious effect in 52% of cases. While previous findings for primary teachers quote reduced self-confidence at just 21% (Donnelly, 2007), the report by the TUI (1999b) describes how 56% of second-level teachers experience loss of confidence as an outcome of being bullied.

Of serious concern also is the finding that nearly half (47%) of bullied principals experience isolation. This is unsurprising as the study has already shown how principals are frequently bullied by those with whom they work closest (deputy principals and special duties teachers). This relationship between bullying and isolation in primary education has already been alluded to by Liddane and Hamill (2007).

Worryingly, the findings also reveal that over a quarter (28%) of respondents actually fear going to work every day. This undoubtedly must have a wide range of implications for health outcomes or ability to perform duties. Nearly a third (31%) of these indicated that they considered the pressure of work to be too great. Fear of going to work is significantly higher (34%) among principals who are bullied by teachers than by any other perpetrator. Poor levels of concentration were identified by a quarter of bullied principals (25%) as a significant outcome of experiencing bullying, with obvious further implications in terms of professional performance.

The 67% of principals who reported feeling anxious stated that the forms of bullying that gave rise to significantly higher rates of anxiety were undermining behaviour, blame for things beyond the principal's control and devaluing of work. Fifty-seven per cent of principals identified unhappiness as an emotional consequence of being bullied. It is of note that principals all rate undermining behaviour as a significant contributing factor in the majority of emotional responses to bullying.

Principals experiencing bullying behaviour also reported negative impact to their health and in some cases serious ill-health. The single most common effect of bullying is lack of sleep or an inability to sleep, according to 57% of principals, corresponding closely with 60% reported for Irish post-primary teachers (TUI, 1999b). In the 1998 INTO study, 6% of bullied primary teachers reported feeling depressed as a result of bullying. In this study, however, the number of principals reporting feeling depressed was five times greater (29%), with male principals significantly more likely to feel depressed. Frequent colds and flus are a consequence of bullying for 16% of principals.

A significant minority blamed ongoing ill-health on bullying in the workplace. A small number (3%) admitted having suicidal thoughts (slightly lower than the 5% reported by the TUI 1999b but still of very serious concern).

Stress was also a factor in terms of bullying and health. Those principals who rated their job as moderately or highly stressful were significantly more likely to report lack of sleep (61%) compared to those in the mildly stressful and stress-free categories. Similarly, stressed principals are significantly more likely to feel depressed (33%) compared to those in lower-stress categories.

Workplace bullying: How principals respond

Respondents were requested to identify what specific actions they took when they experienced bullying in the workplace. In addition, they were asked to reveal which of these actions were effective and ineffective in resolving bullying. Information was also sought regarding work-related responses in terms of their role and performance.

The most common response for nearly three quarters (73%) of bullied principals is to confide in someone outside their work environment, in this case a family member. Principals bullied by deputy principals and post-holders were significantly more likely to discuss the matter with their families. This particular response is high when compared with second-level teachers (23%) (O'Moore, 1999) and the general workforce (64%) (O'Connell et al., 2007), but not surprising given that this study has demonstrated that many principals are bullied by perpetrators close to them and who are supposed to be in a supporting role.

Over two-thirds of victims (67%) respond by confronting the perpetrator – an action recommended frequently in research literature and a response which forms the second step in the policy recommended for primary teachers and principals (INTO, 2000c). This action is more popular among victims in this study than in previous UK studies (41% in Hoel and Cooper, 2000 and 45% in Rayner, 1998). In Ireland, previous research also demonstrated that only 26% of primary teachers (INTO, 2000a) and 53% of second-level teachers (O'Moore, 1999) confronted their perpetrators in school workplace bullying.

Two-thirds (67%) of bullied principals brought their bullying issue to chairpersons of their board of management and discussed it with them. This was most common in the cases of those bullied by parents.

Some colleagues and friends are also viewed as an important resource by the bullied principals. Some 64% of principals discussed matters with colleagues (although exactly which colleagues is not identified), which is higher than the 22% reported by second-level teachers (O'Moore, 1999) but almost identical to the findings in the UK (63%) (Hoel and Cooper, 2000) and among Irish primary teachers (63%) (INTO, 2000a). An equal number of principals (63%) seek support from friends. This is comparable to previous research by O'Moore (1999), where 67% of bullied teachers sought assistance from friends but slightly less than the 76% reported by O'Connell et al. (2007) for the general workforce.

Nearly half (47%) of principals subjected to bullying behaviour contacted their trade union, the INTO. This is considerably higher than the figures quoted for previous research in the UK (13% in Hoel and Cooper, 2000) and Ireland (9% in O'Connell and Williams, 2001 and 21% in O'Connell et al., 2007). Referring specifically to teachers contacting their trade union when bullied, 38% of second-level teachers made contact (O'Moore, 1999) and 18% of primary teachers pursued this action (INTO, 2000a). The 47% revealed in this study is the highest figure observed to date. A third (35%) of principals contacted their professional organisation (IPPN) while a fifth (23%) consulted the Catholic Primary Schools Management Association (CPSMA) – the management organisation for the majority of primary schools.

The number seeking medical help in this study (26%) represented a quarter of victims and corresponds exactly to figures for post-primary teachers (26%) (O'Moore, 1999) but is higher than the 17% of the general workforce quoted by O'Connell et al. (2007).

Similarly a quarter (23%) sought legal advice, which was three times greater than the number of general workers (7%) (O'Connell et al., 2007).

In reviewing the perceived helpfulness of principals' responses the single most worrying finding is that only 29% of bullied principals considered confronting the perpetrator as a useful and productive action. This is ironic given that this is the official recommendation outlined in existing policy (INTO, 2000c) and is followed by 67% of victims. Principals considered discussion with friends (96%), family (94%) and colleagues (87%) a far more beneficial action. Clearly, for those who consulted with these three categories, this was perceived as a far more supportive action. Equally, consulting with the IPPN (86%) or seeking legal advice (83%) were seen as positive responses that were helpful. For 71% of bullied principals, the BOM chairperson provided useful support. The managerial body, the CPSMA, was considered of assistance in over half of cases (57%).

However, less than half (48%) of bullied principals stated that they found consulting their trade union helpful. The qualitative data revealed a significant minority of principals who drew attention to the issue of the same trade union (INTO) representing both parties in a dispute. A small number of respondents suggested a conflict of interest and perceived that the union was not impartial as principals were considered to have legitimate authority and therefore were more likely to be the perpetrators.

While slightly lower than the 58% reported in the general workforce (O'Connell et al., 2007), the findings in this study suggest 44% of principals bullied have considered resignation. These principals were significantly more likely to feel less comfortable in their role, not get on well with colleagues and report deteriorating interpersonal relationships among staff. Those specifically bullied by deputy principals and BoM members were significantly more likely to have considered resignation.

While high rates of sick leave (86%) were reported by O'Moore (1998), much lower rates of sick leave attributed to bullying were noted among teachers. Second-level teachers took sick leave in 16% of cases (O'Moore, 1999), while at primary level only 5% (INTO, 2000a) and 7% (Donnelly, 2007) resorted to this course of action. However, in this study, one-fifth (21%) of bullied principals stated they had taken sick leave as a direct result of being bullied. Work pressure was cited as a significant factor in this course of action.

Seventeen per cent of principals had considered taking a career break as a direct outcome of being bullied. Those who felt less comfortable in the role than twelve months previously and those who perceived that their staff did not hold them in good regard were significantly more likely to consider this option.

The ultimate response by those experiencing bullying is to actually leave their place of work through resignation or early retirement. In general terms, Morgan and Sugrue (2008) noted in their research that over a fifth of principals 'think about leaving frequently.' Cullen (2009) reported that over 300 (about 10% of the total national cohort) of principals were due to retire in 2009. He suggests that this is primarily due to financial considerations but rates stress as a significant factor, and the IPPN (2009) notes that this is a significant increase on previous years. In this study, 16% of principals stated they had considered leaving the workforce completely as a result of workplace bullying, which is comparable to the previous findings of 14% quoted by O'Connell et al. (2007). Principals who felt less comfortable in their role and those for whom work was too pressurised were significantly more likely to consider resignation or retirement. The INTO (2007) noted that 11% of primary teachers had considered leaving the workforce completely as a direct consequence of workplace bullying.

Principals' perceptions of adequacy of procedures

Perhaps one of the most startling findings in this study is that only fourteen principals (5%) consider that current procedures are effective in resolving workplace bullying disputes. The vast majority of principals (95%) have no confidence in current procedures, confirming the IPPN (2006a) view that structures are inadequate to deal with adult workplace bullying in schools. It also confirms the suggestion by Mella (2005) that there exists in schools a lack of respect for anti-bullying policies and effective practical application of these procedures. A significant amount of qualitative data reinforced this belief among principals, which corroborates the suggestion by Herron (2007) that one trade union cannot serve both teachers and principals in disputes simultaneously. Only just over half of bullied principals (54%) have employed the procedures as outlined by the INTO (2000c).

Principals reported very low satisfaction levels with the outcomes of using INTO procedures and therefore continue to be subjected to serious levels of distress and profoundly negative consequences. Those who employ procedures indicated that the bullying stopped in only 5% of cases, with a further 26% stating that the levels of bullying had reduced. Just over half of bullied principals who followed procedures reported that they had no effect whatsoever, with a further 17% claiming that the bullying situation had actually worsened. Such findings establish that current procedures are not effective in addressing the workplace bullying of primary principals.

IMPLICATIONS

The high incidence of workplace bullying reported in this study indicates that the primary school is a work arena in which unacceptably high levels of bullying thrive. For many principals, schools do not provide a safe working environment in which they can discharge their professional duties and lead school communities effectively. Instead, schools are often places where principals are frequently challenged by a wide range of negative behaviours and where fear, anxiety and isolation are not uncommon.

The research findings also highlight a number of serious systemic shortcomings within the primary education system which make principals vulnerable. The fact that the primary perpetrators are often deputies and teachers appointed to support principals raises serious questions in terms of the current in-school management (ISM) structure. Evidence suggests that it is not effective. This combined with the lack of opportunity for promotion and teacher mobility manifests itself in principals being targets of bullying behaviour.

The current system of school management involving voluntary members drawn from a variety of stakeholders is not without its shortcomings. Findings suggest that, within current management procedures, opportunities exist for BOM members to regularly bully principals for a variety of reasons.

Furthermore, the current partnership between schools and parents presents serious challenges for a significant number of principals who perceive that parents have become more demanding. Current procedures for solving disputes appear inadequate as a significant cohort of parents resort to bullying behaviours to resolve issues.

Systemic difficulties are also evident in terms of implementing change and monitoring teachers' performance. The current reluctance to fully engage in existing structures to address issues concerning teachers' under-performance and related matters contributes to circumstances where principals become targets. Ironically, as principals implement change and attempt to monitor performance, some are accused of engaging in bullying by discontented perpetrators. Such a situation leaves a principal in a compromised position.

In addition, despite high levels of personal support, there is widespread lack of confidence in existing structures designed to resolve bullying disputes in primary schools. This combined with the reported perception that trade union support is variable and the fact that using procedures does not resolve disputes in the majority of cases leaves a high number feeling isolated, helpless and unsupported.

Throughout the research there is frequent reference to stress. The findings reveal a strong inter-connectedness between bullying, emotional well-being, ill-health and stress, seriously suggesting that the post of principal is one which regularly faces adversity and serious challenges from a variety of sources.

The workplace bullying of principals has serious individual implications. There exists high levels of distress where the negative emotional outcomes and serious health implications take their toll on principals and schools. For the individual principal, lowered self-confidence, high levels of anxiety and depression all have a psychological impact. Similarly, physical ill-health in various forms adversely affects work performance, quality of leadership and school relationships in addition to negatively impacting on lifestyle and personal circumstances. This study shows that there are many principals for whom this is a daily reality.

From an organisational perceptive, the bullying of primary principals undoubtedly negatively influences their capacity to work and lead their school in a fully effective manner. Absenteeism arising from being bullied affects the school culture and has very obvious financial implications for the Department of Education and Skills. The ultimate response, where bullied principals resign, deprives school communities of their knowledge, experience and leadership skills. This is particularly critical at a time where there is a shortage of applicants for principal posts.

RECOMMENDATIONS

Primary intervention: Reducing the risk

- The education stakeholders should review and evaluate the current cultural climate in primary schools and promote good practice in terms of preventing workplace bullying. This would

involve placing a greater emphasis on creating a positive working environment in which the following would be key elements:
- ○ clear communication structures
- ○ collaboration and collegiality
- ○ democratic management structures
- ○ welcome for diversity
- ○ commitment to dignity at work
- ○ culture of mutual respect and support
- ○ constant monitoring
- ○ commitment to self-reflection
- Key stakeholders should review a number of the general issues pertaining to primary education. Such a review should result in changes relating to levels of work stress, teacher promotion and mobility opportunities, the role and operation of Boards of Management and parental grievance procedures.
- It is necessary to review the current status and operation of in-school management and the desired outcome would be that a revision of present structures would facilitate greater support and assistance to school leaders.
- There is a requirement to increase awareness of bullying among principals. The existing continuing professional development should be extended to all newly appointed and incumbent principals to enhance leadership and management skills. Specific modules addressing bullying, interpersonal relations, conflict resolution skills, and emotional and health issues should be included.
- Specific training initiatives emphasising positive school culture, conflict resolution and dignity at work should be made available to all staff.
- A developmental, supportive and participative appraisal process should be introduced for all principals and teachers.

Secondary intervention: Responding to bullying incidents

Despite emphasis on prevention, bullying incidents will occur and therefore the following recommendations are made:

- The current INTO procedures (INTO, 2006c) are the result of an extensive collaborative process and contain key elements of what is considered best practice. However, a forum needs to be established to examine why these procedures do not currently adequately address resolution of workplace bullying.

- The role and practice of the INTO in resolving bullying disputes needs to be examined from the principals' perspective. A revised structure needs to be established whereby its role in mediation is equally accessible to both parties in bullying disputes.
- It is necessary that disciplinary procedures are revised so as to contain effective sanctions which can realistically prevent perpetrators from persisting in engaging in bullying behaviors.
- While the Health and Safety Authority (HSA) codes of practice require employers to have mandatory policy regulations, the degree to which policies are implemented is variable. While O'Connell and Williams (2001) reject the need for specific bullying legislation, the phenomenon is still endemic and therefore the need for specific legislation should seriously be reconsidered as a matter of urgency.

The above recommendations should incorporate a holistic approach integrating individual, situational, organisational and societal factors in order to effectively address the phenomenon.

Tertiary intervention: Supporting victims and bullies

- While a general employee assistance scheme is in operation through VHI Corporate Solutions, principals require access to a support service specifically designed to meet the needs of those employed in the education sector similar to Educare which was discontinued in 2003.
- This designated support service should provide suitable psychological support and counselling services on an ongoing basis to bullied principals. Similarly, bullies should be able to avail of psychological support together with rehabilitative programmes.
- Management bodies should consider its duty of care towards principals in terms of reducing stress, support of health and lifestyle issues. Where burnout and fatigue prevent the principal from fulfilling his/her duties, a step-down facility should be available similar to the scheme for privileged assistants operating in amalgamated schools.

CONCLUDING REMARKS

This is the first ever research specifically examining workplace bullying among Irish primary principals. The primary objective was to establish incidence and evaluate the consequences of being exposed to negative bullying behaviours.

The study presents strong evidence that a large proportion of primary principals are subjected to workplace bullying on a frequent basis. The findings demonstrate that the majority of perpetrators are from within schools where deputy principals and teachers use a variety of bullying behaviours for differing reasons. Additionally, parents bully principals on a regular basis especially when they have unresolved issues relating to schools. The research also reveals that the insidious effects of bullying have serious emotional, health, work and personal consequences for victims.

Furthermore, evidence presented highlights a lack of confidence in the effectiveness of existing policy structures in resolving bullying disputes between principals and perpetrators. One of the outcomes of this minor study has been to make practical suggestions which, if implemented, could have positive effects in reducing the phenomenon. Moving forward is not simply about the absence of bullying in the workplace but moreover about actively defining and promoting positive school culture and working relationships.

This study should contribute to a continued process of enlightenment and ultimately to a more effective system which addresses the phenomenon in a comprehensive and effective manner. If levels of bullying are to be reduced, key stakeholders must also address broader systemic issues which permit and encourage bullying to thrive. If this is not undertaken, then the Irish primary school will continue to be a work environment which offers little protection to principals and indeed other employees in this education sector.

REFERENCES

Adams, A. *Bullying at Work: How to Confront and Overcome It* (London: Virago Press, 1992)

Archer, D. 'Exploring 'Bullying' Culture in Para-Military Organisations', *International Journal of Manpower*, vol. 20, nos 1/2, 1999, pp. 94–105

ASTI (Association of Secondary Teachers Ireland), 'Bullying at Work' (1999), http://www.asti.ie/pdfs/Info%20Leaflets/Bullying2005.pdf [accessed 25 August 2009]

Begley, T.M. 'Coping Strategies as Predictors of Employee Distress and Turnover after an Organisational Consolidation: A Longitudinal Study', *Employee Relations*, 27, 1998, pp. 160–74

Björrkqvist, K., Österman, K. and Hjelt-Bäck, M. 'Aggression among University Employees', *Aggressive Behavior*, 20, 1994, pp. 173–84

Blase, J. and Blase, J. 'The Phenomenology of Principal Mistreatment: Teachers' Perspectives', *Journal of Educational Research*, 41, 2003, pp. 367–422

Boyle, G.J., Borg, M.G., Falzon, J.M. and Baglioni, J. 'A Structural Model of the Dimensions of Teacher Stress', *British Journal of Educational Psychology*, 65, 1995, pp. 49–67

Branch, S., Ramsey, S. and Barker, M. 'Upwards Bullying: A Theoretical Analysis', *The Abstracts of the 6th Australian Industrial and Organizational Psychology Conference* (2003), pp. 120–1

Branch, S. Ramsey, S.G. and Barker, M.C. 'Causes of Upwards Bullying: Managers' Perspectives', paper presented at the 20th ANZAM Conference, 2006

Branch, S., Ramsey, S.G. and Barker, M.C. 'Managing in the Firing Line: Contributing Factors to Workplace Bullying by Staff. An Interview Study', *Journal of Management and Organization*, 13, 2007, pp. 264–81

Braverman, M. *Preventing Workplace Violence: A Guide for Employers and Practitioners* (London: Sage, 1999)

Brodsky, C. *The Harassed Worker* (Toronto: Lexington Books, 1976)

Capel, S.A. 'A Longitudinal Study of Burnout in Teachers', *British Journal of Educational Psychology*, 61, 1991, pp. 36–45

Carr, A. 'Anxiety and Depression among School Principals', *Journal of Educational Administration*, 32, 1994, pp. 18–34

Cemaloglu, N. 'The Exposure of Primary School Teachers to Bullying: An Analysis of Various Variables', *Social Behaviour and Personality*, 35, 2007, pp. 789–802

CMI, 'One Manager in Three Has Been Bullied at Work, Survey Reveals', *Professional Engineering*, 21 September 2005, p. 9

Coyne, I., Seigne, E. and Randall, P. 'Predicting Workplace Victim Status from Personality', *European Journal of Work and Organizational Psychology*, 9, 2000, pp. 335–49

Cullen, C. 'Mass Exodus of School Principals', *Wexford People*, 1 June 2009

Djurkovic, N., McCormack, D. and Casimir, G. 'The Physical and Psychological Effects of Workplace Bullying and their Relationship to Intention to Leave: A Test of the Psychosomatic and Disability Hypotheses', *International Journal of Organisation Theory and Behaviour*, 7, 2004, pp. 469–97

Donnolly, K. 'Almost Half of Primary Teachers Bullied', *Irish Independent*, 3 January 2007

Edelmann, R.J. and Woodall, L. 'Bullying at Work', *The Occupational Psychologist*, 32, 1997, pp. 28–31

Einarsen, S. 'The Nature and Causes of Bullying at Work', *International Journal of Manpower*, 20, 1999, pp. 16–27

Einarsen, S. 'Harassment and Bullying at Work: A Review of the Scandinavian Approach', *Aggression and Violent Behavior*, 5, 2000, pp. 379–401

Einarsen, S. and Hellesøy, O.H. 'Når Samhandling Går På Helsen Løs: Helsemesige Konsekvenser av Mobbing i Arbeidslivet' ['When Interaction Affects Health: Health Consequences of Bullying at Work'], *Medicinsk Årbog*, 1998 (Copenhagen: Munsksgaard, 1998)

Einarsen, S. and Hoel, H. 'The Negative Acts Questionnaire: Development, Validation and Revision of a Measure of Bullying at Work', paper presented at the 10th European Congress on Work and Organisational Psychology, Prague, May 2001

Einarsen, S. and Mikkelsen, G. 'Individual Effects to Exposure to Bullying at Work', in S. Einarsen, H. Hoel, D. Zapf and C. Cooper (eds), *Bullying and Emotional Abuse in the Workplace: International Perspectives in Research and Practice* (London: Taylor & Francis, 2003)

Einarsen, S. and Raknes, B.I. *Mobbing in Arbeidslivet: En Undersøkelse av Forekomst og Helsemessige Konsekvenser av Mobbing på Norske Arbeidplasser* [*A Study of the Prevalence and Health Effects of Mobbing on Norwegian Workplaces*] (Bergen: University of Bergen, Centre For Occupational Health and Safety Research, 1991)

Einarsen, S. and Raknes, B.I. 'Harassment in the Workplace and the Victimisation of Men', *Violence and Victims*, 12, 1997, pp. 247–63

Einarsen, S. and Skogstad, A. 'Bullying at Work: Epidemiological Findings in Public and Private Organisations', *European Journal of Work and Organisational Psychology*, 5, 1996, pp. 185–210

Einarsen, S., Hoel, H., Zapf, D. and Cooper, C.L. 'The Concept of Bullying at Work: The European Tradition', in S. Einarsen, H. Hoel, D. Zapf and C. Cooper (eds), *Bullying and Emotional Abuse in the Workplace: International Perspectives in Research and Practice* (London and New York: Taylor & Francis, 2003)

Einarsen, S., Matthieson, S.B. and Skogstad, A. 'Bullying, Burnout and Well-Being among Assistant Nurses', *Journal of Occupational Health and Safety – Australia and New Zealand*, 14, 1998, pp. 563–8

Einarsen, S., Raknes, B.I. and Matthiesen, S.B. 'Bullying and Harassment at Work and their Relationship to Work Environment Quality: An Exploratory Study', *European Work and Organisational Psychologist*, 4, 1994, pp. 381–401

Einarsen, S., Raknes, B.I., Matthiesen, S.B. and Hellesøy, O.H. *Mobbing og Harde Personkonflicter: Helsefarlig Samspill på Arbeidplassen* [*Bullying and Interpersonal Conflict: Interaction at Work with Negative Implications for Health*] (Bergen: Sigma Forlag, 1994b)

Einarsen, S., Raknes, B.I. and Matthiesen, S.B. 'Bullying at Work and its Relationship with Health Complaints: Moderating Effects of Social Support and Personality', *Nordisk Psylogi*, 48, 1996, pp. 116–37

Fahie, D. 'Workplace Bullying: What's all the Fuss About?', *In Touch*, 82, Jan/Feb 2007a, pp. 20–2

Fahie, D. 'Workplace Bullying: What's all the Fuss About?', *In Touch*, 83, March 2007b, p. 28

Friedman, I.A. 'Burnout in School Principals: Role-Related Antecedents', *Social Psychology of Education*, 5, 2002, pp. 229–51

Friesen, D., Prokop, C.M. and Sarros, J.C. 'Why Teachers Burn Out', *Educational Research Quarterly*, 12, 1988, pp. 9–19

Hansen, Å.M., Hogh, A., Persson, R., Karlson, B., Garde A.H. and Ørbæk, P. 'Bullying at Work, Health Outcomes, and Physiological Stress Response', *Journal of Psychosomatic Research*, 60, 2006, pp. 63–72

Herron, A.J. 'The Principal and the School: Managing the Challenging Interface', *Leadership*, 44, 2008, p. 12

Hockley, C. *Silent Hell: Workplace Violence and Victims* (Norwood, South Australia: Peacock Publishers, 2002)

Hoel, H. and Cooper, C.L. *Destructive Conflict and Bullying at Work* (Manchester: Manchester School of Management and Umist, 2000)

Hoel, H., Cooper, C.L. and Faragher, B. 'The Experience of Bullying in Great Britain: The Impact of Organisational Status', *European Journal of Work and Organisational Psychology*, 10, 2001, pp. 443–65

Hoel, H., Rayner, C. and Cooper, C.L. 'Workplace Bullying', *International Review of Industrial and Organisational Psychology*, 14, 1999, pp. 189–230

Hubert, A.B. and Von Veldhoven, M. 'Risk Sectors for Undesired Behaviours and Mobbing', *European Journal of Work and Organisational Psychology*, 10, 2001, pp. 415–24

INTO (Irish National Teachers' Organisation), 'Survey on Adult Bullying and Staff Relations in Primary Schools 1998', in INTO, *Staff Relations: A Report on Adult Bullying in Schools* (Dublin: INTO, 2000a)

INTO (Irish National Teachers' Organisation), *Staff Relations: A Report on Adult Bullying in Schools* (Dublin: INTO, 2000b)

INTO (Irish National Teachers' Organisation), *Working Together: Procedures and Policies for Positive Staff Relations* (Dublin: INTO, 2000c)

INTO (Irish National Teachers' Organisation), 'Survey of Newly Appointed Principals in Limerick', unpublished report (Dublin: INTO, 2006)

INTO (Irish National Teachers' Organisation), 'Bullying and Harassment in the Workplace: Results of INTO Survey 2006', presented at the INTO Equality Conference on Dignity at Work, Tullamore, Co. Offaly, 9 March 2007

IPPN (Irish Primary Principals' Network), 'IPPN Survey on Principals' Workload 2004: Executive Summary', unpublished report (Cork: IPPN, 2004a)

IPPN (Irish Primary Principals' Network), 'IPPN Obesity Survey' (2004b), http://www.ippn.ie/index.cfm/loc/6-10/articleid/ba60e8ea-d95b-4f99-9cc13e88dcba98e3.htm [accessed 1 September 2009]

IPPN (Irish Primary Principals' Network), 'IPPN/NAPD Survey on Attitudes & Aspirations towards the Role of Principal' (2005a), http://www.ippn.ie/index.cfm/loc/6-10/articleid/702a3560-9585-42c9-bbe6dcbd69e644f4.htm [accessed 1 September 2009]

IPPN (Irish Primary Principals' Network), 'IPPN Survey of Newly Appointed Principals' (2005b), http://www.ippn.ie/index.cfm/loc/6-10/articleid/86dc3c60-abbb-4dcb-8199aedc96cdda9c.htm [accessed 1 September 2009]

IPPN (Irish Primary Principals' Network), 'IPPN Survey on Principals' Workload' (2005c), http://www.ippn.ie/index.cfm/loc/6-10/articleid/2f2ec5e4-1c37-4128-948160d23afcbc98.htm [accessed 1 September 2009]

IPPN (Irish Primary Principals' Network), 'IPPN Survey of Principals: January 2006(a)', http://www.ippn.ie/index.cfm/loc/6-10/articleid/67f4f5b8-c124-45af-b5e0b790db3d8184.htm [accessed 1 September 2008]

IPPN (Irish Primary Principals' Network), *Investing in School Leadership* (Cork: IPPN (Irish Primary Principals' Network), 2006b)

IPPN (Irish Primary Principals' Network), 'Pre-Conference Survey Report, 2008', http://www.educationopinion.ie/preconf2008.htm [accessed 3 October 2009]

IPPN (Irish Primary Principals' Network), 'The Future of CPD in your School' (2008), http://www.educationopinion.ie/pcsp.htm [accessed 1 September 2008]

IPPN (Irish Primary Principals' Network), 'Mass Exodus of Principals Will Create Leadership Crisis in Primary Schools, press release, 15 May 2009

Irish Independent (2007). 'A Dangerous Place to Work', *Irish Independent*, 12 April 2007

Ironside, M. and Seifert, R. 'Tackling Bullying in the Workplace', in S. Einarsen, H. Hoel, D. Zapf and C.L. Cooper (eds), *Bullying and Emotional Abuse in the Workplace: International Perspectives in Research and Practice* (London: Taylor & Francis, 2003)

Janoff-Bulman, R. 'Assumptive Worlds and the Stress of Traumatic Events: Applications of the Schema Construct, *Social Cognition*, 7, 1989, pp. 113–36

Johns, G. 'How Often are you Absent?' A Review of the Use of Self-Reported Absence Data', *Journal of Applied Psychology*, 79, 1994, pp. 574–91

Jones, N. 'The Real World Management Preoccupations of Primary School Heads', *School Leadership and Management*, 19, 1999, pp. 483–95

Keashly, L. 'Emotional Abuse in the Workplace: Conceptual and Empirical Issues', *Journal of Emotional Abuse*, 1, 1998, pp. 85–117

Keashly, L. and Jagatic, K. 'By Any Other Name: American Perspectives on Workplace Bullying', in S. Einarsen, H. Hoel, D. Zapf and C. Cooper (eds), *Bullying and Emotional Abuse in the Workplace: International Perspectives in Research and Practice* (London: Taylor & Francis, 2003)

Kigotho, W. 'Heads Seek Cover against Mobs', *The Times Educational Supplement*, 21 July 2000

Kile, S.M. *Helesfarleg Leiarskap: Ein Explorerande Studie* [Health Endangered Leadership: An Exploratory Study], Report to the Norwegian Council of Research (Bergen: University of Bergen, Department of Psychosocial Science, 1990)

Kimmel, A.J. *Ethics and Values in Applied Social Research* (Newbury Park, CA: Sage, 1988)

Kitt, J. 'Workplace Bullying in Primary Schools: A Case Study', unpublished MSt thesis, School of Education, Trinity College Dublin, 1999

Kivimäki, M., Elvainio, M. and Vahtera, J. 'Workplace Bullying and Sickness Absence in Hospital Staff', *Occupational and Environmental Medicine*, 57, 2000, pp. 656–60

Lewis, D. 'Voices in the Social Construction of Bullying at Work: Exploring Multiple Realities in Further and Higher Education', *International Journal of Management and Decision Making*, 4, 2003, pp. 65–81

Lewis, D. and Sheehan, M. 'Workplace Bullying: Theoretical and Practical Approaches to a Management Challenge' (Introduction), *International Journal of Management and Decision Making*, 4, 2003, pp. 1–10

Leymann, H. 'Mobbing and Psychological Terror at Workplaces', *Violence and Victims*, 5, 1990, pp. 119–26

Leymann, H. *Fran Mobbning till Utslagning i Arbetslivet* [From Bullying to Exclusion from Working Life] (Stockholm: Publica, 1992)

Leymann, H. 'Ätiologie und Häufigkeit von Mobbing am Arbeitsplatz: Eine Übersicht Über die Bisherige Forschung' ['Etiology and Frequency of Bullying in the Workplace: An Overview of Current Research'], *Zeitschrift für Personalforchung*, 7, 1993a, pp. 271–83

Leymann, H. *Mobbing: Psychterror am Arbeitsplatz und Wie Man Sich Dagegen Wehren Kann* [*Mobbing: Psychterror in the Workplace and How One Can Defend Oneself*] (Reinbeck: Rowohlt, 1993b)

Leymann, H. 'The Content and Development of Mobbing at Work', *European Journal of Work and Organisational Psychology*, 5, 1996, pp. 165–84

Leymann, H. *The Mobbing Encyclopaedia* (1997), http://www.leymann.se [accessed 26 September 2008]

Leymann, H. and Gustafsson, A. 'Mobbing and the Development of Post-Traumatic Stress Disorders', *European Journal of Work and Organisational Psychology*, 5, 1996, pp. 251–76

Liddane, M. and Hamill, N. 'Workplace Bullying: Effects in the Individual in the Workplace', paper presented at the INTO Equality Conference on Dignity at Work, Tullamore, Co. Offaly, 9 March 2007

Matthiesen, S.B., Raknes, B.I. and Rökkum, O. 'Mobbing på Arbeidsplassen' ['Bullying in the Workplace'], *Tidsskrift for Norsk Psykologforening*, 26, 1989, pp. 761–74

Mikkelsen, E.G. 'Workplace Bullying: Its Prevalence, Aetiology and Health Correlates', unpublished PhD thesis, University of Aarhus, Department of Psychology, 2001

McCarthy, M., Mayhew, C., Barker, M. and Sheehan, M. 'Bullying and Occupational Violence in Tertiary Education: Risk Factors, Perpetrators and Prevention', *Journal of Occupational Health and Safety – Australia and New Zealand*, 19, 2003, pp. 319–26

McCarthy, P., Henderson, M., Sheehan, M. and Barker, M. 'Workplace Bullying: Its Management and Prevention', *Australian Master OHS and Environment Guide*, 2002, pp. 519–49

Mccormack, D., Casimir, G., Djurkovic, N. and Yang, L. 'The Concurrent Effects of Workplace Bullying, Satisfaction with Supervisor, and Satisfaction with Co-Workers on Affective Commitment among School Teachers in China', *International Journal and Conflict Management*, 17, 2006, pp. 316–31

McDonald, V. 'Leadership Issues for Principal Teachers', *Oideas*, 53, 2008, pp. 27–40

McElduff, A. 'Workplace Bullying', paper presented at the INTO Equality Conference on Dignity at Work, Tullamore, Co. Offaly, 9 March 2007

Mella, P. 'Bullying among Teachers: Secret, Hidden Trauma', *Irish Independent*, 29 August 2005

Mikkelsen, E.G. and Einarsen, S. 'Relationships between Exposure to Bullying at Work and Psychological and Psychosomatic Health Complaints: The Role of State Negative Affectivity and Generalized Self-Efficacy', *Scandinavian Journal of Psychology*, 43, 2002, pp. 397–405

Minton, S.J. and O'Moore, A.M. 'Teachers: A Critical Focus Group in Both Schools-Based and Workplace Anti-Bullying Research: Perspectives from Ireland', Fourth International Conference on Bullying and Harassment in the Workplace, University of Bergen, Norway, 28–9 June 2004

Minton, S.J. and O'Moore, A.M. 'Results of a Nationwide Anti-Bullying Initiative in Ireland', 13th European Conference on Developmental Psychology, University of Jena, Germany, 21–25 August 2007

Morgan, M. and Sugrue, C. 'The Seven Challenges and Four Rewards of Being a School Principal: Results of a National Survey', *Oideas*, 53, 2008, pp. 8–26

zur Mühlen, L., Normann, G. and Greif, S. 'Stress and Bullying in Two Organisations', unpublished document, University of Osnabrück, Faculty of Psychology, 2001

Murray, N. 'Concern over Rise in Bullying of School Principals', *Irish Examiner*, 14 January 2009

NASUWT, *No Place to Hide: Confronting Workplace Bullies* (Birmingham: NASUWT (National Association of Schoolmasters and Union of Women Teachers), 1996)

Niedl, K. 'Mobbing and Well-Being: Economic and Personnel Development Implications', *European Journal of Work and Organisational Psychology*, 5, 1995, pp. 203–14

O'Connell, P. and Williams, J. *Report of the Taskforce on the Prevention of Workplace Bullying. Dignity At Work: The Challenge of Workplace Bullying* (Dublin: The Stationery Office, 2001)

O'Connell, P.J., Calvert, E. and Watson, D. *Bullying in the Workplace: Survey Reports, 2007. Report to the Department of Enterprise, Trade and Employment* (Dublin: ESRI (The Economic and Social Research Institute), 2007)

Ó'Diomsaigh, S. 'Primary Principals' Perspectives on the Impact of the Middle Management Structure on their Roles', unpublished MEd thesis, St Patrick's College of Education, Dublin, 2000

O'Donnell, V. *Bullying: A Resource Guide for Parents and Teachers* (Dublin: Attic Press, 1995)

O'Moore, M. 'Bullying in the Workplace: Is it a Problem?', *Health and Safety Authority Newsletter*, 106, 1998, pp. 2–4

O'Moore, M. 'Report on Workplace Bullying of Teachers Union of Ireland Members', unpublished report (Dublin: Anti-Bullying Centre, Trinity College, 1999)

O'Moore, M. *Summary Report on the National Survey on Workplace Bullying in the Republic of Ireland* (Dublin: Anti-Bullying Research Centre, Trinity College, 2000)

O'Moore, M. and Minton, S. *Report to the Department of Education on the Project to Evaluate the Effectiveness of a Proposed National Programme to Prevent and Counter Bullying Behaviour in Irish Schools Undertaken in Donegal Primary Schools* (Dublin: ABC, Trinity College, 2002)

O'Moore, A.M. and Minton, S.J. 'An Evaluation of a Whole-School Approach to Prevention of and Intervention against Bullying in Schools in Ireland', XVI World Meeting of the International Society for Research on Aggression, Santorini, Greece, 18–22 September 2004

O'Moore, A.M. and Minton, S.J. 'Violence in Schools in a Culturally Diverse Society', Standing Conference on Teacher Education North and South (SCoTENS) Third Annual Conference, Grand Hotel, Malahide, Co. Dublin, 10–11 November 2005

O'Moore, M., Kirkham, C. and Smith, M. 'Bullying Behaviour in Irish Schools: A Nationwide Study', *Irish Journal of Psychology*, 18, 1997, pp. 141–69

O'Moore, M., Lynch, J. and Nic Daeid, N. 'The Rates and Risks of Workplace Bullying in Ireland, a Country of High Economic Growth', *International Journal of Management and Decision Making*, 4, 2003, pp. 82–95

O'Moore, M., Seigne, E., McGuire, L. and Smith, M. 'Victims of Workplace Bullying in Ireland', *Irish Journal of Psychology*, 19, 1998a, pp. 345–57

O'Moore, M., Seigne, E., McGuire, L. and Smith, M. 'Victims of Bullying at Work in Ireland', *Journal of Occupational Health and Safety – Australia and New Zealand*, 14, 1998b, pp. 569–74

O'Reilly, B. 'Why I Can't Wait to Quit my Job as School Principal', *Irish Independent*, 14 April 2007

Pascal. C. and Ribbins, P. *Understanding Primary Headteachers* (London: Cassell, 1998)

Pervin, K. and Turner, A. 'A Study of Bullying of Teachers by Pupils in an Inner London School', *Pastoral Care*, 4–10 December 1998

Price Spratlen, L. 'Interpersonal Conflict which Includes Mistreatment in the University Workplace', *Violence and Victims*, 10, 1995, pp. 285–97

Quine, L. 'Workplace Bullying in the NHS Community Trust: Staff Questionnaire Survey', *British Medical Journal*, 318, 1999, pp. 228–32

Quine, L. 'Workplace Bullying in Nurses', *Journal of Health Psychology*, 6, 2001, pp. 73–84

Randall, P. *Adult Bullying: Victims and Perpetrators* (London: Routledge, 1997)

Randle, K. and Brady, N. 'Managerialism and Professionalism in the Cinderella Service', *Journal of Vocational Education and Training*, 49, 1997, pp. 121–39

Rayner, C. 'The Incidence of Workplace Bullying', *Journal of Community and Applied Social Psychology*, 7, 1997, pp. 249–55

Rayner, C. 'Workplace Bullying: Do Something!' *Journal of Occupational Health and Safety – Australia and New Zealand*, 14, 1998, pp. 581–5

Rayner, C. and Hoel, H. 'A Summary Review of Literature Relating to Workplace Bullying', *Journal of Community and Social Psychology*, 7, 1997, pp. 181–91

Raynor, C., Hoel, H. and Cooper, C.L. *Workplace Bullying: What We Know, Who is to Blame, and What We Can Do?* (London and New York: Taylor & Francis, 2002)

Romanov, K., Appelberg, K. Honkasalo, M.L. and Koskenvuo, M. 'Recent Interpersonal Conflicts at Work and Psychiatric Morbidity: A Prospective Study of 15,350 Employees Aged 24–64', *Journal of Psychosomatic Research*, 40, 1996, pp. 157–67

Salin, D. 'Prevalence and Forms of Bullying among Business Professionals: A Comparison of Two Different Strategies for Measuring Bullying', *European Journal of Work and Organisational Psychology*, 10, 2001, pp. 425–41

Salin, D. 'Bullying and Organisational Politics in Competitive and Rapidly Changing Work Environments', *International Journal of Management and Decision Making*, 4, 2003, pp. 35–46

Salin, D. 'Ways of Explaining Workplace Bullying: A Review of Enabling, Motivating and Precipitating Structures and Processes in the Work Environment', *Human Relations*, vol. 56, no. 10, 2008, pp. 1213–32

Sarros, J.C. 'Administrator Burnout: Finding Future Directions', *Journal of Educational Administration*, 26, 1988, pp. 184–96

Sheehan, M. 'Workplace Bullying: Responding with Some Emotional Intelligence', *International Journal of Manpower*, 20, 1999, pp. 57–69

Stevens, P.J. 'The Incidence and Consequences of Upwards Workplace Bullying on Primary School Principals in the Republic of Ireland', unpublished MBA thesis, School of Public Policy and Professional Practice, Keele University, England, 2010

Stevens, P.J. 'Primary School Principals as Victims of Workplace Bullying', unpublished MLitt thesis, School of Education, Trinity College Dublin, 2012

Sue, V.M. and Ritter, L.A. *Conducting Online Surveys* (London: Sage Publications, 2007)

Tehrani, N. *Building a Culture of Respect: Managing Bullying at Work* (London and New York: Taylor & Francis, 2001)

Tepper, B.J. 'Consequences of Abusive Supervision', *Academy of Management Journal*, 43, 2000, p. 178

Thylefors, I. *Syndabockar: Om Utstötning och Mobbing i Arbetslivet* [*Scapegoats: On Exclusion and Mobbing at Work*] (Stockholm: Natur Och Kultur, 1987)

Torelli, J.A. and Gmelch, W.H. 'Occupational Stress and Burnout in Educational Administration', *People and Education*, 1, 1993, pp. 361–81

Travers, J. and McKeown, P. 'Leadership of Professional Staff', *Irish Educational Studies*, 24, 2005, pp. 41–53

TUI, 'TUI Launches Major National Survey on Bullying in the Workplace', *TUI News*, 21, 1999a, p. 11

TUI, 'TUI Bullying Survey: Disturbing Reading', *TUI News*, 21, 1999b, p. 15

Vartia, M. 'Psychological Harassment (Bullying, Mobbing) at Work', in K. Kauppinen-Toropainen (ed.), *OECD Panel Group on Women, Work and Health* (Helsinki: Ministry of Social Affairs and Health, 1993)

Vartia, M. 'The Sources of Bullying. Psychological Work Environment and Organisational Climate', *Journal of Work and Organisational Psychology*, 5, 1996, pp. 201–14

Vartia, M. 'Consequences of Workplace Bullying with Respect to the Well-Being of its Targets and the Observers of Bullying', *Scandinavian Journal of Work Environment and Health*, 27, 2001, pp. 63–9

Vartia, M. *Workplace Bullying: A Study on the Work Environment, Well-Being and Health* (Vammala: Finnish Institute of Occupational Health, 2003)

Vickers, M.H. 'Bullying as Unacknowledged Organisational Evil: A Researcher's Story', *Employee Responsibilities and Rights Journal*, 13, 2001, pp. 205–17

Waldman, J.D., Kelly, F., Aurora, S. and Smith, H.L. 'The Shocking Cost of Turnover in Health Care', *Health Care Management Review*, 29, 2004, pp. 2–7

Walshe, J. 'Bullying Taking Toll on Teachers – Study', *Irish Independent*, 14 November 1998

WBI, 'US Workplace Bullying Survey: September 2007', www.bullying-institute.org.360.656.6630 [accessed 12 November 2009]

Zapf, D. 'Mobbing in Organisationen: Ein Überblick zum Stand der Forschung' ['Mobbing in Organisations: A State of the Art Review'], *Zeitschrift für Arbeits- und Organisationpsychologie*, 43, 1999a, pp. 1–25

Zapf, D. 'Organisational, Work Group Related and Personal Causes of Mobbing/Bullying at Work', *International Journal of Manpower*, 20, 1999b, pp. 70–85

Zapf, D. and Einarsen, S. 'Individual Antecendents of Bullying: Victims and Perpetrators', in S. Einarsen, H. Hoel, D. Zapf and C. Cooper (eds), *Bullying and Emotional Abuse in the Workplace: International Perspectives in Research and Practice* (London: Taylor & Francis, 2003)

Zapf, D. and Einarsen, S. 'Mobbing at Work: Escalated Conflicts in Organisations', in S. Fox and P. Spector (eds), *Counterproductive Work Behaviour: Investigations of Actors and Targets* (Washington, DC: APA (American Psychological Association), 2005)

Zapf, D. and Gross, C. 'Conflict Escalation and Coping with Workplace Bullying: A Replication and Extension', *European Journal of Work and Organisational Psychology*, 10, 2001, pp. 497–522

Zapf, D., Einarsen, S., Hoel, H. and Vartia, M. 'Empirical Findings on Bullying in the Workplace', in S. Einarsen, H. Hoel, D. Zapf, and C.L. Cooper (eds), *Bullying and Emotional Abuse in the Workplace: International Perspectives in Research and Practice* (London and New York: Taylor & Francis, 2002)

Zapf, D., Knorz, C. and Kulla, M. 'On the Relationship between Mobbing Factors, and Job Content, Social Work Environment and Health Outcomes', *European Journal of Work and Organisational Psychology*, 5, 1996, pp. 215–37

CHAPTER TEN

Teacher-on-Teacher Workplace Bullying in the Irish Post-Primary Sector

Genevieve Murray

Humanity has always been beset by bullying and until recently, society has tacitly accepted the practice, however as the horrific consequences of abuse now emerge, such resolute consent is now being questioned.

(Field, 1996: xxii)

INTRODUCTION

Bullying in the workplace is acknowledged as a problem in society today both in Ireland and internationally. It knows no boundaries of age, gender, level of education, socio-economic status, types or status of job, whether in the private or public sectors (O'Moore and McGuire, 2001). Workplace bullying is such a complex issue that by the time an individual becomes aware they are the victim of bullying they are psychologically injured. One of the sectors where research studies reveal a high prevalence of this problem is among employees in the education sector. What is more, in Ireland the Economic and Social Research Institute (ESRI, 2007) survey on workplace bullying indicated that the second highest incident rate of this problem existed within the Irish education sector. As no reference was made to specific sections of this sector, the aim of this study is to investigate the incidence of 'teacher-on-teacher workplace bullying' within the post-primary sector. In order to gain a deeper insight into the determinants of workplace bullying in this sector it is critical to determine answers to the following questions:

- Why has the education sector been identified as the sector with the second highest incidence of workplace bullying in Ireland by the ESRI (2007)?

- How prevalent is workplace bullying among the teaching profession in the post-primary sector of the Irish education system?
- What are the causative factors that contribute to workplace bullying in the post-primary sector of the Irish education system?
- Who are the bullies and who are their targets?
- How are complaints of workplace bullying handled within the school?

While describing bullying has been addressed in previous chapters, the emphasis applied in defining the phenomenon in this study stressed the duration and regularity of the negative behaviours involved. This concurs with research in this field which indicates that the negative behaviours must occur frequently over a period of time. Furthermore, bullying is mainly a form of 'psychological abuse' by one or more individuals on another during the course of their work in the place of their employment (Keashly, 1998; Leymann, 1996; O'Moore 2000). An individual may not recognise the nature of the behaviours as bullying, despite realising that they are abnormal and having serious psychological effects. Adams (1992) compares bullying at work to a malignant cancer: 'it creeps up on you long before you – or anyone else – are able to appreciate what it is that is making you feel the ill effects' (Adams, 1992, p. 9). A European research study carried out by Rayner and Hoel (1997) groups bullying behaviours into five categories:

- Threat to personal status (e.g. belittling opinion, public professional humiliation, accusation regarding lack of effort)
- Threat to personal standing (e.g. name-calling, insults, intimidation, devaluing with reference to age)
- Isolation (e.g. preventing access to opportunities, physical or social isolation, withholding of information)
- Overwork (e.g. undue pressure, impossible deadlines, unnecessary disruptions)
- Destabilisation (e.g. failure to give credit when due, meaningless tasks, removal of responsibility, repeated reminders of blunders, setting up to fail)

(Rayner and Hoel, 1997, p. 183)

On the other hand, physical abuse is more obvious in the workplace and thus can be easily recognised as unacceptable behaviour and condemned by others (Caponecchia and Wyatt 2009; Einarsen et al., 2003).

Since workplace bullying is a very complex phenomenon, Liefooghe and Olafsson (1999) emphasise the need for a workforce to be collectively made aware of what 'constitutes' bullying behaviours in their workplace environment. Furthermore, bullying is distinct from harassment in Ireland. Section 8 of the Irish Employment Equality Act (2004) states harassment is 'any form of unwanted conduct related to any of the (9) discriminatory grounds'. The Irish Health and Safety Authority also state that 'bullying is legally distinct from harassment as bullying behaviour is not predicated on membership of any distinct group' (Health and Safety Authority, 2007, p. 5). Moreover, work cultures have a bearing on what could be referred to as abusive behaviours in the workplace. Einarsen et al. (2003) introduce the concept of organisational bullying, where employees are subjected to a work culture that is domineering, undignified and pressurised. According to Harvey et al. (2006), behaviours such as undue pressure or difficulty in obtaining compassionate leave may be considered acceptable 'in certain organisational cultures possessing very formalised rulings' (Harvey et al., 2006, p. 9). As authoritarian management is associated with power, if abused it can create a bullying environment in the workplace. The education sector, according to Crawford (1997), is one of the sectors where a firm authoritarian make-up exists and where bullying in the workplace can flourish as power relations within this type of organisation are dealt with in a non-humanitarian manner.

THE PREVALENCE OF WORKPLACE BULLYING IN THE EDUCATION SECTOR

Research studies carried out internationally and in Ireland have revealed the prevalence of workplace bullying among employees in the education sector. Studies carried out in Australia, Canada, the US, Turkey, Croatia, Finland, Wales, the UK and Ireland indicated that workplace bullying/harassment exists within the workplace of schools and universities. In Australia, two online studies (Duncan and Riley, 2005; Riley et al., 2009) were undertaken to examine the prevalence of workplace bullying among staff in schools. Duncan and Riley (2005) investigated staff bullying in Catholic schools by distributing an online and paper-based format questionnaire to both primary teachers and secondary teachers including their support staff within these schools. Research findings revealed 97.5% of employees alleged they were or had been bullied by other staff members. When referring to the perpetrator, students and colleagues were least represented, while school management and parents were considered to be mostly responsible for the bullying, followed by school principals. Furthermore, when considering the forms of bullying, 87% of respondents referred to 'personal confrontation' whereby their work was criticised and they were subjected to 'unreasonable expectations/deadlines' (Duncan and Riley, 2005, pp. 47, 50), with no acknowledgement of their achievements within their workplace. Research findings from a further online survey on staff bullying (Riley et al., 2009) among staffs in Australian primary and secondary non-government and government schools in all states and territories suggested that 99.6% of respondents maintained they were subjected to some form of bullying at work. The findings identified colleagues (85.8%) as the main bullies and colleagues (97.3%) as the chief targets. These results were unexpected when comparing the findings of the Duncan and Riley (2005) survey. Executives (85.4%) were identified as perpetrators, with parents (80.7%) next, followed by principals. However, when comparing the most common form of bullying, 94.4% of respondents reported being subjected to 'unreasonable targets/deadlines', which was similar to the previous study of Duncan and Riley (2005). The extent of workplace bullying experienced by staff in Australian schools has caused concern for the researchers, who consider the view taken by Richards and Freeman (2002) that the various current strains and workloads involved in teaching may be a factor in the escalation of bullying among staff members. Furthermore, Riley et al. (2009) conclude from these findings that the typical profile of the school staff bully is:

- a secondary school teacher
- an executive staff member in secondary schools
- the principal in non-secondary schools;

and that the typical profile of the target of the school staff bully is a teacher

(Riley et al., 2009, p. 4)

The chief purpose of this study was to assess the prevalence of workplace bullying among teachers, principals, support staff and parents in Australian schools. Data exhibits evidence of the existence of the problem. However, more research is required to determine why the problem is present and to examine the effects it is having on the people concerned (Riley et al., 2009).

In Ontario, three education workers' unions, the Ontario Secondary Schools Teachers' Federation (OSSTF), the Elementary Teachers' Federation of Ontario (ETFO) and the Ontario English Catholic Teachers' Association (OECTA), conducted a study to investigate the prevalence of workplace bullying among their members. The study included a representative sample of equal numbers of members from the three unions and the survey was conducted by telephone interviewing. In total, 62% of members, teachers and support staff were exposed to bullying behaviours, with 51% claiming they were bullied by either a superior, a parent, a colleague or a student and a further 11% stating they witnessed bullying. The incidence of bullying was reported to be higher among support staff (57%) than teachers (50%). Students were the main perpetrators (33%), superiors (to include administrative staff, vice principals and principals) (25%), parents or guardians (22%) and colleagues (19%). Victims maintained that the most frequent type of bullying involved verbal abuse, while the most frequent form of bullying entailed threats of physical violence or assault. The gender breakdown of individuals being bullied by a superior translate into 28% male compared to 23% female, while members being bullied by a colleague are fairly equal – 19% male and 20% female. Overall, 55% of members claim that men instigated the bullying while 33% of members maintain it was instigated by women. However, in the instances of same-sex bullying, both men and women were equal at 47%. In total, 41% of respondents formally reported the bullying, with 69% maintaining that it stopped due to the intervention of school administrators. While this study went into great detail to evaluate the prevalence of workplace bullying among union members, analysis of why members felt they were subjected to such behaviours, to include the personality of both the perpetrator and the victim and the effect it had on their lives, was not carried out.

However, McKay et al. (2008) undertook a study among a subset of employees (faculty members, lecturers/instructors and librarians) at a midsized Canadian university aimed at examining the impact workplace bullying had on their lives. This study included a questionnaire distributed to employees at their university email address. This format allowed the employees give their own definition of what they considered 'bullying'. It was followed by quantitative closed questions as well as qualitative open-ended questions, asking participants if they had been subjected to certain negative behaviours in their workplace in the previous five years. Some 52% of respondents claimed they had been bullied in their workplace, with

21% claiming it was ongoing for more than five years. Respondents linked bullying to issues of 'power, intent, abuse and intimidation' (McKay et al., 2008, p. 86). The main instigators of the negative behaviours were peers (64%), individuals in authority (45%) and students (27%). The two main behaviours that the majority of respondents referred to as bullying were: 'patterns of not taking your concerns seriously' (48%) and 'ignoring or overlooking your contributions' (48%) (McKay et al., 2008, p. 87). Just under half of the respondents (47%) claimed that the bullying took place through email with the majority maintaining the perpetrator intended on causing them harm. This is the first time 'being bullied by email' has arisen in the research literature on adult bullying. Moreover, 16% reported that they were bullied by the disruptive behaviours of undergraduate students who would intentionally interrupt the class. When asked what they felt provoked the individual to behave in such a manner, one respondent stated: 'power games, paranoia, gender discrimination [and] manipulative approach to management', while a second respondent described the motivators as 'misdirected politics, opportunism [and] liberalism' (McKay et al., 2008, p. 87). According to the respondents, the bullying behaviours had a negative effect on their productivity at work, together with the quality and quantity of their work.

Furthermore, the consequences of the effects of the bullying left new staff members and staff on temporary contracts feeling anxious in their workplace, with 13% intending to leave their employment and a further 25% stating they were looking for a new job (McKay et al., 2008). Respondents identified the impact on their health as causing stress (55%), problems/changes in sleep patterns (53%), with 40% claiming the bullying affected their concentration. The bullying also changed the respondents' (71%) outlook of the university. In addition, the university lacked a policy on how to deal with incidents of workplace bullying. According to McKay et al. (2008), respondents' reports of their incidents of workplace bullying indicated an 'unhealthy' work culture within certain sectors of the university and among some staff and students. This study concludes that workplace bullying at the XYX University is started by colleagues, superiors and students, and the impact of such behaviour goes deeper into the work environment, which can escalate further within the work setting.

Research findings from a study in the US (Spratlen, 1995) on the experiences of workplace mistreatment among a random sample of university faculty and staff revealed that 23% believed they were mistreated in their workplace. Some 38% of professional staff reported the highest incidence of abuse, with an equal number of men and women being mistreated. Both colleagues and management were alleged to be the perpetrators. In contrast, Blase and Blase (2003) conducted the first empirical study of the mistreatment of a specific group of employees by 'school principals' within the US education sector. The aim of this study was to explain and understand the 'meanings' teachers linked with being abused/mistreated by their school principals. The researchers used 'snowball sampling', whereby teachers and professors in the US introduced teachers to the study who claimed they had experienced long-term abuse (six months to nine years) by their school principals. The sample included fifty teachers (forty-nine in the US and one in Canada), five men and forty-five women from elementary (twenty-six), junior (ten) and high schools (fourteen) employed in schools with twenty-eight male principals and twenty-two female principals. This in-depth study with teachers was conducted by telephone interviews, with an initial interview outlining the research questions and follow-up interviews to investigate their experiences. Participants were requested to allow the researchers access to any reports, diaries and letters they may have had in relation to their problem.

When considering their findings, Blase and Blase (2003) divided the levels of mistreatment into three: indirect behaviours, direct behaviours and direct (severely). The indirect behaviours teachers referred to included 'discounting teachers' thoughts, needs and feelings together with isolating and abandoning teachers', with some direct forms of behaviour including 'spying, sabotaging, making unreasonable demands and criticism'. Teachers maintained some of the more severe forms of direct behaviours – where teachers maintained that principals 'intended to harm them, even destroy them' and were conscious of their actions – included 'lying, being explosive, threats and unwarranted written reprimands' (Blase and Blase, 2003, p. 6). The overall effect of this mistreatment on teachers' lives left them with feelings of 'humiliation, loneliness and injured self-esteem' plus various psychological/emotional problems and weakened their relationships with their colleagues within their schools. Thus, due to the resulting effects of the mistreatment, teachers felt unable to take action to protect themselves in such circumstances. The gender differences associated with principals' behaviours found that male principals were inclined to be more abusive both verbally and non-verbally in comparison to female principals.

In concluding, Blase and Blase (2003) state that teachers in this study were 'nice people' who fitted into the profile of the victim as outlined in the literature. Furthermore, they maintained that the majority of research on workplace bullying revealed 'abusive bosses' as the main perpetrator. This study focused on teachers' perceptions of how they were mistreated by school principals (bosses) by in-depth interviews conducted by telephone. In a follow-up quantitative study on principals' mistreatment of teachers, Blase et al. (2008) surveyed 172 American elementary, middle and high school teachers on their perception of their mistreatment by principals, the cause of such mistreatment and the harm it caused. This extensive study was conducted by an online questionnaire on the website of the National Association for the Prevention of Teacher Abuse, with 219 in-depth questions concerning the nature, extent and experience of teachers' mistreatment by principals. School-level politics was described by 61% of respondents as the reason for the mistreatment, with 34.9% reporting age and a further 24.2% teachers' gender. However, the majority of reasons reported by teachers were similar to the previous survey (2003). Furthermore, female teachers, teachers involved in unions and divorced teachers experienced more mistreatment than other teachers.

In research carried out among 315 primary school teachers at an in-service course in Turkey using a Turkish adaptation of the Einarsen and Raknes (1997) NAQ (Negative Acts Questionnaire), it was revealed that 50% of primary teachers had experienced bullying in the previous six months. On further investigation, findings determined a negative relationship existed between organisational health and the teachers' exposure to bullying (Cemaloglu, 2007). Research findings from a study using a revised harassment questionnaire on the incidence of workplace harassment among 764 primary and secondary school teachers in Croatia (Russo et al., 2008) discloses that 22.4% of teachers were exposed to harassment at least once in the previous twelve months, while 31.7% witnessed various kinds of harassment. Teachers' ratings of their relationships with personnel within their schools showed they were content with their superiors, a little less pleased with their relationships with colleagues, while least pleased with their relationships with pupils. When taking age and gender into account, younger teachers reported being subjected to harassment more than older teachers and men found some harassment behaviours (e.g., exclusion) less upsetting than women.

In the UK, a study on workplace bullying among 172 members of the Professional Association of Teachers (Edelmann and Woodall,

1997) found a high incidence rate of 18.7%. To further investigate adult–adult bullying in the teaching profession, Maguire (2001) undertook two small-scale studies among secondary school trainees, the first with a half of one full year and the second with a full year. The method involved a 'very simple' questionnaire with no reference to the duration or frequency of the bullying behaviours. Results from the first study indicated that 27% of trainees alleged they had experienced bullying behaviours in their school and 17% in their training institution. Findings from the second study revealed that 43% of trainees maintained they had experienced bullying behaviours in school, with 18% at some time in their training institution. However, in a study carried out by Sewell et al. (2009) among secondary and primary trainees aimed at comparing the findings of Maguire (2001), 12% of secondary trainees and 14% of primary trainees perceived they were subjected to bullying. Female trainees in both primary and secondary schools reported the same level of bullying, 14%, with 11% of trainee males at secondary level and 0% trainee males at primary level. The decrease in findings of Sewell et al. (2009) at secondary level may be attributed to the different methodology of the survey, which referred to specific criteria for frequency and duration in the questionnaire and semi-structured follow-up interviews with the respondents. Primary trainees were not included in the research undertaken by Maguire (2001). Other factors that may explain the gap in these figures are the awareness of workplace bullying by management during the eight years between the two surveys.

Hoel and Cooper (2000) conducted the first nationwide survey on workplace bullying in Britain (excluding Northern Ireland) to include various occupations and industrial sectors. Over 200 organisations were approached to participate, of which 70 responded, including employees in both the private and public sector and teacher unions. In total there was a response rate of 43%, which was considered high due to the sensitivity of the subject. The three sectors of employees who were in the high-risk groups included: prison service, telecommunications and school teachers. However, within a five-year period the teaching profession had the highest incidence rate of workplace bullying, with 36% being bullied in the previous five years. Furthermore, targets of bullying within the teaching profession were workers/teachers (13.5%) and senior management (16.6%). The figures are much higher when taking into account the perpetrator, with supervisor/manager 86.4% and colleague 21.2%. Some of the negative behaviours targets from the various sectors said they were most exposed to were: 'having your opinions and views ignored' (53.6%), 'someone withholding information which affects your performance' (49.9%) with 45.9% being exposed to an 'unmanageable workload'. However, the incidence of workplace bullying in the education sector continued to increase over the next five years in the UK. The education sector is reported as having the highest number of callers to the UK National Workplace Bullying Advice Line. In 2005 the Advice Line received 20% of its calls from the education sector, 12% from Health Care, 10% from Social Services and 5–6% from the Voluntary Sector (National Workplace Bullying Advice Line, UK, 2005).

The Teacher Support Network/Lewis (2008) in the UK revealed that 80% of teachers had been bullied over the previous two years. Respondents held the head teacher or a member of senior management responsible for the bullying. The Negative Acts Questionnaire-Revised (NAQ-R) was applied as a measurement tool listing behaviours connected to bullying and inquiring if respondents had ever been subjected to these types of behaviours in the workplace. Findings from this questionnaire found that:

- Bullying is significantly high among teachers in the UK.
- Bullying is often carried out by the Senior Management Team.
- Bullying has resulted in a variety of health problems and teachers off on sick leave.
- Bullying has resulted in a number of teachers leaving the profession.

(Teacher Support Network UK, 2008)

Furthermore, some participants believed they were 'excessively monitored', while many longed for their weekends and school holidays in order to be away from the environment. Several teachers maintained that the school's senior management team were bullies or permitted bullying by individuals to continue, resulting in teachers contemplating leaving their jobs or changing their careers. The most frequent types of bullying teachers were being subjected to included:

- Being given unmanageable workloads
- Having their opinions ignored
- Having information withheld from them
- Experiencing hostility
- Being persistently criticised in the course of the working day.

(Teacher Support Network UK, 2008)

In Finland, where the term 'harassment' is used, Bjorkqvist et al. (1994) developed the Work Harassment Scale (WHS) to investigate aggression among Finnish university employees. The sample population for the study included 162 males and 176 females, with 19 respondents willing to participate in interviews. Overall findings revealed that 8% stated they had experienced harassment at work during the previous twelve months, with women being harassed more than men. Exposure to harassment was experienced by 55% of women in comparison to 30% of men, with a further 32% of the participants having witnessed others being harassed while 17.8% had observed more than one incident. Envy and job rivalry were noted as reasons for the harassment; however, participants were unsure about features of both the perpetrator and the victim, with 25% referring to the sex of the victim. The effects of the harassment, according to the participants, left them feeling depressed, anxious and affected their sleep, concentration and their social standing. This study concluded that workplace harassment existed among university employees at Abo Akademi University in Finland, with harassment being more frequent among employees in service and administration positions than professors undertaking research and teaching. Furthermore, women were subjected to harassment behaviours more than men, while personality features appeared not to be important. Envy and rivalry of jobs were given as the main reasons for the harassment.

Interim research findings from an exploratory study on workplace bullying in further and higher education institutions in Wales (Lewis, 1999) revealed that 18% of respondents had been directly bullied at work with a further 22% witnessing bullying, while 21% acknowledged that bullying existed within their organisation. The method included structured interviews with personnel professionals and trade union officials, a postal survey of union members and in-depth interviews with a small number of victims/targets of workplace bullying. Respondents maintained that workplace bullying existed due to the lack of training for middle and senior management, and the abuse of the imbalance of power that was present between managers and lecturers.

WORKPLACE BULLYING AND THE IRISH EDUCATION SECTOR

A high incidence of bullying among employees in the education sector in Ireland was exposed in the first survey on workplace bullying (*Irish National Survey on Bullying in the Workplace*, 2000) undertaken by Professor Mona O'Moore, Anti-Bullying Centre, Trinity College Dublin. The effects of these behaviours have been described in O'Moore (2010). According to the findings, some of the behaviours described by victims included: 'severe criticism, devaluing of their work, humiliation by being shouted at and excessive monitoring of their work' (O'Moore, 2000, p. 9). In the Task Force Report on Workplace Bullying (TFRWB) (2001), respondents from the education sector (12.1%) maintained they were subjected to bullying in the preceding six months. Some 81.5% of respondents in this survey reported the most common form of bullying consisted of verbal abuse/insults. A further 3.3% maintained they experienced being sexually harassed. Additionally, respondents referred to being subjected to behaviours such as 'exclusion, verbal abuse/insults, sexual harassment' (TFRWB, 2001, p. 39).

Subsequently, in 2007 the ESRI conducted a survey on workplace bullying in both the private and public sectors, to include both employees and employers. This survey was comparable to the TFRWB (2001) survey. It included a questionnaire and telephone interviews with the participants, inquiring into the frequency, nature and prevalence of bullying within the Irish workplace. Findings revealed that respondents in the education sector had the second highest incident rate (14%) of workplace bullying. According to these findings, the majority of abusive behaviours reported included verbal abuse/insults (76.7%) and undermining (75.8%) and intimidation/harassment (62.5%), with sexual harassment at 4.7%. When comparing the findings to the previous TFRWB (2001) survey, figures revealed a small increase in individuals being bullied by a supervisor. However, there was a 10% increase in respondents being bullied by a single colleague.

This survey also included a similar questionnaire and interviews with employers in both the private and public sector. These included employers involved in such workplaces as construction, industry, services and distribution sectors, and public sectors to include health and education. The survey endeavoured to examine the approach and attitude of these employers in relation to workplace bullying. Since employees from the health and education sectors revealed high incident rates of workplace bullying in the TFRWB survey (2001), it was appropriate to include them in this section of this survey. A similar format as taken in the employees' survey was applied to this part of the survey. The survey incorporated questionnaires followed by telephone interviewing and resulted in a 59% response from the education sector. Over a third (33.7%) of respondents in the education sector reported that workplace bullying was a minor problem. However, a further fifth (19.6%) of this sector maintained that they had some moderate/major problems of bullying.

When addressing gender and the prevalence of workplace bullying, a high incident rate (16%) was reported in organisations employing a high proportion of females compared to organisations where the female quotient was less than a quarter, and male-only organisations. Moreover, respondents (26%) reported being bullied by a colleague, with only one in ten blaming managers. In relation to formal policies and procedures on workplace bullying within the education sector, over three-quarters of the respondents reported they were in place. According to the majority of private- and public-sector organisations, polices and procedures improved morale among employees. However, this issue also created an element of controversy. A third of respondents felt that awareness of the problem could lead to the higher reporting of incidences of bullying, and possibly false accusations.

THIS RESEARCH PROJECT

However, the aforementioned studies lacked a holistic approach to the problem within schools. In particular, there is a lack of in-depth qualitative studies with members of the teaching profession. Thus, this study endeavoured to bridge this gap, by conducting in-depth interviews with teachers/principals in four categories who volunteered through an online nationwide survey to relate their experiences in relation to workplace bullying. The interviewees in this study included teachers, school principals and deputy principals who volunteered to recount their stories on being bullied in their workplace, how some resolved the problem, how others were still working and trying to cope with the problem, as well as staff who worked in a harmonious workplace environment. The primary aim of this research study was to investigate workplace bullying among the post-primary division of the Irish education sector.

When taking into account the findings from this study, it is important to consider how complex this problem is, and the difficulty that exists worldwide in tackling the behaviours associated with the problem. Thus this study endeavoured to bridge this gap, by conducting in-depth interviews with teachers/principals in four categories who volunteered through an on-line nationwide survey to relate their experiences in relation to workplace bullying.

In order to gain access to participants for this study, an original online questionnaire was designed with the advice of the two post- primary teacher union associations, TUI (Teachers' Union of Ireland) and ASTI (Association of Secondary Teachers of Ireland) together with the director of the NAPD (National Association of Principals and Deputy Principals) Mr Clive Byrne. Following on from this questionnaire, twenty-six participants volunteered to take part in the study in the following categories:

1. Teachers/Principals who feel they are subjected to persistent bullying
2. Teachers/Principals for whom the bullying has stopped
3. Teachers/Principals who have had allegations of bullying made against them
4. Teachers/Principals who have not been subjected to workplace bullying.

Preliminary findings from the interviews with the participants revealed that workplace bullying is a serious problem that has resulted in teachers' absenteeism due to ill-health, teachers taking early retirement and, furthermore, teachers' difficulties in their attempt to resolve their problem. Moreover, workplace bullying had serious effects on their mental health, with some mentioning they had suicidal tendencies. Additionally, the financial cost of workplace bullying emerged. However, this differed to other workplaces, as here the student must be educated and thus substitute teachers were urgently employed. Therefore, while a teacher was being paid on sick leave (due to workplace bullying) another teacher was being paid to do their work.

Nevertheless, one of the major findings in this study was the gruelling battle teachers found themselves in when trying to resolve their problem. Teachers expressed how they felt they were misled by the information that was available to them from the education partners regarding agreed resolution procedures. While the infor-mation directing them to address their problem appeared on paper to be workable, when teachers moved to follow up with this material they found themselves up so many 'culs de sac'. For example, participants who maintained they were bullied by their principals felt that they were compromised if they wanted to make a complaint as their principal was secretary of their board of management. Moreover, teachers who took their complaints further found the lack of communication between the individuals involved resulted in the procedures being drawn out, in one case for over four years. The conclusion drawn from this finding is that the support system that teachers felt would help them solve their problem escalated it further. Thus, having policies and procedures in place for workplace bullying on a website is futile unless it has been proven to be effective. In essence, the study found that the approach that was designed to assist school staff who maintain they are being bullied is not only confusing, but does little to resolve the problems in an expedient manner. If anything, it often made matters worse. It is hoped that the Anti-Bullying Procedures launched by Minister Ruairi Quinn in September 2013 will also initiate a debate on school workplace bullying.

REFERENCES

Adams, A. *Bullying At Work: How to Confront and Overcome It* (London: Virago Press, 1992)

ASTI (Association of Secondary Teachers of Ireland), *Survey on Workplace Bullying* (Dublin: ASTI, 1999)

ASTI (Association of Secondary Teachers of Ireland), *ASTI Survey on Stress in Teaching* (Dublin: ASTI, 2007)

Björqkvist, K., Osterman., K. and Hjelt-Back, M. 'Aggression among University Employees', *Aggressive Behavior*, vol. 20, 1994, pp. 173–84

Blase, J. and Blase, J. *Breaking the Silence: Overcoming the Problem of Principal Mistreatment of Teachers* (Thousand Oaks, CA: Sage Publications, 2003)

Blase, J., Blase, J. and Fengning D. 'The Mistreated Teacher: A National Study', *Journal of Educational Administration*, vol. 46, no. 3, 2008, pp. 263–301

Cemaloglu, N. (2007) 'The Relationship between Organisational Health and Bullying that Teachers experience in Primary Schools in Turkey', *Educational Research Quarterly*, 37(2): 3–28

Cemaloglu, N. 'The Relationship between Organisational Health and Bullying that Teachers experience in Primary Schools in Turkey', *Educational Research Quarterly*, vol. 37, 2007

Caponecchia, C. and Wyatt. A. 'Distinguishing between Workplace Bullying, Harassment and Violence: A Risk Management Approach', *Journal of Occupational Health and Safety – Australia and New Zealand*, 25, 2009, pp. 439–49

Duncan, D.J. and Riley, D. 'Staff Bullying in Catholic Schools', *Australia & New Zealand Journal of Law & Education*, 10, 2005

Edelmann, R.J. and Woodall, L. 'Bullying at Work', *Occupational Psychologist*, 32, 1997, pp. 28–31

Einarsen, S. and Raknes, B.I. 'Harassment at Work and the Victimisation of Men', *Violence and Victims*, 12, 1997, pp. 247–63

Einarsen, S., Hoel, H., Zapf, D. and Cooper, C.L. *Bullying and Emotional Abuse in the Workplace* (London: Taylor & Francis, 2003)

Equality Authority, *Employment Equality Act* (Dublin: The Equality Authority, 2004)

Field, T. *Bully in Sight* (Didcot, Oxfordshire: Success Unlimited Publishers, 1996)

Harvey, M.G., Heames, J.T., Richey, R.G and Leonard, N. 'Bullying: From Playground to the Boardroom', *Journal of Leadership and Organizational Studies*, 12, 2006

Health and Safety Authority, *Code of Practice for Employers and Employees on the Prevention and Resolution of Bullying at Work* (Dublin: Health and Safety Authority, 2007)

Hoel, H. and Cooper, C.L. *The British Occupational Health Research Foundation*, Manchester School of Management, 2000

Hoel, H. and Cooper, C.L. (2000). *Destructive Conflict and Bullying at Work*. The British Occupational Health Research Foundation, Manchester School of Management.

INTO (Irish National Teachers' Organisation), *Survey on Workplace Bullying* (Dublin: INTO, 1998)

INTO (Irish National Teachers' Organisation), *Staff Relations: A Report on Adult Bullying in Schools* (Dublin: INTO, 2000)

INTO (Irish National Teachers' Organisation), *Stress in the Workplace* (Dublin: INTO, 2006)

Keashley, L. 'Emotional Abuse in the Workplace: Conceptual and Empirical Issues, *Journal of Emotional Abuse*, 1, 1998, pp. 85–117

Lewis, D. 'Workplace Bullying: Interim Findings of a Study in Further and Higher Education in Wales', *International Journal of Manpower*, 20, 1999, pp. 106–18

Leymann, H. 'Mobbing and Psychological Terror at Workplaces', *European Journal of Work and Organisational Psychology*, 5, 1996, pp. 165–84

Liefooge, A.P.D. and Olafsson, R. '"Scientists" and "Amateurs": Mapping the Bullying Domain', *International Journal of Manpower*, 20, 1999, pp. 39–49

McKay, R., Arnold, D.H., Fratzl, J. and Thomas, R. 'Workplace Bullying in Academia: A Canadian Study', *Journal of Employment Responsibility Rights*, 20, 2008, pp. 77–100

Maguire, M. 'Bullying and the Postgraduate Secondary School Trainee Teacher: An English Case Study', *Journal of Education for Teaching*, 27, 2001, pp. 95–109

National Bullying Helpline, http://nationalbullyinghelpline.co.uk (accessed 18 July 2013)

O'Connell, P. and Williams, J. *Report of the Taskforce on the Prevention of Workplace Bullying. Dignity At Work: The Challenge of Workplace Bullying* (Dublin: The Stationery Office, 2001)

O'Connell, P.J., Calvert, E. and Watson, D. *Bullying in the Workplace: Survey Reports, 2007. Report to the Department of Enterprise, Trade and Employment* (Dublin: ESRI (The Economic and Social Research Institute), 2007)

O'Moore, A.M. *Irish National Survey on Bullying in the Workplace* (Dublin: Anti-Bullying Centre, Trinity College, 2000)

O'Moore, A.M. and McGuire, L. *ABC Workplace Bullying* (Dublin: Anti-Bullying Centre, Trinity College, 2001)

O'Moore, A.M., Lynch, J. and Nic Daid, N. 'The Rates and Relative Risks of Workplace Bullying In Ireland, A Country of High Economic Growth', *International Journal of Management and Decision Making*, 4, 2003, pp. 82–95

O'Moore, A.M. *The Relationship between Workplace Bullying and Suicide in Ireland* (Dublin: Anti-Bullying Centre, Trinity College, 2010)

Osterman, K. *Indirect and Direct Aggression* (Oxford: Peter Lang Publications, 2010)

Rayner, C. and Hoel, H. 'A Summary Review of Literature Relating to Workplace Bullying', *Journal of Community & Applied Social Psychology*, 7, 1997, pp. 181–91

Riley, D., Duncan, D.J. and Edwards, J. 'Investigation of Staff Bullying in Australian Schools: Executive Summary (2009), http://www.schoolbullies.org.au [accessed 7 May 2013]

Richards, H. and Freeman, S. *Bullying in the Workplace: An Occupational Hazard* (Pymble, Australia: HarperCollins, 2002)

Russo, A., Mulic, R. and Mustajbegovic, J. 'Harassment in the Workplace among School Teachers: Development of a Survey', *Croatia Medical Journal*, 49, 2008, pp. 545–52

Sewell, K., Cain, T., Woodgate-Jones, A. and Srokosz, A. 'Bullying and the Postgraduate Trainee Teacher: A Comparative Study', *Journal of Education for Teaching*, 35, 2009, pp. 3–18

Spratlen, P.L. 'Interpersonal Conflict which Includes Mistreatment in a University Workplace', *Violence and Victims*, 10, 1995, pp. 285–297

Teacher Support Network, United Kingdom, *Survey on Workplace Bullying* (London: Teacher Support Network, 2008)

The Ontario Secondary School Teachers' Federation (OSSTF), The Elementary Teachers' Federation of Ontario (ETFO) and The Ontario English Catholic Teachers' Association (OECTA)(2005). *Bullying in Workplace Survey Report*. Ontario.

The Ontario Secondary School Teachers' Federation, *The Elementary Teachers' Federation of Ontario and the Ontario English Catholic Teachers' Association Bullying in the Workplace Survey Report* (2005), http://www.pdfgeni.com/book/bullying-in-the-workplace

CHAPTER ELEVEN

Teacher Aggression: An Attempt at Dialogue

Monica Monahan

I am a teacher. That is my profession. How I practise my profession is something I haven't discussed much with my fellow colleagues during twenty-two years of plying my trade. Whether I behave in a positive or negative manner while delivering subject matter has never been something I have been guided to explore throughout my journey and yet I believe now that how I behave in my classroom is the axis around which all else revolves. I understand now the gravity and magnitude of the responsibility which was bestowed upon me the day my parchment was put into my hands. This awareness, my awareness, came about as a result of a personal journey. It is time that we all, in our profession, were afforded the opportunity to take the journey to awareness … for children's sake.

In recent years there has been an academic shift towards examining and discussing the effects of negative teacher behaviour on students (Sava, 2002; Wubbles and Brekelmans, 2005; Lewis, 2000). That shift has yet to translate into tangible interventions to recognise and deal with incidents of poor teacher behaviour in the school setting. I would suggest, as a teacher myself, that presently, despite the publication of the *Report of the Commission to Inquire into Child Abuse* (2009) in the state's industrial schools and orphanages, negative teacher behaviour and practice is not a concept that the Irish second-level educational community is yet ready to openly discuss. However, in the interests of accountability and balance and as we enter an era of pro-activity and obligation in schools with regard to whole-school anti-bullying policies, child protection policies and behaviour codes, a conduit must be found through which dialogue can be initiated around this subject. I, myself, and the teaching community that I am a part of need to be facilitated towards a discussion on our behaviour in our classrooms and in the general school environment.

THE RATIONALE FOR RESEARCH

My research project explored the concept of teacher/student aggression in Irish secondary schools and the possible effects of such acts on a school community in the context of school policies on anti-bullying. I argued that acts of aggression by teachers against students are perpetrated in our schools despite the existence of the United Nations Convention on the Rights of the Child, 1989, the Teaching Council Act, 2001, the Children Act, 2001, guidelines on Child Protection for Secondary Schools as stipulated by the Department of Education and recommendations made by the *Report of the Commission to Inquire into Child Abuse* (2009). These were documents that I, as a teacher of some twenty-two years' experience, had never before been presented with, nor supported to build and underpin my practice with.

The purpose of my study which formed part of an MEd in Aggression Studies, School of Education, Trinity College Dublin (Monahan, 2010) was to establish a way to discuss teacher/student aggression through the frames of emotional and psychological abuse, to discover whether there is any dialogue on the subject between Irish teachers at school level and what supports exist for teachers and students who find themselves in this dynamic. I also explored how management might deal with such occurrences and parental experiences with school management.

WHAT THE LITERATURE SHOWS

There is evidence to suggest that teachers may be the source of violence in schools. Research literature has frequently focused on three main sources of aggression in schools: interpersonal conflicts, indiscipline and disruption.

Dupper and Meyer-Adams (2002) bring psychological maltreatment of students by teachers into the category of low-level violence in schools. They suggest that although these behaviours are profoundly damaging to students' mental health and school performance, relatively little attention has been paid to these underlying forms of violence which take place in schools every day. Whatever we decide to call this behaviour, be it teacher misbehaviour, teacher bullying, teacher emotional abuse or teacher psychological maltreatment, the aim of my research was to discover whether or not teachers could initiate dialogue around these behaviours in the context of their profession, understand the impact of such behaviours and recognise them within the frame of their teaching code of practice and child protection guidelines for second-level schools and whether there are sufficient supports in place both at school level and at higher levels to deal with such incidents. Put simply, I wanted to know if teachers talked to each other about their negative behaviours or if they understood the potential for damage to students themselves and the far-reaching effects on the whole school community, and ultimately society, by engaging in negative behaviours.

Although auditory and diagnostic tools specifically designed for schools to assess and test emotional climate with all stakeholders – the student, the teacher and the parent – exist (*School Development Plan Handbook*), the practice of measuring the school climate in terms of how the people in the organisation feel about it is an alien one to this author and, as my findings demonstrate, is an undiscovered and unused resource for school managements. It seems there is an avoidance of any dialogue in this area.

How the concept of the school as a *physical place to be* is understood is central to the interpersonal relationships that are formed within it. Conflict between any members of the school community, i.e. teachers, students or parents, can be the precursor to aggression and violence in the school environment and wider social settings. When interpersonal conflict is not resolved by dialogue or mediation, aggressive behaviour ensues (Cowie and Jennifer, 2007).

A PICTURE OF ABUSE

Over the past three decades a substantial body of research has examined various aspects of the teacher/student relationship, particularly the quality of teacher/student interaction and the effects of differential teacher treatment on students' classroom behaviour and academic performance. The concept of teacher aggression or psychological maltreatment of students as an element of this relationship has undergone very little analysis. The uses of aggressive behaviours as a form of classroom management by teachers are rarely highlighted or cause for dialogue among members of the education community at large. I felt at the outset that these behaviours when set against existing policy, statute and guidelines could be a form of emotional abuse perpetrated by the teacher against the student, even though the teacher may or may not be aware of the effects of such behaviour on their students.

> Emotional Abuse is normally to be found in the relationship between an adult and a child rather than in a specific event or pattern of events. It occurs when a child's need for affection, approval, consistency and security is not met.

(Child Protection Guidelines for Post-Primary Schools, p. 9, 2004)

Definitions of emotional abuse towards children given in the above document include:

- Persistent criticism, sarcasm, hostility or blaming;
- Where level of care is conditional on his or her behaviour;
- Unresponsiveness, inconsistent or inappropriate expectations of a child;
- Failure to provide opportunities for the child's education and development;
- Use of unrealistic or over-harsh disciplinary measures.

Barnardos defines emotional abuse as one of four abuses perpetrated against children. The three other categories are neglect, physical abuse and sexual abuse. It states that emotional abuse occurs when a child's needs for affection, approval, consistency and security are not met. Victims of emotional abuse may present as seeming fearful and distressed without obvious reason, or may display unusual behavioural problems.

Often, in schools, the recommended designated staff member to act as liaison between the school and outside agencies and who is responsible for the reporting of allegations of child abuse to health boards and An Garda Síochána is the principal of the school. Barnardos recommends that the person who is responsible for the reporting of incidents of abuse should not be the person responsible for employment issues (Barnardos, 2009).

Teachers do recognise the effects of emotional abuse in their students as academic difficulties in the classroom, higher levels of aggression, low self-esteem and lack of social interaction (Yanowitz et al., 2003). Teachers are generally accurate in their assessment of students who may be vulnerable to and suffering from emotional abuse and have been found to be quite knowledgeable with regard to the effects of emotional abuse on students yet lack the confidence to report their concerns (Cates et al., 2001). But what if the teacher is the perpetrator of the emotional abuse? The research shows that we as teachers are best placed to recognise it and yet we see emotional abuse as something that happens to a child outside our classrooms or as something that is perpetrated by someone else. How have we come to set ourselves apart and outside of the circle?

Either way, there are no tangible or specific supports in place for teachers who do perpetrate such acts – such as specific classroom anger management training – or positive behavioural management training or their student victims. I would go so far as to say that such behaviour is tolerated by school authorities as an accepted cultural norm despite recommended codes of practice and obligatory policies dealing with these areas. Emotional maltreatment or abuse in the school setting has been specifically defined (Hyman and Snook, 1999). There are subtle differences between maltreatment and abuse. Abuse implies an overt act by which the abuser intends to injure and inflict pain; maltreatment is explained as acts of omission where the perpetrator 'ignores, rejects or isolates the victim' (p. 53). Specific examples of this behaviour in the school setting include:

- Discipline and control techniques based on fear and intimidation;
- Low quantity of human interaction in which teachers communicate lack of interest, caring, or affection for students through ignoring, isolation and rejection;
- Limited opportunities for students to develop adequate skills and feelings of self-worth;
- Encouragement to be dependent and subservient, especially in areas where students are capable of making independent judgements;
- Motivational techniques for performance that are overly critical, excessively demanding, unreasonable, and ignore children's ages and abilities;
- Denial of opportunities for healthy risk-taking such as exploring ideas that are not conventional and approved of by the teacher;
- Verbal assaults including the use of sarcasm, ridicule, humiliation and denigration;
- Scapegoating and bullying;
- Failure to intervene when students are teased, bullied and scapegoated by peers.

Hyman and Snook (1999) suggest that practices that constitute emotional maltreatment and abuse are in conflict with the legal and moral obligations of the school in which these acts are perpetrated. They have found, through collecting data using psychometric measurement they devised known as the My Worst School Experience Scale, that between 50 and 60% of citizens vividly remember an 'act by an educator that was abusive enough to implant a vivid memory' (p. 55). This scale measures the effects of all types of school abuses. Through administrating it, 105 symptoms related to all types of maltreatment in schools have been identified. As incidents of abuse are recalled by victims, it is likely that the negative emotions experienced at that time will be re-activated. There were 1 to 2% of victims who developed post-traumatic stress disorder as a result. A large percentage of student victims of educator abuse will develop angry and aggressive responses, re-inflicting their pain on fellow students and their teachers, their misbehaviour having been created by the school as the source. A child who has been abused at school may develop symptoms such as depression or withdrawal and a desire to avoid the abuser in school, oppositional and defiant behaviour, suspicion and hyper-vigilance and alertness for fear of being further abused by the perpetrator.

They also suggest that emotional maltreatment in schools is widespread and at the core of *all other abuses* and that failure by the education community as a whole to recognise this problem lies in a fear of a potential flood of litigation and claims against schools once students and parents become sufficiently aware of its existence and effects. At present school managers could be perceived as reluctant to help in the determining of guilt of a teacher. Those within the school community who are aware of the perpetration of such acts may be reluctant to come forward as a result of political pressure or fears for their own employment if they publicly admit that a colleague is abusive.

THE TEACHER AND THE FRAME FOR POSITIVE PRACTICE

Current Irish educational practice recommends the devising of whole-school anti-bullying policies (see Chapters 12 and 14). Such policies encompass all members of the school community. A teacher's behaviour should be central to any anti-bullying policies and yet there exists a flawed rationale for punishing students for perpetrating aggressive acts against each other while their teachers engage in aggressive acts towards students. Acceptance without question of teacher aggression towards students will undermine any effort to address peer-to-peer aggression. Allied with this, the teacher may also be teaching students the components of aggressive behaviour by modelling it, which is then perpetrated by peer-to peer.

As has been presented, there are a number of guidelines, codes and legal acts which have been put in place to protect children and guide those who work with them. For teachers, the problem lies in the lack of specific enforcement in areas such as psychological maltreatment, emotional abuse and aggression. The code of professional conduct as presented by the Teaching Council of Ireland stipulates the following under section 7(2) (b):

- Teachers should take care of the students under their supervision with the aim of ensuring their safety and welfare.
- Teachers should uphold the reputation and standing of the profession. They should act with honesty and integrity in all aspects of their work.

The Teaching Council also stipulates that teachers should respect students, parents, colleagues, school management, co-professionals and all in the school community. They should interact with them in a way that does not discriminate and that promotes equality in relation to gender, marital status, family status, sexual orientation, religion, age, disability, race, ethnicity, membership of the Travelling community and socio-economic status. They also suggest that in 'recognising the unique and privileged relationships that exist between teachers and the students entrusted to their care, teachers should conduct these relationships in a way that is professional, respectful and appropriate'.

The Teaching Council Act (2001), part five, section 41, Fitness to Teach, identifies the following as teacher professional misconduct:

(a) engaging in conduct which is contrary to the code of pro-fessional conduct established by the Council under section 7(2) (b);
(b) engaging in any improper conduct in his or her professional capacity or otherwise by which reason of which she is unfit to teach.

Section 42 stipulates that the Teaching Council or any person may apply to the Investigating Committee for an inquiry into the fitness to teach of a registered teacher on the following grounds:

(a) He or she has failed to comply with, or has contravened any provision of, this Act, the Education Act, 1998, the Education Welfare Act, 2000, the Vocational Education Acts, 1930 to 1999, or any regulations, rules or orders made under those Acts;

(b) His or her behaviour constitutes professional misconduct;

(c) His or her registration is erroneous due to a false or fraudulent declaration or misrepresentation;

(d) He or she is medically unfit to teach.

The Department of Education and Skills handed over responsibility for the enforcement of Section 42 of the Teaching Act to the Teaching Council in 2006. As of yet the Teaching Council of Ireland has not dealt with a single claim of professional misconduct by any person due to the failure as of yet to agree terms of reference for the Investigating Committee (Section 27) or the Disciplinary Committee (Section 28) as required by the Teaching Council Act, Part 5. These committees would provide the procedural framework through which claims of professional misconduct will be processed. The Teaching Council Act was made statute in 2001 and since then the Council has been negotiating terms of reference with the relevant partners in which the two committees can operate. In the interim, DES circulars 59/2009 (Post-Primary) and 60/2009 (Primary) set out procedures drawn up under Section 24 of the Education Act (1998) and these are the key instruments available to Boards of Management.

CHILDREN ARE STILL VULNERABLE

Currently our children are protected in our schools by the United Nations Convention on the Rights of the Child, 1989, the Children Act 2001, the Education Act, 1998 and safe practice is also supported by guidelines produced by the Department of Health and Children in their Children First programmes and 'Our Duty to Care' document. Whether these statutes and guidelines are central to our practice as secondary school teachers depends on a willingness by management and all its supporting bodies to make them so.

TEACHERS AND THE INEVITABLE STRESS

Aggressive behaviour by teachers has been linked with stress (Kyraciou and Sutcliff, 1978; Maslach and Jackson, 1981). UK studies have found that one-third of teachers surveyed found their jobs stressful, with interacting with students listed as the most common factor that causes stress in the daily work of teachers (Brown et al., 2002). From an Irish perspective, 50% of retiring teachers do so on disability grounds due to work-associated stress, depression and anxiety (ASTI, 2008).

Teachers who suffer from stress can affect how students behave in the classroom and stressed teachers' behaviour can influence problem behaviours in their students (Geving, 2007). Teachers openly displaying lack of regard for school policy, interrupting a student when they are talking and generally displaying behaviours that school behavioural codes encourage students not to display, tend to result in students behaving aggressively towards school property, criticising school policy and behaving disrespectfully towards teachers. Teacher stress emanating from interaction with students can result in a strained, competitive, quarrelsome and sullen atmosphere in the classroom (Vartia, 1996), leaving the way open for repeated acts of stress-induced aggression by the teacher towards the student.

Do stressed teachers become perpetrators of bullying behaviour/abuse? The effects of bullying or abuse at school have been well documented. Survivors of school bullying have been found to suffer similar long-term effects to those experienced by survivors of child abuse (Carlisle and Rofes, 2007). The correlations between the effects of child abuse and bullying can be further reinforced as perpetrators of both rely on 'superior power to violate the child's psychological and sometimes physical integrity' (p. 23). Are some teachers a superior power in their classrooms? Is this power abused? It has been suggested that both forms of abuse exist as a result of the passivity or collusion of adults. Victims in both situations retain a deep sense of anger at the adults in their lives for failing to recognise the abuse and intervene to protect them (Lisak, 1994). Is it the teachers' lack of awareness of what defines these behaviours in their own practice that allows passivity and collusion? Teachers can induce conflictual, aggressive attitudes in their students (Wubbles et al., 2005); when teachers use hostile attitudes and negative methods or misbehave to control a class they teach aggression, and such methods are at present culturally acceptable and unquestioned (Sava, 2002).

The education sector in Ireland has nearly double the national average of reported incidents of bullying in the workplace (ESRI, 2007). In a survey of Irish secondary school teachers by the Association of Secondary Teachers of Ireland in 2007, 61% of those surveyed felt that they had experienced workplace bullying in the course of their careers. Many general comments in this survey allude to bullying by colleagues, students and parents, yet 0% of these teachers see themselves as capable of bullying behaviours. Teachers believe they are bullied but are not bullies, but if teachers are bullying teachers, why would they modify their behaviour when they enter their classrooms? The causal factors of teachers' bullying behaviours may be stress; stressed teachers could then present in their classrooms as hostile to students. Are teachers modelling the wrong behaviours? For more detail on teacher bullying, see Chapters 8, 9 and 10.

THE TEACHER/STUDENT RELATIONSHIP AND TEACHER MISBEHAVIOUR

Riley (2002) suggests that for learning to take place students must be in a healthy, constantly developing relationship with their teachers. He suggests that many students find themselves in unhealthy, toxic classroom settings as a result of unhealthy relationships with their teachers.

Hyman and Perone (1998) refer to victimisation of students by teachers under the guise of discipline. He defines this victimisation as verbal maltreatment, which data suggests the majority of students have witnessed or experienced at some time. There is also evidence to suggest that peer perceptions of the teacher/student relationship based on teacher/student interaction can affect peer inferences with regard to students' likeability and positive or negative attributes (Hughes et al., 2001). They suggest that a conflictual teacher/student relationship has a negative influence on the student-to-student relationship and that students use information they gather on the quality of the teacher/student relationship to guide social choices and perhaps to then justify engaging in bullying behaviour towards another student. Furthermore, it has been found that teacher preference and peer rejection may predict student aggression (Mercer and De Rosier, 2008). Low preference of a student by a teacher has been found to influence peer rejection. It has also been found that teacher preference may influence a student's emotional adjustment and that daily conflict with the teacher is related to higher levels of anxiety in students (Barrett and Heubeck, 2000).

Psychological maltreatment of students by teachers has been categorised as low-level violence (Dupper and Meyer-Adams, 2002). Humphries (1998) takes a softer approach to the same problem in a discussion on the concept of school discipline and focuses on the rights of the victim of ill-discipline in tandem with the identification of the underlying causes of the aggressive behaviour by the perpetrator. He states that when discipline is used to control others it will not succeed; furthermore, he posits that teachers who use authoritarian and aggressive classroom management methods such as dominating, cynical, sarcastic or manipulative behaviours are 'attempting to fight fire with fire and are being abusive' (p. 10). He believes that this results in a teacher-induced cycle of violence. Humphries identifies ill-disciplined behaviour, which could also be defined as misbehaviour, as an attempt by the perpetrator to fulfil unmet needs.

The educational drawbacks and emotional fallout from the use of coercive teaching methods can account for low-quality educational student experiences (Glasser, 1998). Coercive teaching can be theorised as a need for control by the teacher. Glasser posits that even when the need for control is exercised by threatening behaviour, it is rarely successful as the subject of the threat will ultimately choose their own behavioural response. Glasser identifies personal criticism as the most destructive of coercive classroom management practices, which induces anger and often results in attack.

Lewis (2000) describes the problem of teacher misbehaviour as persistent and relatively unexplored. He conceptualises teacher misbehaviour as a response to the integral stress of their profession and cites it as a possible cause of poor educational, somatic and emotional outcomes for students as they become resentful and disengaged from the subject taught by a misbehaving teacher. Stress caused to students during incidents of teacher misbehaviour includes fear responses such as increased arousal and anxiety to fear/flight/ freeze.

> Unfortunately, researchers often tend to overlook teachers as a potential source of problems in the classroom.
>
> (Sava, 2002)

There are terms that have been used by researchers to describe forms of teacher/student aggression, such as teacher misbehaviour, teacher maltreatment and lack of teacher support (Sava, 2002). Consequences of these behaviours in students have been identified as 'lack of self-esteem, anxiety, asthenia, school phobia, conduct disorders and learning difficulties' (p. 10).

Thornberg (2008) sees 'the lack of a common ethical language and knowledge of relevant theories and research in educational and behavioural sciences' (p. 1796) as an impediment to teachers' professional development. He proposes that teachers should have specific training and develop skills in the areas of conflict management, bullying and bullying prevention, moral development, aggression, social influence, ethics and citizenship in addition to knowledge and skills in their own subject areas. He posits that lack of these *essential* skills explains reactive and unplanned teacher behaviour where teachers not in possession of professional behavioural management tools are left to their own, sometimes dysfunctional, resources.

THE RESEARCH

The aim of my research was to initiate dialogue around the problem of teacher/student aggression and emotional and psychological abuse. The hypotheses of the study were that aggressive classroom management techniques may be used by some teachers and that support and intervention are required at school level for teachers to find alternative ways to manage incidents of student misbehaviour in the classroom and also delivery of curricular material. The research was broken into two phases: Phase 1 – a quantitative and qualitative questionnaire for teachers followed by interviews with principals of the schools in which I circulated the questionnaire, and Phase 2 – a series of focus group discussions and interviews with students, teachers and parents.

Phase 1

Sudman and Bradburn (1982) highlight the difficulty of dealing with sensitive issues in questionnaires. I felt that a themed questionnaire for teachers designed around the sensitive issue of teacher aggression/misbehaviour, while providing anonymity to the respondent, would elicit and facilitate responses to sensitive issues. Sudman and Bradburn (1982) address a number of important considerations for researchers when addressing issues which respondents may find threatening or uncomfortable, such as providing open-ended questions to elicit information about socially undesirable behaviour, mixing long and short questions together to elicit information of frequency and using familiar colloquial terms to describe behaviours. The use of data gathered from other informants should be used to frame questions.

I secured the permission of Dr Ramon Lewis, an Associate Professor in La Trobe University Institute of Education, Bundoora, Melbourne, Australia, to use a questionnaire which he authored and employed in his most recent studies into classroom discipline and teacher misbehaviour (Lewis et al., 2008). The questionnaire was designed using data collected from over 5,000 students in three countries who it was found felt that their teachers sometimes yell at them in anger, embarrass them, use sarcasm and punish the whole class as a method to manage student misbehaviour. This research has been published in chapter form in the *International Handbook of Research on Teaching and Teachers* [2009]. The questionnaire is both quantitative and qualitative and allows for participants to reflect on teacher practice and express in words their own version of events in their classrooms and what they may observe in their colleagues' classrooms in addition to answering questions by using five- or six-point Likert scales which will provide a range of responses. Cohen et al. (2000) support the use of rating scales to collect research data as opportunities are created for the respondent to provide a flexible response 'with the ability to determine frequencies, correlations and other forms of quantitative analysis' (p. 253).

The questionnaire consists of seven sections numbered A to G respectively. Sections A, C, D and G are quantitatively designed. Three secondary schools were selected by the researcher as settings to administer questionnaires and conduct structured interviews with the principals of each school. School A was a secondary school for boys with 430 students and 29 teachers (11 male and 18 female). School B was a secondary school for girls with 510 students and 31 teachers (7 male and 24 female).

Kvale (1996) marks the use of the interview, as a move away from research data, as being external to individuals. The purpose of the interview between the principals of the three selected schools in this research was to test the hypothesis that teacher aggression is not discussed at school level between teachers themselves or their principals. A list of questions were drawn up based on the themes central to the questionnaire previously given to the teachers in each school. Lincoln and Guba (1985) suggest that the structured interview is useful when the researcher is searching for knowledge and frames questions that will provide such. The researcher structured questions with regard to the concept of dialogue between the principal and his/her staff around the subject of teacher stress. Questions were also asked with regard to the schools' complaints procedures and the fielding of complaints by students and parents with regard to possible teacher aggression. In an attempt to gauge whether there was an understanding of the concepts of emotional and psychological abuse within the school environment, a number of questions were asked with regard to the schools' anti-bullying structures, the Teaching Council Act and child protection measures at school level. Permission was sought by the researcher to record the interviews with a dictaphone. Principals from Schools A and C gave permission for recording. The principal of School B did not wish to have the interview recorded or notes taken by the researcher. The researcher made notes on this interview immediately after it took place.

Phase 2

Cohen et al. (2000) suggest the use of focus groups to triangulate with the more traditional forms of data collection methods such as interviewing and questionnaires. Therefore as phase 2 of the research, it was decided to conduct two separate focus groups with students and teachers and interviews with two individual parents who had contacted the researcher at the outset of the project. Requests were made to interview the Minister for Education and the Children's Ombudsman, but these requests did not come to fruition.

Cohen et al. (2000) suggest that focus groups are a form of group interview with reliance on the interaction within the group who discuss a topic supplied by the researcher and posit that 'sampling is the major key to the success of focus groups' (p. 289). The data emerges from the interaction of the group. Morgan (1998) advocates the use of focus groups to generate hypotheses that emerge from the insights and data within the group. The researcher made the decision to conduct a focus group with students in order to make the experience less intimidating than individual interviews. Lewis (2000) advocates the use of group interviewing or focus groups with children as a more efficient way to elicit genuine responses from children than individual interviews. Nine students comprised the group, with four girls and five boys. The average age of each student was 16 years and the group was heterogenous, encompassing students from single-parent families, the Travelling community and students with learning difficulties.

Five teachers participated in the teachers' focus group discussion. Each participant was given a selection of stories which the students had told in their own focus group along with a selection of information with regard to the Teachers' Code of Practice, Child Protection Guidelines for Secondary Schools and guidelines for any persons dealing with children from Barnardos (2009). I had been previously contacted by a number of parents concerned with aspects of teacher behaviour in their children's schools. I interviewed two of these parents.

The very sensitive theme of this research project was, in itself, a limitation and obstacle. It was anticipated that there would be a low number of teachers willing to engage in research that may throw up negative aspects of their practice. To the contrary, I found parents and students were more than eager to participate.

Findings: Phase 1 – teacher survey and principal interviews

In the literature review attention was drawn to the fact that one-third of all teachers surveyed in a UK study found their job stressful or extremely stressful (Brown et al., 2002). It was also noted in the literature review that teacher stress has been defined as a 'situation where a response syndrome of negative effects such as anger and depression results from a teacher's job' (Kyriacou and Sutcliff, 1978). With this in mind, it appears that a large number of the teachers surveyed in this research project are suffering from stress, describing feelings of frustration, fear, anger, lack of understanding, exasperation, desperation, lack of confidence and insecurity. Geving (2007) suggests that teachers who suffer from stress affect how students behave in the classroom, influencing problem student behaviour. When asked in the questionnaire why teachers use techniques such as yelling, sarcasm, deliberately embarrassing and punishing the class as a whole, many teachers cited frustration and exhaustion as reasons, along with feelings of exasperation, lack of control and lack of confidence. The most frequently mentioned source of stress in Geving's study was student misbehaviour and poor working environment. On analysis of the data it seems teachers are using these techniques as a response to the stress caused by what they perceive as student misbehaviour and their working environments and in effect, as the literature demonstrates, are creating a cycle of misbehaviour between themselves and the student. Not only will this cycle repeat itself within the classroom, if one applies Geving's theory on the concept of negative teacher actions and their influence on student misbehaviour, students will then tend to behave aggressively towards school property and be disrespectful towards other teachers. Is this evidence of a teacher-induced cycle of aggression, albeit unintentionally initiated by stressed teachers who have not been supported professionally to recognise it? The researcher suggests it is.

Further evidence of negativity within the classroom, which the author feels reinforces the suggestion above, is obvious in responses where teachers are asked why they can be unwilling to notice difficult students behaving well and can be reluctant to talk to difficult students. Respondents cite time constraints, lack of energy, large classes and syllabus pressure as reasons for this unwillingness, giving a lens into less than healthy working environments. Furthermore, teacher stress emanating from interaction with students results in strained, competitive and sullen atmospheres in the classroom (Vartia, 1996); teachers wrote that they felt intimidated, insecure and threatened in their classrooms, which Vartia has found leaves the way open for repeated acts of stress-induced aggression by the teacher towards the student.

Teachers wrote of feeling angry, expecting the worst in their classrooms, bearing grudges and not understanding their students' behaviour, of fearing conflict and not being trained properly to deal with difficult situations. By some, teaching has been conceptionalised as a behaviour displayed in the presence of someone else, with messages passed from teacher to student. How the message is imparted and received is central to effective teaching (Wubbles and Brekelmans, 2005). Are these the teachers Wubbles and Brekelman describe as uncertain and aggressive with low student achievement in their classrooms? Teachers also wrote of not valuing misbehaving students, being suspicious of improvements and of feeling that being nice was giving in to misbehaving students. Could this behaviour be described as Wubbles and Brekelman's drudging, uncertain and aggressive teachers whose students had the worst attitude towards that teacher's subject? If so, data again supports the researcher's view that some Irish teachers are trapped in self-induced cycles of negativity and aggression in their classrooms which are then mirrored by the student. The bearing of grudges and negative judgements of some students that some teachers wrote of may also effect peer perceptions of those students, influencing their likeability and having a negative influence over the student-to-student relationship, often resulting in students engaging in bullying behaviour of those they perceive to be disliked by their teacher (Hughes et al., 2001) and so the cycle continues.

Teachers admit that 'embarrassment works well in dangerous situations', 'deliberate embarrassment stops misbehaviour', 'punishing the class as a whole makes the whole class behave', 'putting responsibility on the whole class makes every student behave', 'yelling is effective as a last resort'.

Can one define the behaviours that teachers admit to in the teacher questionnaire as acts of aggression? Can one define these teachers' use of sarcasm, yelling at students, deliberately embarrassing students and punishing the class as a whole as bullying behaviours? Certainly these behaviours, when viewed in the context of 'Principles of Good Practice' for those working with children – as defined by the Department of Health and Children as being obliged to eliminate as far as possible any threatening violent or degrading behaviour, treating children with dignity and respect and never favouring one child over another – appear not to be in line with such obligations. Furthermore, among the definitions the Department of Health and Children define as acts of child abuse are verbal abuse such as sarcasm, destructive criticism and derogatory remarks and bullying behaviour such as teasing, taunting and threatening. Carlisle and Rofes (2007) highlight a resistance among the school community to classify bullying behaviour as abuse. It could be suggested here that therein lies the reason why it seems the behaviours that teachers describe are absent from dialogue and are, as Sava (2002) suggests, culturally acceptable and unquestioned. Recognition implies condemnation, passivity and collusion.

Teachers write of a need for support from both management and colleagues and of a need for adherence to policies and procedures. A need is also expressed for training or professional development in how to deal with difficult students supporting the view held by O'Moore and Minton (2006a) that teachers are relied upon to deal with problems that society as a whole has yet to deal with effectively. Solutions suggested, such as 'counselling for teachers', 'a sympathetic and uncritical ear' 'support to express anger healthily' and a practice of 'staff comforting each other', imply that teachers need greater professional support with regard to difficult situations in the classroom. It seems teachers need to be supported to initiate dialogue with regard to difficulties in the classroom. Suggestions such as 'developing a positive school ethos where emphasis is put on the quality of relationships', 'teachers modelling good behaviour and being good role models', 'respect for the worth of the student' and 'mediation between student and teacher' demonstrate an understanding of the value of positive interpersonal relationships within the school context, the importance of the rights of the child and positive, mentally healthy methods of resolving conflicts within the school community; opportunities for sharing such understanding with the greater school community should be provided.

Statements from teachers such as 'administration don't care' and 'poor support from management' mirror comments alluding to lack of managerial support in the ASTI 2007 workplace bullying survey, and seem to be thematic in both questionnaire responses and later in the teacher focus group discussion.

Data collected from interviews with principals in Schools A, B and C display a different picture from a principal's perspective. Principal of School A felt supported by his staff and had never been approached by a member of his staff to discuss feeling stressed, though admitted that it was possible that teachers felt that they could not discuss their feelings of stress. Principal B also felt supported in her role but felt that teachers were unaccustomed to discussing negative practice induced by stress. Principal C did not feel supported in his role and had never been approached by a member of his staff to discuss their feelings of stress, and yet teachers from all three schools write of feeling stressed and unsupported by management. Could this demonstrate an absence of dialogue among the school community surrounding these issues that eventually leads to teacher/student aggression and teacher burnout? (O'Moore and Minton, 2006b; Cowie and Jennifer, 2007). Teachers express a lack of managerial support in the teacher questionnaire but for some reason they feel unable to express this to their principals. According to all three principals, students rarely complain of being treated badly by teachers, parents rarely complain of teacher behaviour and yet clear evidence of negative teacher behaviour has been furnished by teachers themselves in their responses to the questionnaire, with further evidence of questionable teacher behaviour in the data collected at the student focus group. According to all three principals, none of their schools have a written complaints procedure to service the school community, nor is there a practice of logging complaints. Could this anomaly further reinforce the possible existence of a cultural acceptance of negative teacher methodology and resistance of school communities to recognise a problem due to fears of litigation and injury claims (Hyman and Snook, 1999; Sava, 2002)?

Principal A admitted that teachers can bully students but may not be aware of it and has never come across a case of emotional abuse by a teacher, and yet definitions of emotional abuse include sarcasm, hostility, use of over-harsh or unreasonable disciplinary measures, verbal assaults, scapegoating and bullying, humiliation and denigration (Hyman and Snook, 1999; Child Protection Guidelines for Post-Primary Schools, 2004; Barnardos, 2009). These behaviours have been described and admitted to by teachers in their responses to questionnaire sections B, E and F. Is Principal A unaware of these guidelines, as it seems are the majority of teachers surveyed, or is this an example of, as one teacher in their response to section E put it, 'a climate of the teacher feeling they are always right'? Principal A suggested that when there are issues between a student and teacher, 'in most cases the teacher is correct'. Is this another example of cultural acceptance of teacher misbehaviour? Not one of School A, B or C has a ratified child protection policy, though, at the time of interview School A was preparing for a whole-school inspection and had been asked by Department of Education inspectors for same. On a more positive note, all principals said that when students come to them with complaints, they enter into a practice of discussing such issues with the teachers under question. All principals said that they did not let aggressive situations between a student and a teacher escalate and would intervene immediately.

Findings: Phase 2 – student focus group, teacher focus group and parent interviews

All students who took part in the focus group discussion agreed that students 'mess' deliberately in class and that teachers can be annoyed deliberately by students. There was an assertion that these behaviours arose more frequently in classes taken by substitute teachers or teachers undertaking teaching practice. How teachers are dealing with this 'messing' seems to be central to whether these situations descend into an aggressive spiral or an opportunity to focus on positive behaviours within the school community. In the literature, older, very experienced teachers over 45 years of age and inexperienced teachers have been discussed as a possible source of classroom disorder and poor classroom management. Older, very experienced teachers and beginning teachers were found to have the worst relationships with their students (Wubbels and Brekelsman, 2005). This may explain why students in the focus group discussion decide to misbehave in such classes, as beginning teachers and student teachers may have unrealistic ideals with regard to classroom management due to lack of practical experience and which students recognise as an opportunity for a bit of 'fun'. Students spoke of enjoying the class and having fun when the teacher lost control. Watzlawick (1967), and Wubbles and Levy (1993) describe a form of aggressive disorder which eventuates as the teacher tries to regain control in a teacher-led opponent-style interaction, resulting in negative behaviours by students such as snatching each other's books, laughing and shouting out loud, unsanctioned moving around the classroom and hitting each other. Is this the fun that the focus group describes?

It is the author's assertion that the majority of teachers at some time in their careers have either experienced this scenario within their own classrooms or heard a commotion coming from a colleague's room. Perhaps if we were guided to a professional discovery of the eventual negative fallout of such situations, teachers would be more willing to make critical interventions in a supportive way, thus arresting the cycle of teacher/student aggression referred to in previous paragraphs and evidenced in the story of Brian, told at the focus group discussion. The incident described ended in an adversarial interaction with the teacher becoming aggressive and Brian harbouring a deep ill will towards the teacher involved. Brian describes himself as feeling like he wanted to 'get' the teacher after the interaction. Brian admits that he brought his feelings of anger home and inflicted them on his siblings. Comments offered in the student focus group such as 'unfairness makes students want to get the teacher' and 'being picked on makes the student have an attitude that will spread' alongside Brian's story seem to be in keeping with the literature and thus may be examples of the teacher-induced cycle of aggression that is thematic in the first part of this chapter.

Furthermore, the students describe their best classes as the classes that they can have 'fun' in and learn at the same time, reinforcing the findings in the study referenced that students distinguish good and bad teachers by the amount of friendly and understanding behaviour they display. Are these the teachers the students describe as 'nice' and 'not nice'? Students in the focus group felt that it was only the 'odd' time that teachers were part of the 'fun'.

Is the conflict that eventuates between Brian and the teacher in question symptomatic of a negative school climate (Freiberg, 1999)? If Freiberg's suggestion that listening to teachers' and students' stories of their school experiences can help to form a picture of the school climate and health of the learning environment could be applied to Brian's story, the listener is given an insight into a situation which becomes unsafe and unhealthy both physically and psychologically not only for Brian but for all those within earshot of the ensuing interaction between them. There are raised voices, signs of aggression and loss of control on the part of the teacher. Brian feels humiliated in front of other students as the teacher responds to Brian's misbehaviour in another teacher's class by shouting at him, calling him names, detaining him in his room while he proceeds to take another class and making derogatory comments with regard to Brian's marks in other subjects in front of this class. Brian asks the teacher what business his marks are to him as he doesn't teach Brian, at which point Brian describes the teacher as putting his face too close to Brian's while shouting at him that he has undermined the teacher's authority.

Principals of the schools (A, B and C) report that they never allow situations to escalate. Teachers in the focus group discussion say that difficult situations should not be allowed to escalate. Who intervened to de-escalate the situation and arrest the negative cycle in Brian's case? Could the conflict between Brian and the teacher be a lost chance for management to reflect on the impact of this incident on the health of the whole school environment and effect change? Would the focus group suggestion of a floating teacher, whose role would be to step into situations like this, be a possible answer? Brian felt his rights were violated (Humphries, 1998) and felt aggrieved at the principal's insistence that an apology to the teacher in question would remedy the situation as Brian felt the teacher misbehaved also and that he himself deserved an apology. Brian was given a three-day suspension from school and tells the focus group that he will never apologise to the teacher. In this situation no adult seems to have displayed the care that Freiberg cites is necessary to overcome the problem of negative aspects of a school climate. Is this indicative of the type of school climate that Freiberg describes as a 'risk factor' in the lives of those who work and learn there? Is this another example of the cultural acceptance of negative teacher behaviour discussed in the opening paragraphs of this chapter? Is the legacy of this incident more aggression as Brian remains resentful at the way he felt he was treated (Glasser, 1998)?

Brian admitted to misbehaviour on his part with regard to the incident but felt his rights were violated by the teacher. Of the nine students who took part in the focus group discussion, none were familiar with the United Nations Convention on the Rights of the

Child (1989). Students who took part in the focus group discussion felt that if a student stood up for their rights in situations in which they feel they are being treated unfairly by a teacher, they would be in 'more trouble' with the teacher, that they sometimes felt powerless when they felt they were being treated unfairly by a teacher and that if their parents complained they would be 'picked on' more by the teacher in question. The students spoke of sometimes feeling degraded by teachers and subject to unsuitable punishments such as being made scrape chewing gum off desks. Comments were also made such as 'some teachers pick on students all the time', and with reference to the techniques examined in the teacher questionnaire such as sarcasm, yelling, punishing the class as a whole and deliberately embarrassing students in Phase 1 of the research, they felt that 'teachers do use the techniques' and that student misbehaviour doesn't have to be bad for teachers to use them.

Stacey's and Mary's stories are harrowing. Both students describe their fear of specific teachers and scenarios which are painful to listen to. At times Mary describes herself as having difficulty with a particular subject and feeling so stressed at the prospect of attending this teacher's class that she sometimes doesn't come to school. She describes the teacher as ridiculing her when she doesn't know the answer to a question by calling her 'stupid' and asking her 'has she no brains'. Mary says this is played out in front of the class on a continuous basis. Mary doesn't want her parents to intervene because she feels the teacher will pick on her more.

Stacey describes being humiliated by teachers because she is a member of the Travelling community. She speaks of times when she sits in class and derogatory discussions about Travellers are initiated by the teacher. She describes being called names by teachers and of being ridiculed by students in front of teachers without any intervention from those teachers. She feels frightened by one teacher in particular who has shouted into her face and, like Mary, sometimes stays out of school because of the way she feels.

Have these students' rights been violated (Humphries, 1998)? Have they been subjected to unlawful attacks on their honour (Article 16.1, United Nations Convention on the Rights of the Child)? Have all appropriate administrative, social and educational measures been taken to protect them from all forms of mental violence (Article 19.1, United Nations Convention on the Rights of the Child)? Has school discipline been administered in a manner consistent with the child's human dignity (Article 28.2, United Nations Convention on the Rights of the Child)?

Are these teachers misbehaving (Humphries, 1998; Lewis, 2000)? Could these teachers' behaviours be the indiscipline/misbehaviour Humphries (1998) describes as shouting at students, cynicism and sarcasm as a means to control, etc? Brian's teacher has engaged in aggressive actions and has caused embarrassment and humiliation to a student (Van Morrow, 1991). Mary is afraid to attend a particular teacher's class because of the difficulties she has with the subject and the way the teacher humiliates and embarrasses her (Sava, 2002). Stacey has felt intimidated by teachers and is afraid because she is a Traveller. Is this student victimisation under the guise of discipline (Hyman and Perone, 1998)?

Are these stories indicative of a negative school climate (Freiberg, 1999)? Are they examples of a cultural acceptance of poor teacher behaviour (Hyman and Snook, 1999; Sava, 2001)? Have these students been emotionally abused (The Children Act, 2001; Our Duty to Care: Child Protection Guidelines for Post-Primary Schools, 2004; Barnardos, 2009)? Are these teachers stressed (Vartia, 1996; Kyriacou and Sutcliffe, 1978; Brown et al., 2002; Geving, 2007)?

The students in the focus group felt that teachers should be calm before dealing with situations like Brian's. They also felt that teachers could get away with anything, always get the last word and that principals will always support the teacher before the student. They suggested that teachers should be given feedback on their behaviour and that a mediator should be brought in to listen to both sides of student/teacher conflict so that situations could be resolved fairly. Who listens? Who decides? Who cares?

McEvoy (2000) suggests that in most schools teachers agree on which of their colleagues are abusive towards students. Teachers who took part in the focus group felt that there was a code of silence among teachers when it came to discussing poor practice and that some teachers may feel defensive if they are asked to discuss their practice. There was also a consensus that teachers have no way of discussing practices they observe by other colleagues which are of concern to them. It was suggested that perhaps teachers 'don't like' discussing their difficulties. Could this be a cultural trend within the profession? One teacher suggested that perhaps the school culture itself influenced a teacher's practice. Barth (2002) suggests that school culture does indeed 'dictate in no uncertain terms "the way we do things around here"' (p. 6). It seems that we do, as a profession, need to be helped to initiate dialogue around our difficulties without fear of feeling we have failed or that we are suggesting someone else has. A cultural norm of expressing our concerns with regard to our own difficulties and those of our colleagues needs to be nurtured, subsequent to initiating an awareness among teachers and management with regard to our ability to create and feed aggressive cycles in our schools.

One teacher suggested that teachers should be able to see beyond difficult student behaviour; however, this statement is subjective in nature. Not all teachers perceive difficulties in the same way. Despite the existence of school behavioural codes defining difficult and challenging behaviour, a teacher's view of breaches of discipline and their methodology in dealing with breaches will differ from classroom to classroom. As the literature shows, teachers can view discipline as a method of control with teacher-instigated behavioural norms and associated rules or it can be viewed as a method of training students in a way that fosters positive values (Munn, 1999). However, the problem that arises when teachers establish their own behavioural norms and positive values in their classrooms is that as teachers we are not trained in how to establish common values and therefore use our own frames of reference such as childhood and adult-life experiences to do so (Thornberg, 2008). The teacher with particularly aggressive frames of reference from life may expose the student to problematic interpretations of value systems. Is this what one of the teachers in the focus group discussion means when they say that teachers' perceptions frame their actions? If we know who is particularly aggressive towards students in our schools, why are we standing by, saying nothing? Are these the 'non discussables' Barth (2002) says are subjects so laden with fear and anxiety that they take place only covertly in the school car park, staff toilets or at the dinner table at home, feedback that Barth suggests we are depriving our principal of and so condemning ourselves to live within the tension and stress that this fear creates? When one of the teachers in the group says that teachers expect difficulties in their classrooms, does this mean that teachers are stressed with anticipation of what may lie ahead of them inside the classroom door or is it possible to countenance that the teacher themselves may be creating the difficulties by presenting with a hostile attitude at the beginning of class? In this case who is initiating the aggressive cycle? Teacher or student? Chapter 8 in this book details reasons why teachers are reluctant to share their concerns with their principal and Chapter 9 deals with why principals are sometimes reluctant to challenge teachers.

It is suggested by one teacher that there should be compulsory refresher courses on classroom management to inform current practice. The assertion was made that teachers are abandoned in the classroom from the moment they begin to practise and that there should be a mentoring system in place to allow for reflection and development of positive methodologies. This begs the question as to why practising teachers are not consulted or audited by educational policy-makers or teacher training programmers in an effort to create a practice based on experiential information from those at ground level.

In tandem with respondents to the teacher questionnaire there are references to being made aware of and adhering to codes and procedures in order to avoid scenarios like Brian's, Stacey's and Mary's. Of the five teachers who took part in the discussion, none of them had at any stage been furnished with copies of their Teaching Council code of professional conduct. How do we know we are instigating negative practice if we are not made aware of the formal boundaries that have been created for us to practice within? In its closing recommendations, the *Report of the Commission to Inquire into Child Abuse* (2009) in state industrial schools and orphanages states that 'a culture of respecting and implementing rules and regulations and of observing codes of conduct should be developed' (Volume IV, Chapter 7). It is also recommended that managers and those supervising and inspecting the services must ensure regularly that standards are observed.

We must learn to practise through our Code of Conduct, Child Protection Guidelines and the United Nations Convention on the Rights of the Child and to apply their standards to particular circumstances as they arise. The principals of Schools A, B and C do not at any stage refer to these documents in their interviews yet teachers in the focus group discussions felt that it was the responsibility of the principal to enforce our code of conduct and that principals had an obligation to inform teachers of relevant guidelines. Thornberg (2008) suggests that teachers as a profession do not have their own 'metalanguage' to practise through. This author suggests that the basis for the formation of such lies within these documents.

Teachers in the focus group discussion were unanimous in their agreement that teachers need parental support. They felt that parents and teachers should work together as part of the greater school community to develop school behavioural codes and create awareness of child protection issues. The scenarios described in both parent interviews show parents, teachers and school management in adversarial positions. Both parents become involved in adversarial interaction with principals and management as a result of what they perceive as poor and aggressive treatment of their children by a teacher. Parent 1 achieves her objective in the end by removing her child from the class of the teacher in question, but the outcome for Parent 2 is not favourable to her and she is forced to send her child back to the teacher that she feels is abusing her child. Both parents speak of classroom environments that they feel are unsafe both physically and psychologically for their children and yet they find that principals and management have difficulty understanding their concerns for their child's safety. Is this yet another example of a cultural acceptance referred to earlier in this chapter?

Parent 1 describes psychosomatic effects on her child which she feels are as a result of attending a particular class (Lewis, 2000). She describes her child as stressed and panicked. She receives phone calls from her daughter crying in the toilet at school because she is afraid to go into this class. Her child describes the teacher as being 'nasty' to her and making her feel small and stupid deliberately in front of the class. A pattern of this behaviour has emerged as Parent 1 says that her older child received the same treatment some time ago but asserted her rights and the behaviour stopped. Parent 1 brought her child to the doctor, who made a note of her stressed state but said that there was nothing more she could do.

She also meets with the school principal and expresses her feeling that her child is being bullied by the teacher in question. Parent 1 says she is told by the principal that 'that's nonsense'. Parent 1 asks to meet with the teacher in question but says the teacher refuses to meet with her. Parent 1 then writes to the board of management with regard to her concerns and says that they reiterated the principal's position. Parent 1 instructs her child not to attend the class and so resolves the situation herself. The parent says the child's symptoms of stress disappear.

Parent 2 is informed of an incident concerning her child by another parent whose child tells her what has happened. Parent 2 is not only shocked at the details of the incident – a table which her son is sitting at is kicked by the teacher, winding him in the stomach – but also her son's acceptance of the situation as a normal school day. Parent 2 chats to her child and discovers that there have been more incidents of concern and immediately removes her child from class for his own safety while she sets about trying to resolve the problem.

There are two common themes running through the stories both parents tell in their interviews. One theme is their perception of management's attempts at dealing with their complaints with regard to the treatment of their children, the second is the lack of availability of written formal complaints procedures and investigative procedures through which the parents can have their concerns addressed and resolved. Both parents are dissatisfied with management's attempts to resolve the situations and they both take matters into their own hands by taking their children out of the classrooms of the teachers that they have concerns about. Parent 2 takes her concerns to the Gardaí. Neither parent feels that the behaviours of the teachers central to their stories have been dealt with in a way that would assure them that there would be no reoccurrence; in fact, in both cases their complaints have simply not been countenanced and have been denied. This situation seems to reinforce the data that has been yielded from teacher questionnaires and focus groups as teachers have expressed a lack of support and absence of dialogue with regard to professional difficulties. It seems before teachers and management can acknowledge the existence of teacher misbehaviour or maltreatment of students, they must be encouraged to recognise the behaviour. Or is it that recognition implies condemnation, passivity and collusion (Sava, 2002)? Is this the resistance of school communities to recognise a problem due to fears of litigation and injury claims (Hyman and Snook, 1999)? Parent 2 refers to what she feels is a deliberate suppression of the details of incidents similar to those her son has experienced. Are these parents highlighting teachers' nondiscussables by discussing them (Barth, 2002)?

Both parents say that other parents in their children's school are also aware of the behaviour of these teachers, which parents 1 and 2 describe as bullying and abusive. Perhaps it is not only teachers who agree on which of their colleagues are abusive towards students but parents also (McEvoy, 2000). The two parents give examples of past scenarios that they have heard about concerning incidents between these teachers and children. Parent 1 feels that parents in general fear coming forward with complaints about a teacher, which is similar, she says, to the way people in the past were afraid of coming forward with complaints about their parish priest. Parent 2 contacts the Parents' Council, who advise her to direct her complaints to the Teaching Council. Parent 2 is informed by the Teaching Council that Part 5 of the Teaching Council Act, the setting up of the complaints and investigatory committee to deal with complaints and allegations of misconduct by teachers, has not yet been signed off, leaving her with nowhere to bring her complaint that is independent of the school. No resolution is arrived at for Parent 2, she remains unsupported, if not isolated, the more she tries to alert people to her concerns and yet the incidents she describes with regard to her son and the teacher, if applied to the literature, do constitute abuse.

What of the teachers in both of these scenarios? It does not appear that there has been supportive intervention for both of them, evidenced by the denial of their managements of the existence of any problem at all. How does management's denial of the problem help them? This denial ensures that they are never afforded any opportunity to explore or discuss their behaviours. Are these teachers stressed? Have they been asked or are they talking about it? It appears the answer is 'No'.

CONCLUSION

My research project was a simple one; it was born out of issues which arose when two concerned parents approached me with regard to treatment of their children by teachers at school. A small part of the data collected was quantitative; much of the data collected was qualitative. In retrospect, my visits to the three schools, A, B and C, and my attempted interactions with teachers in each of the schools were approached with trepidation as I was aware that it was unlikely that these teachers had been asked to reflect on their possible negative behaviours in the classroom in the past. On reflection, students and parents were eager to discuss the issue, teachers and principals were less so, as evidenced in the small sample of teacher questionnaires returned, 35 out of 110.

Questions emerged for me which I felt compelled to find answers to, despite the obvious sensitivities of the subjects that would be discussed. As the journey progressed, which became a personal journey of reflection, discoveries were made which will have lasting effects on my practice in the classroom. Some questions still remain unanswered. Why are teachers largely unaware of their Teaching Code of Practice? Why are teachers given no training in Child Protection Guidelines for Secondary Level (2004) and specifically, the possible opportunities within the context of teaching which exist to inflict abuse on students? Why is a document as important and of such magnitude as the United Nations Convention on the Rights of the Child (1989) not central to school life? Why do we practise without the frame of the Education Act (1998), Children Act (2001) and Teaching Council Act (2001)? At the very least, why was it not mandatory to have certified training in all of the above areas before beginning to practise as a teacher?

At the outset of the project questions were posed with regard to the existence of dialogue between teachers on the subject of negative classroom management techniques, the level of teacher awareness of the effects of such within the school context and within the context of whole-school anti-bullying policies and what supports existed for those in the profession who wished to discuss their own problems or the actions of a colleague which concerned them. The data yielded suggests that teachers don't discuss their aggression or a colleague's aggression towards students and that teachers exist and practise in their own classrooms within their own micro-climate, and no one seems to monitor the health of these climates. It seems as long as teachers are seen to be getting through the course material it is of no consequence as to how the material is delivered or how disruption to delivery is dealt with. The behaviour of students is not viewed within the context of teacher behaviour and only a small percentage of the teacher sample perceive their behaviour as central to how students behave in their classrooms. We seem to expect certain standards of student behaviour in adherence to our schools' behavioural codes and anti-bullying policies but we do not 'culturally' examine our own behaviour within this frame. Furthermore, it seems that either there is no great awareness of this anomaly and therefore no leadership or guidance to affect change or there is an unwillingness to perhaps open a can of worms.

A picture emerged of a profession in need, managements in denial and children at risk; however, I must accept that this is my picture only. The greatest limitation to this research project was the sensitivity of the subject it explored. Evidence of the sensitivities presented itself in the small sample of teacher questionnaires returned and the small number of teachers who attended the focus group discussion. I must acknowledge that data was yielded from very small groups, with the larger part of the research conducted by dialogue and therefore its accuracy is open to question. Furthermore, the theme of the research could have been perceived as an attack on practising teachers; however, this was never my intention. My heartfelt purpose was to simply initiate dialogue around a subject which I felt needed to be outed. I listened to stories by two parents which suggested questionable behaviour by teachers, students then expressed their feelings about issues with teachers, and teachers and principals were invited to discuss their perspectives on the subject also. All members of the school community were given an opportunity to speak freely, without imposition.

Despite the small teacher questionnaire sample, statistical analysis of responses to quantitative sections A, C, D and G do affirm the existence of the use of negative classroom management techniques by teachers when set against the literature. However, there was a strong suggestion through analysis of the data that we as teachers are largely unaware that we may be engaging in behaviour that may inflict damage and could in fact be identified as misconduct. Positive practice may be encouraged through initiating more supportive dialogue on the subject within the profession; this in turn may lead to more structured interventions to deal with a problem that has yet to be given recognition.

For example, when parent 2 was asked by her parish priest if there was a mark on her child subsequent to alerting him to her concerns regarding a teacher's aggressive behaviour which she felt was emotionally damaging to her child, a picture of genuine ignorance of what may constitute abuse emerged. The data yielded would seem to suggest that training in all of the areas mentioned in this chapter be initiated for all stakeholders in the educative process, that is parents, student teachers, teachers, children, and administrative and management personnel.

It is also suggested, as it was by the teachers in the focus group discussion, that teachers could be supported in their practice by being given bi-yearly in-career training in positive classroom management techniques. In line with this, a system of teacher mentoring should be developed. Other models of management within other professions, for example line management, should be examined with a view to narrowing the gap between teacher and principal, thus facilitating the practice of giving supportive feedback on practice and the debriefing of teachers when they have encountered particularly stressful situations in the classroom.

In tandem with compulsory induction into the Teaching Council Code of Conduct for all practising teachers, section 5 of the Teaching Council Act must be brought in to force urgently in order to create accountability and transparency with regard to complaints within the profession, in line with other professions, and that at ground level schools might be supported to devise their own written complaints procedures open to use by the whole school community, also suggested by teachers in the focus group discussion. For students who wish to use these procedures, perhaps the retention of an independent student advocate or mediator would facilitate the process.

In light of the current culture of assessing schools by their ability to produce high academic standards, the development of a quality assurance mark for schools based on principles of best practice with regard to care for those that work and learn within it rather than the results the school produces perhaps could develop healthier climates. As mentioned above, there was a small sample of questionnaires returned. While this project initiated dialogue, further research of the same nature but on a much larger scale is essential to form a clearer picture of what is needed to address the problems highlighted in my research. Observation of teachers in practice over an extended period of time with immediate intervention when situations appear to be escalating would perhaps facilitate a deeper analysis of behavioural cycles in the classroom and the measuring levels of aggression pre- and post-project. It is also recommended that research examine models of management within second-level schools, facilitating exploration of present models and proposals for alternatives. Some analysis should also take place of the gender imbalance that exists within the teaching profession, framed against the findings of this project.

Freire (1970) conceptualised the present model of education as a banking system. The teacher's role is, as the well-intentioned bank clerk, depositing knowledge; the student is the account, receptacle or container waiting to be filled. Through this system, he writes of people themselves being filed away through lack of creativity in the system. The banking concept of education is utilised to avoid the threat of student 'conscientizao' or awareness. Freire speaks of a system that encourages distance between the teacher and the student, where 'the teacher confuses the authority of knowledge with his or her own professional authority, which she and he sets in opposition to the freedom of the students' (p. 54). In contrast to this he proposes the concept of 'problem posing' education where the teacher and student 'become jointly responsible for a process in which all grow' (p. 61). This concept echoes Humphries' (1996) suggestion that in order to avoid conflict between teachers and students the relationship should be equalised, in other words the power is in the interaction between teacher and student, not on the side of one or the other. Freire suggests that through this process arguments based on authority are no longer valid, 'authority must be on the side of freedom not against it' (p. 61). Does the present secondary school education system contribute to the problems highlighted in this research project? Whether this is the case or not will depend on who sincerely wants to know.

REFERENCES

ASTI (Association of Secondary Teachers, Ireland), *Guidelines for Professional Behaviour for Teachers* (Dublin: ASTI, 2005)

ASTI (Association of Secondary Teachers, Ireland), *Bullying of Teachers: Report of the Sub Committee on the Bullying of Teachers* (Dublin: ASTI, 2007)

ASTI (Association of Secondary Teachers Ireland), *Survey of Retiring Teachers* (Dublin: ASTI, 2008)

Barth, R.S. 'The Culture Builder', *Beyond Educational Leadership*, 59, 2002, pp. 6–11

Barrett, S. and Heubeck, B. 'Relationships between School Hassles and Uplifts and Anxiety and Conduct Problems in Grade 3 and 4', *Journal of Applied Developmental Psychology*, 21, 2000, pp. 537–54

Barnardos, 'Definition and Recognition of Child Abuse' (2009), http://www.barnardos.ie [accessed 7 May 2013]

Brown, M., Ralph, S. and Brember, L. 'Change-Linked Work-Related Stress in British Teachers', *Research in Education*, 67, 2002, pp. 1–12

Carlisle, N. and Rofes, E. 'School Bullying: Do Adult Survivors Perceive Long-Term Effects?' *Traumatolgy*, 13, 2007, pp. 16–26

Cates, D.L. and Markell, M.A. 'The Educators' Duty to Report Child Abuse and Neglect: Current Issues in Education Law and Policy', *Child Abuse and Neglect*, 19, 2001, pp. 163–71

Cohen, L., Mannion, L. and Morrison, K. *Research Methods in Education* (New York: RoutledgeFalmer, 2000)

Cowie, H. and Jennifer, D. *Managing Violence in School: A Whole-School Approach to Best Practice* (London: Paul Chapman Publishing, 2007)

Department of Education and Science, 'Guidelines on Violence in Schools', Circular Letter M18/99 (1999)

Department of Education and Science, *Child Protection Guidelines for Post-Primary Schools* (Dublin: Department of Education and Science, 2004)

Department of Health and Children, *Children First: National Guidelines for the Protection and Welfare of Children* (1999), http://www.dohc.ie/publications [accessed 7 May 2013]

Department of Health and Children, *Our Duty to Care: The Principles of Good Practice for the Protection of Children and Young People* (2002), http://www.dohc.ie/publications [accessed 7 May 2013]

Dupper, D.R. and Meyer-Adams, N. 'Low-Level Violence in Schools: A Threat to Students' Mental Health and Academic Performance', *Urban Education*, 37, 2002, pp. 350–364

Freiberg, H.J. *School Climate: Measuring, Improving and Sustaining Healthy Learning Environments* (Abingdon: RoutledgeFalmer, 1999)

Freire, P. *Pedagogy of the Oppressed* (London: Penguin, 1970)

Geving, M.A. 'Identifying the Types of Student and Teacher Behaviours Associated with Teacher Stress', *Teaching and Teacher Education*, 23, 2007, pp. 624–40

Glasser, W. *The Quality School: Managing Students without Coercion* (New York: Harper Collins, 1998)

Hughes, J.N., Cavell, T.A. and Willson, V. 'Further Support for the Developmental Significance of the Quality of the Teacher–Student Relationship', *Journal of School Psychology*, 39, 2001, pp. 289–301

Humphries, T. *Self-Esteem: The Key to your Child's Education* (Dublin: Gill & Macmillan, 1996)

Humphries, T. *A Different Kind of Discipline* (Dublin: Gill & Macmillan, 1998)

Hyman, A.I. and Perone, D. 'The Other Side of School Violence: Educator Policies and Practices that May Contribute to Student Misbehaviour', *Journal of School Psychology*, 36, 1998, pp. 7–27

Hyman, A.I. and Snook, P.A. *Dangerous Schools: What We Can Do About the Physical and Emotional Abuse of our Children* (San Francisco: Jossey-Bass, 1999)

Kvale, S. *Interviews: An Introduction to Qualitative Research Interviewing* (Thousand Oaks, CA: Sage Publications, 1996)

Kyriacou, C. and Sutcliffe, J. 'Teacher Stress: Prevalence, Sources and Symptoms', *British Journal of Educational Psychology*, 48, 1978, pp. 159–67

Lewis, R. 'Classroom Discipline and the Student Responsibility: The Students' View', *Teaching and Teacher Education*, 17, 2000, pp. 307–19

Lewis, R., Romi, S., Katz, Y.J. and Qui, X. 'Teachers' Classroom Discipline and Student Misbehaviour in Australia, China and Israel', *Teaching and Teacher Education*, 21, 2005, pp. 729–41

Lewis, R., Romi, S., Katz, Y.J. and Qui, X. 'Students' Reaction to Classroom Discipline in Australia, Israel and China', *Teaching and Teacher Education*, 24, 2008, pp. 715–24

Lincoln, Y.S. and Guba, E.G. *Naturalistic Inquiry* (Beverly Hills: Sage Publications, 1985)

Lisak, D. 'The Psychological Impact of Sexual Abuse: Content Analysis of Interviews with Male Survivors', *Journal of Traumatic Stress*, 7, 1994, pp. 525–48

Maslach, C. and Jackson, S.E. 'The Measurement of Experienced Burnout', *Journal of Occupational Behaviour*, 2, 1981, pp. 99–113

Mcevoy, A. 'Teachers who Bully Students: Patterns and Policy Implications', unpublished PhD abstract, Wittenberg University, Ohio, 2000

Mercer, S.H. and de Rosier, M.E. 'Teacher Preference, Peer Rejection and Student Aggression: A Prospective Study of Transactional Influence and Independent Contributions to Emotional Adjustment and Grades', *Journal of School Psychology*, 46, 2008, pp. 641–85

Monahan, M. 'Teacher–Student Aggression', unpublished MEd thesis, Trinity College Dublin, 2010

Munn, P. *Promoting Positive Discipline: Whole-School Approaches to Tackling Low-Level Disruption* (Edinburgh: Scottish Office, 1999)

O'Connell, P.J., Calvert, E. and Watson, D. *Bullying in the Workplace: Survey Reports, 2007. Report to the Department of Enterprise, Trade and Employment* (Dublin: ESRI (The Economic and Social Research Institute), 2007)

O'Moore, M. and Minton, S.J. 'Working with Teachers: Module B, Unit B5, A Whole-School Approach' (2006a), http://www.vista-europe.org [accessed 7 May 2013]

O'Moore, M. and Minton, S.J. 'Protecting Children: Making the School Environment Safe', in C. Gittins, *Violence Reduction in Schools: How to Make a Difference* (Strasbourg: Council of Europe Publishing, 2006b)

Report of the Commission to Inquire into Child Abuse (the Ryan Report) (Dublin: Office of the Minister for Children and Youth Affairs, 2009)

Riley, P. *To Stir with Love: Imagination, Attachment and Teacher Behaviour* (Melbourne: School of Educational Studies, La Trobe University, 2002), http://www.ierg.net/confs/viewpaper.php?id=233&cf=3 [accessed 7 May 2013]

Sava, F.A. 'Causes and Effects of Teacher Conflict-Inducing Attitudes towards Pupils: A Path Analysis', *Teaching and Teacher Education*, 18, 2002, pp. 1007–21

Sudman, S. and Bradburn, N.M. *Asking Questions: A Practical Guide to Questionnaire Design* (San Fransisco: Jossey-Bass, 1982)

Sutton, R.E. and Wheatley, K.F. 'Teachers' Emotions and Teaching: A Review of the Literature and Directions for Future Research', *Educational Psychology Review*, 15, 2003, pp. 327–58

Teaching Council Act (Dublin: Government Publications, 2001)

Teaching Council, *Codes of Professional Conduct for Teachers* (2006), http://www.teachingcouncil.ie [accessed 7 May 2013]

The Children Act (2001), http://www.irishstatutebook.ie [accessed 7 May 2013]

The Education Act (1998), http://www.irishstatutebook.ie [accessed 7 May 2013]

The Education Welfare Act (2000), http://www.irishstatutebook.ie [accessed 7 May 2013]

Thornberg, R. 'The Lack of Professional Knowledge in Values Education', *Teaching and Teacher Education*, 24, 2008, pp. 1791–8

Vartia, M. 'The Sources of Bullying: Psychological Work Environment and Organisational Climate', *European Journal of Work and Organisational Psychology*, 5, 1996, pp. 203–14

Watzlawick, P. *Pragmatics of Human Communication* (New York: W. Norton & Co., 1967)

Wubbles, T. and Levy, J. 'Do You Know What You Look Like?' in *Interpersonal Relationships in Education* (Abingdon: RoutledgeFalmer, 1993)

Wubbles, T. and Brekelmans, M. 'Two Decades of Research on Teacher–Student Relationships in Class', *International Journal of Educational Research*, 43, 2005, pp. 6–24

Yanowitz, K.L., Monte, E. and Tribble, J.R. 'Teachers' Beliefs about the Effects of Child Abuse', *Child Abuse and Neglect*, 27, 2003, pp. 438–88

CHAPTER TWELVE

ABC Whole-School Community Approach to Bullying Prevention

Mona O'Moore

INTRODUCTION

Over the years I have received many letters from parents which point out that there are many teachers who not only lack the necessary confidence to tackle bullying behaviour but who teach in schools which do not have effective procedures or guidelines to assist them or the other members of the school community in reporting, investigating and dealing with incidents of alleged bullying. As a result, an unnecessary number of parents feel they have no option but to withdraw their children from the schools and place them in alternate ones.

Anti-social aggression, bullying and violence are everyday occurrences in schools around the world (Smith et al., 1999; Smith and Brain, 2000; Smith, 2003; WHO, 2004). Ireland is no exception, as can be seen from Chapters 1 to 3 in this book which deal with the prevalence of bullying in the Republic of Ireland and Northern Ireland. Naturally the high incidence of bullying throughout Ireland is a cause of great concern in light of the growing scientific and anecdotal evidence of the ill-effects, both short- and long-term, of being bullied and of bullying others (Olweus, 1993; Rigby, 1998; Kaltialo-Heino et al., 1999; O'Moore, 2000; Rigby, 2002; Roland, 2002; Cook et al., 2010).

Norway set a precedent for instigating a national anti-bullying programme in response to bullying-related suicides. The results were encouraging (Olweus, 1997; Roland and Munthe, 1997). Since then many anti-bullying interventions have been developed worldwide (Smith et al., 2004). A recent meta-analysis of school-based programmes to reduce bullying and victimisation by Farrington and Ttofi (2010) found that on average bullying decreased by 20%–23%

and victimisation decreased by 17%–20%. The most important programme elements that were associated with a decrease in both bullying and victimisation were parent training/meetings, disciplinary methods, the duration of the programme for children and teachers. The authors conclude that new anti-bullying initiatives should be inspired by existing successful programmes but should be modified in light of the key programme elements that have been found to be most effective (or ineffective).

The purpose of the present chapter is to present a summary of the process of development, delivery and evaluation of the ABC whole-school community approach to bullying prevention which was delivered in school communities on a nationwide scale in Ireland during 2004–6. It is of note that ABC's pilot programme, referred to as the Donegal Project (O'Moore and Minton, 2005), was included in the Farrington and Ttofi (2010) meta-analysis. In comparing the effect sizes of all the programmes, the ABC pilot programme ranked fourth out of a total of forty-one in its effectiveness to reduce bullying and fifth in its effectiveness to reduce victimisation, placing it ahead of the Olweus New National Programme (Olweus, 2004). The reason for its effectiveness was undoubtedly because the programme had as its guiding framework a multi-level, multi-faceted whole-school approach inclusive of the community. The aim was to have an anti-bullying programme that heightened the awareness of anti-social aggressive behaviour, bullying and violence among the school community and to provide, as had been argued by Byrne (1996), the school management, teaching and non-teaching staff, parents and pupils and representatives of the wider community (e.g. traffic wardens, school bus drivers, shopkeepers and local clergy) with the skills and strategies to prevent and respond to the negative behaviours. It therefore had the key components which Farrington and Ttofi found were critical to programme success.

Details of the programme methodology, implementation and evaluation of the Donegal project can be found in Smith et al. (2004) and O'Moore and Minton (2005). It should be said that the pilot project took its name from its location, but for the purpose of rolling it out nationwide it was renamed the ABC Whole-School Community Approach to Bullying Prevention. The acronym ABC stands for both the Anti-Bullying Centre (Trinity College Dublin) and the programme's fundamental/guiding principles of: **A**void aggression, **Be** tolerant and **C**are for others.

The delivery of the ABC programme on a nationwide scale only became possible with the very generous funding of the Irish government's Research Council for the Humanities and the Social Sciences (2003). The expectation was that the ABC programme, having taken the same framework model as the second nationwide intervention programme in Norway (Roland and Munthe, 1997), would train a network of professionals who would implement the anti-bullying programme in participating schools nationwide. Each of the regional education centres in Ireland, of which there were twenty-two, were asked to nominate two teachers for training, one primary and one post-primary. The trained teachers would form the network of professionals. It was further anticipated that each trainer would initiate the programme in four schools in their region and have four schools (as similar as possible to the programme schools) acting as control schools.

The role of the trainers was to undertake a whole in-service day for the staff of the participating schools as well as to hold a parents' information evening. They were expected also to act in a consultancy role throughout the duration of the programme to the schools that had had them as trainers.

A provision was made for accrediting the teachers who signed up for the training required to be a trainer and thus qualify to be a member of the Network of Professionals. They had the option of gaining a postgraduate Diploma in Aggression Studies with the potential to advance to an MEd in Aggression Studies (awarded by Trinity College, University of Dublin).

It was hoped that the network of professionals, once trained and experienced in implementing the ABC programme, would in time become a valuable resource for our Department of Education and Skills (DES). Seconded to their respective education centre, they could provide the necessary professional development of teachers on the subject of school bullying and violence as well as assist individual schools in their region to put into operation a whole-school approach to bullying.

THE ABC PROGRAMME METHODOLOGY

The programme was carried out in three stages. The first stage involved the training of the network of trainers. The second stage involved the network of trainers providing instruction to a) the teachers and members of the boards of management of the schools aiming to implement the anti-bullying programme and b) the parents and members of the wider community of the schools involved in the project. The third stage involved the implementation of the components of the programme by the participating schools.

Stage 1: The training of the trainers (Professional Network of Trainers)

There were forty-four applications from teachers to undergo training and to implement the ABC programme on a voluntary basis. Thirty-eight were recruited by the programme's Director of Training (Minton, 2007) and thirty-two attended the course. The decision to rely on volunteers was based on financial constraints of the project. However, this did not give rise to too much concern as the voluntary system had worked so well in the Donegal pilot project. The readiness to be involved without monetary gain was undoubtedly influenced by the tradition of volunteerism in Ireland.

However, the trainers realised that there were also benefits to be had. Not only would they be a good resource for the schools in which they worked, they also had the potential to become a national trainer, providing school-based in-service were the government to decide in the same vein as did Norway and most recently Finland to initiate a national anti-bullying programme.

The training programme

The aim of the training programme for the trainers was to provide them with a comprehensive understanding of the theory, skills and strategies needed to be a trainer for members of the boards of management, classroom teachers and non-teaching staff (secretaries, caretakers, catering staff and cleaners), parent, and members of the wider school community. The training consisted of an intensive residential one-week course in August 2004. The areas covered in the training programme for the trainers were: definitions of bullying, the myths of bullying, the extent of bullying, the signs of victimisation and bullying, the ill-effects of bullying, the causes of bullying behaviour, preventative strategies and strategies to deal with incidents of bullying. The rationale for including these elements into the training have been detailed in O'Moore (2000), and they have since found further support in Nicolaides et al. (2002).

A follow-up meeting was held two months later (October 2004) in Trinity College at which the trainers were given a short course on presentation skills. This was an aspect that the Donegal trainers found immensely helpful in spite of all being accredited as professional classroom teachers.

It should be noted that there was considerable unease among the trainers at this meeting as there was uncertainty around whether the DES would sanction the participating schools to close for the half day required for staff training that was central to the implementation of the ABC programme. There was also uncertainty around whether the trainers' replacement teaching costs would be covered by the DES when they left their classrooms to carry out the staff development training in the participating schools.

On leaving the final meeting, the trainers were each given a ring binder containing training materials which consisted of acetates which they could use selectively in their presentations to the school personnel and to the parents. They were also given a ring binder to leave with each of their designated schools. The ring binder contained material on school bullying which the classroom teachers could use to assist them in their awareness-raising sessions with their pupils. In addition to this material and in time for their in-service work with the schools, they were also provided with a copy of O'Moore and Minton's (2004) *Dealing with Bullying: A Training Manual for Teachers, Parents and other Professionals*.

Stage 2: The in-service/professional development day for the school staff (teaching and non-teaching) and members of board of management

The aim of the in-service day was to motivate the school personnel and to provide them with the necessary body of knowledge and skills to take on the challenge of implementing a whole-school approach to bullying. The goal was that the school would work towards achieving a consensus among its members with regard to all aspects relating to their anti-bullying policy.

The active involvement of the school management staff and the commitment of the teaching staff has been found to be a critical factor in determining the success of an anti-bullying programme (Roland and Munthe, 1997; Midthassel et al., 2000; Farrington and Ttofi, 2010). If schools are to accommodate the many recommendations of international best practice that are central to a whole-school approach to bullying and violence (Olweus, 1993; Rigby, 2002; Smith, 2003), then the school principal, management and teaching staff need to strongly support the recommendations. Midthassel et al. (2000) have highlighted in particular the crucial role which school principals play in determining change. Fullan (1992, 2001) has also pointed to many factors that affect a change of policy. Key among these is the necessity to influence a change in beliefs and behaviour.

In some anti-bullying programmes, there is a core group of staff who form an anti-bullying committee or project group whose role is to act as trainers for the staff, to develop the school's anti-bullying policy and to co-ordinate anti-bullying strategies in the school (Lawlor, 2002; Olweus, 2004; Roland and Vaaland, 2003). The ABC programme, on the other hand, encouraged that at the outset all staff be trained. This was to avoid the risk of promoting an elite group, a sort of 'them and us' which is not uncommon when one seeks volunteers or one selects a few key individuals to form a sub-committee. Only at a later stage when everyone who belonged to the school community had been briefed and had had an opportunity to identify with and contribute to the issues under consideration was it recommended that a committee(s) could be formed to initiate, sustain and evaluate the different elements of the anti-bullying policy. See Chapter 13 for an example of this practice.

The trainers independently arranged the half-day in-service training for the staff in the schools designated to them. The areas that the trainers touched on in the training varied somewhat from school to school depending on what anti-bullying work had already been done by the school.

The input to the management and teaching staff was a condensation of the material provided for the trainers. Consideration of the causes of victimisation and bullying was deemed especially important. This was because the evaluation of the Donegal pilot project had shown that it was this aspect that had especially helped teachers to change the commonly held belief that it is the victim's own fault that he/she is bullied. Apprehending the perpetrator was not therefore seen as a top priority by staff (O'Moore and Minton, 2005).

It has been the author's experience that once staff become sensitised to the distinct types involved in bullying, i.e. bullies, victims and bully-victims (Solberg et al., 2007), the need for intervention that moves beyond the punitive to the restorative for both the targeted child and his/her aggressor is more keenly appreciated. Support for both punitive and non-punitive approaches can be gained more recently from Farrington and Ttofi (2010). However in referring to the Finnish anti-bullying programme, KiVa, the evidence suggests that the punitive approach works better with younger children while the non-punitive is more effective with older children. However, more recent research points to the reverse being true, namely that the non-confronting approach works relatively better among younger children whereas the confronting approach had advantages when dealing with adolescents (Garandeau et al. 2011).

In relation to prevention and intervention of bullying behaviour, great importance was attached in the ABC programme to the key elements of policy development contained in the National Guidelines on Countering Bullying Behaviour in Primary and Post-Primary Schools (DES, 1993). In the knowledge that staff did not intervene in bullying incidents as often as they might (O'Moore et al. 1997; O'Moore, 2000), emphasis was placed on the need for staff to develop good reporting, investigating and recording strategies.

Reporting

In an effort to motivate the management and teaching staff to develop good reporting strategies, staff were made aware of the extent to which children worldwide are reluctant to report their victimisation and what reasons there may be for this (Smith et al., 1999; Smith, 2003). It is a particular wake-up call when the figures for Ireland are presented. Staff come to recognise not only the extent of the reluctance to tell but also that the problem increases steadily with age. The Irish nationwide study found that the percentage of children who reported that they would not tell their teachers increased from 54% for 8-year-olds to 92% for 16/17-year-olds. For a detailed breakdown of the level of reporting for each age group, see either O'Moore et al. (1997) or O'Moore (2010, p. 227).

As the Donegal study had shown no significant improvement in the level of reporting in spite of intervention (O'Moore and Minton, 2005), one of the biggest challenges facing the ABC programme was for it to become more effective in promoting the view among pupils that it is safe and beneficial for them to tell. In stressing the importance of developing procedures to promote countering actions such as 'telling', staff members were especially encouraged to become more vigilant of peer aggression and to respond effectively to signs and symptoms that characterise victimisation. James et al. (2006) have showed subsequently that to increase the level of reporting, students need to see incidents being dealt with effectively.

The procedures that the ABC programme recommended for reporting were as follows:

- The complainant's statements, no matter how trivial, should be listened to actively and with no interpretation so pupils gain confidence in telling.
- Alleviate fears by reassuring the complainant/witness that he/she was right to tell and that it demonstrates responsible behaviour. Also, by helping yourself you are helping others.
- Lessen guilt feelings by reassuring the complainant that when the 'bully' is disciplined it is of his/her own doing.
- Offer concrete help, advice and support to the victim.
- All reports of bullying should be recorded in writing using a standardised reporting form.
- If bullying has occurred, the member(s) involved should be apprehended and the appropriate sanctions/interventions applied.
- In addition, if bullying has occurred, call or meet the parents of the pupils involved, explain the actions being taken and why. Discuss also ways the parents can help. This can prevent a later crisis.
- Parents/guardians should be informed of the person(s) in the school to whom they make enquiries regarding incidents that concern them.

Peer support strategies were also encouraged as a way to lessen the victim's need to tell in their effort to have the bullying stop (Cowie and Wallace, 2000; Cowie and Jennifer, 2007). It was also recommended that there should be an address to the entire school body on a repeated and regular basis, preferably once a term, to remind them of the elements of their anti-bullying policy. As has been pointed out by O'Moore and Minton (2005), some schools have successfully used such talks to take the sting or shame out of reporting.

Investigation

When an investigation is necessary, the ABC programme recommended that classroom teachers do the following:

- Investigate the alleged incident as soon as possible to prevent further instances from occurring.

- Alleged perpetrators and victim(s) should be interviewed separately.
- When a gang is involved in bullying, consider using the Pikas (1989) Common Concern Method (the members are interviewed separately before they are interviewed together) or the Robinson and Maines (1997) No Blame Approach (members are interviewed together).
- Talk to potential witnesses of the alleged incident.
- Avoid letting the alleged perpetrator(s) know who reported them.
- Do not criticise the alleged perpetrator(s) in personal terms, only their behaviour.
- When parents bring a complaint, they should be kept informed of the progress that the school is making in dealing with the situation.

Supportive of Olweus (1993), the ABC programme encouraged the involvement of parents. Informing parents of incidents allows them to talk to their child on the subject. For example, information relating to their child's unacceptable behaviour provides parents with a golden opportunity to identify factors that may be causative of bullying. It also sends out a strong message that the school is serious in its efforts to reach a zero acceptance of bullying.

The ABC programme also stressed the need for management and teaching staff to be, in particular, sensitive to those parents who may learn for the first time that their child has been a victim of bullying. Such parents are likely to become upset or angry at hearing that their child may have been suffering in silence, keeping the secret of victimisation from them over a considerable period of time. They should be reassured that the school will follow the procedures which are specified in their school policy and also that they will be kept informed of the steps that will be taken to put an end to the bullying.

All too often the author comes across parents who feel very rebuffed at their efforts to inform the school that their child is a victim of bullying. Schools with a poorly developed anti-bullying policy and a staunch view that there is no bullying in their school tend to respond to parents in a very defensive manner. This adds insult to injury and often causes parents to move their child to another school. As one parent wrote, 'My daughter aged 10 has experienced school bullying in a small town. As the school refused to recognise that she was being bullied and when they finally did, relationships had gone so bad we had no option but to move her to another school where she is now very happy.'

I have also witnessed parents who at the end of a talk stand up and tell the entire audience (mostly parents, a few teachers and members of boards of management of several adjoining schools) of their frustration with the poor response they get when they complain time and time again that their child is being seriously bullied. I remember one father who described how his son had endured bullying for over five years and the negative impact this had had on his whole family. The school, he claimed, refused to take responsibility, passing much of the bullying off as horseplay.

Talking to parents of victims

To avoid upsetting parents and to foster instead their goodwill, the ABC programme recommends that staff when approached by parents who allege that their child is being bullied should:

- Allow the parent(s)/guardians(s) to express their feelings uninter-rupted.
- Accept their feelings (they are real for that parent even if they seem excessive to you). Useful phrases include: 'I realise you're upset' or 'I will try to help you'.
- Assure the parent(s) that you are pleased that they have taken the time to see you.
- State categorically that the bullying is unacceptable and that you intend to act.
- Promise to (and do) keep in touch with the parent(s) as to how the situation progresses.

Talking to parents of children who bully

It is widely recognised that when teachers approach parents of children who have allegedly bullied, they can become very defensive, difficult and uncooperative. Sometimes they are not even prepared to consider that their child might be able to have behaved in the alleged manner. To avoid this and to promote parental support to have the bullying stop, the ABC programme offers the following guidelines to staff:

- Avoid labelling their child as a 'bully'. Begin by offering the parent(s) some positive view/aspect of their child.
- Show genuine concern for their child's bullying behaviour and a concern to help the child fulfil his/her best potential. Useful phrases include: 'I'm sure we both share concern for N's future' and 'we need to help him/her to realise his/her potential and talents'.
- Inquire if there is anything that could be upsetting the child or triggering the bullying behaviour.
- Persuade the parent(s) to agree, if possible, that being aggressive towards a child who bullies is not a positive approach. On the contrary, it is likely to be counter-productive.
- Explain what you intend to do next. If possible, get their consent.
- Promise to (and do) keep in touch to update the parent(s) on the situation.

Correction and support systems for those involved in bullying behaviour

There is no shortage of ways to respond to incidents of bullying behaviour. It is to be recommended that the strategies which class-room teachers choose to use should be in keeping with the school's overall discipline policy. As a result, the staff's attention is once more drawn to the great care that is needed when formulating their anti-bullying policy. They are further reminded that the strategies and procedures to be adopted should not be in breach of any legal, curricular or policy directives that apply to their school community.

While consideration was given to applying behavioural contracts in dealing with incidents of bullying (O'Moore and Minton, 2005), the objective was to have the staff see the virtues of restorative approaches. It is not uncommon to find resistance to restorative approaches as they do not apportion blame or punishment. However, the trainers would emphasise as they themselves had come to appreciate through their own training, that 'no blame' does not mean 'no responsibility', rather the opposite. Perpetrators are made to think through what they have done and to look at the consequences of their behaviour. It provides the perpetrators with an opportunity to develop greater tolerance and respect for individual differences. In addition, it helps them to develop social skills, in particular feelings of empathy. Most importantly, the 'no blame' approach teaches young people to take responsibility for their unacceptable behaviour. The fact that they must offer up suggestions as to how they intend to refrain from hurting their target provides opportunities to learn new social strategies which should help them in future interactions with people for whom they may have little positive regard. It also offers a way to break the cycle of violence, especially when bullying is an escalation of vengeful tit-for-tat behaviour. New ways of managing frustration and anger can be pointed out.

However, all that the trainers could hope to achieve in the restricted time available to them on the in-service day was to awaken the staff's interest in restorative approaches as an alternative to punitive measures and then to familiarise the staff with the procedural steps of conflict resolution and conflict management, the Common Concern Method and the No Blame Approach. Information on how to use these methods was included in the ring binder that was given to the staff on completion of the in-service day. Staff were also asked to consider support systems such as social skills training, anger management and counselling to deal with children and young people who in spite of good teacher intervention repeatedly re-offend.

It was stressed also that such resources should be made available with the help of outside agencies if necessary to victims and provocative/aggressive victims (bully-victims).

Preventative strategies

A critical focus of the ABC programme is preventative strategies. Many of these strategies are practically realised through classroom work with the pupils, such as enhancing awareness of bullying, promoting pro-social behaviour and correcting anti-social aggression, bullying and violence. However, in recognition of the relationship between teachers' management of the class and bullying behaviours of pupils (Olweus, 1997; Roland and Munthe, 1997; Roland and Galloway, 2002), much emphasis was placed on the need for teachers to be sensitive to the quality of the day-to-day management of the class. This principle finds much support in the SAVE project (Ortega et al., 2004) and the Cool School Programme (James et al. 2008).

The staff were introduced in particular to Canter's *Assertive Discipline* (Canter and Canter, 2001), *Positive Teaching* (Merrett and Wheldall, 1990) and *A Whole-School Approach to Behaviour Management* (Rogers, 2004). Reference was also made to the factors that made for a successful school (Rutter et al. 1979). Further and most recent support for the importance of classroom management in reducing school bullying can be gained from Ttofi, Farrington and Baldry (2008) and Farrington and Ttofi (2010).

Essentially the message for staff which underpins the ABC programme was that every opportunity was to be taken to promote a
positive, thoughtful and caring atmosphere, with an emphasis on
incentives and rewards and to avoid threats and punishments. In
addition to this, the attention of the staff was also drawn to the
potential of cooperative learning strategies (Johnson and Johnson,
1991). Working in groups promotes and strengthens children's
propensity to share, to help, to communicate and resolve conflict.

Consideration was also given to teacher–teacher bullying (O'Moore,
1999; INTO, 2000) and teacher–pupil bullying (Twenlow and
Fonagy, 2005; Khoury-Kassabri et al., 2008; James et al., 2008),
encouraging teachers and management to reflect on their own
behaviours and the futility of correcting children's behaviour in a
climate that condones double standards and the misuse of power
among adults. Thus the standards of behaviour that are set for the
pupils should apply also to staff. Pupils need to see adults behaving in
a respectful, tolerant, caring and considerate way in order to reinforce
pro-social behaviour. This view finds support also in *convivencia* by
Ortega et al. (2004) and more recently Monaghan (see Chapter 11
this volume). To gain a greater understanding of adult bullying in
the education sector see Chapters 8, 9 and 10 of this book.

Discussion was held also on the relationship between self-esteem
and bullying (O'Moore and Kirkham, 2001; Farrington and Baldry,
2005). While the scientific literature is still somewhat controversial,
with some researchers advocating that inadequate self-esteem is a
predictor of bullying among girls only, school staff were encouraged
to take every opportunity to provide their pupils with feelings
of positive self-worth in order to reduce the risk of internalising
and/or externalising problems. The key take-home message was that
the more robust the self-esteem is, the more resistant it will be to
victimisation and bullying. Also, good self-esteem is a good predictor
of whether a student will take on the role of defender rather than
that of the more common passive spectator.

Anti-bullying across the curriculum

The attention of the classroom teachers was drawn to how they
can influence attitudes to bullying behaviour in a positive manner
through a range of curricula initiatives. While the compulsory
Social, Personal and Health Education (SPHE) and Civic, Social
and Political Education Programme (CSPE) curricula offer teachers

the opportunity in a very structured way to discuss bullying, so does virtually every other school-based subject. For example, Geography and History offer up valuable opportunities to discuss the negative aspects of power by making references to colonisation and exploitation and to the long line of dictators up to the present day. Anti-bullying work can be further extended into Mathematics, Art, Drama and Religion. In Mathematics, for example, students can apply statistical methods to data collected from a class or school survey on bullying. Physical Education and Sports also provide excellent opportunities for promoting cooperation and for learning to control aggression and violence.

Management and teaching staff's attention was also drawn to the impact that can be had by working with the students towards an Awareness Day or Week on Bullying. This provides an opportunity to formally recognise the creative contributions of students and staff that are expressed through visual art (e.g. posters, pictures and sculpture), poetry, musical compositions, drama or crafts. Most importantly, it has the potential to send out a strong reminder to the school community that the anti-bullying message is taken seriously. While school principals are sometimes reluctant to publicise their campaigns against bullying, they should be assured from listening to parents that they do not jeopardise their reputation by highlighting their policy on bullying. On the contrary, increasingly as parents become aware of potential suffering associated with victimisation they tend to be attracted to schools which draw attention to their anti-bullying policy.

PARENT EVENING

Parent training has been proven to be a critical component in the success of an anti-bullying programme (Farrington and Ttofi, 2010).

The material presented to the parents by the trainers of the ABC programme was in the main similar to that presented to the teachers. Parents were introduced therefore to a discussion of what bullying is, the misconceptions of bullying, the types of bullying, the signs and symptoms, the effects of bullying on victims and aggressors and the risk factors associated with victims and bullies. It was in relation to the latter aspect that particular attention was given so that parents might better understand how they can help to either prevent or modify behaviour that can put their child at risk of being bullied or of bullying others. The factors discussed as contributing to aggression in the home were cruelty, lack of love and care, inconsistent discipline, permissive management of aggressive behaviour, violent emotional outbursts on the part of adults and excessive physical punishment. Parents were also made aware of the importance of self-esteem by making reference to relevant research (Salmivalli et al., 1999; O'Moore and Kirkham, 2001). It is the author's experience that once parents learn that children of medium or high self-esteem tend to be less involved in bullying behaviour either as perpetrators, victims or bully-victims, they are more open to suggestions around safeguarding or building their child's self-esteem.

Among the suggestions that the trainers would give to the parents were: use praise and words of encouragement and give them lots of positive experiences. Play to the child's strengths, help them to achieve and, most importantly, to deal with disappointment and failure.

Empathy, tolerance and respect for individual differences were also singled out for special attention in view of the evidence that links the lack of these attributes to bullying behaviour. Parents were therefore encouraged to take every opportunity to promote tolerance and respect and develop empathic responses in their children. They were encouraged to talk to their children about bullying behaviour and to challenge every incident of mean-spirited and underhand behaviour witnessed in the home. They were reminded also of the importance of leading by example as a preventative and countering measure against bullying. Parents were given examples such as those detailed in O'Moore and Minton (2004) to help them promote empathy and respect in their children.

Another strong focus of the parent evening was to give them to understand that collaboration between home and school was key to a successful whole-school anti-bullying programme. The ABC programme was particularly sensitive to the dilemma that parents so often find themselves in, namely how to deal with the child or teenager who pleads with them not to report a bullying incident. Parents were assured of a sensitive and considered response from the school which would set out to safeguard the victim against reprisals.

Stage 3: Implementation of the Whole-School approach, inclusive of the wider community

On completion of the in-service day and the parent evening, the role of the staff was to work towards creating a zero acceptance to anti-social aggression, bullying and violence. The development of a school policy and school charter was to facilitate this process. In addition all pupils were introduced by their teachers in class time to an awareness-raising programme to counter bullying.

In introducing the pupils to 'What all young people need to know', the classroom teachers were expected to cover the following topics:

- misconceptions about bullying;
- bullying: what is it?
- types of bullying;
- effects of bullying;
- causes of bullying;
- fighting back;
- what to do if you are bullied;
- why tell someone?
- what can you do if others are being bullied?
- how to help prevent bullying in your school.

The class teachers had been given a copy of the material to cover with their pupils on their in-service day. While the above topics for the pupils naturally contain much of the same information as that which has already been reported on for staff, a flavour will be given of the material which is specific only to the students. For example, in discussing with pupils 'what to do if you are being bullied', the disadvantages of retaliation were pointed out while the advantages of reporting were emphasised. The key messages to the pupils were: 'no one can help you unless you let them know' and 'by helping yourself you are helping others'.

Other key messages that were presented to pupils as to how they could help prevent bullying in their schools were as follows:

Don't be a bully yourself

- There is nothing good about bullying others: it is wrong and bullying is an indication of cowardly behaviour.
- Don't pick on others, or let your friends pick on others.
- Try to include people instead of leaving them out.
- Treat other people how you would like to be treated yourself.

Understanding how other people feel

- Not everybody feels the same way as you do about everything!
- It's hard to understand how others feel but it is worth it.
- Think – how do people feel when they are being bullied?

Respecting other people for who they are

- Think about what you have in common with a person, instead of thinking about the differences.
- Don't judge people, or listen to others who judge people.
- Don't treat people badly because of their race, religion, sexuality or nationality.

There was discussion around the causes of bullying, jealousy, envy, the need to exert power, gain status and, as Besag (2006) showed, even boredom. In dealing with the subject of the pupils' own feelings, either as a cause or effect of bullying, teachers drew attention to the fact that many find themselves involved in troublesome behaviour because they don't control their anger. Teachers therefore led on such questions as:

- What does anger feel like?
- How do we behave when we are angry?
- What things make each of us angry?
- Has anger got us into trouble?
- What alternatives do we have to losing our temper?
- How can we calm ourselves down?

The role of the bystander

The conceptual framework of the 'ABC' programme places much emphasis on the role of the bystander. Thus pupils were made aware of the process of bullying and the critical role which they could all play to prevent anti-social aggression from manifesting itself as bullying behaviour (Sullivan, 2000; Sullivan et al., 2004).

Other things which the pupils were encouraged to do in an effort to prevent bullying in their schools were:

- Always play fair in classes, sports, activities, and out of school.
- Treat others how you would like to be treated yourself.

- Ask your teachers if you can do anti-bullying work or have an anti-bullying week.
- Get involved in mediation/mentoring/prefecting where these exist.
- Make a class charter.

EVALUATION OF THE ABC PROGRAMME

The evaluation process was administered centrally from Trinity College's Anti-Bullying Centre by the Director of Training (for details see Minton, 2007). Essentially the evaluation of the effectiveness of the programme was based on a comparison of the pupils' responses at pre-test and at post-test. An adaptation of the Olweus Bully/Victim Questionnaire (1996) was used to measure all third, fourth, fifth and sixth-class pupils at primary-school level, and all first, second and third-year students at post-primary level were asked to complete the questionnaires anonymously in the winter term of the academic year of 2004–5 and again following the implementation of the anti-bullying programme in the winter term of the following academic year. It was their regular classroom teachers who administered the questionnaires according to standardised instructions. All the participating schools (programme and controls) were sourced by the trainers.

Evaluation of the effectiveness of the nationwide initiative was made difficult by the low number of participating schools who returned their pre- and post-questionnaires for analysis. Despite the fact that the eighteen trainers had completed the programme of training in fifty-eight schools (thirty-six primary and twenty-two post-primary), there were only eighteen of these schools (fourteen primary and four post-primary) that returned their pre-programme questionnaires for analysis. With regard to the fifty-three control schools (thirty-three primary and twenty post-primary) only half of them (nineteen primary and eight post-primary) returned them.

At the post-programme stage there were only seven programme schools (five primary and two post-primary) and twelve control schools (eight primary and four post-primary) that returned their questionnaires. Out of these seven programme schools it was possible to match up only five (four primary and one post-primary) with any degree of confidence.

RESULTS

The results which follow will provide only a summary as they have been reported on in detail in Minton (2007) and Minton and O'Moore (2008).

The before and after findings of the ABC programme in relation to the extent of being bullied and of bullying others over the last three months and the last five days of the study showed reductions ranging from 33.8% to 59.8% among primary school children. In relation to post-primary students the decrease in victimisation and bullying of others ranged from 22.4% to 59.3%. Whereas not all these reductions yielded statistically significant values (at the alpha probability level of p< 0.05), the reductions which did (i.e. being bullied at primary level over the last three months and at post-primary over the last five days) indicate that the implementation of the ABC programme at both the primary and post-primary school level had a statistically significant positive effect in reducing the level of victimisation among both primary and post-primary pupils.

There was, however, a lack of strong statistical significance in the 'before' and 'after' reporting rates in respect of the incidence of young people bullying others. However, the reductions which were found, in particular in relation to primary pupils (44% for last three months and 59.8% for last five days), are nevertheless encouraging. Earlier intervention studies have reported post-programme reductions in bullying others at the primary school level of 7% in the Department for Education (DFE) Anti-Bullying Project in Sheffield, England (Smith, 1997; Eslea and Smith, 1998) and a mixed pattern of changes in the anti-bullying intervention in Flanders (Stevens, De Bourdeauhuij and Van Oost (2004). At post-primary level while positive results have been reported (Ortega and Lera, 2000), there are no intervention studies which have succeeded in reporting the original high reduction rates of Olweus (2004).

DISCUSSION

There are many reasons that can be put forward as to why the ABC programme did not deliver the results that were hoped for in view of the promising outcome of the pilot programme in Co. Donegal (O'Moore and Minton, 2004; Farrington and Ttofi, 2010).

When a comparison is made between the ABC programme and its pilot programme, differences emerge. The key differences, some of which have already been pointed out by Minton and O'Moore (2008), relate to a) the way in which the network of professionals were recruited, supported and trained, b) the personnel involved in the training, c) the day-to-day administrative aspects of the implementation and evaluation of the programme and d) the commitment of the Department of Education and Science to the implementation of the ABC programme on a nationwide basis.

In the pilot programme, all the trainers (the network of professionals) were recruited by their regional director of the Education Centre. In the nationwide study, while all the regional directors were invited to help in the recruitment and selection of the trainers who were to implement the programme in their region, not all succeeded in doing this. As a result, some trainers were recruited with the help of the INTO and the Anti-Bullying Centre at Trinity College.

More important than the source of the recruitment was undoubtedly the different approach taken to the training of the trainers and the subsequent ongoing encouragement and motivational support that they received over the course of the project. The Donegal project benefited from the extraordinary dedication of both the regional director of the Donegal Education Centre (Sally Bonner) and the regional Educational Officer (Ann McAteer) of the North Western Health Board. Both were present at all the workshops and seminars held for the trainers and they both continued throughout the project to provide additional support and encouragement to the trainers. The slightest sign of any trainer losing confidence and of dropping out was immediately attended to.

In contrast to the ABC nationwide programme, all the Donegal principals of the pilot programme schools attended a meeting where they learned firsthand about the project from the author. They were also shown presentations by representatives from both the Department of Education and Science and the North Western Health Board. Their blessing, so to speak, gave status to the project. In addition, the principals had the opportunity to experience the exceptional commitment of the trainers when they spoke individually of what the training had done for them and what they hoped to achieve by working as a trainer on the programme. After the information session a social evening was arranged by the Donegal Education Centre so that all who had a training or leadership role in the project would have an opportunity to get to know each other a bit better.

Much of the above was missing in the nationwide project. First of all, the trainers serving the nationwide project were trained intensively over a course of one week during their summer vacation. This contrasted to the pilot project in which the trainers were trained at weekends over an extended period of time – approximately six months. This meant that the 'pilot' trainers had more time than had the 'nationwide' trainers to process and to reflect on the material discussed during training. Also, once the training was over, the nationwide trainers were dispersed throughout the different regions in Ireland. As a result, they did not enjoy as did their pilot counterparts the same level of motivational support from either each other or from their regional Education Centre director. The regional educational officers from the individual health boards did not have a part to play either in the nationwide project. This was through no fault of theirs but the result of an administrative oversight.

Not only were there fewer opportunities to support the nationwide trainers as compared to the pilot trainers, but the nature of the support was different. In contrast to the pilot trainers, the nationwide trainers were for logistical reasons restricted to telephone calls and emails when in need of information or psychological support from ABC's Director of Training. There was also no provision made to have all the principals of the allocated schools come together either on a national or regional scale for an information session. Any communication between the principals and the Director of Training tended to be also of an electronic kind.

Possibly the most critical factor to determine the differences in outcome of the pilot and the nationwide project was the lack of support afforded the project by the Department of Education and Science. The Professional Development Section of the department was unable to sanction the closure of the allocated schools to accommodate the in-service provision and to provide payment for the teaching replacement costs. These decisions greatly affected the status of the project and the morale of the trainers. Not surprisingly, the trainers, in particular those who had hoped to achieve professional status and recognition from the DES on becoming a member of the professional network, lost heart. A programme that did not appear to have the approval/blessing of the DES naturally would give rise to many qualms. It undoubtedly contributed also to the low response rate in requesting and returning pre- and post-test questionnaires.

In hindsight, the hiccups that the project had with the DES should have been anticipated and resolved by the author, as the principal investigator of the project, well before the training commenced. Instead the author naively and mistakenly took the view, given the success of the pilot programme and the award of the government

(IRCHSS) grant to specifically fund the nationwide project, that the DES would be only too delighted to avail of the opportunity to have trainers and school communities sensitised (at minimal cost) to countering bullying throughout every region in Ireland.

While the above reasons may go some way to explain the dropout of trainers and schools in the initial phases of the project, they may not account fully for why those schools that had undergone the training failed to return their material at the pre-programme stage of implementation.

In the absence of any reliable evidence to discern the extent to which the schools had implemented the different elements of the ABC programme it is possible that there were schools who after receiving the professional training considered the programme to be too ambitious or too labour intensive. For these reasons they may have decided not to proceed with the programme of implementation. As there were more post-primary schools than primary schools that did not submit material at both the pre- and post-evaluation stage, it is possible that the former found the programme particularly demanding. This aspect had unfortunately not arisen in the pilot as it had been restricted to primary schools.

In the case of those schools which undertook the pre-programme testing but who omitted to return the post-programme material, it may be that they were not able to follow through on all aspects of the programme. As a result, they may have decided to refrain from post-testing to avoid being recorded as unsuccessful. Of course, on a more noble level they may have thought it unfair that the programme be deemed unsuccessful due to the lack of their school to fully implement the programme. However, most critically, as has been pointed out by Minton (2007), 'had the less than desirable rates of response to the phases of the questionnaire been tracked in an accurate and timely manner they could potentially have been at least partially arrested by a more rigorous following-up of individual schools.'

Taking into account all the shortcomings that have so far been highlighted in respect of the implementation of the ABC programme nationwide, it is undoubtedly true to say that greater attention to the management and the administration aspects of the project would have yielded a more satisfactory outcome. Not only might there have been a greater number of schools that engaged fully with the evaluation process, but the effectiveness of the nationwide programme could have been more confidently determined.

However, valuable lessons have been learned which hopefully may help future intervention programmes based on a 'train the trainers' approach and which have ambitions to implement on a national scale. These are as follows:

- Achieve approval from all the relevant professional sectors and critical stakeholders before commencing the training of trainers.
- Arrange for regional training of trainers over an extended period of time.
- Arrange for regional support for the trainers on an ongoing basis, for example through a mentoring system.
- Provide for an induction course for the principals of the participating schools to sensitise them to the elements of the proposed programme and the criteria as outlined by Samuelson and Ertevag (2006) that make for the successful implementation of a new programme.
- Given that the content and delivery aspects are of high standard, exercise strict care and attention, leaving nothing to chance with regard to implementation strategies and procedures. It would be important to keep a record of the programme elements which are implemented and the time given to them.
- Provide for educational psychologists and professional advisors to help identify organisational factors that may make for the most successful programme implementation (see Maunder and Tattersall, 2010, for details).

In conclusion, it might appear at first glance from the account that has been given in this chapter of the implementation of the nationwide ABC whole-school community approach to bullying prevention that there was much work for little gain. However, in reality much has been achieved. Firstly, the ABC programme has shown itself capable of achieving considerable reductions in the level of being bullied and of bullying others, in particular at primary level. While not all reductions achieved statistical significance, it is as well to be mindful of the viewpoint that a non-significant result should never be interpreted as no difference, no more than a significant result should give total confidence in its conclusions (Field, 2005).

Secondly, the nationwide programme has produced a network of professional trainers who will undoubtedly continue to be an invaluable resource to their own school communities and who can be a further resource to any intervention efforts that may be undertaken at a future date in Ireland on either a local, regional or nationwide basis.

Thirdly, the ABC programme achieved one of its aims, the production of a DVD educational package called *Silent Witnesses*. This was the first Irish-produced DVD designed to raise awareness among post-primary students of peer aggression, bullying and violence. It was kindly launched although post-programme on 11 October 2006 by the Minister for Education, Mary Hanafin. This DVD was sent with the compliments of the Anti-Bullying Centre (Trinity College Dublin) free of charge to all post-primary schools in the country. While it was unfortunate that the DVD was not ready in time to be included in the formal evaluation study reported upon in this chapter, subsequent anecdotal feedback indicates that it is widely used by classroom teachers, especially those teaching the Social Personal and Health Education programme (SPHE). Most importantly and gratifying is that it is reported to be gripping the students' attention in a most powerful way. It has also acted as an inspiration for other schools or youth clubs to develop anti-bullying packs that are specific to their locality or region, for example *Breaking the Silence* (O'Moore, 2008). Copies of *Silent Witnesses* are still available from TCD's Anti-Bullying Centre.

Finally, while the ABC whole-school community approach to bullying prevention did not accomplish all that it set out to achieve, it has nevertheless provided a greater understanding of the conditions which are necessary for effective implementation of anti-bullying programmes. For further details and discussion on the complexity of the delivery process and strategies for implementation see Midthassel et al. (2009). The ABC programme has also provided many school communities around Ireland with knowledge, understanding and skills which they would otherwise not have gained to help them in the prevention and countering of peer aggression, bullying and violence. For this alone it can be justifiably proud.

REFERENCES

Besag, V.E. *Understanding Girls' Friendships, Fights and Feuds: A Practical Approach to Girls' Bullying* (Maidenhead, Berkshire: Open University Press, 2006)

Byrne, B. *Bullying: A Community Approach* (Dublin: Columba Press, 1996)

Canter, L. and Canter, M. *Lee Canter's Assertive Discipline: Positive Behaviour Management for Today's Classroom* (Los Angeles: Canter & Associates, 2001)

Cook, C.R., Williams K.R., Guerra, N.G., Kim, T.E. and Sadek, S. (2010). Predictors of bullying and victimization in childhood and adolescence: A meta-analytic investigation *School Psychology Quarterly*, 25, 2010, pp. 65–83

Cowie, H. and Jennifer, D. *Managing Violence in Schools: A Whole-School Approach to Best Practice* (London: Paul Chapman Publishing, 2007)

Cowie, H. and Wallace, P. *Peer Support in Action: From Bystanding to Standing By* (London: Sage Publications, 2000)

Department of Education and Science, *Guidelines on Countering Bullying Behaviour in Primary and Post-Primary Schools* (Dublin. The Stationery Office, 1993)

Eslea, M. and Smith, P.K. 'The Long-Term Effectiveness of Anti-Bullying Work in Primary Schools', *Educational Research*, 40, 1998, pp. 203–18

Farrington, D. and Baldry, A.C. 'Individual Risk Factors for School Violence', *Proceedings of the IX International Meeting on the Biology and Sociology of Violence, October 6–7, 2005* (Valencia: Queen Sofia Centre for the Study of Violence, 2005)

Farrington, D. and Ttofi, M.M. 'Effective Programs to Reduce School Bullying', in D.W. Springer and A.R. Roberts (eds), *Juvenile Justice and Delinquency* (Sudbury, MA: Jones & Bartlett, 2010)

Field, A. *Discovering Statistics Using SPSS* (London: Sage Publications, 2005)

Fullan, M. *Successful School Improvement* (Buckingham: Open University Press, 1992)

Fullan, M. *The New Meaning of Educational Change* (New York: Teacher College Press, 2001)

Garandeau, C.F., Little, T., Karma, A., Postkiparta, E. and Salmivalli, C. 'Dealing with Bullies at School: Which Approach for which Situations?' in M. Saino and C.F. Garandeau (chairs), Kiva Anti-Bullying Program: Practical Viewpoints on Implementation and Effectiveness and an Innovative Perspective from Social Network Analysis. Symposium Presented at the Biennial Meeting of the European Society for Development Psychology, Bergen, Norway, 2001

INTO (Irish National Teachers' Organisation), *Staff Relations: A Report on Adult Bullying in Schools* (Dublin: INTO, 2000)

James, D.J., Lawlor, M., Courtney, P., Flynn, A., Henry, B. and Murphy, N. 'Bullying Behaviour in Secondary Schools: What Roles Do Teachers Play?' *Child Abuse Review*, 17, 2006, pp. 160–73

Johnson, D.W. and Johnson, R.T. *Learning Together and Alone: Co-Operative, Competitive and Individualistic Learning* (Boston and London: Allyn & Bacon, 1991)

Kaltialo-Heino, R., Rimpelo, M., Martunen, M., Rimpela, A. and Rantenau, P. 'Bullying, Depression and Suicidal Ideation in Finnish Adolescents: School Survey', *British Medical Journal*, 319, 1999, pp. 348–51

Khoury-Kassabri, M., Astor, R. and Benbenishty, R. 'Student Victimization by School Staff of an Israeli National School Campaign', *Aggressive Behavior*, 34, 2008, pp. 1–8

Lawlor, M. 'The Cool School Response to School Bullying', in *Proceedings of the Second National Conference on Bullying and Suicide in Schools* (Dublin: The Irish Association of Suicidology and the National Suicide Review Group, 2002)

Maunder, R.E. and Tattersall, A.J. 'Staff Experiences of Managing Bullying in Secondary Schools: The Importance of Internal and External Relationships in Facilitating Intervention', *Educational and Child Psychology*, 27, 2010, pp. 116–28

Merrett, F. and Wheldall, K. *Positive Teaching in the Primary School* (London: Paul Chapman Publishing, 1990)

Midthassel, U., Bru, E. and Idsoe, T. 'The Principal's Role in Promoting School Development Activity in Norwegian Compulsory Schools', *School Leadership and Management*, 20, 2000, pp. 147–60

Midthassel, U., Minton, S.J. and O'Moore, A.M. 'Conditions for the Implementation of Anti-Bullying Programmes in Norway and Ireland: A Comparison of Contexts and Strategies', *Compare: A Journal of Comparative and International Education*, 39, 2009, pp. 737–50

Minton, S.J. 'Preventing and Countering Bullying Behaviour amongst Students in Irish Schools at a Nationwide Level', unpublished PhD thesis, Trinity College Dublin, 2007

Minton, S.J. and O'Moore, M. 'The Effectiveness of a Nationwide Intervention Programme to Prevent and Counter School Bullying in Ireland', *International Journal of Psychology and Psychology Therapy*, 8, 2008, pp. 1–12

Nicolaides, S., Toda, Y. and Smith, P.K. 'Knowledge and Attitudes about School Bullying in Trainee Teachers', *British Journal of Educational Psychology*, 22, 2002, pp. 105–18

Olweus, D. *Bullying at School: What We Know and What We Can Do About It* (Oxford: Blackwell, 1993)

Olweus, D. *Bully/Victim Questionnaire for Students* (Bergen: University of Bergen, Department of Psychology, 1996)

Olweus, D. 'Bully/Victim Problems in School: Knowledge Base and an Effective Intervention Programme', *Irish Journal of Psychology*, 18, 1997, pp. 170–90

Olweus, D. 'The Olweus Bullying Prevention Programme: Design and Implementation Issues and A New National Initiative in Norway', in P.K. Smith, D. Pepler and K. Rigby (eds), *Bullying in Schools: How Successful Can Interventions Be?* (Cambridge: Cambridge University Press, 2004)

O'Moore, M. 'Teachers' Union of Ireland Bullying Survey', *TUI News*, 20, 1999, p. 5

O'Moore, M. 'Critical Issues for Teacher Training to Counter Bullying and Victimisation in Ireland', *Aggressive Behavior*, 26, 2000, pp. 99–111

O'Moore, M. 'Bullying at School: The Need for Urgent Action', *Kerry Mental Health Association Newsletter*, Spring 2008, pp. 7–8

O'Moore, M. *Understanding School Bullying: A Guide for Parents and Teachers* (Dublin: Veritas, 2010)

O'Moore, A.M., Kirkham, C. and Smith, M. 'Bullying Behaviour in Irish Schools: A Nationwide Study', *Irish Journal of Psychology*, 18, 1997, pp. 141–69

O'Moore, M. and Kirkham, C. 'Self-Esteem and its Relationship to Bullying Behaviour', *Aggressive Behavior*, 27, 2001, pp. 269–83

O'Moore, M. and Minton, S.J. *Dealing with Bullying in Schools: A Training Manual for Teachers, Parents and Other Professionals* (London: Paul Chapman Publishing, 2004)

O'Moore, M. and Minton, S.J. 'Evaluation of the Effectiveness of an Anti-Bullying Programme in Primary Schools', *Aggressive Behavior*, 31, 2005, pp. 609–22

Ortega, R. and Lora, M.J. 'The Seville Anti-Bullying in School Project', *Aggressive Behavior*, 26, 2000, pp. 113–23

Ortega, R., Del Rey, R. and Mora-Merchan J.A. 'SAVE Model: An Anti-Bullying Intervention in Spain', in P.K. Smith, D. Pepler and K. Rigby (eds), *Bullying in Schools: How Successful Can Interventions Be?* (Cambridge: Cambridge University Press, 2004)

Pikas, A. 'The Common Concern Method for the Treatment of Mobbing', in E. Munthe and E. Roland (eds), *Bullying: An International Perspective* (London: Routledge, 1989)

Rigby, K. 'Suicide Ideation and Bullying among Australian Secondary School Children', *Australian Educational and Developmental Psychologist*, 15, 1998, pp. 45–61

Rigby, K. *New Perspectives on Bullying* (London: Jessica Kingsley, 2002)

Roland, E. 'Bullying, Depressive Symptoms and Suicidal Thoughts', *Educational Research*, 44, 2002, pp. 55–67

Roland, E. and Galloway, D. 'Classroom Influences on Bullying', *Aggressive Behavior*, 27, 2002, pp. 446–62

Roland, E. and Munthe, E. 'The 1996 Norwegian Programme for Preventing and Managing Bullying in School', *Irish Journal of Psychology*, 18, 1997, pp. 233–47

Roland, E. and Vaaland, G.S. *Zero: SAF's Program mot Mobbing* (Stavanger: Senter for Atferdsforskning, Hogskolen i Stavanger, 2003)

Robinson, G. and Maines, B. *Crying for Help: The No Blame Approach to Bullying* (Bristol: Lucky Duck Publishing, 1997)

Rogers, B. *Behaviour Management: Whole-School Approach to Behaviour Management* (London: Paul Chapman Publishing, 2004)

Rutter, M., Maughan, B., Mortimore, P., Ouston, J. and Smith, A. *Fifteen Thousand Hours: Secondary Schools and their Effects on Children* (Cambridge, MA: Harvard University Press, 1979)

Salmivalli, C., Kaukiainen, A., Kaistaniemi, L. and Lagerspetz, K.M.J. 'Self-Evaluated Self-Esteem and Defensive Egotism as Predictors of Adolescents' Participation in Bullying Situations', *Personality and Social Psychology Bulletin*, 25, 1999, pp. 1268–78

Samuelson, A.S. and Ertevag, S.K. 'The Whole-School Approach: How to Embed the Whole-School Approach and the Challenge of Implementation', Vista Unit B2 (2006), http://www.vista.org (Accessed 27 June 2012)

Smith, P.K. 'Bullying in Schools: The UK Experience and the Sheffield Anti-Bullying Project', *Irish Journal of Psychology*, 18, 1997, pp. 191–201

Smith, P.K. *Violence in Schools. The Response in Europe* (London: Routledge-Falmer, 2003)

Smith, P.K. and Brain, P. 'Bullying in Schools: Lessons from Two Decades of Research', *Aggressive Behavior*, 26, 2000, pp. 1–9

Smith, P.K., Morita, Y. Junger-Tas, J., Olweus, D., Ratalano, R. and Slee, P. (eds), *The Nature of School Bullying: A Cross-National Perspective* (London and New York: Routledge, 1999)

Smith, P.K., Pepler, D. and Rigby, K. (eds), *Bullying in Schools: How Successful Can Interventions Be?* (Cambridge: Cambridge University Press, 2004)

Smith, P.K. and Sharp, S. *School Bullying: Insights and Perspectives* (London: Routledge, 1994)

Solberg, M.E, Olweus, D. and Endresen, I.M. 'Bullies and Victims at School: Are They the Same Pupils?' *British Journal of Educational Psychology*, 77, 2007, pp. 441–64

Stevens, V., Van Oost, P. and Bourdeauhuij, S. 'Interventions against Bullying in Flemish Schools: Programme Development and Evaluation', in P.K. Smith, D. Pepler and K. Rigby (eds), *Bullying in Schools: How Successful Can Interventions Be?* (Cambridge: Cambridge University Press, 2004)

Sullivan, K. *The Anti-Bullying Handbook* (New York: Oxford University Press, 2000)

Sullivan, K., Cleary, M. and Sullivan, G. *Bullying in Secondary Schools: What It Looks Like and How to Manage It* (London: Paul Chapman Publishing, 2004)

Ttofi, M.M., Farrington, D.P. and Baldry, A.C. 'Effectiveness of Programmes to Reduce School Bullying', Report Prepared for the Swedish National Council for Crime Prevention, 2008

Twenlow, S.W. and Fonagy, P. 'The Prevalence of Teachers who Bully Students in Schools with Differing Levels of Behavioural Problems', *American Journal of Psychiatry*, 162, 2005, pp. 2387–9

World Health Organisation, 'Young People's Health in Context. Health Behaviour in School-Aged Children (HBSC) Study: Intermediate report from 2001/2002 Survey', *Health Policy for Children and Adolescents*, 4, 2004

Action Against Cyber-Bullying (AAC): A Programme for Understanding and Effectively Addressing School-Related Cyber-Bullying

Keith Sullivan

INTRODUCTION

'In cyberspace no one can hear you scream'
(*Irish Times*, 2 February 2013)

Cyber-bullying is a form of psychological abuse created in real space and time then transmitted through cyberspace to selected recipients via a computer, smartphone or computer tablet. As with all bullying, bullying through the medium of cyberspace can have devastating effects. A major difference, however, is that when bullying occurs in real space and time (which I have named RST bullying), although the consequences can be hurtful and damaging, it is still confined within a limited space and timeframe, that is, an act of RST bullying is finite. Cyber-bullying, however, can quickly become 'viral'. The lifespan of even a single incident can be boundless because once launched into cyberspace it can be sent onwards to anyone, anywhere and at any time – 24/7. The initial recipients can add their own spin and bounce it back to the targeted person or on to others who can join in the cyberattack. Each new variant of the initial cyber message can feel like a fresh assault and the result of a single cyber-bullying projectile can turn into a multiple attack process. Furthermore, as the attacks develop 'a life of their own' they can become nastier. As the cyber-bullying perpetrators increase in number, they can elaborate and expand on what they have received before sending off their own particular vicious spin to their cyber venom.

This chapter introduces Action Against Cyber-Bullying (AAC), a programme I have created and offer freely to Irish schools as one instrument for helping to protect our children and hopefully, in the longer term, contributing towards significantly reducing school-related cyber-bullying.

INTRODUCING THE AAC PROGRAMME

Figure 13.1: The Four Components of Action Against Cyber-Bullying

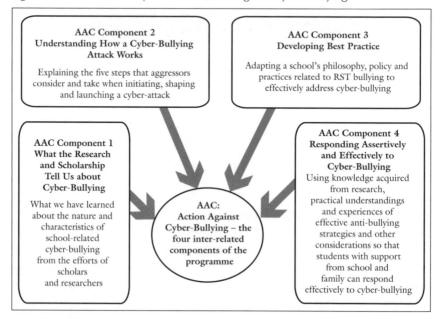

Action Against Cyber-Bullying consists of four inter-related compo-nents, as follows:

i. **AAC Component 1. What the Research and Scholarship Tell Us about Cyber-Bullying** provides a brief but succinct overview of what the literature and research tells us about cyber-bullying.

ii. **AAC Component 2. Understanding How a Cyber-Bullying Attack Works** describes the stages, considerations undergone, and decision points in the creation and transmission of cyber-bullying acts and processes (which consist of multiple acts) (see Sullivan, 2011, pp. 57–71).

iii. **AAC Component 3. Developing Best Practice** examines how best to create policy and practice so that strong foundations are provided for school communities to act fairly and effectively in anticipating and addressing the problem of cyber-bullying.

iv. **AAC Component 4. Responding Assertively and Effectively to Cyber-bullying** is designed to utilise the knowledge, policy and processes developed in the first three components to respond to cyber-bullying so that school communities can effectively support targeted students to respond assertively to cyber-bullying and become confident, assertive and technologically literate cyber-citizens.

These components are discussed more fully as follows:

AAC Component 1. What the research and scholarship tell us about cyber-bullying

a. **Defining and describing cyber-bullying**
   'Cyber-bullying is the deliberate, malicious and repeated use of information and computer technologies (ICT) by an individual or a group to hurt and/or manipulate and/or exclude another person or persons' (Updated from Sullivan, 2011, p. 57). The issue of repetition, which is a fundamental element of RST bullying, is contentious in cyberspace. While an act of cyber-bullying may be instigated only once, its repeated transmission over time and from one recipient to another can have the same effect as multiple acts of RST bullying.

b. **Who gets bullied?**
   According to the chaos theory of bullying (Sullivan, Cleary and Sullivan, 2004, p. 7), bullying can be specific, planned and aimed at a chosen victim(s), can be initiated because of characteristics a person possesses, or it can just happen to anyone for no apparent reason or by someone being in the wrong place at the wrong time. In other words, it may be specifically targeted, or apparently random. Studies of the rates of bullying in schools are a common way of gathering information about bullying. Often, when an anti-bullying programme is introduced into a school, pre-tests are run before the programme has started and post-tests are conducted a while after implementation to see if there has been a decrease in bullying: the accepted conclusion is that if the post-test shows a significant decline in rates of bullying then the anti-bullying programme has been a success. Unfortunately, in 'the real world of the school', there are many variables that are not taken into account when such studies are done. Examples are: i. variable and conflicting understandings of what constitutes

bullying, which can cause individuals to answer differently from each other (even if the students are told what bullying is before they take the pre- and post-test); ii. the mood of an adolescent on the day in question, which may be very different from yesterday's or tomorrow's mood etc.; iii. varying levels of literacy, and differing attitudes towards school, which may influence how students answer; iv. issues of social pressure, bonding, 'dissing' and friendship networks that can colour or determine a student's answers; and v. the ability of manipulative bullies to exercise power but to keep the processes and outcomes hidden. These are just a few reasons why questionnaires can be inaccurate, and also why quantitative approaches to social issues like bullying are never sufficient for getting a complete and accurate picture. Schools and classrooms, after all, are not laboratories; rather, they are often chaotic places where, despite our efforts, many of the 'variables' are hidden or cannot be controlled.

Based upon my own experiences of school culture as a student, a second-level teacher and a classroom and school researcher, after initial observations at the beginning of any school year both students and teachers soon have a reasonable sense of who among the school population is and is not vulnerable to bullying, and also who belongs to the in-betweeners group (where depending on circumstances they could become or escape being victimised). In other words, although research can provide indications of levels and types of bullying, teachers' and students' direct experiences within the lived culture of a school provide the basis for generating both useful knowledge for identifying problems before they occur, and similarly finding practical implementable solutions before things get out of hand. In other words, the knowledge is often 'within' the school population and just needs a reflective process to identify and assist immediate and practical solutions to emerge.

c. **Address 'school-related cyber-bullying'**
   Rather than dealing only with bullying that occurs within the confines of school hours and a school's precinct (school-based), it is more useful to focus on school-related bullying. Although cyber-bullying may not necessarily occur in school time and space, if it impacts upon staff, students and the general atmosphere of a school, it needs to be dealt with. Cyber-bullying can occur at any time and place and affect both students and staff

(for instance, through negative Facebook and Rate my Teacher postings) as well as the effective running and social climate of a school. This approach is also in keeping with the whole-school community approach as described in Chapter 12.

d. **Children and young people initiate and accelerate bullying processes for a variety of similar reasons, whether in real space and time or cyberspace**
    Cyber-bullying processes may result from and give expression to racist, homophobic, sexist, sexual and special needs prejudices, or any other factor that sets a person apart and gives perpetrators of bullying and their supporters an excuse to attack specific individuals or groups (ibid. pp. 48–56).

e. **Cyber-bullying and RST bullying usually contain the following elements:**

    1. They are both abusive and cowardly.
    2. Harm is intended.
    3. They are repetitive and can occur over a short or a long period of time.
    4. The person doing the bullying has more power than the one being victimised.
    5. They are often hidden from people in authority.
    6. Bullies do not expect either to be caught or to suffer any consequences.
    7. Those who bully are often feared for their bullying behaviour.
    8. Bullying can gradually undermine and damage the physical and mental well-being of the person being bullied.
    9. Bullying can be premeditated, organised and systematic, or it can be opportunistic. Once it starts, however, it is likely to continue.
    10. Although bullying may be directed towards one victim, it also may communicate a sense of menace to those who are witnesses but not contributors to it.
    11. Hurt experienced by a victim of bullying can be external (physical) and/or internal (emotional/psychological).
    12. All bullying causes psychological damage (ibid. pp. 10–11).

f. **A brief summary of what we know about cyber-bullying:**
    •   Cyber-bullying is carried out using mobile phones, computers or computer pads.

- Although cyber-bullying affects students' lives in school, it often happens outside of school hours.
- It is a growing problem, with a large percentage of young ICT users being aggressed against. See Chapter 1 for prevalence levels of cyber-bullying both nationally and internationally.
- What is happening face-to-face in schools and in virtual reality is intermingled. Cyber-bullying is a common experience, particularly among heavy users of the internet, and further-more, the forms of online and in-school bullying are more alike than different (Wolpert, 2008).
- Students are reluctant to tell adults. Girls are more prepared to tell adults than boys (O'Moore, 2012).
- In Juvonen and Gross's 2008 online survey of American teenagers, only 10% of the study's cyber-victims reported the bullying to parents or other adults because:
  - They thought their internet access would be restricted (31% overall – 46% and 27% respectively among 12–14-year-old girls and boys).
  - One-third did not tell an adult because they were afraid they would get into trouble with their parents.
  - Wolpert (2008) found that when parental support was high, children experienced less bullying.
- A 2007 study carried out among American high school students by Harris Interactive found that while anonymity may be an initial feature of cyber-bullying, about three out of four targeted students eventually figured out who was doing it.
- In 75% of cases, it was either a friend or someone they knew from school or elsewhere. (Li's 2007 study, on the other hand, found that less than half knew who their tormentor was.)
- High school students in the Harris Interactive research reported the following (sometimes multiple) emotional responses to being cyberbullied:
  - 56% reported feeling angry.
  - 32% said they were hurt.
  - 34% reported being embarrassed.
  - 11% said they felt scared.
  - 58% claimed it did not bother them.
- The same high school students thought their peers cyberbully for one (or more) of the following reasons:
  - They think it is funny (81%).
  - They do not like the person (64%).

- ○ They see the victim as a loser (45%).
- ○ They probably don't see it as a big deal (58%).
- ○ They don't expect any tangible consequences (47%).
- ○ They do not think they will get caught (45%).
- Cyber-bullying occurs in a world where children and teens are more at home than their parents and (older) teachers; however, it is also a world where technical literacy does not equate with the ability to protect oneself from cyber-menace.
- Students sometimes use mobile phones to bully during school hours.
- In most cases, students who are cyber-bullied are also being bullied physically and/or psychologically in the real world, and often at school (Juvonen and Gross, 2008).
- Li (2006), O'Moore (2012) and Wang et al. (2009) found that boys cyber-bully slightly more than girls, and that girls are cyber-bullied more often than boys, especially in their mid-teens (Li, 2006; Wang et al., 2009).
- O'Neil's (2008) Canadian study of pre-teen and teenage girls similarly found that although they had developed an armoury of electronic processes to broadcast hurtful information among their peers about chosen victims, this was part of a process of relational aggression that was an extension of attacks occurring in real space and time.
- American research suggests that school-related cyber-bullying follows the same pattern as RST bullying in that they both occur infrequently at fifth grade (9 and 10 year olds), then gradually increase, peaking at eighth grade (12 and 13 year olds), then gradually fall off and quite significantly so by eleventh grade (15 and 16 year olds) (Williams and Guerra, 2007).
- When students felt more connected to their schools in a trusting, fair and pleasant climate, there was a 9% decline in the odds of internet bullying (ibid.).
- If students perceived their peers to be trustworthy, caring and helpful, the self-reporting of internet bullying decreased by 7% (ibid.).

g. **Cyber-bullying is unlike other more traditional forms of bullying for the following reasons:**
- The anonymity of communicating in cyber-space makes it easier for the bully to engage in hostile, aggressive acts (Johnson, 2009).

- Being able to send a communication through cyber-space at any time, and anonymously, enables the bully to harass their victim twenty-four hours a day (ibid.).
- This new technology allows victims to be attacked at any time, and in any place (ibid.).
- The invincibility and anonymity of cyber-bullies makes this behaviour difficult to manage within the school system and encourages more youth to take part (ibid.).

AAC Component 2. Understanding how a cyber-bullying attack works

The decision to carry out a cyber-bullying attack is a conscious act with malicious intent. AAC Component 2 shows that this entails a five-step process, which includes three steps where selections are made and two decision points, as follows:

Step 1. Decision point i. To initiate (or escalate) a cyber-bullying process or not?

At this point, the potential aggressor(s) has the opportunity to initiate a cyber-attack (or escalate it if a cyber-bullying process has already been initiated) or to decide against it. If initiated or continued (after an earlier attack), this decision starts (or escalates) a process that when enacted will contain all the elements of cyber-bullying. This act of bullying could be restricted to the cyber dimension but is often combined with RST bullying.

Steps 2, 3 and 4 are inter-related choices that are made during the preparation of a cyberattack. They are presented here as sequential but can be decided in a different order or as part of a single process.

Step 2. Selection point i. The technology is chosen (the machine for creating the weapon for firing into cyberspace)

A laptop or desktop computer, a mobile, smartphone or landline (very limited beyond obscene phone calls and easy to trace) or tablets are the hardware. Except for the landline, they all can act as mini-factories both for building cyber-ammunition and firing it into cyber-space. The nature of the theme to be developed and the choice of where it will be placed will decide what mechanism to use. Until recently, the computer was the weapon of choice but now there are more options as constantly improving smartphones transmit not only text messages, but also photos, short videos, email communications and social network messages. Due to the small screens of smartphones, however, computers are still better placed for creating sophisticated and high-quality products.

Figure 13.2: AAC Component 2. Understanding How a Cyber-Bullying Attack Works

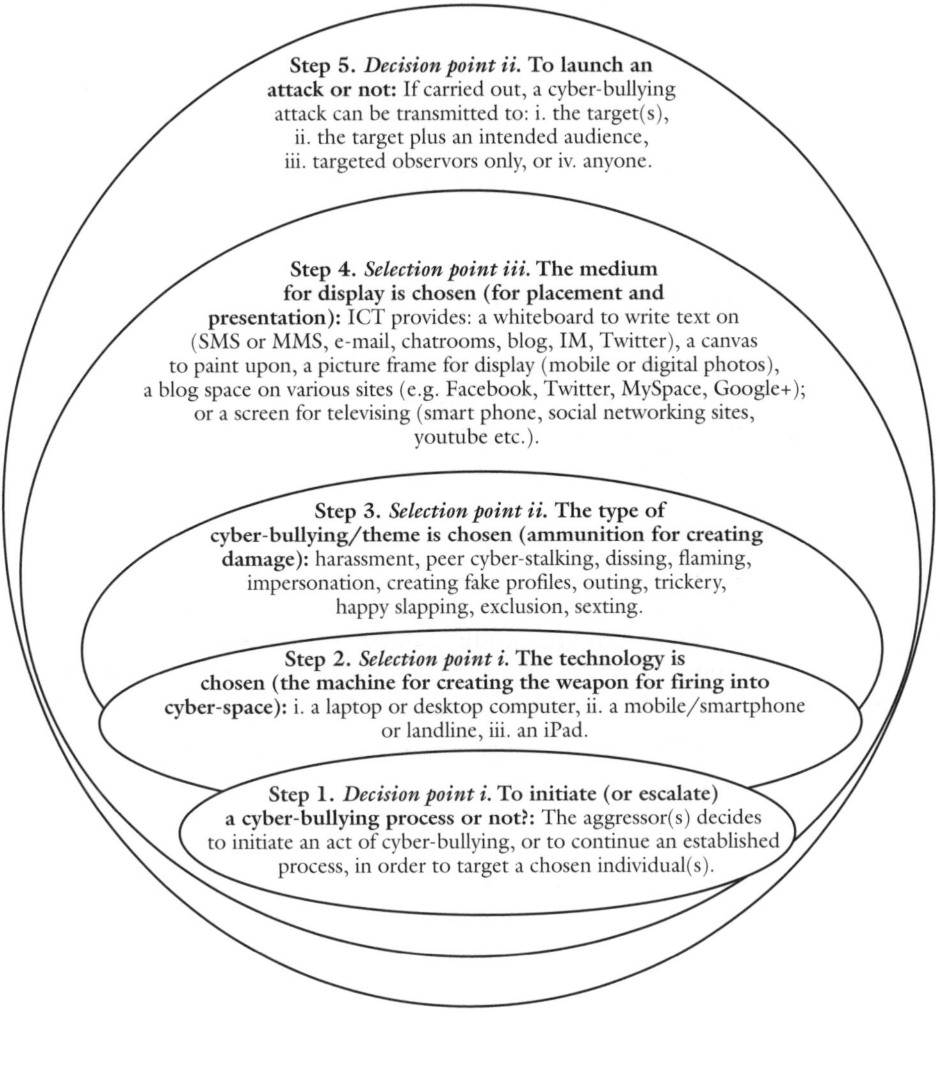

Step 5. *Decision point ii.* **To launch an attack or not:** If carried out, a cyber-bullying attack can be transmitted to: i. the target(s), ii. the target plus an intended audience, iii. targeted observors only, or iv. anyone.

Step 4. *Selection point iii.* **The medium for display is chosen (for placement and presentation):** ICT provides: a whiteboard to write text on (SMS or MMS, e-mail, chatrooms, blog, IM, Twitter), a canvas to paint upon, a picture frame for display (mobile or digital photos), a blog space on various sites (e.g. Facebook, Twitter, MySpace, Google+); or a screen for televising (smart phone, social networking sites, youtube etc.).

Step 3. *Selection point ii.* **The type of cyber-bullying/theme is chosen (ammunition for creating damage):** harassment, peer cyber-stalking, dissing, flaming, impersonation, creating fake profiles, outing, trickery, happy slapping, exclusion, sexting.

Step 2. *Selection point i.* **The technology is chosen (the machine for creating the weapon for firing into cyber-space):** i. a laptop or desktop computer, ii. a mobile/smartphone or landline, iii. an iPad.

Step 1. *Decision point i.* **To initiate (or escalate) a cyber-bullying process or not?:** The aggressor(s) decides to initiate an act of cyber-bullying, or to continue an established process, in order to target a chosen individual(s).

The mobile phone (via text, digital camera, email), computer or tablet provide access to a whiteboard to write upon, a canvas or picture frame for exhibiting, and a screen or stage upon which to create a video representation. (The internet gives access to social networking sites Facebook, Twitter, MySpace, Google+ etc., IM (instant messaging), and chat-rooms and makes it possible to hack into people's email accounts and create anti-teacher postings.) Cyber-space provides the stage or canvas to which items can be sent for display or to be played out. Those in the know can alert others by 'school telegraph'; others can randomly hear about or just come across the displayed item.

Step 3. Selection point ii. The type of cyber-bullying/theme is chosen (ammunition for creating damage)

The aggressor(s) chooses a theme and develops it according to its nature in order to embarrass, humiliate, intimidate or exclude that targeted person(s). The following is an overview of common themes and types of cyber-bullying (adapted from Willard):

Online harassment is one-on-one cyber-bullying and consists of unpleasant texts, sexts, email messages or other forms of posting that are created and sent in the same or a variety of forms to an intended victim and/or others.

Peer cyberstalking. Among teens and young people, this has come to mean the use of the internet or other forms of ICT to stalk a chosen victim, that is, not only to harass but also to threaten and create a sense of fear and impending danger through an ongoing and intense campaign of cyber-attacks. It is similar to online harassment but is more severe. It can include making false accusations, threats of harm, and the seeking out of 'dirt' for harassment and intimidation.

Dissing is the sending of harmful, untrue or cruel information to a chosen victim(s) and to third parties. It can include making nasty and false accusations and/or posting such material online with the intention of damaging friendships and reputations and misrepresenting a person's character. Wiktionary defines dissing as to 'put someone down, or show disrespect by the use of insulting language or dismissive behavior'.

Online harassment, dissing and peer cyber-stalking are similar in that they are forms of direct attacks on a chosen victim or victims. Online harassment and peer cyber-stalking concern cyber-bullying by one person against another but the latter is more sinister. Dissing, on the other hand, consists of both direct attacks on a victim and also orchestrating a wider campaign to include third parties either as observers or as contributors, such as by posting on open sites and/ or asking third parties for comments. The term cyber-stalking refers to a form of child grooming and the predatory practice of adults who use the internet to contact and attempt to meet up with vulnerable minors in order to coerce them into allowing the adult to commit acts of sexual abuse.

Flaming is hostile and insulting interaction between internet users. Flaming usually occurs when people are involved in discussion boards, Internet Relay Chat (IRC), or email or video-sharing websites. It is usually the result of discussion about real-world issues like politics, religion and philosophy, or other similar issues that polarise subpopulations (for example, warring over electronic games or rock bands). Flaming can be considered cyber-bullying if someone carries it out relentlessly or if it is orchestrated so that a group of people make a joint attack against another.

Impersonation is when a person humiliates another by pretending to be that person, either through hacking into that person's email account or otherwise assuming their identity, and sending offensive messages or posting such material on social networking sites, attacking others, and/or appearing to be hostile or stupid.

Creating fake profiles to spread false, malicious and untrue information to embarrass, humiliate and attack a person's credibility is done through creating a website or blog and posting such information there.

Outing is a form of victimisation in which someone is embarrassed and humiliated when sensitive, private or untrue information is posted about them through texts or photographic transmission by mobile phone, email, social network postings, etc. It may also involve making public a person's sexual orientation or suggesting a false sexual orientation in order to demean and embarrass that person.

Trickery is when outing is done through obtaining information by devious means, such as pretending to be a friend and then sending that information to others by posting, texting or emailing in order to embarrass and humiliate. Because of the two steps involved, it is a sort of double-edged bullying.

Exclusion is the mean-minded and purposeful exclusion of individuals from an online group. This is made worse by making sure that the victim and everyone else knows that he or she is excluded and why, thereby causing further embarrassment and humiliation.

Sexting is the sending of sexually explicit photographs or messages via mobile phone. Sexting can be used as a crucial central part of or an addition to any of the above forms of cyber-bullying.

Step 4. Selection point iii. The medium for display is chosen (for placement and presentation)

After the aggressor has chosen the type of cyber-bullying theme and the weapon for firing it into cyber-space, he or she will need to decide how to develop and present it in cyber-space. These spaces allow virtual whiteboards (for writing text messages, emails, chat-room communications, blogs, instant messages or twitter raves) or a canvas (upon which to draw a cartoon), a frame (for mounting pictures) or a screen (for playing video representations).

American website Cyberbullyalert.com has identified the five most utilised means for developing and posting such cyber-bullying creations as follows:

1. **Social networking sites** such as Facebook, Twitter, MySpace, Google+ are currently popular. The social networking carried out here is similar to what young people do in real life as they attempt to make friends and to understand how life and relationships work. The downside of these sites is that they also provide cyber-bullying opportunities where individuals can choose to post hurtful and humiliating items and/or wage a campaign against a targeted person. Theft of user IDs and passwords also occurs, allowing malicious postings to be made by someone posing as the person whose cyber-identity has been stolen.

Twitter serves the purpose of social reporting and allows people to discuss activities, to provide an ongoing narrative from the exciting to the mundane, and to make comment on what others are doing. There has been an increase in the number of nasty and hurtful messages sent 'via Tweet' to as many site users as possible.

2. **Instant messaging (IM)** is a staple of major internet companies such as AOL, Yahoo, Google (through its Gmail service) and MSN (also found on social networks, such as Facebook). IM is made up of a collection of technologies that allow text-based real-time communication to occur between two or more recipients. It differs from chat rooms in that, rather than cyber-talking with a large and often anonymous web-based group, an individual can be chosen from a list of known friends and contacts. Wikipedia compares chat room and IM conversations with a telephone versus a barroom context. With a telephone, you need to know contact details to reach the other person, whereas in a bar, you just show up and see who is there to chat with. Instant messaging facilitates immediate receipt and acknowledgement of and reply to messages and can also use webcams and limited file transfer for its communications. Unfortunately, it is also used as a means of harassment. With IM, individuals have been known to adopt fake screen names and then 'ping' chosen individuals with profanity and threats of violence.

3. **Email** is a relatively anonymous medium, especially if identifiers bear no resemblance to a sender's actual identity, or if a person hacks into an email account and, posing as the account holder, posts whatever they wish to whomever they decide to send to. Threatening messages, rumours, lies, cruel images, etc. have been sent via email with false or stolen identities.

4. **Photoshop.** Tools provided by Photoshop allow the modification of acquired photographs so that harmless and attractive images can be turned into insulting or pornographic ones. These can then be transmitted via mobile phone or internet. Perpetrators can also secretly take embarrassing pictures and then transmit them so as to embarrass, humiliate and expose their targets.

5. **Blogs.** Many teenagers have created Internet blogs with the aim of dissing rivals or enemies and also inviting others to participate

in this process through posting derogatory and insulting comments. Because blogs are easy to set up and the creators are hard to identify, they can become destructive, hurtful and permanent spaces.

Step 5. Decision point ii. To launch or not to launch an attack

When everything is in place, the aggressor must then decide whether or not to activate the cyber-bullying (and initiate or carry on a process). This is the second and more significant decision point since the first decision point is only theoretical. The type of bullying has been chosen, created and turned into ammunition. The mechanism for firing this into cyber-space has been chosen and at this point the trigger is pulled. Cyber-space lacks boundaries, in terms of: i. Observers/participants – all and sundry can potentially witness the bullying materials, and ii. Time – a cyber-bullying act can be played and re-played, as new observers arrive and re-play at will, while others can be alerted to its existence. A cyber-bullying attack can be transmitted to: i. The target(s), ii. The target(s) plus an intended audience, iii. Targeted observers only; iv. All and sundry.

AAC Component 3. Developing best practice

AAC Component 3. Developing Best Practice is the central foundation for addressing cyber-bullying in a school. Relatively speaking, cyber-bullying is a recent phenomenon. Although in some respects it differs from traditional bullying, it is still mean-minded and intended to cause harm to the person being bullied. Once a student has been identified as having cyber-bullied another member of the school, then the school's policy and practice in relation to bullying can be instituted and strategies and programmes can be adapted to address the cyber-bullying, to solve the problem and to provide support to those targeted. In expanding current policy and practice to address cyber-bullying effectively, the following steps are suggested.

Step 1. Establish strong, sensible and inclusive foundations

1. Policies and procedures used by the school for dealing with RST bullying should provide the foundations for creating cyber-bullying policy and practice.

2. In combination with these, it is important also to refer to contemporary research to help respond effectively to the issues and problems that are:
   - Similar to RST bullying;
   - Distinctive from cyber-bullying.

Figure 13.3: AAC Component 3. Developing Best Practice

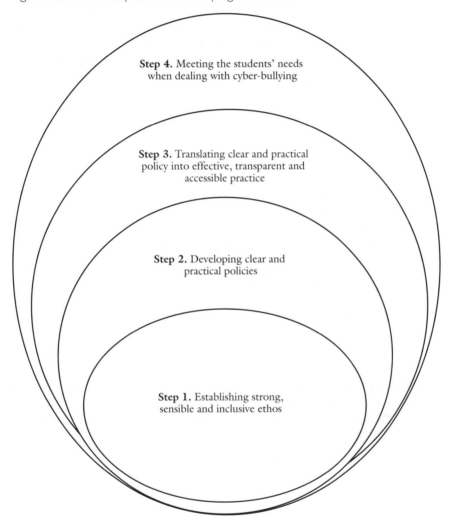

Step 4. Meeting the students' needs when dealing with cyber-bullying

Step 3. Translating clear and practical policy into effective, transparent and accessible practice

Step 2. Developing clear and practical policies

Step 1. Establishing strong, sensible and inclusive ethos

3. Because students are usually much more literate about the technological aspects of ICT than adults, and tend to understand the dynamics of cyber-bullying more, they need to be centrally involved in plans to tackle it in their schools. A partnership

between the school, students, parents and community and a sharing of the varying experiences and expertise is crucial for effectively confronting the problem of cyber-bullying.

4. It is also useful to gather together a cyber-bullying resource kit, with a small collection of books and articles that provide overviews of important central issues, concerns, strategies and programmes. As there are now so many excellent websites (which are constantly being updated), it is useful to have a selection of the best of these, with local ones being particularly relevant, and with a choice from the best of overseas websites, examples of which are found at the end of this chapter.

Step 2. Develop clear and practical policies

1. The policies relating to cyber-bullying should, where appropriate, reflect those used for dealing with bullying in real space and time. New knowledge relating to cyber-bullying should be noted and built upon as it emerges.
2. Legal issues relating to cyber-bullying can be complex, unclear and are still emerging in this largely uncharted area. They also differ from country to country. The bottom line is that the school's duty of care is what is most important when dealing with cyber-bullying, and if a potential threat or danger is present then this should be the first consideration. See Chapter 18 for a detailed overview of the legal perspective.
3. When developing policy, it is important to seek local advice and support in creating the policy. It is also important to have advice from legal and ICT experts in order to anticipate important issues not immediately identified.
4. As this is a new process, it is important to educate members of the school community about content and reasons for inclusion of the various aspects of a programme and to make it clear how they can respond to cyber-bullying, whether it happens to them or to someone else.
5. Members of the greater school community should, where possible and practical, be involved in the process of developing policies, both from the point of view of contributing to the programme and in terms of having a sense of ownership.

Step 3. Translate clear and practical policy into effective, transparent and accessible practice

1. Although schools are becoming aware of the damage that cyber-bullying can cause, it can be difficult to track down and deal with perpetrators as they often hide behind pseudonyms and their anonymity is hard to penetrate.
2. Web pages are difficult to take down and ICT is in a stage of rapid and ongoing innovations within a context of few and largely ineffective controls.
3. It is also true that any new frontier throws up issues and anomalies that lead to the development of rules and regulations.
4. Because of the particular nature and complexion of instances of cyber-aggression, legislation and processes for prosecuting individuals for abuse on the internet are currently in the process of being created and enacted.

Key responses to cyber-bullying may include:
- Discussing and gathering information;
- Providing emotional and psychological support to those being cyber-attacked;
- Attempting to discover the identity of the one who has initiated the cyber-attack.

The cloak of anonymity can be thrown open by:
- Retaining evidence of cyber-aggression and cyber-bullying by downloading and printing the images or text involved;
- Taking screenshots of bullying websites;
- Speaking with a lawyer, or, if a crime has occurred, contacting the police.

Some tactics for proceeding may include:
- Telling the cyber-bully to stop in a non-emotional, assertive message;
- Informing cyber-bullies that threatening messages posted online can be traced to him or her by accessing the nine-digit IP attached to the computer from which the message is sent;
- Ignoring or blocking the cyber-bully;
- Changing the target's screen name or email address;
- Avoiding the website where the victim has been attacked;
- Filing a complaint on the offending website or mobile phone net-work. This might be particularly effective since cyber-bullying is a

violation of the 'terms of use' of most mobile phone companies, ISPs (internet service providers) and websites.

Step 4. Meeting the student's needs when dealing with cyber-bullying

When assisting a student who has been cyber-bullied (and in-school bullied as well), it is important to deal with the situation humanely and clearly, using whatever counselling and listening skills are appropriate, as in any case of bullying. It may also be appropriate to assist/support a student in responding to a cyber-attack in an assertive, clear and empowering fashion.

AAC Component 4. Responding assertively and effectively to cyber-bullying

The need to be vigilant about cyberbullying but to also support child and adolescent development in relation to ICT and digital citizenship. Boyd and Marwick (2011) argue that issues such as cyberbullying need to be addressed calmly and thoughtfully and that the aim should be to provide support in an empowering fashion and within the context of adolescent culture:

> Antibullying efforts cannot be successful if they make teenagers feel victimized without providing them the support to go from a position of victimization to one of empowerment. When teenagers acknowledge that they're being bullied, adults need to provide programs similar to those that help victims of abuse. And they must recognize that emotional recovery is a long and difficult process.
>
> But if the goal is to intervene at the moment of victimization, the focus should be to work within teenagers' cultural frame, encourage empathy and help young people understand when and where drama has serious consequences. Interventions must focus on positive concepts like healthy relationships and digital citizenship rather than starting with the negative framing of bullying. The key is to help young people feel independently strong, confident and capable without first requiring them to see themselves as either an oppressed person or an oppressor.
>
> (Boyd and Marwick, 2011)

Figure 13.4: AAC Component 4. Responding Assertively and Effectively to Cyber-Bullying

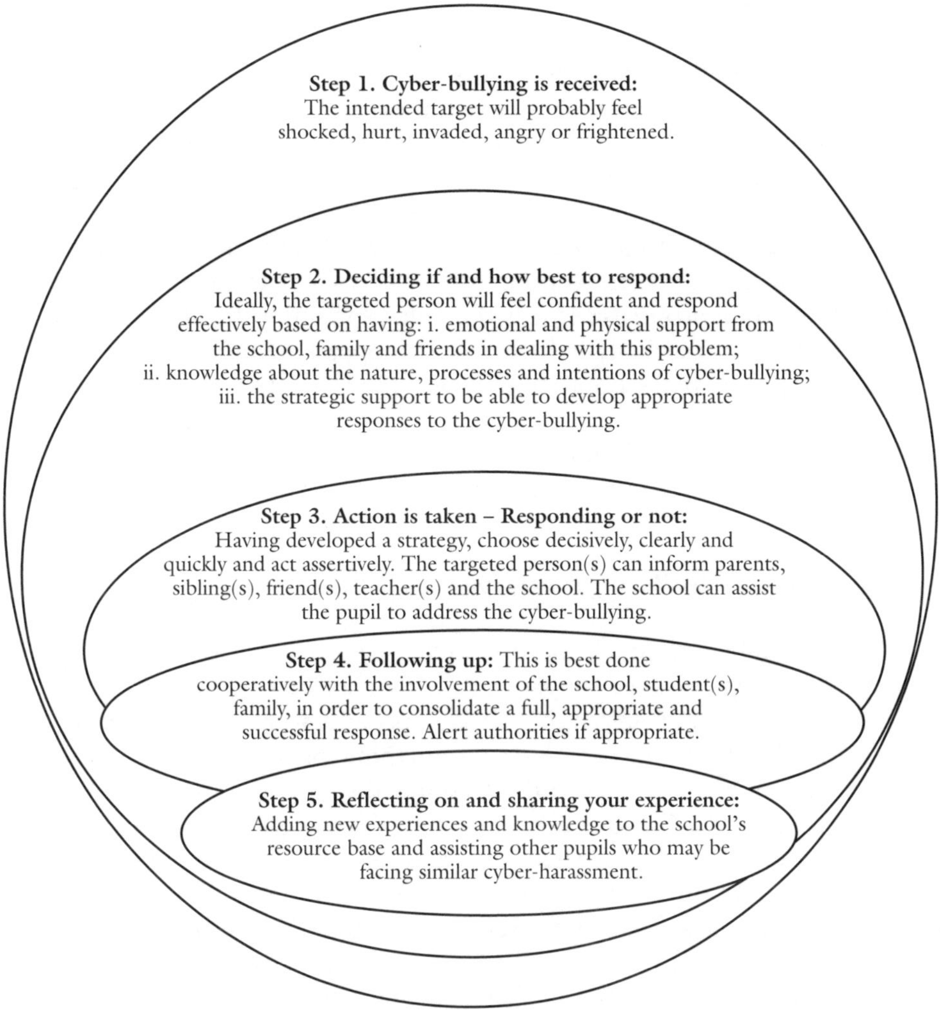

Step 1. Cyber-bullying is received:
The intended target will probably feel
shocked, hurt, invaded, angry or frightened.

Step 2. Deciding if and how best to respond:
Ideally, the targeted person will feel confident and respond
effectively based on having: i. emotional and physical support from
the school, family and friends in dealing with this problem;
ii. knowledge about the nature, processes and intentions of cyber-bullying;
iii. the strategic support to be able to develop appropriate
responses to the cyber-bullying.

Step 3. Action is taken – Responding or not:
Having developed a strategy, choose decisively, clearly and
quickly and act assertively. The targeted person(s) can inform parents,
sibling(s), friend(s), teacher(s) and the school. The school can assist
the pupil to address the cyber-bullying.

Step 4. Following up: This is best done
cooperatively with the involvement of the school, student(s),
family, in order to consolidate a full, appropriate and
successful response. Alert authorities if appropriate.

Step 5. Reflecting on and sharing your experience:
Adding new experiences and knowledge to the school's
resource base and assisting other pupils who may be
facing similar cyber-harassment.

Adopting Component 4 may be a contentious issue. Component 4 is designed to create immediate, long-term and appropriate solutions to cyberbullying attacks. It is also potentially the most rewarding aspect of the AAC programme. It is where the strength of the preparatory foundations of the other 3 components is tested. A firm, unambiguous and strong response to cyberattacks against a school's members (students or staff), is a demonstration of the ability to deal with both immediate and ongoing cyberbullying attacks. It is also a symbolic statement that the school will not tolerate cyberaggression and cyberbullying and is able to handle it, in whatever form it takes. Furthermore, it informs perpetrators that they will be made to take responsibility for their actions, that there will be consequences. Cyberbullying may happen inside or outside of school space and time, but both from and in loco parentis perspective, and in terms of a sense of reponsibility and care boht at school and within its wider community, the school will strive to create and protect a safe and healthy environment. On the other hand, learning to deal effectively and assertively with a cyber-attack could be seen as a useful preparation for life.

As was identified by an NCPC study (Harris Interactive, 2007), in 75% of cases, students could eventually identify their aggressor. Responding here with support and follow-up from the school would seem appropriate. If it is difficult to identify the attacker and the bullying is particularly offensive or appears to be coming from an adult, then the school should take over and the authorities be contacted. Such a process is potentially empowering for the targeted individual and symbolically shows any attacker that the school is able to turn theory to practice and to do so effectively.

Step 1. Cyber-bullying is received

A cyber-bullying attack occurs. The targeted person may feel shocked, hurt, invaded, angry, etc. (this may be the first attack or part of an ongoing onslaught). It is important to take a moment or two, to catch breath, before doing anything further. Emotions will be raised and it is crucial to think things through and to respond as effectively as possible. It is also important that the safety (physical and psychological) of the targeted person is ensured. Unlike bullying in real space and time, where the perpetrator is known, cyber-bullying can involve attack from a stranger, possibly an adult predator.

If possible, it is preferable for there to be a person in the school whose job it is to deal with cyber-bullying, who is an expert on ICT and also has some counselling training. Addressing how best to respond to a cyber-bullying attack could also be the basis for a social studies or health education module, or the school could decide to address it with special sessions outside of any syllabus.

Of course, the cultural divide that can occur between adolescents and the adult world means that the school and parents need to put effort into assuring the students that they are well able to handle such situations and that their approach is a deep one whereby, if a student does respond, he or she will be safeguarded.

Step 2. Deciding if and how best to respond

A recipient of the cyber-bullying may be: a. confident, computer-literate and well able to respond; or b. taken aback, lacking in confidence, 'stunned' and unable to respond; or c. somewhere along the spectrum between these two endpoints. Deciding how to respond may be instantaneous and effective, instantaneous and ineffective, or non-responsive, in that the targeted person hopes that the bullying will go away and not recur. (While this could happen, a successful attack followed by an apparently passive non-response may encourage more attacks.) Either way, the target needs support, from the school and/or family and friends.

Step 3. Action is taken? To respond or not to respond, that is the question

There are essentially two ways to act in response to a cyberattack:

i. **Not to respond but rather to ignore it.** The perpetrator does not get the expected response and therefore there is no fuel with which to send another cyber-rocket of words, images, etc., in effect, an onslaught of further humiliation. The argument goes that the cyber-aggressors want you to respond because no matter what you say, no matter how neutral or articulate you are, 'they' will make fun of it, twist it and send it off into cyberspace for yet another round of humiliation. You can also block anyone who sends offensive messages and not pass them on. You can also discuss strategies with friends and support each other if any of you receive cyber-nasties in any form.

ii. **To respond in a careful and calculated fashion**. One of the major expectations is that all forms of bullying are essentially cowardly behaviour; if you respond assertively then the attacker will back off. For instance, a statement could be made that the cyber-act has been received and photographed/recorded and reported to the school (or the authorities) to deal with and what is more the sender's details have been noted and ISP has been informed. (Facebook, for instance, is known to respond responsibly to requests of censure in relation to cyber-bullying.) A school anti-cyber-bullying committee could draft a standard statement that students could use to respond to cyber-attacks, support the attacked person to write a specific response when an attack has occurred, send a parallel response to the cyber-attacker and/or respond on behalf of the attacked person.

Step 4. Following up

The initial response will need to be followed up. The school can help to address the cyber-bullying by working things through with the student and parents. At this point the school should refer to and possibly develop its policy and practice for dealing with perpetrators of any kind of bullying. Counselling or cyber-mentoring (see Sullivan, 2011, pp. 175–87) may be useful at this point.

Step 5. Reflecting on and sharing your experience

When the cyber-bullying has been successfully dealt with, the experiences of the student could add new and practical learning experiences to the school's resource base and could assist with other incidents.

CONCLUDING REMARKS

Cyber-bullying has become a major contemporary problem, not only in Ireland but internationally. Schools are very busy places and teachers' primary concern is to educate their students and dealing with other issues takes second place. So how schools fully address this primary responsibility and still fulfil their obligation to provide a safe and creative psychological and physical environment can be problematic when there are limited resources. Primary schools are generally smaller than second level, and teachers in these schools, given the nature of the school and the developmental stages of the children, means that teachers get to know their class of children, usually twenty-five to thirty students, quite well. They can therefore more easily help to sort out any problems, such as cyber-bullying, which may arise.

It is in the tween and teen years at the beginning of second level where three major changes occur that disrupt this supportive foundation and which can lead to fractured responses to difficult situations, such as dealing with cyber-bullying. Specifically, i. as adolescence sets in, students start to 'push' against the adult population in their efforts to establish independence (but in so doing they sometimes isolate themselves from adults who could support them), ii. as they move into second-level schooling, despite having homerooms, teachers largely teach their subjects of specialisation to large numbers of students. In the process, knowledge about individual students and the ability to provide guidance and socio-emotional support decreases. Furthermore, the sheer size of many second-level schools further undermines the ability of teachers to know individual students' abilities, personalities, potentials and problems they may be experiencing. This can create students who feel isolated and also at the mercy of those (often older students) who are exerting power and control, in the form of RST bullying and cyber-bullying. Teachers may have the will and the ability to assist those in trouble but these primary blocks can largely stop this from happening. In terms of problem avoidance and solution seeking, in addressing this issue of cyber-bullying I would suggest that a five-part cooperative approach (partnership) is crucial to the development and institution of effective policy and practice and the ownership of it. The five groups are as follows:

1. **The students**

    Cyber-bullying has been developed and carried out largely by the students, who spend so much free time in cyber-space that they are constantly adding to their ICT dexterity and expertise. Administrators, teachers and parents are often estranged from these developments and do not participate in this ongoing upgrading process and its accompanying increased cyber-fluency.

    Although students can be involved in cyber-bullying as participants, targets and observers, they are potentially the most powerful of the anti-bully lobby and can change the dynamics within peer groups that support or reject bullying behaviour.

    Because young people tend to be more literate in ICT than adults, and especially in the social network areas, it is important that they are central to identifying the specifics of a problem and also in helping to identify solutions.

2. **The practitioners: teachers, administrators, counsellors/ psychologists who directly and indirectly deal with bullying on a day-by-day basis**

    On a day-to-day basis, it is the practitioners who are most crucial to the recognition of bullying in all its forms, who repeatedly show the determination to tackle it, and who have the vision and imagination to adopt and/or develop anti-bullying programmes and to implement their use in schools. They have not generally, however, clocked up the time to be fluent or dextrous in the culture of high-speed accessibility and understanding the nature and subtleties of cyber-space. They do, however, have knowledge and experience in problem-solving and providing empathy and support, etc.

3. **The younger teachers**
   Younger teachers in the early stages of their career may lack the experience and understandings of more established teachers but they are closer in age, dexterity, interest and practical ability. Their teaching skills may not be as finely honed as those of more experienced teachers but in ICT skills they may be closer to those of the students and this could act as a creative bridge between teachers and students.

4. **Parents and families of students**
   A partnership between the school, the students and the parents and the students is central to the effectiveness of any anti-bullying programme. This could take bullying out of a murky hidden realm and bring it to the light. Parental involvement can provide support, knowledge, expertise and openness in terms of dealing with the ramifications of bullying in both the school and community environment, and could create a continuum of consistent expectations and safety measures between home and school.

5. **Experts from the wider school community**
   Within any greater school community, there will be those with skills in the areas of ICT, the law and those with management and critical skills who can critique, improve and support creative development. It is important to seek out such people to be part of a full and creative response to dealing effectively with cyber-bullying.

Finally, I would like to state that the Action Against Cyber-Bullying Programme has been created as a process for addressing cyber-bullying in our schools. It is, however, a mute tool that can only come alive in the hands of people with the caring, insights, intelligence and ability to take ownership humanely and creatively and address and defeat this very destructive problem.

REFERENCES

Bissonette, A.M. *CyberLaw: Maximizing Safety and Minimizing Risk in Classrooms* (Thousand Oaks, CA: Corwin Press, 2009)

Boyd, D. and Marwick, A.E. 'Bullying as True Drama', *New York Times*, 23 September 2011, p. A35, http://www.nytimes.com/2011/09/23/opinion/why-cyber-bullying-rhetoric-misses-the-mark.html [accessed 1 February 2013]

Dinkes, R., Kemp, J. and Baum, K. *Indicators of School Crime and Safety: 2008* (NCES 2009-022/NCJ 226343) (Washington, DC: National Center for Education Statistics, Institute of Education Sciences, US Department of Education, and Bureau of Justice Statistics, Office of Justice Programs, US Department of Justice, 2009)

Harris Interactive, *Teens and Cyber-Bullying: Executive Summary of a Report on Research* (Arlington, VA: National Crime Prevention Council, 2007)

Johnson, J.M. 'The Impact of Cyber Bullying: A New Type of Relational Aggression', paper presented at the American Counseling Association Annual Conference and Exposition, Charlotte, NC, 2009

Juvonen, J. and Gross, E. 'Extending the School Grounds? Bullying Experiences in Cyberspace', *Journal of School Health*, 78, 2008, pp. 496–505

Li, Q. 'Cyber-Bullying in Schools: A Research of Gender Differences', *School Psychology International*, 27, 2006, pp. 157–70

Li, Q. 'Bullying in the New Playground: A Research into Cyber-Bullying and Cyber Victimization', *Australasian Journal of Educational Technology*, 23, 2007, pp. 435–54

Ó Dochartaigh, N. *Internet Research Skills*, 3rd edn (Los Angeles, London, New Delhi, Singapore and Washington DC: Sage Publications, 2012)

O'Moore, M. 'Cyber-Bullying: The Situation in Ireland', *Pastoral Care in Education: An International Journal of Personal, Social and Emotional Development*, 30, pp. 209–23

O'Neil, S. *Bullying by Tween and Teen Girls: A Literature, Policy and Resource Review*, Kookaburra Consulting Inc. (2008), www.sacsc.ca/literature%20review_finalSON.pdf [accessed 28 June 2010]

Patchin, J. and Hinduja, S. *Cyber-Bullying Prevention and Response: Expert Perspectives* (New York: Routledge, 2012)

Robinson, G. and Maines, B. *Bullying: A Complete Guide to the Support Group Method* (London: Sage Publications and Paul Chapman Publishing, 2008)

Schrock, A. and Boyd, D. 'Problematic Youth Interaction Online: Solicitation, Harassment and Cyber-Bullying', in K.B. Wright and L.M. Webb (eds), *Computer-Mediated Communication in Personal Relationships* (New York: Peter Lang, 2011)

Sullivan, K. *The Anti-Bullying Handbook* (New York: Oxford University Press, 2000)

Sullivan, K. *A Critique and Formative Evaluation of Kia Kaha: Our Place. The New Zealand Police's Anti-Bullying Programme for Secondary Schools* (Wellington: The New Zealand Police, 2005)

Sullivan, K., Cleary, M. and Sullivan, G. *Bullying in Secondary Schools: What It Looks Like and How to Manage It* (London: Paul Chapman Publishing, 2004)

Wang, J., Iannotti R.J. and Nansel, T.R. 'School Bullying among Adolescents in the United States: Physical, Verbal, Relational and Cyber', *Journal of Adolescent Health*, 21, 2009, pp. 368–75

Willard, N. *Educators' Guide to Cyber-Bullying and Cyberthreats*, http://www.cyberbully.org/cyberbully/docs/cbcteducator.pdf [accessed 28 June 2012]

Williams, K.R. and Guerra, N.G. 'Prevalence and Predictors of Internet Bullying', *Journal of Adolescent Health*, 41, 2007, pp. 14–21

Wolpert, S. 'Bullying of Teenagers Online is Common, UCLA Psychologists Report' (2008), http://newsroom.ucla.edu/portal/ucla/bullying-of-teenagers-online-is-64265.aspx (accessed 12 May 2012)

Websites

Websites are very useful resources because they provide a range of information about various aspects of cyber-bullying. Unlike books, they are in a position to respond to what is happening; consequently, what new knowledge we have gained is contemporaneously presented, as is basic information on the nature of cyber-bullying and the wider cyberworld within which it exists, etc., as well as suggestions about how to deal with and counter the phenomenon. There are a large number of useful Irish-based sites that have been included below, while some useful international sites have also been included.

Irish websites:

http://abc.tcd.ie/ Anti-Bullying Centre, Trinity College Dublin – lots of useful information.

http://www.pcclean.ie/ask-fm-response-to-recent-cyber-bully-victims-in-northwest/ PC cleaning tools to protect and serve computer users.

http://www.scoilnet.ie/pdf_webwise/07_cyber-bullying.pdf Scoilnet, excellent for schools.

http://www.hotline.ie/documents/Cyber-bullying.pdf A Guide to Cyber-bullying.

http://www.dcya.gov.ie/viewdoc.asp?DocID=120 Department of Children and Youth Affairs.

http://www.citizensinformation.ie/en/education/primary_and_post_primary_education/attendance_and_discipline_in_schools/bullying_in_schools_in_ireland.html Bullying in schools in Ireland.

http://www.bully4u.ie/ Bully 4 U: Understanding, Communicating, Empowering.

http://www.thejournal.ie/concerns-about-regulation-of-ask-fm-735597-Jan2013/ Ongoing news.

http://www.cearta.ie/2012/10/combating-cyber-bullying/ A useful discussion board examining cyber-bullying in terms of people's rights.

https://www.childline.ie/index.php/support/internet-safety/cyber-bullying/1639

http://www.barnardos.ie/information-centre/young-people/teen-help/bullying/cyber-bullying.html

http://www.webwise.ie/Cyber-bullyingaguide.shtm Helpful, easy to understand and full of useful information.

http://www.imt.ie/opinion/2012/12/cyber-bullying-the-incurable-online-virus.html *Irish Medical Times.*

http://www.hotline.ie/notices.php?type=archive Irish Internet Hotline – hotline notices.

http://www.internetsafety.ie/ Office of Internet Safety.

http://www.isfsi.ie/#/teacherbom/4553400194 Internet Safety for Schools, Ireland.

http://www.ispcc.ie/uploads/files/dir7/19_0.php ISPCC, Irish Society for the Prevention of Cruelty to Children (a useful site).

http://antibullyingireland.nfshost.com/ Anti-Bullying Ireland.

http://www.spunout.ie/health/Education/Stop-bullying/Cyber-and-text-bullying Irish website giving information to young people on a variety of issues.

International sites

AUSTRALIA

http://www.kidshelp.com.au/teens/get-info/hot-topics/cyber-bullying.ph Kids' Helpline Australia.

http://www.lawstuff.org.au/__data/assets/pdf_file/0006/14883/Cyber-bullying-fact-sheet.pdf
A very useful legal issues site.

http://www.cybersmart.gov.au/Schools/Teacher%20resources/Lower%20secondary/Lets%20fight%20it%20together.aspx A very useful website that includes a short film, *Let's Fight It Together*, developed by Childnet International and the Department for Children, Schools and Families in the UK. *Let's Fight It Together* is a short film based on real events addressing the issues related to cyber-bullying.

http://www.generationnext.com.au/2012/01/top-ten-anti-cyber-bullying-sites/ A useful website that lists its own top eleven anti-cyber-bullying websites and provides access to them. They are listed as:

www.kidshelpline.com.au
www.cybersafetysolutions.com.au

www.netalert.gov.au
www.NetSmartz.org
www.netsafe.org.nz
www.ceop.gov.uk
www.CyberTipline.org
www.iSafe.org
www.bullying.org
www.wiredsafety.org
www.GetNetWise.org

CANADA

http://www.huffingtonpost.ca/tag/canada-cyber-bullyingm Relevant and intelligent articles about important cyber-bullying issues.

EUROPE

https://sites.google.com/site/costis0801/ COST ACTION IS0801. Cyber-bullying: coping with negative and enhancing positive uses of new technologies, in relationships in educational settings.

An excellent website giving access to resources developed as part of an international four-year anti-cyber-bullying collaboration.

http://www.enisa.europa.eu/media/press-releases/new-report-cyber-bullying-online-grooming-18-protective-recommendations-against-key-risks Advice about online grooming.

http://laringsmiljosenteret.uis.no/core-net/ Six leading research centres located in six countries have joined forces in a network called 'Core-Net'. These six research centres are located in Canada, the USA, Australia, Finland, Ireland and Stavanger, Norway.

In Core-Net the activities are meta-studies on methods and results, collaborative research design on identified critical issues, strategies for enhancing collaboration with practitioners and authorities, international research seminars for PhD students, extensive background in research, programme development, collaboration with educational authorities and collaboration with practitioners.

The members in Core-Net are: LaMarsh Centre for Research on Violence and Conflict Resolution, Toronto; the Anti-Bullying Centre at Trinity College Dublin; the Research Centre at Curry School of Education, University of Virginia, Charlottesville, USA; the Research Group at Edith Cowan University, Perth; the Peer Relations Research Group at University of Turku, Finland and the Centre for Behavioural Research at the University of Stavanger, Norway.

NEW ZEALAND

http://netsafe.org.nz/ An excellent comprehensive website.

UK

http://www.nidirect.gov.uk/cyber-bullying-an-introduction

USA

http://www.cyber-bullying.us/ This is the website of leading anti-bullying researchers Patchin and Hinduja.

http://www.danah.org/papers/ Excellent website containing work by social networking commentator Dana Boyd and her colleagues.

http://www.ncpc.org/cyber-bullying US National Crime Prevention Council.

http://www.cyber-bullying.info/resources/report.php Excellent website with reporting procedures for the main social network sites.

http://www.netbullies.com/pages/1/index.htm Netbullies.com – useful general and specific info.

http://www.stopcyber-bullying.org/index2.html A proactive and living website for addressing cyber-bullying procedures (found on Facebook at: https://www.facebook.com/stopcyber-bullying).

http://support.google.com/youtube/bin/answer.py?hl=en&answer =126266 Google support against cyber-bullying.

CHAPTER FOURTEEN

Bullying: Tools for Teachers

Mary Kent and Seán Fallon

BACKGROUND AND RATIONALE

The anti-bullying programme that forms the basis of our *Anti-Bullying Campaign: Tools for Teachers* website was developed in a Catholic all-boys voluntary secondary school in suburban Dublin. It began as a response to a particular situation and continued to develop as we attempted to devise a school-wide system to provide the most positive, healthy and safe environment possible for all our students. While we were motivated by our own observations, experiences and values, we were guided by the research findings of authoritative figures in the field of bullying regarding the effects of bullying on both targeted students and those who bully. These indicated, for example, that among a range of negative outcomes targeted students were ' ... more likely to be depressed and have poor self-esteem' (Olweus, 2001) and also that 'Adolescents who are being bullied and those who are bullies are at an increased risk of depression and suicide' (Kaltiala-Heino et al., 1999). From Chapter 18, it can be seen that under Irish law, the responsibility of a teacher towards students in any situation is to act *in loco parentis* – to act in the way s/he believes a conscientious parent would act in that situation. Naturally, given the possible consequences, any conscientious parent/guardian who became aware that her/his child was being bullied would want to do everything possible as quickly as possible to stop it and this law encourages teachers to approach the issue of bullying with the same level of urgency.

For the purposes of our anti-bullying programme we accepted the Department of Education and Science (1993) definition of bullying as 'repeated aggression, verbal, psychological or physical, conducted by an individual or group against another'. We further accepted that:

Bullying involves a desire to hurt + hurtful action + a power imbalance + (typically) repetition + an unjust use of power + evident enjoyment by the aggressor and a sense of being oppressed on the part of the victim.

(Department of Education, 1993)

We decided that while bullying may involve a particular type of behaviour, for example name-calling, cyber bullying or extortion, or may target a particular type of student, for example racism or homophobic bullying, it was not primarily these kinds of behaviour that had to be addressed. Even if they were prevented, those wishing to bully could easily find other ways to torment targeted students. Rather, it was the underlying 'bullying attitude', the persistent disrespectful attitude that lay at the back of these kinds of behaviour, that needed to be dealt with. After all, if there were no 'bullying attitude' there would be no cyber-bullying or homophobic bullying. To prevent these and other manifestations of bullying, what we really needed to do was deal with the 'bullying attitude'. In our view the best way to achieve this was by raising awareness about the nature, the consequences and the unfairness of bullying and the damage, hurt and misery it causes, and, using this awareness, to persuade students to behave respectfully towards each other.

As practising classroom teachers we set out to create an anti-bullying programme that could be used by teachers with students from first year (age 12–13) through to sixth year (age 17–18). We wanted the programme to be preventative as well as incorporating a structure of formal response to bullying situations. To help discourage and prevent bullying we searched for appropriate resources and materials that we could adapt and use in awareness-raising exercises with students. We hoped that over time, using these exercises with all our students, we could change the culture in the school to one where, firstly, students would be less likely to bully others and, secondly, students would recognise bullying if they witnessed it and would reject it and report it. At the same time we worked to create procedures for dealing with any bullying situations that might still arise.

Our approach being primarily pragmatic, we were conscious that whatever we developed would have to be capable of implementation and would have to be effective within the parameters of normal everyday school life. We were also conscious that a school-wide anti-bullying endeavour would affect every member of the school community, whether student, staff member or management personnel, and that to be effective it would need the cooperation and help of all of these at an appropriate level. It would also have to be compatible with the ethos and mission statement of the school, not only in its objective of seeking fair, equal, respectful treatment of all students by all students, an essential element of the mission statement of the school, but also in its implementation. This meant, for example, that in dealing with bullying incidents the perpetrators of the bullying behaviour would be entitled to the same standard of respectful treatment by investigating adults as they had withheld from the students they targeted.

As a result of our two-pronged approach, our anti-bullying programme developed two distinct but complementary strands, one focused on cultural change through awareness-raising and the other on responding effectively to bullying behaviour. This dual approach complies fully with the 1993 Department of Education anti-bullying guidelines, which aim to:

> (a) ... increase the awareness of bullying behaviour in the school community as a whole ...
> (b) ... assist schools in devising school-based measures to prevent and deal with bullying behaviour ...
>
> (Department of Education, 1993)

It is the combination of these two strands, proactively and very visibly implemented at every level in the school, that we now refer to as the Anti-Bullying Campaign.

Within the first three years of its operation, the Anti-Bullying Campaign proved to be remarkably effective in several respects:

- The number of students targeted for bullying dropped significantly.
- The number of reports of bullying, by student witnesses, increased.
- The number of reports of bullying, by targeted students, increased.
- The severity of bullying incidents before they were reported decreased, suggesting that
- The level of vigilance of students, in watching out for bullying behaviour, increased.
- The number of reports of suspicion of bullying, by staff members, correspondingly decreased.

It is these outcomes that give us the confidence to present to readers what we now believe is a viable and effective anti-bullying campaign for secondary schools.

A WHOLE-SCHOOL APPROACH

On the basis that 'many hands make light work', an effective anti-bullying campaign needs to be driven primarily by a group of teachers, perhaps six, who become recognised in the school as the 'Anti-Bullying Team'. Reflecting the workload that is taken on by the coordinator of a successful Anti-Bullying Campaign, this role could be associated with a post of responsibility or have an associated time allowance.

The enthusiastic support of school management for this endeavour is vital so that whatever needs to be done will be done to facilitate the work of the Anti-Bullying Team. This may include such things as making regular announcements over the school intercom system, making time available for Anti-Bullying Team meetings, at least one per half-term, making prize-money available for student competitions and allowing placement of posters, competition winners and other materials around the school.

Since the campaign is intrusive into other teachers' class time, it needs the wholehearted support of the entire teaching staff of the school. All staff members, including non-teaching staff, need to be made more aware of the nature of bullying, its impact on students and the signs by which to recognise it so that they can become 'the eyes and the ears' of the Anti-Bullying Team. This can be done by making presentations to staff and by regular reports as well as alerts in relation to particular students and what they might be experiencing. Ideally, staff members will then report every suspicion they have of bullying to the Anti-Bullying Team without judgement – leaving the Anti-Bullying Team to carry out an investigation to find out if their suspicions were justified and, if so to deal with the situation.

For the Anti-Bullying Campaign to be effective, then, it is essential that all adults in the school community support it. If they do, and do so visibly, this adds to the persuasiveness of the campaign and its impact on students is significantly enhanced as they more and more come to recognise, respect and support the anti-bullying culture and ethos of the whole school. The addition of the school crest and school name to all worksheets, questionnaires and other materials used in the Anti-Bullying Campaign helps to further emphasise this whole-school approach.

Strand 1: Changing the culture by raising awareness

We cannot assume that every student already knows what bullying is and how unacceptable it is. Some students' experience of the world has made normal for them the kind of behaviour that we define as bullying. It may also be the case that some may not have experienced bullying themselves or noticed any ongoing pattern in the disrespectful treatment of any of their fellow students. Even among those students who have some knowledge of what bullying is there can be a variety of crucial misunderstandings:

- Many students are more conscious of their own actions than those of others around them. Because of this, it may not occur to them that if they tease a student just twice a day (deliberate, hurtful and repeated over time), other students may be doing likewise, each contributing to the targeted student having a more miserable day than any of them realises.
- Some students, whether involved in bullying behaviour or not, do not seem to recognise or understand bullying or the various forms it can take. Some students genuinely think that bullying they observe or carry out themselves is 'just messing' or that the targeted student is an equal participant in the behaviour. They do not seem to understand that for the person on the receiving end it is definitely not 'just messing'.
- Some students seem to 'live in the moment' having compartmentalised their consciousness into a series of instants, each of which engross them fully at the time but are then immediately set aside as the next one takes over, and seem unaware of any pattern linking behaviour in these instants of consciousness. If a boy pushes another in the morning and teases him in the afternoon and then on the following day takes his pen without permission and later, in front of others, makes fun of him, he may be completely unaware of the pattern of his behaviour. On the other hand, the person receiving this kind of treatment may be acutely aware of this pattern.
- Some students who bully may themselves be victims of bullying or subject to other experiences that affect their view of what kind of behaviour is acceptable or unacceptable. Apart from whatever

other supports they may need arising from such circumstances, they may need to have the correct boundaries of acceptable behaviour redrawn for them, with bullying deemed unacceptable, and be given the option (and encouraged) to live within these boundaries.

Students need to be given concrete understandings of the behaviour that constitutes bullying, how to recognise it and what kinds of consequences it can have so they will make a personal commitment not to get involved in this kind of behaviour. They need to be made aware that the consequences of bullying behaviour are always bad for those who are bullied, though this is not always obvious at the time. They need to be told that even if the targeted student appears to make light of the bullying behaviour or to think it is funny or to 'slag' the bullying student back, it is still unfair. That defence strategy may camouflage the serious hurt and unhappiness of the targeted student. It is important that they learn that it is unfair to put a fellow-student in a position of having to work out a defence strategy like this to deal with bullying. Such issues are addressed in the awareness-raising strand of the anti-bullying campaign. It aims to clearly identify what is meant by bullying, to explore with students the effects of the behaviour on all those involved and to consider its inappropriateness, while consistently encouraging students to recognise such behaviour, to reject it and to report it.

Young people are often impulsive and the lessons we teach them in relation to behaviour are best if they are modelled rather than instructed. Rigby (1996) rightly questions 'the value of preaching' and encourages discussing, explaining and supporting respectful behaviour. Outside of the tense context of particular bullying incidents, the vast majority of well-informed students respond well to this and as a result reject and avoid bullying behaviour. There is, sadly, a minority of students who would still bully others if given the opportunity and their tendency to bully must be dealt with. By raising awareness of various kinds of bullying behaviour and their unacceptability, and highlighting some of the signs by which they can be recognised, the majority of students become more aware of bullying behaviour and are more likely to report it. In this environment, those who would still bully become increasingly isolated.

The awareness-raising strand involves a series of exercises for students. These are arranged so that a number can be done in sequence each school year for three years. This avoids being too intrusive into class time in any one school year but yet reinforces by repetition the message that 'bullying is not acceptable in this school'. This kind of repetition is effective in changing the school culture in the same way that repetition of a message is effective in commercial advertising campaigns.

Some of the exercises in the Anti-Bullying Campaign involve the use of worksheets to help students to:

- understand different types of bullying so they will recognise them,
- recognise bullying as behaviour that is deliberate, hurtful and repeated over time,
- understand some of the consequences of bullying so they will avoid bullying,
- understand reasons why students might bully others so they will be constructive rather than vindictive in their response,
- realise how bystanders should respond on seeing bullying so they will not stand idly by while bullying is taking place.

In addition, competitions are arranged that give students the opportunity to present anti-bullying messages to their peers. These involve such things as writing anti-bullying slogans, poems or short stories with anti-bullying messages or drawing anti-bullying pictures or cartoons. If prizes are offered for winning entries in each year group and if, after advance notice is given for preparation, one class period is set aside for completion of competition entries, the participation level by students is very high. If winning entries are then laminated and put on display in the school, they are very effective in supporting and reinforcing the message that 'bullying is not acceptable in this school' because these messages are coming from students rather than teachers.

Campaign materials also include several video or audio presentations about bullying, with associated prepared questions to support their themes. The questions, asked verbally or given to students on prepared sheets, can be used to generate useful discussion on the material in the presentations. Anti-bullying video presentations have been sent to every Irish secondary school including the *Silent Witnesses* video presentation from the Anti-Bullying Centre, Trinity College Dublin (O'Moore, 2006) and the *Anti-Bullying Campaign: Tools for Teachers* DVD that includes four films about bullying. These films are age-appropriate, with some documentary presentations only suitable for students in senior cycle.

As students experience the various stages of this awareness-raising strand of the Anti-Bullying Campaign, potential perpetrators of bullying behaviour forfeit the excuse 'I was only messing' or 'It was only a joke.' They become more accountable for their actions and the impact these have on other students. In this context, if bullying does take place it is now much easier to bring it to an end, as will be described later.

While teachers are unaware of most bullying at the time it happens in schools, students witness almost all instances of bullying. As is clearly shown in the Olweus 'Bullying Circle' diagram (Olweus, 2001), their responses vary and unfortunately are often less than helpful. As they experience the awareness-raising campaign, these witnesses are gradually weaned off the 'easy option' of standing idly by and not intervening in some positive way. They are brought face to face with their responsibility to do what they can to help the targeted student. They are then more likely to intervene by 'shouting stop', and/or report the incident to a teacher or to accompany the targeted student in doing so, or failing that to at least indicate in a subsequent survey what has been happening. Witnesses to bullying are made aware that excuses for inaction in the face of bullying behaviour such as 'It was not me' or 'I did nothing' are neither valid nor acceptable. The awareness-raising strand makes it clear to them that 'doing nothing' when bullying is taking place is, at the very least, offering passive support to the bullying student and the bullying behaviour and this is unacceptable. This change in understanding of witnesses makes the anti-bullying campaign much more effective.

Strand 2: Response procedures for dealing with incidents

Despite the most informative and persuasive awareness-raising campaign, there will still be some bullying incidents in every secondary school. Each year new students arrive, mostly from primary schools where bullying also takes place and some from other secondary schools. These students have not yet been influenced by the Anti-Bullying Campaign. Indeed, a small number of students who have been in the school and have already participated in awareness-raising exercises may still bully others.

If the awareness-raising strand of the Anti-Bullying Campaign, as described above, is effective, students will recognise bullying behaviour for what it is and disapprove of it. However, there are several reasons why most bullying might still go unreported. Without further support and encouragement, targeted students are very reluctant to report that they are being bullied. It seems as if they do not want to admit to adults that they are not able to deal with the situation in which they find themselves, as if the undermining by the bullying student would be exacerbated if adults found out. Indeed, not understanding why they are being targeted, it may sometimes be difficult for students to acknowledge to themselves that they are being bullied. Witnesses too are reluctant to get involved for a variety of reasons. These can include fear that they too might become victims of bullying if they intervene, misguided loyalty to the student who is bullying whom they may admire, or lack of concern once they are not being bullied themselves. School staff members are also unlikely to report bullying because most bullying is cleverly carried out where staff members cannot see it or is of a kind that is very hard to detect if staff members are present. Physical bullying generally takes place out of sight of staff members and when staff members are present something as discreet as a facial expression, eye movement, tone of voice or a sharp intake of breath may be used. Even if they do witness an incident, they may not see the repetition that is a hallmark of bullying behaviour since teachers move from class to class about every forty minutes.

For these reasons an approach to bullying that would merely react to reported incidents would be insufficient to protect students from bullying and an endless series of bullying incidents would go unreported and unresolved. The results of this could be disastrous. Instead, an anti-bullying programme must not only respond to any reports of bullying that arise but proactively seek out and uncover, identify and deal with unreported bullying.

In dealing with cases of bullying among students, the most important objective for the school is that the bullying behaviour stops and targeted students suffer no further abuse. Some responses are unlikely to achieve this. For example:

- Punishment or 'making an example' of the perpetrator is likely to make fellow students reluctant to report bullying. Furthermore, such an intervention might simply result in moving the bullying on to another location. These outcomes would both facilitate recurrence of the bullying.
- Encouraging targeted students to use avoidance techniques, even if necessary in an emergency, would enable perpetrators to turn their unwelcome attention to others. Students should not have to hide in school toilets or skip classes to avoid being bullied.

- Encouraging targeted students to get involved in self-defence courses may only lead to a change in the kind of bullying, for example, from physical to another form like social bullying or cyber-bullying. Also, leaving responsibility for the outcome in the hands of the one person least able to deal with the situation may send out the wrong message – that the bullied student is responsible for his/her own safety.
- Deciding not to intervene on the basis that bullying makes targeted students stronger in the long run is not an acceptable option. Given the misery that bullying causes, the damage it always does and the disastrous consequences that sometimes ensue, intervention is necessary.

The COPS Report advises against relying on strategies such as advising the targeted student to stand up for her/himself, suggesting that this leaves the target open to further bullying and feelings of isolation (Fox et al., 2003). At the other end of the scale, it advises against a zero-tolerance stance which can result in punishments where there may not be full understanding on the part of the perpetrator as to what behaviour needs to be changed and how to change it (Fox et al., 2003). In addition, a zero-tolerance approach ' ... does not solve the problem of the bully, who typically spends more unsupervised time in the home or community if suspended or expelled' (Fox et al., 2003). The need to act on behalf of all parties in a bullying situation is critical. Protection of the abused in order to restore a sense of safety seems self-evident, but findings which show that bullying behaviour in schools 'predicts increased risk of violence and abuse in later life' (Rigby et al., 2004) point to an urgent need to support the bullying student in changing her/his behaviour.

With these types of considerations in mind, the Anti-Bullying Campaign uses a 'no blame' approach of the type suggested by Robinson and Maine (1997). Using non-punitive responses does not mean there are no consequences for students who are found to be bullying but they are afforded the opportunity to recognise that their behaviour is unacceptable and to change it. By adopting and highlighting this method, the goodwill of students on the periphery of bullying situations, whose reason for not coming to the aid of the targeted student might have been fear of getting the perpetrator (or her/himself for reporting it) into trouble, can be harnessed. By promoting the objective of helping both parties – creating a safe environment for the bullied student and at the same time offering the student who is bullying an opportunity to reform – all cases of suspected or reported bullying can be dealt with in a way that is fair and seen to be fair. In this environment, witnesses to bullying are more likely to report the bullying for two reasons. Firstly, they know that this will enable the targeted student to get on with life free from bullying, of which they increasingly disapprove as a result of the awareness-raising strand of the Anti-Bullying Campaign. Secondly, they know they are not getting anyone 'in trouble' but rather are helping someone out of trouble that s/he would in all probability get into if the bullying continued. When students understand this, they increasingly report bullying spontaneously either on behalf of their friends or other targeted students or because they themselves are being targeted.

Whether bullying is already reported or not, students are given the opportunity to report it in regular surveys. These can corroborate reports already received and give additional clarification if such a report is vague as well as uncovering previously unreported bullying. Surveys are carried out at least once per term as well as whenever bullying is reported by students or parents/guardians or suspected by staff members. Usually students complete an anti-bullying questionnaire on average at least once per half term. They are asked to sign their questionnaires. They are thereby held accountable for their responses and can be asked for clarification in relation to them afterwards. The confidentiality of student responses in these questionnaires is guaranteed – only members of the Anti-Bullying Team in the school have access to them and this access is only for the purposes of the Anti-Bullying Campaign. On this basis, and against the background of effective awareness raising, these surveys have a high success rate in bringing any instances of bullying to light and establishing enough of the facts in relation to them to justify interviewing any alleged perpetrators. This approach protects the bullied students and the students who report the bullying from blame and negative repercussions.

At least one experienced member of the Anti-Bullying Team interviews every alleged perpetrator of bullying behaviour. The interviewer is careful not to presume the interviewee is guilty of bullying. There are often two sides to a story. For example, sometimes classmates can mistakenly interpret as bullying what is really retaliation for previous unfair treatment and report it as bullying in a survey. At the start of the interview the student is reassured that if there was any concern that s/he was being bullied the alleged perpetrators would be facing interview rather than her/him and is reminded that everyone is entitled to equal protection from bullying.

Apart from trying to establish the objective facts, the aim of the interview is to ascertain the student's view of the situation. If it transpires, and the student accepts, that the behaviour was 'bullying', s/he is asked to sign a promise to behave differently towards the targeted student in future. By making and keeping this promise, the student is able to avoid punishment and is instead allowed to learn from her/his mistakes. In this case neither parents/guardians nor the school disciplinary authorities, for example year head or deputy principal, need be made aware of the bullying behaviour. S/he is also told that honesty in the interview will be taken as an indicator of whether this promise can be trusted. Once it is clear to the student that this 'amnesty' and confidentiality depend on honesty, the interview can proceed.

The interview is conducted according to a template provided, and involves over fifty behaviour-specific questions under six headings representing different kinds of bullying, for example verbal, social or physical bullying. This enables establishment of the facts regarding what kinds of bullying behaviour, if any, were taking place. If there was no bullying, the student is thanked for cooperating and is free to go. If it is clear that there was behaviour that was deliberate, hurtful to the targeted student and repeated over time, the list of admitted behaviours is then read back to the student. This may be the first time the student realises that the behaviour followed a pattern and s/he really was bullying and is now in a position to take responsibility for it. At this stage, students are often apologetic. (They may need to be told that an apology to the Anti-Bullying Team member is misplaced, in which case some suggest making an apology to the targeted student. The apology may be given later in the presence of the interviewing teacher where students have the opportunity to re-establish relationships, if that is what they want.)

Continuing the interview, further questions are then used to establish whether the student really appreciates the gravity and unfairness of the behaviour and to convince them if they do not. Students who bully may lack empathy, so these questions are designed to be effective even if empathy is to some extent lacking. Based on the response to these questions as well as the previous behaviour-specific questions and the student's history (since all previous Anti-Bullying Campaign documentation is kept on file), the interviewer decides whether a promise form needs to be countersigned by a parent/guardian or not. The promise form is then read in detail to the student and signed by the member of the Anti-Bullying Team. Provided that the student is prepared to keep the promise, s/he is then asked to sign it. Students usually sign this promise enthusiastically, knowing that in doing so they will avoid punishment and will not be reported to parents/guardians or school disciplinary authorities. The majority of those who sign the promise keep it faithfully, which is very good news for targeted students. Having signed, they are usually relieved, too, that they have 'cleared the air', that they are not 'in trouble' and are in a position to make a fresh start with a 'clean sheet'. Those who need to have their promise countersigned by a parent/guardian do not enjoy this kind of closure until they return the countersigned promise to the Anti-Bullying Team member.

While it may be somewhat controversial that neither parents/guardians nor the school disciplinary authorities are informed about the outcome, this only applies to the first occasion on which a student is interviewed and found to be bullying. In sporting parlance, the first interview and promise are like a 'yellow card' and parents/guardians are not informed about every yellow card a child gets in sport provided the child learns from the experience and does not go on to get a 'red card'. If the bullying recurs (or if the bullying in that first case was particularly severe), a promise by the student must be countersigned by a parent/guardian, so s/he knows there has been a problem and can monitor the situation from then on. Usually, there is a good prospect of better behaviour if a child is given a chance to 'turn over a new leaf' without blame after admitting to making a mistake rather than being condemned for it. This arrangement also provides a strong incentive for students not to re-offend.

While the Anti-Bullying Campaign uses a 'no blame' approach, this is not to say that there are no consequences for persistent perpetrators of bullying. Should bullying continue after a promise has been signed to indicate that it would stop, the student has then broken a promise which s/he had signed undertaking to behave respectfully towards her/his fellow students. S/he is also in clear breach of school rules for failing to adhere to her/his written commitment to the school and is thus liable to sanction. The 'amnesty' is now forfeited in this case. If a second promise (countersigned by a parent/guardian as well as a member of the Anti-Bullying Team) is subsequently broken, this is regarded as a refusal to accept both the school's anti-bullying policy and school rules in relation to respectful treatment of others. Apart from the actual bullying offence itself, this is regarded as a very serious matter for which a student may even be liable to temporary exclusion from the school. Only a small number of students ever reach this stage. Such 'possible consequences' of breach of promise can be more effective as a deterrent to further bullying behaviour than actual penalties for bullying itself.

As previously highlighted, in some instances of bullying there is a ringleader as well as others who have varying degrees of involvement, active (e.g. henchmen), or passive (e.g. onlookers who do not intervene). A difficulty arises when many students in the class group support the bullying behaviour or even deny knowledge of it in a survey, for example if the ringleader is feared or enjoys misguided loyalty. Even then, there are usually still enough students who indicate what is happening in a survey, using such expressions as 'everyone does it' to indicate the large number. Once ringleaders and henchmen have been dealt with, the attention of the Anti-Bullying Team then turns to the whole class group. Students are told in detail what has been taking place, the unfairness of it, how intervention could have helped and how failure to intervene actually supported the bullying. They are then invited to complete a 'joining in promise' form in which they can acknowledge their involvement, their 'joining in' or their failure to intervene and sign a promise to avoid such response in future without either interview or penalty, another kind of 'amnesty'. The objective here is to get the bullying to stop – all of it – so students with any level of involvement must make that commitment and they do. Surprisingly for some people, as many as seventeen students from one class group, reassured by the guarantees of confidentiality and 'amnesty' and obviously convinced of the integrity of the process, have completed such a promise and kept it faithfully. If there had been no Anti-Bullying Campaign to deal with this situation, the life of the targeted student would clearly have been quite intolerable.

OTHER SCHOOLS AND THE ANTI-BULLYING CAMPAIGN

Conscious of its success in one school, the Anti-Bullying Campaign is now available to other teachers and schools free of charge through a website. The www.antibullyingcampaign.ie website was launched in September 2008. Materials can be downloaded from this website in formats for which software is widely available in schools and adapted for use by adding the school name and the school crest of each school as well as making any changes teachers in that school think appropriate. In addition, copies of the DVD that includes four films about bullying, for use in the Anti-Bullying Campaign, were sent to every secondary school and Youthreach Centre in Ireland, free of charge, in February 2010. Now every secondary school has access to all it needs to implement the full Anti-Bullying Campaign.

Is there anything teachers do that is more important than creating a safe, happy environment for their students? Maintaining a safe atmosphere in school provides the best setting in which to support students in their personal, social and academic education. A campaign to deal effectively with bullying is essential if such an environment is to be created. This is fundamental to the ethos of our schools and the beliefs of our teachers as well as being enshrined in school mission statements and anti-bullying policies. It is also required under health and safety legislation. Do schools really have a choice in this matter?

This Anti-Bullying Campaign needs an anti-bullying policy to underpin it in a school and make it legally secure. Provided there is no direct conflict between an existing policy and the Anti-Bullying Campaign as outlined, there is no impediment to undertaking a 'full-blown' Anti-Bullying Campaign immediately. The anti-bullying policy can then be modified to match the details of its successful practice rather than vice versa. A sample of a compatible anti-bullying policy is available on the website.

We encourage teachers to register on the website www.anti-bullyingcampaign.ie and try out the Anti-Bullying Campaign, as presented or with local adaptations, in schools. We believe that once you experience its effectiveness and witness the difference it makes to the lives of your students you will recognise and appreciate the benefit of giving the Anti-Bullying Campaign a central role in the life of your school.

REFERENCES

Department of Education and Science, *Guidelines on Countering Bullying Behaviour in Primary and Post-Primary Schools* (Dublin: Department of Education and Science, 1993)

Fox, J.A. et al., 'Bullying Prevention *Is* Crime Prevention', a report by *FIGHT CRIME: INVEST IN KIDS* (2003), http://www.pluk.org/Pubs/Bullying2.pdf [assessed 18 January 2011]

Kaltiala-Heino, R., Rimpela, M., Martutunen, M., Rimpela, A. and Rantanon, P. 'Bullying, Depression and Suicidal Ideation in Finnish Adolescents: School Survey', *British Medical Journal*, vol. 319, no. 7206, 1999, pp. 348–51, http://www.bmj.com/content/319/7206/348.full.pdf [accessed 19 January 2011]

O'Moore, A.M. *Silent Witnesses* (a DVD intended to assist schools and parents/guardians to raise awareness of the problem of bullying and to help them manage the problem) (Dublin: Anti-Bullying Centre, Trinity College, 2006)

Olweus, D. 'Peer Harassment: A Critical Analysis and Some Important Issues', in J. Juvonen and S. Graham (eds), *Peer Harassment in School: The Plight of the Vulnerable and Victimized* (New York: Guilford Press, 2001)

Rigby, K. *Bullying in Schools and What To Do About It* (London: Jessica Kingsley Publishers, 1996)

Rigby, K., Smith, P. and Pepler, D. 'Working to Prevent School Bullying: Key Issues in Bullying in Schools', in *Bullying in Schools: How Successful Can Interventions Be?* (Cambridge: Cambridge University Press, 2004)

Robinson, G. and Maine, B. *Crying for Help: The No Blame Approach to Bullying* (Bristol: Lucky Duck Publishing, 1997)

(School Name Here)

Anti-Bullying Campaign

Strand 1 – Raising Awareness

Tools for Raising Awareness – Explaining the Nature and Unacceptability of Bullying

At least one event per half-term from:

First Year (Age 12–13):
- *Preliminary Lifestyle Survey* and Information re. 'reform, not blame' approach and *Survey of Primary School Bullying*
- *Types of Bullying* and *Recognising Bullying*
- Appropriate film, e.g. *Too Scared for School*, with discussion/questions
- Film with questions, Powerpoint lesson and handout on protecting yourself from cyber-bullying by phone
- At least one Anti-Bullying Competition, e.g. slogans and drawing (sample sheets provided)
- Bullying surveys from Tools/Incidents section (at least one per half-term), with rationale explained.

Second Year (Age 13–14):
- *Feedback Questionnaire Survey* after 1st Year
- *Consequences of Bullying* and *Why Bully?*
- Appropriate film, e.g. *Silent Witnesses*, with discussion/questions
- *Response to Bullying* adapted from Ken Rigby Survey
- At least one Anti-Bullying Competition, e.g. short poem and drawing (sample sheets provided)
- Bullying surveys from Tools/Incidents section (at least one per half-term), with rationale explained.

Third Year (Age 14–15):
- *Bystanders Drama* and *Identifying Bullying*
- Appropriate film, e.g. *Daisy Chains*, with discussion/questions
- Powerpoint lesson and handout on cyber-bullying
- *Caught in the Crowd* music video with discussion/questions
- At least one Anti-Bullying Competition, e.g. drama and drawing (sample sheets provided)
- Bullying surveys from Tools/Incidents section (at least one per half term), with rationale explained.

Senior Students (Age 16–18):
- Appropriate film, e.g. *The Leanne Wolfe Interview*, *Bully for You*, or audio, e.g. *The Leanne Wolfe Diaries*, with discussion/questions

- At least one Anti-Bullying Competition, e.g. short film, story or poem and drawing (sample sheets provided)
- Bullying surveys from Tools/Incidents section (at least one per half-term), with rationale explained.

All Years: (Age 12–18):
- Anti-Bullying activities in *SPHE, CSPE, RE* and/or other classes
- Visiting drama (if available/affordable), visiting speaker (if appropriate) and/or further films

Staff Awareness:
- *Staff Powerpoint Presentation*
- *Symptoms of Low Self-Esteem*
- *One of the following:*
  Too Scared for School (good introductory film on the nature and immediate impact of bullying)
  Leanne Wolfe Interview (extreme impact of bullying and urgency of speaking out or intervening)
  Bully for You (nature and long-term impact of bullying)
  Daisy Chains (drama by Transition Year students that students in other schools could emulate)
  Silent Witnesses (impact of bullying when nobody intervenes compared with when someone intervenes)
  Visiting drama (if available) or other films
- Regular reports and 'Thank You's' at staff meetings, staff days, in-school in-service, etc.

Parents/Guardians:
- Publication of school Anti-Bullying Policy in:
  ◦ School prospectus
  ◦ School website
  ◦ Student journal
- Regular newsletter reports of anti-bullying activities.

Whole School:
Display/Presentation in central, public area of school re:
- Current anti-bullying activities
- Anti-bullying competition winners' names
- Anti-bullying competition winning entries
- Upcoming anti-bullying events
- Current or specific anti-bullying messages.

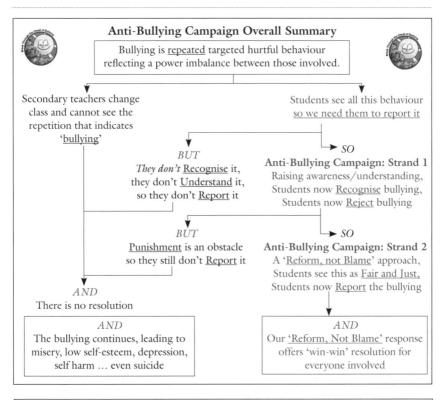

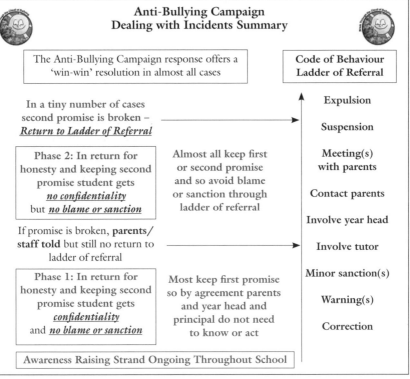

CHAPTER FIFTEEN

A Promising Strategy to Prevent Bullying Behaviour

Orla Murray

INTRODUCTION

The Massage in Schools Programme (MISP) is relatively new in Ireland (introduced here in 2004). It is a peer-to-peer massage programme designed for 4–12-year-old children. Massages are carried out by children on each other while fully clothed. This programme places a strong emphasis on respect and provides healthy touching in a caring, safe environment under the teacher's supervision. Participation is voluntary, and permission from the child is sought prior to each massage.

According to research carried out in America, the United Kingdom and Sweden, there are many benefits to using massage with children: increased listening and attention skills, it builds communication, trust and self-esteem, improved behaviour and learning capabilities, learning about respectful touch, calming in all aspects/less aggression in the class/school, unifies the group, something that every child can do and it gives the child a sense of security and comfort.

Extensive research has shown that there are many positive effects among children who have massage in their lives. This research study carried out in primary schools in Ireland (by the above author) examined the effects of the Massage in Schools Programme as a whole-school approach with a view to promoting positive behaviour. The rationale in undertaking research into this programme was to find out if the effects of peer-to-peer massage found elsewhere could be replicated in schools throughout Ireland. The research study focused on to what extent the Massage in Schools Programme resulted in:

- increasing positive behaviour
- increasing learning

- increasing self-esteem
- developing social skills.

MASSAGE IN SCHOOLS PROGRAMME

The Massage in Schools Programme is an international innovative approach to improving children's quality of life in school. It intends to give children the chance to experience nurturing touch at school in a safe way.

(www.massageinschools.com)

According to the Massage in Schools organisation, massage has benefits not only for the child but for the teacher, school and society.
The benefits for the child are:

- Increased listening and attention skills
- Builds communication, trust and self-esteem
- Improved behaviour and learning capabilities
- Learning about respectful touch
- Calming in all aspects/less aggression
- Unifies the group
- Something that every child can do
- Gives the child security and comfort.

The benefits for the teacher are:

- Quieter, happier classes/more harmonic atmosphere
- Less stress/relaxed teachers
- More attentive/cooperative children
- Great new teaching tool
- Can be used anytime, quickly and effectively
- Keeps children busy and focused.

This can lead to these benefits for the whole-school and learning environment:

- Improved interactions between all grades
- Calmer learning environment
- A practical tool to use against bullying
- Something that remains the same as the child advances from class to class

- An innovative child-centred activity
- Empathy throughout the school
- Positive PR model for the school.

This in turn may have wider benefits for society:

- More respect for each other
- A more peaceful society
- Preventative health care
- Decreased aggression
- More responsive to the needs of others.

(www.massageinschools.com)

According to the www.massageinschools.com website, the Massage in Schools Programme has gained impressive results in reducing bullying and aggression both in and out of the classroom and settling hyperactive children. It maintains that 'it is very hard to hit someone who has made you feel good'. With violence and aggression increasing in today's society and the fear of misinterpretation about the most innocent of interactions between childcare professionals/ teachers and the children they care for, it is no wonder that we are heading towards a no-touch society. According to the Massage in Schools Programme, a no-touch society promotes distrust, suspicion, violence and aggression. A child that benefits from massage will possibly have improved relationships with peers, parents, brothers and sisters, as well as with their teachers. The life-long effects of massage can include calmer, happier children who grow into adolescents and then adults, taking their calmer, happier benefits with them.

The Massage in Schools Programme is being used very successfully in primary schools in the UK as part of Personal, Health, Social and Citizenship Education (PHSCE) and contributes to the Healthy Schools Award (emotional health and well-being). According to the British Department for Health and the Department for Education and Skills (2004), 'Peer massage is an effective tool in promoting child mental health and reducing bullying, aggressive behaviour and stress levels in pupils'.

THE ROLE OF TOUCH

Touch is the earliest and most primitive form of communication that remains fundamental throughout life. The skin is the largest sensory organ of the body and the tactile system is the earliest sensory system to become functional. It is the medium by which the infant's external world is perceived (Montagu, 1986). Following the birth of a baby, early skin-to-skin contact is recommended. Many researchers have suggested that if humans were deprived of the opportunities to touch and to be touched then our psychological, physiological and social development would be adversely affected (Montagu, 1986; Beckwith, 1993). It is the loving touch between a parent and infant that helps the child to establish secure attachment relationships, as well as assisting in many aspects of physical and personal growth, and it is essential for healthy brain development (Bowlby, 1958; Ayres, 1985). Through the use of physical contact, infants establish feelings of security and emotional well-being which allow them to securely explore the world around them (Ainsworth, Blehar, Waters and Wall, 1978). Therefore the role of touch is an important influence on a child's healthy development. The seminal work of Spitz (1945) demonstrated that babies in orphanages who did not have human caring contact often died prematurely. Also in more recent reports about Romanian orphanages – where there was a lack of funding and staff shortages, children were left in their cots all day and only received physical touch when absolutely essential – hormone levels and regulation in these children were found to be abnormal. According to Carlson (1998), abnormalities in stress hormone levels are directly related to delays in mental, physical and motor development.

Each culture has rules on where, how and when touch can be used. The culture of society can be defined as the way of life of its members, the collection of ideas and habits which members learn, share and transmit from generation to generation. Culture, therefore, defines accepted ways of behaving for members of a particular society (Halcon et al., 2003). Within our society touch is the sense which is most neglected; a newborn baby in this country receives less skin-to-skin contact than in 'traditional' or hunter/gatherer cultures. This is partly due to the expectations we have of child development. We value independence in our young as it allows us to continue to some extent with our previous pattern of life, whereas, in African cultures the young child would regularly be carried skin-to-skin. Studies in Uganda show that babies who have been carried in an upright position are quicker to walk and faster to develop in other areas as well (Field, 2003). However, in our society once a child is active, he/she will spend the vast majority of his/her time lying, sitting, standing or walking, with little touch from caregivers. Therefore, it is suggested that the lack of touch can delay or impair the healthy psychological development of infants, with possible long-lasting effects throughout childhood, adolescence and adult life.

The Massage in Schools Programme has recently developed a programme for parents to be involved in the massage process. It recognises the importance of bonding between the parent and child. Teaching parents has a number of benefits: it enables them to be proactive and to have a therapeutic effect on their child. Massage enhances communication through touch, particularly for children with cognitive impairment, and according to Field (1996), carrying out massage has been shown to promote relaxation in children and induce relaxation in their parents too.

THE IMPACT OF MASSAGE AND TOUCH ON THE DEVELOPMENT OF EMOTIONAL INTELLIGENCE IN THE CHILD

Daniel Goleman first used the term 'emotional intelligence' in 1996 in his book *Emotional Intelligence: Why it can matter more than IQ*. Goleman argues that traditionally used 'measures of intelligence', for example IQ tests, are not effective predictors of future success and he states that emotional intelligence (including self-awareness, impulse control, persistence, motivation, empathy and social deftness) is important as it impacts every decision we make. Due to the arrangement of the brain and its associated sensory organs, we tend to make responses first emotionally and act upon them, prior to considering them rationally. The emotional response can be made up with little information, but can produce significant actions. The 'fight or flight' scenario is one where the emotional brain takes over from the rational (Goleman, 1996).

A practical context of this would be where a child comes to school having just had an argument at home; this child may be experiencing a range of emotions and very often is unable to sit down in a chair and pay close attention to one person (the teacher) and learn. Until this child's emotional needs have been met, the child has been hijacked by his/her emotions. Our schooling system does not allow time for this child to calm down or take time out from the class, and so this puts a strain on the teacher and the rest of the class. According to Goleman (1996), emotional responses are triggered by different amounts of chemicals known as hormones which are released in response to the situation we perceive we are in. These hormones act as both messengers to the brain and messengers to the rest of the body from the brain. 'Hormones such as adrenaline, cortisol, prolactin, beta-endorphin and enkephalin are all released when the body is stressed' (Goleman, 1996, p. 168), and therefore cause a plethora of reactions in the body which prepare it to run or fight. Although many of these chemicals will drop back to earlier levels immediately after the stressful situation has been resolved, some do not. Cortisol in particular is known to remain high in the bloodstream for extended periods of time after stressful situations and as a result its effects are longer lasting and it reduces immunity to disease (Goleman, 1996).

In opposition to these hormones are another set which when stimulated activate the parasympathetic nervous system. This is the division of the Autonomic Nervous System which is used when we are learning and therefore is the part we most wish to engage with during the school day (Field et al., 1998b). The parasympathetic nervous system aims to keep our body sufficiently balanced and relaxed; massage stimulates the production of the hormones (in particular oxytocin), which enables the parasympathetic nervous system to maintain the body in a calm state.

Uvnäs-Moberg (1998) has researched the effect of the hormone oxytocin during massage and according to the results of her studies, the levels of oxytocin in the brain rise during massage and remain elevated for a period of time after the massage has ceased. Uvnäs-Moberg (1998) claims that the calming and relaxing effects of massage are the direct result of higher oxytocin levels in the brain which affects the parasympathetic nervous system; however, she acknowledges that further research needs to be conducted to replicate these findings.

EXISTING RESEARCH INTO THE USE OF MASSAGE WITH CHILDREN AND ADOLESCENTS

To date, much of the research that has been carried out into the benefits of massage for children and adolescents has been conducted by the Touch Research Institute at the University of Miami, Florida. Diego et al. (2002) found that aggressive adolescents who received a twenty-minute massage twice a week for a period of five weeks reported feeling less anxious and hostile after the five weeks and they were reported by their parents as being less aggressive than at the start of the five-week period; in comparison, a control group in the same study showed no significant differences.

Khilnani et al. (2003) found similar results for pupils with ADHD. The use of massage has been shown to decrease hyperactivity and fidgeting, and to increase concentration, in children with ADHD (Field et al., 1998b). Field et al. (1997) found that after receiving two fifteen-minute massages per week for a period of four weeks, autistic children displayed a greater attentiveness and response to others than before the massage period; again a control group did not display such dramatic changes. Finally, Field et al. (1998a) found that children with asthma had improved pulmonary function after thirty days of a twenty-minute massage which was given immediately before they went to sleep; again, a control group who received relaxation therapy showed no significant difference.

From this brief review of the academic research it can be seen that there are significant benefits due to massage for children and adolescents with a wide range of medical conditions. It is interesting to note that much of the research that has been carried out about the effects of massage on children and adolescents has tended to focus on specific sub-groups, for example pupils with ADHD, autism or asthma, or on specific difficulties, for example social relationships, learning in maths or learning development. In the Pedersen (2003) study, it found that peer massage was perceived to facilitate pupils' approach to learning and social interaction skills, which in turn had a positive impact on the pupils' behaviour.

In the case of the Woolfson et al. (2005) study, he examined two factors that are claimed to improve following participation in the Massage in Schools Programme – on-task behaviour and self-esteem. Data analysis confirmed that pupils who participated in the MISP over a six-week period made significant improvements in concentration (as measured by on-task behaviour) compared to a control group of children. Although the pupils showed a significant gain in self-esteem following participation in the programme, similar gains were achieved by the control group.

As previously stated, much of the research has been carried out in America; currently there are only findings from two case studies in the UK (Woolfson et al., 2005 and Pedersen, 2003) regarding the Massage in Schools Programme. One of the challenges in this current research project was the lack of evidence about the Massage in Schools Programme, as there are no publications apart from the two case studies mentioned. This research project is the first case study in Ireland examining the effects of the Massage in Schools Programme on children in primary schools.

SELF-ESTEEM

There is value to helping children develop self-esteem. According to Lawrence (1996), children with high self-esteem are less likely to show behavioural problems and more likely to grow into responsible adults.

However, there can be the danger of focusing too much on the learning of skills to the detriment of the education of the whole child, although there is a strong argument for educating for social and emotional development as well as for education of the intellect. 'If we can help children to understand themselves better and to feel more confident about themselves then they are going to be in a stronger position to be able to cope with the inevitable stresses of life and to be better citizens' (Lawrence, 2006, p. xvii).

Humphreys (1996, p. ix) states that 'by the time children come to school their self-image has been largely forged'. Humphreys (1996) and Lawrence (2006) argue that teachers can either add to or detract from children's self-esteem; however, Humphreys states that the sources of children's self-esteem problems lie primarily within the home. Each parent's own level of self-esteem influences that of his/her child. Humphreys (1996, p. ix) maintains that 'children's educational development is also affected by how their parents relate to them and whether the parents know how to develop children's self-esteem'. Parents are the child's first educators and knowledge of what to teach and how to teach are important skills. Parents need to know about behavioural management and they need to understand the nature and purpose of children's problematic behaviours and how to respond constructively to them. According to Lawrence (1996), the child with high self-esteem is likely to be confident in social situations and in tackling school work. He/she will have retained a natural curiosity for learning and will be eager and enthusiastic when presented with a new challenge. The child with low self-esteem, in contrast, will lack confidence in his/her ability to succeed. Carl Rogers (1977) has drawn our attention to the prime need within our culture for self-regard.

Stanley Coopersmith (1967, as cited by Fontana, 1995) undertook research into the development of self-esteem. He selected a sample of 10-year-old boys and followed them through into early adult life. Using a battery of psychological tests and self-ratings, Coopersmith found that his sample could be divided consistently into three groups which he labelled 'high', 'medium' and 'low' self-esteem. The boys selected for this research came from middle-class homes; they were deliberately chosen from the same socio-economic background. Fontana (1995) states that where the boys differed greatly was in the relationship which they had with their parents. Fontana (1995, p. 264) also states that 'the high self-esteem boys came from homes in which they were regarded as significant and interesting people, and in which respect was shown for their opinions and points of view'. Whereas the boys with low self-esteem were 'not as significant and important within the home, and did not count for much as people'. The parents of the boys with high self-esteem had high standards for their children and knew a lot about their children, for example their interests and friends, whereas the opposite was true for the boys with low self-esteem. Another important factor here is that the parenting styles differed greatly. Maccoby (1980, as cited by Fontana, 1995, p. 265) states that the 'authoritarian parental style is certainly a factor in low self-esteem, while warmth in parent–child relationships and secure attachment in the early years of life go with high self-esteem'.

Humphreys (1993) argues that the causes of self-esteem lie principally in the early experiences of childhood and that these experiences are generally of a mixed nature in terms of being positive and negative. According to Humphreys (1993, p. 29), 'Parents, teachers, and others are mirrors for children'; he states that the child who receives love and affection, praise, support, encouragement, positive discipline and who is listened to forms a 'healthy self-image'. In contrast, the child who 'frequently experiences absence of affection, or caring that is unfeeling, ridiculing, scolding, critical, physically abusive and who endures hostile silences, unrealistic demands and standards, negative labelling etc. develops an inferior image of self'. According to Humphreys (1993), no child has all completely positive experiences and as a result there are very few people with high self-esteem; most people have middle self-esteem and a sizeable number have low levels. Humphreys (1993, p. 9) suggests that 'education is not just about academic development, surely of equal importance is the emotional, social, sexual, physical, behavioural, spiritual and creative development of children'. According to Humphreys (1996, p. 1), 'children who have learning difficulties in school frequently have self-esteem problems, and what is most needed is an elevation of their self-esteem before effective academic development can be established'. Lawrence (2006) supports this argument, but he maintains that children will not use their full ability if their self-esteem is low.

RESEARCH CONDUCTED IN IRELAND

The Massage in Schools Programme has only been carried out in a small number of schools in Ireland. This research project has been carried out in an all-girls' primary school in a disadvantaged area in Dublin with forty-six children aged 7 to 12 years. Much of the research that has been carried out previously has concentrated on the benefits of massage and has been qualitative by nature; the quantitative research has focused on the benefits of massage for children and adolescents with a wide range of medical conditions or indeed it has focused on specific sub-groups, for example children with ADHD, autism or asthma, as discussed above. This research project was conducted using both quantitative and qualitative methods, in order to provide a scientific approach and a phenomenological approach (describing people's experiences of the massage programme). In relation to the quantitative approach, the Revised Rutter Parent Scale for School-Age Children (1993) and the Revised Rutter Teacher Scale for School-Age Children (1993) were adminsitered. The LAWSEQ Pupil Questionnaire (1996) was used when assessing the children's self-esteem levels. The Rutter Scales and the LAWSEQ questionnaires were used both pre and post the delivery of the Massage in Schools Programme. In relation to the qualitative method, data was collected through the means of individual in-depth interviews with co-researchers (teachers) and small group interviews with the children. The rationale for these research methods are outlined below.

The research project also used the Revised Rutter Parent Scale for School-Age Children (1993) and the Revised Rutter Teacher Scale for School-Age Children (1993), as they measured the child's behaviour under the following headings:

- total difficulties
- emotional difficulties
- conduct difficulties
- hyperactivity/inattention score
- pro-social score
- supplementary total difficulties
- supplementary emotional difficulties
- supplementary conduct difficulties
- supplementary hyperactivity/inattention.

These questionnaires were used both pre and post the delivery of the Massage in Schools Programme. These behaviours were examined in order to establish the effect the Massage in Schools Programme had on increasing positive behaviour, increasing learning and developing social skills.

Revised Rutter Scales (1993)

The Rutter scales for completion by parents (the A scale) and teachers (the B scale) were developed in a series of studies in the UK as screening and research instruments to detect emotional and behavioural disturbances among children in the age range of 9 to 13 years. The scales also incorporate the assessment of prosocial behaviour, and have been used to investigate the prevalence of behavioural disturbance in children with physical illnesses and conditions, the relationships between behavioural problems and deficits in reading and cognitive abilities, and the effects of social and familial factors on child behaviour. The Rutter scales were deemed suitable for this research study, as they have been established as reliable and valid scales, according to Elander and Rutter (1996). The pattern of findings are in line with similar analyses of other child behaviour ratings scales – for example, a detailed comparison has been made with the Child Behaviour Checklist (CBCL; Achenbach and Edelbrock, 1983). However, this was a much longer instrument which included a number of syndromes of uncertain meaning and was developed primarily with clinical applications in mind (Elander and Rutter, 1996). Reliability was a crucial factor within this research study and was considered important because a reliable measure is one that can produce the same results if the behaviour is measured again by the same scale (LoBiondo-Wood and Haber, 1998).

The Lawrence Self-Esteem Questionnaire (LAWSEQ)

The LAWSEQ Pupil Questionnaire was used to assess the children's self-esteem levels; it was used both pre and post the delivery of the Massage in Schools Programme. It has been tried and tested and is considered a reliable form for capturing data. The research study used the LAWSEQ primary pupil questionnaire (Lawrence, 1996, p. 17) to identify children who felt they had low/medium/high self-esteem. The LAWSEQ is a particularly well-standardised questionnaire and was selected for use in the 1979 National Child Development Study when it was administered to 15,000 boys and girls of primary age.

There are many factors that can affect the reliability of a test when measuring self-esteem. When using the LAWSEQ questionnaire, the quality of rapport established between test and child is crucial in ensuring its reliability. According to Lawrence (2006), the chances of a child being willing to confide intimate feelings are considerably reduced unless there is rapport with the tester. Therefore it is essential that a rapport is established prior to administering the questionnaire. According to Lawrence (2006), the questionnaire is a useful research tool for those who require a before and after measure in relation to measuring children's self-esteem.

In addition to the LAWSEQ pupil questionnaire, each of the co-researchers (teachers) were asked to identify the children in their class within the following categories: high, medium and low self-esteem. This was carried out in order to see if teachers could identify correctly children who have high, medium and low self-esteem, and was conducted pre and post the Massage in Schools Programme. In addition to the quantitative measures, data was collected through the means of individual in-depth interviews with teachers and small group interviews with the children.

FINDINGS FROM THE REVISED RUTTER TEACHER SCALES AND PARENT SCALES FOR SCHOOL-AGE CHILDREN (1993) QUESTIONNAIRES

A statistical test (a paired-samples t-test) was conducted to evaluate the impact of the intervention of the Massage in Schools Programme on the children, in relation to increasing positive behaviour, increasing learning (decreasing hyperactivity/inattention) and developing social skills. From the teachers perspective there is a statistical significant difference in the children's improved behaviour pre and post test, as shown in Figure 15.1 (see next page).

The teachers reported that the massage had an immediate impact on the children; it relaxed them and had a calming influence on them which lasted in some cases for up to twenty minutes, and as a result some teachers found that the children were more attentive. Uvnäs-Moberg (1998) has researched the effect of the hormone oxytocin during massage and according to the results of her studies, the levels of oxytocin in the brain rise during massage and remain elevated for a period of time after the massage has ceased. Although she acknowledges that further research needs to be undertaken, within this study it was found that the intervention of the Massage in

Figure 15.1: Mean score on the Revised Rutter Teacher Scale

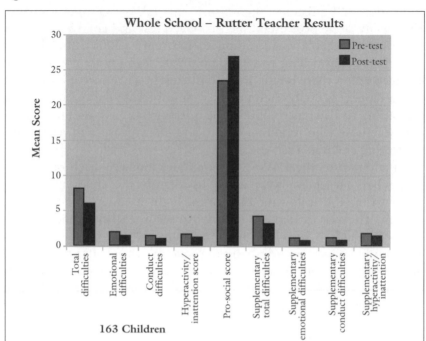

Schools Programme had an impact in reducing the lack of attention and hyperactivity of the children.

In contrast to the teacher scales, the parent scales reflected no statistically significant difference. There is a possibility that the use of the 'train the trainer' concept had a significant impact on the teachers as it provided an effective means for a full understanding of the Massage in Schools Programme. The teachers saw a considerable change and so the intervention of the Massage in Schools Programme had a measurable impact on the children's behaviour. In other words, the teachers reported an increase in positive behaviour, a reduction in hyperactivity and inattention and an increase in the children's social skills. Further support for these behavioural improvements can be gained from the teachers' qualitative responses. The Rutter scales have been used to make comparisons between children with and without a wide range of physical conditions and children exposed to different social and familial conditions. According to Elander and Rutter (1996, p. 71), 'significantly higher levels of behavioural disturbance have tended to be found for conditions that had existed for longer periods and where the expected behavioural changes were general rather than specific'. According to Elander and Rutter

(1996), the teachers' scale has tended to be used more than the parents' scale for studies of this kind, and where both scales have been used, teachers' ratings have produced more positive results. The fact that the parent scales are considered less reliable than the teacher scales may perhaps have had some bearing in this study on the lack of significant differences using the parent scales.

FINDINGS FROM LAWSEQ PUPIL QUESTIONNAIRES (1996) (PRIMARY VERSION) AND TEACHERS' PERCEPTION RESULTS

This research project used the LAWSEQ primary pupil questionnaire to identify children who felt they had low/medium/high self-esteem. A paired-samples t-test was conducted to evaluate the impact of the intervention of the Massage in Schools Programme on the children's self-esteem. From the children's perspective (LAWSEQ Pupil Self-Esteem Questionnaire), there was a highly significant difference in their self-esteem levels, pre- and post-test. This is illustrated in Figure 15.2. Of note was that the control groups in the present one showed a significant gain in self-esteem following participation in the programme. It is possible that the positive feelings the experimental group experienced had a positive effect on the control group and this gave rise to a less aggressive climate in school.

Figure 15.2: Results from LAWSEQ Pupil Self-Esteem Questionnaires

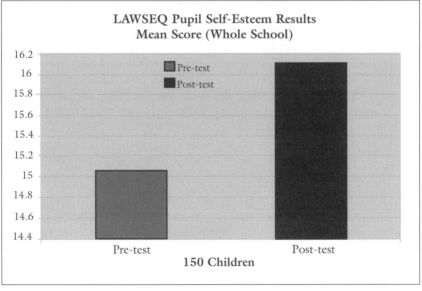

However, no differences were found in the teachers' perception of the children's self-esteem before and after the programme. Analysis of self-esteem as rated by teachers has been found to be unreliable. For example, Miller and Moran (2005) found that only 33% of teachers in Scotland were able to identify correctly the number of children with low self-esteem. A teacher's perception is clearly very subjective, and although the teacher may feel that he/she knows the children in his/her classroom, Lawrence (2006) for example, cautions teachers to be careful of children who display extrovert personalities as sometimes they will have low-self esteem although they may not display it in the classroom.

FINDINGS FROM INTERVIEWS WITH TEACHERS

In using Colaizzi's (1978) method of data analysis, four themes were identified which permeated through all the teachers' and children's interviews. The themes were identified by each of the teachers as being 'true' to their experiences of the Massage in Schools Programme. The four themes identified were:

- Change in children's behaviour
- Conducive atmosphere for learning to take place
- Developing social skills and family bonding time
- Promoting positive self-esteem

Theme 1: Change in children's behaviour

Of the seven teachers interviewed, five believed that the Massage in Schools Programme helped the children to control their aggressive impulses. This was illustrated by one teacher who stated: 'I have found that in my class there are some girls that have not been as aggressive as they were before we started the massage programme.' Other teachers mentioned that it was a good strategy for reducing aggressive behaviour, whereas another stated that it was a useful tool for dealing with conflict resolution. Four of the seven teachers commented on the impact the massage programme had on children with behavioural problems; one teacher expressed her view as follows: 'It worked well for me with a child who had behaviour problems. I found it really helped her, so I would see it as a very positive tool to helping behaviour.'

While acknowledging the limitations of this research, these findings find support from the literature. Diego et al. (2002) found that aggressive adolescents who received a twenty-minute massage twice a week for a period of five weeks reported feeling less anxious and hostile after the five weeks and they were reported by their parents as being less aggressive than at the start of the five-week period; in comparison, a control group in the same study showed no significant differences. In addition, Pedersen (2003) found that peer massage had a positive impact on the pupils' behaviour. However, in contrast, in the Woolfson et al. (2005) study it was found that the MISP did not have an influence on the children's aggressive behaviour. It is interesting to note that much of the research that has been undertaken about the effects of massage on children and adolescents has tended to focus on specific sub-groups, for example pupils with ADHD, autism or asthma, or on specific difficulties. However, within this research study, both from the quantitative data and the interviews with the teachers, there was some evidence to suggest that the massage in schools programme reduced the level of aggression and had a positive impact on the children's behaviour.

Theme 2: Conducive atmosphere for learning to take place

From the thematic analysis of the interviews with the teachers, there was evidence to suggest that the massage in schools programme had a calming influence on the class, which in turn created a conducive atmosphere for learning to take place. The majority of teachers (i.e. five out of seven) believed that the massage programme had a very calming and relaxing effect on the children. This was illustrated by one teacher who stated: 'It calms them, yeah definitely it calms them and settles them very quickly and even after that for maybe about twenty minutes or that, they remain very calm and very, very, quiet.'

According to Field et al. (1998b), the parasympathetic nervous system aims to keep our body sufficiently balanced and relaxed; massage stimulates the production of the hormones (in particular oxytocin), which enables the parasympathetic nervous system to maintain the body in a calm state. Uvnäs-Moberg (1998) has researched the effect of the hormone oxytocin during massage and according to the results of her studies, the levels of oxytocin in the brain rise during massage and remain elevated for a period of time after the massage has ceased. This supports the teachers' views that the massage programme has had a very calming and relaxing effect on the children; some of the teachers found that the massage programme really helped their classes settle prior to lessons or straight after break time.

Of the seven teachers interviewed, five stated that the massage programme was conducive to learning taking place in the classroom. This was illustrated by one teacher who stated: 'I find that they settle down to work more quickly now, I suppose in comparison to the start of the year.' Another commented: 'Before a test, I found it was good because they were much quieter because some of them get a bit hyped up and it calmed them down.' Other teachers commented on how the children's concentration levels improved, one teacher expressing her views as follows: '... really getting them to concentrate, I do maths after break because they are quite weak and I find if I do the massage before maths I am able to do maths for much longer, they don't get as tired. I have really noticed that.'

Previous research would support the teachers' comments above. The use of massage has been shown to decrease hyperactivity and fidgeting and to increase concentration in children with ADHD (Field et al., 1998). Khilnani et al. (2003) found similar results. In addition, Field et al. (1997) found that after receiving two fifteen-minute massages per week for a period of four weeks, children with ASD displayed a greater attentiveness and response to others than before the massage period; again, a control group did not display such dramatic changes. In the Pedersen (2003) study, it was found that peer massage was perceived to facilitate pupils' approach to learning and social interaction skills. Furthermore, the Woolfson et al. (2005) study examined two factors that are claimed to improve following participation in the Massage in Schools Programme, namely on-task behaviour and self-esteem. Data analysis confirmed that pupils who participated in the MISP over a six-week period made significant improvements in concentration (as measured by on-task behaviour) compared to a control group of children.

Theme 3: Developing social skills and family bonding time

From the thematic analysis of the interviews with the teachers, there was evidence to suggest that the Massage in Schools Programme helped develop the children's social skills. Of the seven class teachers interviewed, five believed that the massage programme helped the children to form new friendships and generally get along better with other children in the classroom. Teachers found that 'the massage programme really helped the children to build relationships and make new friends'. Building on the theme of constucting and developing social skills, four out of seven teachers reported that the massage programme assisted in promoting working in pairs and in small groups. This was demonstrated by one teacher who stated: 'I found at the very start of the year my class wouldn't have been able to work in pairs, they weren't able to work in pairs, they weren't able to work in groups, whereas now they can work in groups.' Another teacher commented that 'it helped them with cooperation and working closely together'.

If we examine existing research on the Massage in Schools Programme, for example in the Pedersen (2003) study, it was found that peer massage improved the pupils' interaction skills, which in turn had a positive impact on their behaviour.

From the thematic analysis of the interviews with the teachers within this study it was found that the children brought the massage home into their family life. This was also evident in the Pedersen (2003) study. Other teachers mentioned that they had received positive feedback and comments from parents about the massage programme. One teacher received a letter from a parent to say 'Thank you so much for bringing massage into our home, it had really helped bring the family closer together, and it was something we all enjoyed doing.' In one particular class in the school, there is a child with ASD who would have limited social skills; this child can be quite rough when playing with other children and as a result had difficulties with friendships. Through massage she has learned what level of touch is acceptable to others; prior to this she did not like anyone to touch her, but having taken part in the massage programme she found she really enjoyed it and as a consequence has learnt how to get along better with her classmates and her social skills have developed to a degree. Her mother came in to school to report a change in this child's behaviour, a positive change, and she acknowledged that the massage helped her daughter and asked if she could be trained on the massage programme because she wanted to continue this with her daughter at home as it helped to bond them closer together and it was a positive and enjoyable experience.

Theme 4: Promoting positive self-esteem

There is a statistically significant difference in the quantitative data in relation to an increase in the positive self-esteem of the children.

However, the qualitative findings did not support this increase. Only two of the seven teachers interviewed stated that the massage programme helped the children to become aware of themselves and their bodies and to be able to speak up for themselves and to express their opinions. It could be postulated that the teachers' ratings are not as sensitive to changes as the children's own self-ratings. However, when examining both the quantitative and qualitative data and the finding that the control group's self-esteem also increased, it is not possible to establish with any degree of certainty whether the Massage in Schools Programme has increased the children's self-esteem.

FINDINGS FROM CHILDREN'S INTERVIEWS

Theme 1: Change in children's behaviour

From the thematic analysis of the interviews with the children, there was evidence to suggest that the Massage in Schools Programme had some impact on promoting positive behaviour. Some children spoke about fighting with other children in the class, with one child stating: 'Sometimes if you have had a fight with someone and then you give them a massage in the class, it helps you feel better and you get on better with them.'

There is growing evidence that the Massage in Schools Programme is effective in reducing bullying and aggression both in and out of the classroom and settling hyperactive children. The programme maintains that 'it is very hard to hit someone who has made you feel good'. This view was evident to a degree during the interviews with the children in this study. For example, one child expressed her views as follows: 'Sometimes I fight with others in my class, you know because they just annoy me, and sometimes in the classroom I would have to give them a massage because I was sitting beside them and it was ok … I suppose I got to know them better and it helped me.' The massage programme not only helps children who have aggressive impulses, it also helps the children who are being bullied; one child who has been bullied at school stated: 'it helps you say if you are getting bullied and you are with that same partner well it helps you get along better.' However, this claim needs perhaps to be further explored in a larger-scale research project.

Theme 2: Conducive atmosphere for learning to take place

All the children interviewed (forty-six children) expressed the opinion that the Massage in Schools Programme created a calm atmosphere in the classroom because it helped them calm down and relax. This was a conducive atmosphere for learning to take place. It was interesting to note that even a child who did not have consent to participate in the massage programme but who observed it in her classroom felt relaxed post-massage; she stated: 'I am not allowed to do the massage, but that doesn't matter cause I like to listen and it is relaxing, our classroom is very peaceful when the others are doing massage.' When training children in the massage programme, children who do not have consent to participate are asked to sit quietly and watch; they are not allowed continue their work. According to the massage in schools association, children who observe also get the benefit of relaxation.

When researching the Massage in Schools Programme, one of the factors examined was the impact the programme had on increasing learning by decreasing hyperactivity and inattention; some of the children stated that massage helped them to concentrate better in class, and therefore was conducive to learning taking place. This was illustrated by one child who stated: 'After the massage you just feel like you are ready to do more work because you are relaxed.' Another child stated: 'I found it relaxed me and I was able to concentrate better on my work.' These comments from the children within this research study lend some support to the views of children in the Pedersen (2003) study and to the statistical data from the Woolfson et al. (2005) study. However, given the small scale of this research together with the subjective nature of children self-reporting, these findings should be viewed with some caution.

Theme 3: Developing social skills and family bonding time

Contrary to the Woolfson et al. (2005) study, the children within this research project stated that the massage programme helped them to form new friendships and generally get on better with other children in the classroom. It not only helped children with behaviour issues or special needs but it helped children from all classes, regardless of age. This was illustrated by one child who stated: 'I found it helped me to make new friends in the class; we have two new girls in our class and

I didn't know them and I have made friends with them now and we like to massage each other.' Another child stated: 'I found it helped me to make new friends with girls I don't normally play with.' New children to the school found the massage programme particularly good for getting to know the other children in the class; they commented on how it helped them settle and integrate into school activities. One newly enrolled child expressed her view as follows: 'It helped me make new friends because at first I was scared to talk to people but when we started to do the massage it helped me make new friends because I was talking to them and they told me how to do the massage and I did it and it was really relaxing and I loved it.'

From the thematic analysis of the children's interviews there was some evidence to suggest that the Massage in Schools Programme helped further develop family relationships. All of the forty-six children who were interviewed about the massage programme commented on how they brought massage home to their families. They found the massage an enjoyable activity to do with their mothers, fathers, brothers, sisters, grandparents and even the dog! It was clear from the interviews that the children became more aware of people's feelings and had a positive impact on their lives. Despite the results of the Rutter Parent Questionnaires, many of the parents provided positive feedback about the massage programme to the teachers within the school. One parent even wrote in to the class teacher to say that the massage had helped bring their family closer together and that it was an activity they all enjoyed doing. Building relationships within the family and within school is very important and it has an impact on the child's self-esteem.

Theme 4: Promoting positive self-esteem

While there was a statistically significant difference in the children's self-esteem results, not all of the children commented on their self-esteem. Some of the children reported that the massage programme helped them to become aware of themselves and their bodies. All of the children, including the quieter children, were able to speak up for themselves. Within the school a substantial input was provided to develop the children's self-esteem as some of the children come from disadvantaged families where their self-worth would not be valued.

CONCLUSION/IMPLICATIONS FOR PRACTICE

This small-scale study sought to gain an understanding of the impact of the Massage in Schools Programme in promoting positive behaviour, increasing learning, increasing self-esteem and developing social skills in children within a whole-school context. Extensive research elsewhere has shown that there are many positive effects among children who have massage in their lives. The rationale for researching this programme was to find out if the effects of peer-to-peer massage found elsewhere could be replicated in schools throughout Ireland.

Analysis of the scores from the Revised Rutter Teacher Scale indicated that there was a statistically significant difference within each of the behaviours and there is a very strong likelihood that this is due to the Massage in Schools Programme. There was also evidence to support this from the thematic analysis of the co-researchers and the children's interviews; both the teachers and the children were very positive about their experiences of the Massage in Schools Programme. Therefore the Massage in Schools Programme was found to be a positive tool in promoting positive behaviour, increasing learning, increasing self-esteem and developing social skills in children ranging in age between 7 and 12 years old. It is hoped therefore that schools may consider it as part of their toolkit to help prevent counter-aggression, bullying and violence in schools. In addition, it is hoped that a large-scale, more in-depth study of MISP would further build on this research.

REFRENCES

Achenbach, T.M. and Edelbrock, C.S. *Manual for the Child Behaviour Checklist and Revised Child Behaviour Profile* (Burlington, VT: University of Vermont, Department of Psychiatry, 1983)

Ainsworth, M., Blehar, M., Waters, E. and Wall, S. *Patterns of Attachment* (Hillsdale, NJ: Erlbaum, 1978)

Ayres, A. *Sensory Integration and the Child* (Los Angeles: Western Psychological Services, 1985)

Beckwith, C.A. 'The Concept of Touch as an Aspect of Therapeutic Nursing', *Complementary Therapies in Medicine*, 1, 1993, pp. 211–14

Bowlby, J. 'The Nature of the Child's Tie to his Mother', *International Journal of Psychoanalysis*, 39, 1958, pp. 350–71

Carlson, M. 'Understanding the "Mother's Touch"' (1998), http://www.med.harvard.edu/publications/on the brain/volume7/number1/commentary.html [accessed 21 March 2007]

Colaizzi, P. 'Psychological Research as the Phenomenologist Views It', in R. Valle and M. King (eds), *Existential Phenomenological Alternatives for Psychology* (Oxford: Oxford University Press, 1978)

Diego, M.A., Field, T., Hernandez-Reif, M., Shaw, J.A., Rothe, E.M., Castellanos, D. and Mesner, L. 'Aggressive Adolescents Benefit from Massage Therapy', *Adolescence*, 37, 2002, pp. 597–607

Elander, J. and Rutter, M. 'Use and Development of the Rutter Parents' and Teachers' Scales', *International Journal of Methods in Psychiatric Research*, 6, 1996, pp. 63–78

Field, T. 'Massage Therapy for Infants of Depressed Mothers', *Infant Behaviour and Development*, 19, 1996, pp. 107–12

Field, T., Lasko, D., Mundy, P., Henteleff, T., Kabat, S., Talpins, S. and Dowling, M. 'Brief Report: Autistic Children's Attentiveness and Responsivity Improve after Touch Therapy', *Journal of Autism and Developmental Disorders*, 27, 1997, pp. 333–8

Field, T., Henteleff, T., Hernandez-Reif, M., Martinez, E., Mavunda, K., Kuhn, C. and Schanberg, S. 'Children with Asthma Have Improved Pulmonary Functions after Massage Therapy', *Journal of Pediatrics*, 132, 1998a, pp. 854–8

Field, T., Quintino, O., Hernandez-Reif, M., and Koslovsky, G. 'Adolescents with Attention Deficit Hyperactivity Disorder Benefit from Massage Therapy', *Adolescence*, 33, 1998, pp. 103–8

Field, T. 'Stimulation of Preterm Infants', *Paediatrics*, 24, 2003, pp. 4–11

Fontana, D. *Psychology for Teachers*, 3rd edn (London: Macmillan Press, 1995)

Goleman, D. *Emotional Intelligence: Why it Can Matter More than IQ* (London: Bloomsbury, 1996)

Halcon, L.L., Chlan, L.L., Kreitzer, M.J. and Leonard, B.J. 'Complementary Therapies and Healing Practices: Faculty/Student Beliefs and Attitudes and the Implications for Nursing Education', *Journal of Professional Nursing*, 19, 2003, pp. 387–97

Humphreys, T. *Self-Esteem: The Key to your Child's Education* (Dublin: Newleaf, 1996)

Humphreys, T. *A Different Kind of Teacher*, 1st edn (Dublin: Gill & Macmillan, 1993)

Khilnani, S., Field, T., Hernandez-Reif, M., and Schanberg, S. 'Massage Therapy Improves Mood and Behaviour of Students with Attention Deficit/Hyperactivity Disorder', *Adolescence*, 38, 2003, pp. 623–37

Lawrence, D. *Enhancing Self-Esteem in the Classroom* (London: Paul Chapman Publishing, 1996)

Lawrence, D. *Enhancing Self-Esteem in the Classroom*, 2nd edn (London: Paul Chapman Publishing, 1996)

Lawrence, D. *Enhancing Self-Esteem in the Classroom*, 3rd edn (London: Paul Chapman Publishing, 2006)

Lo-Biondo-Wood, G. and Haber, J. *Nursing Research, Methods, Critical Appraisal and Utilization*, 4th edn (St Louis, MO: Mosby, 1998)

Lorenz, L., Moyse, K. and Surguy, H. 'The Benefits of Baby Massage', *Paediatric Nursing*, 17, 2005, pp. 15–18

Massage in Schools, http://massageinschools.com.au/impactmedia020206 .htm (2001) (accessed 10 January 2008)

Miller, D. and Moran, T. 'One in Three? Teachers' Attempts to Identify Low Self-Esteem Children', *Pastoral Care*, December 2005, pp. 25–30

Montagu, A. *Touching: The Human Significance of the Skin*, 3rd edn (New York: Harper & Row, 1986)

Murray, O. 'The "Massage in Schools Programme" as a Whole-School Approach, with a View to Promoting Positive Behaviour', unpublished M.Ed thesis, Trinity College Dublin

Pedersen, A. 'A Case Study of Pupils' and Teachers' Perceptions of the Effect of Using Peer Massage on the Mathematical Performance and Behaviour of Boys Attending a School for Emotional and Behavioural Difficulties', unpublished Paper, 2003

Regalado, M. 'Primary Care Services Promoting Optimal Child Development from Birth to Age 3 Years', *Archives of Paediatric Adolescent Medicine*, 155, 2001, pp. 1311–22

Rogers, C.R. *Carl Rogers on Personal Power* (New York: Delacorte Press, 1977)

Rutter, M. (1993) Revised Rutter Scale. In Sclare I. (1997) (ed.) *Child Psychology Portfolio*. Berkshire: NFER-Nelson

Spitz, R. 'Hospitalism', *The Psychoanalytic Study of the Child*, 1, 1945, pp. 53–74

Uvnäs-Moberg, K. 'Oxytocin May Mediate the Benefits of Positive Social Interactions and Emotions', *Psychoneuroendocrinology*, vol. 23, no. 8, 1998, pp. 819–35

Woolfson, R., Campbell, L. and Banks, M. 'The Renfrewshire "Massage in Schools Programme" (MISP): An Evaluation of its Impact in a Primary School' (2005), http://www.misascotland.org.uk/pics/ELS-massage-in-schools.pdf [accessed 18 January 2011]

CHAPTER SIXTEEN

Mindfulness and Pre-School Children

Madeleine Young

> Preventing conflicts is the work of politics; establishing peace is the work of education.
>
> (Maria Montessori, 1972, p. 30)

INTRODUCTION

Early childhood is often romanticised with thoughts of play, fun, indulgences and cuddles; images of chubby little individuals who have not a care in the world come to mind. Does behaviour radically change as these pre-schoolers enter middle childhood and adolescence? Much recent media attention has been given to bullying – the victims and perpetrators. According to the charity Beatbullying (BBC News UK, 2010), 44% of suicides of young people in the United Kingdom are attributed to bullying. Schools have adopted anti-bullying policies and codes of discipline and many anti-bullying programmes have been marketed to address the problem; however, a whole-school approach is vital. If we are intent in preventing bullying, we need firstly to promote those positive qualities of empathy and loving-kindness in our children at a very young age as it is in early childhood that the foundations for such qualities are rooted. Once those qualities are present, it may become much more difficult to objectify others by bullying behaviour. We need to counteract the bullying epidemic in our society at a deep level, not by punishing or criticising the perpetrators or bystanders but by encouraging children to pay attention to thoughts and reactions in order to develop compassion. A peaceful mind helps to create a compassionate attitude, while anger and fear create conflict and misery (Warren, 2002). The Dalai Lama (1997) has instructed us that if we accept all experiences in life, whether positive or negative, then we will avoid becoming overwhelmed and losing control. In this way we can learn to manage our emotional responses and avoid out-of-control behavioural outbursts. We need to accept the unacceptable and learn to let go of our tendencies to control, avoid or crave (Rosenbaum, 1999) and work towards wholeness and authenticity (Perls et al., 1998).

Children are constantly told by teachers and parents to 'pay attention', yet they are frequently not shown how (Mann, 2001). The skill of paying attention is at the heart of mindfulness, as by paying attention to the breath, to the body and to the thoughts, children can learn to pay attention to their reactions (Semple et al., 2006). It has been stated by the many advocates who promote mindfulness with children that through mindfulness children learn to pay attention, by improving concentration, developing listening skills and learning how to relax, as they begin to focus their attention on the breath. Focusing on the breath assists children to stay in the present, helps them to acquire an awareness of their feelings and body sensations, without judgement, thus improving their impulse control, so that they become less reactive, and choose instead how to respond (Bien 2006, Thich Nhat Hanh, 2008). The promotion of empathy and kindness is a secondary goal of the mindfulness programme, as children are encouraged to give and receive thoughts of loving-kindness (Kornfield, 2005). Mindfulness may be considered to be a religious practice by many and therefore care should be taken not to influence children's religious beliefs. Although mindfulness is frequently associated with Buddhism, a school programme needs to be regarded as a secular activity (Fontana and Slack, 2007).

It can be difficult to accurately define the term mindfulness. Kabat-Zinn (1994) describes it as paying attention, on purpose, in the present moment, yet without judgement. Essentially, it may be regarded as training in mental discipline. When people learn and practise mindfulness, they begin to stop identifying with thoughts, feelings and body sensations and to cease obsessing with the drama of their own personal narratives. As a result they become more objective and start to observe instead what is going on for them with curiosity and interest (Chaskalson, 2011). Mindfulness teaches us to stop attending to unhappy memories and critical judgemental thoughts and feelings, by witnessing them as they arise with compassionate awareness, thus liberating ourselves from worry, stress and unhappiness (Williams and Penman, 2012).

Mindfulness is a powerful tool in teaching. If a teacher behaves calmly, then students are likely to follow and if a teacher shows respect, then students return the courtesy. Both teachers and students learn through mindfulness to notice thoughts and feelings with conscious awareness, without reaction, observing them as they arise and then as they drift away. Teachers and students learn that a challenging class or a failed test is just that, not a personal failure, and that it need not provide a trigger for unhappy memories. Mindfulness enhances the management of social and emotional skills, such as cultivating kindness and compassion towards self and others and equally acknowledging aggression in order to deal with its energy. Developing awareness of emotions and reactions helps teachers and students reflect that the quality of their actions always affects themselves and others (Schoeberlein, 2009).

The scope of the research I undertook was to study the effects of mindfulness practices on a class of pre-school children (Young, 2009). The pre-school teacher and class were integrated in the study during school hours and a home practice was also encouraged, which involved participation of parents and pre-school children in a recommended programme during out-of-school hours. The purpose of the research was to deliberate whether levels of aggression in the children were reduced as a result.

EARLY YEARS

In today's world, pre-schools encourage young children to learn through discovery, to be spontaneous, to be free thinkers, to be creative, active and to fulfil their potential. Their behaviour is monitored by staff who encourage them to take turns, to share and show kindness towards each other. Their behaviour is likewise regulated by adults, who appear as much larger and more experienced than themselves. Sitting quietly and being contemplative is not really what we would expect of a 3- or 4-year-old. So how feasible is it to teach a very young child to practise self-regulation and to participate in a mindfulness programme when the natural urge is to be active, inquisitive and energetic? Does mindfulness have any real value for a young child, or is it going against the very nature of exploration and inquisitiveness of early childhood and does it indeed make any real difference in assisting them to deal with conflict with calmness and self-control?

A view held is that a child's mind is open and absorbent, without self-consciousness and that a young mind can easily adapt to new habits, such as the power of attention (Levete, 2001). In my recent research I examined whether by learning mindfulness, very young children could learn relaxation skills, discover how to centre themselves and how to be silent, thus acquiring inner stillness and peace and consequently gain a better understanding of their emotional reactions (Young, 2009). This research had been prompted by a fascination with exploring the triggers that direct children's behaviours. Much time is spent unproductively in classrooms in resolving conflict that could instead be directed to teaching. The purpose of the research consequently was to explore if pre-school children, through mindfulness approaches, could find their own inner locus of control. Before embarking on this project I had some reservation whether this approach could be used effectively as a resource for emotional control and self-regulation for very young children. I hold the belief, however, that at pre-school level behaviour problems are at the emergent stage, and consequently the earlier a child can learn to self-regulate and assume some responsibility for behaviours the better chance he/she will have in managing and understanding emotions in older childhood and in adulthood. I propose that impulsivity and poor self-regulation in pre-school years is indicative of aggressive/bullying behaviour in later years. Children indeed can show aggression and others be victimised as early as pre-school level. Aggressive pre-school children are more likely to continue to display social difficulties towards their peers and their teachers throughout primary years (Ladd and Burgess, 1999).

It may be most effective, consequently, to target aggressive behaviour at a very early stage. It may be suggested furthermore that self-regulation is a vital part of development and is concerned with self-control (Harwood et al., 2008). From the third year of life, regulation begins to move from the external control of parents to internal control. It is important for children to begin to regulate their behaviour in order to learn to delay gratification, to avoid what is necessary to avoid, for if not they will be pulled by their reactions in every way and will be at the mercy of their environment (Harwood, Miller and Vasta, 2008). Maria Montessori (1972) believed in directing the children unobtrusively and considered freedom to be the ability to control one's cravings in order to fulfil deep desires and to be able to make conscious choices about behaviour and its consequences. Montessori (1972) had long held the view that in submitting to a responsive environment the young child learns personal autonomy, and she regarded young children as being self-creating, self-actualising and self-enhancing (Gettman, 2004).

EMERGING FIELDS

It is in America and in Canada that mindfulness with children has received most attention and media coverage, and a growing number of schools have been turning to use contemplative approaches, although little research has been completed. An article in *The Greater Good Magazine* (29 January 2008) entitled 'Mindful Kids, Peaceful Schools' by Jill Suttie supports this approach. In this article, Suttie wrote of Susan Kaiser Greenland who introduced a mindfulness approach to Toluca Lake elementary school in Los Angeles with positive effects (Suttie, 2008). Susan Kaiser Greenland founded the Innerkids Foundation through which she taught mindfulness classes in schools and after-school programmes for little or no cost. Kaiser Greenland, under the direction of Dr Sue Smalley, of UCLA, then conducted three school-based, randomised control studies teaching the Inner Kids Programme. The first study designed as a feasibility study looked at pre-kindergarten age children in 2006–7 and confirmed that very young children could take part in a mindfulness group programme. The second study taught second and third-class pupils in 2007–8 and parents and teachers recorded significant improvement in those children with executive function difficulties. They developed an awareness of breath and an ability to notice when their attention had wandered and to bring it back. The third study conducted in 2009 again involved pre-kindergarten children and showed clear improvement for all, not just those with executive function deficits. The three studies showed a positive impact on self-regulation and that the programme also proved to be very enjoyable for the children (Kaiser Greenland, 2010).

A few years earlier, in 1999 Soren Gordhamer, influenced by the work of Kabat-Zinn published in 1991 (Kabat-Zinn, 2007), started teaching meditation at juvenile halls and from this emerged the Lineage Project (2012) for at-risk and incarcerated teenagers, in order to encourage non-violence and reduction of stress. Chen (2012) describes the work of Laurie Grossman who piloted mindfulness approaches in Park Day School in Oakland. Amy Saltzman is conducting ongoing research regarding whether mindfulness affects stress levels in children and teenagers and whether mindfulness enhances emotional intelligence, encourages healthy relating and develops compassion. Saltzman has conducted previous research on a mindfulness-based stress reduction curriculum to elementary school children and their parents. Both parents and children experienced decreased anxiety and increased compassion (Saltzman n.d.).

The Garrison Institute (Jha, 2005) offers an overview of the many approaches used in schools. It reports that the programmes explored drew on various resources, using many techniques in different settings, which assessed behavioural change and urged people to combine and share knowledge. The concept of mindfulness in schools, however, is relatively new, especially in the Republic of Ireland, although people are slowly beginning to recognise and appreciate its benefits.

DIFFERENT MEDITATIVE PRACTICES

The great spiritual traditions have all practised meditation in some way or other and there is speculation regarding its origin. It is probable that it originated in Hinduism and later was adopted by Buddhists, but it has long since been associated with both religions (Fontana and Slack, 2007). Meditation is generally associated with developing a deep sense of relaxation or awareness and quietening of the mind. Breathing deeply has deep significance, it helps us to begin to feel calmer and to be present with our negative feelings and not stuck in them (Bien, 2006). Thich Nhat Hanh (2008) agrees with the statement that correct breathing is more important than food as it builds up the lungs, increases vitality, and improves the blood and every organ in the body. There are many different kinds of meditative practices some including sitting, walking, concentrating on the breath, a mantra, or on an external object, such as a candle, or by visualisation.

Sachs (1998) gives a brief, simple description of meditative practices in order to clarify the major differences.

Tibetan Buddhism concentrates inwardly on the body, or outwardly away from the body to a place of beauty or a Buddha image.

Zen Buddhism concentrates on the breath, without thought interruption, in order to help people deepen awareness so that they respond to life more compassionately (Batchelor, 2001).

Mindfulness has been adapted from other meditative practices by Jon Kabat-Zinn (2007), whereby the practitioner becomes a compassionate observer of the self.

Taoist Meditation uses the symbols of yin and yang to connect and integrate the mind, body and spirit.

Transcendental Meditation. TM was introduced to the USA in 1959 by Maharishi Mahesh Yogi to help all people reach enlightenment. A mantra is used to aid concentration.

Yoga and *Tai Chi* are moving meditations. They stretch and develop
   both mind and body.

All these practices have variations in approach, yet the common
theme is towards an improved state of mind, where concentration,
calmness, balance and clarity are the principal objectives. Much of
our ordinary everyday living is complicated with our gratification of
desire, which is lacking in conscious thought. We tend to ignore the
needs and rights of others if their views conflict with our own. Once
one desire is satisfied, another arises, suggesting that peace is elusive,
which is part of our endless suffering. We see others as objects,
judged by their value to self, which paves the route to social cruelty
and the loss of our humanity (Olendzki, 2005).

WHAT IS MINDFULNESS?

Mindfulness has been practised for over 2,500 years and has been
influenced by both Eastern and Western philosophies. It has
generally been associated with psychotherapy rather than education.
The work in psychotherapy is to alleviate emotional suffering, such as
anxiety, depression, stress, behavioural problems, conflict and despair.
Mindfulness can bring about behaviour change as it is based on a
concept that if an individual engages in unethical activities he finds
peace and tranquility difficult to attain (Fulton and Siegel, 2005).
Practitioners are asked to carefully observe their minds, thus to learn
to be less reactive to the present moment by learning to relate to all
experiences, both negative and positive, in an accepting, non-judging
way. It involves awareness of the present experience with acceptance.
It can be practised with varying degrees of intensity; from the intake
of a long, conscious breath or the performance of everyday tasks
mindfully to sustained periods of time spent in deep meditation
(Germer, 2005).

MEDITATION AND MINDFULNESS

The goal in mindfulness meditation in particular is not to achieve
deep relaxation but to be aware of the state that body and mind
are in and be accepting – to have a deep awareness of the present
moment (Fodor and Hooker, 2008). The unaware mind can be
compared to a chattering monkey or a runaway horse. In meditation,

in contrast, the mind becomes alert, watchful and aware (Fontana and Slack, 2007). What is this awareness all about? Chopra (2004) states it may firstly be helpful to explore what *lack* of awareness is about. Kabat-Zinn (2007) describes our thoughts and emotions as being so overpowering, especially when in crisis, that our present awareness is distorted. Even when in a relaxed state, we can get lost in thoughts, as in a car we can sometimes drive for miles on 'automatic pilot' without being aware of how far we have travelled. In the same way, we may not be really present for a lot of our lives. In practising mindfulness we are willing to walk along life's paths with eyes open and fully conscious without reacting mindlessly (Kabat-Zinn, 2007). Mindfulness is not just about meditating but about performing everyday activities, whether eating, drinking, bathing, cooking or washing dishes, with conscious awareness (Thich Nhat Hanh, 2008).

Visualisation practices are sometimes taught as meditation exercises in order to help people deal with difficult situations in life. The imagination can affect moods and consequently behaviours. By deliberately drawing up a positive, helpful image in the mind and its subsequent associations, people become better able to take control of moods and redirect them for their own benefit and for the benefit of others (Brazier, 1995). A peaceful, calm mind creates compassion and understanding, while emotions like anger and fear cause conflict with others and sickness of mind and body. Visualisation or guided imagery uses the imagination for the body to respond to. The Dalai Lama (1997) states that we need to be aware of the disadvantages of unhealthy negative thoughts and behaviours and acknowledges the advantages of healthy positive ones. Unstable emotions not only affect our own minds but also affect the minds of other people. He describes the untamed mind in which suffering is experienced as a realm of hell.

Mindfulness helps us to be patient and gentle with ourselves, to be open and accepting, without clinging or avoiding. Life is suffering and the root of unhappiness is our desire to control how we want things to be. Craving takes us away from what we have right now and can lead to obsessive addictions. People suffering from phobias are prisoners not to their fears but to the avoidance of them. People with depression are not mourning their lost hopes but instead their attachment to what they longed for. People who are insomniacs are not suffering from their loss of sleep but the terror of being awake in the darkness. If we demand that people are the way we want them to be, then we miss the opportunity of seeing them as they are. Yet there is a connection between sorrow and joy and by meeting all experiences with acceptance we can learn to sing in the rain and, like a child, play in the mud. We can learn to surf those waves with acceptance, instead of being tossed by them and fighting with anger and resentment (Rosenbaum, 1999).

Kornfield (2005) states that there are many good forms of meditative practices and it does not matter what type of meditation is used, as long as it is practised with regularity and discipline. He describes a good practice as one which develops awareness or mindfulness of body, senses, mind and heart. Mindfulness meditation, also known as 'vipassana', helps us to be awake and alive; to live with more wisdom, clarity and compassion. We learn that everything passes, not only painful experiences but also joyful ones; we learn to accept without judgement (Kornfield, 2005). The Dalai Lama (2002) explains that our normal state of mind is made up of wild, unruly thoughts and emotions but through the discipline of meditation and by applying mindfulness continually, we learn to place our minds. Mindfulness enables people to observe with care the consequences of their behaviour, without judgement. The terms 'good' or 'bad' are not used, but replaced with 'wholesome' or 'unwholesome'. Wholesome actions reduce suffering for self and others and unwholesome actions increase it. Formal mindfulness refers to meditation, while informal mindfulness refers to mindfulness exercises that bring attention to the present moment, i.e. slow walking and slow eating. It is not a relaxation exercise, but is about a slow, gradual understanding of self (Germer, 2005). With mindfulness meditation the mind wandering is seen to be an event to be observed and not judged. With the 'raisin exercise', the person is asked to eat a raisin in a mindful way, observing on its appearance, smell, taste and touch, bringing attention to awareness. With the 'body scan' exercise, the person is asked to focus on different parts of the body, while lying on the back. The person is not being asked to relax muscles but to merely observe tension, without judgement (Baer and Krietemeyer, 2006). Mindfulness meditation appears on reflection to be different from other practices, because it involves non-judgemental observation and appears to be a more gentle approach. Mind wandering is not criticised, but is something else to be observed with a curious interest, along with thoughts, sounds, emotions and bodily sensations. The breath, rather than a mantra or object, provides a simple, always available, anchor. Mindfulness brings about insight and insight brings about wisdom and changes us in a deep, profound way (Olendzki, 2005). With mindfulness, the person is encouraged to stay with the sensation, albeit painful, and focus attention on it. The same can be applied to emotional responses; the person is encouraged to observe the emotional response and thus learn to tolerate it, instead of reacting (Siegel, 2005).

TEACHERS

Teachers, unlike many other professions, do their work in isolation, without a division of labour or a collective responsibility. It is considered to be the teachers' roles to apply control, yet any system of hierarchical control is open to abuse. The teacher has the power to judge the behaviour of the child in her class (Senge, 2000). Schools are social systems and consequently the school environment affects the mental health of the child (Somersalo, 2002). 'The leader acts as the group's emotional guide' (Goleman, 2005, p. 5). Leaders who can stay positive and control their impulses even when under extreme pressure can create an environment of trust, fairness and comfort. Some children are emotionally vulnerable; they find difficulty in negotiation and compromise, rely instead on force and are frequently involved in classroom brawls. They have poor impulse control and consequently are disliked by staff and peers. Children need to be taught self-awareness, to recognise feelings and to be able to express them, to see the connection between thoughts, feelings and reactions and work out if it is their thoughts or reactions which are behind their decisions. They need to become aware of alternative choices (Glasser, 1999) and also the consequences of such choices (Dreikurs, 1972). Children need to understand how others feel and respect differences, to question others' opinions and learn how to deal with conflict (Goleman, 1996).

Luxmoore (2006) suggests that we choose the work we do in order to resolve our own issues around authority figures from the past and that children's aggression can provide triggers to teachers' past experiences and relationships and consequently teachers also react inappropriately. Some teachers dance between authoritarian or loving approaches which echo their own childhood experiences. Young people need both approaches. They need to know that a teacher, like a parent can be both authoritarian and loving and to accept the imperfections of both states. Likewise a teacher needs to accept her own imperfections, in order to accept those of her pupils (Luxmoore, 2006). A mindfulness approach can help towards acceptance of the whole self, including the parts that are not perfect. A pilot programme showed that when teachers used mindfulness themselves, it reduced their stress levels and improved their quality of life both in and out of school, as well as creating a positive change in the classroom (Napoli, 2004).

SCHOOLS

Tobin Hart (2004) writes of the need for introducing contemplative practices into the classroom. He states that young children are by their very nature natural contemplatives. They question, they daydream, they reflect on who they are, where they come from and where they will go to. They love secret places. He suggests using journal writing as a contemplative activity, in order to connect with their inner world. Poetry is full of metaphor and images, which also encourages contemplative thought. When we are moved by a poem, it is because it has connected with our own experience and it causes us to step back and look at what is happening to us and helps us to recognise our authentic self (Clarke, 2008). Creating a special silent time, initiated and ended by ringing a bell to add ceremony, can also aid contemplation. Stretching and breathing exercises and simple yoga all release tension and change the energy in the room and help the children to become more centred. He emphasises the benefit of the teacher exploring her own contemplative mind for a better result. Robert Wall's (2005) five-week project on a combined mindfulness and Tai Chi programme with middle school pupils showed positive results. The pupils reported experiencing improved calmness, well-being, a more relaxed state, less reactivity and a sense of connection with nature as a result (Wall, 2005).

CHILDREN

Teaching mindfulness to children needs to be appropriate to their developmental age; it is not helpful to treat them as miniature adults, consequently modifications and adaptations are necessary. Young children cannot be expected to sit for long periods on a mat (Semple et al., 2006). Children are excited by the hope of discovery and see life as a fresh sheet of paper which offers so much limitless potential (Chopra, 2005). Children communicate differently from adults. They express thoughts and feelings in a non-verbal way, through play and body gestures (Harwood et al., 2008). They live more in the present moment than adults do and can often be our teachers in that regard.

Children own many of the qualities of mindfulness, in that they live in the here-and-now, have openness, spontaneity and receptiveness to new experiences and to learning (Goodman, 2005). Metaphors could be used to explain the process. The football team practising penalty kicks is a useful metaphor. When practising penalties, the game is no longer in progress, but practice is necessary in order to play better when the game resumes. In the same way, mindfulness prepares us to live better when under pressure (Thompson and Gauntlett-Gilbert, 2008). In this article, citing Kornfield (2003), the puppy metaphor is described, which explains the process of trying to get a puppy to sit down, by gently bringing it back to its place, much like the wandering mind.

THIS RESEARCH

The main purpose of my research, which formed part of an MEd in Aggression Studies at Trinity College Dublin, was to ascertain whether a mindfulness programme could help pre-school age children gain a better understanding of their emotional reactions. It hoped to reduce aggression in pre-school children by teaching them how to regulate their behaviour, instead of reacting. By creating an awareness of thoughts and feelings, it suggested that the young children would learn to develop empathy towards others and to self-reflect. It intended to promote a sense of calmness in the children, by encouraging them to focus in the present and also by increasing their concentration and attention.

There were two parts to the programme: mindfulness at school and mindfulness at home. The mindfulness at school programme took place over twenty-five days and was supported by the mindfulness at home programme. The duration of each school-based session was approximately forty-five minutes. The pre-school teacher also reminded the class throughout the day to be aware of mindfulness in the daily activities and at times to stop and bring awareness to their breath.

The programme took place over seven weeks in total, was self-facilitated and was influenced by previous research as outlined in Young (2009). The class took place at the same time each day, to provide consistency and a sense of routine in the school day. The daily programme consisted of a turn-taking exercise, followed by active meditation which released energy. This was followed by mindful movement, then an exercise on creating an inner peace with focus on the breath, a short visualisation, a simple yoga exercise, and completed by a brief regrouping closure activity. Short varied activities took place where sitting interchanged with movement, in keeping with the young child's short attention span.

A suitable calm, reverent environment was created by burning incense and playing soft music. The children began by removing their shoes and sat in an inward-facing circle. A bell initiated the start of the session. Emphasis was given to sitting correctly with a straight spine, cross-legged if possible. The programme began by firstly encouraging the children to create silence and stillness of body. Rules were explained: to speak in turn and to treat others present with care and respect. A turn-taking exercise then took place, as the children passed a 'holding object' around the circle as they spoke. This prompted listening and sharing (Mosley, 1998). Active meditation was the next activity. Active meditation is brief emotional release work or bioenergetics which releases agitation in order to prepare for mindfulness meditation (Pearson, 2004). The children found a space in the room and were then encouraged to release energy by vigorous movement, sometimes in keeping with music. They were then asked to move with awareness with mindful walking. Walking meditation is called 'kinhin' by Zen Buddhists, whereby the meditator walks with precision and almost stillness, meditating on each movement, with utmost concentration (Fontana and Slack, 2007).

The children were next asked to sit and cushions were provided. The breath was emphasised throughout as the anchor creating focus. Props such as straws and bubble wands were provided to encourage blowing out the breath. Other focuses such as a sand-timer or a burning candle or stones were also provided at times to aid concentration. Attention was given to the senses of sound, sight, smell, touch and taste. Visualisations were used to create relaxation combined with positive affirmations to create a sense of self-belief. The children were asked to lie down on the floor on their backs with their head on the cushion. 'Visualisation work is focused, active use of imagination. It can be directed, given boundaries or free form' (Pearson, 2004, p. 100). The brain does not differentiate between real and imaginary experiences; we know this when we wake up from a disturbing dream and feel the impact on our bodies (Berkovits, 2005). Imagery depends on imagination; it is not rational and is not restricted to real life. Working with images deserves the teacher's respect, rather than her interpretations. Some people see things very clearly in their imagination, while others have difficulty. Children can be encouraged to visualise problems, dilemmas and feelings, in order to bring about change (Plummer, 2007). Visualisation was explained as seeing pictures in their heads, so children were asked to close their eyes as they visualised. Imagination is not just visual, they were also asked to imagine through sound, touch, smell and taste. Through imagery, it was intended that pupils learned to deal with their struggles and achieve a sense of power and autonomy by themselves (Berkovits, 2005). The visualisations were related using the present tense, to facilitate the children experiencing the images. The children were also taught awareness of body sensations and how to be present in the now, similar to the 'body scan', advocated by Kabat-Zinn (2007). Feelings of fear, sadness and anger were explored. A non-judgemental approach was emphasised towards self and others. The importance of showing loving kindness to self, fellow beings and to the universe was stressed.

A simple yoga exercise was taught to the children, as mindfulness in motion. Children were encouraged to avoid forcing themselves beyond their capabilities, but to observe their bodies and to breathe, with a half-smile. Illustrations of simple yoga exercises were sent home with the weekly homework sheets (Guber and Kalish, 2005; Strutt, 2002). The session ended with the children sitting in a circle, holding hands to create a connection and passing a smile, wink, gentle squeeze, or a word of kindness around the group. One child was then selected to ring the bell to bring closure to the session.

The parents were presented with a home mindfulness booklet and suggestions were added each week so that parents could supplement the programme on a one-to-one basis in the home environment. It consisted of a seven-week programme. The first exercise, Still Quiet Place, encouraged the children to sit and become conscious of the breath (Saltzman, 2004). Additional exercises were described, involving visualisation, discussion of feelings, visual memory, mindful walking, mindful eating, mindful listening, pouring water, blowing bubbles and breathing, thus creating a vital link between home practice and the exercises practised in the classroom. The home mindfulness programme was very much dependent on parental goodwill and willingness to commit.

Both school and home programmes were adapted and extended from the Community Partnership for Mindfulness in Education (2008). Laurie Grossman (2008) was the Community Outreach Coordinator at Park Day School in California and helped pilot a programme of mindfulness with elementary school children. It has also drawn from *Teaching Meditation to Children. The Practical Guide to the Use and Benefits of Meditation Techniques* (Fontana and

Slack, 2007) and Semple et al. (2006). Amy Saltzman's compact disc has also provided inspiration and has added to the programme (Saltzman, 2004). The concept was based on the writings of Kabat-Zinn (2007), Kornfield (2005) and Thit Nhat Hanh (2008).

As the research was a pilot study, it was limited to only one pre-school class in one pre-school in Ireland. It therefore cannot be claimed as being representative of all children who attend pre-school classes. The children were drawn from working parents, so there were no issues of unemployment or obvious poverty to reflect on. No control group was used. The timescale of seven weeks involved five weeks in the pre-school classroom and a further two were conducted solely in the home setting when school was not in operation, during the Christmas break. A proviso was made for this, by means of the home mindfulness programme, yet as previously stressed, it was dependent on parental support. The parents interviewed had made efforts with their children and although there were obstacles, such as time and sibling rivalry, they were very positive about the practice and stated they intended continuing with it.

RESULTS

Both quantitative and qualitative methods were used to measure the effects of the mindfulness programme (Young, 2009). The children's behaviours were examined with the help of the Rutter Behavioural Scale both before and after the start of the programme (1970). The Revised Rutter Parent Scale for Pre-school Age Children and the Revised Rutter Teacher/Nursery Staff Scale for Children were used. Both Rutter scales yielded individual scores for conduct, hyperactivity and social behaviour and a total score. The teachers' scores showed significant differences for social behaviour ($t = 3.443$ for a 95% confidence of not null) and for the total score ($t = 1.835$ for a 95% confidence of not null). There was also a written questionnaire for parents which examined improvement of behaviour, regularity of practice, enthusiasm, awareness of concept and commitment, which were the main themes. In order to provide deeper insight that might not have been covered by the Rutter scales and the parents' questionnaire, two qualitative questions on the written questionnaire and one-to-one interviews were conducted with the pre-school teacher and volunteer parents. The themes that emerged from the Rutter Scales were extended in the qualitative research to include emotional, conduct, hyperactivity/inattention and prosocial. These themes were explored through interviews with the pre-school teacher, parents and by my reflections as facilitator.

The Rutter Parent Scale yielded no significant differences in behaviour; however, the written questionnaire completed by the parents at the end of the project indicated that there was general agreement that the mindfulness programme had improved the children's behaviour. In addition, interviews with the parents produced positive findings, including observing the children's increased confidence and connection with self and feelings, an improvement in dealing with anger and the ability to self-regulate and enthusiasm towards the programme. The parents reported a reduction in hyperactivity and tantrums, an increase in kindness and patience, improved coping skills and a more focused approach. For example, one parent commented that the programme had improved her child's sleeping; nightmares had changed into happy dreams and the breathing had improved the asthma. From the teacher's interview, it was ascertained that the children's positive behaviour had increased and that the programme had a calming effect and helped develop their self-esteem. As facilitator I observed that the session had a calming effect on the children and their concentration improved. It needs to be taken into account that in adopting dual roles of researcher and facilitator, I may have willed the research to produce positive results. The teacher, parents and I were all in agreement that the programme improved the children's social skills, in particular with regard to turn-taking and sharing. The feasibility of such a programme was discussed and teacher and parents agreed it certainly was feasible. The main difficulties which arose in discussion were lack of time on parents' behalf to implement the home mindfulness, lack of information about the concept amongst teachers and parents, lack of prior information regarding the children's backgrounds on the facilitator's behalf and absenteeism.

My research supports previous research in this emerging field and concludes that from this study of a small sample of pre-school children the mindfulness programme did bring about positive change. This pilot study was limited to one small, short experience and should not be seen as a general view representing all pre-schools. It does however demonstrate the potential of such a programme and its feasibility regarding the positive impact of a mindfulness programme on pre-school children's behaviour, in order to self-regulate and reduce hyperactivity and inattention at school and at home.

RECOMMENDATIONS

The findings of this research are consistent with current theory and fit into the existing body of knowledge, yet it needs to be emphasised that it needs to be part of the school programme to show lasting benefit. In future it would be important for adults conducting the programme to have received the eight-week mindfulness training and for parents and staff involved to be informed about the practice before its commencement and to be strongly encouraged to use the mindfulness practices themselves. If undertaking this piece of research again, it might be worthwhile adjusting the variables of size and time. A larger sample could be used and a control group introduced. Different cultural and socio-economic backgrounds could also be explored. The time variable could be lengthened and returning to the pre-school at some point could be considered in order to estimate any behaviour change over time. Further research could explore why the teacher's and parents' Rutter scores were so different, in particular the pro-social skills. The question of how the school and home compare as a good social environment is one which could be explored. An issue to be considered for future research could be how important the quality of the relationship is between the facilitator and the children for the programme's success. Another theme could be the relevance of facilitators of a programme to practise mindfulness themselves in their own lives. A third issue for consideration could be deliberating how much of the success of the programme is dependent on parental support. A final consideration for possible research could be whether a better result would be achieved if parents and teachers had more insight into what mindfulness was about before the commencement of such a programme with their children, perhaps even making a commitment to undertake the eight-week mindfulness programme.

CONCLUSION

Mindfulness with children has generated much interest and enthusiasm in Canada and America and research is still ongoing, yet it has not received the same recognition in Ireland. Using such practices with pre-school children has certainly not been well documented. The Social, Personal and Health Education Programme (SPHE) (Department of Education and Science, 1996) in Ireland recognises the need to explore sexuality and safety, mental and physical health issues, deal with conflict resolution, improve communication and teach children to relate and make decisions. So what are the benefits of introducing mindfulness in early years education and in Irish schools? This research holds the position that mindfulness takes children a step further. It helps children to manage attitudes and reactions and to connect their inner and outer worlds, thus becoming more integrated with themselves (Rozman, 2002). Concentration is associated with focusing to the exclusion of other things, while mindfulness implies paying attention, applying oneself and taking care. A rationale supporting this research is that the mindfulness practice could extend the SPHE curriculum by teaching the children how to relate primarily to themselves, which ultimately helps them to relate more compassionately to others thus reducing bullying and aggressive behaviour. This practice could give children an understanding of their emotional responses and provide them with a choice of how to behave, supported by Glasser's theory (1999). It could also help children gain an understanding of how others feel and to learn to empathise (Goleman, 1996). Through relaxation and breath control, mindfulness can assist children to manage their strong emotions and thereby learn to self-regulate (Mosley and Sonnett, 2007). It is important to stress that in order for mindfulness to effect long-term change, it needs to be built in to the curriculum or pre-school programme, as otherwise it offers a positive taster, but divorced from the process of educating (Levete, 2001). Mindfulness is a way of life, a daily, ongoing practice, a new approach of looking at ourselves and our connection with others in the world we live in, not an 'instant fix'. Mindfulness practice needs to be encouraged by the caretakers of these young children, possibly modelled by them and the philosophy embraced for lasting change to take place.

It is at pre-school stage that many of the learning disorders and inappropriate behaviours can start to emerge. It can therefore be argued that this is an all-important stage for young children to be taught ways of managing their own behaviour, in order for good practices to become integrated into the psyche as a natural way of life. Mindfulness practice develops self-control and acceptance of others, both of which are essential to overcome bullying. It helps individuals to remain centred, to be aware of emotions, to focus and to gain an understanding that some situations in life are inevitable and need to be met with acceptance. The choice of responding to our feelings instead of reacting brings about freedom (Williams et al., 2007). We learn through mindfulness to cultivate patience, compassion, tolerance, empathy and non-judgement both for self and others. When better to initiate this early training of minds than in the highly influential pre-school years?

> If we can observe in ourselves the toxicity of certain beliefs, thought patterns, and behaviours as they rise in the moment, then we can work to lessen their hold on us.

(Kabat-Zinn, 2007, p. 217)

REFERENCES

Baer, R. Krietemeter, J. 'Overview of Mindfulness- and Acceptance-Based Treatment Approaches', in Baer, R. *Mindfulness-Based Treatment Approaches: Clinician's Guide to Evidence Base and Applications* (Burlington, MA: Elsevier, 2006)

Batchelor, M. *Meditation for Life* (London: Frances Lincoln, 2001)

BBC News UK, 'Bullying Link to Child Suicide Rate, Charity Suggests' (2010), http://www.bbc.co.uk/news/10302550 [accessed 20 June 2012]

Berkovits, S. *Guided Imagery with Children: Successful Techniques to Improve School Performance and Self-Esteem* (Duluth, MN: Whole Person Associates, 2005)

Bien, T. *Mindful Therapy* (Boston: Wisdom Publications, 2006)

Brazier, D. *Zen Therapy* (London: Constable, 1995)

Chaskalson, M. *The Mindful Workplace* (Oxford: Wiley-Blackwell, 2011)

Chopra, D. *The Book of Secrets* (London: Rider, 2004)

Chopra, D. *SynchroDestiny: Harnessing the Infinite Power of Coincidence to Create Miracles* (London, Sydney, Auckland, Johannesburg: Rider, 2005)

Clarke, J. (2008) *Poetry and Psychotherapy*, Workshop at the Sligo Psychotherapy Centre, 11 October 2008

Community Partnership for Mindfulness in Education (2008), A Community Partnership Outreach Programme of Park Day School, Oakland, CA. Retrieved from http://www.parkdayschool.org (accessed 8 October 2008)

Department of Education and Science, *Personal Safety Skills for Children with Learning Difficulties. Stay Safe: A Child Abuse Prevention Programme* (Dublin: Stationery Office, 1996)

Department of Education and Science, *Social, Personal and Health Education (SPHE)* (Dublin: Stationery Office, 1996)

Department of Education and Science, *Child Protection Guidelines and Procedures* (Dublin: Stationery Office, 2002)

Dreikurs, R. *Happy Children* (New York: Fontana Paperbacks, 1972)

Fodor, I. and Hooker, K. 'Teaching Mindfulness to Children', *Gestalt Review*, 12, 2008, pp. 75–91

Fontana, D. and Slack, I. *Teaching Meditation to Children: The Practical Guide to the Use and Benefits of Meditation Techniques* (London: Watkins Publishing, 2007)

Fulton, P. and Siegel, R. 'Buddhist and Western Psychology: Seeking Common Ground', in C. Germer, R. Siegel and P. Fulton (eds), *Mindfulness and Psychotherapy* (New York: The Guildford Press, 2005)

Germer, C. 'Mindfulness: What Is It? What Does It Matter?' in C. Germer, R. Siegel and P. Fulton (eds), *Mindfulness and Psychotherapy* (New York: The Guildford Press, 2005)

Gettman, D. *Basic Montessori: Learning Activities for Under-Fives* (Oxford: Clio Press, 2004)

Glasser, W. *Choice Theory: A New Psychology of Personal Freedom* (New York: HarperPerennial, 1999)

Goleman, D. *Emotional Intelligence* (London: Bloomsbury, 1996)

Goleman, D. *The New Leaders: Transforming the Art of Leadership into the Science of Results* (London: Time Warner Paperbacks, 2005)

Goodman, T. 'Working with Children: Beginner's Mind', in C. Germer, R. Siegel and P. Fulton (eds), *Mindfulness and Psychotherapy* (New York: The Guildford Press, 2005)

Gordhamer, S. 'The Lineage Project' (2005), www.lineageproject.org/lineage-project-programs.htm [accessed 8 December 2008]

Grossman, L. (see Park Day School website), www.parkdayschool.org [accessed 10 February 2009]

Guber and Kalish, *Yoga Pretzels: 50 Fun Yoga Activities for Kids and Grown-Ups* (Cambridge, MA: Barefoot Books, 2005)

Hart, T. 'Opening the Contemplative Mind in the Classroom', *Journal of Transformative Education*, 2, January 2004

Harwood, R., Miller, S. and Vasta, R. *Child Psychology: Development in a Changing Society*, 5th edn (San Francisco: John Wiley and Sons, 2008)

Jha, A.P. *Garrison Institute Report. Contemplation and Education: Scientific Research Issues Relevant to School-Based Contemplative Programs. A Supplement* (New York: Garrison Institute, 2005)

Kabat-Zinn, J. *Wherever You Go, There You Are: Mindfulness Meditation in Everyday Life* (New York: Hyperion, 1994)

Kabat-Zinn, J. *Full Catastrophic Living* (London: Piatkus, 2007)

Kaiser-Greenland, S. 'Innerkids' (2001), https://www.innerkids.org/beta/index.php?option=com_contentandview=articleandid=63:susan_kaiser-greenland [accessed 24 October 2008]

Kaiser-Greenland S. and Greenland, S. 'Growing Spirit' (2003), www.growingspirit.org/gs/mindfulness.html [accessed 16 March 2009]

Kornfield, J. *A Path with Heart: A Guide through the Perils and Promises of Spiritual Life* (New York: Bantam Books, 2003)

Kornfield, J. *Meditation for Beginners* (London: Bantam Books, 2005)

Ladd, G.W. and Burgess, K.B. 'Charting the Relationship Trajectories of Aggressive, Withdrawn and Aggressive/Withdrawn Children During Early Grade School', *Child Development*, 70, November 1999, pp. 910–29

Levete, G. 'Meditation to Develop Mindfulness in Daily Life', in C. Erricker and J. Erricker, *Meditation in Schools: Calmer Classrooms* (London: Continuum, 2001)

Luxmoore, N. *Working with Anger and Young People* (London and Philadelphia: Jessica Kingsley Publishers, 2006)

Mann, C. 'Meditation and the Process of Learning', in C. Erricker and J. Erricker, *Meditation in Schools: Calmer Classrooms* (London: Continuum, 2001)

Mosley, J. *Quality Circle Time in the Primary School* (Wisbech, Cambs: LDA, 1998)

Mosley, J. and Tew, M. *Quality Circle Time in the Secondary School: A Handbook of Good Practice* (London: David Fulton Publishers, 1999)

Mosley, J. *Circle Time for Young Children* (London: Routledge, 2005)

Mosley, J. and Sonnet H. *Helping Children Deal with Anger* (Wisbech, Cambs: LDA, 2007)

Montessori, M. *Education and Peace*, translated by Helen R. Lane (Chicago: Regency, 1972)

Napoli, M. 'Mindfulness Training for Teachers: A Pilot Program', *Complementary Health Practice Review*, 9, 2004, pp. 31–42

Olendzki, A. 'The Roots of Mindfulness', in C. Germer, R. Siegel and P. Fulton (eds), *Mindfulness and Psychotherapy* (New York: The Guildford Press, 2005)

Pearson, M. *Emotional Healing and Self-Esteem: Inner-Life Skills of Relaxation, Visualisation and Meditation for Children and Adolescents* (London and Philadelphia: Jessica Kingsley Publishers, 2004)

Perls, F., Hefferline, R. and Goodman, P. *Gestalt Therapy: Excitement and Growth in the Human Personality* (London: Souvenir Press, 1998)

Plummer, D. *Helping Children to Build Self-Esteem* (London and Philadelphia: Jessica Kingsley Publishers, 2007)

Rosenbaum, R. *Zen and the Heart of Psychotherapy* (USA: Brunner/Mazel, 1999)

Rozman, D. *Meditating with Children: The Art of Concentrating and Centering* (New York: Integral Yoga Publications, 2002)

Rutter, M., Yule, W., Berger, M., Yule, B., Morton, J. and Bagley, C. 'Children of West Indian Immigrants: Rates of Behavioural Deviance and of Psychiatric Disorders', *Journal of Child Psychology and Psychiatry*, 15, 1974, pp. 241–62

Sachs, J. *Break the Stress Cycle* (New York: Adams Media Corporation, 1998)

Saltzman, A. *Still Quiet Place* (CD, 2004), www.foryourselfhealth.com/ Dr_Amy.htm [accessed 5 November 2008]

Schoeberlein, D. *Mindful Teaching and Teaching Mindfulness* (Boston: Wisdom Publications, 2009)

Semple, R., Lee, J. and Miller, L. 'Mindfulness-Based Cognitive Therapy for Children', in R. Baer, *Mindfulness-Based Treatment Approaches* (Burlington, MA: Academic Press, 2006)

Senge, P. *Schools that Learn: A Fifth Discipline Resource* (New York: Doubleday, 2000)

Siegel, R. 'Psychophysiological Disorders: Embracing Pain', in C. Germer, R. Siegel and P. Fulton (eds), *Mindfulness and Psychotherapy* (New York: The Guildford Press, 2005)

Somersalo, H. 'School Environment and Children's Mental Well-Being: A Child's Psychiatric View on Relations between Classroom Climate, School Budget Cuts and Children's Mental Health', paper presented to the Hospital for Children and Adolescents, University of Helsinki, Finland, 11 March 2002 (pp. 6–53)

Strutt, M. *Meditating with Children* (revised edn): *The Art of Concentration and Centering* (Buckingham, VA: Integral Yoga Publications, 2002)

Suttie, J. (2008) Mindful Kids Peaceful Schools. *The Greater Good Magazine*, 29 January 2008

The Dalai Lama, *Awakening the Mind: Lightening the Heart* (New York: HarperCollins, 1997)

The Dalai Lama, *The Dalai Lama's Little Book of Wisdom* (London: Element, 2002)

Thich Nhat Hanh, *The Miracle of Mindfulness* (London, Sydney, Auckland, Johannesburg: Rider, 2008)

Thompson, M. and Gauntlett-Gilbert, J. 'Mindfulness with Children and Adolescents: Effective Clinical Application', *Clinical Child Psychology and Psychiatry*, 13, 2008, pp. 395–407

Wall, R. 'Tai Chi and Mindfulness-Based Stress Reduction in a Boston Public Middle School', *Journal of Pediatrics Health Care*, vol. 19, no. 4, 2005, pp. 230–7

Warren, C. 'Guided Imagery/Visualisation: Uses with the Cancer Patron', *Cancer Librarians Section Newsletter*, Spring 1992 (updated 2002), ValleyCare Library Pleasanton, CA, 2002

Williams, M. and Penman, D. *Mindfulness: A Practical Guide to Finding Peace in a Frantic World* (London: Piatkus, 2012)

Williams, M., Teasdale, J., Segal, Z. and Kabat-Zinn, J. *The Mindful Way Through Depression: Freeing Yourself from Chronic Unhappiness* (New York and London: The Guildford Press, 2007)

Young, M. 'A Pure Outcome Study of a Classroom-Based Mindfulness Programme with Pre-School Age Children in an Irish Setting', unpublished MEd thesis, Trinity College Dublin, 2009

CHAPTER SEVENTEEN

Promoting Positive Behaviour with Edward de Bono's 'Six Thinking Hats' Method

Mary Kent

INTRODUCTION

There is no reason at all to suppose that from the start, the teaching of thinking will be easy, or that it will be rapturously received by the pupils.

(de Bono, 1976)

This study set out to investigate what, if any, impact a short programme of thinking lessons may have, first and foremost, on students' self-discipline and behaviour and then on their academic performance. It sought to determine if an improvement in behaviour would occur if students were encouraged to have a more thoughtful approach to issues and situations where conflict or aggression may arise and if this improved behaviour would be likely to facilitate an improvement in academic outcome.

The research project, which formed part of an MEd (Aggression Studies) at Trinity College Dublin, was largely an evaluative study (Kent, 2010). The initial focus was on identifying the attitudes and beliefs of students before and after the teaching programme. Attitudes were expressed by students in surveys which were devised from *Measuring Violence-Related Attitudes, Behaviors, and Influences Among Youths: A Compendium of Assessment Tools* (Dahlberg et al., 2005). The objective of the survey was to identify the attitudes that motivated students' behaviour. Following the completion of the programme, participant students' academic and behaviour reports were studied in order to investigate for changes in performance. Effectiveness was measured, in so far as it was possible, by the extent to which participant students improved their skills with regard to their work efforts and choice of behaviours. Elias and Tobias (1994) emphasise that a main priority and one of the means of measuring the success of programmes such as this is by observing the level of self-control shown by students.

For the purpose of the research, de Bono's Six Thinking Hats method was used as the apparent simplicity of the method, and the non-argumentative style of discussion seemed most suited to the short timeframe available for the project. de Bono asserts that people who have received a brief introduction in the use of this method have been able to work out solutions for their specific problems and have then gone on to adopt his method as a means of dealing with issues as they arise. He states that:

> ... it is an alternative to the argument system, which was never intended to be constructive or creative. With the Six Hats method the emphasis is on 'what can be' rather than just on 'what is', and on how we design a way forward – not on who is right and who is wrong.

(de Bono, 2006)

During these thinking lessons the focus was on the level of student participation, their attitudes regarding the value of such lessons and whether or not they would apply methods presented in these lessons to situations in other areas of their school and social lives.

DE BONO'S SIX THINKING HATS

Dr Edward de Bono has developed many thinking tools or methods. Among those who support and use his methods, his 'Six Thinking Hats' is perhaps one of the most widely used and highly regarded thinking methodologies. The purpose of the Six Thinking Hats method is to provide the framework for thinking and discussing while concentrating on the avoidance of what he frequently refers to as 'time wasting argument'. As with de Bono's other methods, there is an attempt to encourage the users to think laterally and outside the box and to develop a frame of mind which allows them to examine issues from as many different viewpoints as possible. de Bono believes that Six Hat thinking is a powerful and constructive tool with which ideas and solutions can be generated without argument or lengthy discussion.

With the Six Hats method the emphasis in on 'what can be' rather than just on 'what is' and on how we design a way forward – not on who is right and who is wrong.

(de Bono, 2006)

Using this method avoids the pitfalls of clashing egos, often a problem in traditional thinking. The process does not involve defending one's own ideas or attacking the ideas of others. de Bono maintains that there are fundamental difficulties when we attempt practical thinking and that:

… the main difficulty of thinking is confusion. We try to do too much at once. Emotions, information, logic, hope and creativity all crowd in on us. It is like juggling too many balls.

(de Bono, 2006)

De Bono encourages the use of the Six Hats method as a means of examining an issue which enables the users to explore it in a methodical way focusing their thinking on only one aspect at a time. The method involves the participants in a discussion wearing (metaphorically) each of six different-coloured hats which denote a different type of thinking. During the exercise all participants must simultaneously wear the same-coloured hat. Wearing the white hat, participants share factual information – no assumptions or speculation allowed. The available information is set out as completely as possible. Wearing the black hat gives participants the opportunity to explore negative aspects of the issue and voice caution or concern. In a similar way, wearing the yellow hat, participants are encouraged to consider and optimistically speculate on the positive aspects of their issue. The red hat is worn when sharing emotions, feelings or gut reactions with no justification needed for these feelings. Wearing the green hat, participants generate ideas and contribute their views in order to find common ground and identify solutions. Finally, wearing the blue hat, participants review all the thinking that has occurred and, where appropriate, decisions are reached. de Bono stresses that the colour defines the kind of thinking going on and not the individual who wears it.

CONTEXT

The research was carried out in an all-boys Catholic voluntary secondary school in suburban Dublin. The enrolment at the time was 489 students. The student cohort was drawn from a wide socio-economic base, with the registered number of students living in single-parent households standing at 7.8%. Discussion with students would indicate that this figure may have been substantially higher. Students living in second-family structures likewise identified themselves and the school was not otherwise privy to this information. The non-Irish population increases each year. At the time of this study there were students from twenty-seven different ethnic backgrounds, including Irish.

SCHOOL STRUCTURES

The principal and deputy principal are the main authority figures and further to that a year head system exists. The role of the year head is primarily in the area of discipline or personal support and he or she is also the main contact with home when the need arises. A guidance counsellor is available for personal support and career guidance. The school had recently introduced a tutor system to support first-year students. For some years the school has had a very active anti-bullying team and a 'Positive Attitudes' system in place to support and guide students towards improved behaviour with emphasis on self-discipline. When this study was carried out there were five resource teachers and a half-time learning support teacher as well as four special needs assistants, who because of their duties had contact with many students beyond those to whom they had been assigned. The learning support or resource teachers and the assistants, along with the ancillary staff, act as the eyes and ears of the school, alerting the teaching staff to matters of concern.

STUDENT EXTRA-CURRICULAR ACTIVITIES

There has been an active Students' Council and a Green School Committee in operation within the school for several years. Sport has also been a strong feature of school life, with many very successful sportsmen among the present and past pupils. Students are encouraged to participate in the Young Social Innovators and

Student Enterprise Awards competitions and there have also been teams from among the junior cycle classes entered in the Young Scientists Competition. The school also claims several past pupils who are celebrated in the world of business, academia, medicine and science. The ethos of the school has been predominantly a caring one where success is measured not just in terms of academic and sporting outcomes but also in terms of the general well-being, emotional and social abilities of students and, when the time comes, their preparedness for adult living.

AREAS OF CONCERN

Unfortunately, in spite of all the structures in place in the school, there is each year a significant number of students who achieve less well in every sense of the above descriptions and who leave school less prepared to make and take healthy life choices. Many of these students come to school seeming to be 'un-socialised' and resistant to the norms and rules which school attempts to enforce. These students are not enticed by the rewards of the Positive Attitudes scheme and often, to avoid the lowering of morale and of standards of behaviour among the other students, their unruly or defiant behaviour may to some extent appear to be ignored.

An area of particular concern in relation to many students in the latter group is their apparent inability to 'think' – about the options they have in school, where for many school and school work may seem to them to be irrelevant or even something to fight against, and also, very importantly, about how they relate to and treat others.

A consequence of the negative and damaging effects of thoughtless behaviour is how easily it may spill over into violence. Verbal violence among some students and rough or more extreme physical behaviour occurs on a regular basis. de Bono suggests that disagreements which are a normal part of interpersonal relationships are often the result of seeing things differently, wanting different things or even the natural inclination of some people to want to disagree. It is a matter of concern however when disagreement becomes a source of conflict and this conflict becomes violent. Expressing concern regarding ills that may befall young people due to their lack of engagement or boredom with the system, he suggests that whatever their individual path in life, low self-esteem is a common feature.

SUPPORT FOR TEACHING THINKING

Following their review of education programmes designed to reduce youth violence, Tolan and Guerra (1994) recommend teaching programmes which include generic problem-solving and life-skills education. UNESCO, UNICEF, the WHO and other high-profile organisations all recommend that education programmes be put in place which teach towards pro-social and non-violent behaviour, while Nelson-Jones supports the teaching of thinking on the grounds that thinking skills are viewed as a series of choices that may be well or poorly made. To think effectively you require a repertoire of thinking skills that you then apply to your problems and decisions (Nelson-Jones, 1996).

Opinions vary regarding the best approach to the teaching of thinking skills in school. There are those who favour teaching specifically designed programmes, while others support the infusion of thinking in every aspect of the school curriculum. Those who favour the latter approach do so on the basis that thinking as a skill will be internalised by students as they work through their various courses and that transference of this skill into other areas of their lives is much more likely if it is taught in this way. Chance refers to 'thoughtful teaching' as a way of teaching advocated by those who are opposed to explicit programmes for teaching thinking. He outlines the assumption of those who hold this view, that 'thinking is inseparable from content, so thinking is best taught in the context of standard course material' (Chance, 1986).

De Bono's programmes on the other hand are designed to be taught explicitly and applied implicitly. 'If thinking is such a fundamental skill, why should it not be taught explicitly?' (de Bono, 1982). He argues that 'thinking is the deliberate exploration of experience for a purpose' and further observes that 'thinking skills are embedded in subject content' (de Bono, 1976).

With these arguments in mind, a two-stage study was undertaken. For the first stage a short programme of five thinking lessons based on de Bono's (2000) Six Thinking Hats method was developed in which emphasis was placed on finding ways to deal with or resolve possible conflict situations. In the second stage of the research the Six Thinking Hats approach was used as a teaching and learning tool.

PRE-INTERVENTION

Stage one involved the completion of survey questionnaires to determine students' commitment to school and their attitudes to interpersonal relationships. This survey was conducted among all members of the class groups from second and third years. Following this, the programme of five thinking lessons was introduced.

In stage two, the first-year group completed the questionnaire and this was followed by the introduction of the Six Thinking Hats method. In this case the issues discussed were themes from within the Social, Personal and Health Education (SPHE) course. Following the course of thinking lessons and, in the case of the first-year group, at the end of the school year, the survey questionnaire was again completed by all students to compare attitudes pre- and post-intervention.

Survey findings from stage one revealed the most negative attitude to school was among the third-year students, although the majority of students in the second-year group also indicated that they did not like school. In spite of this, a majority of students in each group indicated that they felt they were doing quite well in school. The older students indicated that they were less likely than either the second or first years to engage in physically violent behaviour, the first years showing the greatest inclination to do so. On the other hand, third years were also less likely to intervene and offer help to those in need. First years self-reporting indicated a generally more caring response to others in trouble.

In order to investigate for behaviour changes, students' behaviour and academic reports were examined. Students' behaviour reports which were issued every two months were accessed as well as one academic report pre-intervention and two post-intervention for each participant student. Several weeks after the conclusion of stage one, interviews were held with two participant students from each year group. No interviews were held with members of the first-year group in stage two. The thinking methods applied in the SPHE classes continued to the end of the school year.

STAGE 1: A LESSON-BASED APPROACH TO TEACHING THINKING

During the five-week timeframe of this programme, lessons were given during one class period per week (forty minutes) to each of two sample groups. One group was composed of six third-year students, the other of five second-year students.

The opening discussion in the first lesson concerned the agreement of a set of ground rules by the participants. The rules agreed by students in both groups were:

- I will wait my turn to speak.
- I will not laugh at anyone else's suggestions.
- I will try to avoid argument and follow the thinking rules.

Student worksheets were collected at the end of every lesson and detailed logs were kept of the students' participation, discussion and behaviour during each session.

In stage one, fictional situations and stories were discussed and students were encouraged to consider their topics from as many different angles as possible. Students' participation during the thinking lessons indicated that in general, with encouragement, they were able to explore issues thoughtfully and to draw conclusions in an orderly and civil manner. They accepted the 'no argument' condition of this method and in this respect were able to exercise a self-discipline that was not otherwise evident in other aspects of their lives.

As with all of de Bono's methods for teaching thinking skills, the initial approach in stage one, involving the five standalone 'thinking lessons', was to teach the methods in a direct and deliberate way. de Bono advises that 'the lessons should be tackled in a sober, matter-of-fact manner' (de Bono, 1976) and promotes a fairly fast-paced and business-like approach.

Having devised the set of lessons, the methods and techniques were introduced and explained using a phased approach. Students were offered several situations for consideration, and the thinking methods they applied in each lesson became the basis for the following lesson. Participants were encouraged to see the 'wearing' of the six hats as prompts for the particular type of thinking being used. de Bono (1976) refers to prompts as 'attention directors'. By stimulating and encouraging specific patterns of thought, the aim was to provoke the participants to explore the given situations. By repeatedly using the thinking hats, students were encouraged to consider and discuss situations and to reach conclusions or produce creative alternatives.

The topics chosen throughout the programme were received without criticism by the students and, as Glasser (1969) recommends,

seemed easy to relate to, either through students' experience or observation. Students connected some of the fictional situations to their
own life experiences and conferred among themselves on the facts as
they saw them. While making connections with personal experiences
was helpful, it was sometimes necessary to draw the students back
from their conversations regarding shared experiences as:

> ... the purpose of the lesson is not to provide open-ended, free
> flowing discussion sessions, but to practice deliberately some
> specific thinking processes.

(de Bono, 1976)

The first lesson introduced the concepts of the Six Thinking Hats
with an explanation of the reason for using the method. Cartoon
pictures were used to illustrate some of the motivations behind
arguments where disagreement is often the result of a power struggle
or the inability or unwillingness to see the points of view of others.
Students were encouraged to look for other reasons why arguments
occur and then to consider the benefits of being able to discuss
without the conversation spilling over into argument. Students in
both groups agreed with a colleague who suggested that 'if you really
want something from your parents you want to be able to get them
to agree without making them angry 'cause they won't listen if they
get angry and will just say no'.

In all lessons, the situations or proposals considered were hypothetical. The engagement and response of the students varied depending on the story. In the beginning, a fairly un-contentious issue was
raised when students were asked to consider an announcement from
the principal regarding the use of new portable desks in the school.
Students in each class made many and varied suggestions as to what
problems might arise. Their comments regarding whether or not 'the
desks would fit through the doors', 'they'd be really uncomfortable'
and the fact that the school would have to 'spend loads of money'
in buying new lockers in order to fit the desks indicated that they
related the proposal to themselves and to their school environment
and this appeared to help them in their critical thinking. Several
students from both groups also commented on the 'crush' there
would be in the corridors and doorways and how it would ensure
students would be continuously late getting to class and leaving
school. One student enquired: 'does that mean we can get late slips
in any class?' It was necessary to remind him that this was only a

discussion about a fictional situation. (Late slips are given to students who arrive late to the first class in the morning or to the first class in the afternoon.)

Each new lesson began with a brief review of the previous session. In the second lesson the purpose of the thinking method was recalled and the other coloured hats were introduced and explained. 'White hat' thinking was explained as a fact-finding exercise. 'Red hat' thinking was offered as the opportunity to express feelings of any sort without having to try to explain where these feelings come from. 'Yellow hat' thinking was suggested as being the opposite of 'black hat' thinking. With this approach students were now looking for benefits, rather than exercising caution and taking an optimistic view. Wearing the 'green hat', students were encouraged to be creative and imaginative in seeking solutions, and finally, wearing the 'blue hat', conclusions, if appropriate, were reached.

During lessons, students in both groups were very communicative and again, in situations where they related a fictional incident to one in their neighbourhood, were very forthcoming with suggestions. For example, during the course of a lesson in which students were using 'green hat' or creative thinking, in relation to the situation 'You are awakened in the night by a loud explosion and flash of light. What might have happened?', there was much discussion regarding cars being set alight in their neighbourhood as well as accounts of various other incidents and situations which students had either encountered or read about and which they then put forward as suggested answers.

During this session students were asked to apply 'red hat' thinking to two situations. In the first they were told: 'Your best friend refuses to speak to you' and asked 'How do you feel?' The purpose of this exercise was to encourage them to consider their emotional response to this situation. The fact ('white hat' thinking) was their friend's silence; their 'red hat' thinking (which did not have to be justified) produced the following responses: angry, annoyed, upset, confused, don't care. While reaffirming the message that, using this method, emotions or gut feelings do not have to be explained, students were encouraged to imagine what it would be like for someone who found him/herself isolated or being given the silent treatment. This time, students' suggestions indicated confusion and upset. No one in either group suggested that this person would not care and four of the third years and all of the second years indicated that isolating someone was a form of bullying and was unfair.

The other situation examining the same thought process was stated: 'Someone paints your name in huge letters on a school wall.' Students were asked: 'How do you feel?' Students' responses were again quite varied. They included angry, chuffed, embarrassed, confused, wondering. The third-year student who was 'chuffed' accepted 'black hat' thinking would caution the possibility of trouble with the school authorities but his optimistic or 'yellow hat' thinking was that 'no one is stupid enough to paint their own name on the school wall'. Continuing the exploration of the impact of this behaviour on an individual, it was clear that this kind of highlighting of an individual could be unpleasant for that person. Discussion about students' names on toilet doors and walls developed with examples given. As advised for teaching the method, these conversations were redirected. It was heartening to note that students in both groups had moved from expressing the dismissive view 'it happens to everyone' to the view that it was disrespectful to be targeted in this way and 'probably embarrassing'.

APPLYING THE THOUGHT PROCESS

Students considered decision-making in relation to helping their friends. They discussed their role in a fictional situation where a friend confided in them that they were thinking of running away from home due to friction within the family. The views expressed by second and third years on other issues did not vary too much but in the case of their 'runaway friend', two of the third years were more open to seeking help from an adult, thus, indicating perhaps a clearer sense of reality. In this situation members of both groups related this fictional story to their own experiences. The third-year students were particularly open to considering the dilemma from as many viewpoints as possible. Their 'black hat' thinking, indicating a cautious attitude to their friend running away, included one student suggesting 'he could be in danger – someone could attack him, rob him or give him drugs'. While the other suggested that 'he might be taken into care.'

The exercise entitled 'Building a Government' offered students the opportunity to consider and discuss how best to create an effective system of government for a group of forty individuals who were stranded on a desert island. The main role of this government was to ensure the health and well being of all the group and to seek ways to achieve their rescue. In considering the facts in their given storyline, students, mindful of the emotions ('red hat' thinking) that arise when people are fearful in dangerous situations, set security and safety as priorities. 'They should plan to be safe first – there could be wild animals there' ('blue', then 'green hat' thinking). Within this group, as in the third-year group, it was interesting to note that the initial shared view, that those who could assert their control by forceful means could make the others do menial and even dangerous tasks, changed as students realised that perhaps they themselves might be the weaker individuals. They then reverted, with the exception of one student, to a general consensus that everyone should have equal say in seeking solutions to their dilemma, maintaining it was fairer. This lone student advocated having one person in charge to lead and direct operations. When it was put to the two groups that a sports team has a captain whose role is to lead the team, the responses were that 'someone else picks the captain', 'he's paid to be captain', 'he's put there before the game starts'. Thus the students' considered view was that individual participation in decision-making was preferable to electing a leader in whom to trust the safety and survival of the group.

In the final lesson of the first stage of the study the following definition was given: '*Bystander* is the term we use when referring to those people who watch situations happening. For example they may see others bullying or being bullied and choose for their own reasons not to get involved or intervene'. Students in each group were then asked to apply all Six Hats in considering the brief scenario below:

Paul: That new kid looks a fairly miserable sort. He never smiles and if you greet him he kind of grunts.

Peter: Yeah, I'm feeling miserable just looking at him.

Paul: I saw Joe and his friends shoving him around in the yard at break. But they cleared off when the supervisor came along.

Peter: Did you? I was in early today and I saw Joe throwing his bag out the window into that rain barrel that the caretaker left near our room.

Paul: Hmm, no wonder he's looking sad. I suppose I would too if I was on the receiving end of Joe's bad temper.

Peter: I wonder if there is anything we could do.

During this exercise, students were much more articulate in expressing their thoughts than they had been five weeks before. The third-year students, who were working in pairs, discussed the situation together as though they were involved, stating that the student in question was being bullied and proposals were made as to what interventions they could make. No one, in suggesting support for the bullied student, indicated that they would confront Joe or his friends; instead the general view was that efforts could be made to include him in football with some other friends, walking to and from school and hanging out together. The second years kept their distance, remembering that Peter and Paul were the characters involved but their suggestions regarding how they could help this student were the same.

STAGE 1: REVIEW

Throughout the course of this programme the second-year students were biddable and respectful to each other at all times. They shared their ideas and drew conclusions without any apparent need to assert their own authority or to prove others wrong. The response of the third-year students to the lesson varied much more from week to week. In sessions following classes during which there had be either a specific positive (reward) or negative (staying back for reprimand) experience, several of the students were unfocused and un-cooperative. The most productive lessons were those in which students came directly to their session without any distractions.

For the third lesson the six students had come late following a class period in which they had been awarded time to play football. They were all hot and thirsty; two seemed particularly tired while two others were very wound up. The way they had worked the previous week was forgotten. This session was repeated with the third years by breaking the group up into three pairs. Working in pairs, the students fully engaged with the material, asked and answered questions and were generally more forthcoming with their suggestions.

de Bono (1985) suggests that how the problem is defined and presented can make a huge difference to how it is solved. When working in their pairs, third-year participants were particularly focused and showed their abilities in this area. For example, in the last item to be discussed concerning the challenges around having a disorganised and troubled student within a class whose behaviour impacted on the whole group, diplomacy and understanding were to the fore in student discussions. Joe and Dave were two characters in two different storylines. Joe was being bullied and two freinds were attempting to offer some relief from this, while Dave's challenges in organising himself (the final exercise in the programme) were impacting on teachers' attitude to the whole class. In each case, students were encouraged to think through to the most helpful and inconspicuous means of support. Thus they recognised that in seeking a successful solution for the whole-class dilemma, a tactful or discreet approach was of the utmost importance in this particular case.

STAGE 2: DE BONO'S SIX HATS AS A TEACHING AND LEARNING TOOL

The second phase of the study examined the effect of using the Six Thinking Hats programme as a tool in the teaching of SPHE. The method was employed as a means of considering topics addressed in class, summarising the discussion or reaching a conclusion.

Before undertaking this new approach to SPHE lessons, the class group reviewed the ground rules which had been agreed in their SPHE class at the beginning of the school year where the emphasis had been on mutual respect and the importance of allowing each other to make suggestions without fear of ridicule or teasing. The thinking methods were introduced using the same materials as had been used in stage one. During the second lesson the topic of 'Stereotyping' (an issue considered in the Relationships and Sexuality module) was used to introduce the remaining three thinking hat methods. The feeling ('red hat' thinking) that 'it's not fair' was expressed several times, but also 'great' – explained later with 'green hat' thinking as 'allowing someone to do things, without pressure to succeed or expectations from others'. One student observed: 'I never help in the kitchen, because my mum says boys are useless. When she's not there I cook sausages and rashers for myself.'

Following these introductory lessons a different approach to the exercises undertaken by the students in this stage of the study was adopted. While each lesson for stage one had been designed specifically to draw out the students and encourage their thinking, during this second stage the work was centred on the SPHE modules and diverse thinking methods were encouraged within these lessons.

At some stage during each lesson students were asked to complete a spider diagram, draw a poster or write answers to questions relating to the topic of the day. During the lesson in the Emotional Health module during their discussion on 'feelings', students were very open and honest regarding the things they feared and also very able to identify ways of confronting their own fears. Students were for the most part engaged in the process and there was no criticism or ridiculing of the fears of others. These included fear of water, spiders, the dark and heights.

A student with Asperger's syndrome from among the group who found the thought of death deeply distressing spoke of his feelings, then said: 'I just have to accept that everyone dies and don't let myself think about it'. When asked 'Would you find that difficult?' the student replied: 'Yes, but I just have to say "no" every time the thought comes into my head.'

Module nine of the SPHE programme is concerned with substance use and abuse. Starting from scratch, this module, conscious of the differences which exist among first-year students, where some students have little awareness and others have personal experience of substance use, involved first of all defining what is meant by 'substance'. In the following lesson using their Six Thinking Hats method, students considered how they might persuade someone who might reach for medication for a headache on a regular basis to consider their options. They began with the facts as they knew them ('white hat' thinking), listing off as many medications designed to relieve headache as they could and what these medications claim to do. Recognising 'feeling rotten', 'grumpy' and 'relief' as the feelings which motivate this action, they went on to weigh up, using 'black hat' thinking, the negative aspects 'you could get immune to them' or 'feel you can't do without them (dependency)' with the 'yellow hat' or positive thinking 'like a cloud lifting' or 'helps you sleep and you wake up feeling better'. When it came to offering alternatives, which was the object of the exercise, there were many quite creative suggestions, indicating an awareness of the benefits of 'rest, exercise, sleep, listening to music and meditation' as alternatives to tablet taking.

In the last two SPHE lessons of the year the students addressed the issue of personal safety and the personal responsibility to take care of oneself both inside and outside the home. Following a group discussion on road safety, students went on to rate their own area in terms of safety. Students in the class who lived in areas of heavy traffic were quite clear with regards to the steps that they needed to take to stay safe. The thinking task for this lesson was to consider the facts in relation to traffic in their area, to weigh up the positive and negative safety issues and to consider how they could make use of this knowledge to ensure that they could play a part in trying to ensure that the elderly and the young in their area remained safe.

The final lesson again related to personal safety. Students studied a cartoon scene of a classroom where chaos and indiscipline, including very obvious bullying incidents, featured clearly. The classroom depicted in the cartoon was spacious and bright but very untidy with books, bags and other items strewn around. In the discussion around this scene the feelings expressed ranged from 'tense, just looking at it' to 'agitated'. The fact that was obvious to all the students was 'teacher's not there'. When this was suggested by one student and the class was asked 'how many of you noticed that there was no teacher?', all students raised their hands. During 'black hat' thinking one student was adamant that 'there's nothing wrong with the room that wouldn't be put right by having a teacher in charge'. This seemed to indicate that in the students' view the presence of a supervising teacher goes some way to lessen the likelihood of bullying.

From the introduction of this new teaching and learning style until the end of the school year there were ten SPHE lessons. An essential part of this study was to investigate if students would adopt a more thoughtful approach to situations. For the last lesson, when considering the health and safety aspects of the unruly classroom scene, the author left it up to students to 'think their way' through the situation. The outcome of this exercise was positive, with the majority of students very thorough in their examination of the scene and in suggesting solutions to the situation.

An opportunity arose to apply their thinking skills during the final lesson of the term. A student was given permission to leave the room. When he returned his bag was on the other side of the classroom and it was only at this stage that the teacher was aware of the situation. The student who emptied the school bag acknowledged his responsibility, picked up everything, apologised and returned them to the owner. When the class ended, the students who were sitting around the owner of the bag were asked to remain back after class. The only way for the student who had admitted responsibility for emptying the bag to have done so was if others had passed it to him. Using the Six Thinking Hats method, the students considered the incident:

- The facts were that between them the three students had taken the school bag from under the table and passed it across the room.
- They felt excited or amused – the owner of the bag felt stressed or anxious.

- It was fun to do this.
- There was a possibility of something going wrong – a drink spilling or a book being torn. The student who owned the bag might be in trouble with his parents and that wasn't fair. They would then be in trouble – perhaps even having to pay for the book.
- Weighing up the thinking, their decision was that they would not do this again.

CONCLUSION

In conclusion, it was clear that in both approaches, when offered the opportunity, the techniques and the material, students were able and willing to explore issues in a thoughtful manner. The behaviour issues that arose within the third-year group did not arise with the second-year group and were absent among the third years when they worked in pairs. It was interesting to note that the first-year group, once they had overcome their shyness, were very at ease with using the method and within the class context there were no real behaviour concerns. The second years too, in their smaller group, were also very engaged with the process. It appeared, however, that the older students were better suited to working in pairs. This raised the question as to whether an earlier introduction to this thought process might have produced a different outcome for the older students.

It is important to note that while this research was conducted with the permission and full support of the school, parents and pupils, it was carried out as a standalone project. Without the necessary reinforcement of their thinking skills in other classes, the older students particularly did not assimilate the methods or transfer them to other aspects of their lives. Observation of first-year behaviour showed a slightly different outcome. This group, when they returned as second years, requested that they should continue to consider their SPHE topics using the Six Hats Thinking method.

Although the level of success of this programme was uncertain, the experience of working with the participant students seemed to support the view that teaching young people how to think in a direct and deliberate way with consistent reinforcements could have many benefits and is a worthwhile undertaking. As Chance (1986) concludes when referring to his study of thinking programmes:

Despite the problems and the unanswered questions we must make a new beginning. We must commit ourselves to the goal of teaching students how to think. If our efforts fail we must try again, and then again and again. After all, what alternatives do we have?

(Chance, 1986)

REFERENCES

Chance, P. *Thinking in the Classroom: A Survey of Programs* (New York: Teachers College Press, 1986)

Dahlberg, L.L., Toal, S.B., Swahn, M. and Behrens, C.B. *Measuring Violence-Related Attitudes, Behaviors and Influences among Youths: A Compendium of Assessment Tools*, 2nd edn (Atlanta, GA: Centers for Disease Control and Prevention, National Center for Injury Prevention and Control, 2005)

de Bono, E. *Teaching Thinking* (London: Penguin, 1976)

de Bono, E. *de Bono's Thinking Course* (London: BBC, 1982)

de Bono, E. *Conflicts: A Better Way to Resolve Them* (London: Penguin, 1985)

de Bono, E. *Six Thinking Hats*, revised and updated edn (London: Penguin, 2000)

de Bono, E. *de Bono's Thinking Course: Powerful Tools to Transform Your Thinking* (Harlow, Essex: Pearson Educational Group, 2006)

Elias, M.J. and Tobias, S.E. *Social Problem Solving: Interventions in the Schools* (New York: Guilford, 1996)

Glasser, W. *Schools Without Failure* (New York: Harper & Row Perennial, 1969)

Kent, M. 'A Review of a Programme Designed to Teach Students How to Think Using Edward de Bono's "Six Thinking Hats" Method', unpublished MEd dissertation, Trinity College Dublin, 2010

Nelson-Jones, R. *Effective Thinking Skills* (London: Sage, 1996)

Tolan, P. and Guerra, N. *What Works in Reducing Adolescent Violence: An Empirical Review of the Field* (Boulder, CO: Center for the Study and Prevention of Violence, 1994)

CHAPTER EIGHTEEN

School Bullying and Some Law

Murray Smith

Force not my drift beyond its just intent,
I praise a school as Pope a government;
So take my judgement in his language dress'd—
'Whate'er is best administer'd is best.'
Few boys are born with talents that excel,
But all are capable of living well;
Then ask not, Whether limited or large?
But, Watch they strictly, or neglect their charge?
If anxious only that their boys may *learn*,
While *morals* languish, a despis'd concern,
The great and small deserve one common blame,
Diff'rent in size, but in effect the same.

(William Cowper, 'Tirocinium: or, A Review of Schools'
(1785), ll. 505–16 [Milford, 1913])

INTRODUCTION

This quotation is from a poem, where the poet recommended that a father educate his sons at home rather than send them to school, attacking in general the education system that existed at the time. While huge changes have taken place in education since then, the author's main concern, that a school's proper care of the students entrusted to its charge should be seen in terms of their general welfare, not just in terms of their academic achievement, is still relevant, particularly as far as the law is concerned.

This chapter will look at the more important parts of the legal framework within which bullying in schools happens in this country, and at some issues involving it.

While the law does not deal directly with 'school bullying', it does impose obligations on schools and those running them to, first, deal with bullying in terms of putting adequate policies and procedures in place to deter such behaviour, and act properly and promptly to deal with it when it does happen; and second, when dealing with such behaviour, to act according to fair procedures. Internet service providers and those controlling websites (including social networking websites), due to cyber-bullying, should have proper complaints procedures, and should properly respond within a reasonable time to a complaint made. Parents and guardians may be penalised by the courts for the criminal offences of their children, which can include bullying behaviour; and they can be liable under the civil law for failing to properly control their children's behaviour.

This chapter is divided into three sections. Section 1 details official definitions of school bullying. Section 2 reviews the roles played by certain legal and quasi-legal documents: the Constitution; the European Convention on Human Rights; certain statutes; an EU directive incorporated into Irish law; and certain documents issued by the Department of Education and Skills. Section 3 describes relevant or possibly relevant case law in nine areas. One, those alleging that the personal injuries to a student brought about by bullying was due to the negligence of the school. Two, the lawfulness of actions taken by schools against disruptive students, including suspension and expulsion, where it was argued that fair procedures were not followed. Three, the situation where a school refused to enrol someone as a student due to prior bad behaviour. Four, the situation where a school expelled a student for bad behaviour, including bullying; and when the appeals committee overruled this decision, it was later held to have exceeded its legal jurisdiction. Five, decisions concerning the Equal Status Acts 2000–2011, where actions taken to discipline students for alleged bad behaviour were contested due to alleged discrimination, harassment, victimisation, or any combination of the three. Six, the question of whether a school could lawfully segregate a student from the rest of the student body as a punishment. Seven, the continuing suspension of a student as a precaution beyond what is legally permitted, pending an official decision, and the compatibility of this with the European Convention on Human Rights. Eight, a school's duty of care towards its students when outside of the school, outside of school hours. Nine, the liability of an internet service provider and those controlling websites, as well as that of parents and guardians, for defamatory remarks posted online, important in relation to cyber-bullying.

Before I begin with the above, I have to say a few things. First, what I will discuss are only parts of the legal framework in this country. Second, as soon as this chapter is published, it will begin to go out of date, something that happens with any overview of the law, in any area, and in any country. In the words of one judge, 'The law never stands still. It goes on apace. You have to run fast to keep up with it' (Denning, 1984, p. vi). Third, for that second reason, what I write is not a substitute for you, the reader, getting present-day legal advice.

1. WHAT IS BULLYING?

1. Guidelines on countering behaviour in primary and post-primary schools

An official definition of 'bullying' in a school context was given in *Guidelines on Countering Bullying Behaviour in Primary and Post-Primary Schools*, issued by the Department of Education in September 1993:

> Bullying is repeated aggression, verbal, psychological or physical conducted by an individual or group against others.
>
> Isolated incidents of aggressive behaviour, which should not be condoned, can scarcely be described as bullying. However, when the behaviour is systematic and ongoing it is bullying.

(DES, 1993, p. 6)

This definition was accepted by the High Court in the case of Nicola Mulvey (a minor suing by her mother and next friend Margaret Mulvey) v. Martin McDonagh [2004] 1 IR, 497. In this case, where a student took a case against her school, claiming damages for personal injuries suffered by her from an assault by a follow student or students while attending there, the definition was looked at; and the judge, Johnson J., held that 'I accept and adopt that definition of bullying' given in the 1993 *Guidelines*.

The *Guidelines* then give a number of types of bullying, under two headings. Under 'Pupil Behaviour', nine types are given: physical aggression, up to 'severe physical assault'; damage to property; extortion; intimidation; abusive telephone calls; isolation; name calling; slagging; and bullying of school personnel. Under 'Teacher Behaviour', they say that a teacher might, 'unwittingly or otherwise, engage in, instigate or reinforce bullying behaviour' in three ways:

using sarcasm or other insulting or demeaning language when addressing pupils; humiliating a pupil directly or indirectly; and using any gesture or expression of a threatening or intimidatory nature, or any form of degrading contact or exercise (DES, 1993, pp. 6–7).

2. A guide to cyber-bullying

A more recent type of bullying that has come to prominence is 'cyber-bullying', which has been officially defined in *A Guide to Cyberbullying*, part of the *Get with IT!* series of publications, joint initiatives of the Office of Internet Safety, an executive office of the Department of Justice and Law Reform, Barnardos, O₂, and the National Centre for Technology in Education:

> Cyberbullying refers to bullying which is carried out using the internet, mobile phone or other technological devices. Cyberbullying generally takes a psychological rather than physical form but is often part of a wider pattern of 'traditional' bullying. It can take the form of sending nasty, mean or threatening messages, emails, photos or video clips; silent phone calls; putting up nasty posts or pictures on a message board, website or chat room; saying hurtful things in a chat room; pretending to be someone else in a chat room or message board or text message and saying hurtful things; or accessing someone's accounts to make trouble for them.
>
> (Office of Internet Safety, 2008, p. 3)

So, to have an idea of official definitions of 'school bullying', a person needs to look at both publications. This may soon change; because the January 2013 *Action Plan on Bullying*, the report of the Anti-Bullying Working Group to the Minister for Education and Skills, recommended that the definition of bullying in new revised national anti-bullying procedures for schools include 'a specific reference to the following forms and methods of bullying': deliberate exclusion, malicious gossip and other forms of relational bullying; cyber-bullying; sexual bullying; and identity based bullying (especially including homophobic bullying, transphobic bullying, racist bullying and bullying of those with disabilities or special educational needs). (DES, 2012, p. 128)

I will take these two definitions of bullying, and look at them in the context of such behaviour by primary and post-primary school students against each other, or by those in authority in a school against such a student or students. The bullying carried out by such parties would, in my view, come under what most would regard as 'school bullying'.

2. LEGAL AND QUASI-LEGAL DOCUMENTS

The legal and quasi-legal documents I will review are: the Constitution; the European Convention on Human Rights; certain statutes; an EU directive incorporated into Irish law; and certain documents issued by the Department of Education and Skills.

1. Constitution of Ireland

Two of the Constitution's articles are important in this area of school bullying and harassment (O'Mahony, 2006). While Article 42 is self-evident, as it deals with the education system, Article 40, dealing with the personal rights of the citizen, including the right to a good name, has led to the development by the Irish courts of the right of a citizen to fair procedures.

a. Article 40: Personal Rights: Right to one's good name & Right to fair procedures

This article is important in the educational context, and in terms of dealing with incidents of bullying and harassment, because it contains what the courts have decided is the right to fair procedures. In Article 40.3.1°, the state guarantees to respect, and as far as practicable, to vindicate 'the personal rights of the citizen'. Among the specific personal rights of the citizen specified is the right of the citizen to his or her 'good name' (Article 40.3.2°).

This led the Supreme Court to imply, in the case of In re Haughey [1971] I.R., 217, a right of the citizen to fairness of procedures. In that case, Chief Justice Cearbhal Ó Dálaigh said that 'a person whose conduct is impugned as part of the subject matter of the inquiry must be afforded reasonable means of defending himself'. Earlier he had set out what this meant:

a. that he should be furnished with a copy of the evidence which reflected on his good name;

b. that he should be allowed to cross-examine, by counsel, his accuser or accusers;
c. that he should be allowed to give rebutting evidence; and
d. that he should be permitted to address, again by counsel, the Committee [of Public Accounts] in his own defence.

Article 40.3 he called:

> a guarantee to the citizen of basic fairness of procedures. The Constitution guarantees such fairness, and it is the duty of the Court to underline that the words of Article 40.3 are not political shibboleths but provide a positive protection for the citizen and his good name.

This and other cases have implied that 'fairness of procedures', also called 'natural justice', must be followed by all persons and bodies making decisions affecting the individual and which are fair and seen to be fair. Fairness of procedures contains two basic principles.

First, no one can be a judge in his or her own cause, which means that the person or body making the decision is *not* allowed to have any personal (including financial) interest that might be affected by the decision; and second, to hear both sides, which means that a person against whom allegations are made is entitled to be informed of the allegations against him or her, and to be given an opportunity to answer them.

b. Article 42

According to this article, the family is 'the primary and natural educator of the child', and parents are free to provide education in their homes, in private schools, or those 'recognised or established by the State' (Article 42.1–2).

While the state will not oblige parents to send their children to schools either established or designated by the state, it shall, 'as guardian of the common good', require that children receive 'a certain minimum education, moral, intellectual and social' (Article 42.3).

The state shall provide for free primary education and 'shall endeavour to supplement and give reasonable aid to private and corporate educational initiative', and 'when the public good requires it, provide other educational facilities or institutions with due regard, however, for the rights of parents, especially in the matter of religious and moral formation' (Article 42.4).

In exceptional cases, where the parents for 'physical or moral reasons fail in their duty towards their children', the state 'as guardian of the common good' by appropriate means 'shall endeavour to supply the place of the parents, but always with due regard for the natural and imprescribable rights of the child' (Article 42.5).

While education is delivered in such schools, this system has been increasingly regulated by law since the Education Act 1998, as amended. Education is now seen in Ireland as a state-funded public service, though delivered via a mostly private system. For a historical outline of the Irish education system, see Glendenning (2012). Also worth reading by the same author, on religion, education and the law in Ireland, is Glendenning (2008).

While the law allows parents to educate their children at home if they so wish, the state will insist that the child receives a certain minimum education, under the Education (Welfare) Act 2000, as amended. Also, the state will intervene in the case of an appeal from an expulsion or long suspension of a student from a recognised school, or the refusal of such a school to enrol a student, as we will later see in the 1998 and 2000 Acts, as amended.

2. European Convention on Human Rights

First Protocol, Article 2

This Article reads as follows:

> No person shall be denied the right to education. In the exercise of any functions which it assumes in relation to education and to teaching, the State shall respect the right of parents to ensure such education and teaching in conformity with their own religions and philosophical convictions.

Ireland signed this Protocol, the instrument of ratification deposited on 25 February 1953. The Irish delegate put on record that:

> in the view of the Irish Government, Article 2 of the Protocol is not sufficiently explicit in ensuring to parents the right to provide education for their children in their homes or in schools of the parents' own choice, whether or not such schools are private schools or are schools recognised or established by the State.

Ireland incorporated the Convention, including this Article of the First Protocol, into its domestic law in the European Convention on Human Rights Act 2003. Section 3(1) of the Act says that every 'organ of state' shall 'perform its functions in a manner compatible with the State's obligations under the Convention'.

Section 3(2) says that if a person suffers injury, loss or damage, due to Section 3(1) being contravened, and if no other remedy in damages is available, he or she can sue to recover damages in the High or Circuit Court. Also, section 5 says that the High Court, and the Supreme Court on appeal, where no other legal remedy is adequate or available, can make a declaration of incompatibility of a statutory provision or rule of law with the Convention.

I mention Article 2 and the fact that its provisions are part of Irish law; because there have been cases in the United Kingdom, which has also incorporated the Convention, including that article, into its domestic law in its Human Rights Act 1998. These cases, which I will discuss in detail later, concerned students who claimed that their rights of access to education under Article 2 was denied, when action was taken against them by their respective schools.

It is possible that Irish courts might, in similar situations, regard these cases as *persuasive authorities*. These are court decisions that are not binding on an Irish court, in this case decisions of the courts of other legal jurisdictions in the English-speaking common law world; but they can be considered by the Irish courts when making judgements. By contrast, the decisions of higher courts in Ireland are binding on lower ones in that country, with certain exceptions. The Supreme Court, the highest court in Ireland, is not bound by its own decisions (Hunt and Murdoch, 2007, pp. 899, 928).

3. Statutes

Statutes are formal written enactments of the Oireachtas, Ireland's national parliament, passed by both houses, Dáil Éireann and Seanad Éireann, then signed into law by the president. Here, I divide the ones I will look at under the headings of *criminal law*, the body of law that defines actions (or failures to act) forbidden by the state, and have punishment as a sanction; and *civil law*, the body of law that deals with resolving disputes between individuals, providing a remedy, usually financial, against the wrongdoer by way of compensation, not punishment (Hunt and Murdoch, 2007, pp. 190, 302).

a. Criminal law

While this may seem drastic, some of the most serious types of bullying behaviour overlap on matters covered by the criminal law. While minors, those under the age of 18, are not liable to the full force of the criminal law, they are not immune from its effects. I am going to look at five relevant statutes, then give an overview of how the criminal law treats minors.

i. Post Office Amendment Act 1951

Section 13(1) of this Act has been amended a number of times, most recently by the Communications Regulation (Amendment) Act 2007, Part 2. It now says that any person commits an offence who:

- (a) sends by telephone any message that is grossly offensive, or is indecent, obscene or menacing, or
- (b) for the purpose of causing annoyance, inconvenience, or needless anxiety to another person
    - (i) sends by telephone any message that the sender knows to be false, or
    - (ii) persistently makes telephone calls to another person without reasonable cause.

On summary conviction (conviction after a hearing before a judge only), or conviction on indictment (conviction after a hearing before a judge and jury), that person can be imprisoned for up to twelve months or up to five years respectively, fined or both. The problem with this law is that it only deals with messages sent by telephone, which would include text messages, not by any other media.

Despite this, a case was prosecuted under this Act in the Dundalk District Court. On 31 January 2008, a man of 27 posted offensive and obscene messages on a page of the social networking website Bebo belonging to a 16-year-old girl. He was prosecuted, pleaded guilty, and agreed to pay the girl €3,000. Judge Conal Gibbons placed the defendant under the supervision of the probation service, and the case was adjourned for the compensation to be paid (*Irish Independent*, 2008).

The *Sixth Report of the Special Raporteur on Child Protection* of January 2013, after deciding that 'Existing laws regarding harassment can be used to incorporate cyber-bullying incidents', suggested that 'A review of the Post Office (Amendment) Acts should be undertaken with a view to incorporating emerging means of cyber-bullying'. (DCYA, 2013, p. 96)

ii. Criminal Damage Act 1991

Three parts of this Act are most relevant here:

a. Damaging property

Section 2(1) says that: 'A person who without lawful excuse damages any property belonging to another intending to damage any such property or being reckless as to whether any such property shall be damaged shall be guilty of an offence'. Section 2(2) says that a person shall be guilty of an offence who, 'without lawful excuse damages any property, whether belonging to himself or another':

(a) intending to damage any property or being reckless as to whether any property would be damaged, and
(b) intending by the damage to endanger the life of another or being reckless as to whether the life of another would be thereby endangered.

Section 2(3) says that a person who 'damages any property', whether his or another's, 'with intent to defraud shall be guilty of an offence', while section 2(4) makes it clear that an offence committed under section 2 'by damaging property by fire shall be charged as arson'.

An offence under this section is punishable on a summary conviction by a fine, imprisonment of up to twelve months, or both. On a conviction on indictment, such a crime is punishable in case the person is guilty of arson under subsection (1) or (3) or of an offence under subsection (2) (whether arson or not), to a fine, imprisonment for life, or both. Any other offence means punishment of a fine, imprisonment for up to ten years, or both.

b. Threat to damage property

Section 3 says that: 'A person who without lawful excuse makes to another a threat, intending that that other would fear it would be carried out':

(a) to damage any property belonging to that other or a third person, or
(b) to damage his own property in a way which he knows is likely to endanger the life of that other or a third person

shall be guilty of an offence and shall on summary conviction be liable to a fine, imprisonment for up to twelve months, or both, and on conviction on indictment to a fine, imprisonment for up to ten years, or both.

c. Unauthorised accessing of data

Section 5 deals with the unauthorised accessing of data, section 5(1) saying that a person who 'without lawful use' operates a computer:

> (a) within the State with intent to access any data kept either within or outside the State, or
> (b) outside the State with intent to access any data kept within the State, shall, whether or not he accesses any data, be guilty of an offence.

On summary conviction, that person can be fined, imprisoned for up to three months, or both. This deals with computer hacking, and is relevant regarding cyber-bullying.

iii. Non-Fatal Offences Against the Person Act 1997

There are six offences in particular that bullying overlaps with: assault; assault causing harm; causing serious harm; threats to kill or cause serious harm; coercion; and harassment. There are a number of defences for a person intervening in a violent situation, in terms of protecting persons or property and preventing crime, saving that person from being accused of assault in certain circumstances, something to be taken into account in a school's member of staff dealing with a violent student.

a. Offences

A. Assault

Section 2(1) says that a person 'shall be guilty of the offence of assault who, without lawful excuse, intentionally or recklessly':

> (a) directly or indirectly applies force to or causes an impact on the body of another, or
> (b) causes another to believe on reasonable grounds that he or she is likely immediately to be subjected to any such force or impact, without the consent of the other.

Section 2(2) defines 'force' as including '(*a*) application of heat, light, electric current, noise or any other form of energy, and (*b*) application of matter in solid liquid or gaseous form'. Section 2(3) explains that no such offence is created if the force or impact not being intended or likely to cause injury is in the circumstances such as is generally acceptable in the ordinary conduct of daily life and the defendant does not know or believe that it is in fact unacceptable to the other person. A person found guilty of this offence is liable on summary conviction to a fine, imprisonment of up to six months, or both.

B. Assault causing harm

Section 3(1) says that a person who 'assaults another causing him or her harm shall be guilty of an offence'. Section 3(2) says that on summary conviction, a person can be fined, imprisoned for up to twelve months, or both; or on conviction on indictment, fined, imprisoned for up to five years, or both. Section 1 defines 'harm' as 'harm to body or mind and includes pain and unconsciousness'.

C. Causing serious harm

Section 4(1) says that a person who 'intentionally or recklessly causes serious harm to another shall be guilty of an offence'. Section 4(2) says that a person guilty of such an offence shall be liable on conviction on indictment to a fine, imprisonment for life, or both.

Section 1 defines 'serious harm' as 'injury which creates a substantial risk of death or which causes serious disfigurement or substantial loss or impairment of the mobility of the body as a whole or of the function of any particular bodily member or organ'.

D. Threats to kill or cause serious harm

Section 5(1) says that a person who 'without lawful excuse, makes to another a threat, by any means intending the other to believe it will be carried out, to kill or cause serious harm to that other or a third person shall be guilty of an offence'. Section 5(2) says that a person guilty of this offence shall be liable on summary conviction to a fine, imprisonment for up to twelve months, or both; and on conviction on indictment, to a fine, imprisonment for a term of up to ten years, or both.

E. Coercion

Section 9(1) says that a person shall be guilty of an offence, who 'with a view to compel another to abstain from doing or to do any act which that other has a lawful right to do or to abstain from doing, wrongfully and without lawful authority':

(a) uses violence towards or intimidates that other person or a member of the family of the other, or

(b) injures or damages the property of that other, or
(c) persistently follows that other about from place to place, or
(d) watches or besets the premises or other place where that other resides, works or carries on business, or happens to be, or the approach to such premises or place, or
(e) follows that other with one or more other persons in a disorderly manner in or through any public place.

Section 9(2) explains that watching and besetting under section 9(1)(d) does not apply to 'attending at or near the premises or place where a person resides, works, carries on business or happens to be, or the approach to such premises or place, in order merely to obtain or communicate information'.

Section 9(3) says that a person committing an offence under this section shall be liable on summary conviction to a fine, imprisonment of up to twelve months, or both; and on conviction on indictment to a fine, imprisonment for up to five years, or both.

F. Harassment

Section 10(1) says that any person who

> without lawful authority or reasonable excuse, by any means *including by use of the telephone*, harasses another by persistently following, watching, pestering, besetting or communicating with him or her, shall be guilty of an offence. (My italics)

Section 10(2) says that a person harasses another when:

(a) he or she, by his or her acts intentionally or recklessly, seriously interferes with the other's peace and privacy or causes alarm, distress or harm to the other, and
(b) his or her acts are such that a reasonable person would realise that the acts would seriously interfere with the other's peace and privacy or cause alarm, distress or harm to the other.

As well as imprisonment, a fine or both, whether on summary conviction (up to twelve months) or conviction on indictment (up to seven years), a court may also, or as an alternative, order under section 10(3):

> that the person shall not, for such period as the court may specify, communicate by any means with the other person or

that the person shall not approach within such distance as the court shall specify of the place of residence or employment of the other person.

b. Defences

A. 'Use of Force'

For the purpose of the defences, section 20 of the Act says that a person uses force 'in relation to another person or property not only when he or she applies force to, but also where he or she causes an impact on, the body of that person or that property'. Also, a person is seen as using force in relation to another person if:

(i) he or she threatens that person with its use, or
(ii) he or she detains that person without actually using it.

B. Self-defence and the defence of property

Section 18 of the Act, amended by section 6 of the Criminal Law (Defence and the Dwelling) Act 2011, says that the use of force, within the meaning of section 20, by a person for the following reasons, 'if only such as is reasonable in the circumstances as he or she believes them to be', is not an offence:

(a) to protect himself or herself or a member of the family of that person or another from injury, assault or detention caused by a criminal act; or
(b) to protect himself or herself or (with the authority of that other) another from trespass to the person; or
(c) to protect his or her property from appropriation, destruction or damage caused by a criminal act or from trespass or infringement; or
(d) to protect property belonging to another from appropriation, destruction or damage caused by a criminal act or (with the authority of that other) from trespass or infringement; or
(e) to prevent crime or a breach of the peace.

A 'criminal act' is still 'criminal', even if a person committing it is, frist, if charged with an offence under it,would be acquitted because:

(a) he or she acted under duress;
(b) his or her act was involuntary;
(c) he or she was in a state of intoxication; or

(d) he or she was insane, so as not to be responsible, according to law, for the act;

or, second, that person was one to whom section 52(1) of the Children Act 2001 applied. I will deal with the Children Act later.

For the purpose of this section, property is treated as belonging to any person having the custody or control of it; any proprietary right or interest; or having a charge on it.

C. Use of force in arrest

Section 19 says that the use of force by a person in making or assisting in a lawful arrest, 'if only such as is reasonable in the circumstances as he or she believes them to be', is not an offence. The question on whether the arrest is lawful 'shall be determined according to the circumstances as the person using the force believed them to be'.

iv. Criminal Justice (Theft and Fraud Offences) Act 2001

Commonly known as the 'Theft Act', this statute says in section 4(1) that, subject to a number of exceptions, 'a person is guilty of theft if he or she dishonestly appropriates property without the consent of its owner and with the intention of depriving its owner of it'. Section 4(6) says a person guilty of theft is liable on conviction on indictment to a fine or imprisonment for up to ten years or both.

v. Safety, Health and Welfare at Work Act 2005

This piece of legislation places responsibility for health, safety and welfare at work on all people involved in the workplace. Under section 8(1), an employer has the general obligation to 'ensure, so far as is reasonably practicable, the safety, health and welfare at work of his or her employees'.

Under section 12, every employer shall manage and run the place of work such that 'so far as is reasonably practicable', in the course of the work carried on, 'individuals at the place of work (not being his or her employees) are not exposed to risks to their safety, health and welfare'. This obviously includes the students of a school.

However, the obligations under the Act are not those of employers alone. Section 13 contains a list of the duties of employees, while section 16 also gives duties to designers, manufacturers, and suppliers of articles to be used at work.

Employers are obliged, under section 19, to identify the hazards in the relevant place of work, assess the risks presented by these hazards, and have a written assessment (called a 'risk assessment') of the risks to the health, safety and welfare at work of their employees.

Section 20 then obliges any employer to prepare a written statement (called a 'safety statement') based on the risk assessment carried out under section 19, showing the way in which the health, safety and welfare at work of the employees shall be secured and managed. Section 20(2) deals with what it should contain, including:

(a) the hazards identified and the risks assessed,
(b) the protective and preventive measures taken and the resources provided for protecting safety, health and welfare at the place of work to which the safety statement relates.

This mirrors the obligation on a school's board of management to draw up a school plan under section 21 of the Education Acts, 1998–2007, which will be dealt with later.

A body called the Health and Safety Authority is set up to ensure enforcement of the provisions of this Act.

Section 77(2)(a) makes it clear that a person commits an offence where he or she 'fails to discharge a duty to which he or she is subject by virtue of sections 8, 9, 10, 11(1) to (4), 12, 13 and 15 to 23'. Section 78(2) makes it clear that a person guilty of an offence 'under section 77 (2) to (8) and (9)(a)' is liable on summary conviction to a fine not exceeding €3,000 or imprisonment for a term not exceeding six months or both, or on conviction on indictment to a fine not exceeding €3,000,000 or imprisonment for a term not exceeding two years or both.

Responsibility of young people under the criminal law

In Irish law, a person becomes of 'full age' when he or she reaches the age of 18, under section 2 of the Age of Majority Act 1985. Section 3 of the Children Act 2001 also defines 'child' as 'a person under the age of 18 years', and an 'adult' as a person over that age.

In terms of when a child is responsible for a criminal offence, section 52(1) of the 2001 Act, amended by section 129 of the Criminal Justice Act 2006, states that a child of under 12 years of age 'shall not be charged with an offence'. Subsection (2) says that this subsection (1) does not apply to a child of 10–11 charged with murder, manslaughter, rape, and aggravated sexual assault. Also, subsection (4) makes it clear that if any child under 14 is charged with an offence, 'no further proceedings in the matter (other than any remand in custody or on bail)' shall be taken except by or with the consent of the Director of Public Prosecutions.

Children under 12 do not, however, enjoy total immunity from action being taken against them. Section 53 (1) of the 2001 Act, as amended by section 130 of the 2006 Act, says that where a member of the Garda Síochána has 'reasonable grounds' for believing that a child under 12 has committed an offence (except those detailed in section 52(2) of the 2001 Act, as amended) that member shall 'endeavour to take the child to the child's parent or guardian' or arrange for another member to do so.

Where this is not possible, such as the member taking the child believing, under section 53(2), that he or she 'has reasonable grounds for believing that the child is not receiving adequate care or protection', the member shall inform the health board for the area in which the child normally resides of the name, address and age of the child and the circumstances in which he or she came to the notice of the Garda Síochána.

Section 53(3) says that where 'not practicable' for the child to be taken to his or her parent or guardian, the member concerned may give the child, or arrange for the child to be given, into the custody of the health board for the area in which the child normally resides.

Section 71 says that the District Court, when hearing charges against children or when hearing applications for orders relating to a child at which the attendance of the child is required or when exercising any other jurisdiction conferred on the Children Court by or under this or any other Act, shall be called the 'Children Court'.

Sections 111–114 give the Children Court powers to impose a number of orders on the parents or guardians of a child found guilty of an offence, including a 'parental supervision order' of up to six months, ordering them to undergo treatment, participate in a parenting skills course, 'adequately and properly' control or supervise the child and comply with any other instructions to prevent the child committing further offences (Section 111). Failure to observe such an order may be treated as contempt of court (Section 112), for which a fine or a jail sentence may be imposed. The court can also order the payment of compensation (Section 113) by those it feels 'a wilful failure' to care for or control the child contributed to his or her criminal behaviour; or order instead or as well that a parent or guardian enter a recognisance (a promise to the court) to 'exercise proper and adequate control over the child' (Section 114). Refusal to make this promise may be seen as a contempt of court.

Section 115 also gives the court power to impose a number of orders, under the heading of a 'community sanction', on a child found guilty of an offence. They include: a day care centre order (Section 118); probation orders (Sections 124–126); and a restriction of movement order (Section 133).

In terms of any kind of detention that can be imposed on a child, this is possible under section 142 of the Act. A court can impose on a child a 'children detention order', that is, 'a period of detention in a children detention school or children detention centre specified in the order'. Section 143(1) says that a court will not impose such an order 'unless it is satisfied that detention is the only suitable way of dealing with the child and, in the case of a child under 16 years of age, that a place in a children detention school is available for him or her'.

As we have seen, minors are not immune to the effects of the criminal law; and their parents or guardians may also face legal sanctions due to the criminal offences of their children. Even if criminal charges are not brought, the threat of this happening may be enough in some situations, including school bullying related ones.

b. Civil law

I am looking here at parts of four statutes; because I feel that they are important or could be important in the future, and which have been litigated on, something I will show in more detail in the third section of this chapter.

i. Education Acts 1998–2007

The Education Act 1998, as amended by the Education (Miscellaneous Provisions) Act 2007, deals with the regulation of the primary, post-primary, adult, and vocational education system in general. Among its provisions, section 9 deals with the general functions of a school recognised by the Minister for Education, including its obligations to:

(a) ensure that the educational needs of all students, including those with a disability or other special educational needs, are identified and provided for,

(b) ensure that the education provided by it meets the require-ments of education policy as determined from time to time by the Minister …,

(c) ensure that students have access to appropriate guidance to assist them in their educational and career choices,

(d) promote the moral, spiritual, social and personal development of students and provide health education for them, in consultation with their parents, having regard to the characteristic spirit of the school,

(e) promote equality of opportunity for both male and female students and staff of the school.

The board of management of such a school has to carry out, under section 15, certain functions, and to:

(a) do so in accordance with the policies determined by the Minister from time to time,

(b) uphold, and be accountable to the patron for so upholding, the characteristic spirit of the school ..., and at all times act in accordance with any Act of the Oireachtas or instrument made thereunder, deed, charter, articles of management or other such instrument relating to the establishment or operation of the school,

(d) publish, in such manner as the board with the agreement of the patron considers appropriate, the policy of the school concerning admission to and participation in the school, including the policy of the school relating to the expulsion and suspension of students and admission to and participation by students with disabilities or who have other special educational needs, and ensure that as regards that policy principles of equality and the right of parents to send their children to a school of the parents' choice are respected and such directions as may be made from time to time by the Minister, having regard to the characteristic spirit of the school and the constitutional rights of all persons concerned, are complied with,

(e) have regard to the principles and requirements of a democratic society and have respect and promote respect for the diversity of values, beliefs, traditions, languages and ways of life in society.

Under section 21, the board of management shall draw up and keep updated what the legislation calls a 'school plan'. This plan shall, according to section 21(2):

state the objectives of the school relating to equality of access to and participation in the school and the measures which the school proposes to take to achieve those objectives including equality of access to and participation in the school by students with disabilities or who have other special educational needs.

The principal, and the teachers under the principal's direction, shall have the responsibility 'for the instruction provided to the students in the school', and shall, under section 22(2):

(a) encourage and foster learning in students,
(b) regularly evaluate students and periodically report the results of the evaluation to the students and their parents,
(c) collectively promote co-operation between the school and the community which it serves, and
(d) subject to the terms of any applicable collective agreement and their contract of employment, carry out those duties that
  (i) in the case of teachers, are assigned to them by or at the direction of the Principal, and
  (ii) in the case of the Principal, are assigned to him or her by the board.

While there are no explicit provisions dealing with bullying, sections 28–29 are important in that area. Section 28 empowers the minister, after consultation, to prescribe procedures in cases when:

(a) the parent of a student or, in the case of a student who has reached the age of 18 years, the student, may appeal to the board against a decision of a teacher or other member of staff of a school,
(b) grievances of students, or their parents, relating to the students' school (other than those which may be dealt with under paragraph (a) or section 29), shall be heard, and
(c) appropriate remedial action shall, where necessary, be taken as a consequence of an appeal or in response to a grievance.

No such procedures have, as yet, been prescribed. Section 29 deals with when a board of management, or person acting on its behalf, according to subsection (1):

(a) permanently excludes a student from a school, or
(b) suspends a student from attendance at a school for a period to be prescribed for the purpose of this paragraph [later defined as twenty days], or

(c) refuses to enrol
    (i) a student in a school, or
    (ii) a student to receive instruction on the curriculum through Irish in a school, if the school provides for teaching of subjects on the curriculum through Irish for some or all of its students, or
(d) makes a decision of a class which the Minister, following consultation with patrons, national associations of parents, recognised school management organisations, recognised trade unions and staff associations representing teachers, may from time to time determine may be appealed in accordance with this section.

A parent, or the student if over 18, may appeal the decision to the secretary-general of the Department of Education and Skills. The minister can, under subsection (2), set up an appeals committee in each case to examine the decision and reach a finding, which shall include an inspector and 'such other persons as the minister considers appropriate'. Subsection (3) says that the minister shall appoint one of these people to chair such a committee, who shall have a second or casting vote if there is an equal division of votes. (Two circular letters from the Department set out the appeals procedures to be used when Section 29 is invoked, depending if the school is primary or post-primary: Circular letter 22/02 (Primary), and Circular letter M48/01 (Post-primary).)

Subsection (4) says that the appeal will be dealt with by the appeals committee within thirty days of the secretary-general receiving the appeal, except where it writes to him/her requesting a delay and giving reasons, and he agrees in writing to an extension of the period by fourteen days.

This subsection (4) of section 29 has been amended by section 4(b) of the 2007 Act. This was on foot of some of the recommendations made by the *Report of the Task Force on Student Behaviour in Second Level Schools* (2006). In terms of areas of particular interest to us, the Task Force looked at the legislative framework within which schools now operated, and said that the 'most frequent issue' that came before it was the 'dissatisfaction with certain aspects of the recent [1998] legislation', in particular the operation of sections 28 and 29 of that Act, particularly the latter. Regarding section 29, the dissatisfaction was due to:

1. the cumbersome nature of processing a section 29 appeal,
2. the large investment of time and expense entailed,

3. the consequent inroads on a school principal's other more appropriate role related work,
4. the experience of the actual appeal hearing,
5. the composition of the appeals board,
6. the loss of morale for a school when an appeal is upheld,
7. the sense that schools are now becoming disempowered in their efforts to implement a rigorous code of behaviour,
8. the perception that the pendulum has swung too far in favour of the misbehaving student and away from the rights of the teacher to teach and the compliant students to learn.

(DES, 2006, p. 154)

The Task Force made a number of recommendations to deal with this situation:

1. The amended legislation 'should seek to stress the rights of the compliant majority to learn while at the same time protecting the rights of the persistently disruptive student to an education'.
2. A timeframe for appeals 'less protracted' than the present one.
3. School Boards should be helped in preparing for an appeal by 'a protocol outlining the aspects they need to attend to' before the process.
4. The 'present educational provision' of a student out of school pending an appeal should be improved.
5. The role of the education welfare officer should be promoted as 'agents of support and intervention both for families and for schools'.

(DES, 2006, p. 135)

These recommendations were put into legislation in section 4(b) of the 2007 Act, the new subsection (4) of the 1998 Act now saying that, in relation to an appeal in relation to section 29 (1)(a) and (b), an appeals committee shall have regard to:

(a) the nature, scale and persistence of any behaviour alleged to have given rise to, or contributed to, the decision made by or on behalf of the board,
(b) the reasonableness of any efforts made by the school to enable the student to whom the appeal relates to participate in and benefit from education,
(c) the educational interests of the student concerned and the desirability of enabling the student as far as practicable to

participate in and benefit from education with his or her peers,

(d) the educational interests of, and the effective provision of education for, other students of the school and the main-tenance of a classroom and school environment which is supportive of learning among the students of the school and ensures continuity of instruction provided to students in any classroom concerned and the school,

(e) the safety, health and welfare of teachers, students and staff of the school,

(f) the code of behaviour under section 23 of the [Education Welfare] Act of 2000 and other relevant policies of the school and—

   (i) in the case of that code of behaviour, the extent to which it is in compliance with that section 23 and any guide-lines issued under subsection (3) of that section, and

   (ii) in the case of those other policies, the extent to which each of them is implemented, promotes equality of access to and participation in education and is in compliance with—

      (I) any enactment that imposes duties on schools or their boards,

      (II) any relevant guidelines or policies of the Minister,

(g) the duties on schools or their boards imposed by or under any enactment.

The problem is that this 2007 amendment has not yet come into force, the Minister for Education not having yet signed the relevant order at time of writing (2013). Section 23 of the Education (Welfare) Act 2000 will be dealt with shortly.

ii. Education (Welfare) Act 2000

This Act, as amended, relates to the welfare of students. It is to ensure that they receive a certain minimum education; and it also provides for the compulsory attendance of certain children in recognised schools and for the registration of children not receiving education in those schools. It also covers matters relating to attendance and non-attendance in schools, such activities being coordinated by a National Educational Welfare Board (NEWB).

While, as in the 1998 Act, there are no explicit provisions dealing with bullying, section 23 says that a board of management of a recognised school shall, after consultation, prepare a 'code of behaviour' containing the following:

(a) the standards of behaviour that shall be observed by each student attending the school;
(b) the measures that may be taken when a student fails or refuses to observe those standards;
(c) the procedures to be followed before a student may be suspended or expelled from the school concerned;
(d) the grounds for removing a suspension imposed in relation to a student; and
(e) the procedures to be followed relating to notification of a child's absence from school.

Such a code shall be prepared 'in accordance with such guidelines' as may be issued by the NEWB after consultation with certain parties. This has been done (NEWB, 2008).

The principal of a recognised school shall, before registering a child as a student at that school, provide the parents of such a child with a copy of the code of behaviour and may, as a condition of so registering the child, require the parents to confirm in writing that the code is acceptable to them and that they shall make all reasonable efforts to ensure compliance with it by the child. He or she shall, on a request being made by a student registered at the school or his or her parent, provide that student or parent with a copy of the code.

Section 24 deals with the expulsion of a student from a recognised school, subsection (1) saying that, before the board does this, it shall notify the local education welfare officer employed by the NEWB. Subsections (2)–(3) say that this officer will make 'all reasonable efforts' to ensure that provision is made for the relevant student, and make the same efforts to consult with the relevant and appropriate parties, including convening a meeting of those who agree to attend. Subsection (4) says that a school shall not expel a student before twenty school days pass from the education welfare officer receiving the notification.

Despite this, subsection (5) gives the school's board of management power to take 'such other reasonable measures' it considers appropriate 'to ensure that good order and discipline' is maintained in the school and the safety of students is secured. I will return to this subsection when discussing whether a school may lawfully segregate a student from the rest of the student body, if he or she is violent and disruptive.

Also, under section 26, the NEWB has the power to appeal the decision to expel or to refuse to enrol a student to the secretary-general of the Department of Education, in the same way as a student or a student's parent. It also may make such oral or written submissions to the appeals committee 'as it considers appropriate'.

Where the appeals committee upholds the decision to expel or refuse to enrol, or there is no appeal, section 27 of the Act obliges the NEWB to make 'all reasonable efforts' to have the child enrolled in another recognised school.

iii. Equal Status Acts 2000–2011

These Acts deal with prohibiting types of discrimination, harassment or related behaviour in terms of the provision of services generally available to the public. Section 3(1) defines discrimination as being either:

(a) 'where a person is treated less favourably than another person is, has been or would be treated in a comparable situation' on any of nine discriminatory grounds in subsection (2).

(b) 'where a person who is associated with another person': (i) is treated, 'by virtue of that association, less favourably than a person who is not so associated is, has been or would be treated in a comparable situation', and (ii) similar treatment of that other person on any of the discriminatory grounds would, by virtue of paragraph (a), constitute discrimination.

Section 3(2)(a)–(i), as amended, gives the nine discriminatory grounds: gender; civil status; family status; sexual orientation; religious belief; age; disability; race; membership of the Traveller community. 'Civil status' means being single, married, separated, divorced, widowed, in a civil partnership within the meaning of the Civil Partnership and Certain Rights and Obligations of Cohabitants Act 2010 or being a former civil partner in a civil partnership that has ended by death or been dissolved. (The *Action Plan on Bullying* explicitly suggested that these grounds be listed in schools' anti-bullying prolicies. (DES, 2013, p. 28)).

Section 3(2)(j) then gives a tenth, 'victimisation' ground, which happens when one: (i) has in good faith applied for any deter-mination or redress under the Act; (ii) has attended as a witness ... in connection with any inquiry or proceedings under the Act; (iii) has given evidence in any criminal proceedings under the Act; (iv) has opposed by lawful means an act which is unlawful under the

Act; or (v) has given notice of an intention to take any of the actions specified in (i) to (iv) 'and the other has not'.

Section 4(1) says that for the purpose of the Acts, discrimination

> includes a refusal or failure by the provider of a service to do all that is reasonable to accommodate the needs of a person with a disability by providing special treatment or facilities, if without such special treatment or facilities it would be impossible or unduly difficult for the person to avail himself or herself of the service.

Section 4(2) says that a refusal or failure to provide the special treatment or facilities in subsection (1) would 'not be deemed reasonable unless such provision would give rise to a cost, other than a nominal cost, to the provider of the service in question'.

There is a proviso in section 4(3), that a refusal or failure to provide the special treatment or facilities in subsection (1) is not discrimination if, due to another provision in the Act, 'a refusal or failure to provide the service in question to that person would not constitute discrimination'.

Looking in more detail at the disability grounds of discrimination, among the nine referred to in section 3(2)(a)–(i), section 4(6)(e) says that a 'service provider of a service' includes 'an educational establishment within the meaning of subsection (1) of section 7 in relation to any of the matters referred to in subsection (2) of that section'.

This definition of 'educational establishment' in section 7(1) includes 'a primary or post-primary school'. Also, section 7(2) says that an educational establishment shall not discriminate in relation to:

(a) the admission or the terms or conditions of admission of a person as a student to the establishment,
(b) the access of a student to any course, facility or benefit provided by the establishment,
(c) any other term or condition of participation in the establishment by a student, or
(d) the expulsion of a student from the establishment or any other sanction against the student.

Schools are allowed under section 7(3)(a) and (c), however, to discriminate in admitting students of one gender, if the school only admits students of another gender. Also, if a school 'to provide education in an environment which promotes certain religious values, it admits persons of a particular religious denomination in preference' to those not of that denomination, or refuses to admit the latter, and 'it is proved that the refusal is essential to maintain the ethos of the school'.

Section 11 (amended by section 51 of the Equality Act 2004) defines harassment and sexual harassment as follows:

> (5)(a) in this section –
>> (i) references to harassment are to any form of unwanted conduct related to any of the discriminatory grounds, and
>> (ii) references to sexual harassment are to any form of unwanted verbal, non-verbal or physical conduct of a sexual nature,
>
> being conduct which in either case has the purpose or effect of violating a person's dignity and creating an intimidating, hostile, degrading, humiliating or offensive environment for the person.
>
> (b) Without prejudice to the generality of paragraph (a), such unwanted conduct may consist of acts, requests, spoken words, gestures or the production, display or circulation of written words, pictures or other material.

Under sections 24–25, the Director of the Equality Tribunal appoints equality mediation officers to mediate, or equality officers to investigate, allegations of discrimination, harassment or victimisation under the Acts, made by a person to him or her under section 21(1), or may investigate the matter himself or herself. (The complainant may, in the case of gender discrimination, choose to refer the case to the Circuit Court, under section 21(1A).)

Section 28 of the Civil Law (Miscellaneous Provisions) Act 2011 allows for the determination of a case without a hearing if both parties consent. Section 27 of the Equality Acts says that when an investigation is concluded, the Director may order compensation, direct a person to take a specified course of action, or both.

iv. Defamation Act 2009

Section 6(2) defines the tort of 'defamation' as:

> the publication, by any means, of a defamatory statement concerning a person to one or more than one person (other than the

SCHOOL BULLYING AND SOME LAW

first-mentioned person), and 'defamation' shall be construed accordingly.

Section 2 defines a 'defamatory statement' as:

a statement that tends to injure a person's reputation in the eyes of reasonable members of society, and 'defamatory' shall be construed accordingly.

Section 6(3) says that 'A defamatory statement concerns a person if it could reasonably be understood as referring to him or her'.

Section 6(4) says that there will be 'no publication' for the purposes of the tort of defamation, if 'the defamatory statement concerned is published to the person to whom it relates and to a person other than the person to whom it relates in circumstances where:

(a) it was not intended that the statement would be published to the second-mentioned person, and
(b) it was not reasonably foreseeable that publication of the statement to the first-mentioned person would result in its being published to the second-mentioned person.

Section 2 defines a 'defamation action' as being '(a) an action for damages for defamation, or (b) an application for a declaratory order, whether or not a claim for other relief under this Act is made'. Section 11 says that a person has 'one cause of action only' in the case of a multiple publication, unless the court grants leave 'where it considers that the interests of justice so require'.

In terms of remedies, section 28(1) explains that 'A person who claims to be the subject of a statement that he or she alleges is defamatory may apply to the Circuit Court for an order (in this Act referred to as a "declaratory order") that the statement is false and defamatory of him or her'. Section 33(1) also allows for the High Court, or the relevant court where the defamation case has been brought, to make an order 'prohibiting the publication or further publication' of the relevant statement, if in its opinion the statement was defamatory, and the defendant has no defence that is 'reasonably likely to succeed'.

Section 38(1)(a) makes it clear that a defamation action cannot be brought later than one year 'from the date on which the cause of action accrued', unless the court grants leave for a period of up to two years, where it is satisfied that the interests of justice require it.

Defences under the Act include those of 'Truth' (Section 16, where 'the statement in respect of which the action was brought is true in all material respects'); Privilege, both 'absolute' and 'qualified' (Sections 17–18); 'Honest opinion' (Section 20, where 'in the case of a statement consisting of an opinion, the opinion was honestly held'); 'Apology' (Section 24, not a defence strictly speaking, but can be used as a defence in mitigation (reduction) of damages); 'Consent' (Section 25, where it can be proved that the plaintiff consented to the publication of the relevant statement); 'Fair and reasonable publication on a matter of public interest' (Section 26); and one of interest here, that of 'Innocent publication' (Section 27).

Under this defence of innocent publication, a defendant (such as a publisher) will succeed if he or she can prove that:

(a) he or she was not the author, editor or publisher of the statement to which the action relates,

(b) he or she took reasonable care in relation to its publication, and

(c) he or she did not know, and had no reason to believe, that what he or she did caused or contributed to the publication of a statement that would give rise to a cause of action in defamation.

Aspects of defamation have been dealt with in an EU directive, incorporated into Irish law, which has been the subject of a number of cases, something I will look at later.

This matter is relevant to the question of cyber-bullying, because it is quite possible that an aggrieved student, or someone on his or her behalf, may not just sue another student and a parent or guardian, but also the relevant internet service provider or those responsible for websites, including social networking ones, arguing that they are the publisher of the relevant defamatory statement or statements posted on it.

4. EU Directive 2000/31/EC, incorporated into Irish law

A European Union directive is a legislative act of that entity, binding on its member states (including Ireland), but which allows each state to decide how it incorporates it into its domestic law. The relevant directive here is one of 8 June 2000, 2000/31/EC, commonly called the 'E-Commerce Directive', which created a basic framework for the operation of electronic commerce in the Union's internal market, ensuring the free movement of 'information society services', and providing legal certainty for businesses and consumers. Of particular interest here are Articles 12–14, which deal with the liability of information society services in three particular areas.

- Article 12: Deals with when the 'service provider' (defined as 'any natural or legal person providing an information society service') is a 'mere conduit' for information transmitted. It is not liable for that information transmitted, on condition that the provider:
  (a) does not initiate the transmission;
  (b) does not select the receiver of the transmission; and
  (c) does not select or modify the information contained in the transmission.
  Such acts of transmission and of provision include 'the automatic, intermediate and transient storage of the information transmitted' as long as it is for 'the sole purpose of carrying out the transmission in the communication network', and 'the information is not stored for any period longer than is reasonably necessary for the transmission'.

- Article 13: Deals with 'caching', when the service provider, dealing with 'the transmission in a communication network of information provided by a recipient of the service', is not liable for 'the automatic, intermediate and temporary storage of that information', done for 'the sole purpose of making more efficient the information's onward transmission to other recipients of the service upon their request', on condition that:
  (a) the provider does not modify the information;
  (b) the provider complies with conditions on access to the information;
  (c) the provider complies with rules regarding the updating of the information, specified in a manner widely recognised and used by industry;
  (d) the provider does not interfere with the lawful use of technology, widely recognised and used by industry, to obtain data on the use of the information; and
  (e) the provider acts expeditiously to remove or to disable access to the information it has stored upon obtaining actual knowledge of the fact that the information at the initial source of the transmission has been removed from the network, or access to it has been disabled, or that a court or an administrative authority has ordered such removal or disablement.

- Article 14: Deals with 'hosting', where a service provider, providing a service that consists of the storage of information provided by a recipient of that service, is not liable for the information stored at the request of a recipient of the service, on condition that:

  (a) the provider does not have actual knowledge of illegal activity or information and, as regards claims for damages, is not aware of facts or circumstances from which the illegal activity or information is apparent; or

  (b) the provider, upon obtaining such knowledge or awareness, acts expeditiously to remove or to disable access to the information.

This directive was put into effect in Irish law by <u>S.I. No. 68/2003</u>, the <u>European Communities (Directive 2000/31/EC) Regulations 2003</u>, containing Regulations 16 (Mere conduit), 17 (Caching), and 18 (Hosting). Before that was Regulation 15, which explained that any provisions in those three regulations, which said that the relevant service provider 'shall not be liable for a particular act', shall mean that the provider shall not (a) be liable in damages, or unless otherwise provided, be the subject of an order providing any other form of legal relief 'for infringing, by reason of that act, the legal rights of any natural or legal person or, by reason of that act, for breaching any duty'; or (b) be subject to any civil or criminal proceedings by reason of 'that act constituting a contravention of any enactment or an infringement of any rule of law'.

What this means is that an internet service provider will not be held legally liable in defamation as a publisher if it can invoke any of the defences of mere conduit, caching and hosting. In the last case, the provider will not be liable as long as it has no knowledge of the relevant illegal activity, or is not aware of the circumstances from which the illegal activity is apparent, and once obtaining such knowledge or awareness, 'acts expeditiously' to remove or disable access to the information. There have been a number of cases, mostly UK but one Irish, where the issue was argued on whether the relevant internet service provider could avail of these three defences in the directive, as incorporated into UK and Irish law.

5. Department of Education and Skills documents

I am going to deal with four documents issued by the Department of Education and Skills. They are important, because they can and have been invoked to show what a school's knowledge of matters in this area should be. While not having legal effect in themselves, the fact that they are produced by a government department gives them a certain weight, and what has been called a 'quasi-legal' status. The first document has been recognised in one case (<u>Mulvey</u>) as showing the *general* awareness a school should have of bullying. This is different from a *specific* awareness a school should have, if particular bullying incidents happen there. The second deals with what should happen if there is a violent incident in a post-primary school. The third and fourth flesh out considerably the procedures to be followed in the event of an appeal under section 29 of the 1998 Act.

a. Guidelines on Countering Behaviour in Primary and Post-Primary Schools

These guidelines, already mentioned, issued by the Department in September 1993, are important, and while not compulsory, have added weight since section 23 of the Education (Welfare) Act 2000 came into force. First, they give a definition of bullying, already quoted. They then look at types of bullying, the effects of bullying, characteristics of bullying, and the steps that can be taken to prevent bullying, including the drawing up of a school policy. They point out that:

> it is the responsibility of the school authority in conjunction with staff and pupils to develop a system under which proper supervisory and monitoring measures are in place to deal with incidents of bullying behaviour.

> (DES, 1993, p. 16)

In terms of the procedures for formally noting and reporting a bullying incident, the *Guidelines* recommend:

- All reports of bullying, no matter how trivial, should be noted, investigated and dealt with by teachers.
- Serious cases of bullying by pupils should be referred immediately to the principal or vice-principal.
- The principal or vice-principal should inform the parents and guardians of victims and bullies 'earlier rather than later' of particular incidents.
- Parents and guardians should be told of the appropriate person to whom they can complain of incidents of bullying behaviour.

- Teachers in consultation with the appropriate staff member should 'record and take appropriate measures' regarding reports of bullying behaviour in accordance with the school's policy and Code of Behaviour and Discipline.
- Non-teaching staff should be encouraged to report any incidents of bullying behaviour to the appropriate teaching member of staff.
- A complaint regarding a staff member should be first raised with the person in question, then with the principal.
- Cases relating to a pupil or teacher unresolved at school level should be referred to the school's board of management (DES, 1993, pp. 16–17).

In terms of investigating and dealing with bullying, the *Guidelines* suggest:

- Teachers take a 'calm, unemotional problem-solving approach' when dealing with incidents of bullying behaviour. Such incidents are best investigated outside the classroom to avoid public humiliation. All interviews should be conducted 'with sensitivity and with due regard to the rights of all pupils concerned'.
- If a gang is involved, each member should be interviewed individually.
- Teachers who investigate complaints should keep a written record of their discussions.
- If it is decided that bullying occurred, a meeting should take place with the parents or guardians of the two parties, and the actions of the school explained to them (DES, 1993, pp. 17–18).

b. Circular letter M18/99: Guidelines on Violence in Schools: (Post-Primary Schools)

Unlike the *Guidelines*, this circular does not specifically deal with bullying; but it is obvious, even from the title, that dealing with violence in schools will include bullying. Part 5 describes 'Steps to be followed in the event of an alleged assault', including:

(ii) The incident should be immediately reported to the school principal/deputy principal/manager as appropriate and the person with responsibility for health and safety issues in the school.

(v) The details of the incident should be recorded in an Incident Book kept for this purpose in the school. The information recorded should include personal details (name, age, occupation) of victim and assailant where available; description of what happened; the circumstances giving rise to the incident; when and where it happened; description of any injuries sustained; weapons used; and establish which school procedure failed, if any. Situations in which staff members have been intimidated or threatened with physical violence should also be recorded. Reports should also be made to the Health and Safety Authority as required.

(vii) Where the alleged assault is by a pupil the matter should be dealt with in accordance with the school's Code of Discipline.

(viii) Students who show a tendency to resort to violent behaviour should be discussed with their parents, teachers and the guidance counsellor. In some cases, a psychological assessment may be considered to be appropriate and/or a referral to NEPS (National Educational Psychological Service).

(xi) The implications of incidents of violence for school policies in the areas of discipline, bullying and health and safety and related areas should be considered. In addition, the school should consider the adequacy and effectiveness of support measures in place for victims of violence within the school.

c. Circular Letter 22/02: Appeals Procedures under Section 29 of the Education Act, 1998 (Primary Schools)

Mentioned before, this deals with the details of the appeals procedure to the secretary-general of the Department of Education and Science, under section 29 of the 1998 Act, in terms of primary schools. Appeals need to be generally made within forty-two days of the date the school's decision was given to the parent or student. If there has been no local level accommodation, and if a facilitator has been unsuccessful, and the appropriate Appeals Application Form is received, the appeal will be referred for hearing by the appeals committee.

According to Paragraph 16 of the Appendix to the Circular, the appeals committee shall consist of three persons, a departmental inspector and two others, who in the minister's opinion 'have the requisite expertise, experience and independence' to serve on the committee.

The hearing is dealt with in Paragraphs 22–31. The parties will be told of their right to submit any extra documentation. The parents, student, and NEWB representative if that board has made an appeal, may attend the hearing as, or on behalf of the appellant. The school's board of management may designate two members, or a member and the principal, to attend the meeting on its behalf.

Subject to the appeal committee's consent, either party to the appeal can be accompanied by not more than two persons nominated by them. Such people are not permitted to make statements to the hearing, save in exceptional circumstances when the committee consents.

At the hearing, both parties will be given an opportunity to present their case. Both have the right of reply, and each can question the other through the chair. The committee can question both parties to the appeal, and seek the views of any persons who have been called.

Paragraph 32 says that the following factors will be taken into account by the committee in its determination:

- the established practices within the school for dealing with issues/grievances which are the subject matter of the appeal, including, where relevant and available, any statutory and non-statutory procedures, guidelines, regulations or other provisions in operation at any time,
- the educational interests of the student who is the subject of the appeal,
- the educational interests of all other students in the school,
- the effective operation and management of the school,
- any resource implications arising from the issues under appeal,
- where relevant, the policy of the patrons and the board of managementin respect of the characteristic spirit/ethos of the school, and
- such other matters as the Committee considers relevant.

Paragraph 33 says that the committee can, in making its determination, take advice from such persons 'as it considers appropriate'.

Paragraph 37 says that when the secretary-general, or person deputed by the secretary-general, is notified of the determination, that person will notify both parties of the decision and the reasons for it, and where necessary will issue such directions to the school's board of management he or she 'considers to be necessary for the purpose of remedying the matter' that was the subject of the appeal. The board 'will be bound by such directions'.

d. Circular Letter M48/01: Appeal Procedures Under Section 29 of the Education Act, 1998 (Post-Primary Schools)

This deals with the section 29 appeals procedure in terms of second-level schools. In terms of ordinary second-level schools, it is *exactly* the same as the one used in the previous circular. There is a different procedure, however, for Vocational Education Committee (VEC) schools, where an appeal from the decision of a school's board of management has to be made, *in the first instance*, to the VEC. That Committee shall form an Appeals Sub-Committee to hear the appeal, under section 21 of the Vocational Education Act 1930, that section allowing such sub-committees to carry out any of the VEC's 'powers, duties, and functions'.

The hearing is conducted in much the same manner as that of the appeals committee previously described, the same factors needing to be taken into account by the Appeals Sub-Committee. After its decision is referred to the VEC, then to the CEO, the latter will inform the parties and, if necessary, issue directions to the board of the school, which will be bound by them. However, Paragraph 29 says that the CEO will *simultaneously*, with the notification to the appellant, advise him or her of the right of, and timeframe for, a further appeal to the secretary-general.

3. CASE LAW

I am going to look at a number of judgements by mostly Irish courts and other bodies, which are divided into nine main areas. In looking at them, we have to remember that the judgements hinge a lot on what the court or other body decided happened, a court being willing to give a different judgement if its findings of fact were different. Also, some of the cases took place in the United Kingdom; so while, as I mentioned, the courts in Ireland may find the findings in such cases persuasive, and may follow them, they are under no obligation to do so.

1. Alleged failure to act: Negligence

Negligence is a principal part of the civil law area of tort, which imposes duties by law, the main remedy for breaches of these duties being damages. It is a breach of a legal duty of care where damage is caused to the party to whom the duty is owed (Hunt and Murdoch, 2007, pp. 1213, 818–19).

The standard of care imposed by the courts on schools is that of a 'prudent parent'; or it is sometimes said that schools are *in loco parentis* (in the place of a parent) when children are in their care. This prudent parent standard of care was first developed in an English case: Williams v. Eady 10 TLR (1893–94), 41.

The Court of Appeal heard a case by a schoolboy against a schoolmaster, alleging negligence for an injury caused by the latter leaving a bottle containing a stick of phosphorus in a conservatory, to which the boys had access. The judge in the court of first instance (a court where the case was first considered) directed the jury:

> that if a man keeps dangerous things he must keep them safely, and take such precautions as a prudent man would take, and to leave such things about in the way of boys would not be reasonable care.

The jury then found for the plaintiff (the person who brings a legal action) (Hunt and Murdoch, 2007, p. 905). The schoolmaster appealed the decision to the Court of Appeal, which dismissed it. Lord Esher M.R., who gave judgement for the court, held that:

> it was correctly laid down by the learned Judge, that the schoolmaster was bound to take such care of his boys as a careful father would take of his boys, and there could not be a better definition of the duty of a schoolmaster. Then he was bound to take notice of the ordinary nature of young boys, their tendency to do mischievous acts, and their propensity to meddle with anything that came in their way.

This standard of care was accepted by the Irish Supreme Court in the case of Lennon v. McCarthy (Unreported, 13 July 1966), and in later cases.

The first case I will deal with in detail, already mentioned, is the High Court one of Nicola Mulvey v. Martin McDonagh. This case is important, not just in upholding the existing standard of care of a school towards its students, but also in endorsing the definition of bullying given in the DES 1993 *Guidelines*.

The plaintiff took a case against her school, claiming damages for personal injuries suffered by her from an assault by a fellow pupil or pupils, while attending the school at 4 years of age, on the last day of her first year, in June 1998. She alleged that she had been bullied since the previous October, and that numerous complaints had been made to the school.

The evidence supporting the plaintiff's claim was mostly from herself and her mother. The latter claimed to have made a number of complaints about Nicola being beaten up in the schoolyard. In November 1997, an incident took place when the plaintiff's tracksuit trousers were pulled down.

Her mother reported this to Sister Gemma, the class teacher, who appeared to have resolved the matter.

In December, on the last day of term, Mrs Mulvey complained to Mrs Mularkey, the principal, about Nicola being bullied that term. As Mrs Mularkey was going to retire, she referred Mrs Mulvey to her successor, Mrs Sweeney, who took up her duties the next term. In January 1998, Mr and Mrs Mulvey met Mrs Sweeney, who said that she would take more measures to monitor the schoolyard. At a later meeting, it was agreed that if Mrs Mulvey had any further complaints, she should go directly to Mrs Sweeney.

On 3 February, Mrs Mulvey said that she went to the classroom where Nicola was sitting, asked Sister Gemma for permission to address the class, and berated them for their treatment of Nicola, threatening to 'kick them up the backside' if they did not stop. Mrs Sweeney came into the classroom towards the end of this address.

There were no more communications from Nicola's parents until 25 June, the last day of term, though Mrs Mulvey claimed that Nicola was still being bullied. That day, Mrs Mulvey claimed that Nicola had been beaten up and kicked by a number of people in the schoolyard. She was taken to Crumlin Hospital, her mother claiming that she 'was covered in bruises and that she had been covered in bruises for some considerable length of time, prior to this date'.

The plaintiff gave evidence, which the judge, Johnson J., hinted might be, in his opinion, the result of coaching by her mother, because it:

> agreed in almost every word with the evidence of the next friend [her mother] and despite the fact that she was now ten appeared to have an extraordinarily good recollection of what took place when she was four years of age.

Two expert witnesses supported the evidence of the plaintiff and her mother. The problem about this evidence, in the eyes of the judge, was that 'they only heard the plaintiff and the next friend [her mother] and did not have an opportunity of witnessing the witnesses for the defence or the manner in which they gave evidence'.

The paediatrician who dealt with the plaintiff when she was brought to the hospital on 25 June gave evidence in which, despite the plaintiff's statement of claim, 'there was no damage to the spleen and no rupture of the spleen', and 'there was no bruising whatsoever on any part of the plaintiff's body'.

The judge ruled in favour of the school. There was, he said, in a number of incidents, 'a direct contradiction between the plaintiff's and defendant's evidence'. He preferred the latter, because he had the opportunity in the case of:

> watching the witnesses in court, of seeing them give evidence and of watching their reactions in the witness box under cross-examination. I have also taken the opportunity of visiting the school yard and I am satisfied that it is an open yard, not very large, in which any adult would have no difficulty in observing incidents as described by the plaintiff taking place.

The evidence given by the defendant, which neither of the expert witnesses 'had an opportunity of seeing' was 'extremely convincing and I am satisfied that the defendant and each of the school's witnesses were responsible, caring, alert, concerned and truthful people'. In terms of case law, the judge followed previous precedents that the degree of care to be taken in the case – which was accepted by both sides – was that of:

> a prudent parent exercising reasonable care and I accept that that must be taken in the context of a prudent parent behaving responsibly with a class of 28 four year olds having their first experience of mingling socially with other children.

He was satisfied that this care was taken. In any disputes over the facts, the judge was satisfied, 'having had the opportunity' of watching and listening to both parties, that the defendant's version of the evidence of what took place was 'far more reliable and acceptable'. This, he felt, was borne out by the medical evidence, which showed that there was no bruising. The judge also held that he accepted the definition of bullying in the 1993 *Guidelines*.

There have been two more connected school bullying cases. The first is a Supreme Court one, <u>Kenneth Murphy v. County Wexford V.E.C.</u> [2004] 4 IR, 202, which was applied by the High Court in a second case, <u>Wayne Maher (A minor) v. The Board and Management of Presentation Junior School, Mullingar</u> [2004] 4 IR, 211.

The <u>Murphy</u> case involved a fifth-year student, with his class in the resource area at lunch time. There were about fifty students present. One student arrived with a packet of chocolate bars which he offered to everyone. The bag burst, and the bars started to be thrown around. The plaintiff was struck in the eye by one of the bars, and was seriously injured. A High Court judge awarded him €50,000 for personal injuries, which was appealed to the Supreme Court.

That Court rejected this appeal by a two to one majority. The judgement of the majority was given by McCracken J. He said that both sides accepted the duty of care as set out by the Supreme Court in <u>Lennon v. McCarthy</u>, and followed by the High Court in <u>Flesk v. King</u> (Unreported, 29 October 1996), where the judge, Laffoy J., said, 'the law does not require children in the school playground to be under constant supervision and watched at every instance'. McCracken J. went on to say:

> Quite clearly, school authorities are not insurers of the pupils under their care. However, they do owe a duty to those pupils to take reasonable care to ensure that the pupils do not suffer injury. To do this, some degree of supervision is clearly required. The extent of such supervision will depend on a number of factors, for example, the age of the pupils involved, the location of the places where the pupils congregate, the number of pupils which may be present at any one time and the general propensity of pupils at that particular school to act dangerously.

That judge found relevant evidence that in the defendant's school 'there had been serious disciplinary problems, following which the defendant considered it necessary to ensure that a teacher was present in certain specific areas' including where the present incident took place, during lunch hour. These problems had led to the expulsion of twenty pupils and, following the introduction of the rota system, 'the supervision was reasonable and that for some unexplained reason the rota system did not operate on the day in question and there was no supervision'. In the light of this, the judge concluded:

> I am of the view that the particular circumstances of this case and the history of indiscipline in the school imposed a duty of care on the defendant to provide supervision at lunch time in accordance with its rota system and that the failure to do so constituted negligence on the part of the defendant.

The judgement in <u>Murphy</u> was followed by that of Peart J. in the High Court in <u>Maher</u>. In that case, the plaintiff, a boy of 6, was severely injured in his right eye when in a classroom of the defendant's school another boy of the same age sitting at a table opposite to him used a rubber band to fire a pencil at him, when the teacher had her back turned. The judge concluded that the class was:

> a normal class of six year olds and that there is no evidence that there was any particular or unusual or special difficulty as far as the known behaviour of these children is concerned. I am sure that they were no better and no worse than any other group. I am also satisfied that from the evidence which I have heard that it was entirely appropriate that one teacher should be in charge of this class.

He then looked at what McCracken J. had said in <u>Maher</u>, particularly in Paragraph 27. In applying this, the judge said that:

> for a breach of duty of care to occur, there must exist in addition to the relationship of proximity (which clearly exists in the case of a school and pupil) the requirement of forseeability.

In the present case it meant that:

> before the defendant can be liable, the court would have to be satisfied that it is reasonable that Ms. Shaw [the teacher] should be expected to anticipate that the moment she turned her back (not literally) on the class in order to have a very short conversation with Ms. Fitzsimons at the door of the classroom, it was probable or likely that some behaviour would occur which would cause injury to one or more of the pupils in her charge.

He made the observation that:

> There can of course be situations in any school where the school is well aware of potential dangers, where for example there has been a history of disruptive and even violent behaviour on the part of a pupil or a group of pupils. Bullying would be a case in point. The duty of care of the school in such circumstances would extend to taking appropriate account of these known circumstances when deciding on the appropriate level of supervision in the school, particularly during break and

recreation periods when pupils are outside the more controlled environment of the classroom.

Again confirming that the standard of care required in school was that of a prudent parent, he explained that this meant:

> the school is expected to be no more and no less vigilant of those in its care than a prudent parent would be in his or her own home. In any normal child, if there be such a creature, there is always a certain propensity for horseplay and high spirits. Indeed, if it were not so, there might be some cause for concern.

In the particular circumstances of the case, the judge held that the school was not guilty of negligence, and the student's claim failed.

Looking at these three cases, we can see that the courts have upheld the 'prudent parent' standard of care. The difference is that, from the facts of the cases, certain schools were found to have kept to this standard, others not. Also, the courts have taken into account the school's level of awareness of bullying: first, in terms of *general* awareness, including awareness of the Department's 1993 *Guidelines*; second, in terms of *particular* awareness of incidents that took place at the particular school, something that was an important factor in the decision in <u>Murphy</u>.

In these cases, the incidents complained of all took place in the late 1990s. A court dealing with more recent incidents would take account of more recent developments, including the obligations of section 23 of the Education (Welfare) Act 2000, as amended.

Parents and guardians liable in negligence?

Can parents and guardians of students who bully be liable in negligence, as well as schools, as already discussed? The answer is 'Yes'. McMahon and Binchy's *Law of Torts*, looking at the few Irish cases, and case law in other countries, points out that while there is 'no general rule' for parents being liable for the torts of their children due to being parents, they may be negligent in allowing a child the 'opportunity to injure another' (McMahon and Binchy, 2013, p. 631). Three types of behaviour may result in this liability:

i. Dangerous Things

It may be negligent for a person to have dangerous things within reach of a child where it is foreseeable that they would cause injury to that child or another. <u>Williams v. Eady</u> showed this when phosphorous was left within reach of a child by a schoolmaster exercising parental responsibility. An Irish case showed this regarding a gun: <u>Sullivan v. Creed</u> [1904] 2 IR, 317. The defendant left his gun loaded and at full cock. His 15-year-old son, unaware of this, pointed it at the plaintiff in play and accidentally shot him. The plaintiff successfully sued the defendant (McMahon and Binchy, 2013, pp. 631–632).

ii. Dangerous Propensities

A parent may be liable if he or she knows or ought to know of a 'dangerous propensity' of a child, and fails to reasonably protect others against an injury resulting from it. Examples include a child previously attacking other people, stealing or damaging property. The steps parents will be required to take will depend on the facts of the case, including the age of the child and the nature of the danger. They will not be liable if their reasonable best was not enough to prevent an injury (McMahon and Binchy, 2013, pp. 632–633).

iii. Failure to Control a Child Properly

When parents fail to control a child properly, they may be liable for the child's injuries, or the injuries caused to others. This was particularly stated in the Supreme Court case of <u>Curley v. Mannion</u> [1965] IR, 543, where a 12-year-old girl opened the door of a parked car, driven by her father, in the path of a passing cyclist. In the court's judgement, Chief Justice Ó Dálaigh said:

> a person in charge of a motor car must take reasonable precautions for the safety of others, and this will include the duty to take reasonable care to prevent conduct on the part of passengers which is negligent. In the present case that duty is, it seems to me, reinforced by the relationship of parent and child; and *a parent, while not liable for the torts of his child, may be liable if negligent in failing to exercise his control to prevent his child injuring others.* (My italics)
>
> (McMahon and Binchy, 2013, p. 633)

What this means is that parents and guardians can be liable in negligence of their minor children if they bully, in the same way schools have, who were acting with delegated parental authority.

This can also extend to any tort of defamation carried out by their children, including cyber-bullying, something I will look at later.

2. Acting contrary to fair procedures?

I have discussed fair procedures in the context of Article 40.3.2° of the Constitution, and will show here how this article is put into practice in five cases, which were challenges to school decisions to expel or suspend students, alleging that fair procedures were not taken. The first was The State (Derek Smullen and Declan Smullen) v. Duffy and Others [1980] ILRM, 46, where the High Court, under Finlay P., upheld the decision of a school principal to, after carrying out an immediate investigation, suspend a number of students, divided into two rival gangs, who were involved in a fight immediately outside the school gates, including the two plaintiffs, one of whom had struck another with an iron bar he stole from the school, and the other being wounded in the leg. He informed their mother that she could appeal the decision to the board of management within a certain period.

A meeting of the board later decided, after discussing the principal's report, to suspend the two plaintiffs until the end of the school year. The court said that the general scheme of discipline in the draft articles of management and put into practice by the principal and board was 'fair and wise'. The principal was entitled, after a bona fide investigation, to 'make an immediate suspension of one or more pupils in order to maintain peace and discipline within the school'. Because a 'proper and reasonable opportunity' had been given to the mother of the students to challenge the decision, the board's decision could not be challenged on the basis of unfairness, despite its refusal to permit the mother to be legally represented at that meeting.

The next case was Student A. and Student B. v. Dublin Secondary School [1999] 11 JIC 2501. Two students were caught by bouncers using cannabis in the toilets of a licensed premises, where they were attending a private party. The headmaster told their parents that they had been expelled, as part of the school's zero tolerance policy towards drugs, specified in its code of conduct, which covered students taking 'an illicit drug at any time'. In subsequent meetings, he refused to change his mind, though he told the parents that they could appeal his decision to the board of governors. While correspondence and an account of the representations made on behalf of both boys was passed to the board by the headmaster, no meeting took place between either the parents or students and the board before it confirmed the expulsions.

The students sought from the High Court an interlocutory (temporary) injunction (an order of the court) to restrain the school from expelling them, alleging a breach of fair procedures, and that the severity of the penalty imposed was disproportionate.

The judge, Kearns J., held that one matter was a 'cause for concern', the expulsions being put in place before 'either the students or their parents had an opportunity of making representations prior to the imposition of the most severe penalty to be imposed by a school. This is an essential element of fair procedures.' He decided to adjourn the matter for a week, in order to allow the plaintiffs and their parents to address the board before a final decision was made in terms of penalties. The board could still impose a 'lengthy period of suspension' or expel the plaintiffs, if, after hearing the submission, it feels that it is the 'proper and appropriate course of action to adopt'.

The school in question was not one recognised by the Department of Education and Science, so the provisions of the Education Act 1998 and any guidelines did not apply. Because of this, the judge made a few recommendations such schools should follow:

(a) If long-term suspension or expulsion of a pupil is to take place, rules of natural justice require that the student or parents concerned be given an opportunity of making representations as to penalty.

(b) Exceptional circumstances of the type occurring in The State (Smullen) v. Duffy may justify immediate or even long-term suspension without notice or procedure, e.g. where there is danger to life and property.

(c) In situations where Departmental Guidelines or the provisions of the Education Act 1998 do not apply to a particular school, it is important for such schools to have clear rules of conduct and to ensure that parents and pupils are made fully aware of such rules and disciplinary policy. In addition, it would be prudent for schools to adopt a practice requiring parents to read and sign such rules, particularly where any rule relates to behaviour of students off the school premises and outside school hours.

(d) In the context of any meeting or hearing of the type mentioned in paragraph (a), it is not desirable that lawyers be involved at this stage of the process and indeed in matters of this sort legal intervention should ideally be kept to a minimum.

The third case, again heard in the High Court, was that of James Wright and Alexander Wright v. The Board of Management of Gorey Community School [2000] IEHC, 37. Both plaintiffs were suspended from their school, pending investigation into allegations involving drugs, alleged to have been bought by the first plaintiff and delivered to the school by the second. (The first plaintiff had previously been suspended for admittedly bringing cannabis to the school.) The school's board of management, on the evidence provided, decided to expel one and suspend the other for a specified time.

Both plaintiffs took a case against the board, alleging that it acted in violation of fair procedures; and, in advance of the trial of their case, sought an interlocutory injunction for immediate reinstatement in the school until then. While their parents had legal advice before the relevant hearing of the board, there was an argument about 'whether the charges and details of the evidence upon which they were based became known to them only in the course of the proceedings before the Board itself'.

O'Sullivan J. ruled against the two, holding that the balance of convenience favoured the refusal of their reinstatement. If he were to order reinstatement, 'enormous damage will have been done to the authority and policy of the Defendant school, faced with the grave responsibility of dealing with any threat from drug abuse'; but if he were to refuse the injunction sought, and the plaintiffs eventually won their case, they would 'in all probability in the meantime have had access to appropriate schooling'. Also, they were not facing watershed examinations, and if they won, 'their reputations can be vindicated'.

In the fourth case, McKenna (A Minor) v. Ó Ciaráin (Unreported, 30 November 2001), Ó Caoimh J. of the High Court granted an order directing the principal of a vocational school to readmit a student to that school. The student applicant and others had initially been suspended by the principal, and then expelled from the school by its board of management for smoking cannabis; but the board later decided to reinstate them. The principal had refused to comply with the direction to reinstate the applicant, even though the VEC endorsed the board's decision.

The fifth case, Timothy O'Donovan v. The Board of Management of De La Salle College Wicklow and Others [2009] IEHC, 163, looked at a number of issues, including fair procedures and breach of statutory duty. When the applicant was a secondary school student, he took part in a charity football match, which involved himself and a number of fellow students and two younger teachers, including BG.

After saving the winning penalty, the applicant ran behind BG and pulled his shorts down, causing part of the latter's backside to be exposed to onlookers.

On 29 November 2006, the day after the incident, when the applicant was absent from school due to a rugby injury, BG complained to the principal. The latter rang the applicant's mother to say that he was suspended until the next board of management meeting due to his behaviour. (An exception was later made, his suspension being lifted, for him to grieve with his fellow students when one of their number was killed in an accident.)

On 30 November, the applicant returned to the school, with a letter of apology to BG. The principal rang his mother, saying that the intention was that the suspension be lifted for one day only, and he should remain out of the school until 7 December, when the board would discuss the matter. She said that the matter was 'a very serious one'.

The judge in the case, Hedigan J., said that 'it should be noted that the school's code of conduct was not precisely complied with throughout the dealings between the parties'. He pointed out that Clause D of the school's Code of Conduct 'quite clearly envisages the parents should be advised in writing where serious sanctions are being considered and that they should be invited, also in writing, to discuss the situation with the school principal'. The board of management claimed that any departure from this procedure was due to 'the distraction caused by the tragic death' of the applicant's fellow student; and he was 'not deprived of any material advantage' due to the means of communication used in contacting his parents.

The board met on 7 December to consider the complaint, BG as a member absenting himself, and after it heard a report on the incident given by the principal and the applicant's behavioural history, decided to hold an emergency meeting on 18 December. It advised that BG be offered counselling, and he be invited to make a submission to it for the purposes of the meeting.

In a letter of 8 December, the principal invited the applicant and his parents to the meeting of 18 December, or as an alternative to make a written submission. The meeting went ahead as planned and was attended by the applicant and his parents. BG again absented himself. At the end of the meeting, the principal, the applicant and his parents left to let the board decide on the matter. It decided that the applicant be permanently excluded from the school, the incident being in its view 'a very serious one which had caused considerable distress' to BG. The applicant's parents were told of this decision in a letter of 19 December, which gave details of their right of appeal under section 29 of the Education Act 1998, a right they invoked.

The appeals committee set up under section 29 heard the appeal on 26 January 2007, and rejected it on 15 February. The reasons given were that 'the impact of the incident' on the teacher 'was such as to merit the most serious sanction available to the first named respondent [the board of management]'. While the school had 'not fully complied with its normal procedures and published policies' regarding the student's initial suspension, it 'accepted that mitigating circumstances had pertained at the relevant time'. The local education welfare officer was not contacted regarding the applicant's expulsion until 19 December 2006, the latter being out of school from 1 December 2006 till late January 2007.

Mr O'Donovan sued, by his mother in the High Court, not just the school's board of management, but also the section 29 appeals committee, applying to seek *judicial review* of their decisions and an order quashing his expulsion from the school. A judicial review is a legal remedy given where a body or tribunal that has legal authority to determine rights or impose liabilities has acted outside the authority given to it under the law, or against its duty. It does not deal with the actual decision, but how it was arrived at (Hunt and Murdoch, 2007, p. 677).

The respondents argued that the applicant's mother failed to observe the requirement that those seeking judicial review have to make applications 'in the utmost good faith', because she had not put in the affidavit grounding the application the fact that on 18 December 2006, the board asked the applicant and his parents to attend an emergency meeting, a meeting the three attended.

The applicant claimed that the decisions of both respondents were in breach of the principles of natural and constitutional justice. In particular, the decision not to let the applicant or his parents make representations at the board meeting on 7 December 2006 was a violation of the principal of *audi alteram partem* (to hear both sides), a default not remedied by the later meeting with the board on 18 December. The applicant claimed that he should have been 'permitted to explain his behaviour at the earliest opportunity' before the board considered expelling him. Such an opportunity to make a case was required by Clause B of the school's Code of Behaviour, drafted under section 23 of the Education (Welfare) Act 2000. The board responded that there was 'nothing untoward' in the way it investigated and adjudicated on the complaint made against the applicant. He was 'given more than sufficient opportunity' to make representations and explain his behaviour. Also, 'it was careful to ensure' that his parents were 'kept informed of every step' in the disciplinary process.

The applicant said that the failure of the board to notify the educational welfare officer until after the decision to expel him was a 'clear breach' of its statutory duty under 21(4) and 24(4) of the 2000 Act, dealing with the suspension and expulsion of students.

The judge decided that the omission by the applicant's mother of their invitation to attend a meeting of the board, which they did, was 'to some extent at least, a significant one'. This fact of the invitation and attendance is 'of material relevance to the fair procedures argument alone'. This 'ought to have been clearly revealed' at the original application. He therefore refused to grant any order on the grounds of lack of fair procedures.

He did, however, agree that there was 'a plain and unambiguous violation' of the 2000 Act under sections 21(4) and 24(4) by the board; so he therefore granted a declaration that the decisions of the board and the appeals committee to expel the applicant were 'made in breach of his statutory rights', and granted an order quashing his expulsion for that reason.

In this case, therefore, the question of the school's failure to follow its code of conduct was not dealt with, due to a serious mistake by the applicant's mother in the application for judicial review. However, the school was held to be at fault due to failing to comply with the statutory provisions covering the applicant's suspension and expulsion; so his expulsion was quashed.

3. Refusal to enrol due to prior bad behaviour

The High Court case of County Westmeath VEC v. Department of Education and Science and Others [2009] IEHC, 373, dealt with a community college's refusal to enrol a student in a secondary school, his parents' successful appeal against this refusal under section 29 of the Education Acts, and the judgement of O'Keeffe J. on the matter, following the VEC seeking judicial review of the appeals committee's decision. One of the reasons for the refusal to enrol was the student's prior bad behaviour.

The student was in St Mary's CBS when his mother approached the principal of the community college, saying that her son 'had been told that he would not be "welcome back" to that school'. His parents applied to enrol him in the community college on 12 August 2007, giving the reason as 'change of school'.

The principal said that up to the date of the application she had met the principal of St Mary's 'from which it was clear that the son had a serious disciplinary problem and that the school would not keep him on its rolls "if it could avoid it"'. Such discussions were 'completely at variance with the documentations sent to her by the CBS which supported his application for admission'.

On 14 August the community college's board of management refused the application for enrolment from that student and a second in the same school, who 'are being discouraged from returning in September'. A discussion took place. One member said that unless formally expelled, it was the responsibility of the school they were enrolled in to provide their education. Some members of the board said 'there appeared to be contradictions in the documentation provided by the school'. Two members referred to the duty of care to existing students, and that such students felt that they needed to feel that they had the support of school management. For these reasons, enrolment of the two students was rejected, the reason being that it 'would not be in the best interests of the school community'.

The parents appealed the decision to the VEC on 20 August, which appointed a facilitator, who reported on 12 September. He said that the parents wanted their son to get a place in a school as soon as possible, because while he was a pupil in the CBS till the end of May, 'because the school was not satisfied with his behaviour, he was told to complete his studies for his Junior Certificate at home and look for another school if he wanted to pursue his studies'. At the time of the report he was not expelled and was still enrolled in that school.

The parents were told that the Chief Executive Officer of the VEC could not adjudicate on their appeal, and were told that they had a right of appeal under section 29 of the Education Acts. This they did, and the appeals committee found in their favour. The fourth of the four reasons given by the VEC was that it 'felt that the level of misbehaviour by the son did not warrant a refusal to enrol' him.

The community college's principal later said that, at the hearings of the appeals committee, she raised a number of issues about 'the whole practice of what would be regarded as "offloading" of difficult pupils in the local vocational college'. She pointed out:

> the serious discrepancy between the references received by the school from the CBS in relation to the third party's son, and what appeared to be the true position on the ground. The fact that his parents had canvassed many schools and had

been refused by a number of schools, that appeals had been commenced under s. 29, but either not upheld or abandoned, and the implications that these would have for any suggestion that the community school was the school of choice for the parents, were pointed out to the Committee, she said.

She said that the committee was in 'no position ... to find that the son's level of behaviour was not sufficiently serious, as it did not canvass the issue with the previous school'. Having regard to the number of children with special needs then enrolled in the school, any additional or disruptive pupil represented 'a significant strain on an already strained class/student situation within the school'.

At the appeals committee's hearing the parties were supplied with the community college's Admission and Enrolment Policy, which included that '(d) The Board of Management reserves the right to refuse an application in exceptional circumstances, which might include (i) an established prior record of poor behaviour'.

The VEC sought judicial review of the decision, which was granted. Looking at the four reasons for the decision, the judge held that the first, dealing with the school's enrolment powers, was outside the appeals committee's powers. The second, dealing with the committee saying that he had no school placement, was factually incorrect, as he was still enrolled in the CBS at the time of the decision. The third, that the school had the capacity to accommodate the student, was not 'irrational or unreasonable' as evidence had been presented that this was the case.

About the fourth reason, the student's level of misbehaviour, the judge held that it was not irrational or unreasonable, giving this as explanation:

> Whilst I have been furnished with notes of what was stated by various parties at the hearing of the Appeals Committee, such notes are unofficial and have no status in these proceedings. It is very difficult for the court to conclude, from the wide range of evidence on matters such as the level of misbehaviour of the son, which particular evidence was accepted by the Appeals Committee and formed the basis for the Appeals Committee giving its reason under this heading. However, from the documents submitted and the affidavits sworn, it cannot be said that this reason is irrational or unreasonable. There was evidence to support such a conclusion and the Applicant's witnesses participated at the hearing in the consideration of this issue.

Because of the dispute about the evidence, the judge felt that he could not conclude that the decision was irrational or unreasonable.

4. Exceeded its jurisdiction

In the case of City of Waterford VEC v. Department of Education and Science and Others [2011] IEHC, 278, a secondary school expelled a student due to his behaviour, which included 'name calling, using very unpleasant language, striking another student with his foot, assaulting a student and a failure to engage with school discipline'. Particular incidents were given of throwing a bag at a teacher and calling her 'a very rude name', beating up another student; and when he was caught tripping up another student by a teacher, he threatened to headbutt that teacher, then went on to headbutt and spit on another teacher.

The student's father appealed this decision by the school's board of management to the VEC, and was unsuccessful. He then appealed this on his son's behalf under section 29 of the 1998 Act. The appeals committee upheld this appeal, requiring the school to take the student back, one of its stated reasons being the 'distinct lack of other educational alternatives' for such a boy as a student in Waterford.

The VEC sought judicial review of this decision, and Charleton J. in the High Court ruled in its favour. He pointed out that the appeals committee was a 'statutory creation', which 'can only do what the relevant statute allows it to do'. Also, like any tribunal, it has to give reasons for its decision. While not elaborate, these reasons have to be sufficient (that the parties to the hearing are aware why such a decision was made) and entire (i.e. complete). He held that a school board of management did not, in deciding on a student's expulsion, 'have to consider whether other placements may be available in the immediate area' should the expulsion take place. The appeals committee 'is in precisely the same position'. Also, an additional reason given on affidavit by a member of the committee for its decision, that the student's behaviour did not deserve expulsion, was not part of the document in which the committee officially set down its decision.

That committee 'is concerned with whether or not the expulsion was warranted. This has nothing to do with whether there is an alternative place. The responsibility for that function is elsewhere.' Therefore the judge said that 'jurisdiction was exceeded by the appeals committee and the reasons given were not adequate'.

A school can therefore expel a student without needing to take into account the availability of an alternative placement, the finding of such a placement being seen as the responsibility of the parents or guardians and the NEWB.

5. Equal Status Acts related decisions

A number of decisions have been made, by the High Court and by equality officers, under these Acts that are bullying related. They deal with disciplinary actions taken by schools against students, up to and including expulsion, arising out of alleged bad behaviour, as well as alleged mistreatment of students by school staff. In these cases, the students or their parents on their behalf, alleged that the treatment they received was discrimination, harassment or victimisation under the Acts, or any combination of the three.

a. High Court

The relevant High Court case is that of <u>Richard Clare v. Minister for Education and Science, the South Eastern Health Board, Ireland and the Attorney General</u> [2004] IEHC, 350. Mr Clare sued these parties through his mother, claiming that the defendants failed to provide appropriate education for his needs, as a person suffering from Attention Deficit Hyperactivity Disorder (ADHD), discriminated against him compared to other children, and deprived him of his constitutional rights, in particular Articles 40.1, 40.3.1°, 40.3.2° and 42.4.

While his mother said that when the plaintiff was in national school she was called in every year to discuss his behaviour, and was asked to come and see the teachers regarding this, she had said in a questionnaire in 1993 to the health board that he 'was not falling behind in school, or suffering from any behavioural problems'.

The judge, Smyth J., held that he was 'not convinced' of her evidence, after also hearing evidence of the national school's staff, including the principal, that the plaintiff 'had a defined problem of which the authorities were or should have been aware and that they failed, neglected or refused to do anything about it'.

In sixth class, the principal was aware that the class teacher sent for Mrs Clare and told her that her son's behaviour was 'inappropriate and unacceptable', though the former felt this was 'low-key misbehaviour'. He felt there was nothing to lead him to believe the plaintiff needed any special treatment or psychological assessment.

The plaintiff went into secondary school in September 1998. He was given detention for 14 November, due to removal from class for 'constant disruption' and talking in the study hall. This was followed by a second for 5 December for being 'constantly disruptive' in class. After this his year master requested to see his parents. In early 1999, he was brought by his mother to see a clinical psychologist.

The plaintiff was given notices, on 17 February and 15 April 1999, that he would be suspended for one, later two weeks. The bad behaviour was not just being disruptive in class; it included being disrespectful to a teacher, refusing to obey orders, spitting at another student, deliberately hitting another student with a heavy school bag, use of bad language, and homework missing or incomplete. His parents were warned that he might be asked to leave the school.

Before his second year in the school began, there was 'no evidence' his mother 'ever made good the omissions' in the plaintiff's behaviour. While she claimed before this year that she suspected he might have ADHD, there was 'no evidence' that she contacted the school.

The plaintiff was diagnosed with ADHD by a consultant in September 1999, the school then being told, and the consultant liaising with them. Notices were issued by the school of disruptive behaviour in September and December. On 2 March 2000, the plaintiff's year master wrote to his parents that he was involved in a fight, and that they were 'extremely lucky' that the other boy's parents did not take legal action. He referred to incidents in February where he was so badly behaved that he had to be removed from a number of classes. Therefore, he was 'suspended from school indefinitely'.

On 13 March the plaintiff and his parents met the school authorities and the three signed an agreement with the latter, on which condition he was permitted to return to the school. The judge was satisfied that his mother 'failed to inform the school in advance' of the earlier history of her son's condition.

The agreement said that the plaintiff be expelled from the school if he failed to abide by its conditions. On 15 and 20 March, notices of detention issued. At a meeting with the parents on 23 May, the matter was referred to the next board of management meeting, an alternative suggestion being made that he should seek alternative educational facilities. The board decided in a letter of 29 September not to continue to offer the plaintiff a place in the school. The judge was satisfied that 'by the tone of the notices and the frequency of infringements by Richard [the plaintiff] that any reasonable and responsible Board of Management would not have made any other decision' than to expel him.

Looking at the case law, the judge held that the school 'did not discriminate unfairly, unreasonably or at all' in the context of section 7(10)(d) of the Equal Status Act 2000, in expelling him. It was 'entitled to balance the rights of Richard and the other students in his (intended) class', which was not discrimination under section 7(4)(b). The defendants did not breach his constitutional rights or breach any statutory duty. If he was 'as difficult or as problematical' as his mother stated in evidence, this fact was 'deliberately withheld' from the secondary school, because she wanted him to go there 'with a clean slate'. The principal of his primary school and the teachers of his secondary school should not be faulted 'for failing to ascertain' that he had ADHD. As a matter of fact and law 'the support services and level and quality of education appropriate to Richard to meet his needs was provided to him'.

b. Equality Officers

The first relevant equality officer decision under the Equal Status Acts, on 12 March 2004, in the case of <u>A Mother and Son v. A Secondary School</u>, concerned a complaint by a mother and son that the latter was discriminated against on the Traveller community ground, in sections 3(1) and 3(2)(i), in not being provided with a service generally available to the public contrary to section 5(1) of the Acts. He was 14 at the last alleged incident of discrimination. (This and the other decisions mentioned can be found in a database on the Equality Tribunal's website at www.equalitytribunal.ie/ Database-of-Decisions/.)

When he began school in September 1999, the son was, on the first day, 'involved in a fight in town with a student from another school'. The principal summoned him into his office, and 'warned him about bringing the school into disrepute (the son was wearing the school uniform at the time)'. In December 2000, the principal told the mother in person that her son 'had been involved in a number of unacceptable incidents in the school', and suggested she withdraw him for a short while, as he did not want to formally suspend him. This she did until after Christmas.

In April 2001, the principal told her in person that 'further issues had arisen in relation to punctuality, disruptive behaviour and bullying'. He suggested her son 'be removed from the school and suggested that she might consider enrolling him in a different school altogether'. The mother kept him out of school for the rest of the school year. While arrangements were made for the son to receive additional tuition at home, this was cancelled when he failed to turn up one day.

In October, his mother was asked to remove him from school following allegations, which he denied, that he had 'head-butted a girl' and engaged in 'other disruptive behaviour'. She did so for a week. In December, the principal suggested to her in person that her son be 'removed permanently'. She refused, saying that he would have to expel him. He later told her that he was suspending her son, and that the board of management would discuss the matter at a meeting. The mother wrote to the board before this meeting outlining her concerns. She met the board on 24 January 2002, which told her that her son was welcome back to the school. She told the board that her son did not feel welcome and 'that he felt he was being picked on'. She asked that he be given extra tuition for five subjects for his Junior Certificate, which she was told was not possible as teachers were not available. As no satisfactory solution could be found, the son 'stopped attending the school from then on'.

The equality officer decided that there was 'insufficient evidence' before him to indicate that the mother and son were 'treated less favourably' than non-members of the Traveller community were by the school 'over the years, in similar circumstances'. He decided this after finding that the school's disciplinary rules were 'developed and applied in line' with the Department of Education's guidelines on such matters. Also, he was given reports from the school to show that in twelve other cases over the past number of years, the students were treated the same. There was 'insufficient evidence' before him to indicate that the accusations arose from the fact that he was known to be a Traveller 'rather than the fact that he was known to have been involved in previous instances of misconduct'.

A second decision, of 19 January 2007, <u>Mrs. A on behalf of her son B v. A Primary School</u>, concerned the complaint of a mother that a school's board of management had refused to enrol her son due to him being both disabled and a Traveller (Section 3(2)(g) and 3(2)(i)). She had made a complaint under the Acts against a school her son had previously attended; so she alleged that the present school's refusal to enrol her son was not only discrimination under the previous two grounds; it was also victimisation, the chairman of the board of management of the present school being in the same position in the school the son had previously attended.

The equality officer, while rejecting the complaints of discrimination on the two grounds, and that the school failed to provide 'reasonable accommodation' under section 4 in terms of the son's disability, held that a prima facie complaint of victimisation had been established, which the school failed to rebut, for which he awarded the son €6,350.

This decision was reached because the chairman 'actively participated in the decision making process' leading to the refusal to enrol B. The equality officer concluded that the chairman based his decision to refuse to enrol B 'on matters arising and ongoing at that time in the school at which B had previously attended'. In the circumstances the enrolment process regarding B was 'flawed and not in accordance with fair procedures or natural justice' in that the decision to refuse 'was not clearly and transparently arrived at based on objective criteria' unconnected with B's complaint against the previous school.

The third decision, <u>Ms A (on behalf of her son Mr B) v A Community School</u>, of 30 January 2009, concerned a mother who took a case on behalf of her son, who alleged discrimination against him on the gender ground, due to being suspended by the school after refusing to cut his hair. He also alleged discrimination by the school, when it refused to reinstate him after the appeal committee ruled, under section 29 of the 1998 Act, that he be so reinstated.

The committee ruled that he be reinstated, as long as his hair was 'groomed to collar length'. The equality officer decided that the school had engaged in less favourable treatment of that student compared to female students. Arguments by the school that female students were required by the school's dress code to wear skirts were not an 'appropriate comparison' because girls were free to change their clothing when they left the school; boys 'cannot change the length of their hair at the end of the school day'. Also, he held that the school had put an 'additional obstacle' in place of reinstating him, because it had engaged a barber, and refused admission on the basis of his findings.

The board of management's minutes stated that the barber said that 'it is his opinion' that the student had not complied with the section 29 appeal condition. In fact, the barber was correctly recorded in a note that 'it is your [the board's] opinion', that the student had not complied. The latter was not prepared to comply, so did not return.

The equality officer also made reference to the student being removed from the school band, being asked if he 'wanted to be a girl', being suspended for three months, not being able to sit his mock exams, and not being able to complete his Art project close to the Leaving Certificate, and having to leave his school close to the Leaving. The sum of €3,000 was awarded for this victimisation, on top of €500 for 'the serious upset, disruption and inconvenience caused to him during his final Leaving Certificate year'.

The fourth decision, <u>A Male Student v. A Secondary School</u>, decided on 3 February 2009, was a decision by the same equality officer that a boy of 15 was discriminated against by the 'hair-length requirement imposed on a male student' by the school, because it had a 'much greater impact on him after school', awarding compensation of €1,000; but he rejected a claim by the student that he was 'verbally attacked' by a teacher outside the school, who 'screamed at him' for refusing to get his hair cut. The equality officer found 'insufficient evidence' to substantiate this claim of harassment.

The fifth decision, decided on 15 May 2009, <u>Mrs. A (on behalf of her son B) v. A Boys' National School</u>, dealt with the mother of a student claiming that he had been discriminated against on the disability ground, saying that the school had failed to make reasonable accommodation regarding this. He was suspended from school on two occasions, in May and June 2005, she claiming that it was due to behaviour that was a consequence of his disability.

The school said that it had actively engaged with a 'wide range of professionals' to provide for the complainant's educational requirements. The problem was that as he progressed in the school, 'his behaviour became a serious concern in that it was a danger for himself and others'. It was 'impacting negatively and seriously on the emotional, educational and general welfare' of the other children in the class. Despite this, 'every allowance was made for the complainant' because of his disability, and his parents were told of his striking his 'peers, special needs assistant and teacher'.

On January 2004, he struck his special needs assistant (SNA). It was suggested to his mother that she voluntarily withdraw him for three days, a sanction that would have been automatically imposed had he not been disabled. She refused, and in his seventh and final year in the school 'his dangerous behaviour was becoming so frequent and severe' that the board of management considered it necessary to suspend him in March and June 2005, when on the first occasion he struck his SNA and his teacher, and on the second his resource teacher. Both complaints were investigated, and he was suspended under the school's code of discipline. The school then suggested that a mainstream school was not the appropriate place for her son to be.

The equality officer held that there had been no discrimination by the school, which had engaged in reasonable accommodation of the student's needs. Indeed, he said that the school 'adopted a more lenient application of its code of discipline in this instance' than would have been the case 'if it had been dealing with a pupil without a disability'. He felt the evidence of the pupil's fourth-class teacher 'very compelling regarding the serious difficulties and disruption that the complainant's behaviour presented in the classroom situation' and of the 'extremely disproportionate amount of time that was necessary for him to dedicate to the complainant (as compared to other students in the class)'.

The sixth decision, <u>Mrs X (on behalf of her son, Mr Y) v. A Post-Primary School</u>, of 2 February 2010, dealt with a complaint on the disability, race and Traveller grounds, and in failing to put in place appropriate measures to accommodate his ADHD and special educational needs.

The student, from a few days of starting, 'displayed severe behavioural problems and a lack of ability to concentrate in class'. He was suspended for three days on 8 September 2005, due to an incident 'in which he had assaulted a student and intimidated other students on the basketball court'.

While the school said it had requested a number of meetings with the student's mother to discuss her son's difficulties, she failed to turn up. While efforts were made, Y 'continued to cause severe disruption in classes, was argumentative and aggressive towards others and regularly intimidated and bullied other students'. Y was suspended on two more occasions in 2006, due to incidents 'where he had been involved in the intimidation and bullying of other students'. Also his attendance record of 61 out of a possible 330 days was 'totally unacceptable'. Meetings requested with his mother were not attended by the latter. Through the Visiting Teacher for Travellers (VTT), the mother told the principal in March 2007 that she wanted him to attend the school on a full-day basis. She failed, however, to keep an appointment to discuss this.

No further contact was made with Mrs X till 31 August, when she came to the school to enrol two other students. She also said that she wanted her son to attend on a full-time basis for his third year. The school said that there were problems with this, due to his attending 'on so few days' in the last few years. At a meeting with the mother and the VTT, it was explained that it would not be in his interests or the other students to place him back in a mainstream third-year exam group due to his 'lack of attendance and behavioural difficulties'. An offer of resource teaching for five hours per week was later made. At an unrelated meeting on 7 November, the mother told the school that she was not concerned about her son, and refused to discuss the matter of his possible placement. On 8 November, the mother was written to by the principal, and asked that she set out her reasons for not wanting her son to attend, 'in view of his low attendance and to outline what had since changed'. The mother failed to respond to the letter. The school said its action was such that 'similar action would have been taken in respect of any other student with such a disability and behavioural propensities'.

The equality officer decided that, while the school had not discriminated against the student on the race and Traveller community grounds, he held that it had discriminated on the disability ground, in failing to provide reasonable accommodation in dealing with his absenteeism from school and the request he be returned to full-time education in September 2007.

He held that the measures put in place were 'not sufficient to accommodate' Y's special educational needs, his inappropriate behaviour or absenteeism from school. Also, the school did not fulfil its obligation to notify the education welfare officer under section 24(1) of the 2000 Act in terms of his non-attendance. While the assistant principal, acting as principal at the time, claimed that he had done so, what he offered as proof was 'of very little evidential value'. The equality officer therefore had 'great difficulty' in accepting 'the totality' of Mr Z's evidence that he had contacted the education welfare officer when he did. Also, the offer of five hours of resource teaching per week was not adequate to address his educational needs and comply with its obligations under section 9(a) of the 1998 Act.

He rejected the Traveller community discrimination ground, because there was another child in Y's class, 'a member of the settled community', and 'this student was subjected to the same disciplinary code and sanction of suspension in relation to his inappropriate behaviour'.

He awarded the sum of €3,000, taking into account the measures the school took to deal with Y's special educational requirements and the 'issues that arose in relation to his inappropriate behaviour'. Also, Mrs X 'failed to attend a number of meetings' scheduled by the school to discuss the issues regarding her son.

Also, he ordered that the respondent put in place a 'system that will facilitate the timely compliance' with its statutory obligations under the Education Welfare Act 2000.

The seventh decision, <u>Mr and Mrs X (on behalf of their son, Mr Y) v A Post-Primary School</u>, decided on 14 May 2010, concerned a student against a secondary school. The parents said that their son, Y, was discriminated against in terms of his disability, including contrary to section 7(2), in terms of access to education, failing to put appropriate measures in place to accommodate his special educational needs. They also alleged harassment contrary to section 11(5), and victimisation contrary to section 3(2)(j).

In terms of reasonable accommodation, the equality officer decided that it had been done, accepting the school's evidence that it 'was operating under certain constraints within the mainstream education sphere in terms of the resources available to it'. The special measures and facilities put in place were 'reasonable in the circumstances of the present case'.

Regarding the harassment complaint, the parents claimed 'excessive recording' when he was in the school, and an incident where Y's SNA used her phone to take a photograph of him during a woodwork class. The equality officer accepted the school's evidence that 'it encountered significant difficulties' in terms of Y's behaviour and was 'necessary for it to take appropriate action' to address this behaviour. He concluded he was not 'presented with any evidence' that the actions and measures taken by the school were 'in any way connected with his disability'. Regarding the mobile phone incident, the school said this was because Y was 'disruptive during the woodwork class', and the photo was taken 'as a means of bringing him to apply himself to the work'. The principal said that the SNA was requested to delete the photo from her phone; he acknowledged that the parents had been told that the actions were 'improper and unacceptable', and an apology was issued. The equality officer concluded that the manner in which the SNA acted was 'improper and totally inappropriate', but that it was a reaction to a disciplinary situation, not motivated by Y's disability. The victimisation complaint was dismissed. Two incidents named by the parents were that, first, Y's class was called to a 'special meeting' at the start of the school year in September 2007, in the course of which reference was made to 'the misbehaviour of seven students' during the previous year. Second, Y was not selected for the school hurling team due to the 'behavioural issues' that arose during a trip to Italy in October 2006. The equality officer rejected both, deciding that the meeting was called to deal with 'behavioural issues' that year involving seven students (including Y). Also, the school did not select Y for the hurling team as his 'level of performance on the field of play' did not 'merit selection'.

In the eighth decision, <u>A Pupil v A Primary School</u>, given on 30 July 2010, a student who had Down's Syndrome and verbal dyspraxia complained through his mother that his school treated him unlawfully during the academic year 2006–7, about which a special needs assistant had complained to the Guards.

Such unlawful treatment included the teacher 'regularly' humiliating the complainant student. Also, the SNA said the complainant was not 'complimented or positively encouraged' as other children, without disabilities, were. He was disciplined in 'a very harsh and impatient manner', with no allowances made for his disability.

When the complainant received extra tuition for approximately twenty minutes with the SNA, the latter was instructed to take him and two chairs into an adjacent cloakroom for this activity. As she felt that the cloakroom was quite dark and claustrophobic, she moved the chairs into the corridor. She stated that the school principal would pass by at times and seemed to accept the arrangement.

She also claimed that the complainant would become more relaxed in her company, away from the classroom, because he was 'afraid of his teacher and the regular humiliation he would experience in her presence'.

The school denied such discrimination and lack of reasonable accommodation, explaining that the cloakroom was used as a quiet space with all children because the school had limited space. A number of other SNAs and a resource teacher who gave evidence at the hearings denied that SNA's version of events. That teacher and the principal also refuted allegations against them.

The equality officer found that there was reasonable accommodation of the complainant's disability. The cloakroom was 'used as a quiet space where pupils, regardless of whether they had a disability or not, were taken by SNAs to get extra tuition in their school work'. That space was used 'simply because the respondent school, like many schools in this state, operates in cramped conditions'. The issue of reasonable accommodation only arises where 'it can be shown that without special assistance, facilities and/or treatment it would be unduly difficult or impossible for a person with a disability to avail of the educational service'. The complainant was for most of the time treated 'in a similar manner to the way the rest of the children in his class were treated'.

The equality officer found the SNA's evidence 'not consistent or compelling', also pointing out that ten months had passed before she 'reported an incident that a reasonable person, in this Tribunal's view, would have reported immediately'. The other SNAs who worked with the complainant all denied 'ever having seen the teacher mistreat the complainant or humiliate him'. The complainant's resource teacher's evidence in favour of the class teacher was 'compelling'.

The equality officer found that the complaint was 'entirely without merit', there being 'no evidence' to support discrimination and humiliation of the complainant because of his disability. Also, it was 'remarkable' that the complainant's parent continued to make such an argument considering that she stated he was 'currently flourishing' in the school, in which she chose to keep him and other children.

The ninth decision was <u>Mrs Z (on behalf of her three children) v. A National School</u>, decided on 30 December 2010, which involved a mother claiming that she and her three children were discriminated against by the respondent school on the Traveller and race grounds when she wanted them re-enrolled there in June 2008. Mrs Z also claimed that she was discriminated against by the respondent on the grounds of her gender in terms of section 3(2)(a). She also claimed that she was subjected to harassment by the respondent within the meaning of section 11 of the Equal Status Acts.

Her three sons had been attending the school until the end of May 2008, when the family moved to another town and they were enrolled in another primary school. She returned to the original town, and, as her sons were absent only two to three weeks from the original school, she tried to have them re-enrolled there. She told the VTT that her sons were returning, and the VTT left a voice message on the principal's phone. The complainant stated that she dropped her three sons to the school on 9 June, believing that the school had been informed of their return. Later that morning, she was asked to telephone the school, did so and spoke to the principal, Mr B, who was 'very irate', because he was not informed of her sons' return. She claimed that he spoke to her 'as if she was a dog and not a human being', this being because she was a Traveller and a female parent. The complainant stated that when she went to the school that afternoon to collect her children, she told the school secretary that she was taking her sons out because of the manner in which she had been treated by Mr B. Her eldest son told her that his teacher had said to him 'look at you the cheek of you' during the course of his class. Mr B then took him and put him sitting on a chair outside his office. Also, another teacher left another son sitting on the tiled area of the classroom where the children eat their lunch, with no work during that school day. The complainant claimed that her children were subjected to this treatment by the respondent because of their Traveller identity.

The complainant also stated that her eldest son had been bullied while previously attending the respondent school, though she admitted that this issue had not been brought up at that time.

The respondent denied the allegations, saying it had an inclusive policy in accepting children. Mr B also stated that he had always had a cordial relationship with Mrs Z, and that he had facilitated her in every way with regard to her children's education at the school. He also stated that he was 'very surprised' about their return, since no contact had been made with either himself or the school about this.

Mr B stated that he spoke to the complainant in a normal tone of voice during the relevant telephone conversation. He stated that she did not express any anger with him during the conversation, or make any reference or complaint regarding the manner in which he had spoken to her. The respondent also denied that the complainant's children had been singled out for inappropriate treatment or punished in any way. The issue which caused it difficulty was the manner in which the children were returned to the school. As the complainant had always had a very good relationship with Mr B, it should have been possible for her to call into his office that morning when dropping her children to school, to inform him of the situation.

The equality officer decided against the complainant, saying she failed to establish a case of discrimination on the Traveller, gender and race grounds. The school's evidence that it had difficulty regarding the way the re-enrolment was carried out was accepted, particularly due to the 'good relationship which they [Mr B and Mrs Z] had enjoyed in the past'. He would have spoken to a non-Traveller parent or a male parent in the same manner, due to the circumstances. Mr B's account of the telephone conversation was 'more compelling'; the manner in which he spoke to Mrs Z on this occasion could not be construed as harassment on the grounds of her Traveller identity. The alleged bullying of the eldest son had not been brought to the attention of the respondent during his previous attendance at the school. Furthermore, the complainant gave no evidence to suggest that such bullying, even if it occurred, was in any way attributable to his Traveller identity.

In the tenth decision, <u>Mrs K (and on behalf of her son) v. A Primary School</u> decided on 18 January 2011, Mrs K claimed that both she and her son were discriminated against by the respondent on the grounds of their family status, race and membership of the Traveller community in terms of sections 3(1), 3(2)(c), (h), (i) of the Acts, and contrary to section 7(2), in the way it dealt with her son's application for enrolment at the respondent's primary school during the academic year 2007/8. Mrs K also claimed that she was subjected to victimisation and harassment contrary to sections 3(2) (j) and 11(1) of the Acts.

She sent a formal letter to the school on 16 November 2007 requesting the enrolment of her son; and the VTT later sent a letter on 19 December seeking a formal reply, pointing out that under section 19(3) of the Education (Welfare) Act, written requests for enrolment had to be responded to in writing by the school's board of management, giving its decision, within twenty-one days.

Mrs K later decided to make an appeal, under section 29 of the Education Act, due to this delay, the hearing scheduled to be heard on 8 April. On 2 April she received a letter saying that the school would enrol her son if she withdrew the appeal, which she did.

A number of meetings took place with the principal, Mr B, and the school secretary, involving the correct uniform and books for her son, and the financial assistance to purchase them.

She denied that, one day, she became 'verbally abusive' towards either the school secretary or Mr B. Mrs K stated that she returned to the school with her son on 21 April 2008, as he now had the appropriate books and uniform, and spoke to Mr B. She stated that he spoke to her 'in a degrading manner', referred to a number of errors that she had made in completing the enrolment form, and said that her son could not start at the school that day unless she produced a copy of his birth certificate. She said that her son was excluded from starting classes due to his Traveller identity; and she had been harassed and victimised due to the way her son's enrolment was dealt with by the respondent.

The respondent denied this discrimination, saying it had Traveller students, including the two other sons of the complainant. It said that at one meeting, where she was looking for a letter to state that her son was attending the school, to obtain financial assistance in buying a school uniform, and when the school secretary could not provide such a letter as Mrs K's son was not then attending the school, the latter 'became verbally abusive towards Mr B on this occasion and accused the school of being racist'. At the later meeting, when Mr B spoke about the enrolment form and the birth certificate, Mrs K again 'became verbally abusive and called him "a dirty racist b.....d"'.

The failure to allow the son to start classes was due to his mother's refusal to cooperate and comply with standard requirements for enrolment demanded of all students.

The equality officer's decision was that the school 'failed to provide any reason' why it took four months to decide regarding the application for enrolment of Mrs K's son at the school or why it failed to comply with its statutory obligations under section 19(3) of the Education (Welfare) Act. The reason why was due to his membership of the Traveller community.

The son was not allowed to begin class because he did not meet the requirements for enrolment, not due to his Traveller identity. The respondent's evidence was found to be 'more credible' about the final meeting. That Mrs K called Mr B 'a racist b.....d' was 'undisputed'. Therefore, the equality officer rejected Mrs K's contention that the respondent attempted to obstruct her attempts to enrol her son in the school after it had agreed to offer him a place on 2 April 2008, being satisfied that the reason why he was unable to start school was because of the fact that he did not meet the standard requirements. Accordingly, the complainants failed to establish a prima facie case of discrimination on the Traveller community ground in relation to this element of their complaint.

They also failed to establish a case of discrimination on family status, race and victimisation grounds, or a case of harassment under the Equal Status Acts.

Also found, however, was that the respondent discriminated against the complainants on the Traveller community ground in terms of section 3(2)(i) and contrary to section 7(2) of the Equal Status Acts in terms of the manner in which it dealt with their application for enrolment, that is, the fact that it took four months to make a decision about it. The complainants were awarded €3,500 as redress for the effects of that discrimination.

Also ordered by the equality officer, in accordance with Section 27(1)(b) of the Acts, was that the respondent put in place a system that would ensure 'timely compliance' with its obligations under the Education (Welfare) Act in dealing with applications for the enrolment of pupils.

The eleventh decision, <u>Lee Irwin suing through his next friend William Irwin v Duiske College</u>, of 5 March 2012, involved one of unlawful discrimination on the gender ground in the Acts. The complainant, then a fifth-year student, said that the respondent college discriminated against him by requesting that he remove patches of red hair dye from his hair in accordance with its code of conduct, he being then suspended from the school due to this rule, which prohibited male students from dyeing their hair, and which did not apply to female pupils, some of them attending the school with blue dye in their hair.

The school refuted the complainant's claim that 'girls could do what they wanted' in it. 'Every pupil in the school must abide by the code of conduct.' An alleged demand to have the complainant shave off his hair made by a member of staff was refuted. The complainant's next friend and father was alleged to be 'irate, intemperate and abusive' when the respondent attempted to engage with him about the issue, preferring to go to the media.

The rule in question was changed as soon as the new term began, the matter being addressed at a board of management meeting (at the end of August 2010). The school said that parents who are aware of the contents of a code of conduct and have signed up to it 'must take the school as they find it'. There were other options to solving this issue.

The equality officer found that the complainant was 'in breach of the respondent's code of conduct'. He and his next friend were 'on notice of the rule', and the former had been warned by a teacher the day before the incident not to dye his hair. His actions were 'deliberate and the respondent had no choice but to enforce the rule'. The complainant 'was aware of the potential consequences of his actions'.

While the rule was 'unfair', the equality officer did not find that it 'in any meaningful way oppressed a person's gender identity or made it impossible for a male person to participate in the educational establishment'. There were 'more appropriate means' of challenging the unfairness of the rule. The school's actions were 'reasonable in the circumstances', and while redress would be awarded 'for the impact of the discriminatory rule', the manner in which the complainant and his next friend challenged the issue was criticised. 'It is a well established rule of law that when a parent consents to a code of conduct they are bound by it.'

The equality officer found that the complainant established a prima facie case of discrimination on the gender ground, and awarded him €150.

The twelfth decision, <u>A Mother, on behalf of her Son v Board of Management of a Boys' National School</u>, one of 11 April 2012, involved a mother, on behalf of her son, who had Down's Syndrome with moderate learning difficulties and a speech impediment, who claimed the board of management of a school discriminated against him on the disability ground, and it refused or failed to reasonably accommodate his needs as a person with a disability.

According to his mother, the student was badly treated in September 2009, the first month of his being in sixth class. During the first fortnight, the complainant's class was taught by a substitute teacher, Mr S. During the second fortnight, the class was taught by the class teacher for the year, Ms S.

The mother claimed that the substitute teacher treated her son less favourably than other boys without a disability. A number of incidents were mentioned, his father, who was also his SNA, witnessing one of them.

When the class teacher returned, she spoke to the complainant's father that she had seen an advert in a newspaper for a special school and that his parents should perhaps think about sending him to the school for a day or two a week. His parents regarded this as acting 'way beyond her remit'.

Also, Ms S. asked his SNA to remove him from class for thirty minutes as she wanted to set a test for the other boys in the class. This had never happened before and was discriminatory. The SNA was working on a one-to-one basis with the complainant at the back of the class. Ms S. approached and said in an aggressive manner, 'I can't have this talking.' So the SNA gave the complainant some non-verbal written work and sat him with the rest of the class where he normally did his writing.

The school's board of management later said it 'acknowledges and sincerely regrets any upset, distress and hurt' felt by the parents on behalf of their son. It said a number of factors were responsible. Mr S. did not deny that two incidents happened, but he insisted that it 'wasn't at all like it was reported in the letter of complaint'.

It was also unfortunate that the complainant's resource/support teacher, Ms R., was unavoidably absent from school on sick leave during this time, and the complainant was not in receipt of his allocated resource teaching time of forty-five minutes per day.

The board held that a specific request by the SNA to the principal, when allegations of discrimination were made on 17 September, not to 'look into it further', when the latter asked if he would like him to look at the matter further, put the principal in the difficult position of knowing a difficulty existed but being effectively prevented from intervening at that point.

The equality officer decided that the 'fundamental problem' was because both Ms S. and Ms R. were unavoidably absent during the first two weeks of the school year. While a plan was agreed between the SNA, the class teacher and the principal, on the balance of probabilities, the 'substitute teacher misunderstood his role vis-à-vis the complainant'.

In this case, it was the belief of the school, based on what was agreed, that the complainant was receiving adequate education during the two weeks in question. Matters could have been tackled earlier if the complainant's father (as his SNA) had raised the issue sooner. The lack of engagement by the substitute teacher with the complainant was not discrimination. The reading incident, a one-off event, was not 'a less favourable term or condition of participation' within the meaning of the Act and was therefore not discriminatory.

The equality officer believed that Ms S. asked the SNA to take the complainant outside while she set a test for the class because she understood that: a) the test should be conducted in silence; and b) the complainant would require his SNA to talk him through his test. It was not because of his disability that he was asked to sit his test outside. The allegation that Ms S suggested sending the complainant to a special school was an approach made 'in good faith'.

The complainant alleged that Ms S. discriminated against him or denied reasonable accommodation by demanding quiet from the SNA while she was teaching and by directing him to sit at the back of the class. The board of management considered that the dispute about noise in the classroom could have been better handled by the class teacher. The equality officer did not consider that the actions of the teacher were directly or indirectly discriminatory on the ground of disability, because a teacher must be allowed 'a certain autonomy' under the Acts in how he or she teaches and controls a class.

The equality officer also found that the school made reasonable accommodation for the student. While the standard of education fell below what was usually offered by the school during the relevant period, this was due to 'exceptional circumstances', and was 'not of sufficient gravity' to bring it under the meaning of discrimination under the Acts.

The thirteenth decision, <u>A Parent (on behalf of her son) v. Board of Management of a Primary School</u>, of 12 July 2012, concerned a mother on behalf of her son, who had dyspraxia, over the alleged failure of a school to process an application to enrol him on the disability ground, in terms of sections 4(1) and 7(2) of the Acts.

It was accepted that the son, when in another school, experienced 'persistent bullying'. After he was moved from the junior to the senior school 'the bullying persisted', despite the school management being informed. His parents decided to enrol him in the respondent school, in which his mother was a teacher.

Soon after her request to enrol her son in that school, a letter from the principal was received refusing the application. It referred to 'her son's disability and the requirement for resource teaching and special needs assistance'. The Board of Management supported his decision; so the complainant appealed under section 29 of the Education Act, and was successful. She claimed that the school did not comply with the instruction to offer her son a place 'as soon as possible', offering one only two days before the end of the summer holidays. By that time, she had found him a place in another school.

The equality officer found in favour of the complainant. She took into account the principal's refusal of a place on the stated grounds that the boy 'would require resource help and possible special needs assistance and the staff of the school were not in a position to meet his educational and social needs as the resource and special needs team was overloaded'. This was a refusal on the grounds of the boy's disability and a failure to offer reasonable accommodation.

The maximum sum of €6,348.69 was awarded, the equality officer taking into account the fact that the boy was being bullied in the school 'and he could not move from that school for a considerable period of time'. If the respondent had not discriminated against him 'he could have moved much earlier'.

The fourteenth decision, A Pupil (through his next friend and father) v. A School, decided on 16 July 2013, involved the father of a student, who claimed that his son was discriminated against and harassed due to having a disability. The father claimed that the school was: intimidating his son in front of the class; dismissing the complainant when he attempted to explain matters to his teachers; not compensating him for stolen property; not providing him with a free rugby jersey; leaving him outside the vice-principal's office for hours; and omitting to inform his parents when he left the school without permission.

The equality officer rejected this complaint, finding that the son was not a person with a disability under the Acts; and there was no evidence of adverse treatment to warrant a finding of victimisation.

Conclusion

While these cases and decisions relate to discrimination, harassment and victimisation under nine grounds specified in legislation, they have, in four instances, also taken account of: a school's lack of fair procedures; two schools' non-observance of the Education (Welfare) Act; and the fact that even when a school rule was discriminatory, and compensation awarded for this, the way the student 'deliberately' breached it meant that the school's action disciplining him for this was 'reasonable'. These failures to comply with constitutional and statutory provisions, as well as a school rule, are also relevant in non-Equality Act situations. Schools should comply with the law, and can reasonably enforce their rules. If they do this, they can escape, or at least reduce their exposure to, the case law I have already described and will describe.

6. Segregation

In England, there was an important case: <u>R (on the application of L) v Governors of J School</u> [2003] 1 AER, 1012, that could possibly be followed in Ireland. It involved the expulsion of a student from a school, followed by his reinstatement. Threatened with industrial action by the teachers, the school set up a regime where he was taught separately from the other students. The case eventually came before the House of Lords, based on whether this regime really amounted to 'reinstatement'. The United Kingdom House of Lords was the court of last resort for most UK cases. It was replaced in this role by the Supreme Court of the United Kingdom on 1 October 2009.

Their lordships found in favour of the school. While there has been, as yet, no equivalent Irish case, I believe that, after taking into account our constitution, statute law, and case law, a similar decision might be reached here. Because of this, the details of this case are worth looking at.

A serious assault, involving student L, took place at J School. The head teacher expelled him, a decision later upheld by the school's governing body. L's parents then appealed to an independent appeals panel, which ordered his reinstatement, on the grounds that fair procedures were not followed.

The teaching staff, through their unions, voted for industrial action short of a strike, refusing to teach or supervise L. The latter's parents threatened legal action against the school, following a meeting between them and the head teacher, when he told them of the vote, but that L was reinstated on the school roll.

L later returned to the school, and was subjected to the following regime. He was not brought back into mainstream classes; instead he was taught and supervised separately, during the school day, on his own, by a retired maths teacher who was not a union member. Teachers in the other subjects set him work, which they marked. He was to stay in the room, except for toilet breaks, during the day, and he was not to speak to or associate with any other student (except for another student who joined him, excluded for the same incident and also successful on appeal), or any staff member save his supervisor or those who wanted to visit him. Provisions were made for transport to and from school and for lunch.

This regime lasted for thirty days, ten before the end of the Easter term and twenty before the students went on study leave.

L sought judicial review of the school's actions, arguing that the previously described regime was not 'reinstatement'. Their lordships found by a three to two majority in favour of the school. One of the majority judges, Lord Hobhouse, held:

> It is obvious that a pupil who has committed a serious disciplinary offence for which he was thought to merit permanent exclusion may, when that solution is found to be not available, still have to receive special treatment. Trust may have been destroyed; the capacity and inclination to disrupt may be undiminished; the risk of physical injury to others may still exist. Factors such as these may not unreasonably lead to responses from the teaching staff which, unless accommodated, put at risk the education of some or all of the other pupils of the school.

We have already looked at Irish cases involving the suspension or expulsion of a student from a school: Smullen, Student A and Student B, James Wright and Alexander Wright, McKenna, and O'Donovan.

What could an Irish school do if, after following fair procedures, it expels a student who is violent and abusive; and reinstatement is then ordered, whether by a court order or by a recommendation of an appeals committee to the secretary-general; and the teachers, via their union, decide after a lawful ballot not to supervise or teach the student? Can the school, invoking section 24(5) of the Education (Welfare) Act, set up a scheme of segregation similar to that in the case of R v. Governors of J School?

It is possible that an Irish court might find in such a school's favour, but only on certain grounds. First, all reasonable efforts would need to be taken to keep the student's education up to prescribed standards, and second, the segregation would have to be of a short duration. Even in the circumstances of the English case, J School's policy was only upheld by a small majority.

7. Continuing suspension

There have been two cases in the United Kingdom in this area, where a student's suspension was carried out as a precaution, pending an official decision. First was the House of Lords decision in A v. Head Teacher and Governors of Lord Grey School [2006] 2 WLR, 690, which dealt with the question as to whether keeping a student from school while criminal charges were pending against him, but while he had access to education elsewhere, violated his right to an education under Article 2 of the First Protocol of the European Convention on Human Rights. I have already mentioned that the UK has, like Ireland, incorporated the Convention into its domestic law in its Human Rights Act 1998.

Abdul Hakim Ali was one of three pupils charged with arson, after a fire occurred in the school. All were released on bail. The school judged that Ali should not attend while the criminal investigation and any prosecution were in train, and he was excluded for successive periods.

The forty-five-day cap on a maximum period of exclusions within the school year on 'disciplinary grounds', under the legislation then in force, section 64 of the School Standards and Framework Act 1998, expired on 6 June 2001, the school having under the law either to readmit the claimant or exclude him permanently. The school did not seek to exclude him permanently, as it was awaiting the outcome of the criminal proceedings. The Crown Prosecution Service told Ali's solicitors, but not the school, on 18 June that the prosecution had been discontinued due to lack of evidence. The head teacher received a fax about this on 22 June, and was officially notified of this decision by the police on 3 July.

On the latter date, she wrote to Ali's parents, inviting them to a meeting on 13 July. Neither he nor his parents came to the meeting. The next contact of his family with the school was on 6 November, when his father wrote to the head teacher seeking his son's reinstatement. The school said that, because they had heard nothing from him, the claimant's place had been given to another student, and his year group was oversubscribed, so that the school could not take him back. Ali began attending another school on 21 January 2002.

He took a case that ended up before the House of Lords, invoking sections 6 and 8 of the Human Rights Act 1998, claiming that the school's action was unlawful, violating his right to an education under Article 2 of the First Protocol, and claiming damages.

The court held four to one in favour of the school. The majority judgement of Lord Bingham recognised the dilemma the school faced. Because the fire involved a serious crime, 'Respect for the respondent and for the integrity of the criminal justice process in my opinion required that he should not attend the school until the matter was cleared up'. The problem was that while the legislation made it clear that at the end of the forty-five day period, the school 'had no choice but to re-admit the respondent or exclude him permanently', such re-admission 'with a criminal prosecution in train, was inappropriate'. So was permanent exclusion. If the school 'acted inconsistently with the requirements of domestic law, the inadequacy of the law contributed to that result'.

Looking at the guarantee in Article 2 of the First Protocol of the Convention, he said that it was 'intended to guarantee fair and non-discriminatory access to that system by those within the jurisdiction of the respective states'. He called the guarantee 'a weak one, and deliberately so. There is no right of a particular kind or quality [of education], other than that prevailing in the state'. The test of compatibility was 'a highly pragmatic one to be applied to the specific facts of the case'. Looking at whether, between the dates of 7 June 2001 and 20 January 2002, the school 'denied the respondent effective access to such facilities as this country provides', the judge held that it did not. The school:

> invited the parents to collect course work for the claimant which they did not. It referred the respondent to the LEA's (Local Education Authorities) access panel, which referred him to the pupil referral unit, an education provider; the pupil referral unit's offer of tuition was declined ... The LEA's attempts during the autumn to secure the respondent's readmission to another school were thwarted by the family's uncertainty about what they wanted. As soon as they made up their minds, a place (though not at the school) was promptly found.

Supporting his colleague was Lord Hoffman, who also looked into the question of a 'precautionary exclusion' of a student from a school. While the existing statutory framework did not accommodate this, dealing only with exclusion on disciplinary grounds, he suggested that it was possible that a school had 'as part of its general powers of management, the right to exclude a pupil on precautionary grounds, limited only by the need that it should be reasonably exercised'.

Another majority judge, Lord Scott, argued that the students were kept away by the principal as 'a management decision'. He explained that 'the management powers of a head teacher enable him or her to keep a pupil temporarily away from the school for reasons that have nothing to do with discipline. An obvious example is that of a pupil who arrives at school suffering from some infectious disease.' If the pupil's parents and guardians did not agree to that person being sent home until 'no longer infectious', the head teacher 'would, in my opinion, have power to impose it'. In his opinion, the exclusion was 'at no stage unlawful under domestic law'.

This case was used as a precedent by the Supreme Court of the United Kingdom, the House of Lords' replacement, in the case of In the matter of an application by 'JR17' for Judicial Review [2010] UKSC, 27. The principal of a school in Northern Ireland suspended a Year 12 student for five days on 7 February 2007. The suspension was reviewed for three more periods of five days until 13 March, the student's teachers preparing schoolwork for him, left for him to collect. Between the latter date and 20 April the student was given home tuition, at the end of which period he and other students in that year could attend school or stay at home to study for their GCSE exams. In June, he returned to the school to sit those exams. The student sought judicial review of the principal's decision to suspend him, also arguing that his right to an education under Article 2 of the First Protocol had been breached. His case was rejected by the initial judge and the Court of Appeal and ended up before the Supreme Court.

On 31 January 2007, the principal was approached by two female students at the school, and was told by one, A, that she was terrified of the student's conduct, both inside and outside the school. She did not want to formally complain and did not want the principal to tell the latter that she had done so. Later that day, the other student came to see the principal to say that A was thinking of suicide. He spoke to A's mother, who said that she too was concerned about her daughter's state of mind and the possibility of suicide.

On 1 February, there was a 'multi-disciplinary case conference' arranged by Social Services to consider the student, because allegations had been made against him of 'criminal offences of a sexual and violent nature outside the school'. It was 'not in any way related to the complaint' made by student A. A risk assessment meeting was then held on 6 February, when reference was made to four alleged offences discussed on 1 February. The principal, on hearing of this, said he decided then to protect A's identity and prevent any further deterioration in her mental health, and to not tell the student of her complaint. He decided to suspend him as a precautionary measure and arrange for his education off site, as he did not have enough resources to ensure 'constant monitoring and supervision' of the student in school.

On 7 February the principal told the student in his office that allegations had been made against him regarding his behaviour, but 'he [the principal] could not go into them'. It was decided 'in the interests of everybody' that the student be suspended, which the principal did, with measures being taken to ensure the student's continuing education. There was no evidence that the Social Services' assessment of the student was ever completed, and no risk assessment of him was ever carried out.

All five Supreme Court judges granted the student's appeal, ruling that his suspension was unlawful, but that there was no breach of his Convention rights. In terms of the unlawfulness of the suspension, the law in force was looked at. Sir John Dyson, who gave the most extensive judgement of all the five judges, held that the student was suspended on 'disciplinary grounds', but that this was a clear breach of the scheme in force drawn up by the relevant Education and Library Board. (The scheme made it clear that suspension for a 'prescribed period' should only be 'after a period of indiscipline' and or after 'a serious incident of indiscipline', when the school has investigated and documented the incident, including the pupil being interviewed and that person's version of events given before the decision to suspend is made.) Lord Phillips held that the disciplinary scheme made no provision for a precautionary suspension, therefore the appellant's suspension was unlawful. Lord Rodger held that the principal acted unlawfully, and did not believe it could be implied into a principal's general management powers a power to suspend on 'a precautionary basis'; and if a scheme should have such a power, it was a matter for the Northern Ireland Executive. Lord Brown agreed with Lord Rodger, saying that even if a precautionary power existed, which he said it did not, 'it could never properly have been exercised in this way'.

While four of the judges expressed sympathy with the situation the principal found himself in, one of them in particular, Lord Rodger, was critical of the fact that the principal did not investigate the allegations himself, leaving the matter to an outside agency, who did not. He commented that:

On the basis of an allegation of bullying, not involving physical violence, the appellant was suspended for many weeks. This was, in all probability, a more severe consequence than would have been imposed on him even supposing that the incident had been investigated properly, misconduct on his part had been established and he had been punished for it under the school's current discipline policy.

Regarding his Convention rights, four of the five judges agreed that there was no breach of the Convention. Sir John Dyson agreed with Lord Bingham's judgement at Paragraph 24 in the Lord Grey School case, something followed by his three fellow judges. The fifth, Lady Hale, made no declaration on the matter, saying that the appellant had 'achieved just satisfaction' on the first ground.

As I said, the case could be invoked in an Irish court, Ireland having also incorporated the Convention into its domestic law. The issue would be whether the school and other relevant bodies acted reasonably in ensuring that a student's right to an education was fulfilled, after an official decision was taken not to prosecute, or take any other action.

8. Responsibilities outside school

A school has a duty of care towards its students within the school grounds during school hours, and at other places and times when the students are on school-authorised and supervised activities. But what happens when this is not the case, when a student bullies another student from the same school outside of that school, outside of school hours? What can the school do? May it discipline that student who bullies?

The answer appears to be 'Yes', in certain cases. The case of The State (Derek Smullen and Declan Smullen) v. Duffy and Others, previously mentioned, involved the High Court upholding a principal's decision, after an investigation, to suspend a number of students involved in a fight outside school, 'in order to maintain peace and discipline within the school'. This was followed by another High Court judge in Student A and Student B v. Dublin Secondary School, who held that such 'exceptional circumstances ... e.g. where there is danger to life and property' in Smullen could justify 'immediate or even long term suspension without notice or procedure'.

There was a Supreme Court case which, while not bullying related, did look at the question of where a school's responsibilities lay, in terms of time and distance: <u>Shane Dolan v. Timothy Keohane and Michael Cunningham</u> (Unreported, 8 February 1994). A primary school was 115 yards away at a diagonal from a secondary school. The plaintiff, then 9, was a pupil at the former school. In general, the primary school students would leave their school at 3.00 p.m. and be collected five to ten minutes later, by two to three privately owned buses. The collection point was in the vicinity of the secondary school's entrance.

The latter was a gate of two sections, that could swing in or out. The primary school students had a habit of getting onto a section, and swinging it in, using one foot on the ground and another on the gate. In this case, the section the plaintiff was on moved forward, catching two fingers of his left hand between a pillar and the gate, crushing them.

The High Court judge held that there was 'no evidence' that the teachers in either school knew of the practice of swinging on the gate. He held that it was 'unreasonable' that the primary school teachers had an obligation to supervise the student, when he had 'crossed to the other side of the road and walked an appreciable distance to the gate of the secondary school'. He said that 'children of the plaintiff's then age can get into mischief of various sorts between the time they leave the school grounds and arrive home'. He held that the plaintiff was 'well outside the ambit of any possible duty of supervision on the part of the primary school teachers by the time he reached the gate'.

This decision was upheld on appeal by the Supreme Court, Flaherty J. giving the main judgement. The secondary school teachers, he held, had 'no duty' to supervise the plaintiff at that point. While there were 'clearly cases where the duty to supervise does not end at the school gate', this case was not one of them. Denham J. agreed with O'Flaherty J., saying that the accident occurred outside the primary school's grounds. While she said that there would be liability in other circumstances, such as when 'a young pupil is off the school premises owing to a lack of care of the school', this was not one of these. She went on to say that there was no knowledge of the teachers of either school of the practice of swinging on the gate. While there 'may well be circumstances' where a school 'is responsible for children on their way home, where, for example, the school has knowledge of a dangerous situation, this is not one of those'.

This was in contrast to an earlier Supreme Court judgement, <u>Christina Hosty v. Patrick McDonagh, Canon Hyland and Another</u> (Unreported, 29 May 1973). This decision was given by Fitzgerald

CJ., appealing a High Court award of damages for negligence. The plaintiff, a schoolgirl, then 10 years old, left her school as part of a group of three girls, at around 12.30 p.m., through a double gate. She was struck by a car, both her legs were broken and her scalp lacerated. She made 'a remarkably good recovery' and had 'no permanent disability'. The court reduced the damages awarded to the plaintiff, holding her to be 30% liable, while the first defendant, the car's driver, was 45% liable, and the second defendant 25% liable, for not having a suitable exit from the school, not having it supervised and allowing the plaintiff onto the road unattended.

There have also been two English cases where the duty of the school, in less serious circumstances, has been looked at. In the case of R v. London Borough of Newham and Another ex parte X [1995] ELR, 303, action was taken by a head teacher of a secondary school against a 15-year-old student, X, who 'according to certain versions of events, received insults from another, slightly younger, boy and, in response, he took the boy's trousers and, possibly, his underpants and his socks and shoes off and humiliated him'.

The head teacher, after X admitted what had happened, decided to expel him from the school. While the student's parents came round, after his mother had been telephoned, 'they were not given an opportunity to make representations on X's behalf because the decision [to expel] had already been made' by the governing body. When the mother sought a postponement of the meeting of the governors' panel, to which she had the right of appeal, to discuss her son's expulsion, in order to have more time to gather statements and obtain advice, this was refused, the panel confirming the expulsion.

The parents sought judicial review of the decision to expel, and the judge, Brooke J., of the Queen's Bench Division of the High Court, granted leave to seek such a review, saying even if what happened was 'fair', the 'appropriateness' of the penalty of total expulsion of a 15-year-old boy in his GCSE year, 'without any reliance on previous complaints about his misconduct in relation to his activities outside the school premises' was not.

What is interesting is that the judge rejected an argument that 'the head teacher has no authority in relation to behaviour off the school premises'. He said:

> I think it would be a very sad thing if head teachers did not have authority, in an appropriate case, to use disciplinary action in relation to the behaviour of pupils of the school towards each other off the school premises.

In this case, however, he held that there was 'a strong prima facie case' that there was a breach of the rules of fairness in the way the student had been treated, and that the penalty was 'disproportionate to the offence'.

This case and others was looked at in the Court of Appeal's judgement in <u>Leah Bradford-Smart v. West Sussex County Council</u> [2002] 1 FCR, 425. The plaintiff attended a school maintained by the defendant authority, and claimed that she had been bullied by fellow students both at school and on the way home from school. In particular, in Year 3 (1992–3) there was bullying and threats against her outside of school. While the class teacher, Mrs Ashworth, agreed that this took place, and that this on occasion made Leah fearful of going out into the playground, she was 'adamant' that Leah was not bullied in school.

The Court of Appeal accepted that the bullying which took place during that year, at home or on the way to and from school, 'was not allowed to and did not spill over into school'. Leah was 'closely and affectionately monitored' by Mrs Ashworth.

It held that the school 'does not have the charge of its pupils all the time and so cannot directly protect them from harm all the time. At a day school that charge will usually end at the school gates, although the school will have a duty to take reasonable steps to ensure that young children who are not old enough to look after themselves do not leave the school premises unattended.' There are circumstances where a school's duty 'might go beyond that, for example if it were reasonable for a teacher to intervene when he saw one pupil attacking another immediately outside the school gates'. It would 'clearly extend further afield if the pupils are on a school trip, educational, recreational, or sporting'. But the school:

> cannot owe a general duty to its pupils, or anyone else, to police their activities once they have left its charge. This is principally the duty of parents and, where criminal offences are involved, the police.

While some schools patrol 'areas of concern' outside school to prevent incidents after the students have left, the court agreed with the initial judge that 'this is a matter of discretion rather than duty'.

The school's duty to Leah herself 'cannot be faulted'. The class teacher knew the situation outside school and 'was taking thoroughly sensible and well-balanced steps', to prevent the same happening in school and to counteract any effects on 'her educational performance and development'.

The court pointed out that the nub of the complaint was not what the school did in relation to Leah herself 'but what it did *not* do in relation to the bullies who were pupils in the same school albeit in a different class'. While, in general, A has no duty to prevent B 'deliberately causing harm to C', there are 'exceptions' when A is in control of B. The court agreed with the judgement in <u>R v. London Borough of Newham</u> that 'there are circumstances in which a failure to exercise those [disciplinary] powers would be a breach of the school's duty of care to another pupil. We agree. We also agree that there may be circumstances in which a failure to exercise those powers would be a breach of the school's duty of care to another pupil.'

The question of whether the school breached its duty of care in failing to take action against any of the fellow students she said were bullying her outside school was looked at, in the light of professional opinion on the matter. The court concluded that:

> although we accept that a school may on occasions be in breach of duty for failing to take such steps as are within its power to combat harmful behaviour of one pupil towards another even when they are outside school, those occasions will be few and far between.

Experts agreed that 'where an incident between pupils outside school carried over into school a reasonable head teacher should investigate if it had a deleterious effect on the victim'. In this case there were 'no adverse effects' upon the student's educational performance and development 'clearly attributable' from what was going on. It was clear that 'a responsible body of professional opinion would have agreed that enough had been done'.

To conclude, the school acted correctly in dealing with the effects of the bullying *inside* the school, and had no obligation to deal with what happened outside. If bullying took place outside the school on school trips, that duty of care applies, as it would do if there was a teacher seeing bullying taking place immediately outside of the school. There is also the case where bullying outside school has effects on what happened in school. But absent these situations, the school has discretion to intervene. If it does, the <u>R</u> case indicates that it is protected. It does not, however, have the *legal obligation* to so intervene.

The situation in Ireland appears similar, and there is no reason why the Irish courts could not follow these two English cases. As an example, the case of <u>Student A and Student B v Dublin Secondary</u>

School dealt with the school disciplining two students caught smoking cannabis in a licensed premises where a private party was being held. It could discipline them because its zero tolerance policy towards drugs, specified in its code of conduct, covered students taking 'an illicit drug *at any time*' (my italics). The case dealt with whether the school followed fair procedures when it disciplined them. Its right to do so, even outside of school hours, was not questioned by the court.

9. Defamation online: Who is responsible?

This is a serious matter, due to the level of cyber-bullying in Ireland among school students. A survey carried out in 2008, of 3,004 12-year-old to 16-year-old students from nine post-primary schools, revealed that 13.9% reported they had been cyber-bullied within the past couple of months, and 8.6% confessed to cyber-bullying others. Of that sample, 12.2% reported that they had nasty web postings made about them on internet sites over the previous couple of months (O'Moore, 2012).

I previously discussed the Defamation Act 2009, and EU Directive 2000/31/EC, and promised to discuss relevant or possibly relevant case law. I will look at how it has been used to fix liability on service providers – internet service providers and those controlling websites (including social networking ones) – and suggest that it may also be used against parents and guardians. Also important is that even if those people mentioned are innocent third parties in defamation or other cases, the courts may require them to give information about wrongdoers to the plaintiffs.

a. Service providers

There have been a number of such cases, mostly from the UK, but including one Irish one, which looked at the UK cases, and which was recently itself looked at in a later UK case. I will end with the particularly interesting and important Irish Damien Tansey case.

The first case is the UK one of Godfrey v. Demon Internet Ltd [2001] QB, 201, where the plaintiff brought proceedings for libel against the defendants, an internet service provider, who carried a newsgroup, and stored postings for that newsgroup for a fortnight, within which its customers could read them. Among those postings was one which the plaintiff alleged was defamatory of himself.

The defendants claimed that they were not a publisher, and even if they were, they had no liability under section 1 of the Defamation Act 1996. The judge, Morland J., of the Queen's Bench Division of the High Court, held in favour of the plaintiff, pointing out that the defences under section 1(1)(b) and (c), that the defendants took 'reasonable care' in relation to the statement, and that they did not know and did not believe, that what they did 'caused or contributed' to the publication of a defamatory statement, failed.

He pointed out that when a fax from the plaintiff was received on 17 January 1997, 'the defendants knew of the defamatory posting but chose not to remove it from their Usenet news servers'.

He held that the defendants, 'whenever they transmit and whenever there is transmitted from the storage of their news server a defamatory posting, publish that posting to any subscriber to their ISP who accesses the newsgroup containing that posting'. Every time a customer of the defendant accesses that newsgroup and sees that defamatory posting, 'there is a publication to that customer'. The defendants 'did not play a purely passive role'; they chose to receive the postings 'to store them, to make them available to accessors and to obliterate them'.

He held that the defamatory posting was published by the defendants; and from 17 January 1997, they knew of the defamatory content of the posting, could not avail of the defence under section 1 of the 1996 Act; therefore their defence under it 'is, in law hopeless'. This judgement is interesting in an Irish context, because section 1 of the Defamation Act 1996 is similar to the provisions of section 27 of the Irish Defamation Act 2009 dealing with innocent publication, previously looked at.

The Godfrey case was looked at in a later one, Blunt v. Tilley and others [2007] 1 WLR, 1243, by a judge of the same division. That judge, Eady J., distinguished his colleague's judgement, holding that it did not apply in this case.

In Blunt, the plaintiff brought proceedings for libel against six defendants. The first to third defendants had posted defamatory statements on websites hosted by third parties, doing so by means of services provided by the fourth to sixth defendants, their respective internet service providers. The fourth to sixth defendants applied for orders to strike out proceedings against themselves, saying that they were not the publishers of the statements.

The judge looked at the Godfrey case, saying that it left open for consideration how a court in England 'should approach a situation where', by contrast with the situation in that case, 'an ISP had truly fulfilled no more than a passive role as owner of an electronic device through which defamatory postings were transmitted'.

The judge said that by contrast to the situation in Godfrey, where the ISP continued publication of the defamatory statement after the plaintiff's fax had been received, asking for its removal, in this case the plaintiff was relying on separate postings.

He held that 'as a matter of law that an ISP which performs no more than a passive role in facilitating postings on the internet cannot be deemed to be a publisher at common law'. Looking at the matter in detail, including taking into account EU Directive 2000/31/EC, and the relevant UK legislation, he concluded by agreeing to strike out the proceedings against the fourth to sixth defendants, saying that the claimant's 'remedies lie against the first to third defendants (if he can establish the necessary ingredients in respect of each)'.

The Blunt v. Tilley case was looked at by the Irish High Court in the case of Mulvaney & Ors v The Sporting Exchange Ltd trading as Betfair [2009] IEHC 133. The plaintiffs, who were bookmakers, claimed damages for libel; the defendants carried on business providing a betting exchange, mainly through a website. This website contained a forum, where registered customers could make comments regarding sports, betting and other matters.

Comments were posted on the forum by registered clients of the defendants, the respective third parties to the proceedings. The plaintiffs alleged that the inclusion of the relevant comments were a publication by the defendants of those comments and sued them for libel. This case was not a trial of the action; it was to decide in advance of that trial the applicability of Directive 2000/31/EC to the proceedings.

The judge, Clarke J., agreed with the decision in Blunt v. Tilley, in terms of the definition of 'intermediary service providers'. He held that as:

> the service provided by Betfair, through its Chatroom, clearly falls within the meaning of 'relevant service' as defined by the 2003 Regulations, it follows that Betfair, in providing this service, is a 'relevant service provider' and so an 'intermediary service provider' within the meaning of the 2003 Regulations. Betfair is, therefore, entitled to the benefits of Regulations 15 and 18 of the 2003 Regulations.

The judge therefore accepted that the defendants could seek to rely on the 'hosting' defence in Article 15 of the EU Directive, made part of Irish law by Regulation 18 of SI No. 68/2003. They would need to establish, he said, 'as a matter of fact, in each individual case, that the conditions concerning knowledge and expeditious action set out in subparas (a) and (b) of Article 14 of the E-Commerce Directive are met'.

This judgement was looked at in the UK case of Kaschke v. Grey and Hilton [2010] EWHC 690 (QB). The case was an appeal to the Queen's Bench Division of the High Court by the second defendant, against an earlier refusal to strike out the claim by the plaintiff for damages for libel. The second defendant controlled a website on which was published an article written by the first defendant, in which the latter alleged that the plaintiff was a former member of a terrorist group. He claimed that he took reasonable care in relation to the operation of the website and the publication of the words complained of, claiming that as soon as he was aware of the plaintiff's complaint, he removed the words complained of, and offered her a right of reply.

Stadlen J., the judge, looked at the provisions of the E-Commerce Directive and at Mulvaney, saying that while the decision was persuasive, it did 'provide support for a number of propositions'. The first proposition is the relevant one here, which was:

> There is no reason in principle why the operation of a chat room should be incapable of falling within the definition of the provision of an information society service consisting of the storage of information. Thus in principle there is no reason why it should not be an activity intended to be protected by Article 14 of the E-Commerce Directive and eligible for the exclusion of liability conferred by Regulation 19 [of the relevant UK regulations].

The Irish case of Damien Tansey v. John Gill (a bankrupt), And Vogelaar, Dotster Inc. And (by order) Ann Vogelaar [2012] IEHC 42, is particularly interesting and important with regard to the legal responsibilities in defamation of those controlling websites. The plaintiff was a solicitor, and the four defendants were those alleged to be involved with a website called www.rate-your-solicitor. com. He alleged that defamatory statements were posted on that website, alleging him to be engaged in corrupt, unprofessional and incompetent conduct.

There were four defendants. The first repeated a number of earlier allegations against the plaintiff, as well as against other solicitors and other persons. He later decided to front a campaign against the solicitors' profession as a whole, including establishing the relevant website to facilitate others to make complaints. The second defendant denied any knowledge of the subject matter of the case, and any involvement in the website, something accepted by the plaintiff, who said that he would not seek legal relief against her.

The third defendant had a registered office in the USA, and leave had been given to serve notice of the case's proceedings at that address. The fourth defendant was a daughter of the second, who stated that she was an unpaid volunteer for the website, her job being confined to answering questions sent to it, denying she posted comments on it or was involved in running, controlling or organising it. Her mother was identified as involved because she used her mother's computer regarding the website at one time.

The judge, Peart J., made interlocutory injunctions under section 33 of the Defamation Act against the first and fourth defendants, prohibiting the publication or further publication of the defamatory material, he agreeing that the material in question was 'seriously defamatory' of the plaintiff, and ordering the removal of such material from the internet; requiring those defendants to end the operation of the relevant website; and directing the defendants to give up the names and addresses of the people involved in publication of the defamatory material concerning the plaintiff. The third defendant had judgement given against him because of his failure to make a legal appearance before the court.

To conclude, those involved in running such sites, in particular social networking sites, could find themselves the subject of defamation cases, on the lines of the Godfrey case, involving the cyber-bullying mentioned, if those people were notified of defamatory remarks and did not remove them within a reasonable time of being notified of them, failing to avail of the defences in Article 14 of the E-Commerce Directive. Also, the Damien Tansey case shows that even being an unpaid volunteer for such a website, confined to answering questions sent to it, will not exempt such a person from being liable for defamatory comments posted on it.

b. Parents and guardians

I mentioned earlier that parents and guardians can be liable for the torts, which include defamation, of their minor children, if they allow 'dangerous things' within their reach that can foreseeably cause harm to them or another; if they know of a 'dangerous propensity' of a child, and fail to reasonably protect others against an injury resulting from it; or if they fail to control a child properly.

The last two categories, in particular the failure to control, as outlined in the Supreme Court case of <u>Curley v. Mannion</u>, are particularly relevant in the area of cyber-bullying. If a parent or guardian allows a child to use his or her own electronic device, such as a computer, gives that child an electronic device, or both, in each case setting conditions on how it is to be used, and fails to exercise proper control in ensuring that these conditions are adhered to, that parent or guardian could be liable for defamatory statements posted or sent by the child. This would be particularly the case if it could be shown that the child had a 'dangerous propensity' to post or send such statements.

c. Innocent third parties: Norwich Pharmacal orders

Relevant to this area are 'Norwich Pharmacal orders', a particular type of court order that can be granted to a plaintiff in a case against an innocent third party, who has information about the identity of wrongdoers. This type of court order came out of an English court decision and has been accepted by the Irish courts.

The English case was that of <u>Norwich Pharmacal Co. and Others v Customs and Excise Commissioners</u> [1974] AC, 133. The owners and licensees of a chemical compound had their patent infringed by illicit imports of that compound manufactured abroad. To obtain the names and addresses of the importers, Norwich Pharmacal brought actions against the Customs and Excise Commissioners, seeking orders for disclosing this information. The case came before the House of Lords, who ruled in the company's favour, and ordered that this information be disclosed. One of the judges, Lord Reid, summed up the principle in the case:

> if through no fault of his own a person gets mixed up in the tortuous acts of others so as to facilitate their wrongdoing he may incur no personal liability but he comes under a duty to assist the person who has been wronged by giving him full information and disclosing the identity of the wrongdoers.

This means that if an innocent third party assisted the wrongdoing of another party who commited torts, such as defamation, this party was duty bound to assist the wronged person by disclosing the identity of the other party.

There have been English cases involving online bullying where such orders have been obtained against innocent third parties to disclose the names and addresses of those with the relevant internet protocol (IP) addresses, including against Facebook Inc., responsible for Facebook, a social networking service and website.

Examples include the case of <u>Applause Store Productions Limited, Matthew Firsht v. Grant Raphael</u> [2008] EWHC 1781 (QB), where the Queen's Bench Division of the High Court granted such an order to the plaintiff against Facebook Inc. This was due to a fake profile being created on Facebook, called 'HAS MATHEW FIRSHT LIED TO YOU?' containing information that was admitted to be defamatory of him, the second plaintiff and his company, the first plaintiff. The order was granted for 'disclosure of the registration data provided by the user responsible for creating the false material, including email addresses, and the internet protocol (IP) addresses of all computers used to access Facebook by the owner of those email addresses'.

A more recent similar case concerned a Nicola Brookes, who was targeted by bullies, after she posted online support for a contestant in the talent show *The X Factor*. They set up a fake Facebook profile in her name, called her a paedophile and a drug user, and posted her address online on 30 May 2012. The High Court granted a Norwich Pharmacal order against Facebook to disclose their identities (*The Guardian*, 2012).

Such orders have been accepted by the Irish courts, since the Supreme Court case of <u>Megaleasing UK Ltd v Barrett (No. 2)</u> [1993] ILRM, 497. Chief Justice Finlay said in the judgement that:

> The existing authorities do in fact confine the remedy to cases where a very clear proof of a wrongdoing exists, and possibly, so far as it applies to an action for discovery alone prior to the institution of other proceedings, to cases where what is really sought are the names and identity of the wrongdoers, rather than the factual information concerning the commission of the wrong.

This order has been resorted to in Ireland in three intellectual property cases. In <u>EMI Records (Ireland) Ltd and Others v Eircom Ltd. and Another</u> [2005] 4 IR, 148, the High Court, in the person of Kelly J., ordered that the defendants, two internet service providers, disclose to the four plaintiffs, holders of the Irish copyright of a number of sound recordings, the names, postal addresses and phone numbers of persons, the registered owners of specified internet accounts, who alleged to have infringed their copyright. The judge made clear that any right of confidentiality 'cannot be relied upon by a wrongdoer or a person against whom there is evidence of wrongdoing to protect his or her identity. The right to privacy or confidentiality of identity must give way where there is *prima facie* evidence of wrongdoing. There is such evidence here'.

In the case of EMI Records (Ireland) Ltd and Others v Eircom Ltd [2009] IEHC 411, Charleton J., in the High Court, ruled that the four plaintiffs in the previous case be granted an injunction ordering the defendant, who was innocent of wrongdoing in this matter, under section 40(4) of the Copyright and Related Rights Act 2000, to 'block or disable access by its internet subscribers' to the website PirateBay.org. and related dominion names, a site 'dedicated, on a weird ideological basis, to basically stealing the copyright owned by the plaintiffs in mainly musical works'.

This case was looked at again in a later case, again in the High Court, of EMI Records (Ireland) Ltd and Others v Eircom Ltd [2010] 4 IR, 349. The judge, again Charleton J., referred to the order granted by his colleague Kelly J. in the first case. He said that in that case, the order was 'to enable the plaintiffs to then directly take action against each such illegal downloader'. However, the plaintiffs have here 'left behind what they reasonably regard as an expensive and futile pursuit of the identity of copyright tortfeasors in favour of injunctive relief that has been expressed in the settlement of the case as a protocol to choke off the problem in a three-stage process that never involves the identification of any wrongdoer'. The process was described, which would lead to a termination notice of fourteen days being issued to the bill payer in the event of a third copyright infringement. The case concerned this settlement, reached as a result of the 2009 case. Three questions were raised by the Data Protection Commissioner about the lawfulness of the settlement's terms. The judge answered the Commissioner's questions, and allowed the settlement to be implemented.

This protocol between Eircom and the recording companies was later challenged by the Data Protection Commissioner in EMI Records (Ireland) Ltd. and Others v. Data Protection Commissioner [2012] IEHC 264. On 11 January 2012, the Commissioner issued an Enforcement Notice, directing Eircom to cease the protocol. The High Court, Charleton J. again being the judge, held that the

Notice was unlawful, it not giving the Commissioner's reasons for believing that a provision of the data protection legislation had been or was being contravened. The Commissioner then appealed to the Supreme Court who, in EMI Records (Ireland) Ltd. and Others v. Data Protection Commissioner [2013] IESC 34, rejected the appeal.

CONCLUSION

To conclude, the law I have mentioned, while not dealing explicitly with 'school bullying', makes it clear that those running schools and internet websites, as well as parents and guardians, should look at taking particular measures, in order to deal with bullying.

1. Schools

a. General measures

First, those running schools should put adequate policies and procedures in place to deter such bullying, and act properly and promptly to deal with it when it does happen, and second, when dealing with such behaviour, act according to fair procedures, particularly where long-term suspension or expulsion is an issue, where the student or student's parent should be asked to make representations as to penalty. However, the Smullen decision protects the immediate or long-term suspension of a student by a school in a summary manner, in exceptional situations involving life or property.

The courts, in particular as shown in the Maher case, will not expect perfection of a school and those running it, as long as the standard of a 'prudent parent' is kept. In terms of a school being liable if it does not keep to the terms of its policies and procedures, there is presently no court decision, the O'Donovan case, which raised this question, being decided on other grounds.

b. More specific measures

In terms of more specific situations, first, a school may refuse to enrol a student due to previous bad behaviour. Second, a school that expels a student is under no obligation to consider alternative school places available in the immediate area. Third, it should remember that the Equal Status Acts 2000–2011 have been invoked where actions taken to discipline students for alleged bad behaviour were contested due to alleged discrimination, harassment and victimisation concerning any of the nine grounds: gender; marital status; family status; sexual orientation; religious belief; age; disability; race; membership of the Traveller community. Here, the observation of fair procedures and the Education (Welfare) Act would be particularly important.

Fourth, a school can possibly lawfully segregate a student from the rest of the student body as a punishment, provided all reasonable efforts are taken to keep the student's education up to prescribed standards, and if the segregation is of a short duration. Fifth, a school can possibly suspend a student beyond the legally permitted period, pending a decision of whether criminal charges will be brought against him or her. As long as that student continues to have non-discriminatory access to the education prevailing in the state, such a measure would be compatible with the European Convention on Human Rights. (I use the word 'possibly' here and in discussing the previous measure, as the Irish courts have not yet decided on such issues.)

Sixth, a school may have a duty of care towards its students when outside of school, outside of school hours or school trips, and may take disciplinary action regarding the bullying by a student of another student. The Smullen decision was an exceptional one, involving danger to life or property, and wanting to maintain peace and discipline within the school; but it appears that schools may have a general duty of care in ensuring that bullying and harassment happening outside the school does not carry over into the school. If this is done, it can be argued that the school *may* intervene in outside bullying situations, but it is not *obliged* to do so. Again, this is a situation the Irish courts have not yet decided on. The remarks by Denham J. in the Dolan case, of a school perhaps being responsible if it 'has knowledge of a dangerous situation', could perhaps be used in a bullying context in a later case.

2. Internet service providers and those controlling websites

If such people or organisations control chat rooms or forums, such as on social networking websites, they could be sued in defamation as publishers if defamatory words are published on their websites. They could, if so sued, be found liable if they have, first, failed to give a defence of 'Innocent publication' under section 27 of the Defamation Act 2009; and second, they have failed, as hosts for information provided by a recipient of their services, stored at that person's request, on knowing of the unlawful activity concerned, or the circumstances from which the lawful activity is apparent, to 'act expeditiously' to remove or disable access to that information.

Internet service providers or those controlling websites can reduce their legal liability in these circumstances if they take two steps. First, they have comprehensive and easily accessible complaints procedures, where those who wish to complain know who to complain to, and how a complaint will be dealt with once it is made, and second, that there is a proper response within a reasonable time to a complaint made.

A guide to what could be done can be found in the *Code of Practice and Ethics* of the Internet Service Providers' Association of Ireland (ISPAI), which has a section dealing with 'Complaints Procedure', suggesting, among other things, that its members try and resolve complaints within five to ten working days of their receipt, depending on the complaint and the way it was received (ISPAI, 2002).

3. Parents and guardians

As I mentioned earlier, parents and guardians need to exercise proper control over their minor children's use of electronic devices. If a parent or guardian allows a child to use his or her own electronic device, such as a computer, gives that child such a device, or both, in each case setting conditions on how it is to be used, and fails to exercise proper control in ensuring that these conditions are adhered to, that parent or guardian could be liable for defamatory statements posted or sent by the child. This is particularly the case if it could be shown that the child had a 'dangerous propensity' to post or send such statements.

The steps needed for parents and guardians to exercise proper control will depend on the age of the child and the nature of the injury caused. The impossible is not demanded, because it is a defence if it can be shown that a parent or guardian's reasonable best could not prevent the injury. In terms of guides to parents on how to exercise such proper control, a number of these can be found on the publications part of the Office for Internet Safety's website. They can be accessed at www.internetsafety.ie/website/ois/oisweb.nsf/page/publications-en. Particularly useful ones include *Mobile Phones: A Parent's Guide to Safe and Sensible Use*, published by the Irish Cellular

Industry Association; and, in the *Get With It!* series of publications, as well as the already mentioned *A Guide to Cyberbullying*, there are *A Parent's Guide to Social Networking Websites* and *A Parent's Guide to New Media Technologies*.

REFERENCES

Denning, A.T., Baron Denning of Whitchurch, *Landmarks in the Law* (London: Butterworths, 1984)

Department of Children and Youth Affairs, *Sixth Report of the Special Rapporteur on Child Protection* (Dublin: Department of Children and Youth Affairs, 2013)

Department of Education and Skills, *Action Plan on Bullying: Report of the Anti-Bullying Working Group to the Minister for Education and Skills* (Dubln: Department of Education, 2013)

Department of Education and Skills, *Guidelines on Countering Bullying Behaviour in Primary and Post-Primary Schools* (Dublin: Stationery Office, 1993)

Department of Education, *School Matters: The Report of the Task Force on Student Behaviour in Second Level Schools* (Dublin: Department of Education, 2006)

Glendenning, D. *Education and the Law* 2nd edn (Haywards Heath: Bloomsbury Professional, 2012)

Glendenning, D. and Binchy, W. (eds) *Litigation against Schools: Implications for School Management* (Dublin: FirstLaw Limited, 2006)

Glendenning, D. *Religion, Education and the Law: A Comparative Approach* (Haywards Heath: Tottel Publishing, 2008)

Hunt, B. and Murdoch, H. *Murdoch's Dictionary of Irish Law*, 5th edn (Dublin: Tottel Publishing, 2007)

Irish Independent, 6 June 2008, http://www.independent.ie/irish-news/ man-27-prosecuted-over-obscene-bebo-messages-26451819.html [accessed 12 July 2013]

ISPAI (Internet Service Providers Association of Ireland), *Code of Practice and Ethics* (2002), www.ispai.ie/docs/cope.pdf [accessed 25 June 2012]

McMahon, B.M.E. and Binchy, W. *A Case Book on the Irish Law of Torts*, 3rd edn (Haywards Heath: Tottel Publishing, 2005)

McMahon, B.M.E. and Binchy, W. *Law of Torts*, 4th edn (Haywards Heath: Bloomsbury Professional, 2013)

Milford, H.S. (ed.), *The Complete Poetical Works of William Cowper* (Oxford: Oxford University Press, 1913)

Mohan, H. and Murphy, M.W. 'Defamation Reform and the 2009 Act: Part II', *Bar Review*, 15, 2010, pp. 50–4

Mohan, H. and Murphy, M.W. 'Defamation Reform and the 2009 Act: Part I', *Bar Review*, 15, 2010, pp. 33–7

Murphy, K. 'Defamation Online after the Defamation Act 2009', *Irish Law Times*, 28, 2010, pp. 181–96

NEWB (National Education Welfare Board), *Developing a Code of Behaviour: Guidelines for Schools* (Dublin: NEWB, 2008), www.newb.ie/downloads/pdf/guidelines_school_codes_eng.pdf [accessed 12 July 2013]

Office for Internet Safety, *A Guide to Cyberbullying* (Dublin: Brunswick Press, 2008), www.internetsafety.ie/website/OIS/OISWweb.nsf/page/DPCY-7LYJ4V1343473-en/$File/GWIT-cyberbullying-Dec12 [accessed 12 July 2013]

O'Mahony, C. *Educational Rights in Irish Law* (Dublin: Thomson Round Hall, 2006)

O'Moore, M. 'Cyber-Bullying: The Situation in Ireland', *Pastoral Care in Education: An International Journal of Personal, Social and Emotional Development*, 30, 2012, pp. 209–23

O'Moore, M. and Minton, S. 'Cyber-Bullying: The Irish Experience', in C. Quinn and S. Tawse (eds), *Handbook of Aggressive Behaviour Research* (New York: Nova Science Publishers, 2009)

School of Law, Trinity College Dublin, 'New Legal Issues Facing School Principals and Teachers in 2009: Some Practical Solutions', conference held at Trinity College Dublin on Saturday 23 May 2009

School of Law, Trinity College Dublin, 'Schools and the Law in 2010: Coping with New Challenges', conference held at Trinity College Dublin on Saturday 29 May 2010

School of Law, Trinity College Dublin, 'Defamation and Privacy Law', conference held at Trinity College Dublin on Thursday 7 April 2011

School of Law, Trinity College Dublin, 'Litigation against Post-Primary Schools: All the Recent Developments', Conference held at Trinity College Dublin on Saturday 12 November 2011

School of Law, Trinity College Dublin, 'Litigation against Primary Schools: All the Recent Developments', conference held at Trinity College Dublin on Saturday 24 March 2012

Smith, M. 'School of Hard Knocks', *Law Society Gazette*, 98, 2004, pp. 18–21

Smith, M. 'Mulvey v. McDonagh and Bullying at School', *Bar Review*, 10, 2005, pp. 106–8

Smith, M. 'School's Out', *Law Society Gazette*, 100, 2006, pp. 18–23

The Guardian, 8 June 2012, http://www.guardian.co.uk/technology/2012/jun/08/facebook-revealing-identities-cyberbullies [accessed 12 July 2013]

Index